PATRIOTS

PATRIOTS

National Identity in Britain
1940–2000

Richard Weight

MACMILLAN

First published 2002 by Macmillian
an imprint of Pan Macmillan Ltd
Pan Macmillan, 20 New Wharf Road, London N1 9RR
Basingstoke and Oxford
Associated companies throughout the world
www.panmacmillan.com

ISBN 0 333 73462 9

A CIP catalogue record for this book is available from
the British Library.

Typeset by SetSystems Ltd, SaffronWalden, Essex
Printed and bound in Great Britain by
Mackays of Chatham plc, Chatham, Kent

This book is dedicated with love to

PHIL STRONG
(1945–1995)

Father, friend, mentor and inspiration

Acknowledgements

My greatest thanks go to Professor Nick Black for putting a roof over my head in the three years that it took to research and write *Patriots*. Without his help, the project which Phil Strong inspired would not have been completed. Therefore, in a very real sense, this book and its dedication is as much his as it is mine.

Special thanks go to three people whose love, constant support and practical advice was invaluable: my mother, Angela Weight, Steve Ball and Ashley Chapman. The following friends enabled me to forget my work, and when I could not, endured its presence with humour and understanding. Some also gave me financial and/or intellectual assistance. They are: Jim Hicks, Doug Stewart, Negley Harte, J-C Nowers, Terri Barker, Dave Martin, Guy Patterson, Andrew McIlroy, Fred Keane, Julia Strong, Kathy Rowan, Toby Haggith, Thanmai Bui-Van, Isobel Davies, Jo Marsh and Tom Crawford. Dr Roger Goldberg, the Revd. Robert Atwell, Catherine Aubin, Ewa Kardasiewicz, Gino Della Ragione, Tottenham Hotspur FC and Bertie all, in their different ways, helped me to keep body and soul together.

Professor Peter Hennessy is a mentor and fellow Orwellian who gave me professional support when I most needed it in the years following the completion of my PhD in 1995. Thanks for helping me see the sacramental in the everyday, Peter, and thanks too for all the gossipy laughs. Professor Roy Foster's knack of phoning me at times when the academic world seemed a distant shore also did much to keep me on course. My agent Giles Gordon was, well, Giles Gordon: a stylish but no-nonsense representative and a second editor with an eye for the telling phrase.

I am grateful to three people at Macmillan: my editor, Georgina Morley, for her challenging opinions, delightful lunches and heroic patience; Nick Blake for his expert, witty and exhaustive scrutiny of the text; and Stefanie Bierwerth for all her hard work behind the scenes. Effective historical research depends on the assistance of skilled archivists and I am grateful to the dozens around the United Kingdom who made a daunting task so much easier – in particular

viii *Acknowledgements*

the staff of the Public Record Office in London and the National Archives of Scotland in Edinburgh. Finally, I would like to thank Professor Martin Daunton for overseeing the genesis of this book during my time at University College London. Naturally, I take full responsibility for the final text.

Richard Weight
London, December 2001

Contents

List of Illustrations

The Kingston Bypass at Tolworth in Surrey, flanked by semi-detached houses and their gardens, 1939. *(Hulton Archive)*

Surviving riveters at work in the empty shipyards of Clydebank, c. 1935. *(Popperphoto)*

1914 and 1939: The people of 'England' and 'Britain' go to war against Germany. *(Ronald Grant Archive and Hulton Archive)*

RAF Spitfires race to meet a Luftwaffe attack over the south coast of England during the Battle of Britain. *(Hulton Getty)*

St Paul's Cathedral survives another German bombing raid in the autumn of 1940, thanks to the efforts of clergy, firemen and local volunteers. *(Hulton Archive)*

A Watford woman learns how to kill German invaders from a member of the Home Guard, 1941. *(Imperial War Museum)*

America helps to win the war: GIs take pot shots at a caricature of Adolf Hitler in an amusement arcade, Piccadilly Circus, London, 1945. *(Hulton Archive)*

Humphrey Bogart enforces the American influence on British life, 1951. *(Ronald Grant Archive)*

Jamaican ex-servicemen on board the *Empire Windrush* are welcomed to Britain by RAF officers after landing at Tilbury to start a new life, 22 June 1948. *(PA Photos)*

The Queen lays the foundation stone of the National Theatre on 13 July 1951, twenty-five years before it opened. To the right, the Archbishop of Canterbury, Geoffrey Fisher, looks on approvingly. *(PA Photos)*

The Festival of Britain, South Bank Exhibition. The Dome of Discovery and Skylon face a scaffolded Palace of Westminster, 15 May 1951. *(Hulton Getty)*

List of Illustrations

A train driver wages class war, the British way, during a rail strike in 1971 – as drawn by Giles of the *Daily Express*.

Soldiers arrest a Catholic youth for trying to overthrow the British state in Northern Ireland, Belfast. *(Hulton Getty)*

Members of Scotland's Tartan Army invade the pitch at Wembley Stadium after beating England 2–0 during the Queen's Silver Jubilee, 4 June 1977. *(Hulton Getty)*

Pope John Paul II celebrates Mass in front of 70,000 Britons at Wembley Stadium, 29 May 1982. *(PA Photos)*

Men of 2 Para settle into a sheep pen for the night at Fitzroy in the Falklands, 1 June 1982. *(PA Photos)*

A British family enjoy the sunshine and freedom of Benidorm in Spain, August 1986. *(Hulton Archive)*

Father and daughter celebrate England's first win over Germany since 1966, Trafalgar Square, 1 September 2000.

Introduction

This is a book about why the people of Britain stopped thinking of themselves as British and began to see themselves instead as Scots, Welsh and English who happened to belong to a state called Britain: how three nations on a small island in the Atlantic, who together ruled a quarter of the planet, became minor European powers, divided among themselves and uncertain about where they were going. This transformation took place in little more than half a century after the Second World War. So often seen as a story of decline, it is in fact one of progress and renewal. Scotland, Wales and England had been locked together for four centuries in an uneasy relationship. From 1940 to 2000 they not only rediscovered their core national identities, they also re-imagined themselves, shedding many of the assumptions about class, race, gender, and religion which had once denied millions of people the right to belong to their nation. Many found these changes painful, some effected them unwillingly and some were still resisting them at the end of the century. But Britain did change dramatically in this period. And almost entirely for the better.

The British contributed much to world civilization between 1707 and 1940. Their patriotism was often expressed as much in opposition to the undemocratic regimes under which they lived for most of that period as it was in support of them. But on the whole, the United Kingdom was designed to advance the cause of capitalism, empire and the Protestant faith. It was founded on greed, religious and racial bigotry, fear and contempt. The national identity constructed to unite the four nations claimed that the British were in fact enterprising, godly, tolerant, brave and adventurous. The Union of England, Scotland, Wales and Ireland was created in four stages between the sixteenth and the nineteenth centuries. How, why and when it was established had a direct bearing on British national identity in the twentieth century. The Union of Wales and England was the first. Wales had never been a unitary kingdom, a fact which made its integration much easier. The principality was annexed by Edward I in 1284, following the defeat of Llwellyn, the last of the

Welsh princes. But formal union, in which the remnants of Wales' legal, educational and administrative systems were absorbed into those of England, began only after a Welsh dynasty, the Tudors, assumed the English throne in 1485. Henry VIII's Act of Union of 1536 declared the principality to be 'incorporated, united and annexed to the English realm'. A further Act of 1542 established English rather than Welsh as the nation's official language.

Scotland had been a unitary kingdom since the eighth century, but Edward I was no respecter of history. The so-called 'Hammer of the Scots' meted out the same treatment to them as he did to the Welsh, defeating and executing William Wallace in 1305. Scottish kings and nobles were bought off by successive English monarchs with titles, lands and money in the south. Consequently, for most of the next 300 years Scotland was only nominally independent. But here too it was not until King James VI of Scotland assumed the throne of England in 1603 that the process of formal union began. In both cases, therefore, the smaller nations of Britain were only fully joined with their large neighbour because their own native dynasties took control of the English state and not because the English overpowered them. This did much to legitimize the process in the eyes of Welsh and Scottish patriots. Indeed, many thought they had won the constitutional lottery, symbolized by the bombastic title that James VI took for himself – 'Emperor of the whole island of Great Britain'.

Yet there was a fundamental difference between Scotland and Wales which became clear when the English pressed the Scots to make the Union of the Crowns a full political one in the 1700s. Anglo-Welsh Union might be described as an arranged marriage in which the couple, though not in love, consented to the match, and despite their differences grew to respect each other. That of Scotland and England was more of a shotgun wedding in which two lovers were forced to marry and later regretted it. In 1704, the Parliament of Westminster decided to ensure the Protestant succession after the death of Anne by excluding her Catholic Stuart relatives from the throne and inviting George, Elector of Hanover to succeed her. In order to protect England from a likely Stuart invasion, Parliament proposed to bring the Scots within the full embrace of the nascent Hanoverian state. Over the next three years, England's rulers tried to persuade, then cajole, Scotland's rulers, eventually threatening them with armed invasion.

Many Scots welcomed the idea of Union, disliking the prospect of Catholic Stuart rule as much as their fellow Protestants in England did. And some could also see the economic benefits of merging with their more prosperous neighbour. But thousands of others rioted in the streets of towns and cities all over the country, angry at being bullied by the English and determined to retain their independence. Like previous generations of Scotland's rulers, this one lost its nerve and was bought off. As English dragoons mustered at Berwick in order to concentrate minds in Edinburgh, the Scottish Parliament took a final vote on the Treaty of Union on 15 January 1707 and decided to abolish itself by 109 votes to 69. In 1792, the poet Robert Burns wrote despairingly, 'We're bought and sold for English gold / What a parcel of rogues in a nation!' Nevertheless the parcel of rogues obtained a good deal for their compatriots. Unlike the Welsh, the Scots kept their separate educational, legal and religious systems – thus preserving, as it were, Scotland's maiden name. And in return for relinquishing their monarchy and Parliament they were given a handsome dowry. Customs union with England and Wales provided a larger and freer market for Scottish goods. As a gesture of goodwill, Westminster voted a gift of £398,085 10s. – known as the Equivalent – to compensate Scotland for the loss of its own customs and excise duties. More importantly, Scotland received a share in the spoils of the rapidly growing English empire. Independent attempts at colonization had failed in 1699 with the collapse of the Company of Scotland's Darién Scheme, and its fate demonstrated that Scotland could not build an empire on its own.

Therefore, to a much greater extent than the Unions of 1536 and 1603, that of 1707 took the form of a commercial contract between two national oligarchies, each of which perceived the other to be essentially foreign. The whole arrangement was crowned, so to speak, by a German dynasty foreign to them both. From the start it was a fragile relationship, and it remained so over the next three centuries. While the English came to regard the arrangement as permanent, the Scots continued to see it as conditional upon their getting a good fiscal return on the loss of their sovereignty. The conditional way they viewed the Union was highlighted by the fact that people north of the border called the agreement the Treaty of Union while south of the border it was referred to as the Act of Union.

The more astute Scottish leaders recognized that the value of their share in England's markets could go down as well as up. They also knew that ordinary Scots, who stood to benefit much less from the riches on offer in the Treaty, would need more patriotic reasons for accepting it. In other words, it would take more than pounds, shillings and pence to perpetuate the Union. A new, British, national identity had to be forged. On the afternoon of 25 March 1707, the Commissioner of the Scottish Parliament, Lord Queensberry, wound up its final proceedings with this wish:

> I am perswaded that we and our Posterity will reap the benefit of union of the two Kingdoms, and I doubt not, that . . . you will in your several Stations recommend to the People of the Nation, a grateful sense of Her Majesties Goodness and great Care for the Welfare of her subjects, in bringing this important affair to Perfection, and that you will promote an universal Desire in this Kingdom to become one in Hearts and Affections, as we are inseparably joyn'd in interest with our Neighbour Nation.[1]

Five weeks later, on 1 May 1707, Scotland ceased to exist as an independent nation state. Over the next forty years, Jacobite insurrections took place at frequent intervals. In 1745, the army of Charles Edward Stuart reached Derby before being routed at Culloden Moor by the Duke of Marlborough. A successful experiment in multinational state formation had finally got under way, but with one rather important hitch.

On 1 January 1801, the Union of Great Britain and Ireland took place. From the start, it was 'joyn'd' in neither interest nor affection. In fact, if England's Union with Wales was an arranged marriage and if its Union with Scotland was a shotgun wedding, then the union with Ireland was a date rape. Since the sixteenth century, Ireland had been colonized by the Scots in the north and the English in the south. Following the uprising of the United Irishmen in 1798, the British government moved to abolish the Irish Parliament and fully incorporate the island into the UK. The Irish patriot leader Henry Grattan wrote, 'The two nations are not identified, though the Irish legislature be absorbed, and, by that act of absorption, the feeling of one of the nations is not identified but alienated.'[2] The Union made little difference to Irish life. The Protestant Ascendancy, based around the Viceroy and his court in Dublin, continued to rule the island much as before, implementing legislation now passed at Westminster. Nor, initially, did the Irish economy suffer as a result of Union. But disillusion followed swiftly, as Grattan had predicted it would. Roy Foster has commented, 'The fact of the Union . . . set the rhetorical terms of nationalist politics over the next century.'

'John Bull's other island' as G. B. Shaw once described it, or John Bull's 'other' as historians would now say, united the Scots, Welsh and English by defining who they were not. From the mid-nineteenth century onwards, a new Irish nationalist movement developed. Unlike the United Irishmen, it was based on a Celtic, Catholic and agrarian vision of Irishness. In response, the Irish were seen as an even more backward people. Faced with constant unrest across the small stretch of water that separated the two islands, the largely Protestant industrial peoples of Britain forged a closer bond, particularly in the period 1880 to 1920, when Irish Home Rule dominated the political agenda at Westminster. After Partition, the Northern Irish were welcomed as fellow, if peripheral, Britons. Usually written out of British history, the province is given a central place in this book. *Patriots* does not pretend to be an exhaustive account of Northern Irish identity. There is simply not the space. But it does examine the influence Ulster had on Great Britain. At first, sympathy for Ulster helped Britons define themselves against the Southern Irish. But when war ravaged the province from 1969 to 1999, sympathy disappeared, and mainlanders came instead to define themselves against the Northern Irish. In one way or another, therefore, Ireland was the stranger at the feast of British patriotism in the twentieth century.

Scotland, Wales and the northern part of Ireland benefited materially from the United Kingdom during most of its existence. Moreover, British national identity was largely a Scottish creation, prompted by the need to convince ordinary Scots that England was a benign ally and not a rapacious predator. 'Rule, Britannia' was written by a Scot, James Thomson, in 1740. The concept of 'North Britain' was promoted by Scottish polemicists and gained some credibility north of the border. The idea of 'South Britain' was less popular in England. In fact, until the late eighteenth century, the English were extremely reluctant Britons. Reared on images of Scotland as a barbarous country, they saw the Union as a plank for a parasitic people to feed off England's greater wealth and superior civilization. Protests about the success of Scottish trade and the influence of Scots in public life were common. Consequently, while their partners came to think of themselves as Scottish/Welsh and British, the English refused to adopt a dual national identity. Their scepticism about the Union allowed the Scots the space and time in which to dominate the construction of Britishness in its crucial early years.

In the late eighteenth century the English began to take a more positive view of the Union for four reasons. First, the defeat of the

Jacobites removed the threat of a Scottish invasion and encouraged the English to see the Scots as loyal partners rather than hostile competitors. Second, the danger posed by revolutionary, Catholic France between 1798 and 1815 made the English realize that they would stand or fall in alliance with their fellow conservatives and co-religionists. The threat from a common enemy, whose outlook and way of life was regarded as the antithesis of Britain's own, bound the three nations together as never before. The world's first national anthem, 'God Save the King', was composed in 1745 to rally Britons against the Jacobites, but it did not become a popular and truly national anthem until the Napoleonic Wars. The unifying principle behind Britishness in this period was that which had first moved England's rulers to exclude the Stuarts from the throne and forge the Union of 1707: Protestantism. In her justly acclaimed study of the subject, Linda Colley concluded:

> Great Britain might be made up of three separate nations, but under God it could also be one, united nation. And as long as a sense of mission and providential destiny could be kept alive, by means of recurrent wars with the Catholic states of Europe, and by means of frenetic and for a long time highly successful pursuit of empire, the Union flourished, sustained not just by convenience and profit but by belief as well. Protestantism was the foundation that made the invention of Great Britain possible.[3]

In the half-century following the Battle of Waterloo, victory over Napoleon formed the basis of a sustaining national legend of strength through unity.

In peacetime, the Scots proved that they were neither savages nor parasites. Their entrepreneurs, inventors and workers played a major role in the industrial revolution, while the Scottish Enlightenment provided much of the intellectual basis for British capitalism and the associated idea of Progress which fired the nineteenth-century imagination. The Scots were also ardent imperialists who made a huge contribution to the expansion and maintenance of the British Empire. Throughout the globe, they provided military personnel, civil servants, preachers, doctors, lawyers and engineers on a *greater* scale, relative to Scotland's size, than did England. To take just one example, between 1850 and 1939 almost a third of colonial governors were Scots. In 1888, Sir Charles Dilke wrote: 'In British settlements . . . for every Englishman you meet who has worked his way up to wealth from small beginnings without external aid, you find ten Scotchmen.'[4] Commercial and professional opportunities were not the only thing the Empire offered the Scots and Welsh. It also offered them an unprecedented international role and the chance to be recognized as powerful nations in their own right instead of just the satellites of a larger neighbour. Those who lived and worked together on the imperial margins had a particularly acute sense of Britishness. Surrounded in strange lands by natives most of whom they considered inferior, the Scots, Welsh and English were drawn together by a sense of common purpose *and* by a sense of cultural affinity.

As the UK changed, so too did Britishness. The UK was transformed from an agrarian society into the world's first industrial society. By 1900, Britain had reached its present-day level of 80 per cent of the population inhabiting urban areas; a figure which even Germany, the Continent's most industrialized nation, did not reach until 1960. As a result, the British were also the first people in the West to romanticize the countryside. The squalor caused by industrialization provoked a reaction to Victorian economic liberalism and to urban life. Critics argued that laissez-faire capitalism had spawned a rootless, spiritually bankrupt society where once there had been a nation of organic rural communities. From around the 1880s, this transformed the popular image of the countryside from that of a backward hovel into a picturesque repository of national values. This was not, as historians often assume, a peculiarly English fixation. It was, if anything, stronger in Scotland and Wales.

Imperial expansion made Britishness a more racist consciousness. A shared sense of racial superiority was instrumental in fostering a British national identity during the nineteenth century, particularly among the millions who did not benefit directly from the commercial profits of empire. Because they regarded themselves as a benevolent civilizing force in the world, the British convinced themselves that they were not nationalists like the Europeans but patriots; people who loved their country but who had no wish to oppress others. In reality, Victorian imperialism was a more virulent form of British nationalism than ever before. But the simultaneous growth of democracy in the UK helped to maintain the conceit that the British were merely patriots. The creation of parliamentary democracy between 1884, when most men were given the vote, and 1928 when all women were given it, fostered a national cult of fair play. This was enhanced by the growth of organized games in British schools and of professional spectator sports from the 1860s onwards. How, it was argued, could a sporting nation that valued free speech possibly be an aggressive one? Finally, the fabled reticence of the English and their consequent reluctance to make a song and dance about their nationality was also offered up as an example of Britain's more quietistic identity.

All the means available to nation-builders were used to foster loyalty to the British state between 1603 and 1940. Flags and coinage; weights and measures; music, literature and art; memorials and museums; holidays and festivals; public ceremonial, from the largest royal occasions to the smallest civic pageant – all these played a part. So too did popular studies of the national character. These books became more influential in the late nineteenth century following the start of state education in 1870 and the consequent rise of popular literacy, which gave them a bigger readership than before. The new education system was itself used to promote Britishness through school curricula, organized games and special parades, such as those marking Empire Day. The work of teachers was augmented by the establishment of youth movements such as the Boy Scouts (1908) and Girl Guides (1910). Less deliberately, the transport and communications revolution of the nineteenth and twentieth centuries – the introduction of a postal service, railways, telephones, cinema and broadcasting – all amplified Britishness by bringing the four nations into closer contact.

Integration did not mean the extinction of old identities. In fact, as a result of the Romantic movement in the late eighteenth century, there was an eager search for the arcane customs and traditions of the UK's four nations. As elsewhere in Europe, this led to a good deal of fabrication. The modern kilt was invented in the 1730s by Thomas Rawlinson, a Lancastrian industrialist who clothed his Scottish workers in the garment to save money on breeches. Welsh national costume was invented in the 1830s by Augusta Waddington – a West Country aristocrat married to Benjamin Hall, the government minister responsible for completing the Palace of Westminster and after whom 'Big Ben' is named.

What were the generally accepted national characters of each country? The Dutch academic G. J. Renier, whose book *The English: Are They Human?* was published in 1932 and ran to ten editions by 1945, explained:

I am speaking about the English, not the British. There is no question in this work of the Scots, proud, intelligent, religious and unfathomable. Nor of the Welsh, minute, musical, clever and temperamental. I am not writing about the charming, untruthful, bloodthirsty and unreliable Irish. I shall be exclusively concerned with the English, the unintellectual, restricted, stubborn, steady, pragmatic, silent and reliable English.[5]

He did not get it quite right. Broadly speaking, by the mid-twentieth century, the Southern Irish were seen as backward, untrustworthy and violent; the Northern Irish were thought to be taciturn and uncompromising, but loyal and industrious at the same time; the Scots were considered to be dour and tight-fisted but hardworking, well educated and outward-looking; the Welsh were more insular but as a romantic, idealistic and Godly people, they were seen as the moral conscience of the nation. The English were Britain's pragmatists: private and individualistic with a love of eccentricity, traits which were tempered by a sense of decency, fair play and tolerance towards others.

Renier's book was one of hundreds on the subject of Englishness. The most popular was A. L. Morton's *In Search of England*. First published in 1927, by 1964 it had sold 2.9 million copies and it remained in print until the 1980s. Richly illustrated, it was an impressionistic, intensely patriotic account of its author's journeys around England. 'A buxom wench with a face like a ripe pippin and a waist made for the arm of an eighteenth century gallant' was how Morton described a woman he encountered serving beer and beef in a Rutland inn.[6] From the seventeenth to the twentieth centuries, Englishness continued to be defined and expressed in a separate, though never separatist, form. In the late nineteenth century, that tendency increased as a result of the Irish Home Rule movement. The growing realization that the Union of 1801 was not held together by affection, and that some form of settlement would have to be made, forced the English to look at themselves again. Ireland had perhaps its greatest cultural impact on Britain not through its music, its poets, or even the emigrants who built its roads, but in forcing the English to draw back the red, white and blue veil and look in the mirror to examine their features more closely. During the first half of the twentieth century, a wide range of academics, journalists and politicians pondered what it meant to be English, as distinct from being British, and the public listened.

The main difference between the English on the one hand and the Scots and Welsh on the other was not that the English arrogantly

regarded their nation and Britain as synonymous. The main difference was that in England there was little or no tension between
people's ancient nationality and that which had been constructed
around the British state. Theirs was a cultural nationalism which no
longer required a political dimension because England was the
dominant country in the United Kingdom. The problems which the
English faced when their partners became unhappy with the arrangement arose not from the fact that they had forgotten how to be
English, but that they had forgotten how to articulate their national
identity politically.

However, despite their belated enthusiasm for the Union and their
continuing need to defined their uniqueness, the English were still
disinclined to adopt a dual identity. Instead they invested their
Englishness almost wholly in the idea of Britain, renaming rather
than remaking their national identity. In 1887 the constitutional
expert James Bryce wrote, 'An Englishman has but one patriotism
because England and the United Kingdom are to him practically the
same thing.'[7] The English had come to appreciate the Scots' worth
and the necessity of alliance with them. But with arrogance born of
ancient prejudice, they refused to acknowledge them as equal partners. Despite the disproportionate Scottish influence in the Union,
England remained by far its largest member. Once enthused with the
idea of being British, the English had the power to dominate the
construction and articulation of Britishness and to make economic
and political decisions in affairs of state which often disregarded,
and at times prejudiced, the interests of their partners.

Scholars have been right to challenge the theory of internal
colonialism, which sees the Union as one long saga of deliberate and
brutal English domination. But historians have been far too quick to
absolve the English of any blame for the decline of Britishness. For
most of the UK's history the Scots and the Welsh were viewed by the
English as either junior partners or comical nonentities or both.
There was rarely any malice in this outlook, but the very insouciance
with which the English mocked, patronized or simply ignored the
Scots and Welsh provoked them just as much as if the intent was to
wound. Naturally enough, this served only to reinforce their awareness of separate national identities.

From the 1850s to the 1980s there were regular attempts to
appease the Scots and the Welsh, either through mild forms of
political devolution or, more often, through cultural devolution. The
latter, it was hoped, would prevent the need for the former.

Opponents of devolution argued that it had a ratchet effect, with each concession leading eventually to another. There is some truth in this. Emboldened by the victories they won, the Scots and Welsh pressed for ever more autonomy. But the main reason why devolution never satisfied them was that it was usually followed by another English gaffe. Mistakes not only called for additional solutions; they also wiped out the goodwill engendered by the original concession. Why did the English never learn? Although they gradually became more aware of their partners' discontent, they did not fundamentally alter their Anglo-British identity. What Bryce said of them in 1887 was just as true in 1987.

Therefore, it is impossible to explain why Britishness declined so sharply in the late twentieth century simply by analysing the decline of the beliefs and institutions upon which it was constructed. Scottish and Welsh nationalism did not develop in a vacuum any more than British nationalism developed in one between the eighteenth and the twentieth centuries. Just as wars against the French and then the Germans helped to define and unite Britons against an alien 'other', so England's misrule of the Union allowed its partners to define themselves against the English. Scottishness and Welshness did not survive simply because Britain was a gloriously pluralistic multinational state. They also survived because the Scots and Welsh were provoked into self-awareness at regular intervals by their larger neighbour. The decline of Britishness was neither as sudden nor as surprising as it now seems when one scrutinizes the myopia and complacency with which the United Kingdom was governed.

My central argument, then, is this: from the birth of the Union, cultural differences were allowed to exist within Britain. But because the English never developed a dual national identity and treated their partners accordingly, between approximately 1880 and 1920 those differences formed the basis of a more self-conscious and vigorous cultural nationalism as the Scots and Welsh struggled to preserve and assert their ancient nationhood. From the 1920s onwards, another factor came into play that proved in the end to be fatal: relative economic decline in the north and west of Britain. After the First World War, the heavy industries on which the prosperity of Scotland and Wales had been built since the 1760s began to fail. Because the economic benefits of Union were always central to its success and because the UK's largest nation did not reciprocate the respect of its smaller ones, economic decline came to be seen as the prime example of English misrule.

By 1940, Lord Queensberry's wish that Scotland, Wales and England would become 'one in Hearts and Affections' seemed to have come true. The shared history of the islanders had produced a vast range of British customs, traditions and mores. The four primary stays of Britishness – monarchy, Protestantism, democracy and empire – had survived the upheavals of the first half of the twentieth century relatively intact. The monarchy had been shaken, first by anti-German xenophobia during the First World War and then by the Abdication crisis in 1936, but it had successfully remodelled itself to win back popular support. By changing the family name from Saxe-Coburg-Gotha to Windsor in 1916 and by distancing himself from his Continental dynastic relatives, George V naturalized the institutional linchpin of Britishness. In 1936, Edward VIII's fascist leanings and his openly liberal attitude to sex and marriage led to his swift removal and replacement by George VI, who restored the royal image of homely moral rectitude which their father had promoted during his reign (1911–35). The monarchy also benefited from the rising political tension in Europe, which increased the popular desire for a reassuringly stable figurehead around which the country could unite.

Protestantism was also in fairly good health, despite appearances to the contrary. The process of secularization had begun in Britain around 1900, as it did in most developed countries. Throughout Western societies, religious worship declined as rising standards of living and increasing leisure time, coupled with better access to education and healthcare, made life more enjoyable and the fear of death less acute. Moreover, the militant religious patriotism of the nineteenth century was profoundly discredited by the Churches' unquestioning support of the Great War and to a lesser extent by their refusal to support the General Strike of 1926. Yet the Protestant faith remained a powerful bond between the peoples of Britain. Linda Colley has observed that 'even after the religious power of Protestantism dwindled, its grip on the British imagination remained'.[8] That grip was maintained by the nation's collective memory and by the compact between Church and state. Most other European nations disestablished their churches in the twentieth century. Although the Welsh did so in 1920, the Churches of Scotland and England remained established and played a major part in most state occasions. As a result, British Church leaders still wielded considerable political influence over a wide range of issues.

The mercurial talent of Oswald Mosley dazzled men and women

of all political persuasions. But his British Union of Fascists did not, and democracy survived the Depression. Despite the underlying racism in British society and the tensions caused by mass unemployment, few people shared the fascist sympathies of their deposed King. Nor for that matter did they share the communist sympathies which gripped a large section of the British intelligentsia between the wars. Above all, neither the Welsh nor the Scots were drawn to the nationalist parties that were established in 1925 and 1934 with the aim of winning Home Rule. At most, only 5 per cent of the Scottish and Welsh electorate voted for Plaid Cymru and the SNP. Political divisions still ran from left to right on the island rather than from north to south or west to east. Whatever their core nationality, most Britons turned to a coalition of unionist parties, the National government, to solve the economic crisis of the 1930s. And those who did not – about a quarter of the population – voted for the rump of the Labour Party, which was also heartily committed to the Union.

The Empire remained intact, despite competition from Germany, Japan and the United States and the financial cost of the First World War. In fact, the Treaty of Versailles made it wider still because Britain acquired territories in the Middle East formerly controlled by the defeated Ottomans. Also, Germany's defeat, the loss of its colonial possessions and its subsequent economic collapse temporarily removed one of Britain's main competitors. When Ireland was partitioned in 1920, many people were glad to be rid (as they thought) of the Irish problem; some even believed that a new era of peaceful relations with the island had begun. In *The Foundations of British Patriotism* (1940), Esme Wingfield-Stratford wrote:

> Britain's loss, such as it was, resembled that of a malignant tumour. The degradation of the Parliamentary system by the presence of a disciplined bloc of Irishmen, intent only on wrecking it, was brought to an end, along with the strain and Sisyphean frustration of governing the ungovernable, with all its anti-British repercussions in the Dominions and United States. An Irelandless Britain was in every way a healthier and stronger Britain. And there was at least the chance ... that when the inflamed bitterness of ages had had time to heal, a free Ireland might turn out to be an asset, instead of a liability, to British civilisation.[9]

An Irelandless kingdom did not turn out to be a more united one. The structural foundation of British national identity – the imperial economy – was diseased. Overall, the standard of living in all three mainland British nations rose phenomenally in the twentieth century. But in Scotland and Wales the increase in prosperity was much slower than that in England. It was that disparity which provoked discontent with the Union and led eventually to the erosion of their dual national identities. How did this occur?

From the late nineteenth century onwards, the British economy drifted south and east as it went through a major restructuring. Banks and stock exchanges outside London closed and companies moved their headquarters to the capital. The power of the City grew and the money awash in it began to be invested in new light industries such as electronics instead of the heavy industries like coal-mining on which Scotland, Wales and the north of England had prospered during the first industrial revolution. The economic effect on the north was just as bad, and it fostered a sharper loyalty to the region. But, with the exception of Cornwall, regional identities in England were subsumed within national identity, as they were in Scotland and Wales. Consequently, the political effect of the southern drift on the north was less marked. The reason why the economies of Scotland and Wales were not diversified was as much the fault of their own commercial and financial elites as it was the fault of the English. Like the medieval nobility who accepted money and lands in return for acknowledging the supremacy of the English Crown, so Scottish and Welsh capitalists (many of whom were educated in England's public schools) accepted the quick and easy profits to be had from investing in the south, instead of the riskier option of investing in their homelands.

The Depression made a bad situation worse. Here it is worth comparing the travelogues of two popular English and Scottish writers, written within a year of each other during the 1930s. The first, J. B. Priestley's *English Journey* (1934), found a vibrant nation which, with the exception of the north, was recovering from the Depression. Indeed, it was recovering all too well as far as Priestley was concerned. New affluence was creating, in his view, a passive, trivial people whom he compared unfavourably to the muscular, self-improving industrial society of his Edwardian youth. It was:

> The England of arterial and by-pass roads, of filling stations and factories that look like exhibition buildings, of giant cinemas and dance halls and cafes, bungalows with tiny garages, cocktail bars, Woolworths, motor-coaches, wireless, hiking, factory girls looking like actresses, greyhound racing and dirt-tracks, swimming pools and everything given away with cigarette coupons.[10]

But, for all the triviality Priestley detected, he recognized progress when he saw it. He concluded, 'Care is necessary . . . for you can easily . . . disapprove of it too hastily. It is, of course, essentially democratic. After a social revolution there would, with any luck, be more and not less of it.'[11]

In the course of his *Scottish Journey* (1935), the poet Edwin Muir found an altogether different nation, one dying on its feet with little sign of the regeneration that England was enjoying. Affluent Edinburgh was the exception. But, he observed, Scotland's old capital was now so thoroughly Anglicized that it could no longer be described as 'Scottish in any radical sense'. For the rest, Muir lamented:

> Scotland is losing its industries as it lost a hundred years ago a great deal of its agriculture and most of its indigenous literature. The waste glens of Sutherlandshire and the literary depopulation of Edinburgh and Glasgow were not obvious blows at Scotland's existence, and so they were accepted without serious protest, for the general absorption in industrial progress and money blinded everybody to them. Now Scotland's industry, like its intelligence before it, is gravitating to England, but its population is sitting where it did before, in the company of disused coal-pits and silent shipyards.[12]

It was against this background that the Second World War broke out on 3 September 1939.

The war fostered, defined and powered a new, more democratic Britishness which lasted until the 1980s and, in England, even longer. France, for so long the foreign nation against which the British defined themselves, was replaced by Germany, as the result of two terrible wars against it in the space of thirty years. Moreover, the comforting warmth of Churchillian legends and myths appealed to all classes, sexes and ages, including millions who were not even born during the conflict. Although at the time war against Germany was not welcomed by most Britons, and very nearly resulted in their destruction, it came at a fortunate moment for the United Kingdom. It reminded the British that their similarities were greater than their differences. Nothing unites a people like the threat of invasion from a regime perceived to be utterly inimical to the nation's way of life. And by forcing the state to mobilize every citizen and every square inch of land, the conflict temporarily put the Scottish and Welsh economies back on their feet. Without the Second World War,

Britain would have begun to break up a quarter of a century before it actually did, and we would probably now be witnessing not the beginning of its end but the end itself.

But the war could not halt the decline of Britishness. *Patriots* examines how the growing influence of American, European, black and Asian culture undermined established notions of what it was to be British. This conspired, with the uneven pattern of economic growth in the UK, to force a major re-examination of national identity, the long-term consequences of which are still unclear.

Apart from the decline of Britishness, this book has one other major theme. It examines how the arts and sport replaced religion as the means by which people worshipped an idealized form of their nation. In late Victorian Britain, social reformers worried by class divisions became gripped by the idea that if the lower classes were made to appreciate the sacramental value of art, literature and music, the decline of organized religion might be halted and class warfare averted. The most famous exponent of this belief was the Victorian poet and educationalist Matthew Arnold, who wrote that the 'great men of culture' were those who:

> Have had a passion for diffusing, for making prevail, for carrying from one end of society to the other, the best knowledge, the best ideas of their time; who have laboured to divest knowledge of all that was harsh, uncouth, difficult, abstract, professional, exclusive; to humanise it, to make it efficient outside the clique of the cultivated and the learned, yet still remaining the best knowledge and thought of the time, and a true source, therefore of sweetness and light.[13]

The development of a common culture based on high aesthetic standards became a major concern of Britain's governing elites and it reached a fevered apogee in the mid-twentieth century. *Patriots* therefore examines not only how the British defined themselves but also how the sources of those definitions changed.

Two technical points of explanation. The first relates to nomenclature. What do I mean by a nation and national identity? The most fashionable theory in social science is Benedict Anderson's idea of 'imagined communities'. This is a subtle reworking of the Marxist idea that nationalism is an ideology developed by capitalists to distract the working classes of the world from their revolutionary date with destiny. Anderson argued that nations are the product of sixteenth-century 'print capitalism' – in layman's terms, the beginning of mass communication in vernacular languages with the invention of the printing press.

I depart from this view on two counts. First, there is ample evidence of national consciousness in Europe and elsewhere long before the sixteenth century. Second, I do not believe that countries are artificial constructs. Certainly, I would agree with Ernest Renan's remark that 'getting its history wrong is part of being a nation'.[14] But however ironic and paradoxical the origins of national traditions are, that does not *necessarily* mean they are phoney. Professor Anthony Smith has explained: 'Nations are no more invented than any other kinds of culture, social organisation or ideology. If nationalism is part of the "spirit of the age", it is equally dependent on earlier motifs, visions and ideals.'[15] To which Professor David Cannadine has added:

> Nations may indeed . . . be inventions. But like the wheel, or the internal combustion engine, they are endowed, once invented, with a real, palpable existence, which is not just to be found in the subjective perceptions of their citizens, but is embodied in laws, languages and customs, institutions – and history.[16]

National identity is how people define themselves in accordance with the nation they feel they belong to, whether or not it exists territorially. The term is a post-Freudian version of 'national character', a term invented by the eighteenth-century French philosopher Montesquieu to describe the essential characteristics of a people. It was still commonly used in the period covered by this book, so readers will encounter both terms.

On another point of nomenclature, throughout *Patriots* there are occasions when quoted sources refer to England when Britain is being discussed. This will irritate Scottish and Welsh readers and a good many English ones too. However, because in the past the English regarded their nation and the UK as virtually synonymous, this linguistic conceit is part of the story I am telling. Furthermore, it would be too tedious for the reader to have the distinction noted on every occasion. Where I believe that the source quoted really does mean England and not Britain, I have said so. Also, this book is peppered with quotation. The reason is that the exegesis of national identity lends itself to generalization more than most. Although *Patriots* relates how the British defined themselves by how they actually lived, it is primarily about their perceptions. It is therefore necessary to read precisely what people were saying. For it is only in the tone, fabric and content of the language of national identity that we can begin to understand the reasons for people's patriotism or lack of it.

My second technical point relates to methodology. *Patriots* takes a serious look at the popular culture of Britain. This is not because I think popular culture is *necessarily* of equal value to elite or 'high' culture, though it often is and sometimes it is of far more value. The reason why readers will find as many references to Michael Caine, Tom Jones and Sean Connery in the index as they will to Benjamin Britten, Dylan Thomas and Hugh MacDiarmid is simple. It is impossible to write this or any other history without looking at what the great majority of people were consuming and then trying to assess what they thought about it. How, for example, can anyone hope to understand attitudes to Britain's post-imperial role by poring over ambassadorial dispatches from Washington and Moscow without simultaneously analysing the James Bond films? By popular culture, I do not necessarily mean working- and lower-middle-class culture. I mean that which is popular. Clearly that which is *most* popular usually corresponds to these classes because they make up the vast majority of the population. History without popular culture is not history with a stiff upper lip. It is something much worse. It is history with a cleft palate: incoherent, and quite unable to communicate the full breadth of human experience.

One final word. I have set out to make this book as entertaining as possible. Half a century after A. J. P. Taylor was attacked for writing articles in the popular press, appearing on TV and actually selling books, this approach still horrifies the academic Establishment. Either through genuine disapproval or through mere jealousy, many historians still equate accessibility with poor scholarship. That is not true, and were it so there would be little point to the practice of history. I don't claim to possess all of Taylor's skills and I certainly don't share all his views. But I do share his belief that history, like life, should be entertaining as well as informative and thought-provoking. I leave the reader to judge whether or not I have succeeded.

Our background established, it is time now to begin our journey through the national identity of modern Britain. The story begins in the June sunshine over the fields of Kent in the south of an island threatened with invasion. It was an island whose people were never more certain of who they were and what they were fighting for, nor more united and determined to save it at all costs. The summer of

INTRODUCTION

1940 was one of the warmest on record. Few who watched the dogfights between Spitfire and Messerschmitt or listened to the BBC reporting them realized that it would turn out to be an Indian summer for the United Kingdom.

PART I

WARRIORS

It would be wrong to underestimate the enemy ... The English national character has a flaw of putting tradition above all, retaining for as long as possible what might have been right some decades before. [But] it is possible that in an emergency the British would be capable of letting everything go and becoming surprisingly modern. . . . The British are capable of a complete transformation when thinking that their country [is] in imminent danger, and . . . they are at their most formidable in that situation.

SS General Walter Schellenberg, 1940

The vast majority of the people feel themselves to be a single nation and are conscious of resembling one another more than they resemble foreigners. Patriotism is usually stronger than class hatred ... England is the most class-ridden country under the sun. It is a land of snobbery and privilege ruled largely by the old and silly. But in any calculation one has to take into account its emotional unity, the tendency of nearly all its inhabitants to feel alike and act together in moments of supreme crisis.

George Orwell, 1941

1. All that Britain means

The Second World War prompted a more thorough and far-reaching examination of British national identity than at any time between the formation of Great Britain in 1707 and the start of devolution in 1997. Not since Napoleon's Army of England was camped on the Channel coast in 1803–4 had Britain been so seriously threatened with invasion. Churchill's government knew it had to foster a robust popular sense of Britishness in order to maintain morale. But the need to do so was greater than ever before because the advent of aerial bombardment meant that most of the civilian population would be directly involved in the horror of war for the first time. Fortunately, what also made the war of 1939–45 different was that for the first time the British state had a mass media at its disposal that was capable of reaching the entire population of the kingdom. In Churchill's first broadcast as Prime Minister, on 19 May 1940, he made it plain that Britons were defending not just a piece of rock but an entire way of life. 'After this battle in France abates its force, there will come the battle for our island – for all that Britain is and all that Britain *means* . . . Be ye men of valour.'[1]

What Britain primarily meant to most of its inhabitants and its allies abroad was democracy. Consequently, there was an initial reluctance within the political Establishment to adopt the methods of Goebbels' Reichspropagandaleiter, a reluctance which sometimes led to incompetence but which sprang from a sincere belief that Nazi methods were contrary to the British way of life. Officials were anxious to reassure people of this, and they also saw the propaganda value of doing so. Early in 1940, the writer Harold Nicolson – a governor of the BBC and Parliamentary Secretary to the Ministry of Information (MOI) – told Britons in a radio broadcast that there was a fundamental difference between 'autocratic and liberal propaganda'. The former was 'essentially a smash and grab raid on the emotions' while the latter sought 'gradually to fortify the intelligence of the individual'.[2] Still, the perilous situation Britain was in demanded immediate action.

Not only was the nation faced with total war, it had also changed a great deal since 1918. First, it had become a more fragile constitutional entity. The South of Ireland had gained Dominion status as the Irish Free State in 1922 but still coveted the North; and in 1937 the South's constitution was changed to reflect that fact. The nation now calling itself 'Éire' or 'Ireland' laid formal claim to the North. At the same, the new constitution entrenched the power of the Catholic Church, thus widening the ideological gulf between Éire and the six-county Province it hoped one day to take over. Second, the UK had become a nascent mass democracy. That is to say, not only did all men and women over twenty-one have the right to vote; despite the serious poverty which still existed in the Isles, most of the population was more affluent, healthier, better informed and sceptical about the claims of religious and political leaders. Above all, Britons were more reluctant to fight than they had been when Lord Kitchener's accusatory finger told them YOUR COUNTRY NEEDS YOU.

Although the British later became obsessed with the Second World War, they were not at first enthusiastic about it. Few were pacifists or internationalists, but the shock of the Great War had made their patriotism a more reflective emotion. Determined to avoid another round of mass bloodshed and frankly terrified at the prospect of modern mass warfare, most Britons supported appeasement and deeply regretted that it had failed. On 4 August 1914, cheering crowds took to the streets on hearing the declaration of war. On 3 September 1939, they gathered around radios, listening ruefully to the news. About 2 million people, mostly the better off, fled to relatives and second homes in the country. Conscientious objection was four times higher than it had been during the First World War, with 59,192 people claiming objection, of whom 28,720 were registered.[3] That is not to say Britons shirked from the task ahead. Conscription was introduced on 20 April 1939, but many did not wait for the call-up. By the outbreak of war, 300,000 people had already volunteered for the armed forces and a further 1.5 million for Civil Defence duties. This compares favourably with the 2.5 million who volunteered for service between 1914 and the start of conscription in 1916.

However, and this is the crucial point, the men and women of the Second World War volunteered with little of the fervour that accompanied their predecessors' rush to the colours a quarter of a century earlier. In March 1940 Bishop Hensley Henson lamented:

The prevailing temper of our troops is a half cynical boredom, as remote as possible from the high crusading fervour which their situation authorizes and requires . . . Religion makes little appeal, and patriotism no appeal at all. They have neither the enthusiasm of youth, nor the deliberate purpose of age, but just acquiescence in an absurd and unwelcome necessity.[4]

As a result, few in Whitehall believed that either a German 'smash and grab raid on the emotions' or the jingoistic exhortations of the First World War would suffice to explain 'what Britain means'. It was clear the government needed a tough but imaginative strategy to promote national culture, a strategy that would embed in the British consciousness the common heritage which people were once again being asked to defend but one that also took account of Britain's transformation in the first half of the twentieth century and the despondency with which the outbreak of war was greeted. What resulted was the biggest informational exercise ever undertaken by the British state.

During the Phoney War, in December 1939, Josef Goebbels noted in his diary: 'The Führer is fully determined to go for England's throat. I tell him a few anecdotes about characters in the English Information Ministry. He laughs until the tears flow. These gentlemen are totally inferior to us. As they will soon learn.'[5] Not everyone in the German High Command was so cocksure. After several attempts to parley with the British government, in June 1940 Hitler accepted that they would not make peace and plans for an invasion got under way. SS General Walter Schellenberg was ordered to write a handbook on Britain to assist 'the invading troops and the political and administrative units accompanying them'.[6] A lawyer by training, Schellenberg was a committed Nazi. He had been a protégé of Himmler's since the 1930s and had risen rapidly through the ranks of the Gestapo, coming to know Hitler fairly well. He did not share the Führer's romantic admiration for the British. And, like many senior officers, he was dismayed at Hitler's obvious reluctance to 'go for England's throat'. Nonetheless, Schellenberg sounded a note of caution in his advice to German invasion forces:

It would be wrong to underestimate the enemy . . . The English national character has a flaw of putting tradition above all, retaining for as long as possible what might have been right some decades before. [But] it is possible that in an emergency the British would be capable of letting everything go and becoming surprisingly modern. . . . The British are capable of a complete transformation when thinking that their country [is] in imminent danger, and . . . they are at their most formidable in that situation.[7]

How right he was. Churchill's War Cabinet was so determined to defend democracy that on 16 June 1940 it approved the merger of the British and French nations.

The Proclamation of Franco-British Union created a single government with complete power to decide the domestic and foreign policies of both countries and common citizenship for both peoples. This extraordinary plan was an attempt to keep France in the war by making it harder for its leaders to conclude a separate peace with Germany and to reassure those who wanted to fight that Britain would not flinch in her support. The plan was mooted by the French Economic Mission to Britain led by Jean Monnet, the future architect of the European Union. It was supported by the young Military Attaché Charles de Gaulle, who twenty years later, as President of France, vetoed Britain's first attempt to join the EEC. Churchill told the Cabinet 'in this grave crisis we must not let ourselves be accused of a lack of imagination', but he emphasized that it was merely an emergency measure. De Gaulle, a staunch nationalist, agreed.[8] Had the British people been told about the Union, they would have accepted it only on a temporary basis because, however much they saw the need to rescue the Continent from fascism, they did not consider themselves to be European. Only Monnet regarded it as a blueprint for a European Union which must necessarily involve Britain.

The Proclamation was drafted in a frantic but elated session at 10 Downing Street. No comparable claim to sovereignty had been made by either country since the dynastic disputes of the medieval British and French monarchies. Amused by the proceedings, Churchill's Private Secretary, Jock Colville, observed that 400 years of history were being reversed without the King's knowledge. 'The King does not know what is being done to his Empire. The Lord President is going to see him and will break the news. We may yet see the Fleur De Lys restored to the royal Standard'.[9] Churchill obtained the King's approval and that of the Labour and Liberal Party leaders, Clement Attlee and Archibald Sinclair.

The Prime Minister was then driven to Waterloo Station with Attlee and Sinclair beside him. At 9.30 p.m. the three men secretly boarded a special train for France. They were bound for Bordeaux, where Paul Reynaud's government had fled the advancing German army. Once in France, Britain's leaders hoped to persuade their allies to accept the Proclamation and fight on. But as Churchill and his colleagues sat in silence, anxiously waiting for the train to move, a Downing Street official ran up the platform and through the window of the carriage handed Churchill a message from the British Ambassador in Bordeaux. It said that Reynaud had cancelled the meeting due to a 'ministerial crisis'. Churchill knew immediately that this meant the belligerents in the French government were being deposed. He got out of the train and returned to Downing Street with, he said, 'a heavy heart'.[10] There, a few hours later, news came through that General Pétain had formed a government and had asked the Germans for an armistice. Britain was on its own.

The departure of Britain's leaders from the platform at Waterloo that June night marked the end of any direct political involvement in Europe for twenty years. It also marked the start of the patriotic legend of the Finest Hour, according to which the British – standing alone and defiant on their island home – saved the world from tyranny. The phrase was coined by Churchill in a speech broadcast to the nation on the evening of 18 June 1940, twenty-four hours after the fall of France:

> I expect that the Battle of Britain is about to begin. Upon this battle depends the survival of Christian civilisation. Upon it depends our own British life, and the long continuity of our institutions and our Empire . . . Let us therefore brace ourselves to our duties and so bear ourselves that, if the British Empire and its Commonwealth last for a thousand years, men will still say, 'This was their finest hour.'[11]

The Finest Hour dominated the popular idea of Britishness for nearly half a century after people switched off their radios that night. It formed the basis of a new post-imperial identity, one that was more inclusive of Britain's diverse citizenry. But it also fostered a more insular attitude to the world, reinforcing ancient prejudices about the Continent and undermining attempts to develop a European community. How exactly was the legend constructed and why did it take such a hold on the British imagination?

2. Christians who happened to be British

For the first time in the nation's history, the Protestant religion did not play a major role in sending Britons into battle. The Church historian John Wolffe has observed that by the early twentieth century Protestant patriotism made claims on the individual 'which led it to the threshold of a nationalism that equated the cause of Britain with the cause of God'.[12] By the Second World War, that was no longer the case. Throughout the West, religious faith had begun to decline in the 1900s. In Britain, it accelerated after the First World War thanks to disillusionment with muscular Christianity and anger at the Churches' uncritical enthusiasm for the war. The Churches' response during the 1930s was an equally uncritical enthusiasm for appeasement and a gradual shift in their whole approach to war. Increasingly, the island's theologians justified war as a terrible trial to be endured for a greater good rather than a thrilling opportunity to make a blood sacrifice for God and Great Britain.

Consequently, when Britain's leaders discussed religion between 1940 and 1945 they rarely spoke about a struggle for the national faith, but referred instead to a generic struggle for 'Christian civilization' in which all Europeans were involved. Churchill used the term, not least during the speech in which he heralded the Battle of Britain. In 1940, George VI personally approved the holding of a multi-denominational National Day of Prayer on 26 May which involved Catholic and Jewish leaders as well as those from the Protestant Churches. The event was used to put clear blue sky between God and the Union Jack. The Archbishop of York, William Temple, led prayers on the BBC and afterwards made the following statement: 'When we turned to prayer it could not be as Britons who happened to be Christians; it must be as Christians who happened to be British. Otherwise we fall into the error of our enemies, whose distinctive sin it was that they put their nationality first.'[13] Thus shorn of jingoism, Christianity remained central to the definition of war aims. Indeed, there were widespread calls (in the press as well as the pulpit) for Britons to recover their faith so that they could better defend their national values.

These calls met with some success. Although Christianity inspired few Britons to join the battle, it did sustain many when they got there. In February 1942 Churchill appointed Temple Archbishop of Canterbury, telling him, 'Few in the long succession since St Augustine can have received the summons to Canterbury at a time when the burden of the Primacy was heavier'.[14] Together with his associates in the Churches of Scotland and Wales, Temple presided over a brief religious revival as millions turned to God in order to cope with the anxiety, terror and grief caused by military conflict. BBC religious broadcasts trebled during the war and many churches staged extra services to meet popular demand. They gave material as well as spiritual assistance. During the Blitz, the clergy increased their presence in Britons' daily lives (particularly in urban areas where it was weakest) by providing food, shelter and entertainment to bomb victims. In 1942, the Commander-in-Chief of the Home Fleet wrote to the Archbishop of Canterbury stating his 'firm conviction that throughout the Service and on shore there is a deeper religious feeling and a longing to live a more Christian life than ever before in my lifetime.'[15]

People who did not experience that longing still valued the Church as an important aspect of their nationhood. The most famous poem of the war – T. S. Eliot's *Little Gidding* – placed the idea of England the eternal nation in an Anglican chapel: 'So, while the light fails / On a winter's afternoon, in a secluded chapel / History is now and England'. Church bells were silenced during the war, to be rung only in the event of an invasion. When they did ring again in 1945, by all accounts Britons found it the most moving symbol of their triumph. During the war, *the* symbol of British resistance to Hitler was the survival of St Paul's Cathedral during the Blitz. Churchill knew how important the 'parish church of the Empire' was for morale and sent a message to the Lord Mayor of London on the night of 29 December 1940 ordering it to be saved at all costs. The Dean, W. R. Matthews, supervised a team of aged helpers on the cathedral roof using only stirrup pumps and pails of water to extinguish the fires started by the hundreds of incendiary bombs that fell upon it. 'St Paul's belongs to the people and they know within themselves that somehow it binds them to God,' wrote Matthews. Like many, he concluded that its survival was a miracle.[16] *The Times* later declared:

It was at all times a living spiritual centre in the life of the City, of the nation, and, indeed, of the entire free world. There were long

months when the way in which the dome of St Paul's emerged
from the smoke and darkness after each successive raid, apparently
indestructible however great the devastation around it, seemed like
a miracle.[17]

The celebration of such escapes as acts of Providence was a direct
echo of pre-twentieth-century Britishness. The rescue of the British
Expeditionary Force from Dunkirk was seen as the greatest deliverance of all, and it gave rise to a new phrase in the English lexicon,
'the Dunkirk Spirit', which denoted British pluck and a determination
to win despite the odds. The reaction to Dunkirk demonstrated that
the idea of Britain as a righteous nation under God's special protection still influenced the national imagination long after church pews
had begun to empty.

Certainly, the British were left in no doubt that they were fighting
evil. For example, the creator of *Winnie the Pooh*, A. A. Milne,
argued in his book *War Aims Unlimited*, 'In fighting Hitler we are
truly fighting the Devil, Anti-Christ, the negation of every spiritual
value which separates mankind from the rest of creation.' It was
Britain's duty, he said 'to bring salvation to the rest of humanity'.[18]
Jock Colville compared the subterranean existence that blitzed Britons were enduring in the shelters to that of the early Christians: 'I
begin to understand', he wrote, 'what the early Christians must have
felt about living in the Catacombs.'[19] Most people supported the
RAF's carpet bombing of German cities such as Cologne. They
warmed to the biblical spirit of vengeance expressed by Air Chief
Marshal Sir Arthur 'Bomber' Harris when he remarked that the
Germans had sown the wind and would 'reap the whirlwind'. When
the Bishop of Chichester, George Bell, condemned carpet bombing
as immoral in 1943 he was heavily criticized. Few people still thought
God was actually British but most believed him to be firmly on
Britain's side. Consequently, the inhabitants of the United Kingdom
expected their religious leaders to bless their struggle and chafed
when they did not.

Furthermore, despite all the lofty rhetoric about the unity of
Christian civilization, many Britons were conscious that they were
leading its defence *as Protestants*. Arthur Mee's *Nineteen-Forty: Our
Finest Hour* was the first book to translate Churchill's phrase into an
extended treatise on the national character. Its publication in 1941
marks the formal point at which a moment in history began to
crystallize into a British legend. Mee was born near Nottingham in

1875 to a family of devout Baptists and Liberal voters, and he inherited their belief that the English were a people chosen by God to better the world. His multi-volume guidebook to the English counties, *The King's England*, was one of the most popular works of the era. *Nineteen-Forty* was roundly praised in the national press and it too became an instant best-seller. Advertised as 'A Book To Lift Up the Heart', it was infused with the romantic Protestant patriotism which had helped to make Mee famous before the war:

> Nineteen-forty will probably be remembered in all history as our finest hour. We suffered incredible disasters . . . We took upon ourselves overwhelming burdens . . . But we carried on. Guided by the Hand of God and sustained by our own right arm, we came through the shadows of defeat into the sunlight of a nobler dawn . . . Never has the English spirit knit our people so closely into one, never has it stirred the heart and captured the imagination of the world as now. A thousand years have cemented us more firmly to the Island, and set us invincible on the rock of human freedom . . . We fight to drive back from our Island the paganism overthrown twelve hundred years ago by King Oswy in the last English battle for Christianity . . . We fight to save Europe from the foul spectacle of virtue dethroned and Hitler set up as the god of vice; and for ourselves we fight to save from destruction all that is noblest in our way of life. It is our abounding glory that it has fallen to us to save it. We who live through 1941, consecrating our souls to God and His purposes, pledging our lives to our country and its needs, will see the turning of the tide and know that for our children and our children's children the world will be a free and decent place again.[20]

Anti-Catholic prejudice did not form a significant part of wartime Britishness. Government relations with the Vatican and with Britain's Catholic hierarchy were polite and the Axis powers were never overtly cast as a Catholic enemy. Nonetheless, key public positions from the monarchy downwards were still regarded as out of bounds for Catholics. If anything, that view became more prevalent in wartime because of the perceived need to be vigilant about any deviance from the national norm. When Sir John Reith retired as Director-General of the BBC in 1938, Cecil Graves was vetoed as his successor because, said the Governors, 'it would be quite impossible that the supreme executive control of one of the most important organs of public education in this country should be placed in Roman Catholic hands.'[21] The man chosen instead was F. W. Ogilvie, a former Oxford don who proved incapable of running a large corporation and had to be removed in 1942. But as a high-minded Presbyterian Scot he was in the same ideological mould as Reith and that counted for much.

Furthermore, wartime ecumenicism was severely strained by widespread awareness that the Continental Catholic Church had close links with fascist movements and actively participated in maintaining totalitarian regimes. In 1943, Temple expressed his reservations in a letter to an army chaplain:

> An authoritarian organisation of religion is always bound to find itself lined up on the whole with authoritarian politics. I think the Church of Rome will always stand in its support of democracy in politics for emphasis on the rightful power of the majority, without which there is no democracy, but will make very little of the moral rights of the minority, without which democracy cannot be wholesome. Their whole attitude to freedom of thought is, to my mind, quite unsatisfactory ... the Roman Catholics treat grown-up people permanently as children and that is inevitably a frame of mind which inevitably overflows into politics ... I believe that all the doctrinal errors of Rome come from the direct identification of the Church as an organised Institution with the Kingdom of God.[22]

Temple's view of Catholicism was not altered by Pope Pius XII's shameful collusion in the Holocaust, nor by the support he got from the British Catholic hierarchy (until the end of the war, their view was that the Jews could save themselves if they converted to Christianity). In the absence of moral leadership from the Vatican, Temple became the first Church leader in the world to publicly condemn the Final Solution. In a speech to the House of Lords on 23 March 1943 he said, 'We stand at the bar of history, of humanity and of God'. His incessant pleas for government action sprang from a long tradition of British Protestant empathy with the Jews which stretched back to the seventeenth century. This was partly based on a belief that the British were God's chosen people, latter-day Israelites who had a duty to protect the original chosen people. But Temple's outlook was no less sincere for being a product of British nationalism, and Jewish leaders appreciated his support.[23]

Temple could not, of course, prevent the Final Solution. But his equally vocal support for social reform in Britain did meet with some success. *Christianity and Social Order* (1942) – which he wrote with the assistance of John Maynard Keynes – endorsed the idea of a welfare state, became a bestseller and earned him the sobriquet 'the People's Archbishop'. The book not only contributed towards the demand for a just postwar settlement. It also improved the status and popularity of the Church of England, decisively shaking off its reputation as the Tory Party at prayer and giving real substance to the historic claim that Anglicanism was the national faith. Temple dreamed of creating a single British Protestant Church. Although he failed to do so, his high personal standing with other Protestant leaders in the UK resulted in the Churches being more united during the Second World War than they had ever been. When Temple died prematurely of a heart attack in October 1944, the grief expressed by prelates and the public was profound and unprecedented.

However, these important qualifications do not alter the fact that British Protestantism was in decline. Despite the wartime anxiety which led people to begin or renew a relationship with God and despite the Churches' successful attempt to shed their jingoistic past, the number of regular communicants continued to fall from 1940 to 1945. The rate of decline was slower than before but relentless nonetheless, and in 1945 a Committee on Evangelism appointed by Temple concluded:

> Seen from a distance, Britain is the country which seems most nearly to approach the ideal of a Christian community. The ceremony of the Coronation, the regular openings of the sittings of Parliament with prayer . . . the provision for religion in the services and in all State institutions, the religious articles in popular periodicals, the Religious Department of the British Broadcasting Corporation, and many similar phenomena, go to show that . . . the English are still more deeply influenced by Christianity than they themselves know . . . But behind the façade the situation presents a more ominous appearance . . . There is a wide and deep gulf between church and people.[24]

All of which rendered any sustained appeal to Christianity, still less Protestantism, much less potent than it had been in previous conflicts. It is against this background that wartime propaganda should be viewed. Religion could no longer mobilize the British as it had once done and the nation's leaders needed to find a substitute. They found it in the idea of national culture.

Who and what embodied that culture? The monarchy remained central to the popular idea of Britain. Indeed, the Second World War restored the Windsors' reputation after the damage done to it by the

Abdication crisis. By appointing the Duke of Windsor Governor of the Bahamas, Churchill removed the volatile ex-King to a safe distance from the UK, giving George VI and Queen Elizabeth the opportunity to establish themselves as national figureheads. First, they were able to erase memories of their keen support for appeasement (they had appeared on the balcony of Buckingham Palace with Chamberlain on the night he returned from Munich to announce 'Peace in our time'). Unlike the Duke of Windsor they did not admire Hitler, but they had not wanted Britain to go to war with Germany partly because, like him, they regarded the Nazi regime as a bulwark against communism. Second, the war also enabled the Royal Family to shake off what remained of their German associations and become more visibly British than ever before.

How was this achieved? As well as carrying out their wartime duties conscientiously, the royal family paraded an equality of sacrifice with their subjects. In doing so they reprised the concept of monarchy as an idealized version of Everyman which George V had perfected earlier in the century. The most famous example of this took place on the morning of 13 September 1940, when the Ministry of Information sent forty journalists to cover the bombing of Buckingham Palace on the theme 'The King with his people in the front line'. Treading gingerly through the rubble with her husband, the Queen remarked 'We can now look the East End in the face', a comment which came to represent the bond between Crown and people in the British mind for decades after. In 1941, Churchill wrote to the King:

> This war has drawn the Throne & the people more closely together than was ever before recorded, & Yr Majesties are more beloved by classes & conditions than any of all the princes of the past.[25]

Away from the cameras, the King and Queen relied on the black market to maintain their living standards. Smarting from wartime lavatory paper, George VI asked the British Ambassador to the US, Lord Halifax, to send some soft Bronco paper which, sighed the King, 'is unprocurable here'.[26] Here too, in a sense, the Windsors shared the experience of their subjects, even though the spivs they used were found in embassies rather than on street-corners. In 1945 an official survey, *The Royal Family in Wartime*, concluded:

> We have come to think of the King as the supremely representative man, the most English Englishman, the most British member of the British Empire. We expect him to set an example of living in the

English manner, to live the normal English life at its best . . . And since the fullest natural life of an Englishman is a home life, with his wife at his side . . . there is an indispensable part for the Queen and her children to play in fulfilling the royal task of representative living.[27]

But loved though he was as 'the most English Englishman', the shy, stuttering George VI was no warrior king. It was Churchill who assumed that role.

To a great extent, Winston Churchill *was* Britishness during the Second World War. The personality cult which developed around him underpinned the legend of the Finest Hour, matching that enjoyed by Stalin and Mao in less democratic circumstances. While Neville Chamberlain never shed the image of a kindly provincial undertaker, Churchill was every inch a national leader. His bullish features and defiant rhetoric came to symbolize resistance to Nazi Germany throughout the world. He had a strong, if paternalistic, love for the British people which often brought him to tears and he had a cheeky, irreverent wit, which the British count as an essential part of their national character. His ability to communicate with ordinary people without talking down to them was most apparent in his radio broadcasts, which were religiously listened to by seven out of ten Britons. The speeches he made contained a sweeping knowledge of the island's history framed by a romantic patriotism. From 1940 to 1945, he took the British on a series of express rides around their national identity, crystallizing and embellishing it as the scenery of 1,000 years flashed past. When they alighted at the other end, he gave the impression that he was personally embracing every one of them.

Having heard Churchill, it was difficult not to feel part of a great nation on an heroic enterprise that would inevitably end in victory. In surveys conducted between 1940 and 1945, never less than 78 per cent of the population supported him as Prime Minister. Seven months before he entered 10 Downing Street, in October 1939, Mass Observation (a pioneering body established in the 1930s to monitor public opinion) recorded this conversation between two men in Bolton.

1ST MAN: Ah bet tha heard Churchill.
2ND MAN: Aye – I did.
1ST MAN: He doesn't half give it to them. I corn't go to sleep when he's on. He's the best talker we have.[28]

It was said by the American journalist Ed Murrow that Churchill 'mobilized the English language and sent it into battle'.[29] If so, the BBC was the tank corps which took it there.

The Corporation smashed its way into the nation's consciousness with talks, concerts, features and comedy programmes that were expressly designed to elucidate Britishness. The total cost of the BBC's wartime output was £50 million, less than the cost of one week's fighting. This represented, according to one observer, the 'government's most effective investment in the hostilities'.[30] Since its foundation in 1922 by the Scotsman Sir John Reith, the BBC had done more to foster British national identity than any other institution. It not only brought people closer together from Inverness to the Isle of Wight through a shared experience around the wireless. Under Reith's stern regime it broadcast a mixture of high- and lowbrow programmes that sought to bring the classes together in a common culture, with the ultimate aim of raising popular taste.

At first, news dominated the schedules. An MOI survey in 1940 noted with concern that only 0.4 per cent of the corporation's output dealt with the arts and that 'positive talks are confined to military rather than cultural strength . . . culture is spoken of in general terms . . . rarely is something told of British achievements'.[31] This was rectified by broadcasting executives as the war got under way, their minds concentrated by Churchill's threat to take over the BBC if it did not mentally mobilize the population. Peter Ritchie-Calder, a Scottish journalist, was appointed the corporation's first Director of Campaigns. One of the biggest he and his team launched was 'The Projection of Britain'. The document's authors, who included the historian Alan Bullock, defined the national character in what might be called the Holy Trinity of Britishness: first, a love of tradition and order; second, a belief in tolerance and fair play; and third, that redoubtable bulwark against tyranny, a sense of humour.

'The Projection of Britain' concluded: 'in British intellectual achievements we can find an almost inexhaustible supply of palatable and nourishing food'.[32] Unlike First World War propaganda, that of the Second did not equate German culture with the regime against which Britain was at war. For example, in Humphrey Jennings' documentary Heart of Britain (1941) the Hallé Orchestra plays Beethoven's Fifth to a packed Free Trade Hall while the narrator says 'in Manchester today, they still respect the genius of Germany'. But such tributes were little more than a device to emphasize the nation's open-minded character.[33] The genius of Britain was always in the foreground. Music was thought especially important. A British renaissance which had begun in the 1860s, and which produced Edward Elgar, the Royal College of Music (1894) and the Proms (1895), had been driven by a desire to challenge German supremacy in the musical field. During the 1930s, the BBC had played its part by broadcasting the Proms and commissioning work from young British composers. That role was seen as paramount during the war and in 1942 BBC executives issued the following ruling:

> Music is an international 'language', which through the medium of broadcasting is heard and understood all over the world . . . [But] in spite of this recognition of the international factor, the BBC regards it as a matter of first importance to develop a strong sense of pride in British music in order to exorcise the long-standing national sense of inferiority . . . and rid music of its status as a foreign art.[34]

During the 1940s, a third of the classical repertoire broadcast to the UK was British, an estimated rise of 20 per cent on the prewar level.

Despite America's growing influence, British popular music was still dominated by native writers and performers, and during the war it became more overtly patriotic. The star of the show was a plumber's daughter from the East End of London, Vera Lynn. In 1941, BBC Governors passed the following judgement on her radio show: '*Sincerely Yours* deplored, but popularity noted.'[35] Just as well, because more than any other figure apart from Churchill she came to personify the British at war. Her success was attributed to her homely sincerity which turned sentimental numbers like 'White Cliffs of Dover' into 'precious old folk songs', a view she herself endorsed.[36]

Important though music was, literature and the spoken word dominated the BBC schedules. Approximately 80,000 words a day were directed at the British people during the war. There was a specific reason for this. Since the late sixteenth century, literature was the art form at which they had excelled, and though Protestant dislike of 'graven images' was a thing of the past, the idea of the British as a people of the Word was still a powerful one when it came to assessing their achievements. Indeed, the Reformation was often referred to as the foundation of British culture and the writers of the sixteenth and seventeenth centuries as its finest exponents. In a letter to his brother, Clement Attlee described his favourite wartime reading thus: 'Milton and the more sonorous Elizabethans seem to match the hour'.[37] To mark the tercentenary of Milton's essay on the freedom of speech, *Areopagitica*, the BBC asked E. M. Forster to give a talk which emphasized that 'British patriotism isn't based on the idea of the soil like French patriotism or on race, like the German kind.' The novelist responded by telling listeners that he was proud 'of the variety of opinion incidental to our democracy [which] exalts our national character'.[38] The religious origins of British literary culture were apparent in a speech delivered by the Archbishop of Canterbury at the Caxton Hall, Westminster, in 1943. Addressing the first meeting of the National Book Council (a charity set up to distribute books among the population), Temple said: 'When you come to the higher range of beauty in literature, you are always on the edge of religion [and British literature is a] store of inspiration to patriotism and courage.'[39]

Back at Bush House, the Director of European Broadcasts sounded a note of caution about 'The Projection of Britain'. He warned that when broadcasting to the Continent it was important to stress 'the virtues of the European heritage [because] any arrogance behind the helping hand of . . . British liberalism [might] seem worse than the jackboot'.[40] His colleagues took note. But this reservation did not apply to the BBC's domestic audience. The Director-General was adamant that 'We are as a nation too modest about our achievements.'[41] Britons were thought capable of digesting an endless diet of programmes about their way of life – and so it proved. The BBC's popularity soared. One million additional licences were sold between 1939 and 1945 and the readership of *The Listener* rose from 49,692 to 131,425. Through a combination of relatively truthful news reporting and a more sophisticated promotion of Britishness than hitherto, the corporation came to be seen as an emblem of democracy, the epitome as well as the conduit of what the nation was fighting for. Novelist Antonia White's conclusion in the pamphlet *BBC at War* was an accurate one: 'Before the war, most people thought of the BBC as an aloof and impenetrable organization . . . [Now] it is an integral part of their lives'.[42]

The film industry complemented the work of the BBC, producing hundreds of features, shorts and documentaries which celebrated the British character and way of life. Cinema attendance in the UK reached a peak in the mid-1940s, with 30 million people going every week out of a population of 49 million. Most films shown on British screens were still made in Hollywood (the most popular of the period was *Gone With The Wind*), but thanks to government support the

British film industry was in excellent health and it found a ready audience for high-quality patriotic productions. The Ministry of Information advised film-makers to display 'our independence, toughness of fibre [and] sympathy with the underdog'.[43] Film-makers obliged. But they also made a point of showing the social classes working together as equals. The film historian Jeffrey Richards has noted that there was a 'significant change in the national image as projected by film'. Heroic individualism gave way to 'the people as hero, learning tolerance of each other and building cooperation, comradeship and community through it.'[44]

Three films that were universally liked by officials, critics and audiences were Carol Reed's *The Way Ahead* (1944), about a group of army conscripts; Anthony Asquith's *The Way to the Stars* (1945), set on an RAF base; and David Lean's *In Which We Serve* (1942), which dramatized the naval exploits of Lord Mountbatten and the crew of his ship, HMS *Kelly*. The latter was scripted by Noël Coward, a friend of Mountbatten and an ardent patriot who believed the war had brought out the best in his fellow countrymen. 'Would not have missed this experience for anything', he wrote in 1941, 'It certainly is a pretty exciting thing to be English'.[45] Despite government reservations that his 'dressing gown and cigarette holder' image would not inspire the muscular patriotism necessary to win the war, his work did much to define Britishness in this period. Reviewing *In Which We Serve*, the *Observer*'s Dilys Powell wrote that he 'took a handful of typically British men and women and made from their stories . . . a distillation of national character'.[46] It not only tapped into the nation's seafaring tradition. The understated heroism of each man, from Captain Kinross (Coward) to Ordinary Seaman Shorty Blake (John Mills), and their stiff upper-lipped comradeship, set the tone and style of the genre for the 1950s and 60s, making it the quintessential British war film.

3. Art for the people

If the BBC and the film industry were the tank corps in the promotion of British national identity, the Council for the Encouragement of Music and the Arts (CEMA) formed a colourful cavalry charge. One result of the new approach to propaganda was that the British government overcame a century of opposition to state patronage of the arts. What had once seemed to be a waste of taxpayers' money on minority pursuits now seemed an ideal way to foster a more refined Britishness. CEMA was established in December 1939 by the President of the Board of Education, Lord De La Warr. Christened Herbrand Edward Dundonald Brassey Sackville, and known to his friends as 'Buck', he was a left-leaning Tory grandee who had been a conscientious objector during the First World War before embarking on a long ministerial career which began in the 1924 Labour government and ended in the Conservative one of 1955. De La Warr's lifelong concern was to improve the leisure opportunities of Britain's working classes, a mission he pursued with less condescension than most social reformers of his background. CEMA was designed to complement the work that ENSA (the Entertainments National Service Association) already did in the field of popular entertainment; and, like ENSA, its purpose was to augment the work of the BBC by staging live concerts, plays, talks and exhibitions, many of them new works by British artists commissioned especially for the occasion.

The organization took off in February 1940 when Sir John Reith became Minister of Information. As founder of the BBC, he was no stranger to the politics of national identity. His vision was summed up in a comment he made to the Chairman of the British Council, Lord Lloyd, who still had gentlemanly reservations about dirtying his hands with propaganda: 'It is impossible to say', Reith told him, 'where cultural activity ends and propaganda begins.'[47] In that spirit, he wrote to the Treasury in March 1940 requesting a permanent grant for CEMA. Reith bluntly argued that total war required a total identity:

> We are engaged in a war to defend civilisation. Such a policy can only have meaning if the people behind it believe intensely in the value and reality of their own cultural roots. It might be possible to make the country aware that its traditions are indeed bound up with conceptions of democracy, tolerance and kindliness. These things have little meaning in the abstract but are actual and concrete when expressed through national literature, music and painting; and such consciousness might become the spearhead of national effort, both as a weapon of war and as a means of implementing a constructive peace.[48]

The Chancellor of the Exchequer needed no further persuading, and Treasury policy towards the arts was overturned with an initial grant

of £50,000. The *Listener*'s judgement was that 'in this curious war
. . . the arts have been added to the crafts of policy in the creation of
prestige, or, if we must use that much-abused word, propaganda'.[49]
It was more significant than that. The decision marked a revolutionary acceptance by Britain's political elites that the state had a duty to
foster national culture.

The first meeting of the CEMA executive took place on St George's
Day 1940. It included three figures who would be among a dozen or
so to dominate cultural policy in postwar Britain, a Welshman and
two Scots: W. E. Williams, Director of the Institute of Adult Education and one of the founders of Penguin Books; Sir Kenneth Clark,
Director of the National Gallery; and the Earl of Crawford and
Balcarres, soon to become Chairman of the National Trust. The
Daily Express was outraged, asking, 'What madness is this? There is
no such thing as culture in wartime?'[50] But the rest of the press was
supportive, thanks partly to Clark's connections. He was a friend of
Chamberlain, an especially close one of the Queen, and he was on
good terms with Ogilvie of the BBC, having been tutored by him at
Oxford in the 1920s. Chamberlain warmly approved the project.
Churchill was indifferent to it and in addition detested Reith, whom
he thought vain, pompous and sanctimonious (the feeling was
mutual). He sacked the great Scot in May 1940, moving him to less
sensitive ministries before getting rid of him altogether in 1942. But
CEMA had got the kick-start that it needed.

From 1940 to 1945, the Council organized thousands of events
across Britain in factory canteens, army camps and air-raid shelters,
as well as more traditional venues for the arts. The Welsh composer
Sir Walford Davies, who had succeeded Elgar as Master of the King's
Musick in 1934, was appointed the organization's Director of Music.
On his initiative, the first CEMA concert, with a programme of
Purcell and Elgar, took place in a Midlands works canteen on 22
February 1940. Ernest Bevin was enthusiastic about the scheme and
his Ministry of Labour helped to run it. The Principal of RADA, Sir
Kenneth Barnes, became the Council's Director of Drama. Barnes
persuaded the Old Vic to alter a constitution which forbade it to
leave the Waterloo Road and the company began the first of many
national tours in the autumn of 1940. Looking back, the actor
Bernard Miles wrote: 'for the first time in history the State recognised
the drama as one of the sinews of the national soul, and this was the
most important thing that had happened to the British theatre since
the birth of Shakespeare'.[51]

The most lasting achievement was Kenneth Clark's. CEMA's Director of Art revived the War Artists' Advisory Committee (WAAC) and commissioned 325 artists to record Britain at war. By 1945 they had produced almost 6,000 paintings, drawings, prints and sculptures. Clark used the scheme to promote the distinctively British 'Neo-Romantic' school led by John Piper, Graham Sutherland and Henry Moore. Rejecting the full force of twentieth-century European modernism, Neo-Romantic artists re-engaged with British landscape painting of the eighteenth and nineteenth centuries. 'As a race', wrote Piper, 'we have always been conscious of the changeable climate of our sea-washed country . . . This atmosphere has sunk into our souls. It has affected our art as it affects our life'.[52] The results of Clark's patronage were hailed as a victory for national culture. In the *New Statesman*, Raymond Mortimer wrote: 'In this country never before [has there been] such an interest in painting . . . Crowds flock to good contemporary shows because French pictures have fled, giving at last a fair chance to native artists'.[53]

Before the war, Clark's deputy, W. E. Williams, had pioneered an adult education scheme called 'Art for the People', and this was revived to take works around the country. Among the places 'Art for the People' showed was the pie-and-mash ambience of British Restaurants, which were established in 1940 to provide cheap, traditional British food for civilians and troops on the Home Front. The *Daily Herald* testified to the subtle power of CEMA's work: 'Not one artist', it declared, 'waves a flag or makes a boast, yet you come away refreshed and reassured, confident in the future of the British race'.[54] By 1942, 500,000 people annually were visiting the Council's art exhibitions, and 10,000 in one week saw an exhibition of British landscape art in Bristol. Even at full stretch, the Council only reached approximately 1 per cent of the population at any one time, but with the BBC covering many of its events, CEMA became an important subsidiary of the propaganda effort.

Mention should also be made of wartime concern for the natural and built environment. The destruction wrought by the Blitz and the threat of invasion highlighted public concern for Britain's heritage. A consensus emerged that the state had a duty to protect it from unscrupulous developers as much as from Hitler's bombs. The 1944 Town and Country Planning Act and its more stringent 1947 successor were designed to regulate new building developments. They were augmented by the National Buildings Record, a project founded in February 1941 by the architectural critic Sir John Summerson and luminaries of the Royal Institute of British Architects. The NBR established for the first time a detailed record of Britain's most splendid buildings, in particular those which required state protection, and it formed the basis of the listing system developed after the war.[55] Kenneth Clark was heavily involved in the NBR and in a related project, 'Recording Britain'. Established in 1939 with royal approval, Recording Britain was intended as 'a pictorial Domesday' of Britain from Norman times to the present. Clark commissioned artists from the WAAC to travel the country painting and drawing Britain's architectural heritage and by 1942, 727 had been executed and purchased. Exhibitions of the work toured the UK to remind Britons once again what they were defending.[56]

4. Patriotism and intelligence

If a total war required a total identity, it also needed the nation's best creative minds to implement it. This posed a serious problem, because the British distrusted intellectuals, a tendency encouraged by theorists of national character since the eighteenth century. The British, they argued, were a practical, straightforward people for whom the Continental predilection for systematic theorizing about society was partly responsible for the extremism which had started the war in the first place. In *British Life and Thought* (1940), the former Conservative Prime Minister Stanley Baldwin wrote: 'We are not intellectual . . . the ordinary Englishman has a distrust of political theory, of being what he calls "academic", and he has no confidence in logic . . . the result of the efforts of so-called intellectuals to turn him into a pink communist have been just what might have been expected'.[57] As this comment indicates, a specific cause of anti-intellectual feeling in this period was Britain's left-liberal 'highbrows' who were blamed by conservatives for encouraging popular scepticism about the value of patriotism.

During the First World War, the government had found it easy to enlist figures such as Rudyard Kipling and H. G. Wells to do propaganda work, but as a result of the conflict a new generation of intellectuals had condemned the patriotic assumptions of 'My country right or wrong'. The Bloomsbury Group saw the British as parochially immune to Continental artistic developments and simultaneously vulnerable to what they regarded as the vulgar American mass culture which emerged in the 1920s. The trend was exacerbated by the Depression and the rise of fascism. The group of poets and writers which became loosely known as the Auden Generation were dissatisfied with the aesthetic detachment of the Bloomsbury Group. They argued that patriotism had led not only to vulgarity but also to poverty and dictatorship. They moved to the left, adding internationalism to the cosmopolitanism of the Bloomsbury salons, and in many cases flirting with communism. The influence which this *trahison des clercs* had on a generation of British youth was thought to be malign and extensive.

Following the Oxford Union's infamous vote in 1933 not to fight for King and country, Churchill told the annual meeting of the Royal Society of St George that 'The worst difficulties from which we suffer ... come from the unwarrantable mood of self-abasement into which we have been cast by a powerful section of our own intellectuals'.[58] Early in the war, George Orwell published his classic account of Englishness, *The Lion and the Unicorn: Socialism and the English Genius*. Oft-quoted but never bettered, here is his description of the nation's intelligentsia:

> England is perhaps the only great country whose intellectuals are ashamed of their own nationality ... It is a strange fact but unquestionably true that almost any English intellectual would feel more ashamed of standing to attention during 'God save the King' than of stealing from a poor box ... All through the critical years, many left-wingers were chipping away at English morale, spreading an outlook that was sometimes squashily pacifist, sometimes violently pro-Russian but always anti-British ... [However] the Bloomsbury highbrow with his mechanical snigger is as out of date as the cavalry colonel. A modern nation cannot afford either of them. Patriotism and intelligence will have to come together again. It is the fact that we are fighting ... a very peculiar kind of war that may make this possible.[59]

The emphasis which both men placed on England was neither accidental nor narrow-minded. The trend for self-abasement had gone further there than in Scotland or Wales – not because the Scots and the Welsh were any less shaken by the Great War, but because their intellectuals reacted to it more constructively. During the 1920s they refashioned patriotism into an anti-imperial sentiment directed against the English. Like the Irish, they developed a cod-Celtic cultural movement that laid the foundations for a re-examination of Scottish and Welsh identity later in the century. These nuances were of little interest to propagandists in 1940. At one of the first meetings he chaired as Minister of Information, Lord Reith wearily observed 'the greater number of persons likely to be of use . . . in a creative capacity would be of left-wing tendency'.[60] The literary critic John Lehmann thought that many 'Members of Parliament, influential Civil Servants and Generals' wished to 'put us in front of a firing squad, or at least clap us in prison for the duration'.[61] To everyone's relief this did not prove necessary.

The war was a turning point for the British intelligentsia. Disillusionment with communism had been spreading since news of Stalin's purges reached the West in 1938 and it intensified after the signing of the Nazi–Soviet Pact a year later. The fascist victory in the Spanish Civil War was an even heavier blow to morale. On the day Barcelona fell to Franco's army, W. H. Auden flew to America. From there, on the outbreak of war seven months later, he watched, as he put it, 'the clever hopes expire of a low, dishonest decade'. Auden's escape was heavily criticized at the time because it appeared to symbolize his generation's betrayal of their country. What it actually symbolized was a disillusionment with left-wing politics which enabled those who remained in the UK to regain a position of influence in British society.

As the Wehrmacht swept across Europe in the summer of 1940, and the threat of invasion became a terrifying probability, British intellectuals were forced to appreciate that the survival of Western liberal civilization upon which their artistic and critical freedom depended lay in the hands of Britain. Consequently, a nation which they had previously dismissed as the most parochial and class-ridden in Europe came to be celebrated as the torchbearer of democracy. Kingsley Martin's *New Statesman* editorial at the height of the Battle of Britain was typical of the time. 'Britain', he wrote emphatically, 'is the bridgehead of freedom which unites the New World and the Old.'[62] Such sentiment sprang partly from a sense of satisfaction that the appeasers had finally woken up to the struggle against fascism which they, the intelligentsia, had been carrying on for a decade or more. It was also the result of circumstance. Stranded on a besieged island, unable to travel abroad, artists and intellectuals were forced back to the British scene for inspiration, whether they liked it or not. And some simply jumped at the chance to avoid active service or penury.

But the work they carried out sprang from a dramatic change of attitude towards their country. There was an overwhelming realization that Britain, for all her inequalities, could no longer afford to be cast into a 'mood of self-abasement' when so much depended on her victory. Very few doubted that the conflict was a just one. A few pacifists – notably the composers Benjamin Britten and Michael Tippett – refused to become directly involved in the war effort, but pacifists formed a tiny minority of the population. Some leading figures from the conscientious objection movement of the previous war like the MP Fenner Brockway found it difficult to sustain their principles. 'I was too conscious of the evil of Nazism and fascism to be completely pacifist', he wrote.[63] Vera Brittain travelled the country giving lectures on the evil of war, but she too felt the patriotism of the time. She wrote an account of her travels, *England's Hour* (1941), in which she celebrated the compassionate nature of its people which, she hoped, would eventually forge a world without war.

As well as the artists who took commissions from the WAAC, film-makers such as Harry Watt from the left-leaning documentary movement were pressed into service as the Crown Film Unit, producing shorts which extolled the British character. Authors did their bit too. Stephen Spender and Leonard Woolf joined the Auxiliary Fire Service, George Orwell the Home Guard. Virginia Woolf returned to journalism, in what Quentin Bell described as 'a kind of patriotic gesture' towards the nation whose resistance to Hitler ensured that her husband did not have to wear a yellow star in the streets of London.[64] The former communist and future Poet Laureate Cecil Day-Lewis wrote pamphlets for the MOI, discovering a deep love of country which, he admitted, 'takes a seismic event such as war to reveal to most of us rootless moderns'.[65] Louis MacNeice flew back from the United States to become a talks producer. Perhaps the most symbolic change of heart was that of the philosopher C. E. M. Joad, who had proposed the Oxford Union motion not to fight for King and country in 1933. When war broke out, he publicly recanted in the pages of the *News Chronicle* and became a regular panel member on *The Brains Trust*, the BBC's popular wartime discussion programme.

In May 1940, as the recusants of the interwar years queued up for propaganda jobs alongside conservative counterparts like T. S. Eliot, Reith gleefully observed that 'converted left-wing speakers have undertaken to help on the Home Front'.[66] The ex-communist writer Arthur Koestler noted later that 'The intelligentsia has to a large extent been absorbed as temporary civil servants in the Ministry of Information [and] the BBC.'[67] The Blitz intensified this change of heart. As the full force of Nazi aggression was brought to Britain's major cities by the Luftwaffe in the autumn of 1940, more and more intellectuals not only suspended criticism of their native culture, but fully embraced it. 'Old slogans will have to be scrapped', wrote John Lehmann, surveying the intellectual scene in March 1941, 'everywhere . . . a new consciousness is stirring.'[68] Even English conservatism was celebrated as a virtue in time of war. Writing in Lehmann's periodical, *Penguin New Writing*, the novelist Robert Pagan argued that 'to be conservative . . . may actually be a sign of vitality . . . the Englishman is not famous for imagination . . . but for tenacity, obstinacy and doggedness. Get him in a corner with his back to the wall, and then see if he is alive or not'.[69]

What effect did wartime propaganda have on national identity in Britain? The British were not empty vessels into which their leaders poured an official definition. Mistakes were made and had to be rectified. The Scots and Welsh were riled by the tendency to equate England with Britain; women everywhere were less keen than men on gung-ho military themes (particularly in films); the working classes objected to the haughty, hectoring tone of some attempts at morale-boosting, notably the infamous poster which read 'YOUR COURAGE, YOUR CHEERFULNESS, YOUR RESOLUTION WILL BRING US VICTORY'. However, there can be no doubt that Churchill's government managed to ignite the latent patriotism of a nation that had gone to war reluctantly. By 1942, the British people were not only determined to see the end of Hitler, they had a much clearer idea of who they were – their history, traditions and character – than they had had in 1939.

Even the ambitious attempt to improve their understanding of British culture met with some success. The number of books sold in the UK almost trebled, up from 7.16 million in 1939 to 20.24 million in 1946. Publishers reported record sales of the British literary classics that were being read and discussed on the BBC. The Corporation's drama ratings doubled between 1940 and 1941 and continued to rise thereafter. And although two men misunderstood the aims of 'Art for the People' by stealing a Blake and a Turner from a travelling exhibition, there was evidence of a more constructive popular interest in painting. In July 1942, the *Listener* reported that a group of working men had written to CEMA complaining that the selection of works by Duncan Grant and Paul Nash displayed in their area 'were not the best that might have been chosen'.[70] Many Britons who did not possess such critical acumen were deeply moved by experiencing the arts for the first time. The communist writer Jack Lindsay carried out a survey of the response to government initiatives, published in 1945 as *The Arts In Wartime*. At a series of subsidized London Philharmonic concerts at Portsmouth, he described the scene as if it was an Evangelical meeting:

> The concentration of attention was almost unbearable to watch
> . . . even after the final chord had been hammered out there was
> a moment's silence. Then there came a volley of applause which
> nearly lifted the roof. Standing by me was a tough ordinary seaman
> with a scarred face and gnarled hands. His eyes were wet with
> tears . . . he had never heard an orchestra until the Festival began,
> and now he couldn't keep away from it. 'It's worse than the drink
> or women, the way it gets you,' he said.[71]

Lindsay was so excited by what he saw at similar events all over the UK that he declared: 'We have . . . creat[ed] for the first time since folk-days a genuine mass-audience for drama, song, music. The British people . . . have begun powerfully . . . to claim their cultural heritage. A cultural revolution has been initiated.' He was not alone in his excitement. The apparent refinement of popular taste led many to believe that the national culture was starting to reflect the progress of British democracy in the twentieth century.

Cultural propaganda is only part of the story. It gave British patriotism a structure and a depth once provided by the Protestant faith, and which it would have lacked had the government not acted so decisively and with such imagination. But whatever form propaganda took, it did not and could not generate patriotism on its own. What did? The Second World War united the four nations of the United Kingdom for four reasons which can be summarized as follows: first, acute fear of the nation's enemies; second, mass mobilization, which revived the economies of Scotland, Wales and the north of England; third, unprecedented solidarity between classes and sexes, which led to the creation of social democracy; and fourth, the factor least discussed by historians, national guilt about appeasement. The widespread feeling that they had not acted quickly enough to prevent the spread of fascism caused the British to romanticize their war, turning it from one heroic episode in their history into a legend which underpinned their national identity.

5. I'm not English

The first thing which united the British was the simplest and most powerful of all: the fear of death and the human will to survive. The war was fought by a citizenry sharply aware that they were defending a country under siege from a foreign aggressor. In this respect, national divisions were not only a distraction but could, if they were indulged, threaten the safety of Britain. It is significant that when the First World War began, newspapers and their hoardings said 'ENGLAND DECLARES WAR ON GERMANY'. In 1939 they said 'BRITAIN DECLARES WAR ON GERMANY'. During a parliamentary debate of 2 September 1939, Leo Amery famously implored Arthur Greenwood to 'Speak for England' when he rose to address the House about the war to come. But before Greenwood could do so, a chorus of MPs, many of them English, shouted 'Speak for Britain.' This new sensitivity was not just the result of invasion fever. It also sprang from a growing realization that the loyalty of the Scots and Welsh could not be taken for granted.

Although membership of the SNP and Plaid Cymru remained small compared to the main unionist parties, both were becoming steadily larger and better organized and they were significant enough to concern Britain's leaders. Tentative comparisons were even drawn with Irish nationalism. On 7 July 1940 the Chiefs of Staff discussed the threat of a German invasion via Ireland, concluding (rightly) that the IRA would assist the Nazis in such an event. They agreed there was also a possibility that if there were an invasion the Germans would be given active support in Scotland and Wales by opportunistic nationalist sympathizers as well as by committed fascists in each country. These concerns were based on concrete intelligence. Although he wisely didn't publicize the fact, the SNP leader Douglas Young relished the prospect of a German invasion, telling friends that he hoped to run a Vichy-style government north of the border. Plaid Cymru was less circumspect, sending an official delegation to Berlin in the summer of 1940 to convince Hitler that in return for some measure of Welsh independence they would support a Nazi regime elsewhere on the island. The Führer decided that the Welsh were not vital to his plans for world domination and declined to support Plaid. But the Nazis did encourage Welsh and Scottish discontent with the Union. Goebbels' New British Broadcasting Station (from which the treacherous 'Lord Haw Haw' spoke) was supplemented by Radio Caledonia and the Welsh Freedom Station. These called on the Scots and Welsh to throw off English hegemony and make a separate peace with Germany.

Taking all this into consideration, Churchill agreed with the Chiefs of Staff that a close eye should be kept on Scottish and Welsh opinion. He was careful in his speeches to talk of the 'British nation'. On 9 February 1941, for example, he compared the resilience of blitzed civilians to the infantry who had helped defeat Napoleon:

> They remind me of the British squares at Waterloo. They are not squares of soldiers; they do not wear scarlet coats. They are just ordinary English, Scottish and Welsh folk – men, women and children – standing steadfastly together. But their spirit is the same; and, in the end, their victory will be greater than far-famed Waterloo.[72]

The day before that speech, he appointed the sixty-year-old Labour MP Tom Johnston as Secretary of State for Scotland. Johnston was a hardline Clydeside socialist, but like many socialists of his generation he also had strong Home Rule sympathies. He commended his people thus: 'The strong self-respect of the Scot may at times intensify into undue individualism and a certain touchiness . . . But self-respect, loyal comradeship, and a passionate love of justice are traits inseparably bound up with his fine qualities as a worker.'[73] He accepted the post on condition that a Council of State for Scotland was set up, comprised of former Secretaries of State and assorted worthies. MPs for all Scottish constituencies were invited to attend its meetings. The Council was poorly attended throughout the war and ceased to exist four weeks after Johnston left office, its last meeting taking place at St Andrew's House on 16 February 1945. Nor was it taken seriously at Westminster. Whenever Johnston entered No. 10, Churchill was apt to bellow, 'Here comes the King of Scotland!' Sir John Reith recorded a conversation he had with his disgruntled compatriot in 1943: 'He is very bothered by Bevin and other ministers who do things affecting Scotland without consulting him. He thinks there is a great danger of Scottish nationalism coming up and a sort of *Sinn Fein* movement as he called it.'[74]

Still, Johnston did manage to wring concessions out of the Cabinet by constantly raising the spectre of nationalism. He obtained greater Treasury investment in Scottish industry (of which more later) and he had symbolic victories, like that over Scottish banknotes. In the 1820s, Sir Walter Scott had headed off an attempt by the Bank of England to abolish them, but the English had continued to treat them as foreign currency even though they were legal tender throughout the UK. To make matters worse, in 1942 letters appeared in the national press complaining that the circulation of different notes was hampering the war effort and calling for Scottish ones to be abolished forthwith. The Scots were outraged, particularly troops and factory workers who brought the notes south when they were posted to England. The *Scotsman* later said, 'English organisations have forgotten that the parliament at Westminster is a Union of parliaments. This is a matter of primary concern to the Scottish public'. Thanks to Johnston's intervention, in 1943 the Treasury stopped the historic practice of English banks charging customers to change Scottish notes. But because other organizations were not obliged to accept them, the issue continued to be a source of irritation in the postwar years. Given how paranoid the English became about losing the pound to a European single currency, their disdain for Scottish banknotes epitomized their disdain for Scottish autonomy in general.

Welsh devolution never got off the ground – not because there was no demand for it, but because the principality was taken even less seriously than Scotland as a nation. In June 1943, Churchill was petitioned for a Welsh Office by 107 local authorities. This was followed four months later by a petition from every MP representing the principality. It was supported by the Welsh press, Churches and trade unions, which together marshalled public opinion in favour of change. The petition declared:

> The paramount fact is that the Welsh People are a distinct British Nationality and have so regarded themselves from time immemorial . . . We, the Representatives of Wales in Parliament, pray for this recognition of our nationality. . . . The Welsh People, who hope to amplify and make fruitful those special moral qualities which are inherent in their distinctive character claim that their Province shall be henceforth recognised as a National entity and that they, as a people, must be given the opportunity of exhibiting in full nationhood what definitely pertains to their own genius. The Welsh People, ever conscious and proud of their long British traditions, now ardently aspire to obtain an authoritatively proclaimed position amongst the National Divisions of Britain . . . At the present moment there is everywhere much concern for the common welfare when victory shall have been achieved . . . The

Welsh People, more deeply than at any time in recent history, feel
that they are entitled to distinct and separate representation in His
Majesty's Cabinet, where the welfare of the People of Wales will
be discussed and determined.

The petitioners reassured Churchill that their aim was to strengthen
not weaken the Union:

> Not only would such recognition of their nationality confer on the
> Welsh People a status, both at home and abroad . . . but we are
> confident that it would still further strengthen the attachment
> which binds the Welsh People to their fellow Britons of the other
> Nationalities. We further believe that such a recognition as we
> now beseech would inspire in the Welsh People a loftier pride, a
> wider and more responsible interest in the British Empire and
> would widen the conception of citizenship among this intensely
> loyal people. Finally, and on this we lay exceeding stress, we
> profoundly believe that it would have a deep and far-reaching
> effect in strengthening and exalting the national character of the
> Welsh people, who . . . have now for so many ages past continued
> to suffer the subtle, but still very real, injury of national belit-
> tlement.[75]

This extraordinary five-page document was a testament to the extent
to which the Welsh thought of themselves as British and the extent
to which the Second World War intensified a roundly British
patriotism.

But the petition also stands as a memorial to that patriotism.
Never again would Welsh discontent with the Union be expressed in
such an effusively loyal way, with so much emphasis placed on the
importance of the country's unity. Churchill was unmoved and he
refused to meet a deputation to discuss it any further. He made a
token gesture by introducing an annual 'Welsh Day' in Parliament,
in which only Welsh matters were debated, the first of which took
place on 17 October 1944. It was a poor return on their contribution
to the war effort, but they had more success in the cultural field.

Shortly after the war, T. S. Eliot wrote: 'it would be no gain
whatever for English culture, for the Welsh, Scots and Irish to
become indistinguishable from Englishmen – what *would* happen, of
course, is that we would all become indistinguishable featureless
"Britons" '.[76] The wartime government realized the importance of
maintaining the nation's varied features; and in a strategy established
since the nineteenth century, the cultural distinctiveness of Wales and

Scotland was celebrated in the hope of dampening demands for political devolution. Officials made a serious attempt to suppress the tendency to think of Britain as Greater England. Early BBC features such as *Forever England* provoked a number of complaints. One Welshman wrote, 'Is the war being fought by English people only and to safeguard their interests only?'[77] In the *Listener*, the Scottish critic Grace Wyndham Goldie warned that Britain would not be mobilized with 'the speeches of Queen Elizabeth ... linked by snatches of Elgar to the sonnets of Rupert Brooke'.[78] In November 1940, the MOI formally told the BBC to avoid using England as a synonym for Britain because, it archly observed, 'it causes irritation among the minorities'.[79] The Corporation then issued a ruling to producers stating, 'England is acceptable if England is really meant ... otherwise Britain should be used except when it sounds absurd'.[80]

Britain's broadcasters not only policed the language of national identity more effectively, they also made more of an effort to depict Scotland and Wales as nations in their own right and to celebrate their particular contribution to the war effort. The aim was to educate the English as well as to pacify their partners. Among the fruits of the policy were talks by poets Edwin Muir and Dylan Thomas and one delivered by the actor Emlyn Williams, simply entitled 'I'm Not English'. The BBC extended its Gaelic and Welsh language service. Scotland and Wales enjoyed twice-weekly plays, concerts and religious services in their ancient tongues, while the Welsh also had a nightly news service. Because Forces Radio took over the frequency on which *The News in Welsh* normally appeared, it was broadcast on the Home Service to the whole of the UK. Although people listened more by accident than design, it was the first time most Britons had ever heard Welsh being spoken, making the programme one of the more curious examples of the way in which the war amplified the plurality of Britishness.

However, since legislation could not easily alter a national identity, a memorandum had little chance of doing so. There remained a tendency, from the War Office to the sub-post office, to see 'the minorities' as loyal but subsidiary to the war effort. In 1940, Reith decided to commission the nation's leading composers to write patriotic music for the BBC. Sir Adrian Boult wrote to Ralph Vaughan Williams requesting a 'lay hymn with orchestral accompaniment, the theme patriotic but not necessarily warlike; an *air* theme especially welcome; caveat – the word "England" to be avoided as a synonym for Britain'.[81] Vaughan Williams defied this

instruction by setting W. E. Henley's *England My England* to music.
The project was quietly shelved after a token performance of the
piece in November 1941. The UK's Poet Laureate, John Masefield,
seemed not to notice that the whole of Britain was at war when he
wrote:

> Through the long time the story will be told;
> Long centuries of praise on English lips,
> Of courage godlike and of hearts of gold
> Off Dunquerque beaches in the little ships.

Cinema suffered from the same tunnel vision. The title of the feature
This England (1941) was tactfully changed to *Our Heritage* for
release in Scotland. Little else changed. When the Scots and Welsh
appeared in films they were usually portrayed as brave but subsidiary
comic characters.

The story was a similar one at CEMA. Kenneth Clark came from
a family of Scottish textile magnates and had fond memories of
Harry Lauder singing to him as a boy. He was an urbane, Anglicized
Scot who became the darling of London society in the 1930s as the
youngest ever Director of the National Gallery. Clark had a commen-
surately Anglocentric approach to the task of commissioning war
artists, and the Royal Scottish Academy was enraged when it put
forward the names of fifty artists and only three were commissioned.
The most famous scenes of the Scottish Home Front were painted by
Stanley Spencer. A shy, diminutive English rural romantic who
dreamed of the Second Coming happening in his Berkshire village,
he was sent north to sketch the shipbuilders of Govan. His nature
made him popular in the yards and the result of his stay, *Shipbuilding
on the Clyde*, is one of the great works of twentieth-century British
art. But the origins of its creation lie in a less generous vision of
national culture and the Scottish Office lodged a formal complaint,
scorning Clark's insistence that all commissions were based on merit.

The Anglocentricity of the organizations charged with promoting
national identity reflected that of the English people as a whole.
Wartime reading habits are one example. The most popular works
were those which scrutinized the national character, ranging from
simple picture books to more learned treatises, and the bestselling
books were those which focused unashamedly on England. Antholo-
gies of patriotic verse and speeches such as Penguin's *Portrait of
England* (1942) were extremely popular. Among the notable original
works were A. L. Rowse's *The English Spirit* (1944) and Arthur

Bryant's *English Saga 1840–1940*, a Book Society Choice, which ran to a dozen editions by the end of the war. It concluded: 'An island fortress, England is fighting a war of redemption not only for Europe but for her own soul. Facing dangers greater than any in her history she has fallen back on the rock of her national character.'[82]

Official publications by HMSO charting the progress of the war were scrupulously British in scope, and authors who had previously examined the English broadened their attention. The most respected scholar of Englishness in the mid-twentieth century was Ernest Barker, Professor of Political Science at Cambridge. In 1942, he wrote a pocket volume, *Britain and the British People*, which extolled the virtues of all the Isles' inhabitants. Esme Wingfield-Stratford's 1913 *History of English Patriotism* was rewritten to become *The Foundations of British Patriotism*. But the text within still reverenced England and the occasional mention of Scotland and Wales displayed a rosy vision of the three nations' relationship. This is how he described the formation of Great Britain in 1707:

> A free union, by mutual consent … on the basis of common patriotism and common freedom, expressed in the same Parliamentary way of government, though with an agreement to diverge in the ways of law. And this without leaving the faintest tinge of bitterness on either side, or anything that could become the seed of a national inferiority complex.[83]

The tendency to equate England with Britain was also displayed in the attitudes to England's patron saint. According to legend, St George was a Greek officer in the Roman army of the early fourth century, martyred during a purge of Christians. He was adopted as England's patron saint in the fourteenth century during the Crusades, at which time the blood-red cross on a white background became the national flag. After the Battle of Agincourt, the Church declared 23 April to be a public holiday in his honour and it became a religious festival as important as Christmas or Easter. His was the only saint's day to be retained after the Reformation. Although official observance of St George's Day was ended during the Cromwellian Interregnum, England's patron saint remained popular among working people, and during the nineteenth century he once more enjoyed official acclaim, when thanks to the Victorian Gothic revival and the associated cult of the gentleman he was celebrated by Church and state as an exemplar of muscular Anglo-Saxon Christianity. By the 1890s, he was *the* expression of that intense English patriotism which both subsumed itself in Union and Empire yet left no doubt which nation ruled the world. In 1894, the Royal Society of St George was founded with the Queen as its Patron; Elgar composed *The Banner of St George* for Victoria's Diamond Jubilee; school classrooms were adorned with his image; and in 1918 Vice-Admiral Roger Keyes led British destroyers into action at Zeebrugge with the signal 'St George for England!' But, on land, the rat and the howitzer succeeded where the Reformation had failed. St George became associated with the militaristic, imperial Englishness which steadily fell out of public favour after the First World War.[84]

During the 1940s his fortunes declined further. Because the Church of England was wary of linking patriotism and Protestantism too overtly, it distanced itself from the cult. When Good Friday fell on 23 April in 1943, the Prime Minister and Archbishop of Canterbury agreed that St George's Day should be shifted to 3 May to emphasize that 'we are fighting above all for the Christian faith'.[85] In a BBC broadcast on Easter Sunday, the naturalist Peter Scott reminded listeners that St George's Day had just passed and he claimed that what England meant for most people was the countryside. Despite Scott's talk the verdict of the Home Service Controller was that observance of this once great national festival was 'a pretty complete flop' all round.[86] Another producer was more blunt: 'nine people out of ten haven't the least idea who St George was and don't care anyway'.[87] Thereafter, the corporation began to downgrade the event. One of the few who did care about St George was sixty-year-old Clara Milburn, a housewife from the Midlands, whose wartime diaries capture a certain type of middle-class English pluck. In 1944, she felt confident enough about victory over Germany to celebrate the nation's patron saint:

> St. George's Day and a prayer for the Nation. A lovely day too – warm, even when cloudy – and I rode off to the 11am service at St Peter's. Afterwards I decided to thin the parsnips and, of course, went 'hoeing round elsewhere and mucking abart the garden' . . . the Union Jack bought for (my) Jack's birthday in 1942 – very optimistic I was to buy it then – has been flown for the first time today, St George's Day. It looked grand, and he has found a new way of arranging the pulley and halliard.[88]

Cycling to communion, observing the weather, doing some gardening, raising the Union Jack – Mrs Milburn's celebration of St George's Day captures not only the texture of middle English life but also the tendency of her southern compatriots to regard England and Britain as synonymous. That conceit explains why the iconography and narratives of the Finest Hour legend were constructed in such an Anglocentric way.

The most celebrated images of Britain's defiance, reproduced in hundreds of posters, films, newspapers and magazines, were St Paul's Cathedral, the South Downs, the White Cliffs of Dover, and the East End of London. Partly, this reflected the fact that England was closest to the main theatre of war. And the south-east was, after all, where an invasion of the UK was most likely to happen. But it was England's singular national identity which ensured that the war was memorialized in such a one-dimensional way. The Battle of Britain and the Blitz were a convenient base for the English to construct a patriotic legend which foregrounded themselves. Like a bossy father who shoves his way to the front of a family photo and presses the shutter before anyone can protest, the English created an image which annoyed the Scots and Welsh at the time and thoroughly alienated later generations who hadn't lived through the war. When Scottish and Welsh discontent with the Union intensified in the second half of the twentieth century, it was difficult for the English to regenerate British patriotism by appealing to the spirit of 1940 because that spirit was associated, in younger minds at least, with a time when the Scots and Welsh were peripheral to the English world view.

However, in the short term, the defence of the Isles was so important that English self-aggrandizement was a secondary concern to even the most sensitive inhabitant of Scotland and Wales. The English might think they were winning the war almost single-handedly but it was quite clearly a Battle of Britain. The litmus test of Scottish and Welsh loyalty was the response of each country to military conscription. The SNP opposed the call-up on the grounds that the war was England's and that unilateral conscription by the British state was a breach of the Act of Union. Their countrymen ignored them, answered the call, and vented their anger on nationalists who claimed conscientious objection. Nearly all nationalists had their applications rejected (with the exception of a few who backed up their case with evidence of religious principle) and the tribunals often took place amid angry clashes with the public. Subsequent protests against the war inflamed public feeling still further. After a summer show on Aberystwyth promenade in August 1941, three Plaid Cymru activists pointedly walked away during the playing of

'God Save The King'. The largely Welsh crowd watching the show turned on the three men and the police only prevented a lynching by arresting them for provoking a breach of the peace.

Nationalists argued that the only reason Scotland and Wales were threatened by Hitler was that the English-dominated state which encompassed the island had declared war on Germany. On the island of Ireland, they pointed out, Éire had remained neutral while the North had not. This was nonsense for two reasons. First, the idea that neutrality would guarantee the safety of Scotland and Wales was, to the say the least, a naive view of Hitler's intentions and integrity. Given modern military capabilities, no part of Britain could rely on the good will of an invader. The days were long gone when armies halted at Berwick because the northern terrain made conquest difficult. The basic geopolitical necessity for the Union had been apparent during the Napoleonic Wars. It was even more apparent in 1940, and it acted as a significant brake on nationalism until the 1960s when nuclear weaponry rendered conventional military concerns obsolete. In 1940, a threat to one part of Britain was a threat to the whole. When defences were placed around the islands' 2,000-mile coastline, concrete and steel were laid on 113 Scottish beaches and 27 Welsh ones for good reason. The second reason why the nationalist argument was not accepted was that Irish neutrality *did* hinder the British war effort. Not for the first time since the creation of the UK, a shared dislike of the Irish bound the Scots, Welsh and English together and helped to define their common identity.

6. The mackerel are fat on the flesh of your kin

Twenty years after southern Ireland won its independence, the British had not yet come to regard Éire as a foreign country with the right to self-determination. It remained a member of the Commonwealth, and consequently it was expected to support the war as willingly as Australia, Canada or the West Indies did. But even when Churchill offered de Valéra reunification in return for participation, the Taoiseach refused to budge. Neutrality directly affected the UK's war effort, because the inability of the Royal Navy to use Ireland's ports shortened the range at which armed vessels could protect merchant ships carrying supplies from the US.

Few Irish people celebrated the deaths of British servicemen. But most were heartily proud of neutrality. George Bernard Shaw wrote, 'That powerless little cabbage garden called Ireland wins in the teeth of all the mighty powers'.[89] When Harold Nicolson visited Dublin to drum up support for the UK, he recorded the following conversation with Daniel Binchy, a former Irish Ambassador to Germany:

> He [Binchy] says that a visiting Englishman is apt to be taken in by blarney and to imagine that the feelings of this country towards us are really friendly. Not in the least: at the bottom of almost every Irish heart is a little bag of bile, and although their hatred of us may die down at moments, it is there, even as our Protestantism and puritanism are there subconsciously . . . 'Neutrality' has thus taken on an almost religious flavour; it has become a question of honour; and it is something which Ireland is not ashamed of but tremendously proud.[90]

The visiting Englishman he had in mind was the poet John Betjeman, posted to Dublin as the Press Attaché at the British Embassy because it was thought he was 'the sort of whimsical person the Irish will like'. In a broadcast to the UK, he said, 'Ireland is the breeding ground of eccentrics . . . [it] is still the most hospitable country in Europe, where every inhabitant is a wit and every other inhabitant a poet.'[91]

However, Betjeman could not convince his compatriots that the Irish were anything other than duplicitous peasants, no different from those who had led the Easter Rising of 1916 during Britain's last war with Germany. Approximately 40,000 Southern men and women defied de Valéra and volunteered to serve in the British armed forces during the Second World War. Because they were an embarrassment to the Irish, the volunteers were not officially honoured in their own country until 1995. They were at least praised by Churchill for '[keeping] alive the martial honour of the Irish race'.[92] But uppermost in the British mind was the bombing campaign which the IRA conducted in Britain from 1939 to 1940. One bomb left five dead in Coventry before de Valéra helped Churchill put a stop to it all by arresting the ringleaders (among those imprisoned was the writer Brendan Behan). But the Irish threat remained a clear and present one in the first three years of the war. The Joint Intelligence

Committee of the War Office described the IRA as 'a very formidable band of revolutionists; violently anti-British and many of them pro-German'.[93]

Northern Ireland, in contrast, was seen to be a loyal and valiant member of the UK. The war reinforced the North's British identity just as it reinforced the South's sense of Irishness: the Protestant majority didn't know about Churchill's secret offer to abandon them to their fate and they waved the Union Jack with unequivocal vigour.

The Northern Irish government was based at the magnificent neo-classical Stormont parliament buildings opened by the Prince of Wales in 1932, and from there it led the North's war effort with varying degrees of efficiency. Its intentions were clear, however, as this letter to Churchill from the Prime Minister, John Andrews, demonstrated: '[There will] be no slackening in [Northern Ireland's] loyalty. There is no falling off in our determination to place the whole of our resources at the command of the Imperial government . . . anything we can do here to facilitate them . . . they have only just got to let us know.'[94] Andrews refused to establish a Home Guard, because he did not want to arm the Catholic minority; but he did want to send them into the front line to enforce loyalty to the UK and he asked the British government to impose conscription on the province. Churchill wisely refused, and consequently Northern Irish servicemen and women were volunteers like their Southern counterparts. There were a few Catholics among Ulster's volunteers and the only Victoria Cross awarded to a citizen of the North went to one of them.

However, the difference between the two countries was manifold. A larger proportion of the Northern population volunteered (38,000 in all) and they did so with an ostentatious patriotism absent among volunteers from the South, most of whom felt they were fighting against fascism rather than for Britain. The desertion rate among Southern Irish troops (estimated at 12 per cent) was one of the highest in the British armed forces, while Ulster's was among the lowest. Furthermore, Northern Ireland made a substantial material contribution to the war effort which the South did not. As well as providing a key base for the British navy during the Battle of the Atlantic, the shipyards of Belfast produced 10 per cent of the UK's merchant shipping, 140 warships and 1,500 heavy bombers. Ulster was described as 'The British Bridgehead' in pamphlets distributed to schoolchildren in Great Britain in an effort to make them more aware that Northern Ireland was an integral part of the United Kingdom.

The fact that John Andrews' successor as Prime Minister, Basil Brooke, was the nephew of the Chief of the Imperial General Staff, Alan Brooke, symbolized the wartime bond between Ulster and the mainland. So too did the Blitz. Several thousand people were killed when Belfast was bombed in April 1941. Although fire engines from Éire went to help, the effect of German bombing was to foster a greater sense of comradeship with Northern Ireland. Thus, for many Ulster Protestants, there was a perverse delight in the destruction which Hitler wrought on their country. In 1945, Churchill told Brooke: 'The stand of the Government and people of Northern Ireland . . . for the great cause of freedom, for which we all risked our survival, will never be forgotten by Great Britain . . . A strong, loyal Ulster will always be vital to the security and well-being of the whole Empire and Commonwealth. Linked with us, Ulster must also share in the happier days to come.'[95]

In contrast, the South was bitterly attacked. *Picture Post* declared in 1940: 'the Ulstermen are adult; they do not behave like overgrown infants'.[96] David Low traduced Irish neutrality in a series of cartoons for the *Daily Mirror*. Intellectuals engaged in the war effort were also scathing, none more so than the Anglo-Irish poet Louis Mac-Neice. A liberal to the core, there was little love lost between him and his native Ulster, but the South's position moved him to fury. In the poem 'Neutrality', he attacked 'The neutral island facing the Atlantic' as 'The neutral island in the heart of man'. The closing verse reminded the Irish that while they were busy admiring their Celtic heritage their British cousins were dying in the defence of democracy – not least the merchant seamen drowned by U-boats during the Battle of the Atlantic:

Look into your heart, you will find fermenting rivers,
Intricacies of gloom and glint,
You will find such ducats of dream and great doubloons of ceremony
As nobody today would mint
But then look eastward from your heart, there bulks
A continent, close, dark, as archetypal sin,
While to the west off your own shores the mackerel
Are fat – on the flesh of your kin.[97]

The Ministry of Information received regular complaints from communities in Scotland, Wales and England that Irish workers were lazy and drunk, and made unpatriotic comments (complainants found anti-royalist sentiment the most offensive). The government took these reports seriously. Though grateful for Irish volunteers in the armed forces, Churchill was less enthusiastic about civilian workers. He saw them as potential fifth-columnists and they were not allowed to work on the south coast near sensitive military installations. British opinion was unnecessarily inflamed in 1945 when de Valéra drove to the German Embassy in Dublin to deliver a personal message of condolence on the death of Hitler.

The Irish had a good war. De Valéra judged rightly that Churchill could not deliver reunification, and neutrality was a chance to prove that Éire was an independent nation no longer under the British yoke. It poisoned Anglo-Irish relations for a generation and, by driving another wedge between North and South, it hampered the cause of reunification. But in a curious way it served the British well too. They began to accept that Éire was a foreign country and not a recalcitrant satellite state. Northern Ireland got the chance to dem-onstrate its loyalty and its practical use to the rest of the UK. The international standing of the province had never been as high, nor would it ever be again. Above all, Éire's refusal to fight helped the British regain some of the patriotic pride which they had lost during the appeasement era. Looking across the water, they saw a nation which even at the eleventh hour had failed to put the past behind it and shirked the call to save civilization. It was not an entirely fair judgement, but it stuck nonetheless. However, for all Northern Ireland's loyalty, Britons regarded its people as cousins rather than siblings. Wartime Britishness was ultimately based not on a vision of the United Kingdom but of the island of Britain – alone, self-contained and redoubtable.

7. No more bloody allies

The siege mentality of Britons was not just the result of invasion scares. For centuries geography had been at the heart of their national identity. They thought themselves to be influenced by the Continent but set apart from it by the sea and, consequently, different to it in character and custom. The poet Alfred Noyes was born over a hundred miles from the sea, in Wolverhampton, one of the innermost towns in Britain. In 1939, a few months before the outbreak of war, he wrote: 'The City of God will be built in every land, but it may come eventually by way of the sea. The life of England lives by the sea almost as the human frame lives by the air it breathes . . . We are isolated for a very good purpose [for] the sea position of Great Britain may help her to save the world by example.' The poet got his wish, and the image of a people single-handedly defying Europe's tyrants reinforced the self-righteous isolationism already embedded in the British consciousness.

Of course, the UK was not self-reliant because it still had the resources of a huge empire at its disposal. As Noyes acknowledged, 'The sails of the islanders were the wings that made them more than islanders . . . The very conditions which made the British the most characteristically insular people in the world, led them also into the widest world-wide relationships and gave them the most deep-set outposts and far-ranging frontiers'.[98] Thanks to those outposts and frontiers, 5 million men and women from over fifty different nationalities joined the British armed forces during the Second World War, a figure that nearly doubled the total number who fought under the Union Jack between 1940 and 1945. Of these, 170,000 died or were missing (compared to 230,000 Britons). The Australian Prime Minister Robert Menzies rallied his people with the motto 'One King, One Flag, One Cause', but in the UK few hearts were lifted or pulses quickened by such declarations. The plain fact is that by 1940 the British people were not terribly interested in the Empire.

Since the end of the First World War, huge efforts had been made by the monarchy, voluntary organizations and by governments of every political hue to maintain pride in *Pax Britannica*. Consequently, imperial patriotism was still alive when war broke out. But, like the Protestant patriotism with which it had been closely associated since the eighteenth century, it was not in the best of health. Most historians place the end of popular imperialism in the late 1950s after the humiliation of the Suez Crisis. In fact, it was in terminal decline over a decade before. By 1940, the First World War and the Depression had robbed the Empire of its romantic allure, colonial independence movements were steadily eroding faith in its invincibility, and British radicals were beginning to call into question its moral validity. Britons were shocked by the dramatic fall of the UK's Far Eastern colonies to the Japanese in 1942, but the real impact of that shock was not a revival of imperial sentiment. Abroad, it emboldened nationalists to challenge British rule with force. At home, it made the British realize that the Empire did not put them at a decisive advantage over their enemies in a modern world war.

If Britons looked beyond their shores for salvation, it was to the two nations which had started to emerge as the world's new super-powers: America and the Soviet Union. When the latter replaced France as the UK's main ally in 1941 and soaked up the onslaught of Operation Barbarossa at the cost of millions of lives, it won admiration and gratitude. That said, the government's attempt to humanize Stalin through 'Uncle Joe' propaganda was not as success-ful as some historians have claimed. The Russians remained widely distrusted because they had signed a pact with the Nazis in 1939, and above all because they were communists. In any case, for all their bravery they could do little more than mount a holding oper-ation against the Wehrmacht. It was to America that most Britons looked to help win the war. The planet's richest nation was also the one that Britons felt the greatest affinity with, thanks to the huge impact that Hollywood and Broadway had had on British popular culture between the wars. Therefore, both the romantic idea of the UK standing alone indefinitely *and* the more realistic idea of holding off Hitler until the cavalry arrived were testaments to the fact that British imperial identity was waning.

So much so, in fact, that after the fall of France there was widespread relief that the UK was on its own. George VI famously told his mother he was happier 'now that we have no allies to be polite to and pamper'.[99] A tugboat skipper shouted to MPs across the Thames, 'Now we know where we are! No more bloody allies!' Some Britons included the Empire in that 'we', not least the King. But most did not, a national mood summed up by the cartoonist David Low of the *Evening Standard*, who drew a soldier standing on Dover's cliffs and shaking his fist at the vanquished Continent. The caption read 'Very well, alone.'[100] Given the gravity of the situation Britons were in, their stated relish for isolation said as much about their insularity as it did about their bravery. Wartime propaganda encouraged that insularity. The Empire did not figure much in the projection of Britain. This was partly because, in order to persuade the US to enter the war, Americans had to be convinced that they would be freeing the world and not just rescuing the British Empire. But the government also recognized that its own people would not be rallied by calls to defend far-flung parts of the globe about which they knew little and cared less. A joint MOI/BBC plan for an 'Empire Crusade' in the autumn of 1940, designed to enthuse the public about their imperial mission, had to be abandoned because of indifference and a good deal of complaint.[101]

The focal point of propaganda was the UK's struggle with Europe. Politicians, poets, historians and journalists drew explicit parallels with the Elizabethan and Napoleonic eras. They portrayed Hitler and Mussolini as the latest in a long line of jumped-up, power-crazed Continental dictators and they emphasized the unshakeable continuity of 'the island story', stiffening morale by showing the British how their ancestors had defeated previous Continental aggressors against the odds. Broadcasting to the nation on 11 September 1940, Churchill said of the Battle of Britain: 'It ranks with the days when the Spanish Armada was approaching the Channel, and Drake was finishing his game of bowls; or when Nelson stood between us and Napoleon's Grand Army at Boulogne.'[102] Churchill always portrayed the British as an island people: outward-looking; in need of Imperial and American aid; but ultimately self-reliant. The most memorable phrase of the speech he delivered – the promise to 'fight them on the beaches' – resonated for precisely that reason. So too did Vera Lynn's song 'The White Cliffs of Dover'. So too did the Dunkirk evacuation. 'BLOODY MARVELLOUS', the *Daily Mirror* said of Dunkirk, ignoring Churchill's insistence that 'wars are not won by evacuations'.[103] The manner of the BEF's 'deliverance', as much as the deliverance itself, was seen as quintessentially British. Most troops were rescued by large ships from the Royal and merchant navies, but the legend of Dunkirk was constructed around the hundreds of small boats that chugged over to France to lend a hand, in particular the pleasure boats of south coast resorts. J. B. Priestley told BBC listeners, 'Our great-grand-children, when they learn how we began this war by snatching glory out of defeat ... may also learn how the little holiday steamers made an excursion to hell and came back glorious.'[104]

This was the patriotism of a maritime people. But the emphasis they placed on the seashore differed from that of their ancestors, who had sailed across oceans to enrich and aggrandize the nation. These were Britons for whom the sea was primarily a frontier, a natural barrier against the outside world rather than a route to foreign glory. The change in emphasis owed a lot to the fact that since Nelson's day the British had colonized much of the island's coastline. By the late 1930s they had turned it from the windswept haunt of fishermen and smugglers into a site of mass leisure and one of *the* components of domestic culture. Priestley's broadcast succeeded because he celebrated the tenacity of a cosy world of seaside holidays, in which neither people nor boats strayed too far from the shore unless they absolutely had to. A popular history of the British seaside written shortly after the war concluded: 'Never was the seaside so important in English life as during the years 1940 to 1944. Never had it seemed so much the edge of our island: it was more than the edge, it was a dead end.'[105] Eventually, it proved to be a dead end for Britishness too. But in the meantime, the geography of the UK and the mentality it spawned drew the Scots, Welsh and English closer together.

Although the sea remained central to Britishness as a protective moat, the sky was the main arena of battle in 1940–41 and it generated the most potent legends of the war. Both the Battle of Britain and the Blitz created a sense of being a fundamentally small nation rather than a world power. The British fondness for the underdog, previously directed at countries like Serbia and Belgium, was now directed at themselves. Churchill's notion of 'the Few' encapsulated that David and Goliath sentiment. The 2,917 Battle of Britain combatants were romanticized as Knights of the Air. Accounts of fighter pilots' exploits combined the chivalric derring-do of Victorian imperial stories with the technology of the aeroplane, still an object of awe in the days before mass passenger travel. Carpet bombing notwithstanding, aviation was seen throughout the war as a return to a nobler form of combat, in which individuals duelled with each other far above the bloody mire of land warfare. This outlook was apparent not only in fictional accounts like *Biggles' Spitfire Parade* (1942) and memoirs like Richard Hilary's *The Last Enemy* (1944), but also in the letters pilots wrote to their loved ones. In September 1940, Nigel Rose, a twenty-one-year-old pilot in a Scottish squadron, wrote to his parents: 'Yesterday we were directed into a raid coming towards Beachy Head, and had an absolutely superb scrap about 15 miles out at sea . . . Boy! This certainly is the life!'[106] Aviation sparked a revival of the sporting approach to war which liberals thought had been left behind at the Somme. The BBC frequently reported RAF kills like cricket and soccer scores. *New York Times* correspondent Drew Middleton was astounded to see a press hoarding in London saying 'England 112 not out'. 'I asked the man what it meant, and he said, "We got 112 of the fuckers, cock, and we're still batting." A strange people.'[107]

Like millions of others, Middleton's newspaper salesman saw himself as part of a national community, represented by a team of

airmen notching up a winning score for Britain with every Messerschmitt that plummeted to the ground in flames. Dashing young men
and their flying machines set female and schoolboy pulses racing as
well as any innings by Dennis Compton. But the truly iconic power
of the Few was that they symbolized the nation itself: small but
perfectly formed and prepared to fight to the last.

Some RAF pilots dissented. Paul Richey was coming back from
a sortie when, far below, he saw a game of cricket being played in a
village near the Dorset coast. He wrote, 'I was seized with a sudden
disgust and revulsion at this smug insular contentedness and frivolity that England seemed to be enjoying behind her sea barrier.
I thought a few bombs would wake those cricketers up, and that
they wouldn't be long in coming either.'[108] German bombers weren't
long in coming, but they only reinforced the island mentality of the
British.

A mass spirit of resistance was conjured up by the Blitz and
captured in the phrase 'Britain Can Take It', which resounded in the
press and in Parliament at the time. Some people resented the cheery
invocations of their leaders, but the majority did not and felt pride
in the fact that Göring's attempt to crush their morale had failed.
Humour was one of the reasons why the nation was so resilient. In
Vera Lynn's hit song 'We'll Meet Again', the lines 'Keep smiling
through just like you always do / Till the blue skies drive the dark
clouds far away' expressed a certain optimistic stoicism which the
British people recognized in themselves and acted upon.[109] Humour
was also regarded as an expression of British democracy. Unlike
barbed French wit or German sledgehammer humour which mocked
human weakness, the native variety, it was claimed, celebrated
human diversity. In *The English Genius* (1939), Hesketh Pearson
wrote: 'Our true Patron Saint is not St George but Sir John Falstaff
. . . we are the most civilised people in the world, the reason being
that we are the most humorous people in the world.'[110] The *Listener*
commented that Hitler's problem was that Göring had never made
him an apple-pie bed:

> Bravery of the devil-may-care variety is not peculiar to the English.
> Where we do differ from other peoples is in our natural capacity
> for laughing at ourselves. The patriotic employer who embellished
> the firm's air-raid shelter with a placard saying 'God Save The
> King – and us' was expressing a typically English attitude to life.
> And this is an attitude that in the days to come will stand us in
> good stead. Whatever other noises will assail our ears, it is safe to

predict that the sound of English laughter will not cease to echo around the world.[111]

The national suicide rate actually *fell* during the war, from 12.9 per hundred thousand in 1938 to 8.9 in 1944.[112] This statistic was partly attributable to the fact that the war made many people who had previously thought their lives were meaningless feel that they were now doing something of vital importance to their country.

Tea lubricated the war effort. Its popularity was a by-product of the Victorian temperance movement as well as the colonial plantations where it grew. For 250 years after its introduction to Britain in 1612, it was a predominantly middle- and upper-class beverage which lubricated the genteel intercourse of the nation's sitting rooms. Then, in 1863, William Gladstone slashed import duties on it to encourage the working classes to drink less alcohol. Queen Victoria lent a hand, founding the annual Buckingham Palace Garden Party in 1868, at which only tea was drunk. By the 1880s 'the cup that cheers but not inebriates' had replaced beer as the favoured breakfast drink of the working man and woman. In 1940, Churchill's government realized the drink's psychological importance to the British and made strenuous efforts to maintain supplies, with some success. Annual consumption per person from 1940–45 was about 9lb – not much less than prewar levels. In 1945, an official account of the Home Front concluded, 'People could not run a village dance, raise money for Spitfire Funds, get married or maintain morale in air raids without tea.'[113]

Perhaps the most visible sign of British defiance were the signs placed outside bomb-damaged shops saying 'Business as Usual' or, with a twist of humour, 'More Open Than Usual'. They were not the invention of propagandists; they went up spontaneously and remained in place once the cameras had gone. Though press reports of men carrying umbrellas into battle to shield themselves from enemy fire were fabricated, the national obsession with the weather did typify a certain kind of stoical British approach to adversity. One Mass Observation survey in December 1940 found that winter weather came well above air raids as a source of depression in blitzed cities. No doubt some of those respondents felt they had to conform to accepted notions of Britishness, but the fact that they did so is an indicator of the power of that identity to perpetuate itself. Angus Calder wrote: 'heroic mythology fused with everyday life to produce heroism. People "made sense" of the frightening and chaotic actualities of wartime life in terms of heroic mythology . . . But acting in accordance with this mythology, many people helped make it more true.'[114]

The British love of animals is a further example of that tendency. The treatment of everything from zebras to budgerigars was seen as proof that the UK had not been brutalized by violence. To earn much-needed funds, London Zoo director Julian Huxley set up an Animal Adoption scheme. People contributed towards the upkeep of their chosen beast and in return their names were displayed on its cage. The scheme was a success, with rich and poor contributing alike. Elsewhere in Europe, zoo animals were the first victims of starving civilians and, had the British been faced with starvation, they would probably have tucked in to tiger stew as well. As it was, they prided themselves on their superior sensibilities. When officials at the Ministry of Food complained that people were feeding domestic pets rationed food at the expense of human health, the Ministry was heavily criticized. The Canine Defence League argued that dogs were good rat-catchers (a boon in towns and cities with bombed sewers) and that they were morale-boosting companions. But the really telling protests were those from people who did not advance utilitarian arguments for having pets. One man from north London, whose Labrador refused to accompany him to the air-raid shelter, told *The Times*: 'Sir – My dog is completely useless and I intend to keep him. He slept on my bed all through the Blitz . . . People are very keen on other people making sacrifices I notice.'[115]

When military victories finally came, the underdog patriotism of the British gained a new intensity. Despite the fact that victory could not have been achieved without Russian, American and Commonwealth and Imperial help, it was the period 1940 to 1941 when Britain stood alone that figured most in the public mind. This testimony from a woman working at an aircraft factory in the north of England on D-Day captures the mixture of raucous patriotism and phlegmatic pride which characterized the British in the later stages of the war:

> Suddenly the Managing Director came on to the stage and everything stopped. 'Ladies and Gentlemen', he said quietly, 'we have landed in France'. There was a stunned silence, then a quavering voice started to sing 'Land of Hope and Glory'. In a moment everybody had joined in a great crescendo of sound . . . some of the women who had sons and husbands away were singing with tears running down their faces, while the men were trying to

control their emotion. Then we went quietly back to work – for
victory.[116]

Working for victory was as important as fighting for it and few were
untouched by the experience.

8. Millions like us

The second thing which united the UK was that the people and
material resources of every part of the UK were harnessed on a
greater scale than ever before. Six million men and women were
enlisted in the armed services, but altogether half the population –
23 million people – were called up in one capacity or another.
Countless other millions did their bit for the war effort, from housing
evacuated children to raising money for the government's Spitfire
Fund. The most important impact that mass mobilization had on
national identity in Britain was economic.

State-directed industrial production revived the economies of
Scotland and Wales and in doing so it quelled a good deal of
nationalist discontent. In Wales, unemployment fell from 24.1 per
cent of the population in 1938 to 2.7 per cent in 1951. In Scotland,
it fell from 15.7 per cent to 2.5 per cent.[117] At one point, in 1944,
unemployment virtually disappeared in both countries. Despite the
failure of the Scottish Council of State to become an engine of
devolution, Tom Johnston squeezed every financial benefit from the
war that he could. He persuaded the Treasury to spend £12 million
on Scottish industry, investment which created or significantly
enlarged 700 enterprises and produced 90,000 new jobs. This compared to 121 enterprises and 14,900 jobs created in the whole of
the UK by government investment in the 1930s.[118] Johnston also
harnessed Scotland's natural power for the benefit of its people. In
January 1943 he piloted a Bill through the House of Commons
which set up the North of Scotland Hydro-Electric Board. It was
the first Scottish Bill to be passed without a division since 1832.
The scheme lacked tartan romance, not least because Scotland's
electricity was fed into the UK's national grid. But by the early
1950s the extra power generated by Highland turbines had literally

electrified huge tracts of Scotland, significantly improving its standard of living as a result.

People followed the movement of capital. Economic investment, coupled with the strategic deployment of manpower, prompted one of the most rapid migrations in British history. Between 1939 and 1941, 1.75 million civilians moved from eastern and southern Britain to the north and west, the same number that had moved in the opposite direction between 1924 and 1939.[119]

Plaid Cymru opposed the evacuation of English children to rural areas, arguing that the 'Anglo-Saxon' influx would undermine Welsh language and culture. The party's leader, Saunders Lewis, condemned it as 'one of the most horrible threats to the continuation and to the life of the Welsh nation that has ever been suggested in history'.[120] No children were evacuated to Scotland during the war; instead, Scots complained when they were posted to England or Wales. In 1941, some 13,000 young unmarried women were moved from the central belt to the Midlands to work in munitions factories. This aroused traditional resentment about English domination and a rather older belief that women belonged at home. Scottish leaders protested and forced the government to concede that only those over the age of twenty would be taken in future. The women themselves were less irate. Many liked the Midlands and settled there permanently after the war.

The economic revival and repopulation of Scotland and Wales were short-lived, with disastrous consequences for British national identity. But during the war it seemed as if the southern drift of the previous half-century had at last been halted. The establishment of some degree of equity with England underpinned the unionist patriotism which the simple fear of invasion had sparked. In his memoirs, Tom Johnston credited the war with fostering 'A new spirit of independence and hope in [Scotland's] national life. You could sense it everywhere, and not least in the civil service. We met England now without any inferiority complex. We were a nation once again.'[121] Thus it was a spirit of friendly rivalry that once again characterized Anglo-Scottish relations. During the war peaceful crowds averaging 60,000 watched the annual football match between the two countries, and when the Scottish team received an 8–0 drubbing in 1944 it did not prompt a wave of national self-flagellation, such was the renewed confidence of the Scots. The broad cultural impact of mass mobilization on British national identity is harder to pinpoint statistically than its economic impact. But it seems clear from oral evidence that the millions of troops and civilians who moved around the island in wartime were, as a result of their travels, made more aware of the rich variety of national and regional cultures contained within the United Kingdom.

Relations between the north and south of England also flourished. Most historians claim that the dominant vision of Britain promoted during the Second World War was the rural south of England, or 'Deep England' as Angus Calder has memorably described it. That is simply not the case. The gritty, self-improving northern personality, which the Victorians had celebrated, remained a key element of the good-humoured stoicism that was so central to British national identity in this period. The Lancashire entertainers George Formby and Gracie Fields were the most popular box-office stars in the UK from 1936 to 1943. In all their films, they struggled successfully against poverty and snobbery, delivering a message of courage and cheerfulness to their millions of fans. Formby's catchphrase 'Turned out nice again!' was put to especially good use in *Let George Do It* (1940), in which he parachuted into Nuremberg to punch Hitler on the nose. The film was judged to have been one of the most morale-boosting of the whole war. The war actually improved the north's status; as in Scotland and Wales, shipyards and factories which had closed during the Depression were reopened to maximize production. With the return of full employment, the north's qualities were once more set against a background of enterprise and industry rather than dole and deprivation.

Without doubt, the countryside was one of the main things that people felt they were fighting to save. In any nation threatened with invasion, land is a more immediate and tangible source of patriotism than ideologies. As Britain's cities were heavily bombed for the first time, the countryside – unscathed, peaceful and apparently timeless – became an especial symbol of continuity. H. E. Bates, author of the bucolic idyll *The Darling Buds of May*, told a BBC audience, 'As I was gathering mushrooms [this morning] it occurred to me that the field and the landscape surrounding it . . . hadn't changed much for a hundred years. It was 1940; but it might just as easily have been 1840 or 1870, or 1900 or 1910'.[122]

However, this was not a peculiarly English fixation. The roots of rural romanticism lie in the late-eighteenth-century reaction to indus-trialization; consequently, the countryside had an equally totemic place in the national identities of other developed nations, from the US to Germany. Scotland and Wales were no different, a fact demonstrated by the countless books, songs and paintings which celebrated the Scottish and Welsh countryside. The English celebrated their land a little more self-consciously; not because they were more arcadian or utopian in temperament but because doing so was one of the few ways they felt able to express their uniqueness. Love of the countryside was a form of patriotism which did not undermine Britishness. It rarely challenged the economic and political institutions on which the Union was built and it was something that the Scots and Welsh could relate to. Furthermore, it must be emphasized that the English did not romanticize their rural landscape to the extent that historians commonly assume. In fact, like other Britons, they had a rather functional attitude to it which became even more pronounced after 1939.

Agriculture, no less than heavy industry, enjoyed a revival during the war. The attempted German blockade of Britain meant that every available piece of land was required to grow food. Between 1939 and 1945, 5.75 million acres were reclaimed in a venture that substantially reversed the agricultural depression of the interwar years. The 'Dig for Victory' campaign accounted for some of this figure. Flowerbeds and lawns, golf courses and football pitches were turned over to vegetables by a beleaguered citizenry and produced over 3 million tons of extra food.[123] Most reclamation took place in rural areas – for example in the South Downs of Sussex, large tracts of which were ploughed for the first time since the Anglo-Saxon age. Ploughshares *were* swords as rural Britain became a site of production essential to the nation's survival and not just a picturesque playground for day-trippers.

A few Britons hoped that agricultural mobilization presaged a mass movement 'back to the land', something that left- and right-wing ruralists had dreamed of since the late nineteenth century. In 1943, the rural commentator Richard Harman wrote: 'Farmsteads that were neglected are busy centres of man and beast. England has become a well-kept land again. Of all the evidence that her soul is being reborn this is perhaps the strongest.'[124] A particular source of hope was the Women's Land Army. Founded in 1917, it was re-established by the Ministry of Agriculture in 1939 to make up for the expected shortfall in male farm workers. Its Patron was the Queen and its Director was the Women's Institute Chairman, Lady Denman. The WLA's 87,000 recruits were mostly young, single urban women. Their uniform – brown breeches, tight-fitting green jerseys and Wellington boots – did not escape the attention of

Britain's most famous lesbian gardener, Vita Sackville-West. In her official account of the WLA, Sackville-West recorded her feelings after watching recruits on parade:

> It made me feel very English indeed, when one after the other stood up and announced herself not by her own name but by the name of the county she represented – 'Norfolk! Devon! Warwick!' ... it reminded me of the map one used to have in the schoolroom, showing one's little triangular island cut up into jig-saw patches of different colours, only here the patches were suddenly personified, dressed in honest tweeds and rather strong shoes. I felt how much, how very much, I liked the English; how much, how very much, how painfully much, I loved England.[125]

Most people were not so excited by the rural fecundity of the period. If the war had any effect on popular attitudes, it was to improve the understanding between town and country through a more realistic and *less* romantic appraisal of each other's way of life.

City people who regarded their rural cousins as quaint but mentally backward bumpkins learnt that intelligence quotients were just as high in the lanes of Britain as they were on its streets. The *Land Girl* magazine helpfully told recruits, 'The countryman is a lot more civilised, intelligent and better-mannered man than you are inclined to think at first glance ... They may seem slow, but it is the slowness of people who always look before they leap.'[126] The better-off learnt of the squalor in which so many town *and* country people lived. The sight of lice-ridden city children urinating on the floors of stately homes was not the only culture shock administered by the war. The damp, dark (un-electrified) tenanted cottages found on countless landed estates, and the poverty of the labourers who inhabited them, made many city-born migrants realize that the picturesque social harmony they been told existed in Britain's green and pleasant land was a nationalist fiction. One book in the series 'Home-Front Handbooks', *How To See The Country*, told new arrivals that rural workers had been the victims of 'callous oppression' by aristocratic landlords over the centuries. 'It is fortunate', the book reassured its readers, 'that unlike his Irish cousin [the British countryman] does not hug a grudge about the past, and flame into anger about something that happened eight hundred years ago.'[127]

In the end, whether Britons chose to romanticize the countryside or not, hardly a soul was under the illusion that it would determine their survival against the Germans. In *Out of the People* (1941), J. B. Priestley made the point plainly:

> This is a war of machines . . . They do not manufacture fifteen-inch guns or Spitfires down at the old family place in Devon . . . It is industrial England that is fighting this war, just as it was industrial England, those scores of gloomy towns half-buried in thick smoke, with their long dreary streets of little houses, that produced most of the wealth which enabled this other fancy little England to have its fun and games . . . The hard centre of world resistance to the Nazis is found in the real . . . industrial England.[128]

To conclude, rural Britain – Scottish, Welsh and English (northern or southern) – may have been one of the things that Britons felt they were fighting for. But it was far from being the only thing, or even the most important. And, despite increased agricultural productivity, people knew that the defence of Britain depended first and foremost on the productivity of the ugly factories spattered across the great conurbations of the UK.

The public response to the launch of the Spitfire Fund in July 1940 highlights the theme of this section. The aeroplanes fought most of their battles over the south coast of England. But communities in every part of the UK contributed to the Fund, which by April 1941 had reached £13 million. One of the biggest collections was raised in the Outer Hebrides. The people of Cardiff raised £20,000. Their Lord Mayor explained how:

> Collections were made in the clubs, pubs and places of work. A dance, arranged by the Tongwynlais wardens, raised £50 and another substantial sum was raised when villages at Castleton organised a sale of their fruit and vegetables. Two Cardiff lads spent their August holidays collecting golf balls which they sold to raise ten shillings for the fund, while school children sent in their pocket money. Such was the spirit of 1940.[129]

Two aspects of mass mobilization caught the national imagination so much that they came to form an essential part of the Finest Hour legend: the enlistment of elderly and female Britons.

The Home Guard was a part-time force formed in May 1940 with men aged between seventeen and sixty-five who had not been conscripted, most because they were too old to fight. Half were veterans of the First World War, and if Hitler had invaded they would not have held the mighty Wehrmacht up for long; nor would they have waged much of a guerrilla war against a German occupying force. But the force did serve two purposes, one practical, the other emotional. First, by keeping watch for invaders in town and country, its members released younger troops for front line duty. Second, the fact that all of its 1.75 million men were volunteers, and that they came from all walks of life and every part of Great Britain, boosted national morale by highlighting the depth of British patriotism in a crisis. An official study, published in 1945, summarized the Home Guard's popularity in hyperbole not far removed from Britons' actual view of it:

> It was an outward and visible sign of an inward unity and brotherhood, without distinction of class or calling, begotten of great danger . . . but essentially as natural and rightful a phenomenon of the British landscape as the oak or the elm, the cow-byre or the suburban back-garden, the pub on the corner or the village cricket ground.[130]

The Home Guard was an object of affectionate mirth for the rest of the century, thanks largely to the BBC sitcom *Dad's Army* (1968–77). But here too it struck a chord in the British: the idea of a poorly equipped, aged militia appealed to a nation that prized amateurish but dogged 'muddling through' as a feature of its democratic culture. Jimmy Perry, the co-writer of *Dad's Army* and himself a veteran of the force, captured that spirit in the programme's very first episode. Mr Mainwaring, the pompous bank manager and captain of the Walmington-on-Sea platoon, aims a firearm out of his office window at imaginary Germans in the High Street. After a great deal of huffing and puffing, he exclaims: 'The machine-guns could have a clear field of fire from here to Timothy White's if it wasn't for that woman in the telephone box.'

In reality, women didn't get in the way. Indeed, the mobilization of women had a far greater effect on British national identity than that of aged men. Women had played an important part in the First World War but on nothing like the scale they did in the Second. And, having since won the vote, their contribution was taken more seriously than before. Female citizens were conscripted in 1941, and the number reached a peak in 1943 when 7.25 million were employed in industry, transport, civil defence, and the armed forces. By that date, 90 per cent of all single women between the ages of eighteen and forty, and 80 per cent of married women with children over the age of fourteen were working. Churchill acknowledged that 'this war effort could not have been achieved if the women had not marched forward in millions'.[131]

Economic survival was their main motive, but a new form of patriotic feminism accompanied it. Mrs Mary Clara Evans, a munitions worker in Birmingham, told *Woman's Own* in 1942, 'Every time my leg goes up and down I feel I'm giving Hitler a kick in the pants.'[132] The magazine urged its readers to seize the opportunity war had offered them. 'House-pride is no longer the virtue it was. Carry on in comradeship with the women who have put it in their pockets to make munitions, work on the land, hold down a man's job . . . do anything in your capacity to the utmost of your power to hasten victory.'[133] The BBC series *Women at War*, which led to the launch of *Woman's Hour* in 1946, celebrated their contribution to the war effort; so too did the film *Millions Like Us* (1943). Perhaps the most significant change was the expansion of the women's armed services in 1938–9: the ATS (army), and the WRNS (navy) and WAAF (air force), originally formed in the First World War (the WAAF as the WRAF). They were not intended to be directly involved in armed combat and, with make-up packed in kitbags, British women were at pains to show they had not lost their femininity by donning military uniforms. But many did find themselves in the thick of battle, not least the 180,000 members of the WAAF some of whom won medals for extreme bravery when air bases were bombed during the Battle of Britain.

A large number – 8.77 million – remained full-time housewives. And many who were conscripted were not happy about it. Women in traditionally male occupations like shipbuilding or bus conducting had to contend not only with lower rates of pay but also with chauvinist hostility. For married women, the strain of working and keeping a family together with inadequate child care and a husband on active service was too much, and wartime rates of depression were highest among this section of British society. But mobilization was a liberating experience for most women. First, it led to greater sexual freedom. Fear of death, and the 'live for today' attitude that war fostered, loosened inhibitions. The anonymity of war helped too. Not only were husbands and boyfriends away fighting; women posted around the UK were able to temporarily escape the twitching net curtains of family, friends and neighbours. Divorce rose by 150 per cent during the war; veneral disease by 139 per cent; and illegitimacy doubled, with a third of all babies being born out of wedlock by 1945 (the highest figure ever recorded). Of course, these could be traumatic events, particularly when women returned home to face the music.

Attitudes to women's work changed quicker than attitudes to their sexuality. The proportion of British women who had jobs rose steadily, from 34 per cent just before the war to 75 per cent by the end of the century, the biggest rise taking place among married women. Career opportunities increased too. The collapse of domestic service and the growth of office work liberated working-class women from the more ignominious effects of the British class system. Between 1931 and 1961, the number of women in domestic service fell from 2 million to 200,000.[134] As millions exchanged pinnies for skirts and trousers, their former employers were forced to experience the joys of scrubbing lavatories for the first time. In 1937, working-class women spent twice as many hours doing housework as middle-class ones; by 1961, there was no difference between the two groups.[135]

Wartime mobilization gave British women a glimpse of a more independent, fulfilling life and few of them forgot it. Historian Penny Summerfield writes: 'the British woman was never after the Second World War debarred from paid work in the way she had been before, despite a strongly marginalizing rhetoric. While she remained central to the family, during the war there had been a redefinition of what that meant: the housewife was now a financial as well as a moral and emotional cornerstone'.[136]

I would go further. Their visible contribution to saving the UK from destruction led to women being seen as Britons on the same terms as men. The Victorian ideal of a benign, maternal Florence Nightingale tending to the wounds of heroic men was replaced by a more dynamic image of female patriotism. In the Victory Parade of 1946, British women not only waved Union Jacks at passing soldiers, sailors and airmen, they also marched alongside them. Their right to belong was legally recognized by the Nationality Act, passed by the Labour government in 1948. Previously, a woman who married a foreigner automatically lost her British citizenship because nationality was seen to reside in the male. After 1948, a woman's Britishness was no longer dependent on *her* choice (if any) of a partner. Property law was not reformed until the next Labour government twenty years later, and in everyday social relations male prejudices were slow to thaw. But the Second World War did begin a fundamental improvement in women's lot and in the process it made Britishness a more inclusive national identity.

9. At home you don't wear shoes anyway

Mass mobilization also revealed how exclusive British national identity still was. There were riots against Germans and Italians early in the war in England, Scotland and Wales. But the 1939 Aliens Act and the consequent internment of 26,000 Continentals proved to be unpopular, particularly when people realized that most so-called aliens had either been loyal residents of the UK for many years or else had come to Britain to escape fascism. As a result, the Act was modified, leaving only 25 people interned by 1944. In addition, almost 1,600 British citizens of Continental descent were imprisoned under Defence Regulation 18B, on suspicion of 'endangering the safety of the realm'. But here too common sense prevailed and by 1941 only 400 were left in captivity. Black Britons fared less well.[137]

Despite the fact that one of the nation's central war aims was to defeat the most pathologically racist regime Europe had ever seen, the British had a clear and certain belief in their own superiority as white people. Political enthusiasm for the Empire may have been in decline, but the racial understanding of Britishness was alive and well. And during the war it was nourished by the country's leaders. Churchill's speeches were full of references to the glory of the British race, and it was not merely a rhetorical device. The Prime Minister was both an ardent imperialist and an Atlanticist who believed it was the destiny of Britain and her white diaspora to lead the world. He often used the more respectable twentieth-century euphemism of 'the English-speaking peoples' to describe that diaspora, but skin colour and not language was its defining characteristic. Moreover, skin colour denoted fixed moral qualities in Churchill's mind. In 1943 he told an audience at the White House, 'Why be apologetic about Anglo-Saxon superiority?'[138]

During the war, the British did not apologize for their sense of racial superiority. But they were conscious of the need to present it in a better light. The British emphasized how, in contrast to the Germans, they were proud of their racial diversity. However, in doing so, no mention was made of the island's small yet centuries-old black, Asian and Oriental population. Proof of Britain's racial diversity was instead found in the ancient history of the islands' white tribes. Britain, it was argued, was made up of Celts, Anglo-Saxons, Danes and Normans who had intermingled for so many centuries that no clear racial type could now be identified. This pluralism of whiteness had been a feature of racial theory since the Victorian era. It was not designed to foster a multiracial sense of Britishness but to unite the Scots, Welsh and English by demonstrating that they had more in common with each other than they did with the coloured peoples over whom they ruled. And although the Empire was justified as a multiracial family of nations, a clear moral distinction continued to be made between the inhabitants of the 'Motherland' and the white Commonwealth on the one hand and those of the black Commonwealth on the other.

The Army Bureau of Current Affairs (ABCA) ensured that the message reached those in the front line of the battle for democracy. ABCA was run by the Welshman W. E. Williams, who had also helped to set up CEMA. The barrack-room discussions on citizenship which the Bureau staged under the title 'The British Way and Purpose' were credited with radicalizing the armed forces and so delivering the service vote to the Labour Party in the general election of 1945. But that was not the extent of its influence. One of the Bureau's pamphlets, *You and the Empire*, expressed regret that 'To many people nowadays, the very word "Empire" has a nasty sound. It reminds them of Nazi ideas of a master-race ruling others'.[139] Another, written by the geographer C. B. Fawcett, outlined the qualifications for being British. He acknowledged that due to invasions and migrations from Europe over the course of two millennia 'the British peoples are not a distinctive race'. Then he asked: 'Are all British subjects members of the British nation – the Irish, the Jamaicans, Indians and so on? Legally and politically, they are members beyond question, but do they belong to it in feeling and culture?'[140] He left the question open, but it was clear he thought the answer was no. Emphasizing that the British were mongrels did not therefore remove race from the DNA of national identity. If anything, quite the opposite. Ancient racial differences within Britain were played down in order to promote a unitary whiteness among the Scots, Welsh and English.

Tragically, black Commonwealth citizens who joined the armed forces did feel that they belonged to Britain in 'feeling and culture'. Unlike inhabitants of the UK, they were nearly all volunteers not conscripts. Over 3.5 million black and Asian Commonwealth citizens volunteered to fight for Britain. In India, 1.5 million swelled the ranks of the 200,000-strong professional army. India's Scottish Viceroy, the Marquess of Linlithgow, put down the biggest nationalist uprising since the Indian Mutiny of 1857, killing over 2,000 people and imprisoning 60,000 in 1942. But the vast majority of Indians defied nationalist calls to topple the Raj because they realized that defeating Germany and Japan was a more urgent task. In Africa, 374,000 people joined up. Countless other Africans voluntarily helped with the war effort. The people of Kano in Nigeria, for example, raised over £10,000 and sent it to Britain for the purchase of a Spitfire. But this goodwill was soon abused. Forced labour was imposed on the black population in several colonies. From 1942 to 1944, 100,000 Nigerians were set to work in the tin mines of the Jos Plateau, prompting the *Nigerian Eastern Mail* to ask: 'What purpose does it serve to remind us that Hitler regards us as semi-apes if the Empire for which we are ready to suffer and die, for whom we poured our blood and drained our pockets in 1914 and for whom we are [doing] the same today, can tolerate racial discrimination against us?' West Indians, whose islands were outside the main theatres of war, travelled thousands of miles to the UK to enlist. They rallied to the Union Jack not only from a desire to fight fascism but also because they felt a patriotic duty to assist a nation of which they believed themselves to be citizens. A thousand skilled technicians were employed in munitions factories in Lancashire and the central belt of Scotland; many others joined the merchant navy, where there had long been a black presence. Approximately 12,000 Caribbean people joined the armed forces: most went into the RAF, stationed in Nottingham and the south of England. Despite their profound sense of Britishness and the comradeship which the war inspired, the majority endured persistent racism.

Many factory owners (supported by trade unions) publicly refused to take black workers, while the armed forces operated a more insidious scheme of discrimination. Black women were unofficially barred from the WAAF and the WLA. The less prestigious ATS took them, but once in uniform they encountered hostility. One woman was refused a new issue of shoes by her officer on the grounds 'At home you don't wear shoes anyway'.[141] For some, the only escape was in the sky. Jimmy Hyde, a much decorated Trinidadian RAF pilot, wrote: 'No friend, no girl, no one in all England. I am alone and the only time I feel happy is when I am in my Spitfire alone in the clouds.[142] Others fought back. In 1943, the cricketer Learie Constantine (then serving at the Ministry of Labour with responsibility for black Britons on Merseyside) was given four days off to captain the

West Indies against England at Lords. He and his team-mates were refused admission to the Imperial Hotel in London because, said the manageress, 'we're not going to have all these niggers in our hotel'.[143] On repeated occasions over the next fifty years, black citizens would learn that cricket was no guarantee of fair play nor of Commonwealth brotherhood, despite the claims made for it by celebrants of English culture. Constantine took the Imperial to court where his case was heard by Lord Justice Birkett, later a judge at the Nuremberg War Crimes Tribunal. Birkett awarded him £5 damages.

Even stars like Constantine could do little to change attitudes because racism was actively encouraged by military and civil authorities. Army guidelines on 'Relations With Coloured Troops' advised white personnel to mix with them as little as possible, concluding 'While there are many coloured men of high mentality and cultural distinction, the generality arc of a simple mental outlook.'[144] Miscegenation had always been at the forefront of racial hostility and the Second World War was no different. Opprobrium was heaped upon white women who associated with black men and many regional police forces prosecuted them for doing so. The men themselves risked beatings and intimidation.

When the US Army arrived in 1942, Britons were shocked by the formal segregation of black and white GI units, but it was merely a question of degree. The dislike of America's more naked racist culture should not disguise the plain fact that a majority of Britons did not regard black people as equals, still less as compatriots. In daily intercourse, they rarely distinguished between black troops from the US and those from the UK. To solve the problem, Harold Macmillan (then Under-Secretary of State for the Colonies) suggested that black Britons should be issued with little Union Jack badges. He did not make the suggestion in order to alter popular attitudes but because he shared them. When the Duke of Buccleuch complained that Honduran foresters sent to work on his Scottish estate were enjoying intercourse with local women, Macmillan replied, 'It is of course obvious that if you bring coloured men to this country for war purposes, there will be the risk of some undesirable results . . . All we can do is mitigate the evil.'[145] It was the same desire to 'mitigate evil' that twenty years later led Macmillan, as Prime Minister, to limit black immigration by Act of Parliament.

Ethnic minorities who were born and bred in the UK were also excluded from the prevailing definition of Britishness. Hostility towards evacuees was not only based on a fear of the urban working classes among the rural elite. There was a strong racial element to it as well. Jewish evacuees were frequently subjected to anti-Semitic abuse and many pretended they were gentiles to avoid it, eating pork and attending church with the families on whom they were billeted. Sometimes the level of hostility was so great that it drove gentiles from country and town to put aside their other differences. Twelve-year-old Gloria Agman and her four-year-old brother were sent from London to a village in the Midlands. 'Both groups united to attack me as a "rotten Jew",' she remembers. 'My closest friend during much of my stay in the village was a half-Chinese girl from London who was exposed to the same experience as mine, except that she was called a "dirty Chink". We had a pact. I never called her "Chink" and she never called me "Jew".'[146] As late as 1947 there were anti-Semitic riots in several British cities. The main cause was a popular belief that Jews were deliberately exploiting the economic austerity of the time by running the black market.[147] Those who physically attacked Jewish people and property were simply the most vociferous members of a society which still saw Jews as second-class Britons. In 1949, by which time the Holocaust was common knowledge, polls showed that approximately half the population of the UK had strong anti-Semitic opinions.[148]

The issue of race is rarely confronted in histories of the 'People's War', perhaps because it is a reminder that a belief in democracy was not the only thing that bound the Scots, Welsh and English together. Much older, darker and contradictory ties of racial unity did so too. In a war against fascism it was impolitic for those ties to be overtly celebrated, but they existed in millions of minds nonetheless. One of the reasons why the Finest Hour legend had such nostalgic potency after the war was that it came to stand for a culturally homogeneous and self-sufficient nation which Britons felt had been sullied by black immigration. What enabled that lie to stand was the ease with which the contribution of black Britons to the defeat of Hitler was ignored and then forgotten.

What the British preferred to celebrate was the improvement of class relations. In *Out of the People* J. B. Priestley wrote:

> It was not until the bombs fell and the people stood up undaunted that the world began to admire Britain again. What had there been to admire about us before that? Pleasant manners and an easy good temper, and what remained, after greed and stupidity had done their worst, of a beautiful island. It was a nice place to be rich and rather silly in, but few outsiders envied us our ordinary

life, which seemed to them ugly and complacent and dreary, shocking in its inequalities, too often bound up with trivialities, an attempt to live without passion and gaiety, without art and philosophy, even without real politics.[149]

We have now looked at four reasons for national unity between 1940 and 1945. But there was a fifth force at work (to some a fifth column), hinted at in the quote above, which over the following thirty years was instrumental in maintaining a popular sense of Britishness: the emergence of social democracy.

10. All in the same boat

The war raised national consciousness in Britain by prompting a closer look at what it meant to be British, and because the Home Front was a battleground for the first time, it also fostered a more cooperative spirit, softening class barriers and creating a sense of common purpose in the 'People's War'. Most conflicts have this effect on nations but in 1940–45 it was more pronounced. John Betjeman told BBC listeners that 'War divides us into where we really belong. Class nonsense and incomes and possessions become of no importance. The cake is cut at right angles to the way it was cut before . . . [War] teaches us to consider other people and to value a man not according to his income but according to his heart.'[150] Betjeman's response was an essentially spiritual one: for him, the war simply made class seem less important than the all-embracing nation 'where we really belong'.

But, for many others, the war was an opportunity to transform the nation by confronting inequality and ensuring that the cake would always be cut differently. In her study *Life Among the English* (1942), the novelist Rose Macaulay wrote: 'It was a life which tended to resolve class distinctions; taxi-drivers [and] shop assistants . . . and young ladies and gentlemen from expensive schools and universities, met and played and worked on level terms . . . English social life is, in these curious, dark, troubled years, moving a few steps nearer that democracy for which we say we are fighting and have never yet had.'[151] The best-known herald of class unity was J. B. Priestley. His

Sunday night *Postscript* broadcasts attracted audiences second only to Churchill's, and on 21 July 1940 he told listeners:

> Now, the war, because it demands a huge collective effort, is compelling us to change not only our ordinary, social and economic habits, but also our habits of thought. We're actually changing over from the property view to the sense of community, which simply means that we realise we're all in the same boat. But, and this is the point, that boat can serve not only as a defence against Nazi aggression but as an ark in which we can all finally land in a better world.[152]

When Mass Observation asked people what long-term effect the war would have, the most common belief was that there would be fewer class distinctions.[153] The Blitz was instrumental in fostering comradeship. During the war, 130,000 civilians were killed, 43,000 of them between the start of the Blitz in September 1940 and its abatement in July 1941. Amidst the terror, blood and fire of total war, human differences melted as quickly as flesh. People were also forced closer together physically, in the air-raid shelters where, night after night, millions from Glasgow to London huddled. The experience was not a pleasant one and many preferred to risk dying in their own homes than surviving with a stranger's foot pressed against their nose in cramped, dark tunnels drenched with urine and excreta. Nonetheless, the experience of the Blitz was an inspiring one for many. One survey of the Home Front, *Ourselves in Wartime*, observed: 'The greatest lesson perhaps of all was the lesson of the shelters – the lesson that neighbourliness, understanding and unselfishness were the birthright of the British people.'[154]

The comradeship of men in the face of battle also left a mark on millions, including those who were literally in the same boat. Former Etonian and future TV broadcaster Ludovic Kennedy served as a sub-lieutenant in the navy. In 1943, he wrote, 'the greatest gift the war has brought me is a sense of comradeship, which I did not know existed between men. On a ship . . . you work with them, eat with them, play with them; your lives are interwoven; on the fate of the ship depends the fate of each one of you.'[155] Infantry officer Anthony Irwin's platoon included a docker from Belfast, a fireman from Dublin, a hawker from the East End of London and a theological student from Glasgow – all of whom, he said, were 'instilled with the will to fight and a damn clear idea of what they were fighting for'.[156]

It was that clear idea, maintained through the worst carnage, which made the difference between the First World War and the Second. The death rate among the upper echelons of British society was proportionately greater than that of servicemen from ordinary backgrounds. Indeed, Britain's officer class suffered more in 1939–45 than it had in 1914–18 (150 per cent higher than average casualties compared to 80 per cent higher in the previous war, according to one estimate). Once again, the worst hit were junior officers – the subalterns of British military legend.[157] Yet the later conflict did not foster a legend of 'the Lost Generation' among the officer class because there was a greater sense that their sacrifice was for a worthy, common cause. What also made a difference in the Second was that British victories were achieved relatively quickly and with tolerable loss of life. Moreover, generals led their men from tank turrets and not from drinks cabinets miles behind the fighting. The most popular, Bernard Montgomery, regularly toured the front lines speaking to his troops in a patriotic but informal way, and keeping them informed about what they were being asked to do. Monty believed that ordinary troops were not cannon fodder but 'a measure of the greatness of the British character'. The fact that he was Britain's most successful general made him a national hero. But it was his ability to convey his admiration of his troops which made him especially popular on the front line.[158]

The war showed that state planning could make the UK more efficient and more equitable. But it was the cooperative spirit of the period and the material benefits ordinary people hoped would flow from that spirit, rather than the mechanics of how it would be done, which excited public opinion. The national mood was given a focus and a fillip by the Beveridge Report, published on 2 December 1942, shortly after Monty's victory with the Eighth Army at El Alamein. The report put forward a blueprint for the welfare state, promising to abolish 'the Five Giants' of 'Want, Disease, Ignorance, Squalor and Idleness'. Beveridge's biographer has written that 'his mingled tone of optimism, patriotism, high principle and pragmatism exactly fitted the prevailing popular mood'.[159] The comedian Tommy Handley dubbed the plan *Gone With the Want*, and it soon became as popular as the Clark Gable blockbuster. An unprecedented 635,000 copies of the report were sold; by early 1943 a survey carried out by the British Institute of Public Opinion found that 86 per cent of Britons were in favour, with only 6 per cent opposed.[160] Beveridge's proposals were complemented by Butler's Education Act of 1944, which established free secondary education for all, and several other reports which laid the foundations for a planned economy and a much greater role for the state in British life.

In later years, historians questioned whether there really was a consensus for reform. Were they right? Up to a point, yes. The idea that if Johnny foreigner drops a few million tons of explosives on Britain, dustmen and debutantes will spontaneously link arms and sing 'Knees Up, Mother Brown' is sentimental nonsense. Many Britons did not want to learn the lesson of the shelters. The Ritz avoided them altogether by providing comfortable bedding in the basement. Observing one group sitting in the lobby of a Mayfair hotel, Ed Murrow remarked, 'It wasn't the sort of protection I'd seek from a direct hit . . . but if you were a retired colonel and his lady, you might feel that the risk was worth it because you would at least be bombed with the right sort of people.'[161]

Throughout the UK, social inequality and snobbery were still rife, a fact which amid the suffering of war sometimes intensified class hatred. During the Blitz, when 90 per cent of the bombs dropped on London were falling on the East End, some air-raid wardens deliberately let houses in areas like Knightsbridge burn. When Churchill visited Camberwell in south-east London, he made a brief speech that concluded with the words: 'We can take it,' to which a voice shouted back, 'What do you mean "we", you fat bastard!'[162] A decline of deference was widely commented on during the war. Those who complained about it not only thought the trend undermined the British tradition of politeness, they also saw it as a disturbing sign that social hierarchies were collapsing. The Liberal MP Robert Bernays was disturbed by

> a growing lack of consideration and courtesy in the ordinary relations of civilian life. Parents, for instance, thoughtlessly allow children in railway carriages to take up the room of an adult, while youths on holiday will occupy first class seats with third class tickets . . . I have noticed, too, in some cases in the shops a marked deterioration in the hitherto high standard in the manners of shop assistants, particularly in relation to goods that are in short supply.[163]

Crime in the UK rose by 40 per cent during the war, and looting in London became so frequent that Scotland Yard had to set up a special division to deal with it. Strikes were common. Although in 1940 the number of days lost to industrial action fell sharply, once the invasion crisis receded the figure started to rise again. By 1942 it exceeded prewar levels and by 1944 the figure – 3.7 million days – was nearly treble what it had been in 1938.[164] Even in the forces, the bond between officers and men was not always close. In 1943 Evelyn Waugh was demobbed. Ostensibly this was so that he could complete his novel *Brideshead Revisited*, which lamented the decline of aristocratic power; in fact, he was allowed to leave the army because he had been unable to hide his snobbish contempt for the men under his command and it was thought he would be shot by them in battle.

Deep-seated resentment therefore fuelled much of the desire for change. Equally, the opposition to change was often uncompromising and, at times, apocalyptic in its prognosis of what a welfare state would do to the nation. The letters page of *The Times* has often been described as the bush telegraph of middle England. The following letter was published in December 1942:

> Sir – In my opinion the way of the Beveridge Report is the road to the moral ruin of the nation, it is the way tending to weaken still further the initiative and adventure, the stimulus of competition, courage and self reliance. It substitutes emphasis on rights for emphasis on obligations, and collective impersonal charity for private personal charity. It is a blow at the heart of the nation with the weapon of a seductive opiate. It is the way of sleep, not a symptom of the vitality of our civilisation but of its approaching end.[165]

The idea that Britain was becoming a dependency culture in which enterprise and individual responsibility were forfeited in the bid to redistribute wealth never entirely vanished, even at the height of Labour's moral authority in the 1940s.

At Westminster advocates of state control and advocates of the free market were still divided on most areas of policy. Churchill bitterly resented the Labour Party's decision not to continue the coalition government in peacetime and, worse still, to go to the country before the war was completely over. He was so angry that in the general election campaign which followed he impugned the patriotism of the Labour Party, describing socialism as 'this continental conception of human society . . . abhorrent to the British idea of freedom', and, in a comment that caused much offence, he warned that a Labour government would have to resort to 'some form of Gestapo' to establish socialism in Britain.[166]

However, none of these qualifications should obscure the fact that from the 1940s to the 1980s there was widespread agreement about the general direction Britain should take in the future. The subsequent questioning of that agreement says more about the period historians were writing in than the period they were writing about. During the 1980s, scholars of the left and centre were so disillusioned by the ease with which Mrs Thatcher dismantled the postwar consensus that some found it easier to argue a consensus had never existed in the first place, instead of confronting the reasons why social democracy, through its own failings, had lost so much of its popular appeal. The originator of consensus theory, Professor Paul Addison, remarked in his defence that despite the differences between parties and people in the 1940s, their 'comparative moderation lowered the ideological temper and opened the door to the politics of the centre'.[167]

The British agreed to open that door because of the patriotism which the Second World War generated. George Orwell described its power in *The Lion and the Unicorn*:

> The vast majority of the people feel themselves to be a single nation and are conscious of resembling one another more than they resemble foreigners. Patriotism is usually stronger than class hatred . . . England is the most class-ridden country under the sun. It is a land of snobbery and privilege ruled largely by the old and silly. But in any calculation one has to take into account its emotional unity, the tendency of nearly all its inhabitants to feel alike and act together in moments of supreme crisis.[168]

Like many Western theorists of the subject, Orwell pictured the nation as a family: 'it has its private language and its common memories, and at the approach of an enemy it closes its ranks.' But he then famously concluded that Britain was 'a family with the wrong members in control'.[169] Because the country was so united from 1940 to 1945, there was a widespread feeling that Britishness was in full bloom for the first time since the creation of the Union. Some observers put this down to a dramatic empowerment of the people; a feeling that already the right members of the family were in control. In 1945, for example, the historian Raymond Postgate wrote that 'patriotism has come back into its own [as] the people take over the defence and running of their country'.[170] The real reason was more prosaic.

A great deal of the patriotic consensus of mid-twentieth century Britain was due to the Labour Party's success in positioning itself for the first time in its history as *the* patriotic party of Great Britain. Having chosen not to join the National governments of 1931 to 1940, Labour leaders had struggled before the war to convince Britons that they truly loved their country. Until Attlee succeeded George Lansbury in 1935, the party was avowedly pacifist. Even after Attlee took over, their justification for not joining the National government – that true patriots wanted to improve their country and not rest on its laurels – seemed to many to be self-indulgent tosh at a time when Britain was struggling to overcome the worst domestic and international crises it had experienced for nearly a century.

The war changed that view because the party was instrumental in Chamberlain's downfall and because it had joined the coalition government led by Churchill. This not only gave its leaders valuable administrative experience; more importantly, it removed the stigma of disloyalty which had stuck to them during the previous decade, just as it had stuck to the nation's intellectuals. In Labour Party offices, no less than in Bloomsbury salons, the war provided a stiff breeze which fluttered ragged Union Jacks into life again. From this base, Labour and its sympathizers were able to exploit the cooperative mood of the country and convince a majority of Britons that social democracy *was* patriotism; that a new Britain would simply be a better Britain; the fulfilment of its finest traditions and not a betrayal of them. The Party's 1945 election manifesto even described its proposals as 'the practical expression' of 'the spirit of Dunkirk and the Blitz'.[171]

Socialists also argued that those who were marginalized or excluded altogether from society could not be expected to love their country. They had to be given a stake in it. This reassured the middle classes that radical reform would heal rather than aggravate social divisions, thereby maintaining the national unity of war in a more effective way than the election of Churchill as a figurehead would. In 1944 the MP and future Minister for War, John Strachey, confronted the question of 'On Loving One's Country' thus:

> The appeal of patriotism, of devotion and sacrifice to one's country, is a very high and noble one; but it is also one which can be most shamefully abused . . . We who want to make our country a fair and just place love her much better and more truly than those people who pretend that nothing in Britain needs altering . . . Almost all of us have some stake in the country . . . because of this we feel . . . that this is *our* country, which we must, and will, defend . . . When the people of Britain get control of their country,

by getting control of its real economic life, they will become the strongest and best champions that Britain has ever known.[172]

Labour finally succeeded in convincing enough people that it was neither a puppet of communist Russia nor a clone of Continental socialist parties. It respected Britain's traditions; indeed, it sprang from them, applying common-sense solutions to problems instead of imposing ideological ones. It was the party, Attlee rebuked Churchill, of Robert Owen and not that of Karl Marx.

The basis of Labour's message was a concept that went to the heart of British national identity: fair play. Although Labour's proposals were genuinely radical, at the time they were not presented as a dramatic redistribution of wealth and power in which the world would be turned upside down. Instead, they were presented as 'fair shares for all', a victory for decency rather than a defeat for conservatism. In his reply to Churchill's 'Gestapo' broadcast, Attlee told Britons:

> The Labour Party is . . . the one Party which most clearly reflects . . . all the main streams which flow into the great river of our national life. Our appeal to you, therefore, is not narrow or sectional. We are proud of the fact that our country in the hours of its greatest danger stood firm and united, setting an example to the world of how a great democratic people rose to the height of the occasion and saved democracy and liberty . . . We call you to another adventure which will demand the same high qualities as those shown in the war; the adventure of civilisation.[173]

Much has been made of Attlee's public school background when explaining why the middle classes voted for Labour in 1945. But it was as a keen follower of cricket, rather than as a Haileybury boy, that Attlee was able to deliver a message of fair play which attacked privilege without raising the spectre of class conflict; a message which invited people not to revolt against their country but to prove their love for it in a different way. The essence of the social democratic revolution of the 1940s was that the Labour Party rewrote the rule book of Britishness while convincing the nation that it was simply abiding by it.

11. Building a new British culture

Creating a consensus for reform did not simply entail pressing the right buttons on the console of national identity. Beyond the patriotic rhetoric so effectively employed by the country's liberal elite from 1942 to 1945, there was a commitment to promote Britishness in peacetime by adapting methods used in war. Once the beleaguered Island Fortress began to turn into a victorious one in 1942, the Nazi threat to the British way of life receded, but the task of reconstruction was daunting. The belief grew that Britons could be more effectively mobilized for that task if they had a still deeper understanding of who they were. By subsidizing and publicizing British culture, the state could awaken the latent sensibilities of the people. Armed with those sensibilities, Britons would then be able to appreciate what in 1940 Lord Reith had called 'the value and reality of cultural roots'. The result, reformers hoped, would be a nation of mature, patriotic citizens, a social unity never before achieved in peacetime and a renewed sense of purpose in a dramatically changed world.

In short, national culture was the foundation on which postwar reform was seen to rest. The critic Robert Hewison has explained the point well:

> The most useful way to manufacture [consensus] – that is, a general acceptance that certain concepts or courses of action are right and natural – is through a society's culture, through the ideas, images and values which are embodied in its rituals and its historical memory – in its mythology. Culture puts the flesh on the bones of national identity, and a sense of national identity is one of the prerequisites of political consensus.[174]

By 1945, it was no longer a peripheral issue. Though to a contemporary eye it may seem extraordinary, to the leaders of mid-century Britain it was second in importance only to the economy and it was on a par with welfare, health and education, to the last of which it was closely linked. At one time or another the debate over national culture involved most of the leading figures in the arts, sciences, politics, Churches, and the media. They frequently disagreed on how to achieve their goal. But, broadly speaking, they all saw that goal as the democratization of Britishness.

The two men responsible for cementing the consensus were key figures in the wider attempt to reform Britain. The first was the Conservative President of the Board of Education, Rab Butler. As a policymaker and minister he laid the foundations of a more liberal Conservatism. The second was the economist John Maynard Keynes. Though he died of heart failure at Easter 1946, he was the architect of the planned economy which, in one shape or another, dominated British politics until 1979. Butler appointed Keynes Chairman of CEMA in 1942 and secured more money for the organization, and shortly after the invasion of Normandy they began discussions about making the organization a permanent body, called the Arts Council of Great Britain. A proposal for it to be called the Royal Council of Arts was vetoed by Butler on the grounds that such a title would not be 'consistent with the main object of CEMA which is a popular appeal' – a telling sign of the political mood of Britain in the mid-1940s. A short, sharp debate took place about whether Scotland and Wales should have their own organizations. Tom Johnston pressed for one but Keynes found the subject 'tiresome' and set up toothless Scottish and Welsh Advisory Committees instead. One of his officials believed they were a 'mean and puny piece of machinery for carrying out what the Scottish and Welsh feel should be national programmes in their own right'.[175]

The Council's strategy was not decided as easily as its new name. Three different groups contested it. Keynes and Kenneth Clark led those who believed it should concentrate on the fine arts in order to raise popular taste. Keynes deplored what he called 'the welfare racket' who wanted to dole out culture like so many insurance stamps. The 'welfare racket' was led by the composer Ralph Vaughan Williams, who criticized Keynes for turning the Council into 'little more than a commercial concert agency'.[176] He saw amateur activity not merely as a wartime stopgap but as the basis of a new folk culture which would fan out from the village halls of Britain to embrace the whole nation. The last group was led by W. E. Williams. The most visionary of the three, he too was sceptical about amateurism. But unlike Keynes and Clark, he envisioned a pluralistic national culture in which the arts were integrated with the entire spectrum of popular leisure.

In an article in *Picture Post*, Williams asked 'Are We Building a New British Culture?'. His reply was an emphatic 'Yes' because, he argued, the war had made it 'really national' for the first time. To harness this change, he advocated building civic centres in every town with a population of over 10,000, where everything from string quartets to the jitterbug could be enjoyed. Williams had an 'unfettered capacity for hedonism'. He also knew that while his counterparts in health and education only had to compete with dank Victorian hospitals and schools when framing their plans, he would have to compete with all the excitement the mass-entertainment industry had to offer, particularly once it was in full flow again after the war.

He was therefore adamant that the centres should not be earnest temples of high culture but bright, glamorous places of entertainment which combined the pleasures of the art gallery with those of the music hall, cinema, dance hall and pub. He was supported by a number of people, among them Ivor Brown, the Council's first Director of Publicity and editor of the *Observer*. Brown argued for a 'a cordial home of all the reasonable pleasures, and not some austere factory of uplift, betterment and grim educational routine'.[177] Aware that the work of Victorian social reformers had been hampered by the myopic puritanism of the temperance movement, Williams was particularly keen that the centres should have a good supply of alcohol.

> We must no longer be content with the Calvinist notion that any old upper room will do for cultural purposes – an attic over the Co-op, or an Infant's School classroom ... Let us so unify our popular culture that in every town we have a centre where people may listen to good music, look at paintings, study any subject under the sun, join in a debate, enjoy a game of badminton and get a mug of beer or cocoa before they go home.[178]

Both men were also adamant that amateur activity was not the root of a healthy popular culture. This was not snobbish disdain on their part but a pragmatic assessment of what would attract audiences. Most people wanted to be entertained by professionals as a release from the rigours of working life rather than spend valuable leisure time staging their own productions. However novel it might be to see the local butcher dressed up as the Lord High Executioner, it was clear that a constant round of ropy productions of the *Mikado* cast by the vicar's wife would do little to form queues outside a box office when Stewart Grainger, Henry Hall or Max Miller were appearing nearby. Ivor Brown acidly observed, 'The association of the arts with stale buns, the tea-urn and tepid lemonade is a dreadful curse of

British community life . . . Let the people sing by all means . . . but let them sing in tune'.[179]

Keynes was having none of it. The thought of a drunken game of bingo taking place after a poetry recital was anathema to him. In November 1945 he was in America negotiating financial aid from the US in order to fund reconstruction when he heard the idea of arts centres was being touted round Whitehall. He wired London, demanding to know 'Who foisted this rubbish on us?'[180] It was not the end of the project. But in the six months of life left to him, Keynes stamped his vision on the Council by pumping most of its money into prestigious metropolitan bodies like the Royal Opera House in Covent Garden. Dogged for ever after by accusations of elitism, the Opera House was symbolic because during the war it had been leased to Mecca Cafés and the sounds of Verdi had temporarily been replaced by those of Joe Loss and his Orchestra. When Keynes emerged victorious from the first round of the debate, he told the Cultural Attaché at the Soviet Embassy, 'it is the kind of State cultural establishment which you have long known in Russia', and he boasted, 'I am Commissar for Fine Arts in my country!'[181]

The Arts Council's concentration on the fine arts helped to ensure that within a few years the initiative in remaking national identity slipped away from the state as Britons rejected the persistent call to improve themselves. At the same time, the power to do anything about that mistake was surrendered because a Ministry of Culture was not created. The idea was roundly vetoed on the ground that it was a Continental notion which did not conform to British political traditions. Keynes' boast to the Russians was therefore a hollow one. Lord Esher, a member of the Council's Executive, wrote: 'The patronage system has been destroyed by the war . . . [We] have no alternative but to throw ourselves into the arms of socialism [but it is] important that our infant steps in socialism should not be led away by that wretched German Karl Marx into the desert of tasteless bureaucracy.'[182] This was a widely held view, even among those who disagreed with the elitist strategy the Council had adopted. A 'nationalisation of the arts' would 'bind the muses in red tape' was Ivor Brown's conclusion.[183] Keynes' self-satisfied judgement on it all was that 'State patronage of the arts has crept in. It has happened in a very English, informal, unostentatious way – half-baked if you like. A semi-independent body is provided with modest funds to stimulate, comfort and support the arts.'[184]

On 12 June 1945, the official launch of the Arts Council of Great

Britain was made by a Scot, Sir John Anderson, Chancellor of the Exchequer in Churchill's caretaker government and Keynes' patron at the Treasury. It was while setting up Civil Defence as Minister for Home Security in 1940 that he gave his name to the Anderson shelter, the small, robust DIY structure erected in gardens and backyards which saved so many lives during the Blitz. He regarded the Arts Council in a similar light; a sort of Anderson shelter of the mind in which people might find refuge from the vulgar bombs of mass culture dropped by the Heinkels of the entertainment industry. He had a habit of talking down to people (something which on one occasion in Parliament prompted an MP to shout 'Don't talk to us as though we were a lot of niggers').[185] In many ways, therefore, Anderson was just the person to announce that the state would henceforth strive to create better Britons. Praising CEMA for maintaining 'the national traditions of the arts under war conditions', he assured MPs of the 'lasting need' for a permanent body.[186]

There was little opposition from the press or Parliament, and a month later Keynes spelt out *The Arts Council: Its Policy and Hopes* in a Home Service broadcast. He offered Britons 'the possibility of learning ... new games which only the few used to play' and continued:

> We look forward to a time when the theatre and the concert hall and the art gallery will be a living element in everyone's upbringing ... the purpose of the Arts Council is to ... breed a spirit ... to such purpose that the artist and the public can each sustain and live on the other in that union which has occasionally existed in the past at the great ages of a communal civilised life. There could be no better memorial of a war to save the spirit of the individual.[187]

Keynes knew that in peace as in war the success of the Council's work depended on the BBC's ability to prepare a mass audience for it. Soon after his broadcast, he invited the new Director-General, William Haley, to his Treasury chambers in Whitehall. A Scotsman in the Reithian mould, Haley agreed to cooperate in the adventure which lay ahead.

The Labour Party kept a close eye on these developments. In March 1945 the Chairman of the Fabian Arts Group, Philip Noel-Baker, submitted a paper to the party's National Executive Committee which argued that a cultural policy would be a vote winner: 'There is a large and growing public in Britain who take an interest in the arts ... There is great scope for [the] development of that

interest and there are many people who attach the greatest importance to it, and would be prepared to cast their votes for a party
which had a definite and comprehensive programme.'[188] It was as
much principle as electoral gain which made Labour the first British
political party to adopt a coherent cultural policy. The party's
intellectual founders, Beatrice and Sidney Webb, saw the improvement of British sensibilities as one of socialism's main aims. 'The
kitchen of life', they wrote, 'must be collectivised so that all may
have freedom for the drawing room of life'.[189] Although the Webbs
died in 1943 and 1947, the Fabian Society, which they set up to
promote their ideas, still had a strong influence on the party (more
than half of the Labour MPs elected in 1945 were members). Clement
Attlee, Herbert Morrison, Ernest Bevin, Stafford Cripps, Aneurin
Bevan were as enthusiastic as party intellectuals like G. D. H. Cole
and Michael Young. The result was the following clause in the
party's 1945 manifesto, *Let Us Face the Future*:

> National and local authorities should co-operate to enable people
> to have opportunities for healthy recreation. By the provision of
> concert halls, modern libraries, theatres and suitable civic centres,
> we desire to assure to our people full access to the great heritage
> of culture in this nation.[190]

Only one thing still had to be settled before the communal civilized
life could begin: the cooperation of the British intelligentsia. As the
director of one repertory theatre said, 'Without the artists' goodwill,
our scheme will be unworkable: without the bees our beehive will be
derelict.'[191]

At first, it looked as if the government might have trouble filling
the beehive. The experience of wartime propaganda had not been a
happy one for all those involved and there was some apprehension
at the prospect of it continuing after the war. The documentary film-
maker Humphrey Jennings wrote to his wife from one shoot lamenting that '[some] intellectuals are still afraid of becoming patriots'.
Those who had taken the plunge were rounded on by the few who
had not. In 1941 they were the subject of a verse attack in *Tribune*
by the pacifist poet Alex Comfort, who later found fame and fortune
by writing *The Joy of Sex*. He accused them of betraying their ideals
and becoming a 'Laureate of Monkeys' who 'beat up every buzzard,
kite and vulture / and dish them up as English culture'. Orwell
replied in verse, lambasting those for whom it remained 'so black a
crime . . . to love one's country'. He reminded Comfort that 'in the

drowsy freedom of this island / you're free to shout that England isn't free'.[192]

A harder charge to answer was that propaganda was aesthetically worthless. Cyril Connolly, editor of the journal *Horizon*, which was the main forum for the contemporary arts in the 1940s, observed that 'The B.B.C. pumps religion and patriotism into all its programmes; mediocrity triumphs.'[193] He also argued that propaganda was killing the very culture that British intellectuals were trying to defend because it was draining their creative energies:

> We are becoming a nation of culture-diffusionists . . . The appreciation of art is spreading everywhere, education has taken wings, we are at last getting a well-informed and inquisitive public. But war artists are not art, journalism is not art, the BBC is not art, [nor] all the CEMA shows, ABCA lectures . . . MOI films and pamphlets . . . We are turning all our writers into commentators until one day there will nothing left to commentate on.[194]

As the war progressed, others came to have doubts because they felt that the artistic freedom they defended against fascism was being stifled by their own government's utilitarian attitude towards the arts. Most famously, the political interference in some of Orwell's broadcasts caused him to leave the BBC in 1943 and begin writing *Nineteen Eighty-Four*, basing the Ministry of Truth of his totalitarian dystopia in part on the Ministry of Information.

However, the success of Orwell's classic novel has fostered an exaggerated view of the level of censorship which he and others had to endure. The Censorship Division at the MOI was mainly concerned with ensuring that military details were not divulged to the enemy rather than with preventing a radical message getting through to the population. Peace aims were increasingly discussed on radio, in film and in print after the Beveridge Report, a factor which contributed to the public's desire for reform. This did not mean that all intellectuals came out with guns blazing for the Labour Party. Much as the majority supported social democracy, the disillusionments of the prewar era had left them wary of overt political involvement. Their support for the Labour Party was almost wholly contingent upon the extent to which it was committed to assisting the arts. In 1943, the Town and Country Planning Association gathered together government officials and representatives of arts and amenities groups from across Britain to discuss the way forward. The most telling speech was that made by the zoologist Julian

Huxley: 'In order to fashion a general social consciousness . . . [we must] have a national culture in which people feel that . . . they can look to contemporary writing, music and painting and so on to help them understand where they are in the universe [and] where the nation is heading.'[195] The conference closed with the slogan 'Our Goal a National Culture'. It was this aspiration which propelled a wary intelligentsia into the world of postwar reconstruction.

In the 1940s the British intelligentsia turned to culture as the pursuit of politics by other means. For writers, artists, composers, critics, film-makers and actors, bringing culture to the masses in order to unite Britain was what survived of prewar ideals. The view put forward by Harold Nicolson at the start of the war that British propaganda was essentially educative made it easier for them to overcome any doubts they had about working for the government. Even after his resignation from the BBC, Orwell believed that 'the microphone is the instrument by which poetry could be brought back to the common people'.[196] Part of the reason for the intelligentsia's enthusiasm was that they enjoyed the status war work had brought them. 'Highbrow' was no longer a term of abuse. They had no political power but they had been given a place of influence at the heart of the state to an extent which even their Victorian predecessors had not enjoyed. And they were now being offered the chance to retain that position by helping to turn warriors into citizens. In 1945 John Lehmann caught the mood of British intellectuals as surely as he had in 1941:

> Cultural diffusion has come to stay . . . [It] involves a state intervention and a national self-consciousness in artistic matters which is less characteristic of our country than any other in Europe . . . [But] this development of agencies to sustain the arts, to give [the artist] a place of respect in the community . . . all this is the fulfilment of the dreams of thinkers and idealists for generations.[197]

Hugh David has remarked that Lehmann was 'inviting them all to eat in the BBC canteen'. It was 'a sort of literary protocol to the Beveridge Report holding out the hope of a nationalised gas-and-water aesthetic'.[198] So it was. But the most interesting thing about Lehmann's comment was the yearning he expressed for intellectuals to overcome their alienation from ordinary Britons. Many came to realize during the war that if they were ever to win the esteem that their Continental counterparts enjoyed, they had to follow Orwell's lead and re-engage with British culture in all its forms. In short, they had to function as most Continental intelligentsias had done since the nineteenth century: that is, without losing their vision of mankind as a whole and without losing touch with their international influences, they could nurture their own national culture and so find a permanent role in society. Over the next decade, the prospect of doing so gripped many of Britain's finest minds.

The first majority Labour government was elected to power on 26 July 1945 with 393 seats to the Conservative's 210, an overall majority of 146. Three weeks later, on Victory over Japan Day, forty-four-year-old William Haley took his family out onto the streets of London. There they joined the hundreds of thousands celebrating the cessation of all hostilities. Haley's diary entry captured the elation of the time and the caution of a generation who had lived through both world wars. Theirs was a patriotism made up equally of nostalgia, expectation and fear. He wrote:

> Yesterday all England celebrated final, absolute victory and the first day of total peace. Late last night and well into this morning London's millions were out rejoicing. St Paul's, floodlit, looked indescribably beautiful ... we have come through six hard and bitter years and none of us can be quite the same again. And the halcyon Edwardian days of 1910 have gone for ever and ever. Tomorrow the British people face a new world. They face it with eagerness and with a tremendous determination to get things done. If only this Labour administration can cope ... with the mountains of problems awaiting them, they can bring in as new an age as did Gladstone's first government.[199]

The coming of the new age had more than one sting in its tail. Before moving on to the postwar period, we must look at the sixth and most lasting effect which the war had on national identity in Britain: the British attitude to Europe.

12. Let us be kind to the Germans

In a broadcast to British schools on 'The Idea of Patriotism' in October 1940, the popular historian A. L. Rowse asked: 'Is it too much to hope that ... one day after these present troubles are over we may . . . attain something like a European patriotism?'[200] He was to be badly disappointed. The Second World War soured Britons' view of their Continental neighbours, and for half a century afterwards it undermined the faltering attempts of the country's leaders to reposition Britain as a post-imperial, European nation. Henceforth, the Continent was perceived as a thoroughly alien place, at best troublesome and at worst hostile. The British did not regard all Europeans as tyrants or cowards, but the war confirmed their belief that the Continent was the place where most of the tyranny and cowardice in the world originated. It was this belief, far more than any sentimental attachment to the Empire, which caused the British to be sceptical about European Union in the postwar era.

The war not only honed the island identity of the British, it also intensified their dislike of the Germans. In the late nineteenth century Germany had begun to replace France as the prime 'other' by which the British defined themselves, and the Second World War completed that process. Any sympathy the Germans had gained as a result of their harsh treatment after the First World War was erased by the international suffering Hitler caused. Now blamed for two world wars, the Germans were seen as an innately militaristic people and the main carriers of the nationalist virus to which the British thought themselves immune. Shortly after Rowse's plea for a new kind of patriotism, Lord Vansittart made a series of broadcasts called *Black Record*. Vansittart was Chief Diplomatic Adviser to the government, a long-standing opponent of appeasement, and one of the figures involved in the drafting of the abortive Franco-British Union. He argued that 'envy, self-pity and cruelty' were fundamental traits of the German character; all modern wars were the fault of a 'breed which from the dawn of history has been predatory and bellicose'; Hitler 'gives to the great majority of Germans exactly what they have hitherto liked and wanted.'[201]

Historians in the UK have played down the extent of Germanophobia in this period because it does not tally with the conceit that tolerance is a British virtue. Vansittartism, as it became known, was dismissed as 'the creed of a vocal minority'.[202] Such commentators point to two things: the fact that during the Second World War there was less of the knee-jerk jingoism that characterized the First World War and that after 1945 the lessons of Versailles were learnt with the consequence that the Allies helped Germany to rebuild herself rather than seeking to punish her.

Relatively speaking, both of these points are true. Mention has

already been made of the Churches' less jingoistic approach to the
war and of the government's celebration of German culture in official
propaganda. Two further points are worth making here. Military
experience in Europe, particularly after D-Day, had an enlightening
effect on some troops. The liberation of Europe was also a personal
one, offering an unprecedented opportunity to meet and sleep with
people from other nations. One estimate has it that a soldier who
survived from D-Day to Berlin slept with an average of twenty-five
foreigners along the way.[203] Most liaisons were consensual, including
those with enemy civilians – a fact which the War Office condemned
but which troops relished. In May 1945, one officer in Germany
wrote home to his wife: '[My] men [have] endured a year's fighting
. . . [and] it's sheer lunacy to imagine that the one thing filling their
minds and bodies isn't the dire necessity for a thumping good bang.
The Army's solution is P.T. and games. Dear God give me patience
with the English'.[204] For those less interested in corporeal pleasures,
the war engendered a profound sense of Britain's historic links with
the Continent. When Edward Heath witnessed scenes of death and
destruction as a young colonel in the Royal Artillery during the
advance towards Germany, it cemented his belief that some form of
European Union was necessary to prevent the conflict happening again.
He was not alone. His reading in this period included contemporary
tracts on the subject like W. B. Curry's *The Case for Federal Union*,
a Penguin Special of 1939 which sold 100,000 copies.

It is a myth that federalism is a European import. There was a
great tradition of federalist thought in Britain, promulgated by
leading political thinkers and statesmen between 1870 and 1950 and
which Continental leaders acknowledged as an influence when forming the European Union. Its initial motive was to bind the British
Isles and their Empire closer together. But by the late 1930s the
movement had turned its attention to the Continent. In September
1938 a pressure group, Federal Union, was formed which by June
1940 had 225 branches around Britain with 12,000 members. Those
who joined included an impressive array of Britain's left/liberal elite:
J. B. Priestley, C. E. M. Joad, Arnold Toynbee, Lionel Robbins,
William Temple, the future Labour Prime Minister Harold Wilson,
and Sir William Beveridge. Beveridge chaired the Federal Union
Research Institute in Oxford, a hive of intellectual activity in the
1940s, producing pamphlets and books that were widely and sympathetically reviewed in the national press, and he wrote *The Price
of Peace* (1945), in which he posited a middle way in the solution to

European conflict. He rejected the Marxist idea that war was a by-product of international capitalism and he also rejected the view that it was the product of peculiarly aggressive national characters.

> No nation and, with a few lunatic exceptions, no individual desires war, just as no man desires venereal disease. But, in order to avoid venereal disease, it is necessary to avoid desiring things which involve risk of disease ... The seeds of modern war are not now the natural pugnacity of mankind, the economic system or conditions, or the special wickedness of Germans. The seeds of modern war are ambition of rulers, revenge and fear ... Abolition of international anarchy means setting up a super-national authority.[205]

Beveridge considered federalism to be so vital that he regarded *The Price of Peace* as the third part of a trilogy which had begun with *Social Insurance and Allied Services* and *Full Employment in a Free Society*, the books in which he provided a blueprint for the welfare state. Unfortunately, the British did not respond with as much enthusiasm to his plans for a United States of Europe as they did to his plan for a welfare state. In fact, by 1942 the Federal Union's support had slumped. This was because it was seen by a nation, battle-hardened and bitter towards Germany, to be naive. A Foreign Office report on the FU stated that while its theories had 'many attractions', the organization was hampered by 'an inebriated optimism [and] opaque miasma of belief in the perfectibility of man ... Unless Federal Union can purge itself of this element it will not easily catch the popular imagination, nor having done so will it be able for long to put its theories into practice.'[206]

In the end, no amount of Christianity, classical music or casual sex could overcome the popular belief that once again Britain had been forced to sort out the mess in which the Germans had left Europe, and that it had suffered greatly in the process. As the Blitz took its toll on the civilian population, Churchill became more virulently anti-German. He talked regularly about the need to 'abolish' Germany. In September 1940, after a bomb exploded in south London causing heavy casualties, he told his staff that the German people would have to be physically castrated after the war. Jock Colville recorded:

> He is becoming less and less benevolent towards the Germans (having been much moved by the examples of their frightfulness in Wandsworth ...) and talks about castrating the lot. He says there

will be no nonsense about a 'just peace'. I feel sure this is the wrong attitude not only immoral but unwise. We should aim at crushing them and then being firm but magnanimous victors.[207]

In June 1940, BBC executives approved an 'Anger Campaign' which aimed 'to heighten the intensity of the personal anger felt by the individual British citizen against the German people . . . in such a way that it appears to come quite spontaneously from the people themselves'.[208] Those who think that xenophobia is an elite phenomenon implanted in the minds of ordinary people should not get too excited at this point. Although wartime propaganda sharpened British national identity, there is no evidence that the British needed to be roused into a self-righteous fury against the Germans. The war achieved that on its own.

In September 1939, Gallup polls showed that 90 per cent believed that their enemy was not the German people but Hitler's regime. By 1945 the reverse was true.[209] A series of Mass Observation surveys carried out between 1940 and 1944 asked what should be done with Germany after the war. No less than a third wanted the Germans to pay economic reparations of the kind meted out after the First World War. Another third also wanted the country to be militarily and politically neutered in order to prevent it ever making war again (the preferred option was to break it up into several small states, thus dismantling the nation state created by Bismarck in the nineteenth century). Anecdotal evidence supports this picture. The Dean of St Paul's made a point of sounding out opinion wherever he went in the country. Some of his interlocutors denied that they were fighting for democracy at all. 'When I asked, "What then are you fighting for?" they replied simply "England". It may be', the Dean concluded, 'that the dominant motive in the people of England was simply a deep-rooted objection to being pushed around by Germans'.[210]

The end of the war did not temper anti-German feeling. If anything, it grew worse as Britons paused to reflect on the enormity of their suffering. On VE Day, the *Daily Express* proclaimed: 'ALL GERMANS ARE GUILTY!' In the same paper, Noël Coward wrote, 'It is certainly victory over the Nazis . . . but it remains to be seen whether or not we have really conquered the Germans.'[211] His song 'Don't Let's Be Beastly to the Germans' was not a plea for forgiveness but a satire on appeasement and those who thought restraint was still called for; and it became a hit for that reason. Churchill was eventually persuaded that castrating the Germans was not a sensible peace aim. His dictum, 'In war: resolution. In defeat: defiance. In victory: magnanimity. In peace: goodwill' was frequently repeated in the press as evidence of Britain's tolerant character. But the rhetoric of Britishness differed from reality as it so often did. Churchill made no attempt to distinguish between Germans and Nazis. Addressing a jubilant House of Commons at 3.15 p.m. on VE Day he begged to move 'That this House do now attend at the Church of St Margaret, Westminster, to give humble and reverent thanks to Almighty god for our deliverance from the threat of German domination.'[212] After the service, Churchill, Attlee and other members of the War Cabinet moved on to Whitehall where, from the balcony of the Ministry of Health, Churchill made this speech to a crowd of 30,000:

> My dear friends, this is your hour. This is not victory of a party or of any class. It's a victory of the great British nation as a whole. We were the first, in this ancient island, to draw the sword against tyranny. After a while, we were left all alone for a whole year. There we stood alone. Did anyone want to give in? 'No!' [the crowd replied]. Were we downhearted? 'No!' [the crowd replied]
>
> The lights went out and the bombs came down. But every man, woman and child in the country had no thought of quitting the struggle. London can take it. So we came back after long months from the jaws of death, out of the mouth of hell, while all the world wondered. When shall the reputation and faith of this generation of English men and women fail? I say that in the long years to come not only will the people of this island but of the world, wherever the bird of freedom chirps in human hearts, look back to what we've done and they will say, 'Do not despair, do not yield to violence and tyranny, march straight forward and die if need be – unconquered.' Now we have emerged from our deadly struggle – a terrible foe has been cast on the ground and awaits our judgement and our mercy.[213]

The men and women who heard that speech then sang 'Land of Hope and Glory' until they were hoarse.

The popular image of VE Day is of a magnanimous people having a street party, with women flashing Union Jack knickers and smiling children drinking Ribena under red, white and blue bunting. Celebrations were generally good-humoured and in many cases completely abandoned. The Old Etonian jazz trumpeter Humphrey Lyttleton mounted a handcart and led a huge swaying conga of revellers from Trafalgar Square to Buckingham Palace. There, he blasted a rendition of 'For He's a Jolly Good Fellow' towards the balcony when the

King, Queen and Churchill appeared to greet the crowds. Drunken men and women openly kissed and hugged on the streets and the bushes of Britain's parks rustled with copulating couples. Some thought this communal display of emotional physicality was un-British in its abandonment of reserve. The *Birmingham Mail* said: 'We are not much given to mass gaiety. We are gardeners, family men, artificers and very individualistic at that . . . The war's hazards and chances will be lived again over drinks in the "local" [and] high tea in the family parlour.'[214] The British were never as reserved as they liked to think. Like most great public events before and since, on VE Day they showed themselves to be a match for any nation when given the chance for revelry.

However, there were darker emotions lurking just underneath the joy which greeted the coming of peace. In Andover in Hampshire, a swastika was pinned up outside a shop in the High Street to be kicked and spat at by passers-by throughout the day and later it was torn to shreds (a Soviet hammer and sickle got the same treatment). The burning of effigies of German leaders took place in thousands of communities across the UK and the patriotism which accompanied them was as strident as the burning of Guy Fawkes effigies in the seventeenth century. In the Herefordshire village of Stoke Lacy, S. J. Parker, Commander of No. 12 Platoon of the Home Guard, lit an effigy of Hitler in the car park of the Plough Inn. As the flames crackled and Hitler's arm, propped up into a Nazi salute, fell off, a crowd of 300 roared into a chorus of 'Rule, Britannia!' and 'There'll Always Be an England' before linking arms for 'Auld Lang Syne'. In Hanover Road, north London, the whole community took part in preparing effigies of Hitler and Göring, hanging them from gallows in the street before burning them next to a battered child's doll, its face and body painted blood red to symbolize the pain that the Germans had caused. When the bonfire became too fierce, an angry crowd shouted 'Let him linger!' and the area's Chief Fire Watcher applied a hose to the effigies to prolong the spectacle.[215] Broadcaster Richard Dimbleby compared the fires to those which once ringed the British coastline warning of Spanish or French invasion. He watched flames lick round an effigy of Hitler at Hope Cove in Devon and found it 'a bright and warm and comforting signal that no ship but a friendly ship should ever again come to the shores of this island'.[216]

The clergy played their part in the orgy of Germanophobia that swept the country. William Temple's successor as Archbishop of Canterbury, Geoffrey Fisher, was a deeply conservative man who did not share Temple's view that a welfare state was a necessary step towards a Christian society. But Fisher was keen on Anglo-German reconciliation. In May 1945, he reminded readers of the *Daily Telegraph* that 'there are good Germans' and he also circulated forms of service for use on VE Day which emphasized the importance of forgiveness.[217] They were immediately criticized. The Vicar of Mapledurham, Dr E. L. Macassey, told the press: 'There is nothing manly or British about them. They are in the tone of the whining mendicant, the general trend is "Let us be kind to the Germans".'[218] Macassey was widely praised for speaking out in this way and millions of Britons crowded into churches and chapels to hear preachers like him extol the virtues with which the British had defeated Teutonic evil. On VE Day, 35,000 people attended services of thanksgiving in St Paul's; in other cities, the demand was so great that services were provided on the hour every hour throughout the day. Only one cleric in the whole of Britain's established Churches, the Dean of St Albans, refused to conduct one.

Even those with a liberal bent found it difficult to resist a feeling of moral superiority over the defeated enemy and a desire for retribution as strong as any felt in 1918. On a visit to Paris in November 1944, the photographer Cecil Beaton was shown around the former Gestapo headquarters in the Avenue Foch. On the walls of its bleak cells he found messages written by captured British pilots and secret agents about to meet their death. 'These scrawled, desperate messages', he said, 'are now a writing on the wall for all the world. They ought to be preserved so that future generations read them in order to realise that Germans are capable of perpetrating such brutality.'[219] The philanthropist Violet Markham returned from a visit to Germany in the summer of 1945 having witnessed the poverty, homelessness and despair in Germany's occupied cities. She was unmoved, writing to an American friend:

> There is a great streak of sentimentality in both our countries . . . and I have come home feeling little patience with the people who want to be kind to the Germans. Eventually of course they must be given a chance to win their way back into the European family, but for the moment there has got to be very stern treatment until they show some signs of repentance and horror for the enormities that have been committed in their name.[220]

When it became clear that reconstruction rather than reparation was Allied policy towards Germany, hostility turned to anger. In a letter to her husband, Vita Sackville-West wrote, 'The reconstruction of Germany [means] shaking hands with blood-stained murderers, who would start it all up again if they saw the chance.'[221] Relatively objective reportage also played a part in hardening attitudes. British anti-Semitism notwithstanding, the nation was deeply shocked when newsreels displayed the results of Nazi prejudice. Pictures of the emaciated corpses in Europe's death camps seemed to prove that the scare stories circulated during the First World War about baby-eating, nun-raping Huns had not been far off the mark after all. In his moving radio account of the liberation of the concentration camp at Belsen on 19 April 1945, Richard Dimbleby said, 'I have never seen British soldiers so moved to cold fury as the men who opened the Belsen camp this week'.[222]

It was, above all, the terrible first-hand experience of front-line battle that left a bitterness towards the Germans. The actor Hugh Williams, a star of early wartime propaganda films like *Ships With Wings* (1940), became a captain in the army in 1942. The letters he wrote to his wife Margaret became angrier after his regiment entered Belsen:

> It is unutterable balls to pretend that the whole German race did not know of the existence of these camps and the horrors and agonies they contained ... Before the war I thought that anyone who said the only good German is a dead one, was hateful, stupid, unimaginative, a fool, a blimp ... but now I believe it absolutely.[223]

His wife replied, 'everyone who I've met recently who has just returned is filled with the same loathing and determination not to be soft [on them] this time'.[224] Ordinary troops were as hostile as officers and didn't mince their words. Jim Wheeler, a private in the Parachute Regiment, was assigned to guard POWs. When a group of committed Nazis executed a fellow German prisoner for criticizing the Third Reich, the British guards did not intervene because they saw no moral difference between the two groups: 'The name German was bad enough for us. They were vermin as far as we were concerned. We really hated them', Wheeler recalled.[225]

Of course, nothing matched the anger of men and women who endured Japanese POW camps. The Bishop of Singapore, J. L. Wilson, was imprisoned in Changi camp from 1943 to 1945. He forgave his tormentors, and the repeated floggings he endured as a boy at public school helped him to survive. 'Well, thank heaven I went to St John's, Leatherhead', he thought as he was led away for another savage beating by his captors.[226] But few were as forgiving as Bishop Wilson. Japan's capitulation after Hiroshima and Nagasaki was greeted with universal relief by the British people. Even if one allows for contemporary ignorance of the full after-effects of nuclear fission, the gratified awe that characterized the public reaction to the dropping of the atom bomb gives a measure of the antipathy felt towards the Japanese. Still, that antipathy was a fresh one. The collective anger of the British people was directed almost entirely at the Germans, built as it was on decades of enmity. Therefore, instead of analysing the Myth of Consensus, historians would be better occupied analysing the Myth of Magnanimity. For without under-standing how the British really felt about Germany in the 1940s, it is impossible to understand their national identity in the second half of the twentieth century.

It might be argued that Germanophobia was an excusable emotion in the immediate aftermath of a patently just war. But the British sense of moral superiority also extended to allies who had been invaded in 1940. Troops rumbling through ruined towns in France and the Low Countries, their streets lined with the relieved smiles of the liberated, felt fraternity but not always equality towards people who had endured Nazi occupation. Sybil Eccles, whose husband David became a prominent Tory Cabinet minister in the 1950s, shared his belief in European integration. But in 1942 she wrote to him in Lisbon, where he was stationed, warning that the quick collapse of the Third Republic had aggravated the perennial Franco-phobia of the British:

> At the time of Dunkirk we told ourselves too often that we bore the French no grudge – patting ourselves on the back for a magnanimity that was not genuinely felt. Beneath the skin and in the guts, age-old resentments seethed and bubbled anew – and the wound has festered ever since. It will take a good deal of skill and education to put things right.[227]

Michael Denman, an official at the Board of Trade in the 1940s who later joined the diplomatic team that negotiated Britain's entry into Europe, made this assessment of the nation's outlook:

> Britain had won the war. The continentals had not. Those who had fought Britain were wicked; those who had not were incom-petent, for otherwise they would not have been defeated . . . For a great victorious power to abandon its world role, its leadership of

the Commonwealth, and its favoured position with the United States in order to throw in its lot with a bombed out, defeated rabble south of the Channel seemed to the British unthinkable.[228]

At the root of this hubris was the fact that the British had not been invaded. Nor had their national character been questioned by subsequent defeat and collaboration. Jean Monnet believed that this above all else explained the British reluctance to become involved in European integration after the war. 'Britain', he said in his memoirs, 'had not been conquered . . . she felt no need to exorcise the past.'[229]

The Channel Islands were the only British territory to be occupied by the Nazis. Although they are Crown Dependencies and not formally part of the UK, most of their 60,000 inhabitants thought of themselves as Britons and were regarded as such by mainlanders. Yet collaboration in the Channel Islands was just as extensive as it was in other territories under German rule. Some historians have argued that it was actually *more* extensive and point to the fact that armed resistance on the islands was utterly negligible in comparison to that on the Continent. But that is not how the British chose to remember the episode. Films depicting a German invasion, from *Went the Day Well?* (1942) to *The Eagle Has Landed* (1976), were set in imaginary villages in England and their inhabitants were shown almost without exception to be actively resisting the enemy. After the war, strenuous efforts were made by UK governments to play down what really happened in the Channel Islands. No one was formally accused of collaborating; in fact, leading members of Island administrations received knighthoods and other honours, something that happened in no other country the Germans occupied.

Behind the facade of loyalty which the British erected, vengeance was meted out. As elsewhere in Europe, women who had slept with the enemy bore the brunt of the population's anger. However much equality female Britons had won during the war, they were still primarily seen as guardians of hearth and home. This was especially true of the Channel Islands, which were more socially conservative than Britain (divorce was still unlawful, for example). Female betrayal of the nation was therefore regarded as the ultimate betrayal. Known as 'Jerrybags', their very personal fraternization with the Germans helped to mask that carried out for more mercenary reasons by the male population. *Jersey under the Jackboot*, written in 1946 by one who lived through the Occupation, condemned the 'widespread licentiousness' among women after the

Germans' arrival, while explaining away economic collaboration as 'realisation of the fact that there was money to be made from the Hun'.[230] Overall, the picture painted was one of a valiant people defying a ruthless enemy: 'True to tradition,' the book began, 'the Hun prefaced his march-in by a wanton and savage assault on the defenceless towns . . . [This] is a simply told narrative of the courage and fortitude of the Islanders.'[231] There was actually no need to reassure the nation that the Islanders had been staunch patriots because most Britons simply didn't want to know. Military occupation of UK soil was an acute embarrassment. It challenged the image which Britons had constructed of themselves as a uniquely incorruptible nation of brave and decent warrior/citizens. Which leads us on to the fourth major reason why the Second World War strengthened the national identity of the UK: it made the British feel better about themselves.

13. Guilty men

The conflict restored the national pride which the British had lost during the later stages of appeasement. Like most forms of patriotism, it concealed a good deal of insecurity among its celebrants. A Mass Observation survey published after D-Day, *The Mood of Britain 1938–44*, found that two-fifths of those interviewed said they still felt guilty about appeasement, a figure that probably underestimated the true extent of popular feeling since it is a difficult thing to own up to. Although the British looked down their noses at the French for capitulating so easily, in ideological terms the Finest Hour came to function in much the same way as the legend which de Gaulle constructed of 'La France Résistante'. He offered the French absolution through the pretence that most of them had in some way participated in the resistance movement and had therefore never really surrendered to the Germans. In a similar way, Churchill convinced the British that they would never have surrendered and that the occupation of the Channel Islands was an aberration.

However, the two legends differed crucially. Wildly inaccurate though it was, de Gaulle's version of events allowed room in the French *mentalité* for postwar cooperation with other Europeans. The history of the resistance movement was one that could be shared with other nations occupied by the Axis powers. It could even be shared with the Germans, who lost no time exaggerating their own opposition to Hitler. The French resistance movement therefore became part of a common European heritage of democratic struggle that stretched from Ancient Greece to the present establishment of the EU. Churchill's version of events, on the other hand, vaingloriously emphasized Britain's uniqueness as the only combatant European nation to remain undefiled. This outlook led the British to claim the moral leadership of Europe while at the same time reserving the right to remain distant from it. There was no shortage of French Anglophiles ready to proclaim the UK's moral leadership in the 1940s. The writer and Free French spokesman Pierre Maillaud spent the war in London with de Gaulle. Looking back on the summer of 1940, he wrote: 'a people was passing, within a few hours, from armed indolence to moral heroism . . . and was to take into its care, at the moment when Europe was collapsing, the conscience, the mission, the last hopes of Europe'.[232] But, like de Gaulle, Maillaud was acutely aware that Britain's amoebic European identity was based on a sense of superiority towards the Continent and that, as such, it would not be so productive in peacetime. In *The English Way* (1945), he wrote:

[Britain's] European sense lies more deeply buried in her national consciousness than that of Continental nations . . . It is a singularity of England's modern history that in peace she should so often fail in her European duties and yet afterwards stand as Europe's champion at the eleventh hour; that she should by turns help loosen the European fabric and decisively contribute to save it *in extremis*.[233]

The socialist writer and MP Michael Foot was a lifelong opponent of European Union. Recalling the war in 1990, he wrote:

All of us who lived through those times had a special instruction in the meaning of patriotism. The sense of the community in which we had been born and bred suffused all else, made everything else subordinate or trivial. And one essential element in the exhilaration was the knowledge that the shameful Chamberlain era had at last been brought to an end, and that English people could look into each other's eyes with recovered pride and courage.[234]

What exactly enabled Britons to look each other in the eye once more? Apart from resilience on the Home Front and victory abroad, two factors can be identified. First, a belief that the British had come late to the struggle against fascism because they were not a naturally martial people; and second, 40,000 words that Michael Foot wrote in four days during the summer of 1940, published under the title *Guilty Men*.

The memorialization of the First World War had been dominated by the Unknown Warrior. An anonymous corpse was interred in Westminster Abbey in 1920 to symbolize the blood sacrifice of millions of troops and the suffering of their loved ones; and in the same year Lutyens' cenotaph, or 'empty tomb', was erected in Whitehall. The concept of the Unknown Warrior retained its symbolic potency in the second half of the twentieth century. But to it was added the concept of the Reluctant Warrior. During the 1940s, the British explained away appeasement by claiming that they were not a warlike people but a peaceful community of individuals who minded their own business unless forced to save civilization because others had failed to do so. A. L. Rowse's *The English Spirit* concluded:

> The English . . . are lazy, constitutionally indolent. They are always being caught lagging behind, unprepared – again and again in their history it has been the same; and then, when up against it – they more than make up for lost time by their resourcefulness, their inventiveness, their ability to extemporise, their self-reliance.[235]

Diaries and letters of the time tell a similar story. Sybil Eccles wrote to her husband: 'The English have led lazy, self-indulgent lives of late – and have forgotten God and country. But they can still be aroused quickly and easily to ferocious displays of energy and patriotism that one can't lose faith in them. Oh No! – we're all right.'[236]

In *The Lion and the Unicorn* George Orwell described the British as 'an eleventh hour nation of reluctant warriors'.[237] Like the lion, this composite Briton was a slumbering beast who was slow to anger but when roused knew no fear. The idea served two purposes: it helped the British to distinguish themselves from the more militaristic Germans and it incorporated appeasement into the legend of the Finest Hour. Churchill's celebration of a martial, 'bulldog spirit' was underpinned by the conceit that the British had come late to the war not because they were indifferent to the suffering of Europe and reluctant to fight for democracy but because they were Europe's greatest democrats. Their natural indolence, said critics, may have caused their tardiness but that same indolence was the basis of their love of moderation. It was a compelling and popular argument.

However, for Britain's absolution to be complete, the nation needed a Judas, a scapegoat who could take the blame for not rousing it sooner. The British found their Judas in the Conservative politicians they had voted for during the 1930s – or rather, it was found for them. The left/liberal reforming rhetoric of the 1940s did not rest content with the claim that the Tories were naive incompetents who had sleepwalked into another world war, it actually implied they were guilty of treason. The left argued that almost the entire conservative political Establishment had been ready to sell Europe to the Nazis in order to preserve social inequity at home and imperial plunder abroad. A lot of fuss was made about the 'Cliveden Set' – the pressure group of well-connected German sympathizers who had gathered at Lord Astor's house in Buckinghamshire during the 1930s. They epitomized, it was claimed, Britain's ancien régime of gentlemen-racketeers who had led Britain to poverty and near oblivion. Liberal-minded Conservatives adhered to this political cosmology, but the left was primarily responsible for it.

Guilty Men, which Michael Foot wrote under the pseudonym 'Cato', named fifteen, led by the former Prime Ministers Baldwin and Chamberlain. Like Émile Zola's *J'Accuse* (1898), which denounced the French military Establishment over the Dreyfus affair, *Guilty Men* exonerated the rest of the nation: 'This land of Britain is rich in heroes', it began – men and women who had proved their heroism as soon as they were given the chance to do so, at Dunkirk.[238] Whether appeasement was a disgrace or a noble attempt to preserve British lives is irrelevant. As far as national identity is concerned, what matters is that the British agreed with Foot's view that they were not responsible for the war. After the book was published, he wrote to his mother: 'At last the British people are awakening to the fact that they have been ruled by traitors. When they are fully awakened their wrath will be terrific'.[239] And so it was. W. H. Smith refused to stock the book in order, said the company, 'to preserve national unity'.[240] It still sold 217,000 copies.

The popular embrace of Foot's specious theory was an extraordinary act of collective amnesia. It demonstrates that the forgetting of history is just as important in shaping a nation's identity as the retrieval of long-forgotten facts or the invention of traditions. The stark truth is that Chamberlain's Cabinet and the tuxedoed guests who rolled up to Cliveden's Palladian portals were not the only ones to blame for the war. The guilty men (and women) were the millions of ordinary Britons who had supported appeasement – just as the guilty men and women of Germany were not simply the cadre of revolutionary Nazis who had burned down the Reichstag in 1933 but the millions who voted the Nazi Party into government a week later. Until 1938, approximately 70 per cent of the public were in favour of the National government's foreign policy. Even after the Munich agreement, right up until March 1939, it continued to command the support of over 50 per cent of the nation.[241] The idea of the 'Guilty Men' was the flipside of the idea of the 'Few'. A small number of young RAF pilots were celebrated because they were seen to represent the collective bravery of an underdog nation. At the same time, a handful of elderly politicians were vilified in order to erase memories of the national mood which had propelled and legitimized their sickly diplomacy in the first place.

Labour leaders never explicitly endorsed the idea, but neither did they challenge it, and Attlee's victory in 1945 owed a lot to the fact that the left constructed a myth of betrayal around which the British could unite. By linking the failure of the Conservatives to prevent the Depression with their failure to prevent war, the left exploited the nation's desire for political change and its hunt for scapegoats. In vain, Conservatives protested that the Labour Party had supported non-intervention in the Spanish Civil War. In vain they protested that under Attlee's leadership between 1935 and 1939 the party had voted against rearmament on ten different occasions. Paradoxically therefore, while Labour gained electoral credibility for ending its self-imposed exile from government in 1940, that exile also worked in its favour. Those years of opposition enabled the party to distance itself from appeasement, and blur a political record that was as chequered as that of the British people. This, combined with Attlee's consensual rhetoric of fair shares for all, completed the left's reappropriation of patriotism in the mid-1940s. And here was Churchill's tragedy. As the most consistent opponent of appeasement he was not the focus of popular anger towards the conservative Establishment. Hence the regret which many Labour and Liberal voters expressed when he ceased to be Prime Minister in 1945. But, by becoming leader of the Conservative Party in 1940, and by failing to endorse the Beveridge Report enthusiastically enough, he became the victim of a myth of betrayal which he himself had helped to generate.

14. Advance, Britannia!

The Second World War had more influence on British national identity than any other event in history. The extent of that influence and its many nuances stretch throughout this book. In the meantime we can sum it up as follows: the dread threat of invasion, greater than at any time since the Napoleonic Wars, arrested the development of Scottish and Welsh nationalism; it brought ages, classes and sexes closer together because it was a total war involving virtually the entire population and therefore required more social cooperation for it to be effectively prosecuted. This led to the creation of the welfare state and an attempt to improve the fabric of national culture. In the long run, Spitfires proved to be a more durable image of the war than free spectacles. However, 'the Finest Hour' and 'the People's War' were not entirely different political narratives of the period 1940 to 1945, they were patriotic legends which reinforced each other, and it was because they did that the Second World War became such a fulcrum of Britishness.

The threat of invasion made Britons think intensely about their way of life and what they stood to lose if Hitler won, from freedom of speech to more mundane things like village fêtes and football matches. Had Britain been defeated and occupied, its inhabitants would still have sold home-made jam and turned out in the rain to watch Spurs lose at home because of a slipshod defence. Once Jews, blacks, homosexuals, gypsies, communists, trade union leaders and any other public figures who opposed the new regime had been rounded up; once they had been imprisoned, brutalized and murdered; once Hitler had made a triumphal procession from Parliament Square to Buckingham Palace; once the swastika was fluttering over every major building from Cardiff Arms Park to Calton Hill and the Albert Hall; once children were learning German language and history in schools (as they were forced to do in the Channel Islands) – once all this had happened, the country would have settled down to Nazi occupation just as it had once settled down to Roman, Danish and Norman occupation. A few brave souls would have escaped to mountainous regions like the Pennines, Brecons and Highlands. From there, they would have continued the struggle, perhaps sabotaging the *Flying Scotsman* on its way from London to

Edinburgh or assassinating the occasional Nazi officer as he was being driven to a rural posting. Another minority would have actively collaborated, either for ideological reasons or simply to profit materially from the invasion. But most people would just have got on with their lives as best they could.

Eventually, the unavoidable intimacy a conquered people has with its conquerors would have led thousands, perhaps millions, of Britons to enjoy friendships and sexual relationships with members of the occupying forces, even falling in love and having children with them. Many Germans, especially those who felt a cultural bond with the English, would have settled permanently on the island. Over time, as the descendants of these settlers commingled, the distinct lines that the British had mentally drawn between themselves and the enemy would have become blurred and a new nation evolved from the old. Examining the national character in 1939, the writer William Gerhardie made a similar point. He questioned why the British were making such a fuss about the prospect of a German victory:

> What is this unreasonable fear of . . . invasion? If Hitler invades England to-day, somebody will boast two hundred years hence: 'We Goerings are a very ancient English family; our ancestor came over with Hitler'. And some [Scottish] fighting cock, Sir Somebody Mackenzie, will, at another date, prove to be the first of a proud line of patriotic Prussians calling themselves von Mackenzen.[242]

It is a clever point. But here we must leave our counterfactual reverie to the novelists. Because however the British people would have reacted to the invasion of their country, we do know for sure that they did not want it to happen in the first place. Few believed, as Gerhardie did, that the Briton was simply 'a carefree German'. And they certainly did not think he was a simply a carefree Nazi.

Between 1940 and 1945, almost every man, woman and child knew that the British way of life would be fundamentally altered by a German occupying force, perhaps out of recognition and certainly not for the better. Consequently, they worked and fought as hard as they could to prevent their island being invaded. The British knew they had been appeasers and that their recent past was not one to be proud of; and they constructed a myth of betrayal by a small elite in order to disguise their collective shame. Throughout the war, their patriotism was peppered with irony, paradox and downright hypocrisy. And after the war this mingled with the hubris victory brought to create a pathological distrust of Europe. But, however belated their resistance to fascism was, the fact remains that Britons *did* fight, even when the odds against them seemed ridiculous. As General Schellenberg had suspected, they were capable of a complete transformation when their country was in great danger. That transformation was motivated primarily by a deep love of country. And the success of their struggle to defend it, from Dunkirk to the Battle of Britain, the Blitz to El Alamein, D-Day to VE Day, restored their pride in themselves.

Therefore, to understand the intensity of wartime patriotism and the prejudices which it fostered one has to go beyond the fading memoranda of Whitehall, beyond the delicate calculations made by politicians and bureaucrats about which form of economic management was best for the country, how many houses and hospitals should be built and what sort of education system would increase opportunity. One has to see into the minds of the British in the mid-twentieth century. To do so does not require a romantic flight of the imagination. The evidence, written and oral, is thick on the ground. The fact is that mentally and emotionally, one might even say spiritually, the Second World War brought the people of this small nation together as no event had ever done. Quite naturally, on 5 July 1945, most Britons voted as they always did: in order to improve their standard of living. But perhaps more than other elections, they felt they were going to the polls not as socialists, liberals or conservatives but as patriots. How postwar governments attempted to capitalize on the profound sense of Britishness which the war created, and how they failed, is the subject of the following chapters.

PART 2

CITIZENS

I have a Vision of the Future, chum,
The workers' flats in fields of soya beans
Tower up like silver pencils, score and score:
And Surging Millions hear the Challenge come
From microphones in communal canteens
'No Right! No Wrong! All's perfect, evermore.'

John Betjeman, 1945

[The Festival of Britain] is a gauntlet flung in the face of disbelievers, a call to men of spirit, a moment to take courage from the past in order to look forward to the future.

BBC Home Service, 1951

1. A kind of smouldering pile

When the Labour Party came to power in 1945, the United Kingdom appeared to be more united than ever before. The Chancellor of the Exchequer, Hugh Dalton, captured the optimism of the moment when he wrote: 'after the long storm of war . . . we saw the sunrise'.[1] The sunrise which has transfixed most historians is that of public ownership of essential industries and services. After eighteen months of debate in Parliament and the press, on the morning of 1 January 1947 National Coal Board signs went up at pit-heads across Britain, declaring the newly nationalized mines to be under common ownership. According to the *Daily Herald*, they were now 'THE PEOPLE'S PITS'. At Penallt in the Rhondda, hundreds of miners, their wives and children (many asleep in their parents' arms) walked to the colliery an hour before dawn, their lanterns making them look like 'chains of glow-worms' in the dark according to one observer. As dawn broke, they gathered under the massive pitshaft, and with the colliery band playing, the blue flag of the National Coal Board was hoisted in the early light. To loud cheers, the local trade union leader dressed in khaki battledress shouted into a microphone: 'Private enterprise has had it!' Then, as the night-shift reached the surface to be greeted by the crowd, the Last Post was sounded.[2]

The event which transformed the lives of most Britons was the creation of the National Health Service on 5 July 1948, in the teeth of opposition from George VI and the medical profession. It was the first service in the world to offer free health care at the point of delivery to everyone 'from the cradle to the grave'. For the majority who believed in it and used it, the NHS was *the* concrete symbol of the welfare state. It was a visible reminder of the social democratic revolution in a way that no dog-eared pension or child-benefit book ever could be, and it was a more meaningful and lasting reminder of that revolution than the nationalization of industry. Nationalization did little to increase workers' control of production or their prosperity, and after forty years of mismanagement in the boardroom and militancy on the shop floor the tottering structure erected by the Attlee government was largely dismantled. Why did the NHS last?

Death is more of a taboo in Britain than most countries, but the moral authority of the NHS lay in the fact that mortality is the greatest leveller in any society. The right to health care was therefore the easiest to assimilate within the British idea of fairness and the hardest for its opponents to contest. National institutions are the frames and joists of a national identity. Some can be removed and new ones added as the structure of the building is modernized and embellished over time, but without them the building will collapse. In the National Health Service, the Attlee government created an institution that became so wedded to Britons' notion of themselves as a decent, fair-minded and compassionate people that no government could afford to abolish it any more than they could afford to abolish the monarchy. Peter Hennessy wrote that it 'is the nearest Britain has ever come to institutionalising altruism'; July 1948 'was the second of Britain's finest hours in the brave and high-minded 1940s. Like the Battle of Britain it was a statement of intent, a symbol of hope in a formidable, self-confident nation'.[3] By 1949, the levelling effect of the Labour programme prompted *Picture Post* to ask: 'IS THE MIDDLE CLASS DOOMED?' They 'cling to their culture', it said, 'but the education and medical treatment that were once their prerogative is now available to all'.[4] But all was not well.

Discontent in Scotland and Wales had not been erased by the war, merely suspended by the need to beat Germany. The contribution which the Scots and Welsh had made to victory led many to believe they had earned the right to greater self-determination. The English were oblivious of the fact. George Orwell was one of the few to recognize it. In 1947, he wrote:

> The Scottish nationalist movement seems to have gone almost unnoticed in England . . . In the past, certainly, we have plundered Scotland shamefully, but whether it is *now* true that England as a whole exploits Scotland as a whole, and that Scotland would be better off if fully autonomous, is another question. The point is that many Scottish people, often quite moderate in outlook, are beginning to think about autonomy and to feel that they are pushed into an inferior position . . . I think we should pay more attention to the small but violent separatist movements which exist within our own island. They may look very unimportant now, but, after all, the Communist Manifesto was once a very obscure document, and the Nazi Party only had six members when Hitler joined it.[5]

In April 1945, Robert MacIntyre, the SNP leader, won his party's first seat in Parliament at a by-election in Motherwell. Harold Nicolson recorded his arrival at Westminster with the weary hauteur of a man addressing a naughty adolescent:

> He refused to be introduced by any sponsors, since he does not recognise the Mother of Parliaments and wishes to advertise himself . . . Members rose offering to sponsor the cub and put an end to the shaming incident, but he refused. He was therefore told to go away and think it over, which he did, shrugging vain shoulders. Next day he thought better of it and accepted sponsors; but even then, as he reached the box, he said, 'I do this under protest', which was not liked at all. He is going to be a sad nuisance and pose as a martyr.[6]

So began the formal campaign to undo the Union of 1707. Nicolson could perhaps be forgiven for not taking MacIntyre seriously enough. After all, the Scotsman did not remain long at Westminster, losing the seat to Labour two months later at the general election. But Nicolson's attitude was indicative of a political elite which believed that all the answers to Britain's problems could be found in the debating chambers and offices which sat in mock-Gothic splendour beside the Thames, and which had learnt little or nothing from the Second World War. Far from demonstrating the need for greater sensitivity towards England's partners, the patriotic unity of 1940–45 seemed to show that Scottish and Welsh aspirations were a passing fad. From 1945 until 1997, discontent in Scotland and Wales was unnecessarily exacerbated by complacency at Westminster. The English underestimated the conditional nature of Scottish and Welsh unionism and the cultural pride of both countries upon which relative economic decline acted to produce demands for political autonomy. The result was a tendency to equate Scottish and Welsh nationalism with the size and electoral success of nationalist parties. Since those parties were regarded as 'picturesque and articulate but negligible', the constitutional alarm clock of Britain's leaders had its snooze button permanently switched on.[7] Scottish and Welsh discontent was addressed haphazardly and ham-fistedly, with concessions often accompanied by gaffes which wiped out what little goodwill had been earned. When these measures failed to halt the growth of nationalism the response was surprise and exasperation.

Scotland and Wales were Labour strongholds. At the 1945 election, Scotland returned thirty-seven Labour MPs and twenty-nine

Conservatives, Wales twenty-five and four, plus six Liberals. But from the outset, Attlee's revolution was itself the source of discontent. By expanding the remit and size of the state, Labour's reforms led to a greater centralization of power, with Britain's banking, coal and shipbuilding (to name a few) now entirely managed in London. For England's partners, nationalization meant, in another sense, denationalization. This was exploited by the Conservative Party, which offered to review the constitution when it returned to power. 'Scotland is a nation,' declared Churchill in 1949, 'it is only since 1945, under the first socialist majority, that we have seen the policy of amalgamation superseding that of Union.'[8]

Early postwar nationalism was moderate in tone: the existence of the British state was never questioned, merely the way in which it was managed with apparently little regard for Scotland and Wales. The motive behind the desire for devolution was partly pragmatic – a desire to make sure that they got a fair share of the welfare cake being baked in London – and partly a principled belief that the democracy which Britons had defended during the war was becoming more remote and unaccountable. Socialists in north and west Britain feared the rise of radical nationalism if they were not given more control over their own affairs. Two-thirds of Scottish and Welsh MPs at the general election in 1945 pledged support for some form of devolution.

Despite the investment and employment which wartime mobilization created, the British economy had been weakened by the massive cost of the war. John Maynard Keynes wrote, 'we threw good housekeeping to the winds. But we saved ourselves, and helped to save the world'.[9] True enough. But who would now save Scotland and Wales? They remained the most vulnerable sectors of the economy. Their dependence on heavy industry grew rather than diminished after 1945. Pits and shipyards may have been owned by the people but as they became less and less profitable the gulf between England's more diversified economy and those of her partners widened still further. At first Regional Aid ameliorated this trend. The expanded public sector enabled the government to locate more government offices and factories in areas of high unemployment. Circuses were added to this airy bread, with block grants to local authorities to improve civic amenities. However, the severe economic crisis of 1946–7 led to aid being cut by a third so that it was actually lower in real terms than during the 1930s. Furthermore, in a departure from wartime practice, Labour's regional aid programme was managed almost entirely from Whitehall. The failure of the Attlee government to arrest economic decline exacerbated resentment about political centralization. The Scottish and Welsh Labour Parties decided to act.

Kenneth Morgan has stated that 'In 1945, and for several years afterwards, Welsh nationalism seemed to be as dead as the druids'.[10] In fact, it was coming to life again. The Welsh were the first to request devolution in the postwar era, formally approaching the Prime Minister in 1945 and again in 1946. Unlike the petition that Welsh leaders delivered to Churchill in 1944, those delivered to Attlee contained no effusive declarations of loyalty to the rest of Britain. Instead, they flatly told the Prime Minister that anxiety about the economy was growing and with it a distrust of those making decisions on their behalf in London:

> There is ever present in the minds of the Welsh people the bitter experience passed through during the inter-war years when unemployment ruled and nearly half a million of the population had voluntarily or forcibly to be removed to England. It seems now that that the full cycle has been turned. Once again the people of Wales are filled with anxiety. Dread and fear of the future are widespread, while, in turn, their elected representatives are made profoundly uneasy and apprehensive.[11]

Like petitioners to an absolute monarch they pledged loyalty to their party while at the same time warning of the consequences of a refusal. 'The advent of a Labour government was nowhere hailed with more satisfaction than in Wales . . . [but] a negative reply will cause intense disappointment to our own people, and will be exploited by all our political opponents on the Left and the Right'.[12] In order to emphasize the danger, they brought an all-party deputation to Downing Street to meet the Prime Minister on 6 March 1946. A year later, on 16 June 1947, the Scots followed suit, expressing similar fears and demanding devolution as redress.[13]

Attlee was even more dismissive than Churchill had been. This marked a radical change in the political philosophy of the labour movement. Since Keir Hardie's day, devolution had been one of Labour's articles of faith. In 1917, party leaders agreed that the old Liberal idea of 'Home Rule All Round' would make the UK more democratic, and it became official party policy shortly before the general election victory of 1929, but like most of the policies of that brief minority government, Home Rule proved impossible to implement. Although the idea lingered on in Scottish and Welsh circles of the labour movement during the 1930s and 1940s, by 1945 Attlee and most of his colleagues had gone off the idea. Having finally scaled the ramparts of the British state, they had no wish to cede any of their newly won power to Celtic nationalists. They also feared that the extra bureaucracy created by devolution would be a waste of precious resources. In addition, those on the left of the party had an abiding suspicion of nationalism as a chauvinistic diversion from the struggle of the British working classes.

The Welsh cause was hampered by the fact that Britain's most famous Welshman was against devolution. Aneurin Bevan, founder of the NHS and standard-bearer of the left of the Labour Party, was something of a folk hero in the principality, as Lloyd George had been before him. At a Cabinet committee called to discuss the matter in October 1945, Bevan summed up his views on the issue:

> THE MINISTER OF HEALTH thought the demand had passed its peak. It had been due to political considerations which had now ceased to be important. The appointment of a Secretary of State for Wales ... was misconceived. There was no Welsh problem that was not also an English problem and separation would be inimical to Welsh interests. There was no case for a transfer of Ministerial functions unless it were accompanied by some devolution from the Imperial Parliament to a separate Welsh body. Nor would any exceptional measure of administrative devolution in Wales be justified unless, for instance, Local government as a whole were radically reorganised to provide for regrouping on a regional basis. Even such administrative devolution as existed at present – e.g. through the Welsh Board of Health – did not always conduce to efficient administration.[14]

In the discussion that followed, ministers agreed that 'Wales was not a coherent unit', its northern region having closer links to Lancashire and its southern region to south-west England and the Midlands. The full Cabinet endorsed the decision in February 1946.[15] The idea that Wales was not a coherent unit had some economic validity but it did not appease national sentiment. Welsh MPs protested that Attlee had 'repudiate[d] entirely the claims of Wales as a nation'.[16]

Bowing to pressure, Attlee agreed to the establishment of a Council for Wales. It first met in May 1949, chaired by the trade union leader Huw T. Edwards. Edwards was a tireless agitator for Wales, a staunch unionist who defected from Labour to Plaid Cymru in 1953 and a man whose gradual loss of patience with Britain's political elite mirrored that of millions of ordinary people. The Council was toothless and Edwards recorded that no other body 'in the history of our nation ever had such a cold reception'.[17] This was the result not of popular indifference to devolution but enthusiasm for it. The failure to win a Welsh Office provoked a more radical demand. In 1950, the Campaign for a Welsh Parliament began. It was chaired by Lady Megan Lloyd George, Deputy Leader of the Liberal Party and a daughter of the former Liberal Prime Minister. Over the next ten years it attracted cross-party support, with every-one from Conservatives to communists involved, and popular sup-port from the more Anglicized communities of the south and east as well as from the Welsh-speaking north and west. Such was its moral authority that Bevan had to step in to prevent a witch-hunt of its members in the Labour movement. It was disbanded in 1959 as a result of internal divisions but not before it delivered a petition containing 250,000 signatures, approximately a tenth of the popula-tion, to Downing Street.

Meanwhile, Attlee attempted to placate the Scots with piecemeal administrative reforms. To Herbert Morrison, the Deputy Prime Minister, he suggested: 'while I think our Scots friends are apt to be unduly alarmed at Scottish Nationalism, I think it might be wise to have some kind of enquiry'.[18] Morrison in turn told the Secretary of State for Scotland, Joseph Westwood, 'there is a big public relations job here which ought to be tackled before it is too late'.[19] The result of this public relations exercise was a White Paper in January 1948 which proposed that legislation that affected Scotland would be given more parliamentary time.[20] The report's author was Arthur Woodburn, who succeeded Westwood as Scottish Secretary in 1947. A Home Ruler before the war, Woodburn had since recanted and he commended the White Paper to his Cabinet colleagues. But he also issued a prophetic warning against complacency:

During the war years party politics were in abeyance and the patriotic sentiment was concentrated on the war effort ... [Now there is a] widespread feeling that Scotland is held to be of no account by British governments. The matter is of some urgency. There is a powerful upsurge of Scottish spirit at the moment ... [It] is a kind of smouldering pile that might suddenly break through the party loyalties and become a formidable national move-ment.[21]

Less than two years later, the smouldering pile ignited and the monarchy had to be marshalled to put out the blaze.

The 'Scottish Renaissance', first heralded by nationalist intellectuals in the 1920s, regained its momentum in the 1940s. There was a flurry of books and articles on Scottish culture in this period, most of which emphasized its Celtic nature. 'The true outline and identity of Scotland are at last taking shape through the haar', concluded one critic in 1945.[22] In art, two alcoholic homosexual Glaswegians, Robert Colquhoun and Robert MacBryde, led the way. They were part of the British-wide Neo-Romantic movement which included the Welsh painter David Jones and England's Graham Sutherland, but they were the most nationally minded of the Neo-Romantics. They had 'a paranoia, a fear of being contaminated by English culture', writes David Mellor. 'Dour and vengeful', many of their paintings were 'elegies for a Celtic Scotland'.[23] Colquhoun and MacBryde had struggled to gain government commissions during the war. But in the mid- to late 1940s they flourished, striding around Glasgow and London in kilts, successfully persuading dealers of their worth before their premature deaths in 1962 and 1966.

One of their admirers was the undisputed leader of the Scottish Renaissance, the poet and essayist Hugh MacDiarmid. Born Christopher Murray Grieve, he was the son of a Borders postman, a communist and a nationalist who dreamed of an independent cosmopolitan Scottish republic taking its place in a Europe of small nations. MacDiarmid spent his long life (1892–1978) railing against the Anglicization of his native land. He chastised poets like Edwin Muir for helping bankers and politicians sell out to the English by not writing in Scottish dialect as he did. They were, he said, 'the touts and toadies of the English Ascendancy'. In 1950, Attlee gave him a Civil List pension – a rare honour for a poet in Britain – and he rewarded the state which rescued him from poverty by continuing to attack it for oppressing his country:

> The extraordinary consensus of opinion [in Scotland] against the English on the score of their greed, stupidity, their cruelty, their snobbery . . . is thoroughly well-founded and arises basically from the fact that the English, like their cousins, the Germans, have a 'herren volk' tradition and are intolerably arrogant and overbearing. There is a silly disposition in many quarters to attribute any such complaint to an 'inferiority complex' . . . I believe the English are finished as a world power and must be forced back upon their own 'right little, tight little island', or rather that part of it which

is their own ... Surely there is no need to slobber kisses on the
feet that are trampling us down. We have nothing to be grateful
for to the English ... The leopard does not change his spots. The
English are as they have always been.[24]

In response, the *Times Literary Supplement* argued that 'the desire
to write Scottishly at all costs' often led to 'affectations, absurdities
and sterile pedantic tricks.'[25] But MacDiarmid's ravings did reflect a
growing disillusionment among ordinary Scots which in 1949 took
a dramatic political turn.

The SNP, which MacDiarmid had helped to found, was in a bad
way. Demoralized by its lack of electoral success and riven by
internal feuds, the party had split in 1942, its leader, John Mac-
Cormick, a professor of law at Glasgow University, arguing that
contesting elections as a separate organization had failed and that
nationalists should work within the main parties to achieve their
goal of Home Rule. Taking the bulk of the SNP with him, he
formed a pressure group, the Scottish Covenant Association, similar
to the Scottish Home Rule Association of the 1880s. The radical
rump of the SNP came out in favour of complete independence and
followed MacIntyre, whose rapid exit from Westminster seemed to
confirm MacCormick's prognosis, and over the next few years it
was to the Scottish Covenant that disaffected Scots looked for
leadership.

On 29 October 1949, 1,200 delegates gathered in the Church of
Scotland Assembly Halls, Edinburgh, for the third annual meeting of
the Scottish National Assembly, organized by MacCormick. Led by
the Duke of Montrose, the delegates signed a Covenant calling for
Home Rule in which a Scottish Parliament with tax-raising powers
would have control over the nation's domestic affairs. The document
declared:

> We the people of Scotland who subscribe to this Engagement,
> declare our belief that reform in the constitution of our country is
> necessary to secure good government in accordance with our
> Scottish traditions and to promote the spiritual and economic
> welfare of our nation.
> ... With that end in view we solemnly enter into this Covenant
> whereby we pledge ourselves in all loyalty to the Crown and within
> the framework of the United Kingdom, to do everything in our
> power to secure for Scotland a Parliament with adequate legislative
> authority in Scottish affairs.[26]

The Covenant was supported by the Scottish press, and within days there were queues in the streets of Scotland's major cities to sign the Covenant. By spring 1950 the government estimated that approximately 1.25 million signatures had been collected. The figure eventually reached 2 million, two-thirds of the electorate in a population of 5.17 million. The Covenant was the first serious tremor in the body politic of postwar Britain. It proved that Scottish nationalism was no longer the obsession of a few romantic intellectuals.

Eminent Scots were concerned for the UK's future and tried to press home Arthur Woodburn's warning on a complacent English elite. One of them was Sir Robert Bruce Lockhart, who had run the Political Warfare Executive from 1941 to 1945, responsible for covert propaganda in Axis countries. He was born in Fifeshire, a descendant of James Boswell. A moderate Covenanter, his diaries record a furious but unsuccessful attempt to make English friends like Richard Crossman and Anthony Eden realize the true nature and extent of the problem. In December 1949, he wrote:

> There must be no hatred of England and the English . . . We must avoid at all costs the impression that Scotland is seeking to desert England when she is in difficulties and that Home Rule can be achieved wholly at the expense of the English Exchequer . . . [But] if nothing comes of the Covenant . . . the extremists will get hold of the movement and create something akin to Sinn Fein and hatred of England.[27]

Support for the Covenant did not translate into votes for the SNP at the general election of February 1950, despite the party's pragmatic support for the campaign started by its former leader. Consequently, English unionists thought that no constitutional surgery was needed.

Instead, the Labour government diagnosed a further programme of invigorating exercise in the form of a continuation of the social democratic revolution of the previous five years. Given that the revolution had virtually ground to a halt by this time as a result of economic crisis, in practice this meant that little would be done. In May 1950 the new Secretary of State for Scotland, Hector McNeil, circulated a lengthy memorandum to his colleagues laying out the arguments against Home Rule. These arguments formed the basis of the unionist position over the next half-century. Broadly, they were: that Scotland could not afford to go it alone economically; that she lacked 'the political talent' necessary to maintain representation in two Parliaments; and that 'a corollary of Home Rule for Scotland is

Home Rule for England', which would necessitate a reduction in the number of Scottish MPs who sat in Westminster to compensate the English for the loss of say over Scottish affairs, and would, he argued, inevitably lead to further separation since 'conflicts would easily arise' between the Westminster and Edinburgh Parliaments. He concluded that in every sphere of life the Labour government had worked 'with the fullest regard to Scotland's sense of nationhood' and would continue to do so.[28] The Cabinet agreed.[29]

Attlee believed that the Covenanters had no mandate to negotiate Scotland's Union with England. He refused to see the movement's leaders at Downing Street and left McNeil to explain the government decision at a meeting in Glasgow on 17 June. There, MacCormick reassured the Secretary of State that they were seeking not separation from England but merely equal status within the Commonwealth along the lines of Northern Ireland, Canada or Australia. But he warned McNeil that if the government did not give in, the Covenanters 'would be forced to take political action'.[30] That political action turned out to be one of the most daring publicity stunts of the twentieth century. It angered the King, severely embarrassed the government and brought the whole issue of Celtic nationalism to the attention of the English public for the first time since Ireland announced its neutrality in 1939.

2. The Stane's awa'

Early on Christmas morning 1950, four of MacCormick's students from Glasgow University removed the Stone of Scone from underneath the Coronation chair in Westminster Abbey and drove it north in the boot of a Ford Anglia. The Stone, upon which, reputedly, the Kings of Scotland had been crowned since the tenth century, was removed by Edward I after defeating the Scots in 1296. He took it to London, where English, and latterly British, monarchs were crowned on it. The Stone was therefore a potent symbol of Scottish nationhood and for some a symbol of the country's ongoing subjugation by the English.

The event spawned a number of rousing folk songs by nationalist groups, such as 'The Stane's Awa' '.[31] The leader of the group who

stole the Stone, a twenty-three-year-old law student called Ian Hamilton, believed that 'the raid' on the Abbey 'was at once a sign and a
result of the reawakening of a people which, in two thousand years
of war and invasion and betrayal, has clung to its liberty and refused
to surrender'.[32] Some senior Church of Scotland figures agreed and
publicly said so, but the majority of respectable Scottish opinion was
deeply embarrassed by the event. The Lord Provost of Perth, in
whose jurisdiction Scone Abbey lay, and Scottish politicians from the
main parties condemned the theft. The *Glasgow Herald* called it
'publicity-seeking vulgarity', by a minority who were out of touch
with the Scottish people, and it defended the housing of the Stone at
Westminster as a symbol of the Union.[33] The writer and Home Ruler
Compton Mackenzie condemned the reaction of his compatriots as
that of an unscrupulous elite betraying their nation for English gold.
It was, he said, 'the usual chorus of protest from the North Britons
with hard heads and weak knees who lose no opportunity to fawn
on England in the sacred cause of Big Business'.[34] The feelings of
ordinary Scots lay somewhere between the two camps. Few saw the
incident as a rallying point for Home Rule but a majority would
have liked the Stone to have been kept north of the border. Mackenzie described the popular mood, probably accurately, as one of
'cautious elation'.[35]

What was the reaction of the English people? Many were amused
by the theft and would have accepted some form of compromise to
satisfy Scottish opinion. The English continued to view the Scots as a
quaintly eccentric variant of themselves; loyal Britons whose
occasional truculence could be indulged at little cost to the Union.
This view was encapsulated by the Ealing comedy *Whisky Galore*
(1949). Written by Compton Mackenzie and directed by another
Scot, Alexander Mackendrick, it dramatized the true story of how
the people of Barra in the Hebrides rescued a consignment of whisky
from a sinking ship during the Second World War and fought to
keep it. They are opposed by the English leader of the local Home
Guard, Captain Waggett – self-proclaimed governor of the island
and a pompous stickler for rules (a character strongly prefiguring
Captain Mainwaring of *Dad's Army*). An exasperated Waggett
declares: '[The Scots] are so unsporting! They don't do things for the
sake of doing them like the English. We play the game for the sake
of the game. [They] play the game for the sake of winning it . . .
Once you let people take the law into their own hands, it's anarchy,
anarchy!'[36] Waggett is defeated not only by the canny islanders but

also by his Cockney sergeant, who wants to marry a local girl and is welcomed into the community. The film is not therefore about Anglo-Scottish hostility but a dislike, common among all Britons, of a certain kind of English authority. Like most Ealing films, it was equally successful south and north of the border. *Whisky Galore* therefore captured a period when Britishness still rested on a good-humoured understanding between Scots and English.

But the Stone of Destiny highlighted a change in the relationship once lubricated by the whisky of Barra. Although many people in England were amused by the Stone's removal, a good many were deeply angered by it and saw the Scots as ingrates to whom no quarter should be given. The Korean War had started six months earlier and some saw Hamilton's escapade as an irresponsible, disloyal act at a time when the country should be united to prosecute a conflict that threatened to be the start of a Third World War. The *Times* letters page was filled with exclamations of 'Sacrilege!' and the Dean of Westminster made an emotional appeal for the Stone's return on the BBC, telling his listeners that the King was 'greatly distressed'.[37] The attitude of the English press was an early warning to Scottish nationalists that they risked a corresponding reaction south of the border. 'Cassandra' of the *Daily Mirror* argued that the Stone should be given back to these 'ludicrous cranks' and hoped the gift would 'serve as a remembrancer for that long-overdue movement which someone will soon have to start – Home Rule for the English'.[38] The *Manchester Guardian* said:

> Apart from the childish stupidity of these Nationalists, which deserves sharp punishment and no extenuation, need we English be much wounded by the loss of the Stone if it is never recovered? We have a far better one of our own, the King's Stone, now at Kingston on Thames, on which the Saxon kings were crowned. There is a better tradition behind that than behind the miserable piece of Scottish stone used as magic by barely civilised Irish and Scottish kings in an age of barbarism. Why not England for the Saxons?[39]

The Attlee government took the matter extremely seriously. A twenty-four-hour guard was mounted on the Stone of Kingston, in case the Scots decided to give the English a taste of their own medicine by carrying that back to Scotland as well. Meanwhile, a nationwide hunt was launched for the Stone of Scone, involving roadblocks on the borders and the dredging of the Serpentine in Hyde Park. Nearly four months later, on 11 April 1951, the

Covenanters handed the Stone into the care of the Church of Scotland at Arbroath Abbey, scene of the Declaration of Scottish Independence in 1320.

Now awake to the possibility that Scottish nationalism could get out of hand and facing a general election with a narrow majority, the government was more wary of public opinion north of the border. On the advice of the Attorney-General, Hartley Shawcross, it was decided not to prosecute Hamilton and his associates.[40] Some ministers worried that unless an example was set, foreign nationalist movements might try to repatriate all sorts of state treasures which the British had 'collected' over the centuries, such as the Elgin Marbles, but Shawcross argued that a public prosecution 'would produce a very adverse reaction' in Scotland, with conviction making them martyrs and acquittal making them heroes.[41]

What to do with the Stone was a more difficult decision. Speaking for the Covenanters in the House of Lords, the Duke of Montrose suggested a compromise whereby the Stone would remain in Scotland but would be brought down to England for Coronations. When the House debated the issue a majority backed him,[42] but the Cabinet was less enthusiastic and when it met to discuss the issue the Secretary of State was the only one who argued for it. Although opposed to Home Rule, Hector McNeil, like Woodburn, knew his country well enough to realize that unless some gestures towards Scottish feeling were made, and made fast, unionist sentiment north of the border would continue to erode.

> There is a strong feeling in Scotland, among moderate opinion as well as among those who are vocal in support of some form of home rule, which favours the transfer of the Stone . . . my own feeling is that Scotland would respond to [such] a decision by The King . . . [it] would, I am sure, be regarded by moderate opinion in Scotland as a generous gesture and I think that once it had been made, interest in the matter would quickly die down. If the Stone remains in the Abbey we must expect a continuing agitation not only by the nationalist movement but by the Church of Scotland.[43]

But Attlee had already been swayed by two things: the dying George VI was utterly opposed to the move; and the Cabinet Secretary, Norman Brook, had advised him not to panic. 'The extreme nationalist movement is of no account', he wrote. In the coldly self-assured tone of the Whitehall mandarin, Brook added 'symbolism does not make much appeal to the Presbyterian mind'.[44] Attlee postponed a decision, hoping the issue would die down. It did not. The Presbyterian mind showed itself to be alive to the symbolism and the substance of English domination over the following years.

Anger about Scottish and Welsh nationalism did not lead to an awakening of a distinctly English consciousness until the 1990s. In the early postwar period there were calls for St George's Day to be properly celebrated once again, amid claims that England's fabled tolerance was being abused by her partners. The philosopher C. E. M. Joad mounted a campaign for the saint in his *Sunday Dispatch* column, beginning with an article in 1951 claiming that 'St George is the patron saint of England, and having been deafened by the clamour and ground under the heel of Welsh nationalism, Irish nationalism, above all of Scottish nationalism, all these many years, this English worm is going to turn and voice the distinctive claims of England.'[45] But the worm did not turn. Despite the fact that 23 April was also Shakespeare's birthday, the English continued to take little notice of the event, in stark contrast to the Scots and Welsh who celebrated their saints' days with increasing fervour.

Why the reluctance? Faced with the end of empire, the English lost some of their former swagger, but they continued to place their faith wholeheartedly in the Union. Indeed, they subsumed their identity in the concept of Britain more than ever before, because 'Great Britain' carried with it echoes of glory, however faint, with which 'Little England' could not compete. The entrenchment of Anglo-Britishness between the 1940s and the 1980s and the failure to develop a dual national identity similar to that of the Scots and Welsh widened the gulf between the three peoples of mainland Britain. At Westminster, the myopic view of the ideological changes taking place on England's borders handicapped efforts to understand and contain 'Celtic' nationalism.

In the meantime, two events occurred which reminded the Scots and Welsh what they had in common with the English: the repeal of Ireland's External Relations Act in 1949, as a result of which British monarchs ceased to be head of state in the South of Ireland; and the arrival of West Indian immigrants in 1948. Each event, in its own way, bolstered Britishness by defining who the inhabitants of the UK were not. The UK's rejection by Ireland reinforced the British belief that, unlike the Irish, they were a progressive people with no hangups about the past. In the second instance, the British demonstrated that they were indeed shaped by their past, rejecting the idea that they ever were or could be a multiracial people.

3. You found England with its pants down

On 21 June 1948, Lord Kitchener stood on the dockside at Tilbury, dressed in a snap-brim trilby and double-breasted suit, guitar in hand, singing 'London Is the Place for Me'. Born Aldwyn Roberts in Trinidad in 1922, he was the West Indies' most successful calypso singer. Kitchener was one of 492 passengers on the *Empire Windrush*, which had arrived from the Caribbean that morning. Together, they changed the course of British national identity. They came to the UK for a better life, encouraged by a change in the law which made them equal citizens of Britain for the first time in their history.

The bulk of postwar black immigration was facilitated by the British Nationality Act, enacted on 30 July 1948. It created a new form of citizenship shared by all those resident in a newly designated area, the United Kingdom and Commonwealth (UKC). Theoretically, the Act placed every UKC citizen from Neasden to Nairobi on an equal footing, giving each citizen and their dependants the right to settle anywhere within the UKC. Since the nineteenth century, champions of empire had argued that all subjects of the Crown in the imperial 'family of nations' were Britons. But *civis Britannicus sum* had been little more than a rhetorical device to celebrate the extent of British imperial power. Now, for the first time, subjects had become citizens and had acquired equal rights under the law regardless of their race or creed.

The Conservative Party fiercely opposed the Act on two main grounds – that defining people as citizens encouraged republicanism, and that the coloured races were not and could not become equally British. The shadow Home Secretary, David Maxwell Fyfe, argued that 'the ordinary citizen' did not have 'a feeling of special unity with the inhabitants of a colony',[46] and in the other place, Lord Altrincham denounced it as 'a departure into complete and utter unreality' which ignored the bonds of 'like to like'.[47]

In fact, the Act was designed to strengthen the Commonwealth. It came about as a result of changes to Canadian law in 1945 which made Canadian citizenship paramount and British citizenship merely a fringe benefit. Fearing that this would encourage nationalist movements around the globe to press for independence, Attlee decided to expand the formal parameters of British citizenship. The 1948 Nationality Act accepted that Commonwealth states could define their own citizenship but at the same time made sure that this could not take place without reference to the UK, so by legally codifying the concept of a far-flung British family, the Act was in a sense the high point of British imperialism. The labour movement contained many committed and vociferous opponents of imperialism, certainly more than the Conservative or Liberal Parties did.[48] But despite granting Indian independence, the Attlee government was not anti-imperial. Its desire to maintain what was left of the Empire was highlighted by the establishment of the Colonial Development Corporation in 1947. Most Labour leaders also shared the Conservative view that some Britons were more British than others. The Home Secretary, Chuter Ede, said the change would place 'the coloured races of the empire' on a legal par with people of the motherland. But equality would not begin with royal assent to the Bill. The government's purpose was to 'raise them to such a position of education, of training, and of experience that they too shall be able to share the grant of self-government which this House has so generously given during the last few years to other places'.[49] The Act was therefore based on the idea of a racial hierarchy which reserved Britain's right to define 'civilization' and to decide when it had been attained by the people under its tutelage.

There was a labour shortage in the early postwar period (a government survey of 1946 estimated a shortfall of between 600,000 and 1.3 million people). Various Ministries, particularly Transport and Health, had encouraged Commonwealth citizens to come to Britain to make up the shortfall, but they had envisaged something similar to the Gastarbeiter scheme run by the West German government to employ Turkish labour: blacks would find employment through a registered agency before coming to Britain; once there, they would be monitored; and when their labour was no longer required, they would be returned to their country of origin. But the passengers on the *Windrush* and those who followed them were more au fait with the implications of the Nationality Act than the officials who had drawn it up. They simply exercised their new right as full British citizens to migrate permanently to England and booked their passage without any reference to the government. Many who made the journey were ex-servicemen who had been demobbed in the West

Indies against their wishes, and took advantage of the Act to return
to the UK.

Until recently, historians argued that white Britons rejected the
new arrivals on racist grounds, forcing a liberal political Establishment to introduce legislation curbing immigration in order to restore
public order after serious race riots and (though it never said so)
to win votes. This view underpinned a nationalist myth of betrayal
in which the wishes of the British people were ignored, then recognized due to public pressure. Recent research has shown that
governments discouraged and resisted black immigration. Most
recruitment drives were directed at Europeans because it was thought
those groups were, according to one Whitehall official, 'full of the
spirit and stuff of which we can make Britons'.[50] Not only could
they be made into Britons; politicians believed that they could also
improve the country's racial stock by marrying Britons. Miscegenation with Europeans was positively encouraged. In a parliamentary
debate on the subject, one MP enthused about 'the infusion of
vigorous new blood' which European females would bring.
Altogether, 345,000 European Volunteer Workers were recruited. As
well as being provided with proper accommodation on arrival – not
to mention tea and buns – they were given free language tuition and
books such as *How to Help you Settle In Britain*. Crucially, an effort
was also made to educate the British people about the new arrivals.
Leaflets such as *What the Poles Have Done for You* were distributed,
which reminded people of their heroic efforts during the Battle of
Britain. No such arrangements were made for their black counterparts.

The arrival of black Britons caused alarm and panic. In June 1948
the Prime Minister chaired an emergency meeting of the Cabinet
Economic Policy Committee to discuss the situation. Ministers briefly
considered moving the *Windrush* passengers on to East Kenya to
work on one of the government's colonial development projects, the
Groundnuts Scheme, but they were forced to accept that the new
arrivals had come to Britain legally and, having no wish to return to
their African 'roots', they could not be deported. The Committee
demanded a report from the Colonial Secretary, Arthur Creech Jones,
Attlee in particular wanting to know who the 'ringleaders' of the
'incursion' were.[51] This view of black British immigration as an
invasion by foreigners became central to the rhetoric of racism. As
well as revealing the limits of British democracy, it was also indicative

of the extent to which the siege mentality generated by the war remained a key element of Britishness.

When the Colonial Secretary's report was submitted to the Cabinet, it 'had a distinct air of the battle station about it'.[52] Creech Jones argued that 'the problem' had to be tackled without the usual red tape in order to avoid a 'public scandal'.[53] The passengers of the *Windrush* were hastily billeted in an old air-raid shelter under Clapham Common. The nearby Brixton Employment Exchange found some of them jobs, so beginning Brixton's transformation into the biggest black community in Britain and the place synonymous in the national mind with immigration. Although the 'public scandal' was contained, MPs on both sides protested that because black people could not be truly British, their presence threatened the 'British Way of Life' and, therefore, the 'profound unity' of 'the British people'. A group of eleven Labour MPs wrote to the Prime Minister stating that 'an influx of coloured people . . . is likely to impair the harmony, strength and cohesion of our public and social life and to bring discord and unhappiness among all concerned'.[54] In Parliament, the Minister of Labour, George Isaacs, reassured Members that 'no encouragement will be given to others to follow their example'.[55] But follow they did.

The United States was equally concerned about black immigration, and in 1952 Congress passed the McCarran–Walter Act reducing the number of West Indians who could go to America. This resulted in a sharp rise in Caribbean traffic to Britain, up from approximately 3,000 people in 1953 to 28,000 in 1955 and 66,300 in 1961. The demographic nature of immigration also changed. Until the mid-1950s, most newcomers were skilled or semi-skilled from urban areas of the West Indies. After that, they tended to be unskilled people from poorer rural backgrounds. The same was true of their Asian and African counterparts. Also, the numbers of those coming to the UK from Africa and Asia rose dramatically – from 7,700 people in 1955 to 49,000 in 1961.[56] In later years, Asians were thought to be more industrious than Afro-Caribbeans, but when they first arrived, the opposite was the case. While officials grudgingly acknowledged the 'English ways' of Afro-Caribbeans, their attempts to assimilate and their 'skilled character and proven industry', Indians and Pakistanis, most of whom were initially from lower castes, were considered 'lazy . . . feckless individuals who make a bee-line for National Assistance'. The Colonial Office concluded that Britain had no obligation 'to act as a dumping ground for the rag-tag and bob-tail of Asia'.[57]

The public reaction to the new arrivals was predominantly one of fear and loathing. As one Trinidadian man recalled, 'You found England with its pants down.' What this unedifying sight revealed in the working-class areas where most immigrants settled was a people who had little knowledge or love of the Commonwealth but who retained a crude imperial view of its inhabitants. That view buttressed their sense of national greatness in a period during which the hubris of victory over Germany mingled with anxiety about British decline:

> They didn't know where the hell Trinidad was. They never knew anything about geography. They had no education period. They were shell-shocked from all the bombing and still they had this air of prejudice or fear, difficult to say what it was, a sort of dislike. Probably because they realised that you didn't have a tail . . . you dressed in beautiful clothes and . . . you were better appointed than they were. You could speak English to them and they seemed very shocked that you could understand the language. People in the lower echelons knew nothing about anything. All they knew was that Britain was great and they ruled over many territories.[58]

The litany of discrimination which black Britons suffered in jobs, housing and day-to-day life has been well documented. A brief survey will suffice here.

With a few exceptions (notably NHS recruitment of black doctors and nurses), skilled immigrants were unable to obtain jobs for which they were qualified. One study in 1958 estimated that 55 per cent had suffered occupational downgrading since arriving in the country. Such was the buoyancy of the economy in the 1950s that few Britons were unemployed, but this did not stop the welfare state becoming one of the areas where national identity was contested on racial grounds. There was widespread resentment of black people receiving state benefit. Indeed, it was frequently claimed that they had come to England simply to receive benefit and that the innate decency of the British was therefore being exploited. In housing the situation was worse still, with adverts openly proclaiming 'no coloureds'. One survey of Birmingham in the 1950s showed only 15 out of 1,000 people prepared to let accommodation to coloured people, and of that small number, most charged extortionate rents, forcing immigrants to share rooms that were already dilapidated, thus causing overcrowded and sometimes insanitary conditions. This contrasted with Welsh and Cornish resentment of English migration to west Britain, when the affluence of the new arrivals drove property prices up rather than down.

Endemic racism towards black Britons led whites to move out of areas when they moved in. Although entirely voluntary, this was widely seen as a forced exodus. It also increased the concentration of immigrants in certain areas. Added to which, black people stuck together even more as it became clear that white society did not want them. Their material way of life was not the only source of hostility. Complaints about their cultural habits ranged from 'flashy clothes' and 'florid gesticulations' to 'smelly cooking' and 'feeling food before buying it'. What caused most concern was drug-taking, playing loud music, holding frequent parties and regarding the streets as an arena of leisure. These were real cultural differences but again they were not without irony, because the colour bar operated by pubs and dance halls was partly responsible for the number of private parties.

In conclusion, the inability of so many black Britons to get skilled jobs and decent accommodation fuelled existing beliefs that they were stupid, lazy, dirty people who were unwilling to mix with the indigenous population. The racial basis of British national identity was therefore viciously self-perpetuating, and it came as a shock even to those who had experienced it during the war. A West Indian who had been a pilot in the RAF put it simply: 'They didn't mind us fighting for them but when it came to living with them under one roof the iron gates slammed shut.'[59]

This leads us to back to the Irish Question. Even when the Irish proclaimed themselves to be foreign, they were still seen to be more British than black people.

4. This is the land of Frankenstein

The repeal of Ireland's External Relations Act in 1949 was the first major constitutional change within the Isles in the postwar period and the last until the Parliament of Northern Ireland was suspended in 1972. In 1937, the South had issued a new constitution, but the External Relations Act, under which the King theoretically remained head of state, had remained in place and was an irritant to nationalists. The Fine Gael Party returned to power in 1948, led by John Costello. In 1920, Fine Gael had agreed to the partition of Ireland and since then it had continued to be more conciliatory than de Valéra's Fianna Fáil. However, the new Taoiseach, John Costello, was anxious to prove his nationalist credentials and announced the repeal of the Act in September, to take effect on the anniversary of the Easter Rising in 1949. To cap it, he also announced that, unlike India, the new republic would be leaving the Commonwealth.

Shortly after the war, the diplomatic relationship between the two countries had improved slightly. The Labour government was suspicious of right-wing Northern Irish Protestant leaders and there was a corresponding willingness in Whitehall to bury the hatchet with the South. The British Ambassador to Ireland, Sir John Maffey, told the Cabinet that despite 'lively resentment' in Britain over neutrality, it had been a great improvement on the insurrection which occurred during the First World War. 'The old slogan of Irish patriotism . . . "England's difficulty is Ireland's opportunity" had been replaced by "England's difficulty is none of our business." . . . For the first time in history, the British Cabinet have been able to conduct a long war without any anxiety about Ireland.'[60]

In the late summer of 1946, Herbert Morrison used a holiday in Éire with his wife to have friendly talks with de Valéra. When he returned to Britain, he wrote a report for the Cabinet on his visit. It observed that the links of history and language between the two nations were still apparent everywhere. He noticed, for example, that postboxes had not been blown up but simply painted green, and still bore royal insignia. He also noticed that although buses bore their company's name in Gaelic, 'Gaelic did not appear to be useful when people wanted to know where the bus is going.' His report lamented that 'the Irish government have done their best to make Eire a foreign country' and that this was a fact which the British had to face. But he concluded that the potential was there for healthy Anglo-Irish relations. The good humour did not last long.[61] Two years later, de Valéra's successor declared Ireland to be a republic and all the rancour of the war returned.

Despite heartfelt reassurances from Costello that the change would improve relations between Britain and Ireland, the announcement was greeted in the UK with horror. Most British governments were instinctively against any constitutional tinkering unless forced to do so, and in this case it was presented with a fait accompli which, like the Rhodesian Unilateral Declaration of Independence twenty years later, offended British pride. But more than pride was at stake. In November 1948, Sir John Maffey (now Lord Rugby) sent a dispatch to Attlee entitled 'The Writing on the Wall'. In it, he warned that Éire's move would lead to renewed bloodshed on the island. The letter is chillingly prescient and deserves to be quoted at length:

> It is my view that this rivalry between the parties in an anti-Partition crusade will bring the gun-man back again . . . On the surface there are here the same friendly people, for the most part generous admirers of England, cordial and helpful. But in the blood stream there is a malignant virus . . . We go from celebration to celebration inspired by the half conscious cult of hatred. The indoctrination of the younger generation by press, radio, platform and pulpit has been intense. Some people in England think that the repeal of the External Relations Act has automatically put the Partition question to sleep. There could be no greater mistake. All it has done is to destroy the best chance of a friendly solution. The establishment here of an independent Republic will stimulate national sentiment and inflame opinion about the Border on both sides of it . . . My forecast is that unless a move is made now on our side to . . . disperse the forces and influences now gathering we shall have bloodshed in Ireland, a grave state of disorder in the North, with world opinion once again only too ready to believe that England is misbehaving herself in Ireland . . . We know, or should know, by bitter experience what Irish opinion . . . in the Catholic world can do. It may not take the first trick but it wins the rubber. I am not suggesting that Mr. Costello would approve a violent solution to the Partition question . . . But Irish leaders are not free agents and they know it. This the land of Frankenstein . . . The rebels of 1916 were loudly cursed in Dublin, but in three months' time they were heroes. The blood sacrifice worked its *mystique* and changed or hastened the course of history. We may perhaps feel some sympathy for a government which has to control a vendetta-minded people who have had no outlet for their tribal passions during the years of war. Unionists in the North, and perhaps elsewhere, may be tempted to say 'Let them do their worst. The forces of the Crown will soon teach them a lesson.' This view has no element of wisdom in it. It will be a day of triumph if the forces of the Crown are actively employed against patriotic elements in Ireland. British bayonets are Ireland's secret weapon.[62]

Rugby suggested that the Irish Question should be referred to international arbitration, arguing that the moral standing of Éire was low as a result of the war, and that Ulster had a better chance of getting a good deal than it had ever had. It was not to be. Dublin's action had sent Unionists into a tailspin. Since 1937 the South's claim to the North had been written into its constitution (Article 2), but so long as Éire remained under Crown and Commonwealth, the threat contained within Article 2 was less immediate. Genuinely fearful of insurrection, the government of Northern Ireland pressed Britain for a guarantee of its sovereignty by Act of Parliament. Attlee willingly gave it.

The Ireland Act was passed on 2 June 1949, and included the provision 'any change made in the relationship between the two governments in Ireland shall require the consent of both'. This became a mantra of unionists on both sides of the Irish Channel over the next half century. In Britain, it fossilized a consensus that change in Ireland would come about only with the consent of the North, which meant in effect that the Catholic population would have to be larger than the Protestant. However, given the higher Catholic birth rate, it was a distinct possibility that this would occur and that a future plebiscite in the province would result in a vote for reunification, a prospect which politicians in Northern Ireland and Britain privately viewed with alarm. Costello and his colleagues were furious. A message of goodwill from George VI on the day the republic came into being calmed feelings only temporarily. Meanwhile, in the North, the Prime Minister, Brookeborough, held an election on the single issue of nationality. In February 1949, he asked people to decide 'whether we are King's men or not'. The result was a resounding yes, the Ulster Unionists gaining another 12 per cent of the vote.

The British roundly agreed that the Act had been precipitated by Irish politicians seeking short-term electoral gain and that Ulster had to be defended. In the Commons, Attlee said that the Irish thought cutting ties with Britain 'a more important objective than ending Partition'. Churchill agreed: 'It is evident that a ditch has been dug . . . which invests partition with greater permanency and reality than it ever had before . . . the maintenance of the position of Northern Ireland becomes all the more obligatory upon us.'[63] The *Manchester Guardian* urged Parliament to abolish dual Irish citizenship, which guaranteed free passage and the right to live, work and vote in Britain. 'If Eire breaks, we should see no reason for pretending that she is not as much a foreign country as Albania or Bolivia. She and we will have to take the consequences'.[64] This proposal was considered by the government, but was rejected for two reasons. First, it was simply thought to be unworkable. Given the immense traffic between the Republic and the UK (more Irish people migrated to Britain than any other nationality) and the fact that much of that traffic came via the unpoliceable border with the North, it would be impossible to enforce.

The second reason why the Irish retained the privileges of dual citizenship was that the British considered the two islands to have ancient cultural links which could not and should not be broken. By this, they did not mean the glories of Anglo-Irish literature; the Irish were seen to have racial links with the British and benefited from the fact. Consequently, the Irish presence did not give rise to the same forebodings as the presence of black people. A brief prepared by senior Whitehall officials for the Prime Minister in 1949 argued that they were an 'unpredictable and inconsequent people' but should be allowed to retain their rights by virtue of the 'outstanding' fact of their race. The Irish, 'whether they like it or not are not a different race from the ordinary inhabitants of Great Britain'. In fact, said officials, 'the population of the whole of the British Isles is for historical and geographical reasons essentially one'.[65] This despite the fact that, throughout the postwar era, the number of Irish people moving to the UK outstripped the number of black people doing so (in the period 1953 to 1962, for example, an average of 60,000 foreign Irish nationals arrived each year compared to only 48,000 coloured UK nationals). Hostility towards black Britons also bene-fited the Irish because much of the animus previously directed at them was diverted towards the new arrivals. It should be noted that Irish immigrants were guilty of some of the worst racism themselves, since they saw the opportunity to raise their standing by stigmatizing others.

In short, the arrival of large numbers of black and Asian immi-grants was instrumental in changing the way that the British saw the Irish. It breathed fresh life into the Victorian belief in the common racial ancestry of Saxon and Celt, and took the heat out of Anglo-Irish relations from street corners to Whitehall meeting rooms. At the same time, it helped to consign the black and Asian population to the outer peripheries of Britishness.

Still, one cannot ignore the fact that the Irish experienced prejudice in mid-twentieth-century Britain. Although they were white, they were still viewed less sympathetically than the patriots of Northern Ireland. Southern Irish immigrants were discriminated against in housing and employment both by the general public and by the state. Addressing the problem of poverty in the Irish community, the Ministry of Labour concluded in 1955 that most of those who lived in squalor did so through choice. They were, it said, 'accustomed to living in their own country in conditions which English people would not normally tolerate'.[66] Even devout British Catholics viewed the South with some disdain. Evelyn Waugh, who was embittered by the creation of social democracy after the war, briefly considered emigrating to Ireland in 1952. He decided not to, and wrote to Nancy Mitford to explain why:

> Among the countless blessings I thank God for, my failure to find a house in Ireland comes first. Unless one is mad for fox hunting there is nothing to draw one. The houses, except for half a dozen famous ones, are very shoddy in building . . . the peasants are malevolent. All their smiles are as false as Hell. Their priests are very suitable for them but not for foreigners. No coal at all. Awful incompetence everywhere. No native capable of doing the simplest job properly. No schools for children.[67]

The main manifestation of popular prejudice was telling Irish jokes. Originating in the late Victorian period, they portrayed the Irish as quaint people with a childlike stupidity. Sometimes – as in the 1953 collection *Have You Heard This One? Best Scottish, Irish and Jewish Jokes: A Picked Collection of Really Funny Stories about these Delightful Folk* – tales of Irish stupidity were mixed with those about Scottish and Jewish meanness. But the Irish joke was the most common and it reached its high point (if that can be said) with the one about the Englishman, the Scotsman and the Irishman.

Ireland's backwardness was viewed not simply in terms of social conditions and religious belief. It was also seen as a nation neurotically obsessed with the island's ancient conflicts. In the latter half of the century, this trait came to be firmly associated with Unionism, but in this period Éire was seen as the country that would not let go of the past. One incident, widely reported in 1951, was thought to be typical: in January the Irish government complained that two squadrons of the Dutch navy had been stationed in the North for a NATO exercise. This extra affront to the sovereignty which the Republic claimed over the island caused Dublin particular offence because it was a reminder of the defeat of James II's army by William of Orange's Dutch Protestant troops at the Battle of the Boyne in 1690 and the lifting of the Siege of Derry. With some irritation, Attlee told the First Lord of the Admiralty that 'memories of Dutch William III are very much alive'. The Commonwealth Relations Secretary, Patrick Gordon Walker, was dispatched to tell the Irish Ambassador 'there was no distinction between foreign forces going to Northern Ireland and going, for example, to Kent'. And there the matter rested.[68]

The Southern Irish therefore had an ambiguous status in mid-twentieth-century Britain. On the one hand, they retained extraordinary rights of citizenship given to no other foreign country and which were not reciprocated by the republic, and the prevailing racial definition of Britishness enabled them to be more readily accepted into British society than coloured people. Yet the Irish continued to be viewed with scorn and suspicion. When Eamon de Valéra toured mainland Britain in 1958 he was regularly booed, and in London on St Patrick's Day bottles were thrown at him by an angry crowd, leading to the arrest of forty people. Public hostility was provoked by the start of a new IRA campaign in 1956, which fuelled existing bitterness about its campaign of 1939–40 and about the neutrality of Éire during the war.

In contrast, Northern Ireland and its people were warmly regarded. It was not merely seen to be strategically important. Ulster's moral standing was at its height in the mid-twentieth century because it had fought side by side with Britain during the war. The republic's withdrawal from the Commonwealth highlighted the North's loyalty. On Empire Day 1949, Princess Elizabeth and Prince Philip visited the province to reassure its inhabitants that they would remain a part of the United Kingdom, bound not simply by Act of Parliament but by culture and sentiment. The visit was also designed to reaffirm the Britishness of the province in the eyes of the mainland. According to the Princess, their common Britishness was based around loyalty to the monarchy. After being given the Freedom of Belfast, she declared:

> The warmth of an Irish welcome, the loyalty which the very name of Ulster recalls, removes any thought of separation and makes us feel as much at home in your midst as in any other part of the United Kingdom. We know this springs largely from the fact that the Crown is the focus of our unity, comradeship and moral standards . . . We are and cannot help being a Mother Country . . . yet the great self-governing countries which are our children have not forgotten us.[69]

For the Protestant majority, the period of Lord Brookeborough's Premiership at Stormont (1943–63) was a golden age. 'Ulster used to be a great wee place. Really lovely and always very quiet', recalled one pensioner from County Down.[70] Although the siege of Derry remained central to Protestant mythology, popular accounts of it published in this period lacked the polemical edge of those published during the Home Rule crises of the late nineteenth and early twentieth centuries. As Ian McBride has observed, 'they reflect the more confident position of Ulster Unionism in the middle of this century.'[71]

Few Britons were aware of the institutionalized discrimination against Catholics in every walk of civil life over which Brookeborough presided. Nor was it raised diplomatically by British governments, content as they were to have an obliging regime on their doorstep. Northern Ireland was seen as a thriving part of the United Kingdom throughout the 1950s. Despite initial fears that the welfare state would be resisted by Stormont it was introduced with some success. This, together with other subventions, meant that the North's standard of living, on a par with the South in 1930, was 75 per cent higher by the late 1940s. In 1951 an official guidebook for British travellers to the province said:

> Their loyalty to the British crown, staunchly protested and often demonstrated, is charged with emotions quickened by the separatist movement south of 'the border' ... The six counties ... are closely bound to the larger island by political and personal bonds and by ties of economics and sentiment which were tested and strengthened in the crisis of the Second World War.[72]

Parts of Britain had more than a passing admiration for Northern Ireland. In Glasgow and Liverpool, particularly, Orange Lodges retained strong links with those in Ulster during the 1950s. They bore testimony to a pan-British Protestant identity which, though in terminal decline on the mainland, was nonetheless still a feature of Britishness in this period. Thousands of people travelled each summer to the province to participate in the 12 July marches and associated festivities, often staying with relatives and making it their annual holiday. It was then thought to be little more than a colourful patriotic tradition, as harmless as the Last Night of the Proms and with little bearing on contemporary politics. It was against this mixed background of discontent in Scotland and Wales, peace in Ireland, and complacency towards all three in England that the UK's rulers attempted to reform British culture.

5. In trust for the nation

The Attlee government never perceived the health of the nation solely in material terms. The party manifesto of 1945 promised 'to assure to our people full access to the great heritage of culture in this nation'. A report on the arts in Britain compiled shortly afterwards by the party intellectual G. D. H. Cole explained, '[Our aim is] not to produce more and better works of art but better people and better communities.'[73] In the short term, the Labour government wanted to maintain public morale during a period of economic hardship in which the cost of the welfare state was being compounded by the cost of the Cold War. In the long term, Labour sought to change the very fabric of national culture, turning Britons from subjects into citizens by developing their mental faculties.

Creating better people meant encouraging them to use their spare time more productively. Leisure became a fiercely debated issue after the war thanks to the 1938 Holidays With Pay Act, which gave Britons a statutory right to a holiday for the first time. It had been effectively suspended from 1939 to 1945 due to mass mobilization, but started to take effect when people were released from war service. In 1931, only 1.5 million people received a paid holiday; by 1946 the figure was over 12 million (about 80 per cent of the workforce; much of the rest funded unpaid leave by subscribing to holiday saving clubs).

Conscious of public concern about Soviet communism, Labour leaders went out of their way to reassure the electorate that theirs was a very British socialism, based on a pragmatic respect for the individual. They were especially keen to show that cultural reform was not simply a decorative cufflink on the long arm of an autocratic state.

The Deputy Prime Minister, Herbert Morrison, was in charge of selling the New Jerusalem to the British. He was a short man with spectacles, a jutting chin and a little quiff of hair which made him look like an ageing version of the Belgian cartoon character Tintin. Born in Brixton in 1888, he cut his teeth in local government as Leader of the London County Council. But he became a truly national figure during the 1940s, and in a BBC broadcast he explained the nature of his patriotism:

The working and middle classes love their country with a love that is real and enduring. Their patriotism is the patriotism of service and not that of possession. We love our country so much that we want to free it from the disgrace of ugliness and poverty. We love it so much that we want its great resources to be the common inheritance and the common joy of every citizen. That is the patriotism of the Labour Party. It is a patriotism that seeks to elevate the honour and well-being of our own country without doing damage to the other peoples of the world.[74]

Half a century later, his grandson, Peter Mandelson, sold Blair's 'Third Way' to the British in similar terms. The two men had much in common aside from a prominent chin. Both were egotistical, vain and loathed by senior party figures. Above all, both realized the importance of the media and knew how to manipulate it. In July 1946, Morrison submitted a memorandum to the Cabinet called (like its wartime precursor) *The Projection of Britain*. In it, he argued that 'British culture is as alive as ever' and should be used to promote 'the greatest experiment in a planned economy in a free society that the world has ever known'. On his advice, the Cabinet agreed to create a permanent state propaganda body, so they stripped the wartime Ministry of Information of its executive powers and renamed it the Central Office of Information (COI). One of the COI's first briefs was to promote legislation designed to improve public access to one of the things Britons had fought to preserve from Nazi invasion: the countryside.

A year after the war ended, Clement Attlee decided to present the leaders of twelve European nations with a gift to symbolize the nation which had stood alone in 1940–41 in defence of Western democracy. He chose *Recording Britain*, a large volume illustrating the paintings commissioned by the coalition government in 1940 to record Britain's historic architecture in town and country. Attlee was determined to protect that heritage by Act of Parliament.

The minister at the forefront of his initiative was Hugh Dalton, Chancellor of the Exchequer from 1945 to 1947, responsible in that short time for the biggest redistribution of wealth ever undertaken by an occupant of No. 11 Downing Street. Aside from taxing the rich, his favourite pastime was rambling. In April 1946 he created the National Land Fund, which set aside £50 million to reimburse the Treasury for country estates left to the nation in lieu of death duties. He presented it to the House of Commons as a memorial to those who had been killed during the war:

Much of [Britain] has been spoiled and ruined beyond repair . . .
the best that remains should surely become the heritage, not of a
few private owners, but of all our people, and above all, of the
young and the fit, who shall find increased opportunities of health
and happiness, companionship and recreation in beautiful places.
There is still a wonderful, incomparable beauty in Britain in the
sunshine on the hills, the mist adrift across the moors, the wind on
the downs, the deep peace of the woodlands, the wash of the
waves against the white, unconquerable cliffs which Hitler never
scaled . . . it is surely fitting in this proud moment of our history
. . . that we should make a thankoffering for victory, and a war
memorial which, in the judgement of many, is better than any
work in stone or bronze. I should like to think that through this
Fund we shall dedicate some of the loveliest parts of this land to
the memory of those who for our sake went down to the dark
river, those for whom already 'the trumpets have sounded on the
other side'. Thus let this land of ours be dedicated to the memory
of our dead and to the use and enjoyment of the living for ever.[75]

Dalton was also involved in the National Parks and Access to the
Countryside Act of 1949. Britons were theoretically given the right
to roam wherever they liked. The Act also designated twelve areas of
England and Wales as National Parks where the right to roam was
guaranteed by the state. The idea for National Parks came from the
United States, which had begun to establish them in the 1870s.
    Introducing the Bill to Parliament, the Town and Country Plan-
ning Minister, John Silkin, described it as a 'People's Charter':

The enjoyment of the countryside is just as much a part of our
health and well being as are the building of hospitals or insurance
against sickness . . . This is not just a Bill. It is a people's charter
for the open air . . . for everyone who loves to get out and enjoy
the countryside. Without it they are fettered, deprived of their
powers of access and facilities needed to make holidays enjoyable.
With it the countryside is theirs to preserve, to cherish, to enjoy
and to make their own.[76]

Millions enjoyed the new parks and elsewhere a total of 130,000
miles of public footpaths, many of them ploughed or overgrown
since the enclosures of the eighteenth century, were reclaimed as a
result of the Act. But Scotland did not get its own national parks
until 1967 and Northern Ireland had to wait until 1983. Moreover,
in all four nations, the onus remained on the citizen to prove that
recreational access to private land was in the public interest. The

opposition of landowners, and the equally Conservative leaders of rural local authorities, was dogged. Consequently, by the end of the century, less than 0.5 per cent of the UK's countryside was covered by access agreements. Another barrier stood in the way of the tourist: the National Trust for England and Wales. Country estates purchased with the Land Fund would be managed by the Trust and much of its existing property fell within the areas designated as National Parks. Everything looked green and pleasant. It was not.

Analysing the decline of the British aristocracy, David Cannadine has observed their 'gradual shift from political activism to cultural stewardship' after the First World War. 'As aristocrats ceased to be the governing class', he concluded, 'they sought to carve out a new role for themselves as the self-appointed guardians of the national heritage . . . [they] were no longer the exclusive owners of "the land" but became instead the altruistic proprietors of "the countryside" on behalf of the community as a whole'.[75] The Trust, more than any other British institution, was the product of that development. It was founded in 1895 by middle-class Victorian social reformers and was charged by Act of Parliament in 1907 to 'preserve places of historic interest and natural beauty for the benefit of the nation'. Its leaders became more aristocratic during the 1920s and by 1945 it was led by a Scot, David Lindsay, twenty-eighth Earl of Crawford, and an Englishman, Oliver Brett, third Viscount Esher. The two men, respectively a Conservative and a Liberal, had come to run most of Britain's cultural institutions after unsuccessful spells in politics. Because of its unique ability among preservation societies to hold property, the Trust had become one of the biggest private landowners in Britain and a pressure group to be reckoned with. Moreover, unlike its Scottish counterpart, which was not established until 1931 and in 1945 was near bankruptcy for lack of support, the Trust had enjoyed the patronage of the Queen Mother and notables like Stanley Baldwin and Rudyard Kipling. A British Council pamphlet summed up its status in 1943: 'From small beginnings has sprung a noble edifice. So great a movement embodying in visible form Englishmen's love for their country and pride in their national heritage has no parallel in history.'[78] The strength of the Trust and of the class that ran it was demonstrated when it rejected an attempt to nationalize it by one of its own men.

The end of the war in Europe fortuitously coincided with the Trust's fiftieth anniversary. Amid the celebrations, in December 1945, its secretary, George Mallaby, predicted that it was about to 'go the way of voluntary hospitals and the Liberal Party', and advised the organization to achieve its objects as a government department rather than sacrificing them to preserve the voluntary principle. Mallaby said that a consensus now existed about the role of the state in British society: 'No one believes that the next government, whatever its colour, will de-nationalise the Bank of England and the coalmines; and it seems to me to be better to take time by the forelock ... than await elimination in pride and reserve.'[79] A horrified committee rejected the idea and Mallaby departed soon after to join the Ministry of Defence.[80] One of his fiercest opponents was James Lees-Milne, an aesthete whose job it was to assess the worth of country houses offered to the Trust. In his diary, Lees-Milne recalled Viscount Esher explaining why they had rejected Mallaby's proposal:

> He began by saying he never believed in hari-kiri. Many people after 1911 thought the House of Lords was doomed and gave up the struggle, whereas it still survives. He believes it fulfils today another but no less necessary function than it did in 1910. The same could be said of the Monarchy, now that it is constitutional. That is why he believes the National Trust will survive. Mallaby's ... memo ... advocates defeatism. Esher said this attitude is typical of the Civil Service mind, which is perfectionist. He said the aristocratic mind was quite different. It was pragmatical.[81]

What Mallaby had failed to realize was that for men like Esher, voluntary service was not simply a justification for their continuing role in British society, it was central to their vision of Britishness itself. For they believed that the pragmatism which had ensured the peaceful evolution of the state was a peculiarly aristocratic trait. The Trust's leaders therefore saw themselves not only as guardians of the nation's physical heritage but also as guarantors of its national character.

After a brief honeymoon, the Labour government and the National Trust locked horns in a fight for the right to manage the nation's heritage, and, with that right, the power to shape Britain's collective memory. As a result of Labour's taxation policy, the destruction of country houses accelerated to unprecedented levels after the war as many aristocrats found it impossible to maintain their properties, and the Land Fund proved to be inadequate to save them. In the five years to 1955 demolitions reached a peak of 204, but by the late 1940s it had already become a major public issue and was being widely compared in the press and in Parliament to the destruction of the monasteries in the sixteenth century. Realizing that a public-relations triumph was turning into a disaster, not least among the English middle classes upon whose support Labour's survival depended, the government set up a committee to examine the problem. It was chaired by Sir Ernest Gowers, who had begun his career as private secretary to Lloyd George in 1911.

The government's officials argued that country houses should be looked after by the state and as far as possible turned into training colleges for nurses and teachers or holiday homes for industrial workers. James Lees-Milne shuddered at the prospect of splendid symbols of aristocratic civilization being given over to 'a little folk-dancing, some social economy and Fabianism for the miners and their wives ... at a time when this country is supposed to be bankrupt they spend (our) money on semi-education of the lower classes who will merely learn from it to be dissatisfied'.[82] The Trust argued that the owners of country houses were their best custodians and that they should be given tax concessions to remain in their property in return for allowing public access to them. Preserving 'the historic link between families and their houses', it said, would prevent them 'from becoming mere lifeless museums'. In addition, owners would be more likely to give their property to the Trust than to a state 'to which they attribute their present impoverishment'.[83]

The Trust's assurance that it merely sought to preserve family homes was a compelling one. Not only did it cloak the organization's conservatism in populist language; it did so by very neatly turning a key component of English national identity on its head: if an Englishman's home was his castle, then his castle must surely be his home. This encouraged human sympathy for aristocrats faced with eviction from their homes, and encouraged people to see them not only as connoisseurs but also as emblems of a happier age when Englishmen and women were presided over by caring squires. A BBC broadcast produced with the Trust's cooperation in 1947 promoted that idea. It interviewed the Fairfax-Lucys and their staff about the recent loss of their estate at Charlecote, near Stratford-on-Avon, as a result of death duties. Against the backdrop of what the presenter called 'Shakespeare's England', a succession of faithful retainers were wheeled on, culminating in the park-keeper who loyally opined that 'The early days were better [when] gentlemen weren't taxed so much.' The programme concluded with Major Fairfax-Lucy lamenting the loss of Charlecote because 'Homes such as these were the centres of rural life, and their owners the friends of the people, sharing their interests and taking care of them in sickness or misfortune . . . it was a privilege, but it carried with it a strong sense of obligation out of which the traditions of leadership of the so-called "leisured classes" were born.'[84] The Major then compared the loss of his estate at the hands of the Treasury to the loss suffered by ordinary people when their homes were bombed by the Luftwaffe. Like Churchill's infamous speech during the general election of 1945, in which he compared the Labour Party to the Gestapo, the Major's speech presented the state and, by implication, socialism, as something dangerously alien to the traditions of the English people.

Whether or not such sentiment swayed Anthony Blunt, the art historian and Soviet spy who sat on the Gowers Committee, we do not know. But to the dismay of the government, when it reported in June 1950 the Committee blamed excessive taxation for the problem. Quoting the words of the Duke of Wellington, Gowers described the stately home as 'the greatest contribution made by England to the visual arts . . . [an] achievement . . . which is irreplaceable, and has seldom been equalled in the history of civilisation'.[85] The report recommended that a government body, the Historic Buildings Council, should be set up to administer sweeping tax concessions to the aristocracy. Many public figures sprang to its defence. Sir Eric Maclagan, former Director of the Victoria and Albert Museum, pleaded that the plan would not be 'a form of indulgence to the few, but an investment on behalf of the many'.[86] Attlee was unmoved and dropped the report like a hot potato. Hugh Gaitskell, the Chancellor of the Exchequer, told the Cabinet: 'stately homes are an important part of our national heritage [which] give very widespread pleasure . . . [but] I need not stress the political difficulty of giving specially favourable treatment to the owners.' He proposed instead a system of discriminatory building grants which, on St George's Day 1951, the Cabinet agreed were 'more consistent with Labour Party principles'.[87]

Access to land also provoked a bitter conflict. Fears were rife that the countryside could not cope with the number of Britons now taking their holidays in it. The combined effects of paid leave, demobilization, the end of petrol rationing and the rise in car ownership raised the spectre of a land devoured by the people whose soul it was thought to represent. In its Annual Report of 1947, the National Trust had warned: 'The enrichment of life for the masses [is] not incompatible with the preservation of the best of our natural scenery and architecture. But if these movements are not carefully

watched and guided, irreparable harm can quickly be done.'[88] Preservation groups like the Trust justified their antipathy to uncontrolled
access in terms of social responsibility, arguing that as custodians of
the nation's heritage they had a twofold duty: to preserve its fabric
for future generations and to ensure that the spiritual refreshment of
individuals among the present generation was not spoiled by over-
crowding. However sensible this argument appeared to be, it masked
a fundamental distinction between the 'nation' and the 'people'
which lay at the heart of British political discourse. When the Trust
refused to submit to compulsory purchase orders of land it owned
that was not open to the public, a Ministry of Town and Country
Planning official remarked, 'I do not think the nation as a sort of
entity independent of its citizens can be said to benefit from the mere
existence of something locked up.'[89]

Schemes for limiting the numbers of visitors to Trust property that
was open to the public ranged from the mean-minded to the absurd.
Until the 1950s, it did not properly advertise where and when its
land and buildings were open, nor did it signpost them terribly well.
In the *Spectator*, Harold Nicolson likened the National Trust to a
gentlemen's club whose properties belonged to subscribing members.
He lamented that 'living as we do in a Welfare State, the adjective
"national" possesses for the public associations with "nationalised".[90] One of the Trust's senior officials considered National Parks
to be 'wholly pernicious'.[91] The government was told that accommodation for holidaymakers 'should be monastic, hardy . . . and
uninviting'.[92] One of the Trust's more progressive leaders was Buck
De La Warr, who later led the battle to introduce commercial
television to Britain. He advised the Trust to become more commercial and got the same frosty reaction from his colleagues as Mallaby
had for suggesting nationalization. The rural historian Howard
Newby concludes, 'The countryside had to be preserved for the
"nation" but *from* the "public" [because] only a self-appointed
minority possessed the qualities to appreciate fully the cultural
enlightenment which the experience of the countryside could
bestow.'[93]

The resistance to public access sprang not only from a lingering
nostalgia for aristocratic Britain, but also from a more widespread
dislike of mass culture. Working- and lower-middle-class holidaymakers were frequently portrayed in this period as invaders of the
countryside – an ironic image, because these were the people who, as
Dalton said in his Land Fund speech, had formed the greater part of

those who prevented Britain being invaded by Hitler. Fear of the masses, however, was not the preserve of diehard Tory landowners; it was shared by many ordinary farmers with smallholdings, and by liberal intellectuals. Indeed, the most trenchant attack on public access to rural Britain came from C. E. M. Joad. In an influential book, *The Untutored Townsman's Invasion of the Country*, published in 1946, he lamented that industrialization had divorced the common people from the countryside, and argued that they must once again 'have intercourse with beauty'. But, he observed, 'the lover long deprived of his beloved finds that the first raptures of sexual renewal are brutish'. Consequently:

> In fifty years' time either the tides of modernity will have engulfed us completely or begun to recede . . . there is laid upon the men of my generation a peculiar responsibility . . . we are the high priests of a half-forgotten cult, the tenders of a sacred but dying flame. Upon us is placed the obligation to keep it alight . . . it falls, in short, to us to hold the pass until democracy can safely be let through.[94]

The pass could only be held, he concluded, by 'educat[ing] the invaders . . . and canaliz[ing] their inflow until they are educated'. In other words, nationhood was not a natural right. It was a state of mind which had to be learnt and, since this was a long process, the people had to be effectively policed in the meantime. On one occasion he argued that Butlin's holiday camps were a good thing because, like sewage farms, they contained the nation's effluent until it could be treated.[95]

The attempt to educate the public was usually more tactful and not without success. The BBC programme *Nature Parliament*, fronted by Charles Maxwell Knight ('Uncle Max') and the naturalist Peter Scott, informed children about the delicate ecological system they were being loosed upon. When not appearing on *Nature Parliament*, Knight (known to his listeners as 'Uncle Max') worked as an MI5 agent rooting out communist subversion around Britain. A more lasting initiative than kids' radio shows was the Countryside Code. Published by the government in 1950 and targeted at the young with the aim of promoting 'good citizenship',[96] by the end of the decade it had sold 90,000 copies. Also worth noting is the establishment of local authority field study centres where city schoolchildren could have a short holiday while learning about the countryside. A kind of Scout Camp for the post-imperial age, the first centre opened in 1946 at Flatford Mill in Sussex – an appropriate location given that it was the subject of one of Constable's most iconic paintings of rural England. The promotion of responsible recreation appeared to be a success. Membership of the Youth Hostel Association rose from 50,000 in 1940 to 230,000 in 1958, its patriotic ethos encapsulated by the bestseller *Camping for All*, written by the editor of the *Boy's Own Paper*, Jack Cox, in 1953.

The biggest success was country-house visiting, which became one of the most popular British pastimes. At its peak in the early 1960s, over 300 houses were open to the public. Although few hearts bled for the aristocracy, prejudice against it waned as its power declined. As the National Trust had predicted, many people did prefer properties to be lived in by the owners because it made them more homely. A glimpse of a lord scuttling past a guided tour prompted murmurs of delight in many a coach party. But the most successful properties were those whose owners bowed to commercialism and augmented the aesthetic appeal of their homes and gardens with miniature railways or wild animals. Others staged re-enactments of famous battles. One of the pioneers, Lord Montagu of Beaulieu, told the House of Lords: 'We must abandon the pretence that the world still owes us a living. We must adopt the attitude and method of the Impresario ... unless we can adapt ourselves to the times and conditions in which we live we shall suffer a fate as final, if less dramatic, as the French feudal aristocracy at the end of the eighteenth century.'[97] Eventually, the National Trust moved with the times and its membership shot up, from 8,000 in 1945 to 157,000 in 1965, making it one of the most popular British institutions. By the time of its centenary, the figure had reached over 2.2 million, more than the active membership of the Church of England.

The critics of mass culture continued to muster on a regular basis. The cry of 'No Popery!', shouted by Britain's leaders a century before, now became 'No Pot-pourri!'[98] What was later known as the 'heritage industry' was condemned for peddling a sanitized view of British history which encouraged and profited from a growing national predilection for nostalgia. When a Conservative government steered the Historic Buildings Bill through Parliament in 1953 (in all essentials, the system Labour agreed on in 1950), the Minister of Works, David Eccles, warned MPs:

> I would be sorry to see us turning ourselves into a nation of sub-sidised museum keepers. We have to strike a balance between the

past and the future, between the structures of bygone ages and the creations of our own generation ... [Too great a concern for the former] is a mark of decline in the nation.[99]

How justified were these fears? Not very, is the answer. The British loved their countryside and tended to romanticize it. Take, for example, the UK's first soap opera, *The Archers*. First broadcast in 1950, the programme hit its peak audience of 20 million in 1955. Its appeal was captured by BBC publicity, which described the fictional village of Ambridge as 'a gentle relic of Old England, nostalgic, generous, incorruptible and (above all) valiant. In other words the sort of British community that the rootless townsman would like to live in and can involve himself in vicariously'.[100]

However, the extent of British – and especially English – rural romanticism has been grossly exaggerated. Most people still preferred other destinations for their summer holidays. The 1940s and 1950s were the golden age of the seaside resort and holiday camp; both were a cheaper, more convenient way for people to enjoy themselves, with accommodation and entertainment provided in one location, and when flying became more affordable towards the end of the century, most Britons preferred to travel abroad. Folk music had little impact on English culture. In Scotland and Wales it became more popular in this period because it was driven by nationalist fervour and drew on contemporary life for inspiration; in England it remained defiantly arcane. Despite attempts to reform the English Folk Song and Dance Society by introducing American line dancing, it still favoured activities like morris dancing, a medieval ritual with pagan origins but irredeemably silly in the eyes of the nation. And, despite a craze for protest song among the left-leaning middle classes from 1950 to 1970, most English people did not respond to earnest celebrations of the Tolpuddle Martyrs by men and women in Aran sweaters with a hand clasped over one ear.[101]

The British were day-trippers, happy to enjoy the occasional brief visit to the countryside, but with no desire to live there and faintly amused by those who did. Few Britons who were posted to the countryside during the Second World War wanted to stay after 1945, any more than the 150,000 German and Italian POWs who worked with them on British farms. Having experienced the boredom, bigotry and back-breaking work which characterizes so much of rural life, the vast majority of Land Girls and evacuees returned to their bombed-out towns and cities as soon as they could. Government schemes like 'Lend A Hand on the Land' attracted 400,000 people in the late 1940s, but these were mainly the poorest families who could not afford a Butlin's holiday and who, like the hop-pickers of Kent, had a tradition of working breaks in the countryside.

Gardening, of which more in Chapter 4, was the greenest most Britons wanted to get to get their fingers on a regular basis. But even this was not the product of a frustrated ache for ancient rural origins. The garden was a picturesque space which was thought to harbour a number of British characteristics: a love of self-improving hobbies, of privacy and of nature. But it was an end in itself and not a substitute for a return to the land, a place where the outdoors could be enjoyed but with all the amenities of the city close at hand. Britain's suburbs were a testament to that modernity. Their dominant architectural style, mock-Tudor, with its wooden beams and sloping roofs mimicking the sixteenth-century manor house, was derided as off-the-peg Lutyens. But, far from being an example of ersatz ruralism, the suburbs were a beacon of mass culture and were loathed for precisely that reason: the cinema and not the church was their main institution; the urban transport system was their economic lifeline to jobs in the cities; they formed the world's first conurbations; above all, they marked the beginning of lower-class home-ownership, and in England the popularization of that key phrase 'an Englishman's home is his castle'.[102]

This brings us to the main point about the British attitude to the land in the twentieth century: consumption. In the end, considering the lilies took second place to cheap food, power and new homes. The Attlee government preserved what it could for leisure activities and voters approved. But Labour's mandate was to improve the nation's standard of living. Hence the fact that preservationists still had so much to cry about in the second half of the century. Their vociferousness was in direct proportion to Britons' indifference to the fate of the countryside.

Rightly or wrongly, the public rarely made the mental link between consumption and destruction, even when the point was forcefully made by the more radical environment movement which emerged in the 1960s. Britons' priorities can be seen in the lack of support they gave the National Trust when it objected to rural development. For example, in 1949, it tried to stop the building of a council estate near Birmingham on the grounds that it would spoil the view from one of its stately homes ('estate' is a peculiarly British term for public housing which reflects the cultural legacy of the nation's land-owning classes). The Trust was shouted down in the local press and the estate rose up. Most Britons were happy for the resources of their countryside to be exploited if it improved their standard of living. Preservationists were, as the geographer David Matless remarks, 'a self-consciously embattled minority setting themselves against the dominant vision of a simultaneously planned and preserved nation'.[103] Consequently, despite the curtailing of agricultural depression, the social gulf between town and country remained as wide as it was in 1945. Asking 'Who Cares For England?' in 1964, James Lees-Milne answered that those who did should promote 'The sanctity of historic buildings and beautiful scenery, and a reverence for nature and wild-life – in other words a proper love of one's country. Patriotism in the Kiplingesque sense is rightly out of date . . . [We] love England because of its beautiful buildings and its surviving woods and fields'.[104] Then, as in the 1940s, Lees-Milne's voice was a bitter one, few echoes of which could be heard among the great mass of his compatriots.

6. A people's civilization

The second strand of the government's strategy was to promote British artistic achievement and disseminate it more widely. This project also revealed a conflict between what the people wanted and what reformers wanted to give them. At the end of the war, radicals had battled with John Maynard Keynes to place the Arts Council on a more populist footing and lost. F. M. Levanthal has written, 'The Arts Council which emerged after the war bore the imprint of Keynes' conception of public patronage. Unabashedly elitist, he disdained those, mainly on the left, who extolled the merits of popular culture or sought to revive participatory folk traditions.'[105] Ellen Wilkinson, the Minister of Education, protested, 'There is no representative of the working-class point of view, although the appeal of CEMA has been so largely to the mass of people',[106] but little changed after Keynes's death from a heart attack on Easter Sunday 1946. When the Arts Council Charter was formally approved by George VI in Privy Council on 10 July 1946, it stated a commitment to 'develop a greater knowledge of the fine arts exclusively'.

The main parties and the press welcomed it as an enlightened act. *The Times* predicted it would 'substitute a permanent and organic relationship of the State to the fine arts for the haphazard policies of the past . . . the day of the aristocratic patron is over. Here too, the few have given way to the many'.[107] The consensus was striking, considering that Labour was busy destroying the aristocracy's remaining ability to buy and commission works of art. As well as hiking up death duties, Dalton had abolished tax relief on donations to charities, once a major source of private arts funding. Still, there was a widespread feeling that the aristocracy had failed the nation: patronage had been sporadic and often conservative in taste, and Britons rarely had access to the work bought by the upper classes.

The new British culture was national not only because the many were gaining access to what had once been available to the few. It was also seen as national in the sense that the people were reclaiming a heritage which had been betrayed by the upper classes' patronage of foreign art and music, a betrayal supported by a cosmopolitan intelligentsia. The idea that the upper classes were cultural traitors had been a feature of nationalist discourse in most European countries since the mid-eighteenth century. But while it enabled mid-twentieth century reformers to present their attack on privilege as a patriotic act, it was actually rather a misnomer. Although few aristocrats could still afford to be private patrons they continued to sit on the governing boards of Britain's museums, theatres and orchestras, as well as running the National Trust. Second, the middle classes had long since equalled the aristocracy's cultural role. In order to enhance their prestige with a view to joining the upper ranks, Victorian business leaders formed private collections of their own. And in order to aggrandize the towns and cities they ran, from the 1870s to the 1920s, they financed the building of most of Britain's libraries and museums. It was therefore appropriate that the launch of Labour's initiative should take place at the Tate Gallery. Dedicated to modern British art, it had been founded in 1897 by the sugar magnate Henry Tate (of Tate and Lyle) after successive governments refused to provide funds to house the collection he had left the nation.

On 11 April 1946, Ernest Bevin, now Foreign Secretary, took up Sir John Rothenstein's invitation to re-open the Tate following the restoration of its severely bomb-damaged buildings. Announcing the event on the Home Service, Rothenstein welcomed the revival of a national spirit in painting. Before 1940, he argued, artists had slavishly conformed to Continental fashions. As a result of their enforced isolation from Europe during the war, they had 'drawn upon their own traditions to a degree unparalleled for generations [and] recovered a sympathy with the peculiar qualities of the English genius'.[108] According to the *Observer*, the Tate 'was mobbed by a crowd of cup-tie size'.[109] Bevin brought with him George Tomlinson, the Minister of Works and the man responsible for museums and galleries. Bevin told the audience that Labour was committed to the arts. 'Art', he declared, 'has no greater friend than the Minister of Works. Because he began as a Lancashire cotton worker, he knows what it is to have a childhood deprived of art.'[110] The speech received enthusiastic reviews in every section of the press.

The centrepiece of the government's initiative was the creation of a national theatre. It had been the Holy Grail of culture reformers since the Victorian era (Matthew Arnold himself had been involved in the first campaign during the 1870s). In 1944, the LCC offered a prime site on the South Bank of the Thames to the Governors of the Old Vic and the Shakespeare Memorial National Theatre Company. The two charities joined forces under the leadership of Lord Esher (he who ran the National Trust). After intense lobbying, in 1948 Stafford Cripps pledged £1 million of taxpayer's money to the project. The patriotic impulse behind the decision was confirmed when Bevin told a gathering of theatre managers: 'In this mechanical age we look to the theatrical world to preserve the national characteristics of our people.'[111] The real launch of the project took place at the British Theatre Conference, organized by J. B. Priestley, in February 1948 and attended by representatives from almost every corner of the dramatic profession. Though his plays did rather well by the system, Priestley was fond of attacking West End theatres as 'nothing better than tipster's pitchers at a racecourse' run for profit and serving up 'dirty rubbish' for the 'country house' set. This, he argued, was prostituting the 'native genius' of 'the most dramatic people on earth'.[112] Praising the Soviet system, Priestley called for complete state control of the theatre. But neither the profession nor the Labour government had any wish for such control. Stafford Cripps promised instead to build a National Theatre.

Meanwhile, Aneurin Bevan's Local Government Act of 1948 enabled local authorities to spend 6d. from the rates on the arts. Releasing a potential £50 million, it was an attempt to kick-start a public sector version of nineteenth-century philanthropic civic patronage. Bevan's declared intention was the 'emancipation of the arts' from the ruling class; he wanted them 'restored to their proper relationship with civic life'.[113] The Ministry of Town and Country Planning drew up 'Plans for an Arts Centre', an exhibition which toured the town halls of Britain encouraging them to erect buildings similar to those suggested by W. E. Williams during the war – bright, colourful modern spaces that would include bars and dancefloors as well as stages and exhibition space. Again, the government emphasized that the popular reclamation of British culture would be a memorial to those who had died saving it. 'At a moment when our hearts are filled with gratitude that the war has been brought to a successful conclusion, what better form of memorial could be devised than a centre where present and future generations can enjoy in comfort their rightful heritage?'[114]

When the National Theatre Bill was presented to the House on 21 January 1949, MPs from all sides clamoured to praise it. Among them was the Conservative MP Oliver Lyttleton. Uncle of the jazz trumpeter Humphrey Lyttleton, who had led the VE-Day crowds to Buckingham Palace, he was Chairman of the National's board from 1962 to 1971 and eventually had one of its three auditoria named after him. He told the House that only a philistine would oppose the initiative. If there were philistines present they kept quiet, and the Bill was passed without a division. The reception was equally enthusiastic in the House of Lords. There the Lord Chancellor, William Jowett, said that Britain had produced the best dramatists in the world. Yet, he argued 'we [have never] used our national heritage to the best advantage' because since the eighteenth century its audience had been confined to the ruling class. Jowett argued that because the people were now better educated, they were able to reclaim their heritage: 'Britain can now show, with the coming of age of her working-classes, that they can emulate . . . the standards given them by their guardians . . . By the building of a national theatre we shall, I hope, make a real contribution to the idea of a people's civilisation.'[115] The press was unanimous in its support, and the acting profession was no less enthusiastic. Michael Redgrave described it as the beginning of 'a truly national culture'.[116]

The launch of the National Theatre project also gave an early indication that British culture, far from being a spur to national renewal, was in fact going to be a compensation for national decline; a mental bulwark against further encroachment by the new superpowers of the Soviet Union and America. Addressing the Lords, Esher said:

I have an optimistic view of the future. This country has had a great loss of military power and wealth. These things have passed to those remote monsters who live to the east and west of Europe. Their way of life, though very different, has no real appeal to us. But I am convinced that Shakespeare's countrymen are about to enjoy an Athenian summer of great interest and charm.[117]

The idea of Britain playing Athens to America's Rome gained ground in this period. Since the days of Gibbon, the British ruling elite had looked to the classical world for political inspiration and as a moral pointer to the nation's fortunes. As the British Empire declined, the idea that Britain was a latter-day Athens – smaller but perfectly formed – helped to rationalize its decline as a world power. Discussing America's leadership of the Allies in 1944, Harold Macmillan said to the Labour intellectual and politician Richard Crossman:

> We, my dear Crossman, are Greeks in this American empire. You will find the Americans much as the Greeks found the Romans – great big, vulgar, bustling people, more vigorous than we are and also more idle, with more unspoiled virtues but also more corrupt. We must run [Allied Forces Headquarters] as the Greek slaves ran the operations of the Emperor Claudius.[118]

As he rose to become Prime Minister and manage decolonization in the 1950s, Macmillan returned to this theme again and again, implanting it in the minds of the British as a worthy justification of the UK's changing role.

In the meantime, the heralds of Britain's 'Athenian summer' turned their attention to music. Although drama and literature had become largely middle- and upper-class pursuits, they were seen to have remained essentially national in spirit, partly because of an enduring notion of the British as a people of the word, and partly because of the continuing proliferation of world-class British poets, novelists and playwrights. Music, on the other hand, was thought to have been given over to the French, Italians and Germans since Purcell's day. The renaissance of British orchestral music during the late nineteenth and early twentieth centuries had improved the situation, but opera remained defiantly foreign. Gilbert and Sullivan's work was overtly patriotic but it was condemned by the musical Establishment as middlebrow entertainment. Reformers therefore directed their energy at this particular art form. In January 1946, Ralph Vaughan Williams drew up a policy statement for the Arts Council which bluntly asked the question 'Nationalism or Internationalism?'. He attacked the 'snobs and prigs who think that foreign culture is the only thing worth having'. Their aim, he said, was to 'establish a little Europe in England'. But only a distinctively British opera would 'touch the *people*, those who are eventually going to make opera in this country'.[119]

This policy was pursued by the Council for two reasons. First, it was hoped that if opera was sung in English it would be easier for people to understand. The reluctance of the working classes to embrace opera was officially blamed on the claim that 'audiences do not . . . respond favourably to the use of foreign languages'.

Second, it was hoped that the use of English would encourage composers to respond more deeply to their national characteristics. In *The National Ballet: A History and Manifesto*, the Director of Sadler's Wells summed up how ballet could be similarly nationalized. 'Jingoism of any kind is abhorrent,' he wrote, 'the public would not long stand for an unvaried diet of balletic roast beef and Yorkshire pudding.' But by encouraging native artists 'the national theme will arise naturally and spontaneously'.[120] In an age when culture was replacing religion as the focal point of national identity in Britain, the idea of opera in English seemed almost as important to mid-twentieth century reformers as the translation of the Bible into English had been to reformers in the mid-sixteenth century.

The Covent Garden Trustees made commissioning works in English their priority, and the policy bore fruit with the première of Benjamin Britten's *Peter Grimes*. The work was hailed as a 'People's Opera' by the press, and Britten was rewarded with a seat on the Arts Council's music panel to help encourage other British composers. *Picture Post* hailed it thus:

> In years to come, June 1945 may well be remembered as the date of the reinstatement of opera in the musical life of this country. The absence of opera in British music was a void which could be filled only by a national work in the true sense. Without a truly British production, opera remained an exotic bird which never rested here . . . the fisherman's opening chorus and those little tunes in the pub scene, they are all English. The storm could blow nowhere but on the English coast, the Sunday bells could ring only from an English village church.[121]

Music critics agreed that the renaissance of the early twentieth century had finally matured, one critic writing: 'It is permissible to ask, without being chauvinistic, whether any other single country can claim so strong a school of native composers.'[122] By the concert season of 1948–9, over a quarter of all works played by domestic orchestras were British in origin – a continuation of wartime levels. The canon was drawn mostly from a septet of composers: Elgar, Delius, Vaughan Williams, Holst, Walton, Tippett and Britten.

To conclude, the mid-twentieth century 'nationalisation of culture' was not simply driven by a belief that the state should make the arts – like health and education – more widely available. It was also a concerted attempt to encourage Britons to see drama, painting, music and literature as belonging to everyone, using state patronage of native artists and performers to make the arts more distinctively British.

7. A broadly based cultural pyramid

The Attlee government quibbled, as all governments do, that the BBC's reporting was politically biased. But this did not stop Labour using it to ensure that as many people as possible embraced the new British culture. On 21 May 1946, Herbert Morrison launched a White Paper which renewed the BBC's charter on the grounds that it had a responsibility to improve public taste. Morrison proposed to further that aim by introducing a new channel devoted entirely to the 'serious-minded listener': the Third Programme.[123]

It was the brainchild of William Haley, the BBC's Director-General from 1944 to 1952. Haley was born in Sussex in 1901 to Scottish parents and throughout his life thought of himself as a Gladstonian Liberal. He was an avid reader and a shy man, but tough with it and respected by his staff. On the one hand, he was less autocratic than Reith – during a period when organizations such as the London Symphony Orchestra were being purged of communists, he fought off suggestions that they be banned from the air – yet, in other ways, he was firmly in the Reithian mould. A deeply religious man of Presbyterian origins, he was received into the Church of England in 1949, and like Reith, his commitment to the idea of a robust, uplifting national culture was an extension of his religious beliefs. He had been involved with Keynes and Butler in setting up the Arts Council and took a dim view of popular entertainment. After dutifully watching a recording of Britain's favourite comedy show, *The Crazy Gang*, at Victoria Palace in 1950, he confided to his diary that he found it 'stale, tawdry and vulgar'.[124]

At the end of the war, the corporation was at the zenith of its reputation as the 'Voice of Britain' and herald of a new British culture. Haley told BBC Governors it was no longer necessary to surreptitiously slip high culture in with entertainment on the Home and Light Programmes. According to the critic Anthony Smith, 'the Third Programme was a response to the change in the cultural climate brought about by the wartime popularisation of music, arts and letters, to which the BBC had itself contributed'.[125] In the *Listener*, Haley said the Third would make Britain 'the best-informed democracy in the world' and its launch, on 29 September 1946, was evidence of continuing 'national vigour'.[126] In the *Picture Post*, Edward Sackville-West declared it to be 'the greatest civilising force England has known since the secularisation of the theatre in the sixteenth century'.[127] The Education Minister, Ellen Wilkinson, wanted Britain 'to become a Third Programme nation'.[128]

The Third's greatest achievement in its early days was to lure Dylan Thomas back to Wales, which he had left for London in 1934. The result, *Return Journey*, a typically melancholic celebration of the poet's roots, became the most repeated programme in Welsh broadcasting history. Thomas returned for good in 1949, living in a boathouse in Carmarthen Bay which was the inspiration for his monumental radio play *Under Milk Wood*, starring Richard Burton and first broadcast on the Third Programme on 25 January 1954. A recording and subsequent book became best-sellers and despite his premature death at the age of thirty-nine, *Under Milk Wood* established him as the best-known Welsh poet of the twentieth century, comparable in stature to Scotland's Hugh MacDiarmid and England's John Betjeman.

The new service was criticized for being elitist as soon as it began. In the *Observer* Ivor Brown worried that it would lead to 'a closed shop in the dissemination of culture', alienating those whose sensibilities were still in a fragile, embryonic stage.[129] Conservatives, on the other hand, condemned state interference on the grounds that it would lower standards. In 1948, T. S. Eliot wrote:

Nowadays culture attracts the men of politics; not that politicians are always men of culture, but that culture is regarded as an instrument of policy, and as something socially desirable which it is the business of the State to promote ... [But] in the headlong rush to educate everybody, we are lowering our standards ... destroying our ancient edifices to make ready the ground upon which the barbarian nomads of the future will camp in their mechanised caravans.[130]

Reformers pressed ahead. Shortly after Sidney Webb's death in 1947, Ernest Simon, the man with whom he had founded the *New Statesman* in 1913, became Chairman of the BBC Governors. Simon encouraged George Barnes, the Director of Talks, to hold regular dinners for writers, artists and composers to involve them not only in the writing and production of features, but in the policy-making process itself. The dinners lasted from December 1946 to February 1948. Those present included Louis MacNeice, Graham Greene, Michael Tippett, V. S. Pritchett, Herbert Read and the man who had invited them all to eat in the BBC canteen, John Lehmann. The aim was to encourage intellectuals to see the corporation not just as a temporary employer but as a permanent patron. Here was the clearest recognition yet that that the British intelligentsia had done its bit for the war effort and was being rewarded with a new position of influence. A new cultural establishment had been born, and it took its baptismal vows with the launch of the Third Programme. The *Times Literary Supplement* summed up what had changed since 1940. The interwar trahison des clercs was finally over; intellectuals, it said, were 'more intimately involved today than at any time before in the changing relationship of the individual towards the authority of the State'. Britain now had an 'Artist caste'.[131]

The most epochal definition of what Britain's elites were trying to achieve came from Haley himself. Delivering the Lewis Fry Memorial Lectures at the University of Bristol on 11 and 12 May 1948, he told the assembled academics that broadcasting should 'seek the good, the beautiful and the true'.

Since the war we have been feeling our way along a more direct approach. It rests on the conception of the community as a broadly based cultural pyramid slowly aspiring upwards ... The listener must be led from good to better by curiosity, liking, and a growth of understanding. As the standards of the education and culture of the community rise so should the programme pyramid rise as a whole.[132]

William Beveridge agreed. In 1949, still glowing from the implementation of his blueprint for the welfare state, he took the chair of a
Committee of Enquiry into Broadcasting. Its main task was to
consider the introduction of commercial television, an issue which in
a few years would split the country from top to bottom. It received
223 memoranda from organizations throughout the UK over two
years. Haley's view that broadcasting should be used 'to develop true
citizenship' was accepted on the proviso that the BBC became, in
Beveridge's phrase, a 'Hyde Park of the Air', airing as many opinions
as possible. A dissenting report by the Conservative MP Selwyn
Lloyd – condemning what he called 'compulsory uplift' – was
rejected. The BBC's monopoly had survived – for the time being.

8. A less uniform patriotism

One important feature of cultural reform that left and right agreed
upon was the need to encourage English regional cultures. 'Regionalism' as a political movement has a chequered history in the UK.
The term came into common usage among the political classes in the
1880s when the Liberal Party tacked English devolution on to its
proposal for Irish, Scottish and Welsh Home Rule. The aim was to
enhance British democracy, but it was also designed to contain an
English nationalist backlash to the granting of autonomy to the rest
of the UK. For a brief moment, in 1940, the movement's time seemed
to have come. As a result of the national emergency, the United
Kingdom was divided up into twelve regions to coordinate civil
defence. The nine designated English regions were the North West,
the North East, Yorkshire and the Humber, the West Midlands,
the East Midlands, the South West, the South East, the East, and
London. Each area was headed by a regional commissioner responsible to the Minister for Home Security. Meanwhile, town planners
busied themselves with grandiose schemes for postwar reconstruction, many of them hoping that this would form the basis for full
regional autonomy.

But the 1940s also revealed the political limits of regional identity.
Quite simply, the English disliked the new authorities. Commissioners

were seen as dictatorial Hitlerian Gauleiters leading armies of petty-minded bureaucrats. Critics pointed to the fact that the last time England had been regionally administered was during Oliver Cromwell's republican Protectorate. Socialists and conservatives were reluctant to cede any power to the regions because they feared it would undermine their control of the British state, a fear similar to that which coloured attitudes to Celtic nationalism and European federalism. In a study of the subject published in 1948, G. D. H. Cole argued that the English would learn to love regionalism if it was given a chance. 'I am not saying that [regional] feelings . . . are equally strong in all parts of the country', he admitted, 'but only that they exist as a foundation on which regional sentiments attached to Regional Authorities could be built'.[133] His words fell on deaf ears. Regional initiatives by Labour and Conservative governments in the postwar era were primarily economic. The Attlee government's 'Development Areas', the more corporatist 'Development Councils' of the Macmillan, Hume and Heath governments and the 'Regional Economic Planning Boards' of the Wilson governments were all directed by the Board of Trade. Some Byzantine tinkering was carried out to the structure of local government in the postwar period, notably in the Local Government Acts of 1949 and 1972, but it was done separately and usually on the grounds of administrative efficiency with little regard to the identity of the areas.

The political failure of the regional movement did not lead to its demise. From 1945 to 1995, regionalists met with some success on the battlefields of English culture because England's diversity was seen as proof of its democratic spirit. The expansion of the British state after 1945 provoked concern about the importance of regional life in England, just as it did about the national cultures of Scotland and Wales. But whereas the latter raised the spectre of political nationalism and led to extreme caution in policy-making circles, the evident lack of enthusiasm for regional government in England led to a more relaxed, even breezy approach to cultural devolution. And as a result, it met with rather more success. If regionalism had a clear political aim in the postwar era, it was in seeking to restore popular interest in the existing structures of local government rather than in creating new ones. Engaging people in cultural activity was seen to be the best way to do this. Left/liberal political theorists argued that only by encouraging participation in local organizations, whether Women's Institutes or cycling clubs, would mass democracy truly flower. In 1952, Michael Young wrote: 'in peace we need a more relaxed atmosphere, less fervour, a less uniform patriotism, allowing more variety and divergence.'[134]

From 1945 onwards, a concerted attempt was made to decentralize English life. The BBC led the way out of the metropolis. In July 1945, Sir William Haley restored the corporation's six regional Home Service Departments, which had been set up by Reith in 1936 but suspended during the war, and gave them more editorial freedom than before. He told readers of the *Radio Times* that it would help to foster 'those national and local cultures which are an enduring part of our heritage.'[135] The initiative was a success. Local news and features were popular, and the regions produced a number of entertainment programmes which went on to reach a national audience. Among them was a light-hearted quiz show, *Down Your Way*, first broadcast from Bradford on 11 February 1946, in which the audience participated for prize money. A sort of Butlin's competition of the airwaves, it was hosted by Wilfred Pickles, who had made his name during the war as one of a new breed of BBC announcers with a northern accent. A jovial Yorkshireman, he and his wife Mabel invited people to 'have a go'. Within six months the programme was networked, 'Have a go' became a national catchphrase and Pickles was employing two secretaries to deal with his fan mail. The closing ditty at the end of the show captured its spirit:

> That's the show, Joe, tha's been and 'ad a go;
> Now tha can tell thi friends as well
> Tha's been on't radio.[136]

However, the corporation's belief that popular culture was a necessary evil hampered its efforts to reflect regional differences. The North Regional Director, John Coatman, had been one of the driving forces behind regionalization, but before joining the BBC in the 1930s he had been a civil servant in Bengal, on the North-West Frontier of India, during the period when Sir John Anderson had been governor. Coatman's attitude to the natives of the northern frontier of England was little different to those he had benignly administered in India. As a result, the popular culture he reluctantly purveyed remained as quaint, folksy and unrepresentative of working-class life as before the war.

The Arts Council was also devolved in 1946. John Maynard Keynes had told Home Service listeners: 'nothing can be more damaging than the excessive prestige of metropolitan standards and fashions. Let every part of Merry England be merry in its own way.'[137] The postwar decline of provincial repertory theatre was a concern. J. B. Priestley, whose bestselling novel *The Good Companions* (1929) had celebrated it, was a tireless campaigner for rep, arguing that taking Shakespeare and Shaw to the provinces was not enough; playwrights should be encouraged by those commissioning them to 'suggest the character of their several regions' in order to 'nurture local patriotism'.[138] Having fought hard to ensure that the Scots and the Welsh did not get their own Arts Councils, Keynes enthusiastically established ten regional Councils in England and pumped money into ventures such as the Bristol Old Vic.

The bulk of the English intelligentsia were also keen advocates of regionalism and responded to such appeals. They had deeper reasons for doing so than the desire to win commissions from the Arts Council. A debate had been rumbling in the salons and journals of England since the late nineteenth century about the dominance of a metropolitan 'intellectual aristocracy' which operated in a 'golden triangle' between Oxford, Cambridge and London. Writing in 1948, T. S. Eliot argued 'it is important that a man should feel himself to be, not merely a citizen of a particular nation, but a citizen of a particular part of his country, with local loyalties'.[139] Eliot defined Englishness as: 'Derby Day, Henley Regatta, Cowes, the Twelfth of August, a cup final, the dog races, the pin table, the dart board, Wensleydale cheese, boiled cabbage cut into sections, beetroot in vinegar, nineteenth-century Gothic churches and the music of Elgar.'[140] But he allowed that 'the reader can make his own list' and concluded that 'a national culture, if it is to flourish, should be a constellation of cultures'.[141]

Benjamin Britten was among those who agreed with Eliot. In December 1947 the Arts Council approved a grant to him, his librettist Eric Crozier and the Earl of Harewood to establish an annual festival devoted to East Anglian culture, held in the Suffolk fishing village of Aldeburgh. The first festival took place from 15 to 18 June 1948. The programme included lectures by E. M. Forster on the Norfolk writer Henry Williamson and Sir Kenneth Clark on Constable and Gainsborough as Suffolk painters, and a concert of English music, culminating with the world premiere of Britten's new opera, set in Aldeburgh, *Billy Budd*. The BBC broadcast much of the festival on the Third Programme and it received enthusiastic reviews in the press, all of which led Lord Harewood to conclude that 'local patriotism' had found its 'point of contact with the national'.[142]

The most enthusiastic comment came from the *Times Literary Supplement*, which used the occasion to muse on the growth of 'Regionalism' since the war. The journal noted that while Scotland, Wales and Ireland had all had their cultural revivals in the nineteenth century, England was now having hers. But she was doing so in a quintessentially English way by being localized and 'not nationalistic'. Therefore, regionalism was used by the English to promote the conceit that they were patriots rather than nationalists. The *TLS* also remarked that regionalism was reversing the cultural effects of the economic boom of the interwar period which had ravaged the country:

> Poor, road-scarred, villa-pocked, wire-strewn England, that once so diversified country, is recovering its regional sense. A love of his own parish or town has been the inspiration of many of the best English writers in the past and at last, after a sterile period mainly devoted to criticism and economics, it looks as if that love may come to life in England again.[143]

A number of similar festivals were started in this period, among them the Cheltenham Festival of Literature and the Assembly of West Country Artists at Penzance in 1949, patronized by the BBC's biggest and most successful regional department, in Bristol. These festivals not only provided a minor boost to local economies; they were also, by taking the west and east of England seriously, an important attempt to place regions which had been marginal since the industrial revolution nearer to the centre of English culture.

But therein lay their limitation. Important new works were premièred every year and Britten's own was in no way confined to Aldeburgh, but on the whole, regional arts festivals were symptomatic of a belief that Englishness and modernity were incompatible. As the *TLS* comment quoted above highlighted, they were a reaction to the world of Northcliffe and Marconi, the arterial road and the electricity pylon. What cultural regionalists celebrated, in other words, was not the participatory mass democracy championed by Michael Young but an England unspoilt by mass democracy altogether. It was, as Keynes had declared it to be, an attempt to resuscitate 'Merry England'. In the end, the main function of regional arts festivals was to provide a refreshing break in the country for the metropolitan elite once or twice a year.

9. Death to Hollywood

While all this was going on, a powerful force had been chipping away at the base of William Haley's pyramid since the 1920s: American mass culture. Popular anti-Americanism had broken out during the GIs' stay in Britain from 1942 to 1945, largely because they aroused sexual jealousy among British men (feelings similar to those of aristocratic women in the nineteenth century when American heiresses came to court titled men). But this had subsided when the GIs left to open up the second front in 1944. In September 1945, Sir Godfrey Haggard, Head of American Forces Liaison at the Ministry of Information, took the view that 'a noticeably more intelligent attitude towards the Americans exists among the people of this country than when they arrived, [and in particular] an unmistakable interest in America has been aroused [among the young]',[144] and a 1946 Mass Observation Survey confirmed this. It showed that older Britons tended to dislike Americans, citing as character traits boastfulness, immaturity, materialism and immorality – what MO called 'the less pleasing qualities of adolescence', while younger respondents cited traits such as energy, enterprise, generosity and efficiency.[145]

Ross McKibbin has written of 1918–51 that 'the history of England in this period is also the English idea of America'.[146] The same could be said about the whole of the UK until 1964, and with even more justification. One result of full employment and rising wages in the mid-twentieth century was that Britons' consumption of American culture and lifestyles increased. Yet US influence was never as great as its critics claimed. In whole areas of national life, such as sport, it had no influence at all. Women were generally more Americanized than men because they were keener on films, music and fashion than they were on sport, but neither of the sexes was a passive consumer. In whatever form American culture crossed the Atlantic, the British incorporated it into their own way of life, sometimes altering it out of recognition, as they did, for example, with popular music in the 1960s. Why then did the anti-Americanism of Britain's elites become so bitter in this period?

The answer is that increasing consumption of American culture coincided with the United States' supplanting of Britain as a world superpower. The UK was already in hock to the US for wartime

('Lend-Lease') aid. The Marshall Plan, launched in June 1947, added billions more to the tab. The Attlee government accepted the necessity of American aid, both to maintain living standards at home and to maintain military commitments abroad (by 1951, defence accounted for a tenth of Treasury expenditure, more per citizen than America). But it did not accept this as a change in the course of world history. Ernest Bevin told the House of Commons in 1947:

> His Majesty's Government do not accept the view that we have ceased to be a Great Power . . . We regard ourselves as one of the powers most vital to the peace of the world and we still have our historic part to play. The very fact that we have fought so hard for liberty, and paid such a price, warrants our retaining this position.[147]

Britain's leaders resented having to lose economic and political power to what they regarded as a vulgar, arriviste cousin. The defence of national culture seemed to be one way that this humiliating process could be halted or at least slowed down. On the left, anti-Americanism was made worse by a hatred of modern American capitalism. Radicals who had once seen the US as an inspiration for political reform lamented that the nation of Benjamin Franklin had become that of Henry Ford.

Anti-Americanism did not foster a more positive attitude to Europe. Despite pleas from Continental leaders for Britain to join Robert Schuman's plan for a Coal and Steel Community, in May 1950, the Attlee government rejected the proposal. What eventually evolved into the European Union began without the UK and was shaped without it. The British rejected the Schuman Plan because, as Bevin said, they still regarded themselves as a great power. The Labour Party was especially opposed to joining, seeing the Community as a banker's club which would undermine British socialism, a view reinforced by American enthusiasm for European integration. The Attlee government had no wish to cede political power to Continental federalists any more than to Celtic nationalists. The British Occupied Zone was not given over to German administration until 1949 and, as Noël Annan once said, it was regarded as 'Britain's New Colony'. The main purpose of the occupation was to 'stamp on the tradition on which the German nation was built' by re-educating its people.[148] Robert Birley, a former headmaster of Charterhouse, coordinated the distribution of literature that celebrated the British way of life. Sympathy for Berliners during its siege by the Soviet

Union in 1948 did not last and was characterized more by anti-communism than a desire for rapprochement with Germany.

There was a small European Movement in the UK at this time, founded in 1947 by Churchill and dominated by Conservatives. But it bore no relation to the radical Federal Union led by William Beveridge. The European Movement believed that Britain's job was to sponsor foreign rapprochement rather than to become part of a United States of Europe. Even this was too much for most Britons, who still regarded Germany as an untouchable. Publisher Victor Gollancz, one of the Movement's few supporters on the left, received abusive letters from the public such as this one: 'As distinct from 1918, there is now a generation that has heard it all before . . . The Europe you profess to want to save believes in letting the crapulent swine go on Heiling Hitler'.[149] But however much the British people detested the Germans, neither they nor the nascent European Union was regarded as a serious danger between 1945 and 1960. America, on the other hand, was thought (at least by Britain's leaders) to be eroding national culture and with it the UK's way of life.

The canteens of the BBC and other cultural institutions became as strong a fortress to prevent American supremacy as the committee rooms of the Foreign and Colonial Office. Indeed, an almost McCarthyite atmosphere prevailed in this period. BBC programmes were constantly vetted for their American content. When Haley noticed a US variety show on the schedules in 1946 he halted it, telling the controller responsible, 'we don't want to be ultra nationalistic but . . . we don't want to end up just a pale copy of American radio'.[150] Yet Haley signed up to the European Broadcasting Union, which was formed in Brussels in 1946. The results were not spectacular: when the first cross-Channel broadcast was made in 1950, the few Britons who owned TV sets were able to see live, blurry pictures of smiling French citizens waving at them from Calais. Still, the BBC's membership of the EBU highlighted the extent to which Europe was seen as positively benign in comparison to the US.

The real hand-to-hand fighting took place over the cinema. Launching the Arts Council, John Maynard Keynes had concluded his broadcast with the battlecry 'Death to Hollywood'. Where British anti-Americanism differed from McCarthyism was that it did reflect the true extent of alien influence, at least in the cinema. Because there was no language barrier, Britain was the world's biggest importer of American films. Cinema was at the height of its popularity in the late 1940s, and in its peak year, 1946, British cinema audiences accounted for 30 million out of a world total of 235 million – a figure out of all proportion to the country's population of 46 million (1,635 million visits were made that year – 54 per person). To add insult to injury, the Americans themselves publicly admitted the ideological intent of their work. In 1950, Walter Wanger, a senior American producer, dubbed Hollywood's influence overseas a 'Marshall plan of ideas'.[151]

The government's attempt to halt the Americanization of Britain was the one area where its economic and cultural policies met, because films had the potential to generate a huge income for the nation. The policy-makers were the Chancellor, Hugh Dalton, and the President of the Board of Trade, Harold Wilson. The war had shown conclusively that film could be used by the state to promote national culture. In 1942 Dalton set up a committee to examine how this could be continued in peacetime, and its report, published in 1944, recommended state subsidy to the film industry: 'The screen has great influence both politically and culturally over the minds of the people. Its potentialities are vast, as a vehicle for the expression of national life, ideals and tradition, as a dramatic and artistic medium, and as an instrument for propaganda.'[152]

In 1945 the need seemed to be even more pressing. Although the Crown Film Unit continued to make documentaries under the auspices of the COI after the war, it no longer sponsored feature films;[153] by 1947 the clamour for something to be done was immense. Michael Young advised the Labour Party that the main threat to Britishness was the 'perversions' of the cinema – its escapist 'pre-occupation with an unreal world of wealth and trivial emotions [and] its concentration on the stars'. 'The British film industry', he concluded, 'has a cultural as well as an economic importance . . . the party must see to it that an appropriate proportion of British films are seen on our screens.'[154] John Grierson, father of Britain's documentary movement, went to see Dalton and told him that if British culture was to be saved the government had to directly intervene in the industry. Dalton agreed, memorably commenting that Britain wanted 'bacon but not Bogart' from the United States.[155] It was this attitude which led Americans to see the British in the second half of the twentieth century as a nation of whingeing freeloaders.

The initial solution was to set quotas on the number of American films which cinemas could show every month. In spring 1947, Dalton introduced a 75 per cent levy on American films, a move which it was hoped would recoup $57 million of the $70 million which they earned annually. The levy failed because it merely provoked Hollywood into a boycott of the British market, leaving distributors with only old films to show. When Cripps replaced Dalton as Chancellor, thirty-one-year-old Harold Wilson was appointed President of the Board of Trade and given charge of film policy. He took a more sensible course of action, reducing the levy to 30 per cent, which proved acceptable to Hollywood and which remained in place for the next thirty years. Labour also began to subsidize the British film industry. In January 1949, Wilson announced the Cinematograph (Special Loans) Act, which set up the National Film Finance Corporation (NFFC), a semi-independent state body, answering to the Board of Trade. The money it distributed came from the Eady Levy on cinema tickets introduced the same year.

Wilson made Labour's intent clear when he announced the plan to the House of Commons. He extolled the innate decency of the British people, which the government hoped would dampen opposition to effectively paying more for native films. He also criticized the tendency of British films to be set in the south of England.

> Speaking as an ordinary cinema-goer, I should like to see more films which genuinely show our way of life. I am tired of the sadistic gangster . . . films [made by] diseased minds which occupy so much of our screen time. I should also like the screen writers to go up to the North of England, Scotland and Wales and the rest of the country and to all the parts of London which are not so frequently portrayed in our films.[156]

To promote the work commissioned by the NFFC, the government turned to the British Film Institute. The BFI had been founded by the British Institute of Adult Education in 1932 'to promote the film as a contribution to national well-being', but its own well-being had depended on charity and occasional grants from the Treasury. Herbert Morrison appointed a committee of inquiry into its funding chaired by Sir Cyril Radcliffe, a key figure in the wartime MOI, and his recommendation, that the BFI be given a regular quinquennial grant to promote British film, was implemented by the government in 1949.

The plan backfired. Once the NFFC gave its money to production companies, the government had little control over the content of the films produced, a situation which the BFI was powerless to alter. Over £3 million was sunk in Alexander Korda's British Lion, which Korda then used to launch an assault on the American market by mimicking transatlantic mores. Ironically, the films which Korda and others made for the American market *were* accurate reflections of early postwar Britain, though not the Britain of hard-working, decent citizens which the government wanted to create. *They Made Me a Fugitive* (1947) was one of many films which celebrated the black market and that peculiarly English version of the Chicago gangster, the spiv. Dilys Powell of the *Sunday Times* complained of the 'taste of blood' that was pervading the cinema. To the dismay of Caroline Lejeune of the *Observer*, these 'sordid dramas' became box-office hits at home. *Sight and Sound* believed that the spiv was the 'personification of decent humanity demoralised by war and unfitted for peace'.[157]

Not all British films of the period were of the kind condemned by Wilson. Gainsborough Studios continued to produce lavish romantic costume dramas, which had been a feature of the British cinema since its early days. And Ealing Studios entered its golden age in this period. From its creation in 1938 to its demise in 1955, Ealing was run by Michael Balcon. He described its purpose to be 'projecting Britain and the British character', and in 1945 he set out his vision for the postwar era, arguing that cinema could maintain morale at home and improve Britain's image abroad:

> Never, in any period of its history, has the prestige of this country, in the eyes of the rest of the world, mattered so much as it does now ... Clearly the need is great for the projection of the true Briton to the rest of the world ... Britain as a leader in Social Reform in the defeat of social injustices and a champion of civil liberties; Britain as a patron and parent of great writing, painting and music; Britain as a questing explorer, adventurer and trader; Britain as the home of great industry and craftsmanship; Britain as a mighty military power standing alone and undaunted against terrifying aggression.[158]

In his autobiography, Balcon wrote, 'My ruling passion has always been the building up of a native industry in the soil of this country ... films, to be international, must be thoroughly national in the first instance ... there is nothing wrong with a degree of cultural chauvinism.'[159] Ealing produced films covering a variety of subjects, but they shared one theme: the nation's celebrated tolerance, eccentricity and love of liberty. And, unusually in British culture, they did so without smugness or pomposity. The heroes and heroines of Ealing films were usually small, tightly knit communities of ordinary people whose canny self-reliance laughed at then overcame authority, whether it sprang from greedy industrialists or well-meaning state officials. They were the 'mild anarchists, little men who long to kick the boss in the teeth', as Balcon once said.

The 'little men' in Ealing films often tried to get away with crime, from Stanley Holloway's and Alec Guinness's attempt at a gold heist in *The Lavender Hill Mob* to Dennis Price's murder of his aristocratic relatives in *Kind Hearts and Coronets*. The films could also be explicitly critical of the social-democratic revolution of the 1940s, pitting the little man (and woman) against the paternalistic officiousness of 'Men from the Ministry' seeking to control the lives of ordinary Britons, notably in *Passport to Pimlico*. But the Men from the Ministry were presented as misguided rather than malevolent. They were usually played by Basil Radford and Naunton Wayne, actors for whom pin-stripes and bowler hats seemed to have been invented, but whose insouciant club-room charm made their eventual reconciliation with the people almost believable. Furthermore, serious crime was never depicted as glamorous or remunerative. The Ladykillers were a gang of seedy freaks defeated by a loveable old lady, and spivs were run out of town by communities in *Hue and Cry* and *Passport to Pimlico*. But, popular though Ealing films were, the studio did not have the capacity to halt the tide of American productions flooding into Britain. In 1950, of the 400 films distributed, only 72 were made in the UK.

Surveys confirmed that Britons wanted to see more British films. The most authoritative, carried out by the sociologist J. P. Mayer for *Picturegoer* magazine, found that native productions 'speak their language'.[160] Said one thirty-four-year-old typist, 'I love the English films which have been made since the war; never before has English character, with its humour, pathos, stoicism etc., been so perfectly portrayed'.[161] The problem was that most cinemagoers were not so content. They disliked the tendency of British films to be 'instructive or morally uplifting'. What they wanted was sex, glamour, adventure and violence, preferably in a native setting but, failing that, in an American one.[162]

Disillusionment with the New Jerusalem began to set in within a year of VE Day. The government organized a Victory Parade in London on 8 June 1946. For the first time, civilian forces like the air-raid wardens and the Women's Auxiliary Ambulance Corps marched with soldiers, sailors and airmen; so too did black and Asian Britons who had served in those forces. Evelyn Waugh, who had considered emigrating when Labour came to power, expressed in his diary the misanthropy which had brought him close to being shot by his platoon during the war.

> At home, having refused an invitation from the *Empire News* to report a masquerade which Mr. Attlee is organising in London. He is driving round in a carriage with Churchill, behind the Royal Family, at the head of a procession of . . . Naafi waitresses and assorted negroes claiming that they won the war. It has rained most of the day. I hope it rained hard in London and soaked Attlee.[163]

Even *Picture Post* reported that the mood had changed since VE Day. Its reporter overheard an argument on the train going home from the event. 'If we hadn't won, we wouldn't be here on the seven-fifteen travelling home . . . we might be in a concentration camp,' said one man; but another observed, 'Victory celebrations . . . £1,000,000 it cost, 226,000 man hours . . . and I can't get a man to come and fix my boiler.' The *Post* concluded, 'We celebrated because we are alive and like parties. Because we won the war, and wanted to cheer those who helped win it . . . but whatever else it was, this was not a day of unquestioning celebration'.[164]

The attempt to rally the country with patriotic appeals became more intense as Britain plunged into economic crisis in the vicious winter of 1947/8, with fuel shortages and a huge balance of payments deficit which eventually led to the devaluation of sterling in September 1949. An international Gallup Poll revealed that a massive 42 per cent of Britain's population (58 per cent of those under thirty) would emigrate 'if free to do so' – a much higher proportion than any of the other seven developed countries surveyed and a figure that was spread evenly across income groups. Britons endured 'Go To It' exhortations such as the COI poster campaign 'We're up against it! WE WORK OR WANT. A challenge to British grit.' Worse still were the requests for people to voluntarily cut consumption, such as the 'Four-Inches-Only-in-the-Bath' campaign. The 1948 Olympics were held in Britain, the first time since 1908 during the heyday of British power, and a cracking chance to demonstrate that all was well. But after uninterrupted progress from Mount Olympus across a war-ravaged Continent the Olympic flame went out as soon as it touched British soil. The lights, it seemed, really were going out all over the UK.

Britain's intellectuals were called to put them on again. When the government published its *Economic Survey for 1947* (sales of 300,000), the *Times Literary Supplement* placed culture at the forefront of Britain's drive for recovery. 'Statistics, sociology and citizenship' were no match for patriotism; by which it meant:

> Plain national pride; the pride of great literature, music and painting . . . the pride of noble traditions, the belief that England, with these intact, has still much to share with the world . . . Austerity is certain to be our portion for a long time to come. Let it be the austerity of a lean, athletic people passionately reforging a great destiny . . . The country of Shakespeare and Milton is not going under.

Maintaining British culture, concluded the journal, 'is the role of the Intellectual in an epoch of crisis'.[165]

However, the intelligentsia did not respond to the crisis quite as willingly as they had in 1940. Their support for the government was provisional upon the extent to which it funded the arts. Between 1945 and 1951 the Arts Council's grant nearly trebled, rising from £235,000 to £675,000, but as the economy collapsed, money for the arts, like everything else, was cut, prompting accusations that the government was betraying its commitment to democratize British culture. The economic crisis – what Attlee called the 'Second Battle of Britain' – wiped £800 million off the government's capital expenditure programme. Bevan's plan for Local Authority Arts Centres remained just that, with only two built by the end of the 1940s.

The casualty that attracted most attention was the decision to put the National Theatre project on hold less than a year after it had been announced and only a few weeks after the Queen had laid the foundation stone in a ceremony by the Thames. The theatre did not open until 1976, largely as a result of cost-cutting by less culturally minded governments. Meanwhile, the foundation stone was moved to a less prominent part of the South Bank to minimize government embarrassment, a decision which prompted the Queen to suggest that it should be put on castors.[166] Analysing Labour's whole cultural programme, Cyril Connolly wrote: 'A Socialist government besides doing practically nothing to help artists and writers . . . has also quite failed to stir up either intellect or imagination; the English renaissance, whose false dawn we have so enthusiastically greeted, is further away than ever.'[167] In the summer of 1946 he sent a questionnaire on state patronage to Britain's leading writers, artists and composers. Most echoed Robert Graves' reply that 'he who pays the piper plays the tune'.[168] The government could not win: if it cut funding of the arts it was accused of philistinism, and if it increased funding it was accused of sinister designs on intellectual freedom and the British democratic tradition which that freedom embodied. Suspicion of the state was partly an intellectual hangover of the 1930s – disillusionment with communism; and partly a hangover from the war – frustration at the aesthetically restrictive nature of propaganda work. As Robert Hewison put it, 'The prewar conflict between Communism and Fascism gave way to the postwar conflict between the individual artist and totalitarianism of any kind.'[169]

On a less principled note, intellectuals, like most of the population, simply disliked economic shortages, bureaucracy and the grey egalitarian levelling which Austerity Britain seemed to bring with it. In the bleak midwinter of 1947, J. B. Priestley gave a lecture to the Fabian Society on *The Arts under Socialism*. In it, he warned that discontent was putting the government's cultural policy at risk. The intellectual, he said,

> Is ready to reject the devil of commercial exploitation but cannot look forward to the deep sea of Arts Council committees. He cannot help feeling that he may be called upon to sacrifice too much for this socialism ... he wonders dubiously about the socialist atmosphere of co-operation and common-sense; asks himself how he will like it when splendid patrons are replaced by earnest and dreary town councillors; he is doubtful about a society that no longer has either magnificent palaces or picturesque hovels but only tidy communal flats and he regrets the dramatic values that will disappear from a society abolishing all terrific social inequalities.

Priestley advised the government to 'be patient with him [and] spoil him a little'.[170]

Disillusionment with the New Jerusalem spread to Labour supporters at the very top. Like many members of Britain's liberal middle classes, William Haley watched in horror as the cost of progress became apparent. His diaries in this period reveal a man and his family squeezed by heavy taxation and growing increasingly bitter that there was no return on their money in the shape either of economic recovery or class harmony. In August 1949 he detected a deep-seated British malaise:

The ills of the country into which she has sunk through the cupidity, laziness and class snobbishness of its workers, all make one despair. Bevin and Cripps are off to America next weekend to buy still more dole from Washington. To such straits in four years has this great nation come. England is sick; sick of a wasting fever; with deep political roots. Nothing can now be done straightforwardly; committees confer endlessly; the individual who wants to do anything is swamped in a sea of formalities, forms and other papers. The press is trivial, mean-spirited; Parliament is just a lot of Party hacks; government endlessly consults the Trades Union Congress before it makes up its mind. Wasteful and anachronistic working arrangements slow up production and block progress because they are a vested interest of the Trades Unions. They are the calamity of twentieth century Britain. If in years to come all this looks better, it will be well to recall the sickness of Britain's soul that induced such bitterness. The country is not done, if only we can break these shackles. But they are the shackles of the mob, grasping, stupid, ignorant, grudging – and the mob is in control. And now back to work, to keep free speech going at least on the ether, and to preserve and to recreate the BBC's tradition in the years to come. Wisdom, patience and serenity allied to imagination, vigour and authority. Amongst us all, can we call them forth?[171]

It seemed not. To add to his worries, the Third Programme was failing to attract the million listeners he had hoped for. Although sales of The Listener peaked in 1949 at 151,350, the Third's average audience was 100,000 – 0.2 per cent of the population. Successes like Under Milk Wood were rare, and the whole venture came to stand as a symbol of the failure to create better Britons.

By the late 1940s, Arts Council regional offices were all reporting that the promised 'renascence of taste' had failed to appear. One wrote despairingly to the organization's grand headquarters in Piccadilly, London, saying that activists were 'desperately worried' by 'their failure to establish contact with the ordinary folk in their towns'.[172] In a confidential report of 1947, executives concluded that council activities 'do not . . . touch the mass of the working-class, even to the extent they did during the war'. Reformers continued to put a brave face on the situation. In 1951, the social scientists Rowntree and Lavers published their survey English Life and Leisure, in which they concluded: 'Britain has become increasingly conscious of books, of music, and of the natural beauty of the English countryside. These yearnings . . . constitute a search for beauty which . . .

could not appear in a decadent or thoroughly materialistic generation.'[173] The memoirs of Charles Landstone, the Council's drama
chief, were more realistic. From the same vantage point of the early
1950s, he looked back on a revolution that never was: 'At the end of
the war, all of us thought that all that remained to be done was to
provide buildings for this vast audience, but, unfortunately, an
extraordinary thing happened. The audience disappeared from their
hostels, camps and their war centres, and in a flash appeared to have
left their interest behind them.' Landstone estimated, probably accurately, that the Council had retained only 20 per cent of its wartime
audience.[174] Why had the reformation of British cultural life failed so
spectacularly?

10. We may be disgusted at the choice which the public seems to make

There were five reasons. The first was chronic underfunding in
comparison to every other European nation, West and East. The
failure to build modern arts centres meant that many of the smaller
repertory companies and orchestras were all dressed up with nowhere
to perform; nor could they attract big names, as some had in wartime
when patriotic stars were eager to do their bit by entertaining troops
and workers. In fact Britons who in war had accepted substandard
performances from companies put together on a shoestring were not
prepared to do so in peacetime, just as they were not prepared to
tolerate the indefinite rationing of food and clothing. Indeed, the
continuation of economic austerity made people seek out more
glamorous entertainment to relieve the gloom. As Landstone's predecessor warned in 1946, 'with the coming of peace, people expect
higher standards all round. In wartime a play in a school hall was
part of the strange new life we all led. In peace it smacks of "welfare"
and is unlikely to increase the public's respect for the theatre, or its
popularity'.[175] However, the lack of funding does not explain why
even glamorous metropolitan venues failed to attract working-class
audiences; nor does it explain why the audiences for the Third Programme remained so small.

It is usually argued that this was because of the elitism of those running the project. That is true up to a point. Like the religious missionaries of the Victorian era, the cultural reformers of the 1940s fell upon their quarry with a wide-eyed utopian zeal that sent most Britons running to the Blackpool Tower, the Clapham Odeon or the Dog and Duck. Reformers made strenuous efforts not to appear patronizing, didactic or regimental, claiming that this went against the grain of British democracy. But this was usually no more than a waiting game, behind which lay a deep revulsion from popular culture. Announcing the creation of the National Theatre in 1948, Stafford Cripps told theatrical dignitaries:

> We can educate and persuade the public to adopt the tastes which we believe to be right, but we have no more right to impose taste upon them than we have to impose propaganda. Sometimes we may be disgusted at the choice which the public seems to make, but we must be patient to prove to them that our views of what are good are better than theirs.[176]

This attitude was present at the grass-roots too. One Arts Council regional director told headquarters: 'we positively alienate sympathy because we give the impression of being intellectual superiors'.[177] However, the twin charges of underfunding and elitism which bedevilled Britain's cultural leaders for the rest of the century do not sufficiently explain the failure of the cultural experiment of the 1940s.

The third reason was more directly related to the question of national identity. Since Keynes had refused to create autonomous Arts Councils for Scotland and Wales, the national organization reflected the knowledge and outlook of the southern metropolitan elite. The Edinburgh Festival, established in 1947, is a case in point. The government claimed that it was an example of how Scotland was 'achieving a fuller way of life, spiritually, culturally and socially'. In fact, the Festival was deliberately established as an international arts festival because it was believed that Scottish culture was incapable of sustaining such an event on its own. Rudolf Bing and the Glyndebourne set were sent north to organize the first one with specific instructions that 'the level [of artistic merit] was not to be accommodated to meet native claims'.[178] Native events that were squeezed into the programme were afterwards condemned as proof of the decision to keep them to a minimum. According to the Arts Council's Director of Publicity, a concert by the Scottish National

Orchestra was 'not up to the Glyndebourne standard' while an exhibition of native art staged by the Royal Scottish Academy was 'nothing short of a scandal'. In general, he concluded, the Scottish events were 'bad enough to have brought home to everyone the need to . . . extend [it] in scope outside Scotland'.[179] Hugh MacDiarmid protested that although the Festival was popular with tourists and Edinburgh's Anglo-Scottish middle classes, an opportunity to create a Scottish 'People's Culture' had been missed. It was, he claimed, a 'snob culture jamboree . . . for the delectation of the decadent bourgeoisie and . . . entirely opposed to the cultural requirements of the bulk of our people'.[180]

The Welsh already had a national festival, the Eisteddfod, a ritual celebration of Welsh music and poetry founded in the twelfth century, but its existence only encouraged a belief that the summit of Welsh nationhood was dressing up once a year in white robes and pointy hats and singing loudly without instrumental accompaniment. The Arts Council operation in early postwar Wales was run by a native of the principality, Huw Wheldon. Wheldon's connections were impeccable. His father, Wynn, was the Permanent Secretary in Whitehall responsible for Welsh education and he was a friend of W. E. Williams, arguably the most influential Welshman in mid-twentieth century Britain after Aneurin Bevan. But Huw regarded Wales as a backwater, a view he expressed in the following memorandum to London:

> There was a fabulous period when coal streamed like gold into the coastal ports and wealth and authority gathered in Cardiff . . . It looked, for a brief moment, as if there was being created in Cardiff the kind of environment in which the metropolitan arts could flourish and thrive. Those days are gone, and massive and flyblown restaurants tell their own sad tale.[181]

Wheldon had no time for the principality's tradition of amateur music-making and marked his file on choirs 'B.T.B.H.O.', for 'Bawl Their Bloody Heads Off'.[182] He helped to get the Welsh National Opera Company off the ground in 1948 but vetoed the creation of a national orchestra on the grounds that 'the Welsh are good at singing but exceptionally unmusical where orchestras are concerned . . . [they] cannot play any instruments other than a harp or brass band.'[183]

The fourth reason for the decline of public interest in the arts was that the return to normal life in peacetime meant that the bulk of wartime audiences simply dispersed. Troops were demobilized; air-raid shelters, church halls and other relocation centres were closed; civilians who had been relocated by the Ministry of Labour left their temporary factory and farm hostels and rejoined their communities; those who had remained behind wanted to get back home after a hard day's work to be with friends and relatives and resume the social life which had been disrupted by the war. The Arts Council observed:

> Working people, both industrial and rural, who welcomed concerts and plays when life was abnormal and private duties and pleasures had been shelved, are often too busy now to seek entertainment out-side the accepted round of cinema and sport, unless the attraction is very great . . . [They] want to get back to family life rather than to linger in canteen or recreation room when work is done.[184]

In short, reformers no longer had a captive audience. This, and not elitism, was the reason why factory concerts – that great symbol of the People's War – were wound up by the Minister of Labour, George Isaacs, in 1945. Despite the many crises which beset the nation after 1945, the spiritual comfort provided by the arts was not needed to the same extent. People who during the war had, for example, eagerly pocketed the latest Penguin paperback edition of a Dickens novel while sitting bored and anxious on a camp bed far from home returned to more digestible recreation when it became readily available again.

This leads us on to the fifth and final reason for the haemorrhaging of popular support for the cultural revolution which began in 1940. The full employment and affluence of the 1950s, coupled with shorter working hours and the arrival of paid holidays, gave people a far greater choice of leisure pursuits than they had ever enjoyed before. As early as 1947, the Labour Party acknowledged the threat which affluence posed to the creation of a common culture. 'In modern civilisations', it concluded, 'there is an infinitely larger choice of types of leisure pursuits and the community inevitably splits up into small groups as individuals make their own personal choice.'[185] Sometimes Britons chose pursuits that had once been largely the preserve of the well-to-do, like country-house visiting; sometimes they did something new, such as watching television or going to a pop concert. The phenomenal youth culture which emerged in the 1950s probably did more than anything to short-circuit the attempt to enhance popular sensibilities. It was already making an appearance in this period, with the first Teddy boys emerging from the rubble of south London and the modern jazz craze appealing to more middle-class youth. Whatever Britons did to enjoy themselves, they did not usually choose to visit art galleries, concert halls or bookshops.

By the early 1950s, the more far-seeing reformers were coming to terms with these painful facts. In 1951, W. E. Williams became Secretary-General of the Arts Council, and until his retirement he virtually ran the operation. He remained committed to a broader vision than its charter would allow. It made little difference. Williams knew that underfunding and elitism, terrible though they were, were not solely to blame for the failure to reform Britishness and he decisively turned his back on the idealism of the 1940s. He replaced the Council's motto of 'The Best for the Most' with 'Few But Roses'. Submitting financial estimates to Chancellor Hugh Gaitskell, in July 1951, he mocked the 'sentimentalists willing to send tatty little troops out into the provincial wilderness to perform in village fit-ups – when the villagers have gone off in droves to see a film twenty miles away. Our provincial Saharas are littered with the bones of these good companions'.[186]

The following year he held a conference at Manchester Town Hall with the leaders of Britain's local authorities. It followed a survey which showed that 45 per cent of those who replied did not fund the arts at all, while 39 per cent spent only a fraction of the money allowed. When asked why this was, the reply from the Mayor of Chester was blunt: 'Why should we spend the public's money on something that only a very small section of the public wants?'[187] The delegates fell silent. Nearly half a century later, an adequate answer to the mayor's question had still not been found. In the meantime, the Attlee government staged a patriotic event which encapsulated the optimism and the disillusionment of the early postwar years – an event which, temporarily at least, silenced the complaints of citizens, intellectuals and political opponents: the Festival of Britain.

11. A gauntlet flung in the face of disbelievers

The Festival of Britain was designed to do three things. First, the government aimed to cheer up a country heartily sick of austerity – in Barry's famous words, it would be 'A Tonic to the Nation', offering an enjoyable escape from queues and rationing; a time of 'fantasy and colour', of 'the fun and games which the bitter circumstances of the last few years have denied us'; a year to 'let ourselves go, and in which the myth that we take our pleasures sadly will finally be disproved'.[188]

Second, by trumpeting British achievements, the government aimed to show people at home and abroad that Britain had recovered from the war and that she was still a force to be reckoned with. The BBC declared it was 'a gauntlet flung in the face of disbelievers, a call to men of spirit, a moment to take courage from the past in order to look forward to the future.'[189] More than any figure except perhaps George Orwell, J. B. Priestley was the voice of the 1940s. He had recently joined the ranks of the disbelievers, saying, 'We are revolutionaries who have not swept away anything.' But he found enough to inspire him in the Festival to tell listeners to the BBC:

> If we British do not deserve to show off and enjoy ourselves, then who in the name of thunder in this mad world does deserve it? We have fought the two worst wars in history from beginning to end: we have been burned, blasted and battered: we have pawned, scraped, saved and queued up patiently for all manner of scrag-ends: we have set the world an example of public spirit, tolerance, self-discipline and patience; so – by Jupiter! – either there must be *no* enjoyment in this world, which is ridiculous, or we British are now entitled to our own slice of it. So – on with the Festival![190]

The third purpose of the Festival was not publicly heralded but it was no less serious: the government hoped to restore its ailing popularity.

The Festival began life in 1943 when the Royal Society of Arts suggested that an event should be staged to celebrate the centenary of the Great Exhibition of 1851. Staged against a background of economic recession in the 'Hungry Forties', the Great Exhibition had crystallized the Victorian idea of progress and came to symbolize Britain's ascendance as the world's most powerful nation in the nineteenth century. Since then, exhibitions had been staged on an ever grander scale by the Western powers. But, with the exception of the British Empire Exhibition of 1924, they had become more international as well as more opulent events, particularly since the First World War. As part of the strenuous efforts made to avoid a second such conflict, in 1928 ninety-two nations including Britain had met in Paris and signed a convention designed to prevent countries from using exhibitions for political ends. At the Paris Exposition of 1937 and the New York World's Fair of 1939 there had been intense competition between the participants (not least the aggressively monumental German sections designed by Albert Speer). But they had been self-consciously multinational events.

Though no one took any notice, the Attlee government contravened the agreement of 1928 and decided to make the Festival an exclusively national event. In 1946, a Committee of the Board of Trade had recommended that some form of international exhibition should be held 'to demonstrate to the world the recovery of the United Kingdom from the effects of the war in the moral, cultural, spiritual and material fields';[191] the ostensible reason for the change to a national exhibition was that Britain could not afford to stage an international one, but the real reason was political: by the winter of 1947, the government was painfully aware of the effect the economic crisis was having on national morale and the Labour Party's popularity.

It was also encouraged by a bit of recent flag-waving by the Board of Trade: in 1946 it had sponsored a 'Britain Can Make It' exhibition at the Victoria and Albert Museum of new designs in home furnishings and domestic appliances. In yet another echo of wartime patriotism, the catchphrase of the Blitz, 'Britain Can Take It', was adapted to show that the country could design its way out of austerity just as it had fought its way out of the threat of Nazi subjugation. Reviewing the exhibition, however, the art critic Herbert Read complained: 'Public taste is deeply corrupted, and it will need some action more drastic than an exhibition to retrieve it.' Taste, he said, 'must be imposed on the public by a few exceptional individuals'. But he concluded that 'Britain Can Make It' showed that 'as a nation (if not yet as a people) we have become design-conscious'.[192] In fact, while Britons had less inclination to absorb the arts than before, they *were* eager to consume material goods. The expectation of a better standard of living after the war led people to see the acquisition of a decent home as a possibility and many of those who already had one wanted to modernize it. The exhibition was a success, almost comparable in its impact to the 'New Look' in fashion launched by Dior in February 1947. Over the course of three months, 500,000 people – as tired of Utility furniture as they were of Utility clothing – visited and went away inspired.

Buoyed by the success of 'Britain Can Make It' the Cabinet gave Herbert Morrison the task of overseeing the project. In December 1947 he told Parliament that the government intended to stage 'a national display illustrating Britain's contribution to civilisation' at a cost of £12 million. The centrepiece of the Festival would be an Exhibition mounted on twenty-seven acres of bomb-damaged riverfront near Waterloo on the south bank of the Thames. Morrison appointed Gerald Barry, the editor of the liberal *News Chronicle*, as Director-General of the Festival. He and his team took up residence in offices next to the Savoy Hotel which during the war had been occupied by de Gaulle's Free French government-in-exile.

It was not long before the wolves began circling. In the run-up to 1851, critics had predicted that the Queen would be assassinated at the event and the country overrun by Papists and vagabonds spreading schism and venereal disease. Criticism in the late 1940s was less alarmist, but claims that the event was a costly frivolity which the nation could not afford were repeated. *The Times* (which had led the critics a century before) observed that in contrast to the 'strident showmanship' which had characterized the Great Exhibition, the organizers of 1951 were 'a generation on which the clutch of circumstance grips harshly'.[193] Others were less charitable. Over the next three years, Conservative MPs, egged on by the Beaverbrook press, attacked the government for wasting valuable resources when the nation was in crisis. Inevitably, there were also accusations that the Festival was merely an elaborate piece of socialist propaganda. The cost of the Korean War provoked a further outcry. But although dental and spectacle charges were controversially introduced by Hugh Gaitskell, the Festival survived with a cut of only £1 million.

The government did all it could to stifle criticism. Morrison told Parliament: 'There is plenty to be anxious about in the state of the world ... and in this situation, it is profoundly important that we should keep the self-respect and morale of the British people on a high level.'[194] He also vetoed any overt reference to Labour's achievements. Demands that the National Health Service should be celebrated got nowhere. More importantly, Morrison co-opted as many Conservatives as he could. Lord Ismay, Churchill's Chief of Staff during the war, was made Chairman of the Festival Council, a coordinating body, set up to emphasize the cross-party nature of the event. Ismay persuaded Churchill to lend a cigar box to the main exhibition on the South Bank in London, and in a series of press conferences, he likened his job to Operation Overlord, telling the snipers that 'it was not in the British tradition to spoil the ship for a ha'porth of tar'.[195] The government's coup, however, was to get the King and Queen to act as patrons to the event. Consequently, in May 1950, Rab Butler told the Conservative Party Chairman, Lord Woolton, that the party had no option but to support it, and Beaverbrook relented.

The Opposition's change of opinion, together with a huge publicity campaign, led the Central Office of Information to report with some relief in November 1950 that 'British opinion is slowly coming round to support the Festival.'[196] By the following January, a Gallup Poll showed 58 per cent of the population in favour of the event going ahead, with only 28 per cent believing it should be postponed because of the Korean war. Noël Coward wrote a song for the 1951 Lyric Revue called 'Don't Make Fun of the Fair'. Despite its characteristically barbed tone, it captured the popular willingness to give the whole enterprise the benefit of the doubt:

> We down-trodden British must learn to be skittish
> And give an impression of devil-may-care
> To the wide wide world,
> We'll sing 'God for Harry',
> And if it turns out all right
> Knight Gerald Barry . . .
>
> We've never been
> Exactly keen
> On showing off or swank
> But as they say
> That gay display
> Means money in the bank,
> We'll make the dreadful welkin ring
> From Penge to John O'Groats
> And cheer and laugh and shout and sing
> Before we cut our throats,

> We know we're caught
> And must support
> This patriotic prank
> And though we'd rather have shot ourselves
> We've got ourselves
> To thank.
>
> Peace and dignity we may lack
> But wave a jolly Trades Union Jack,
> Hurrah for the festival,
> We'll pray for the festival,
> Hurrah for the Festival of Britain![197]

Once again, the BBC proved how valuable it was at times of national anxiety, helping to shape as well as amplify the Britishness being mapped out at the Festival Office in Savoy Court. Gerald Barry told readers of the *Radio Times* that 'broadcasting will be the means by which the event can be spread throughout the kingdom and so help to create a sense of community'. As well as bringing people closer together through live broadcasts from around Britain and encouraging them to take part in the whole event, the actual content of the corporation's output was also seen as a 'potent vehicle for expressing the national spirit'. *The Archers* and *Test Match Special* were some of the regular programmes designated as 'Festival of Britain Specials' because, said Barry, they were 'part of the life-stuff of the British people'.[198] Altogether, a total of 2,700 programmes relating to the Festival were produced. As well as the usual rota of town planners like Sir Patrick Abercrombie, the Festival Council included several figures responsible for the promotion of national culture since 1940: Rab Butler, Sir Kenneth Clark and Sir William Haley. Even T. S. Eliot, who had condemned the levelling effect of their policies, joined them, together with other notables like Sir Malcolm Sargent, John Gielgud and Noël Coward. For three years, the event occupied the energies of the nation's leading artists, writers, composers, architects and designers as well as Church and civic leaders. If the new cultural Establishment had taken its baptismal vows with the launch of the Third Programme, the Festival was its vow of confirmation.

Gerald Barry told the press that it was 'the People's Show, not organised arbitrarily for them to enjoy, but put on by them, by us all as an expression of the way of life in which we believe'.[199] The playwright Michael Frayn offered a contrary opinion in what has become an oft-quoted essay. It was staged, he said, by the 'Herbivores'. These were

> the radical middle classes – the do-gooders; the readers of the . . .
> *Guardian* and the *Observer*, the signers of petitions; the backbone
> of the BBC . . . There was almost no one of working class
> background concerned in planning the Festival and nothing about
> the results to suggest that the working classes were anything more
> than the loveable but essentially inert objects of benevolent admin-
> istration.[200]

Frayn had a point. The photographs of the Festival's organizers
released to the press showed a series of earnest pipe-smoking men in
double-breasted suits frowning at architectural plans. Billy Butlin,
Britain's premier showman, was notably absent from the line-up.
Even the folksy view of the indomitable Cockney peddled by Herbivores and Carnivores alike during the war was absent. When the
Pearly King and Queen asked if they could make an official visit to
the South Bank, Gerald Barry snidely remarked that they should not
be treated as royalty.

Hugh Casson, the man responsible for the architecture and design
of the whole event, later asserted that it was 'the usual charade of
Hampstead wets teaching the working classes to have fun.'[201]

> The whole smell of the place was rather like the Workers Edu-
> cation Association. We all had, I suppose in a way, rather naïve
> views that England could be better and was going to be better –
> that the arts and architecture and music and healthy air and Jaeger
> underwear and all these things . . . were in fact keys to some sort
> of vague Utopia.[202]

There were also a number of strikes over pay by construction
workers which nearly delayed the opening of the South Bank site. At
one stage, construction was halted completely for two weeks, the
only sign of activity being strikers playing football on the main
fairway by the Thames and rats chewing newly laid electricity cables.
Clerical staff stayed at their desks, but they were not afraid to
express the jaded mood of the country. Hugh Casson was told that
the switchboard woman at the Festival Office usually answered the
phone with the greeting, 'Festering Britain here.'[203] To make matters
worse, during the first few months of 1951 it rained more heavily
than it had done since 1815.

The Festival was a testament to the insularity of the British in the
early postwar period. There was little in it to indicate any links with

the Continent. Bevin had opposed the original idea of an international trade fair on the grounds that it might raise the question of European cooperation. On the other hand, the government wanted to attract tourists for political as well as economic purposes. The Foreign Office was keen for Germans to visit the UK, and instructed the COI not to tone down its 'hard selling' of the event for German audiences.[204] In the summer of 1950, potential visitors were wooed by four London buses which made a 4,000-mile tour of the Continent in convoy, stopping at major cities to give information about the Festival. According to Gerald Barry, 'the sight of these four scarlet monsters . . . caused the good citizens of Europe to rub incredulous eyes'.[205] Indeed they did. The lead bus had a gramophone which continuously played 'God Save the King' and other British anthems while a huge Union Jack fluttered over its entrance. Not surprisingly, it got a muted reception when it parked in the ruins of Berlin and other German cities (3,750 Germans visited compared to 62,750 French). Nor were Anglo-French relations promoted when the bus crews were given lavish banquets by French mayors, only for the crew's leader, Frank Forsdick, to complain that the 'strange dishes' they'd had weren't 'up to English standards'. Forsdick and his seven men demanded 'a bit of old English roast beef or a plate of fish and chips' and beer instead of wine. (They didn't get their food but by the time they reached Paris a keg of English beer had been found for them.)[206]

The Cabinet also decided to exclude the Empire from the event, except 'where it was relevant to British culture', though more out of tact than anti-imperial sentiment.[207] The British Empire Exhibition held in Wembley in 1924–5 had used the lion as a symbol of the might of the nation. 'Walk up, Walk Up and Hear the Lion Roar' had been its motto. But with India gone and others beginning to follow, the lion was not roaring quite so loudly in 1951. The Colonial Relations Office warned Morrison, 'there are powerful nationalistic elements in many of the Dominions and it would be at least doubtful whether they would welcome the idea of an exhibition . . . emphasizing the British contribution to civilisation'.[208] At Wembley in 1924, model African villages were constructed and Africans were shipped over to show how happy they were under Britain's benevolent rule. Topless black women stood outside mud huts demonstrating native handicrafts. Having had their interest in empire aroused, gentleman visitors could then proceed to the West Indies pavilion where, the programme informed them, 'a Negro mixer of cocktails is to be

found in the North Porch'.[209] In 1951 there were no topless women
or cocktail mixers. Even a tasteful exhibition of 'Primitive Art in the
Colonies' was vetoed – on the grounds that 'so many native people
are touchy about it'.[210] The government was also conscious of
American hostility to the Empire and did not want to provoke the
country which by 1947 had the nation's purse strings firmly in its
grasp.

So how exactly did the Festival of Britain celebrate Britishness?
The dominant theme was that the national past was the touchstone
to the future. In order to emphasize this, the two institutions which
most symbolized the historical continuity of Britain – Church and
Crown – opened the Festival on 3 May 1951. They did so, appropriately, at a service in St Paul's, symbol of the nation's survival during
the Nazi onslaught of 1940–41. The rains had stopped but it was a
dismally grey day. On the steps of the cathedral a fanfare by the
Household Cavalry announced the King's opening speech. George VI
was already dying of cancer. A pale and gaunt figure, he stepped
forward and told the nation:

> Two world wars have brought us grievous loss of life and treasure;
> and though the nation has made a splendid effort towards recovery
> new burdens have fallen upon it and dark clouds still overhang the
> whole world. Yet this is no time for despondency; for I see this
> Festival as a symbol of Britain's abiding courage and vitality.[211]

Morrison had asked the Established Churches to play a central role
in order 'to emphasize that the Festival is not a stunt but a solemn
act of national reassessment'.[212] The official handbook stated categorically 'BRITAIN IS A CHRISTIAN COMMUNITY, The
Christian Faith is inseparably a part of our history'.[213] In reply to the
King's speech, Archbishop Fisher declared that the Festival's purpose
was to reaffirm 'our belief and trust in the British way of life, not
with boastful self-confidence but with sober and humble trust that
by holding fast to that which is good . . . we may continue to be a
nation at unity in itself and of service to the world'.[214] Holding fast
to that which is good included banning foreign food from cafes on
the South Bank. And at the opening of the new Festival Hall,
attended by the King and Queen, Sir Malcolm Sargent conducted a
concert of British music which ended with Arne's 'Rule, Britannia'
and Elgar's *Pomp and Circumstance Marches*.

Brightly coloured pavilions celebrated different aspects of British
life, taking the visitor on a lengthy tour through the island story on

what the government called 'the Autobiography of a Nation'. The Lion and the Unicorn pavilion, with captions written by Laurie Lee, set out to illustrate the British character. Above large effigies of each beast were the words

We are the Lion and the Unicorn
Twin symbols of the Briton's character
As a Lion I give him solidity and strength
With the Unicorn he lets himself go . . .

The national character was summed up as 'the fight for religious and civil freedom [and] the idea of Parliamentary government; the love of sport and the home; the love of nature and travel; pride in craftsmanship and British eccentricity and humour.'[215] Early editions of the King James Bible and Shakespeare's complete works stood on pedestals as icons of that Britishness, while the 'Eccentrics Corner' hymned the country's love of hobbies, displaying feats of native genius such as a violin made entirely from matchsticks. Outside, organizations such as the incomparably British Bicycle Polo Association of Great Britain put on sporting displays to entertain the public and to prove 'how great a feature of British life is the voluntary organisation'.[216] All of this was meant to illustrate British individualism and to emphasize that the state was not the centre of Labour's political universe.

At the Land and the People pavilion, Britons were told that 'the land has nurtured and challenged and stimulated us'.[217] Souvenir stalls offered commemorative 1951 horse brasses. Trowell, a picturesque village in Derbyshire mentioned in the 'Domesday Book', was nominated as the 'Festival Village' in order to emphasize the organic national unity which the countryside represented. Yet, overall, emphasis was placed on the productive capacity of rural Britain, not its beauty. The Seaside also had a pavilion, celebrating the traditional British holiday. 'Give the British a mile of warm, sea-scented beach,' it said, 'and they don't feel, or seem, so sad and frigid, after all.'[218] On a more serious note, the idea of Britain as an island, maritime nation was conveyed by an exhibition ship, the *Campania*, which travelled the coastal ports of Britain from Southampton to Dundee showing 'how closely our history, our achievement and our destiny is linked with the sea'.[219]

Against this background of thriving tradition, the Festival celebrated modern industry and technology. At the centre of the South Bank was Ralph Tubbs' huge aluminium Dome of Discovery, which looked like a spaceship that had just landed. Further downriver, at South Kensington, a large science exhibition was staged by Jacob Bronowski. He was Director of the Coal Research Establishment, where he developed smokeless fuel in the early 1960s. Throughout the postwar era, Bronowski was the great popularizer of science on radio and television. A poet as well as a mathematician, he also sought to bridge the gulf between his profession and the arts. In the exhibition programme he said that science, like the arts, was international but that it was also an exemplar of national characteristics.

> There is nothing which is fiercely British about this exhibition. Science is international, and the ideas and discoveries which are shown here belong to all mankind. Yet it is right to take pride that some of the greatest names in this exhibition are British: Newton and Darwin, Faraday and Rutherford. Their work is our heritage; it is our ambition to continue it.[220]

Bronowski also reassured Britons that science was not 'something remote or frightening' which made the individual a powerless cog in a soulless technocratic society. Rather, it was 'part of the fabric' of everyday life which served the community. 'Nothing in this exhibition', he concluded, 'is meant to puzzle or astonish . . . Here is the modern world itself, standing straight and handsome on its base of science'.[221]

The main symbol of this bracing yet homely British futurism was the Skylon, a stunning vertical structure designed by Hidalgo Moya which looked like a ballpoint pen suspended in midair (Biro produced souvenir Skylon pens for the occasion). Many, including *The Times*, saw it as 'the engineering idea of the century'. With no visible means of support, *Punch* joked that what it actually symbolized was the essential weakness of Britain's postwar recovery. The truth behind the joke was embarrassingly brought home when the royal family toured the South Bank with the Prime Minister, Churchill and other VIPs in May 1951. Within minutes of entering the 'Interior Lighting' section of the 'Homes and Gardens' zone, the royal party was plunged into darkness, prompting George VI to turn to Attlee and remark, 'Another of your power cuts, Prime Minister?'[222] This did not stop them being impressed with the bracing modernism of the Exhibition. Later in the tour, Churchill broke off from the royal party in order to ride on an escalator in one of the pavilions. According to General Ismay, the seventy-six-year-old Conservative leader had never seen one before and was 'fascinated' by it, going up and down half a dozen times with a boyish glint in his eye, before Ismay could persuade him to return to the King's side.[223]

Meanwhile, the faltering 'People's Culture' was celebrated by a season of music, drama, painting and sculpture which Arts Council directors unanimously decided should include no foreign works. Given an additional grant of £400,000, it commissioned works from John Piper to Victor Passmore which were then incorporated into the rest of the event to make them as accessible as possible. For instance, sculptures were placed in the middle of Battersea Park, which was now host to a Festival Fun Fair, so that visitors were able to enjoy the delights of a Henry More reclining nude before going on to the open-air Victorian Music Hall. Over 100 plays and pieces of music were commissioned, including the première of Vaughan Williams' new opera *John Bunyan* at Covent Garden (in English, of course). The Festival briefly revived hopes that the battle to improve the fabric of Britishness had not been lost. The Archbishop of Canterbury even issued a Form of Divine Service to be used during the five-month-long Festival, which contained a thanksgiving for 'the growing interest in the arts and for wider education and greater culture among our people'.[224]

The dominant metaphor of Britishness during this period lay in the notion that the British were a family. The implication was that – *pace* Orwell – the right members were in control at last. At the same time it conveyed the idea that no one, even those guilty of past misdemeanours, was excluded. It therefore reflected Labour's attempt to reassure the middle and upper classes that they were participating in a patriotic adventure. J. B. Priestley, for example, likened state planning to a family getting its affairs in order. 'Wives, husbands, parents [and] children draw closer to the fire, one of you has paper and pencil . . . You are intent on getting things done . . . and the whole business is securely . . . rooted in a deep personal relationship.' This, he said, was 'Cosy Planning'. The Archbishop of Canterbury described the Festival itself as a 'family party'[225] and the COI commissioned a film from Humphrey Jennings called *Family Portrait*. It began with these words:

Perhaps because we in Britain live on a group of small islands, we like to think of ourselves as a family (and of course with the unspoken affection and outspoken words that all families have). And so the Festival of Britain is a kind of family reunion. To let us

take a look at ourselves . . . to let the young and old, the past and
the future meet and discuss. To give thanks that we are still a
family.

What made the family work together as a unit were 'tolerance,
courage, faith – the will to be disciplined and free together'. The film
ended on a more expansive note, observing that 'the Elizabethan
journey ended with the Battle of Britain' and that Britain could no
longer stand alone but had to look to America and Europe for
support.[226]

If the Festival was a family reunion, then it was partly designed to
calm the children down. Addressing the first national conference on
juvenile delinquency in 1949, the Minister of Education, George
Tomlinson, told delegates:

> I am convinced that most of what we call juvenile delinquency is
> nothing more than what my mother used to call naughtiness . . .
> [We need to] divert 'glamour' from badness to goodness . . .
> Children need to feel that they 'belong' – that they have a part in
> the grown-up world. Here in the 1951 Festival it seems to me we
> have an opportunity to give full play to that ambition.[227]

Festival exhibitions struck a distinctly 'BBC for Schools' note, offering up clean-cut modern heroes in order to attach glamour to
goodness. In the Dome of Discovery, children were informed that
'the great heritage of Drake and Cook has passed to the marine
scientists who yearly are adding to our knowledge of the sea'.[228] As
well as giving British youth something to imitate, the government
gave them something to do. Volunteer bands of young workers were
enlisted to paint fences and clear up rubble on bomb sites, thereby
turning 1951 into a sort of state-sponsored Bob-a-Job year.

The family reunion was also designed to celebrate the idiosyncra-
sies of every member in order to prove that the British were a tolerant
people whose unity was founded on diversity. Gerald Barry declared,
'We hope to draw upon the rich diversity of local patriotism and
local genius which in sum make up the pattern of our British
democracy'.[229] Northern Ireland was presented as a thrusting, modern province. As well as being applauded at the South Bank Exhibition, a 'Farm and Factory' exhibition was staged near Belfast. It
trumpeted the linen and shipbuilding industries, and Ulster's farmers,
who had created 'a tremendous increase in production' using the
latest agricultural techniques.[230] Belfast also hosted an arts festival,
showcasing the works of contemporary dramatists, painters and

composers from Ulster. In Wales, a music festival was held in Cardiff and a play was commissioned from the leader of Plaid Cymru, Saunders Lewis. Nationalists were less pleased with the result of the Poetry in Welsh competition, which had to be abandoned due to a lack of entries.

Scotland got its own permanent exhibition at the Kelvin Hall in Glasgow, organized by the former Secretary of State, Tom Johnston, and designed by the Scottish architect Basil Spence. True to Johnston's roots in Labour's working-class, central belt heartlands, the 'Exhibition of Industrial Power' presented a straightforward picture of urban Scotland, decorated by sculptures of heroic shipbuilders and steelworkers which could have graced a Soviet hall of *proletkult*. The event did not appease militant nationalists, who stole the Festival emblem from the Kelvin Hall in protest at what they regarded as another exercise in English colonialism. Nor did it stop the general demand for devolution. But Labour's careful celebration of the kingdom's different identities did at least mean that the Festival was reasonably popular in Scotland, Wales and Northern Ireland and so played no part in actually worsening tension within the Union. The regions of England were also well served. As well as the Festival Ship, a Land Travelling exhibition (a miniature version of the South Bank) visited Birmingham, Leeds, Manchester and Nottingham, while arts festivals were staged in twenty-two towns and cities.

What the government called 'calculated displays' like those described above were not the only means of involving the whole country. Morrison also aimed to inspire 'spontaneous expressions of citizenship', with Britons (or, at least, their civic leaders) organizing their own festivities. He succeeded. British pluralism was put into action in over 900 local authority events staged in 2,000 towns and villages across the country, from gymkhanas to swimming galas and historical pageants. This mammoth operation was fictionally recreated in J. B. Priestley's turgid novel *Festival at Farbridge*, published to coincide with the Festival. Its 600 pages contained 129 characters, such as Ernest Saxon the college lecturer, and Lettice Church the secretary. *The Times* gently mocked the element of invention in many of the events organized locally. 'Villages', it said 'are now convincing themselves that Queen Elizabeth slept at the old house and so might, without offence to historical truth, ride on her horse in the pageant'.[231] But there was more to it all than pageants.

The government used 1951 to stimulate an ad hoc programme of public works which went far beyond the Bob-a-Job year for British youth. Indeed, the Festival was the dying gasp of Labour's reconstruction programme. On 8 June 1949, Ismay and Barry gathered the mayors and chairmen of every local authority in England and Wales at the Guildhall to exhort them to do their bit. It was the first such gathering since 1916, when civic heads met to inaugurate the National Savings Movement. Doing their bit, Barry told them, meant anything from 'the removal of an eyesore to the . . . planting of trees, the cleaning of public buildings' or simply the completion of work in hand.[232] The government gave a lead by building a model housing estate in Poplar (the Lansbury, named after the former Labour leader). But it made no extra cash available for other projects, hoping that local rivalries would spur authorities to carry out the work. The meeting was a public acknowledgement that in the face of economic collapse reconstruction depended more than ever on patriotism. For the time being, it seemed as if patriotism was enough. Thousands of projects were successfully carried out and in a broadcast to the nation marking the end of the Festival, Archbishop Fisher judged that a 'brightening up of the family home' had been achieved at little cost.[233]

12. A bite of lemon at half-time

For all the criticism hurled at it, the Festival was an undoubted success. Huw Wheldon had escaped the 'flyblown' restaurants of Wales by getting a job running the Arts Council's contribution to the event. On New Year's Eve, 1950, he made a dramatic entrance to a party. 'At midnight the French windows opened, and Wheldon, wearing a ballet skirt and bra, was driven into the drawing-room, perched on top of a car. He was ringing a bell and throwing confetti. He announced he was the Spirit of 1951.' His biographer writes that the Festival succeeded because 'confident, mainly youngish men were let loose to indulge themselves at public expense'.[234]

In fact, much of the nation indulged itself too. Various official events across the country had 18 million visitors; 8.5 million visited the South Bank alone, with many travelling from all over Britain (on the busiest day, it received 158,365 people). Many more attended locally organized events. Though no precise figures exist for these, judging from the number and the extensive coverage in local newspapers, the final total of Britons who participated in the Festival was probably around half the population of 48.9 million (a higher proportion than in 1851 when only a third of the country took part in the Great Exhibition). In a Gallup Poll, only 15 per cent said they were not impressed with what they had seen, younger Britons being the most enthusiastic. The Pavlovian stoicism of the British was also highly visible, with South Bank attendants noticing that people would sometimes form queues for absolutely nothing, simply because they saw other people standing around at certain spots.

But the Festival was not about stoicism. More than anything, it prompted a widespread feeling that the nation was finally emerging from the doldrums. 'People in joyous mood', reported *The Times* when the Festival began. The police reported a drop in crime levels during the summer of 1951, in particular among juveniles in the capital. On the last night, Saturday, 29 September, thousands from all over the country danced in the floodlights by the Thames on the main South Bank Fairway, led by Gracie Fields and her orchestra. The night ended with a mass rendition of 'Abide with Me', the national anthem and 'Auld Lang Syne'. The mood of optimism did not end there. Britain may have been festering when Hugh Casson and his design team were struggling to give shape to the Festival, but their work, from the Dome of Discovery to the litter bins, helped to establish modern design in Britain. G-Plan took off where the South Bank ended, as homes, offices and shopping centres across the country mimicked what became known as the 'Festival Style'. Casson concluded: 'Architecture in its fullest sense – i.e. places not buildings – so long the Cinderella of the arts, became the true Princess of the Festival . . . But the real achievement of the South Bank was that it made people want things to be better and believe that they could be'.[235] Referring to the expensive London furniture store frequented by the metropolitan elite, one journalist dubbed it 'all Heal let loose'.[236] Given that Herbert Morrison always bought his furniture at the Co-op, it was an ironic comment. But, in any case, the Festival did give everybody a glimpse of a more colourful, affluent lifestyle on a much grander scale than the 'Britain Can Make It' exhibition five years earlier. As one visitor recalled, '[After] the rat-infested ruins created by the war, the clarity of the South Bank came like a bite of lemon at half-time.'[237]

Herbert Morrison accurately described the whole event as 'the people giving themselves a pat on the back'. But shortly afterwards they gave Labour a slap in the face, voting the Conservatives back into power a month after the Festival closed, on 30 October 1951. Much has been made of the fact that the new Conservative government levelled the South Bank within months, leaving only the Festival Hall and the Telekinema (later the National Film Theatre) standing, even ignoring an offer from the Marquess of Bath to resurrect the Skylon in the grounds of his estate at Longleat. Sad though it is that the Skylon no longer graces the London skyline, records show that most of the buildings were never intended to be permanent. Yet this levelling has been seen as a symbol, like the whole event, of an era's end. Michael Frayn wrote that it was 'a gay and enjoyable birthday party, but one at which the host presided from his deathbed'.[238]

In fact, the Festival was both the end of an era and the harbinger of a new one. Its success was indirectly part of the Attlee government's downfall. People voted Conservative in 1951 in order to put the Homes and Gardens pavilion into the high street, within their financial reach and without the flickering lights which had greeted the King when he entered it. The fact that the Festival site was turned into a car park was, therefore, wholly appropriate, because within a few years mass car ownership became the exemplar of Britain's newly affluent, mobile society. The nation *was* given a patriotic boost by the event. Much of the Festival's appeal was that it brought together the various strands of Britishness celebrated during the 1940s in an entertaining and instructive way. But at the same time, the material vision of Britain which the Festival offered reminded an already disillusioned nation of the comforts and pleasures they were missing in their everyday lives. It was a vision against which jolly appeals to national character illustrated by violins made of matchsticks could not compete.

Another element of the Festival's success was that it gave a boost to the tourist trade; tourist earnings were up by £19 million in 1951, a rise of 15 per cent. Not everyone saw this as a good thing. Charles Plouviez, an administrator in the Festival Office, argued that it marked the beginning of Britain's decline into a backward-looking nation of entertainers: '[It] was the beginning of our English disease – the moment at which we stopped trying to lead the world as an industrial power, and started being the world's entertainers, coaxing tourists to laugh at our eccentricities, marvel at our traditions and wallow in our nostalgia.'[239] Plouviez' conclusion is meretricious. The event displayed thoroughly modern aspects of British achievements. Moreover, it did not celebrate tradition for tradition's sake. The purpose of reminding Britons of their heritage in this period was to unite the nation and inspire it to future endeavour. A fairer, if florid, assessment was made by Harold Nicolson on the BBC in November 1951:

> The first motive [was] to dissipate the gloom that hung like a pea-soup fog above the generation of 1951 ... Britain for various reasons was feeling rather humiliated. It was with regretful sadness that we looked back to 1851 and the time when Europe was the centre of the world and we the greatest power in Europe ... We would show the world ... that we were not down and out but up and in ... not a back number, but front-page news. And we did show them. We were worried by all this internal dissension, by that unnatural malady of class animosity. Let us therefore emphasise our unity ... Let us show the world that we were after all a people, cemented together by the gigantic pressures of history, being amused by the same sort of silly little things. One thing, an indestructible if indefinable thing, we all had in common, whether capitalist, bourgeois or proletariat: we had the same sort of character underneath ... We are an ancient people, formed of many obscure strands. We take a pride in this wonderful fusion of tradition and invention, of precedent and experiment, of uniformity with eccentricity. Surely that also was one of the motives of the Festival, to remind us that we were very, very old and very, very young; and thus to fortify our pride ... Such were the motives of the Festival: to assert our energy, our resource, our unity, our intelligence, our antiquity and our eternal youth.[240]

The Attlee years were an attempt to marry patriotism and social democracy, and in doing so to remake the popular idea of Britishness. To some extent the Labour government succeeded. Despite its defeat at the polls in 1951 and the subsequent undoing of much of its work, the welfare state remained in place. And, although it was perennially attacked for creating a nation of un-enterprising sloths, the welfare state gave some credence to the view that the British had of themselves as a fair-minded and compassionate people for whom a social conscience was not a sign of weakness nor a barrier to enterprise. By turning the rhetoric of decency into reality, the government deepened a key aspect of British national identity. Britain remained one of the most class-ridden societies in the world, its main institutions, from the monarchy to Parliament and the BBC, at best paternalistic and at worst downright reactionary. Labour leaders, just as much as their Conservative counterparts, remained wedded to an essentially late-

Victorian view of Britishness; their civilizing mission to the natives
of Britain based on the same sense of innate superiority as their
mission to the natives of the Empire. Yet, despite this handicap, the
changes effected in the period 1940–51 made the idea of the nation
more closely synonymous with that of the people. For all the
disillusionment of the era, ordinary Britons gained a sense that they
had a stake in Britain; a sense not only that they were a part of its
heritage but that fundamental reform for their benefit was possible;
a sense, in short, that patriotism need not be a substitute for change
but the vehicle for it.

– PART 3 –

VIEWERS

The Country and the Commonwealth last Tuesday were not far from the Kingdom of Heaven.

Geoffrey Fisher, Archbishop of Canterbury, 1953

There is nothing that brings you closer to eternity than making an advertisement for television.

Eamon Andrews, 1955

1. A union in space and time

From 1951 to 1964, British national identity was assailed by forces more powerful than any it had undergone before: Americanization, decolonization, black and Asian immigration, Scottish and Welsh nationalism and a drive towards European integration. Despite a desperate and often successful struggle to cling on to national traditions, the period marked the beginning of the end of the relatively homogeneous Britishness mapped out during the Second World War. Yet it began with a powerful affirmation of extant Britishness which seemed to suggest that all was well: the Coronation of Elizabeth II.

Churchill became Prime Minister again on 26 October 1951, promising to end austerity and 'Set the People Free'. On 6 February 1952 George VI died, and the country virtually came to a standstill. Churchill paid tribute to the late King in the House of Commons:

> Never in our long history were we exposed to greater perils of invasion and destruction than that year when we stood all alone and kept the flag of freedom flying ... the late King lived through every minute of this struggle with a heart that never quavered and a spirit undaunted.

The result was that Britain had survived the 'fearful convulsions of the terrible twentieth century'. 'We stand erect both as an island people and as the centre of a world-wide Commonwealth and Empire.' Churchill looked forward to the new reign:

> A fair and youthful figure, Princess, wife and mother, is the heir to all our traditions and glories ... and to all our perplexities and dangers never greater in peacetime than now. She is also heir to all our united strength and loyalty. She comes to the Throne at a time when a tormented mankind stands uncertainly poised between world catastrophe and a golden age. That it should be a golden age of art and letters we can only hope – science and machinery have their other tales to tell – but it is certain that if a true and lasting peace can be achieved ... an immense and undreamed of prosperity, with culture and leisure ever more widely spread can come ... to the masses of the people.[1]

At the time Churchill spoke, Britain was in the midst of a financial crisis, with a budget deficit of £700 million thanks largely to the Korean War. The Minister for Works, David Eccles, had overseen the destruction of the Festival buildings on the South Bank. He explained why the Coronation was vital: 'The argument is unsound that because we are forced to cut the people's bread we should also cut their circuses. Whether one thinks of the stability of our institutions, or of morale in a difficult year, or of the earnings of the tourist trade, a fine show is justified.'[2] The Coronation cost almost £1 million, twice as much as that spent on George VI in 1937. It was subject to cost-cutting. Eccles complained that the Treasury 'turned down everything I asked for except a new ladies lavatory in St. James' Park'.[3] In the event, though, it turned out to be a lavish spectacle. It was, Eccles said, 'showbusiness' with the Queen as his 'leading lady'.[4]

The British monarchy, assisted by the government of the day, has frequently legitimized itself, when it has been unpopular or at moments of national anxiety, by inventing traditions in which it is shown to be the symbol of national continuity. The professional orchestration of royal ceremonial at state occasions from the 1870s onwards rescued the monarchy from the torpor into which Victoria's dotage had cast it and helped to stymie a republican revival. As the political power of the monarchy has waned its cultural importance has increased. In a memorable phrase, David Cannadine described the Coronation of 1953 as 'a cavalcade of impotence'.[5] Yet there was more to it than that, because the cultural power of the monarchy rested not only on nostalgia but on its ability to continually reposition itself as the embodiment of *contemporary* Britain. Mid- to late-twentieth-century British monarchism was as much about the invention of modernity as it was about the invention of tradition.

On the one hand, the Coronation of 1953 *was* a more conservative version of British national identity than the one articulated in the 1940s, and as such it symbolized Churchill's return to power. Where Herbert Morrison's Festival had celebrated British social democracy, the event organized by the Duke of Norfolk celebrated a hierarchical society at the apex of which stood a hereditary monarch who embodied through her ancestral lineage 1,000 years of history: myriad personalities, events, customs and traditions coming together in one person to form a seamless picture of the nation. Whereas the Festival had been largely staged by the Herbivores, the Coronation was very much a Carnivorous affair. In the office of the Earl Marshal, the Dukes of Norfolk had organized English and British coronations since that of Richard III in 1483. The sixteenth Duke, Bernard Marmaduke Fitzalan-Howard, was a forty-five-year-old gruff, reactionary Tory with 'a mouth like a prune in a face like a poker'.[6] The Commission he set up to organize the event included the Prime Minister, the Archbishop of Canterbury, the Lord Chancellor, the Home, Foreign and Commonwealth Secretaries, the Leader of the Opposition and the Prime Ministers of the Commonwealth. Of the nineteen senior members of the Queen's Household who liaised with the Commission, fourteen were peers, of whom twelve were Conservative, one Independent and one Liberal; nine were company directors, holding twenty-three directorships between them; and thirteen were Old Etonians.

The discussions at their meetings centred almost entirely around previous coronations. George VI's was used as a model, because it had helped to restore the reputation of the monarchy after the Abdication crisis. Memos were passed backwards and forwards between constitutional experts in a painstaking attempt to ensure that the minutest ceremonial precedents were observed so that the Coronation of Elizabeth II could be as near to a repeat of her father's as possible. Clement Attlee's suggestion that the Speaker of the House of Commons should do homage to the Queen 'on behalf of the Common Man' was rejected.[7]

Much of the publicity which accompanied this event reflected the concern for stability. In the official programme to the event, Arthur Bryant wrote:

> A Coronation is a nation's birthday . . . [for] a nation is a union in both space and time. We are compatriots not only of those who live a long way away, but of those who lived before us . . . we are as much the countrymen of Nelson, Wesley and Shakespeare as of our own contemporaries. Our Queen . . . is the symbol of that union in time. She is descended from a long line of those who have represented . . . our country through every hour of [its] history.[8]

More than any other Coronation in the modern era, that of Elizabeth II was seen as a religious event. Although the Duke of Norfolk was the lay leader of Britain's Catholic community, he played no symbolic role in the Coronation he organized, which remained a thoroughly Protestant event. The Archbishop of Canterbury wondered whether it was necessary for the Queen to take an oath upholding the

Protestant religion, but his theological adviser, the Oxford Professor of Divinity, Edward Ratcliff, told him that the nation ought to be reminded that 'English kingship is still a Christian Kingship, for all that left-wing politicians and Fellow Travellers may wish to the contrary'.[9] In the Coronation programme, Fisher stressed that the Anointing of the Queen was a sacrament that originated with King David. The British Churches, as the agents through which God consecrated the monarch, thus claimed to provide a metaphysical link between the Kings of Israel and the Kings of the United Kingdom, implying therefore that the British were a chosen people.

The Queen was shown to be the embodiment of traditional Christian family values. Bryant wrote, 'She represents in her person the abiding virtues – of hearth, home and service – which are the foundation of society.'[10] Pictures of the Queen surrounded by her children were used, like those of Victoria a century earlier, to emphasize that she was also a wife and mother, her homely femininity undiminished by being the monarch. Commentators made much of the fact that while she wore the Crown of State and held the Orb and Sceptre in the procession back from the Abbey, she also kept her handbag with her – 'something no woman, not even a Queen, likes to be without', trilled the *Daily Mirror*.[11]

The event also demonstrated the extent to which the British were increasingly reliant on their cultural heritage to assert their status in the world. Europeans, both East and West, were mocked for throwing away their monarchies. Assessing foreign reactions to the event, the Foreign Office told the Queen and the Prime Minister: 'Europeans found solace in the realisation that the glories of old Europe . . . were not all extinguished . . . they watched . . . and thought of all that they themselves, fooled by empty intellectual doctrines, had thrown away.'[12] The United States was given even shorter shrift, for it was seen never to have had such glories. The US might have superseded the UK politically and economically, but Britain's cultural superiority was apparently evident in the ancient traditions on display. In the *Sunday Dispatch*, Richard Dimbleby wrote: 'Visitors from abroad were envious of everything they saw, and none more so than the Americans – a race of such vitality but so lacking in tradition – who know that they must wait a thousand years before they can show the world anything so significant or lovely.'[13]

The wider cult of New Elizabethanism rested on a romantic vision of the late sixteenth century as a national Golden Age, in which the reign of Elizabeth I had brought peace and prosperity, together with a heightened national self-consciousness based on religious self-determination, cultural achievement and overseas expansion. As such, it made monarchism in this period a more English affair. The phrase 'United Kingdom' had only replaced 'England' in the Coronation Oath in 1937. The Proclamation of the Accession of Elizabeth II in February 1952, when she was only Elizabeth I of Scotland, provoked fury north of the border and provided further evidence that the unionism of England's partners could no longer be taken for granted.

2. Thoughtlessness, lack of tact and disregard of sentiment

In the spring and summer of 1952, postboxes bearing the insignia 'EIIR' were set alight, and in some cases bombed, in a series of incidents throughout Scotland greeted with delight by most of its inhabitants. The act was particularly symbolic because the creation of the postal service in 1840 had been one of the early improvements in communications by which the peoples of Britain had been brought into closer contact and their sense of Britishness amplified as a result. The fact that 1952 was also the centenary of the Post Office's introduction of postboxes added still more resonance to the Scots' protest.

Churchill's initial response could best be described as affectionate exasperation and it revealed how little the English had grasped what was happening to Scottish national identity. In a statement to the press, he said: 'If I think of the greatness and splendour of Scotland and her wonderful part in the history not only of this island but of the whole world, I really think they ought to keep their silliest people in order.'[14] It was left to Scots to provide an accurate picture. The journalist and broadcaster Fyfe Robertson wrote a reply to Churchill in *Picture Post* called 'Are Two Million Scots Silly?'. Fyfe Robertson was an admirer of the English, among whom he had spent most of his life. But like many of his compatriots he was losing patience with them. Nationalism, he explained, had been spawned not by overt

English oppression but by England's complacent indifference to its fellow islanders. 'Most English people [see] Home Rule [as] a thing too fantastically nonsensical to take seriously ... Their indifference to the national feeling of the smaller and largely Celtic peoples who share these islands is so massive that Irish, Welsh and Scots have despaired of shaking it.' Robertson argued that English attitudes had led to a lower standard of living for the Scots, an Anglocentric media and regular Government slights like the EIIR controversy – all of which were helping to 'set the heather on fire'. 'Today', he concluded, 'you can find Home Rulers where you couldn't find them even five years ago'.[15]

The long-term response of the Churchill government between 1952 and 1955 was simultaneously emollient and belligerent. First the Prime Minister decided that in future the Royal Style in Scotland would be simply ER, a clever compromise which avoided the anger provoked by EIIR while avoiding the separatist emotions which EIR would have encouraged. Second, Churchill decided to return the Stone of Scone to Westminster Abbey. The imminent Coronation made a decision imperative, and Churchill was determined not embroil the Crown in constitutional controversy during an event in which the government was hoping to demonstrate Britain's unity to people at home and abroad. Churchill still saw the Scots as imperial partners and it was on this basis that he and his Secretary of State, James Stuart, advised the Cabinet to defy nationalist opinion. On 11 February 1952, the Cabinet agreed that 'The Stone has been in the Abbey for 600 years and has now acquired from its use at Coronations an Imperial significance.'[16]

Scottish peers' suggestion that the Stone should be temporarily returned so that the Queen could be crowned separately in Scotland was dismissed by Churchill's Private Secretary, Jock Colville, in terms which revealed how seriously the government regarded Celtic nationalism and how much Ireland continued to haunt the minds of the British political elite.

> One does not want to undo the good work of James VI and, still better, of Queen Anne, in linking the two kingdoms of England and Scotland. In order to crown the Queen as Queen of Scotland you would have to undo the act of Union of 1707. This is, of course, what a lot of Scottish nationalists would like to see, but I think the government feel, and a great many ardent Scots with them, that this would be a very dangerous step and that even Wales might want to follow suit. Before we knew where we were

we should have Scotland and Wales going the way of Ireland and
that would not really be either to their interest or to ours.[17]

Colville added that Canada, Australia and New Zealand would also
want separate Coronations if the Scots got one; in other words, the
creation of a federal Britain would lead to a federal system of
government for the Commonwealth – something which was then
unthinkable.

In 1951 Churchill had set up a Royal Commission under the
Chairmanship of the Earl of Balfour to examine how Scotland might
have more control over its affairs. Home Rule was excluded from its
remit, and when the Commission reported in 1954 its recommendations led to a modest increase in the powers of the Scottish Office
with responsibility for electricity and roads being ceded. The motive
for setting up the Royal Commission was pragmatic and its results
were cosmetic. But it was significant because for the first time an
official body of the British state publicly acknowledged that there
had been a serious deterioration in Anglo-Scottish relations. What is
more, it argued that the cause of Scottish discontent was due to long-
term and deep-seated cultural problems which underlay the political
structure of the Union: namely the English tendency to regard Britain
as 'Greater England'. A 'harmonious relationship does not depend
only upon efficient administration', the report warned. There was in
Scotland a growing 'emotional dissatisfaction' due to the 'thoughtlessness, lack of tact and disregard of sentiment' of the English. This
situation had been made worse, it said, by the centralization and
economic problems which had occurred since the war. The result
was: 'A widespread feeling that national individuality is being lost,
that the Treaty of 1707 is no longer remembered as the voluntary
union of two proud peoples each with their own distinctive national
and cultural characteristics and traditions, but rather as the absorption of Scotland by England.'[18] The report concluded that the situation was redeemable. Scottish pride had been wounded, but it had
not yet turned into a rejection of the Union. Balfour detected 'a
feeling of frustration, rather than a new-found nationalism' among
the Scots. Their frustration could be quelled, he argued, given minor
devolution, economic recovery and a more respectful understanding
of them as a nation. In other words, the writing was on the wall for
the Union and it was not in Gaelic. Did the English read it? Yes, but
it didn't sink in.

At Westminster, it was another decade before the problem was taken seriously. As for the English people, they remained heartily oblivious to it. The Parliamentary debate on the Royal Commission's Report, which should have been one of the most important of the era, was poorly attended by English MPs and not a single Cabinet minister or Shadow minister turned up. His voice echoing in a half-empty chamber, Labour's Arthur Woodburn condemned the Balfour Report for not doing enough.

> It must be recognised that in the marriage between England and Scotland the words 'I obey' did not occur. It was a marriage without any obedience being introduced. That has to be under-stood . . . We have no objection to our English friends remaining English and being proud of their heritage and destiny . . . [But] this cold war which has gone on for a couple of hundred years between English people and ourselves is due to the lack of appreciation of [our] national feelings.

Woodburn admitted that the Scots were a 'touchy' nation. But he argued that if they didn't get more respect *and* the British economy worsened, England would lose Scotland as she had once lost Amer-ica, India and Ireland.[19] The half-empty chamber was not the only sign of complacency. There was a limit to how far the unionist Establishment was prepared to go in order to contain nationalism, and it was reached in 1955 over the postage stamp.

Weights and measures, coinage, and other means of trade and distribution like the stamp lie at the heart of a nation's identity. They facilitate the smooth running of a customs union and they are laden with images of the nation. Postage was particularly important because since the 1920s stamp-collecting had become a popular hobby in the UK. It was approved of by educationalists as a means of geographical instruction and, in particular, as a way of promoting monarchy and empire: children collected an array of colourful designs depicting British territories around the world, all of which had one thing in common: the monarch's head in the top right-hand corner. Yet, while the Post Office sanctioned imperial designs, it never issued any domestic stamps depicting the nations of the British Isles, apart from those which commemorated entirely national events like VE Day or the Festival of Britain.

In 1955, shortly after a Burns Night dinner in his Essex constitu-ency, the Assistant Postmaster-General, Cuthbert Alport, argued that separate stamps should now be issued for Scotland, Wales and Northern Ireland bearing the symbols of each country next to the

Queen's head (thistle, leek and red hand). Despite Scottish Office
warnings of an English backlash, no proposal was made to create
English stamps with a rose, a telling reminder of the extent to which
Anglo-British identity remained indivisible in this period. Anthony
Eden was opposed on the ground that it would stir up nationalism.
But eventually, in the summer of 1956, the change went ahead. The
idea of displaying national heroes next to the Queen was less
acceptable and demonstrated just how central the monarchy still was
to the maintenance of Britishness. Over the next two years, the Burns
Federation petitioned the government for a special stamp to commemorate the bicentenary of the poet's birth in 1959. The Postmaster-General, Ernest Marples, told the Cabinet, 'It is unthinkable that
we should put a portrait of a private person alongside that of the
monarch . . . the Monarch's head has been accepted throughout the
world as standing for the United Kingdom.' He predicted trouble
if the petition was granted: 'With the number of famous people in
our history [it] would result in strongly pressed demands for commemorating other Scots, Welsh, Irish as well as English notabilities.
It would quickly become a political issue.'[20] The Cabinet agreed, and
it was not until 1968 that pictorial stamps were introduced,[21] after
intense pressure from the Labour left-winger Tony Benn.

Wales also felt the cold hand of Westminster descend on its
shoulders in the 1950s. In the spring of 1948, Enoch Powell had
been sent there on a fact-finding mission by Tory Central Office,
optimistically clutching a copy of Hugo's *Welsh in Two Weeks*. The
result was a *Charter for Wales*, published on St David's Day 1949.
It acknowledged the principality's 'separateness as a national entity'
and promised that a Cabinet minister would be given special
responsibility for it.[22] For the first time, in 1950, the Conservative
Party entered a general election with a more devolutionary manifesto
than the Labour Party. But the depth of Tory commitment was
shown at Anglesey in 1951, when Party Chairman Lord Woolton
said, 'a country for the whole of which the product of a penny rate
fetches less than the City of Westminster cannot be expected to pull
itself up by its bootstraps'.[23] Wales was added to the brief of the new
Home Secretary, David Maxwell Fyfe. But neither he nor his successor, Gwilym Lloyd George (son of the former Prime Minister), had
any real power. The decision not to publish separate public accounts
for Wales, following their introduction for Scotland in 1952, was a
typical case. Nationalists hoped they would show that Wales could
stand on her own two feet. In fact, the Treasury warned, they would

show conclusively that 'Wales is a deficiency region' and 'less richly endowed by nature'.[24] The government therefore decided that publication would encourage discontent. When Welsh affairs were shunted to the Ministry of Housing and Local Government in 1957, the Minister responsible, Henry Brooke, found the Whitehall files on Wales to be virtually empty.

Despite this, nationalist parties remained small and electorally unsuccessful. At the general elections of 1955 and 1959 Labour's huge majority in Wales was untouched. In Scotland, the Conservative vote not only matched the Labour vote; in 1955 for the first time since 1900 they took the most seats. Throughout the decade, the Scots and the Welsh remained wedded to the idea of Britain: to the collective memory of the wartime struggle against fascism; to the increasing prosperity it brought; and to the institutions which bound the UK together. Although Scotland and Wales still lagged behind England economically, for the time being the disparity was still masked by the fact that both shared in the affluent boom of the period. And although the monarchy had been the focus of discontent during the EIIR controversy, it was still embedded in Welsh and especially Scottish national identity. Unlike Wales, Scotland had been an independent kingdom before 1603, and its royal dynasty, the Stuarts, was still the object of romantic affection.

At first glance, Jacobitism might not seem to be a solid basis for Britishness in the 1950s. The last Pretender was a Bavarian prince chosen by a nationalist pressure group in 1891. He reduced his chance of succeeding to the British throne by fighting for the Kaiser during the First World War and thereafter Scots had left well alone.[25] However, a heroic defeat is central to most national identities. The Jacobite movement was no longer a threat and could therefore be comfortably assimilated into Britain's history while still acting as a focus of Scottishness. It therefore functioned in a similar way to the story of the American Confederacy in the United States. As Jeffrey Richards has pointed out, Jacobitism 'involves war and rebellion but the war and rebellion are safely located in a romanticised past on which Scotland turned its back in the eighteenth century to become full and enthusiastic partners in the British Empire'.[26] In addition, since the 1780s, the once savage treacherous Highlands had been repackaged as a picturesque emblem of Scottish culture. Within this context, the legend of 'Bonnie Prince Charlie' promoted a sentimental view of monarchy north of the border and, since there was no latterday Pretender to the throne, monarchist sentiment was transferred to the Windsors, thereby ensuring that support for the Crown was stronger in Scotland than would it would otherwise have been. It is no coincidence that the mid-1950s saw a spate of hugely popular films with a Jacobite theme, *Rob Roy* (1953), *The Master of Ballantrae* (1953) and *Brigadoon* (1954), replete with all the props of tartanry, kilts, pipes and claymores. Jacobitism appealed to the most extreme left-wing nationalists like Hugh MacDiarmid, who described Bonnie Prince Charlie as a 'symbol of the Gaelic Commonwealth'. This tendency, together with a more sensible concern for Scottish public opinion, tempered the republican wing of the SNP.[27]

3. Not far from the Kingdom of Heaven

Protestantism was also crucial in maintaining the Scots' sense of Britishness. The militant Orangeism present in Scotland's industrial 'central belt' and particularly on the west coast around Glasgow remained a significant force until the late 1960s. Cutting as it did across class and national divisions, it maintained the working-class Tory vote north of the border, even during periods of economic hardship. The relationship between the Orange Order and the Conservative and Unionist Party (as it was called until 1965) was always strained. The Order was suspicious of the Tory Anglican Establishment in England, particularly after the partition of Ireland. The feeling was mutual. Orangeism was increasingly seen, like the Orangeism of Ulster from which it sprang in the 1830s, as a hybrid, illiberal faith and an embarrassment to Britain's unionist elite at Westminster. Nonetheless, write Scots historians Graham Walker and Tom Gallagher, 'Orange ideology, with its stress on Crown and Parliament as guardians of civil and religious liberty, inspired a fundamentally British patriotism and loyalism.'[28] Mainstream Presbyterianism also played a part. The Church of Scotland was a predominantly middle-class institution, but, like its Anglican counterpart, it had a patriotic appeal within all social groups, including those who were not even churchgoers. As an Established Church, it provided a direct link between the Scots' religiosity and the Crown in a way that the free Churches of Wales could not.

Given the centrality of monarchism and Protestantism to Scottishness in the mid-twentieth century, manipulating popular loyalty to both offered the best chance for placating nationalist sentiment. Among those who grasped the opportunity was the Dean of Westminster, Alan Don. Don was an austere Scot from Dundee, whose condemnation of the Covenanters' 'theft' of the Stone of Destiny had inflamed opinion north of the border and increased support for it to be left there permanently. Realizing his mistake, in 1952 he told the Archbishop of Canterbury that 'nationalist feeling is very strong in Scotland at the moment'. It would, he said, be a good idea if the Moderator of the General Assembly of the Church of Scotland was given a role in the Coronation service.[29] Fisher regarded the union of the British Protestant Churches as a task of his Primacy so he had no hesitation in agreeing to the Dean's suggestion. The result was an important innovation in Coronation ritual, in which the Moderator, J. Pitt-Watson, stood next to Fisher and handed the Queen a Bible before she made her oath to uphold the Protestant religion. The televised sight of the two nations united in the Word through the Crown was a potent one that was well received in Scotland.

Before retiring to bed in Lambeth Palace after the most exhausting but uplifting day of his life, the Archbishop contentedly wrote in his diary, 'the religious significance of the Coronation has been much more generally appreciated than at the last'.[30] Broadcasting to the nation a few days afterwards, he declared 'the Country and the Commonwealth last Tuesday were not far from the Kingdom of Heaven'.[31] This oft-quoted comment is usually seen as an example of the arrogant failure of Britain's leaders to grasp postwar realities. The Coronation, they argue, simply proved that monarchism had become an ersatz expression of British religiosity, superseding the Protestant faith in an age of agnosticism. An influential 1953 article by the sociologists Edward Shils and Michael Young encouraged this view. 'Much like Christmas', it concluded, 'the Coronation was the ceremonial occasion for the affirmation of the moral values by which the society lives'.[32] Monarchism was undeniably the lay religion of Britons in the second half of the twentieth century. However, for millions more, the crowning of Elizabeth II demonstrated how vigorous traditional religion still was. Fisher's speech was not mocked at the time, because Protestantism continued to form an integral part of Britishness – not only in the Orange heartlands of Northern

Ireland and Scotland but also in England and Wales. The idea that the British were close to the Kingdom of Heaven was greeted with a chorus of approval in the press, with many commentators predicting religious revival on a Wesleyan scale. In fact, a revival was already taking place when the Archbishop placed the crown on Elizabeth's head.

The period 1945–1960 was the Indian Summer of British Protestantism, and 1950–56 a particularly warm time. Nonconformism continued to lose believers at a steady rate. Its decline was symbolized by the demolition of Manchester's Union Chapel in 1950, a vast Victorian Baptist auditorium, once known as 'the Nonconformist Cathedral of Lancashire'. But the number of communicants in the Established Churches of Scotland and England actually rose, as did the number of confirmations and ordinations. The Church of England enjoyed the biggest revival, with a 23.6 per cent rise in active membership, compared to 2.3 per cent for the Church of Scotland. By 1961, the readership of the *Church Times* had reached a level not achieved since its heyday in the 1900s. Also in 1961, the *New English Bible* became the year's runaway bestseller and Guildford Cathedral was consecrated – the first cathedral to be built on a new site in the south of England since the Middle Ages. Another event seen as evidence of Protestant vigour was the ordination in 1955 of the captain of the English cricket team, David Sheppard, who went on to become a much-loved Bishop of Liverpool. 'It was', writes Adrian Hastings, 'a most satisfying moment, symbol of what the fifties seemed all about'.[33] Yet this was not a time of insularity. The 1958 Lambeth Conference was the most successful ever. Held every ten years since 1888 and attended by bishops from every corner of the earth, on this occasion it was judged to have turned the Anglican Church from a missionary agency of the British Empire into a truly international and multiracial fellowship. As he closed the proceedings after five weeks of productive discussion, the famously rigid Archbishop Fisher burst into tears of joy and hurriedly left the chamber to weep in private.

Why the revival? In Britain, the Protestant faith provided solace for those bereaved and traumatized by the Second World War, reassurance for those bewildered by accelerating social change and an ideological framework for anti-communist thought of all kinds. The Churches took advantage, combining doctrinal conservatism with a more dynamic approach to pastoral care and to saving souls. The formation of the Samaritans in 1953 by a London curate called

Chad Varah was an example of the former. An example of the latter was the welcome given to American preacher Billy Graham in 1954. A dinner was held for him by MPs in the House of Commons and at his final rally at Wembley Stadium he was flanked by the Lord Mayor of London and the Archbishop of Canterbury. Graham promised 'a sweep for God through Britain' when he arrived. Accurate figures do not exist for the number of converts, but over 1,300,000 heard him preach during his three-month stay and newsreels captured thousands going forward nightly to be received into the Church.[34]

Intellectually too, Anglicanism enjoyed its biggest lay support since the mid-nineteenth century. The poet and broadcaster John Betjeman became a household name during the 1950s. His very human religiosity – his good-humoured passion for the sights, sounds and smells of the Anglican Church and the liberal national culture which it embodied – appealed to people searching for a moderate spiritual antidote to materialism. The painters John Piper and Stanley Spencer, and the writers Dorothy L. Sayers and Rose Macaulay were but a few of those whose work exuded the faith in this period. The author C. S. Lewis was in the prime of his creative life during the 1950s. Born in Ulster in 1898, he was an Oxbridge don who rejected the Presbyterianism of his youth and converted to Anglicanism in the 1930s. But Ulster never entirely left him. He had an evangelical temper and a reluctance to compromise on fundamental principles. These characteristics, evident in books like *Mere Christianity* (1952), gave the Anglican revival the theological muscle it needed. Lewis also reached a mass audience with his septet of allegorical 'Narnia' stories for children. Their central character is Aslan, a very British lion who embodies muscular goodness and its triumph over evil. Published between 1950 and 1956, the Narnia stories achieved an almost catechistic status among the middle classes as moral primers for the young.

In 1942, Bishop George Bell began a bestselling illustrated history of *The English Church* thus:

> The Church of England is the most venerable and the most influential of all the factors which have gone to the making of English history and English character. Broadly and deeply planted in the land, mixed up with all our manners and customs, one of the main guarantees of our local government, and therefore one of the prime securities of our common liberties, the Church of

England . . . is part of our history, part of our life, part of England itself.[35]

A decade later, few people would have disagreed. If Anglicanism was dying, it was not readily apparent to Britons in the first half of the 1950s. Critics like Bertrand Russell who gathered around its wrinkled frame eagerly awaiting the end not only found it breathing steadily; to their amazement, they also saw it get off its deathbed and wander round the house and garden speaking as lucidly as ever.

It was this renewed confidence which led Geoffrey Fisher to visit Rome and meet the Pope on 2 December 1960 – the first time an Archbishop of Canterbury had done so since the fourteenth century. The talks were friendly, but Fisher stoutly told John XXIII that *Ecclesia Anglicana* had no need to return to the Catholic fold and that the two would continue to travel on 'parallel lines'.[36] Fisher also came closer than any of his predecessors to creating a united Protestant Church of Great Britain. After a decade of friendly and often excited discussion, in 1957 an agreement was reached between Presbyterian and Anglican leaders whereby their members would be able to worship freely in each other's churches. Formally, the Churches of Scotland and England would still exist. But they would be doctrinally 'in full communion', and organizationally in ever closer union. Known as 'the Bishops' Report' it came unstuck over the proposal that bishops, consecrated as Anglicans, should be appointed as moderators of the Presbyteries. The Scottish press erupted in fury, one observer calling it a piece of 'coarse Anglican imperialism'. Four-fifths of the Scottish people were found to be opposed.[37] The issue touched much rawer nerves than the EIIR controversy because both religious and secular Scots saw the Church as an institution, like law and education, which preserved their separate identity. An apocryphal story widely circulated at the time had a churchgoer asking an atheist why he was so upset about the Report, to which the man replied, 'I'm a Presbyterian atheist.'[38] In England, *Crockford's Clerical Directory* lamented that 'the old unhappy Anglo-Scottish conflicts of the seventeenth century have been recalled and there has been blatant appeal to the prejudices of national feeling'.[39] But in Edinburgh, the General Assembly (itself riven over the issue) bowed to national feeling and rejected the Report.

In 1959 the Scottish Episcopalian leader, Thomas Hannay, stiffly rebuked Archbishop Fisher in a letter to Lambeth Palace: 'I wish

English folk would realise that the Border is a reality, and not a mere figure of speech or a line in a map ... The whole outlook and ethos is different here'.[40] The English were given the chance to atone a year later when the General Assembly invited the Queen to attend the four hundredth anniversary celebrations of the Scottish Reformation. When Buckingham Palace consulted Fisher about whether Elizabeth should go, he replied that she should do so because Christianity was a question of 'good manners' or else it was nothing. His comment encapsulated the gentlemanly ethos of Anglicanism which was both its strength and its weakness.[41] After a service in Edinburgh's St Giles' Cathedral on 11 October 1960, Elizabeth II became the first monarch of the United Kingdom to address the General Assembly of the Church of Scotland. Her speech emphasized the bond between Scots and English which the Reformation had forged and which she, as Head of both Churches, symbolized. Speaking, she said, 'as one who loves this country of Scotland', the Queen concluded:

> In spite of the bitter quarrels of the past and the divided religious loyalties which still remain with us, I believe that what happened at the Reformation can be stated in terms on which [we all] may agree. Holy writ was liberated to the people, and as a result the Word of God was revealed again as a force to be reckoned with in the affairs of both public and private life.[42]

The Queen's speech was well received by the 1,200 dignitaries present and by press and public alike. The whole event demonstrated that even when the Scots were provoked by English tactlessness into asserting their unique nationality, it was still framed by a belief in a historic community of Britons.

However, for all the emphasis placed on religious and secular history in New Elizabethan ideology, the Coronation was not an orgy of nostalgia. Like most Golden Ages, that of the sixteenth century was seen as a spur to progress. Elizabeth II, said commentators, was a medium through which the spirits of Shakespeare and Drake could be invoked to inspire a similar renaissance in the twentieth century – one that would benefit the whole of the UK. Consequently, New Elizabethanism was not so much a celebration of tradition per se as a conservative definition of how progress could be achieved in postwar Britain.

4. Set the enfettered spirit free

Sincere though the public mourning for George VI was, it was accompanied more than in most reigns by an openly breathless anticipation of the reign that had just begun. Sombre pictures of Elizabeth returning to Britain from Africa for the Proclamation of the Accession, swathed in black, were swiftly followed in the popular press with gushing columns heralding the New Elizabethan Age. Since their marriage in 1947, Elizabeth and Philip had been celebrated as young, attractive and sexual individuals. Now, with the help of Cecil Beaton's technicolour portraits and the full weight of the Palace and press behind them, they were turned into pin-ups. The Queen's sexual magnetism was such that the homosexual journalist Godfrey Winn of the *Sunday Express* thought 'a woman on the throne [will give] back to a nation its manhood'.[43] A young MP called Margaret Roberts wrote an article in the *Sunday Graphic* – 'Wake Up, Women!' – which argued that the new Queen was an inspiration to female Britons fighting for a place in public life and that family and career could be successfully combined. 'Women can – AND MUST – play a leading part in the creation of a glorious Elizabethan era', she wrote. 'Should a woman arise equal to the task, I say let her have an equal chance with the men for the leading Cabinet posts. Why not a woman Chancellor – or a woman Foreign Secretary?'[44] It was a radical thought for the time, and an ironically prescient one because, as Prime Minister Margaret Thatcher thirty years later, the writer would establish a monarchical style of Premiership which helped to undermine the allure of the Crown.

Democracy was overtly celebrated in New Elizabethan propaganda. Churchill saw to it that government publicity about the event emphasized that the Crown was not simply above politics but was a symbol of democratic progress. Rejecting suggestions that Arthur Bryant should do the job, the Prime Minister drafted the Queen's Coronation Day broadcast to the nation himself. It ended with a flourish of Whiggery. 'Parliamentary institutions, with their free speech and respect for the rights of minorities, and the inspiration of a broad tolerance in thought and its expression – all this we conceive to be a precious part of our way of life and outlook'. 'We can go forward together', she continued, with the assurance that democracy was 'as sacred to the Crown . . . as to its many parliaments and peoples'.[45]

Nor did the event's religiosity rest solely on the arcane patriotism of ancient ritual. Fisher emphasized that when the Queen was consecrated to the service of God, her subjects were called to His service by paying her homage. 'Her peoples', he told the public, 'must dedicate themselves with her to seek the righteousness which makes a nation at unity in itself.'[46] The point of the Coronation was to establish a Christian contract between the Crown and the people which would make Britain great again. The contract was sealed in a grand act of national communion which reunited Britain. A testament to this was the government amnesty for wartime deserters. Churchill thought 'there is a very grave evil . . . in having so many thousands of "outlaws" dwelling among us'.[47] He told the Cabinet: 'The national rejoicing at the time of the Coronation would provide a suitable occasion for an act of mercy towards these men'.[48] The Coronation therefore became a sanctification of Britain, an event in which every Briton was purified and made fit for national service. Here was the true meaning behind Fisher's apparently complacent comment about the nation being so close to the Kingdom of Heaven.

There was another, more bullishly Conservative strain of New Elizabethanism than the notion of a dutiful, organic, Christian democracy. Many believed that the values of 'hearth, home and service' – though necessary in personal life to maintain the social fabric – were not, if applied to the public world of business, the arts and science, enough to create a national renaissance. What was needed instead was a revival of private enterprise, individualism and hard work. The reassertion of these values went hand in hand with an attack on social democracy. The Conservative government, like its predecessor, was careful to avoid being seen to exploit a national event for political purposes. In July 1952, the Conservative Party Chairman wrote to party agents instructing them not 'to appear to be making political capital out of the Coronation'.[49] Nonetheless attacks were made on the Labour legacy which revealed that Conservatives were prepared to use the Queen to challenge the postwar consensus. Indeed New Elizabethanism was the first concerted attempt since Disraeli's reinvention of Victoria as an empress to make the monarchy the foundation of a wider ideological movement.

The Poet Laureate, John Masefield, raised the royal standard in his 'Prayer for a Beginning Reign', published in *The Times*:

May this old land revive and be
Again a star set in the sea
May she re-establish standards shaken,
And set the enfettered spirit free.[50]

A book written by Richard Dimbleby, *Elizabeth our Queen*, was distributed through local authorities to schoolchildren. It made a pointed contrast between the unaccountable, faceless bureaucracy of the state and the accessible, human, yet spiritual nature of the Crown: 'The Crown is truly a nationalised service belonging to the people more than any other politically nationalised undertaking. With that personal sense of ownership which no man feels towards the railways or the Bank of England . . . the Crown is an instinctive outlet of patriotism that borders on the religious.'[51] The royal family's charity work was celebrated, emphasizing that voluntarism rather than state provision was still the noblest form of welfare. The National Playing Fields Association (patron, the Duke of Edinburgh) launched a campaign with the slogan 'The battle for recovery will be won on the playing fields of Britain' and an informational film directed by Carol Reed – both deliberate echoes of the muscular patriotism of the Edwardian era. The sixteenth-century Golden Age was also pressed into the service of Cold War propaganda, for example in Phillip Gibbs' popular book *New Elizabethans*, which presented the Soviet Union as a latter-day Spain, and the Labour Party by implication as a group of Catholic agents provocateurs.

On Coronation day, *The Times* bluntly argued that the cost of socialist reform was too high. The Labour Party had mortgaged the nation's future by squandering resources on welfare instead of 'replac[ing] the industrial equipment on which [our] life depends'. The paper also condemned the rise of class-consciousness under Labour. 'Amidst the incessant and strident talk of rights, the voice of duty is only half-heard. Meanness of spirit, envy and jealousy sour too much of our national life'. In moral terms, it argued that the welfare state had sapped the work ethic of the British and developed a culture of dependency. Britons, it acknowledged, had deserved a brief 'holiday from reality' as a reward for the sacrifices they made during the war. But the result was that they no longer 'have the will to prosper'. *The Times* laid the blame for this partly at the door of the Conservative Party, which had become embroiled in a postwar consensus in which no one was 'facing the facts'. One example given of this malaise was that the litter in the Mall had not been cleared up straight after the event. 'The British', it concluded, 'are a good people grown careless.'[52] This forthright leader was written by the paper's new editor, Sir William Haley. Haley had resigned as Director-General of the BBC in 1952, partly because he could not face the threat of commercial TV. Much as he thought the nation needed a shot of free enterprise in the arm, he was adamant that it had no place in broadcasting. His former colleague, Third Programme boss Harman Grisewood, wrote to congratulate him: 'It is a true comprehensive analysis of our malaise ... the article has the true spirit of leadership and provides what the politicians cannot.'[53]

Government gave a lead by exploiting the commercial potential of the Coronation. The Commonwealth Secretary, Lord Salisbury, told the President of the Board of Trade, Peter Thorneycroft, that it offered 'opportunities for making substantial sums of money', a view endorsed by the Cabinet.[54] £648,000 was recovered from the sale of seats; an unaccounted sum was made by selling film rights and by licensing the usual range of royal knick-knacks, from mugs to medallions. Objections were raised. During a debate in the Commons the Conservative MP for Buckingham, Major Frank Markham, asked Churchill to put a stop to 'entirely objectionable' goods such as 'Coronation ladies underwear, ornamented with the Union Jack at the rear'.[55] The Prime Minister obliged, instructing the Council for Industrial Design to advise companies on the taste of their products. The idea that the national flag could be informally yet patriotically displayed became an accepted feature of British culture in the 1960s. That it was not so in 1953 was a measure of how narrow the official parameters of Britishness still were in this period.

The Empire was also vigorously celebrated. In the Coronation procession there were none of the civilian contingents which Attlee had allowed to march in the Victory Parade of 1946. The Earl Marshal ordered it to be an uncomplicated display of imperial military might with units from British territories all over the world (Commonwealth representation was double what it had been at the 1937 Coronation). The *Daily Telegraph* rejoiced in the loyalty shown by 'all her scattered family, from sheep-farmers of New-Zealand to fuzzy-haired dancers of Fiji', and the smiling, rotund figure of Queen Salote of Tonga became a national heroine for braving the torrential rain in an open-topped carriage.[56] Some British troops stationed abroad were inspired by it all. John Smith, serving in the Suez Canal Zone in Egypt with the Royal Artillery, remembers:

With the temperature along the Canal 100F in the shade, uniforms starched and creased, boots gleaming in the sunlight, with due pomp and ceremony we fired our guns twenty-one times at precisely (so we were told) the moment of the crowning . . . A strange transformation came over us. We became immensely proud of what we were doing and why we were doing it . . . [Back at Woolwich Barracks on 21 June] I saw all the decorations and flags . . . every house, store and street still bore testimony to a rare event, the crowning of a monarch. I know I had a lump in my throat and watery eyes as the significance of what I saw slowly sank in. Then I remembered sweltering in the hot Egyptian sun doing my duty and paying homage to a person and a tradition that made and kept Great Britain the nation it was, and I felt very proud of the small part I'd played.[57]

By a godsend, a New Zealander, Edmund Hillary, and a Tibetan, Tensing Norgay, conquered Mount Everest on 29 May. Thanks to careful news management the news was broken on the day of the Coronation. *The Times* compared it to Drake's circumnavigation of the globe. 'BE PROUD OF BRITAIN ON THIS DAY' ran the *Daily Express* headline. It was 'a stroke in the true Elizabethan vein, a reminder that the old adventurous, defiant heart of the race remains unchanged.'[58] Although more scientific equipment was used than in the previous seven British expeditions, there were echoes of the Victorian cult of the gentleman amateur. Umbrellas were carried to 13,000 feet. Sir John Hunt, who led the expedition, diverted himself by reading the *Oxford Book of Greek Verse* in sub-zero temperatures in rest periods during his phlegmatic organization of the climb.

More revealing still was the reaction to the nationality of the climbers. Though the climbing team treated Tensing as an equal and no one divulged who had reached the summit first, it was Hillary who got most of the glory. When Tensing visited London he was portrayed as a loveable naif, his lack of sophistication evidenced by his wearing two wristwatches while shaking hands with everyone.[59] Ordinary Britons were in no doubt who had conquered the highest mountain in the world. One schoolboy, Howard Palmer, was told by his father, 'The British are the best in the world, we are the only ones who could have done it.' When, a few days later, he was told at school that the climbers were a Tibetan and a New Zealander, he confronted his father, who replied: 'The Sherpa didn't count as he was only doing his job, and Hillary was as good as English as he came from New Zealand.' 'At the age of seven,' said Palmer, 'this made sense to me.'[60]

The Queen herself declared that there was substance to the pomp and circumstance. In her Coronation day broadcast she told the country that the ceremony was 'not a symbol of a power and splendour that have gone but a declaration of our hopes for the future'.[61] In her Christmas broadcast that year she said:

> Some people have expressed the hope that my reign may mark a new Elizabethan age. Frankly, I do not feel at all like my great Tudor forebear, who was blessed with neither husband nor children, who ruled as a despot and was never able to leave her native shores. But there is at least one very significant resemblance between her age and mine. For her kingdom, small though it may have been and poor by comparison with her European neighbours, was yet great in spirit and well endowed with men who were ready to encompass the earth. Now, this great Commonwealth of which I am proud to be the Head, and of which that ancient kingdom forms a part, though rich in material resources, is richer still in the enterprise and courage of its peoples.[62]

What New Elizabethanism did was to dress up Victorian laissez-faire capitalist imperialism in the colourful doublet and hose of the sixteenth century to make it more palatable. This was nothing new. Imperial apologists of the late nineteenth century had seen the Elizabethan era as the harbinger of Victorian overseas expansion, a view which had found its way into school textbooks. An aestheticized version of this Golden Age – 'Tudorbethan' semis – had dominated interwar suburban development, housing a new generation of middle-class owner occupiers and making an Englishman's home not his castle but his ersatz manor house.

However, the royal cult of the 1950s was not simply a lace ruff on the brass neck of conservatism. From the start, the royal couple were directly associated with modern technology. On Elizabeth's return from Africa, it was noticed that she was the first British monarch to arrive in her capital by aeroplane. In an era when passenger air travel was only open to a few, this was a potent symbol of modernity. The *Sunday Express* praised the Queen for 'crashing precedents' by flying because 'that is the way to bring in a new age'. There were also hopes that Elizabeth would usher in a more informal monarchy. The *Express* warned that 'The court machine will oppose any change. They always do. But the destinies of a nation are no longer shaped by a limited circle surrounding the throne. This is the age of the common man and woman.'[63] The identification of the Court as a reactionary body was part of a tradition of blaming the monarch's advisers rather than the monarch himself. But on this occasion it also expressed a determination that a long-overdue modernization of the monarchy would begin; that Elizabeth would combine the probity of the Georgian Court with the dash of the disgraced Edward VIII. Though the Queen kept her uncle well away from the Coronation, Edward observed approvingly from his home in France, 'She intends to rekindle among her compatriots something of the spirit of adventure of the first Elizabethan reign.'[64]

It was not long before the Queen was given the chance to demonstrate her commitment to change. In October 1952, a cabal decided that the Coronation should not be televised. It comprised the Prime Minister, the Archbishop of Canterbury, the Duke of Norfolk and the Queen's Private Secretary (and cousin), Sir Alan Lascelles. The four men believed that television would demystify the monarchy, turning a sacramental event into an entertainment. They also feared that the whole edifice of Britain's political system which the monarchy supported would eventually have daylight let in on its own magic. Sir Norman Brook prophetically told Churchill that if the cameras were allowed in, 'No argument will remain for refusing television facilities of . . . proceedings in the House of Commons.'[65] There were no dissenters in the Cabinet. But it rubber-stamped the decision only for the BBC to leak it to the press and a furore to erupt.

The Beaverbrook press led the charge. 'So mighty an occasion belongs to the whole British family', it said, pointing out that the Coronation rite included the phrase that the Queen was crowned 'in the sight of all her people'.[66] The *Manchester Guardian* commented, 'It was the sort of decision that might have been taken in Victoria's day and by the same sort of people. This obviously will not do nowadays when nobody is terribly overawed by the dignity of office of Earl Marshal or Lord Chamberlain or even Archbishop of Canterbury.'[67] There were also protests from some clergy on the grounds that the cathode-ray tube was a tool for bringing Protestantism to the people, just as the vernacular Bible had done in Elizabeth I's reign. Attlee forced a Commons debate on the matter, at the height of which Churchill protested that a religious event 'should not be presented as if it were a theatrical performance'.[68] But only *The Times* agreed and an opinion poll showed that 78 per cent of Britons wanted to see the ceremony. The Queen and the Duke of Edinburgh were reported to be in favour and the Cabinet was forced to overturn its original decision on 28 October 1952. The *Listener* said the event was a victory of the people over the Court, concluding, 'The directness of the relation between the citizen and the Crown is something contemporary . . . it belongs to an epoch in which the court is less substantial.'[69]

The Coronation of Elizabeth II became the 'TV Coronation'. A total of 56 per cent of the adult population, 20.4 million people, watched the event while a further 32 per cent, 11.7 million, listened on the radio. Because few people had TV sets, many gathered in friends' and neighbours' houses to watch. Elizabeth appeared to be more in touch with her people than any previous monarch by using modern technology to give Britons a better view than the peers in Westminster Abbey. The *News Chronicle* said: 'It is rarely that a great people feels and acts in perfect unity. But yesterday . . . the sense of fellowship was everywhere . . . Television wrought the miracle . . . For once "the people" was no legal fiction.'[70] The *Evening Standard* simply said it had 're-educated this people with pride in their nationhood'.[71] Even the Archbishop of Canterbury was converted by 'the liturgical stage-direction' of the BBC and Richard Dimbleby's reverential commentary. Fisher wrote to thank the corporation for bringing 'God's presence' into 'countless homes'.[72] He noted that even godless socialists like Aneurin Bevan and the Soviet Ambassador had followed the service intently.

How did the monarchy contribute to the cult of New Elizabethanism? First, a serious attempt was made to present the monarch as a patron of the arts for the first time since the Victorian era. David Eccles commissioned the architect of the Festival of Britain, Hugh Casson, to design the decorations for the processional route; the Arts Council promoted a series of concerts of British music at the Festival Hall, among them one by William Walton, who wrote *Orb and Sceptre* for the event. And Frederick Ashton was commissioned to produce a special Coronation ballet for Sadler's Wells, *Homage to the Queen*. The centrepiece of the Coronation was Benjamin Britten's new opera, *Gloriana*. Britten had already been hailed in the 1940s for creating a distinctively British opera; *Gloriana* was the result of a specific conversation about national identity between Britten, his companion Peter Pears, and the Queen's cousin, Lord Harewood, when the three were on holiday together in 1952. Harewood recalled:

What was 'national expression' in opera we asked ourselves? . . .
'For the Italians undoubtedly *Aida*,' said Ben. 'It's the perfect
expression of every kind of Italian nationalist feeling – but where's
the English equivalent?' 'Well, you'd better write one.' The next
few hours were spend discussing a period – the Merrie England of
the Elizabethans? Highly appropriate! What about a national
opera in time for next year's Coronation?[73]

Harewood put the idea to the Queen through her Private Secretary,
Sir Alan Lascelles. The House of Windsor is not known for its
aesthetic acumen and Elizabeth II was no different, her main interests
being dogs and horses. But she was keen to emulate her illustrious
forebear and so approved the project. A speech she made to the
Royal Society of Arts in 1947 gives us an indication of her cultural
viewpoint. 'A nation', she said, 'whose level of good sense in art was
once reflected in the furniture of Chippendale . . . cannot rest content
with slavish imitations of foreign styles.'[74]

Though not a slavish imitation of foreign styles, Britten's opera
was not the success Elizabeth had hoped it would be. The composer
told his librettist, the poet and critic William Plomer, that he wanted
'lovely pageantry'. But he also warned, 'It's got to be serious. I don't
want to do just folk dances and village green stuff.'[75] With Lytton
Strachey's *Elizabeth and Essex* as the basis for Plomer's libretto,
John Piper providing a distinctly melancholic set, and Britten making
no musical concessions to the assembled dignitaries, the opera was a
critical disaster and was quickly dubbed 'Boriana' by most of the
press. The portrayal of Elizabeth as a vain old woman, prone to the
flattery of dashing, self-styled adventurers was seen to be offensive,
for it contradicted the image of Elizabeth as a moral, dynamic youth.
Plomer blamed the opera's failure on the jingoistic philistinism of an
elite still trapped in the Edwardian era:

> Were these chatterers interested in anything beyond a plenteous
> twinkling of tiaras . . . in the auditorium? Did they perhaps expect
> some kind of loud and rumbustious amalgam of *Land of Hope
> and Glory* and *Merrie England*, with catchy tunes and deafening
> chorus to reproduce the vulgar and blatant patriotism of the Boer
> War period? If so, they didn't get it.[76]

There were deeper reasons for the opera's failure than jingoism and
the refusal of artists to produce an unambiguous national culture
that accorded with it. In a telling act of collective amnesia, the press
forgot that the Queen had personally commissioned the opera. The

Arts Council was blamed instead and attacked as a symbol of all that was wrong with state interference in British life (there were even calls for its abolition to atone for the slighting of the monarchy).

A more successful attempt to sponsor a New Elizabethan age was the monarchy's association with science and technology in the 1950s. Prince Philip, frustrated by playing second fiddle to his wife and by the fustiness of her Court, carved out a role for himself as a Prince Albert for the jet age (Albert's interest in science had been spawned by similar frustrations). Philip's new role was launched with his appointment as President of the British Association for the Advancement of Science. In February 1951 he made his inaugural speech at Edinburgh University, which celebrated 'The British Contribution to Science and Technology in the Past Hundred Years'. The speech was rapturously received by the press, relieved that after fourteen years of being saddled with a shy and unhealthy king they had a consort with some charisma and a brain. According to *The Times*, 'old courtiers marvelled at his unprecedented action in composing his own address . . . The British public can be profoundly thankful that . . . the Queen . . . should be supported by a personality of outstanding vitality who is in step with the march of the modern world.'[77] In fact, most of the speech was written by leading scientists. In a letter to the Secretary of the Association, Sir Harold Hartley, the Duke confessed, 'The more I read the material you have been sending me the more confused I get.'[78] Moreover, the real impetus behind British scientific progress came from the state. From 1945 to 1964, government spending on civil scientific research and development rose from £6.58 million to £151.6 million, a tenfold rise allowing for inflation.

Nevertheless, it was the Duke of Edinburgh who turned statistics into patriotism and made the British see themselves as a progressive people. Over the course of the next decade, he travelled the UK visiting research centres and industrial sites and making speeches, which were collected in book form at an affordable price. The Duke had two main themes. The first was that more investment in science and technology was needed if Britain was to be a world leader and not simply muddle through. Second, he reassured people that the rapid transformation of Western life was not something to be afraid of, that science was not a 'black art' but a boon, providing central heating, washing machines and all the other life-enhancing goods that Britons were starting to consume. Philip made sure the press were never far behind. At a colliery in the north of England he examined new mining techniques, after which Richard Dimbleby said (in an account reminiscent of *Pravda* covering a visit by Stalin to a Ukrainian coalfield), 'the Duke gave such an impetus to the miners that the pits in the area broke all production records in the ensuing weeks'.[79] His most notable photo-opportunity was a visit to de Havillands, where he flew a prototype Comet, the world's first passenger jet aeroplane. Until it crashed in 1953, the Comet was hailed as proof that Britain was leading the technological revolution just as she had once led the industrial revolution. *Picture Post* said, 'this was no royal chore, no concession to the spit and polish brigade. He wants to see for himself how Britain goes to it'.[80] The *Sunday Dispatch* predicted, 'He will galvanise British industry . . . to put Britain back on her feet.'[81] In 1956 the BBC asked English licence holders how they thought the nation had changed since the war, and 65 per cent thought the UK had become a world leader in science and technology, compared to only 35 per cent for the arts. The 'Two Cultures' debate of the late 1950s – in which scientists accused literary intellectuals of being Luddites and they accused scientists of being Philistines – filled the columns of august journals. But it did not vex most of the population, for whom science was a greater source of patriotic pride because it impacted more on daily life.[82]

What was the significance of the Coronation? Though it was far from being a politically neutral event, it demonstrated how essential the monarchy still was to British national identity and how much the institution was able to unite the country. Oral evidence suggests that people were specifically uplifted by the memories of wartime camaraderie which the event evoked. The sight of the three party leaders standing side by side at the funeral of George VI brought back memories of the coalition government. The huddled bodies photographed by the press sleeping in a rain-swept Mall the night before the Coronation were compared to the pictures of bodies, similarly huddled, in Underground stations during the Blitz. As well as gathering round TV sets, people staged thousands of street parties and pageants throughout Britain; bonfires were lit, fireworks were set off, the national anthem and other patriotic songs were sung over and over again and people danced into the night. It was the largest public demonstration of patriotism since VE Day. Even the Scots forgot the slight of the Accession Proclamation and celebrated.

Despite the Conservative propaganda which accompanied the event there was little criticism of the monarchy itself. Only the Communist Party openly attacked the institution. 'These "patriots" are not really patriotic . . . Their loyalty is not to country or crown.

It is to their wealth and their privileges. They love themselves not their country,' said a pamphlet issued for the occasion.[83] But when the TUC sent a message of congratulation to Buckingham Palace, only the National Union of Railwaymen complained that it was 'toadying to the Queen'. Nor was there much criticism from the liberal intelligentsia, some of whom were involved in staging the event. Most saw it either as harmless pageantry or as an antidote to nationalism. This view was summed up by the Dutch writer G. J. Renier, whose study of national character *The English: Are They Human?* was a bestseller before the war:

> The Queen is . . . a perpetual reminder of the national consciousness of each individual member of the nation. And this, at present, is a vital matter. Nationalism, which is the morbid exaggeration of national sentiment, is dangerous . . . But the feeling of an ordinary person, that he is part of a population which is homogenous and belongs together . . . *that* feeling is indeed normal, healthy, and good for the world . . . sane patriotism . . . becomes a clearer issue when it can, as in Britain, find a concrete human symbol in the form of a beloved ruler.[84]

The architectural critic John Summerson's attack on Hugh Casson's decorations was the most damning criticism of the event. With characteristic hauteur, he observed, 'We shall not be sorry to see the end of decorated London . . . Tom-toms cannot din louder than the pelmets so unrhythmically hung in some of our streets.'[85] Shils and Young asked, 'Who criticises Britain now in any fundamental sense? . . . Great Britain on the whole, and especially in comparison with other countries, seems to the British intellectual of the mid-1950s to be all right and even much more than that. Never has an intellectual class found its society and its culture so much to its satisfaction.'[86] The writer and former anarchist James Joll explained why in an article in the journal *Twentieth Century*: 'If we were in revolt in the thirties it was because there was something to revolt against: if we accept English society in the fifties it is because there has, after all been a revolution.'[87] Shils and Young were therefore right to conclude, 'The central fact is that Britain came into the Coronation period with a degree of moral consensus such as few large societies have ever manifested.'[88] If there was a conflict, it was more between popular and elite expressions of the same form of patriotism. The Coronation therefore legitimized the postwar consensus far more than it undermined it. Like the Festival of Britain, it was a state celebration of a culturally homogeneous nation, one desperately seeking inspiration from its past in order to revive its fortunes.

As the royal entourage set off on a successful tour of the Commonwealth in the autumn of 1953, it seemed to many Britons that a New Elizabethan Age really had begun. But to many outsiders, and a good many insiders, the event was the final, colourful celebration of a nation in irreversible decline. In his memoirs, *Confessions of a European in England*, the Dutch historian J. H. Huizinga confessed to having 'Coronation Blues' shortly after leaving the Abbey:

> I found myself jerked back to the reality of the times we lived in by the cold shower that, only too symbolically, poured down on the patiently waiting subjects of her with whose Coronation we had just inaugurated the second Elizabethan age . . . I grieved for the British because during those unforgettable hours in the Abbey I had understood . . . their belief that history would not deal with them as it had dealt with all other nations that had strutted their brief moment of power and glory on the world's stage. For it had indeed been unique, this spectacle we had just witnessed . . . unique in the splendour of its colours, the beauty of its language . . . the exquisite good taste and flawless organisation which no Cecil B. De Mille could ever hope to equal . . . [and] sitting side by side with their Colonial subjects who had come from the four corners of the globe . . . how could these English help but feel that [their] power [was] a reality warranting the highest expectation of the glories that yet lay in store for it . . . But the more sympathetic comprehension one had for the high hopes with which they embarked on the second Elizabethan era, the more acutely one realised what a painful era it would be for them, how rich in disillusionment, frustration and humiliation.[89]

Britain's sense of world power had yet to be fully tested. But anxiety about her cultural fate was already coming to a head when Huizinga stepped out of the Abbey into the rain. It focused on what had been the central issue of the Coronation: television.

5. Coronation blues

C. P. Scott of the *Manchester Guardian* once remarked, '*Television?* The word is half Latin and half Greek. No good can come of it.'[90] His comment captured the hostility among Britain's ruling elites to the media revolution that took place in the 1950s. The revolution began to rumble on 15 May 1952, when Churchill's government published a White Paper announcing its intention to break the BBC's monopoly. The debate which ensued was much more than another contest between advocates of state control and advocates of the free market. The battle to decide who should have responsibility for this powerful new medium was a battle for the future of British culture. The Festival of Britain and the Coronation had promoted slightly different versions of national identity. But the issue of commercial TV reached into the engine room of national identity itself: the pumps, hammers and pistons of broadcasting which had done more than any other machinery to foster Britishness in the twentieth century.

Opening the Parliamentary debate on the White Paper, the Assistant Postmaster-General, David Gammans, attempted to play down the significance of the issue:

> The great questions that matter today are those of peace and war, of national security, the balance of trade, full employment and housing. We shall not earn our daily bread, nor save ourselves from being bombed by looking at a television set . . . television, to the majority of our people, will always be primarily a means of entertainment. I hope that, even in the Welfare State, we believe that the bread must come before the circuses.[91]

Gammans failed to dampen passions. Opening for the Opposition, Herbert Morrison said:

> It is, perhaps, the most important debate that we have had since the war. An enormous amount depends upon it as to the future of our country, the thinking of our people and the standard of culture of the people.[92]

TV broadcasting began in 1936. It was suspended during the war and resumed in 1946, but the corporation did not invest much in the

medium. When the Controller of Television, Norman Collins, protested, he was sacked and replaced by the Third Programme director,
George Barnes. The BBC could not have sent out a clearer signal.
The man responsible for 'compulsory uplift' believed 'you can't put
thought on television' and contemptuously regarded his new charge
as 'a kind of *Daily Mirror*' of the air. The BBC Chairman, Sir
Alexander Cadogan, proudly announced to the press that he did not
own a TV set; William Haley told his senior staff that if they were
doing their jobs properly, people would be watching less TV not
more.[93] When Haley left the BBC in 1952 to become editor of *The
Times*, he was replaced by Sir Ian Jacob, another committed Reithian. Like all opponents of commercial TV, BBC executives were
not simply opposed to the destruction of their monopoly. They
regarded television per se as a threat to popular literacy.

Opponents could not stem the growing dissent in Parliament nor
the country at large. The Conservative Party was then in the throes
of modernization, with liberal Tories led by Rab Butler having
pressed Churchill into accepting the welfare state. But there were
other modernizers who wanted to circumvent the postwar settlement
and appeal to working-class voters by launching a populist free-
enterprise programme. For them, British society was not a community sharing a common culture but a loose conglomeration of
consumption-oriented individuals. One group saw that commercial
television could be a driving force behind the 'people's capitalism' by
providing a new arena for advertising. The group was led by Selwyn
Lloyd, who had repudiated Beveridge's confirmation of the monopoly in 1949 and set Tory agitation in motion. He was joined by
the Home Secretary, David Maxwell Fyfe, and two rising stars of the
party, Duncan Sandys and John Profumo, the future War Minister.
They represented, in other words, the more bullish strain of New
Elizabethanism. Churchill had never lost his dislike of John Reith
and thought the BBC was 'honeycombed with socialists'. Furthermore, 90 per cent of Conservative MPs were in favour of commercial
TV. Opinion polls showed that approximately 60 per cent of the
population were too. The go ahead was given.

Since the initial debate in 1952, the Coronation had raised the
stakes in two ways. First, the number of television licence holders
rose sharply, giving TV a potential mass audience which it had never
had before. Second, the success of the BBC's coverage of the event
enhanced its reputation. It was now seen not only as an organ of free
speech and cultural dissemination, but also as a means by which the

British were brought together and *spiritually* prepared for service to the nation. The media historian John Corner has noted, 'Television was now in the process of becoming the principal instrument both of public information and of national cultural identity.' The success of the Coronation had made BBC chiefs take television more seriously, but only in order to confirm the necessity of the corporation's monopoly. Third, the failure to protect the British film industry from Hollywood made reformers determined to protect television from American influence.

A fortnight after the crowds had left the Mall, the Establishment marshalled its forces for the battle. On 18 June 1953, a meeting was held at the home of Lady Bonham Carter, only daughter of Herbert Asquith, close friend of Churchill and a former BBC governor. Those who gathered at her home included William Beveridge, E. M. Forster, Julian Huxley, Harold Nicolson, Bertrand Russell and the head of Ealing Studios, Sir Michael Balcon. They formed the National Television Council (NTC), which soon won support from fourteen of Britain's Vice-Chancellors (including those of Oxford, Cambridge and London), the National Union of Teachers, the Workers' Education Association and the Archbishop of Canterbury. The NTC's manifesto, *Britain Unites against Commercial TV*, argued that the media revolution would destroy the entire fabric of British culture: in the pursuit of profit, television companies would produce lowbrow entertainment because only that would get the large audiences necessary to attract advertisers. As a result, popular taste would be debased and the nation's fragile social cohesion shaken. Most of the Labour Party was also opposed. *Dear Viewer*, a pamphlet written by Christopher Mayhew MP with the support of Sir Ian Jacob, sold 60,000 copies. It concluded: 'If our TV standards are good, Britain can enjoy standards of entertainment and citizenship never before known. If they are bad, they can undermine . . . our whole national culture and way of life.'[94] In Parliament, Herbert Morrison warned that commercial TV was 'totally against the British temperament, the British way of life and the best or even reasonably good British traditions'.[95]

Much of the opposition to commercial television sprang from anti-Americanism. The Labour Peer Lord Macdonald asked: 'Surely there are some things which are too sacred to be commercialised? Nothing gives me more satisfaction as a Briton than that we in this country have not trod that path very far.'[96] Many Conservatives had a dislike for the unapologetic American capitalism which the young Turks of the Tory Party were seeking to mimic. They included Anthony Eden,

Rab Butler and Lords Hailsham and Waverley. Eden's Press Secretary, William Clark, argued that the Tories were throwing away the reforming reputation which they had worked so hard to attain since their defeat in 1945:

> Between the wars the whole trend of 'intelligence' was to the left; Mr. Butler . . . has already succeeded in reversing that trend . . . it is the oldest and easiest cry of intellectuals that the Conservative Party is the stupid party; if [it] plays the role of Philistines it will be a severe blow to [its] attempts to change the climate of opinion from Left to Right.[97]

Anti-Americanism not only cut across the party divide. It also undermined established loyalties to the US. Like earlier critics of Hollywood, most of those opposed to commercial TV were Atlanticists. They valued the Special Relationship but they disliked American mass culture in equal measure. Anxiety about its influence on the British people intensified towards the end of 1953 as a result of international developments. In December, Churchill's failure to mediate in the Cold War reached a humiliating climax at a meeting with Eisenhower in Bermuda, where the President dismissed the ailing Prime Minister's pleas for a summit with the Soviet Union. Bermuda showed that the United States' political supremacy had become unstoppable. Consequently, Britain's retention of its cultural supremacy became even more important than it had been when J. M. Keynes cried 'Death to Hollywood!' in 1945. Harold Nicolson believed that anti-American feeling was 'a dangerous and quite useless state of mind', but he couldn't help himself. In September 1953, he wrote, 'Gradually they are ousting us out of all world authority. I mind this, as I feel it is humiliating and insidious . . . they are decent folk in every way, but they tread on traditions in a way that hurts.'[98]

American comics, which began to arrive in Britain during the early 1950s, were one source of concern. Publications like *Corpses Monthly* glorified sex, drugs and violence. One issue gave its young readers the following advice: 'One needleful of joy-juice and you'll get so satisfied with the world you'll forget your obligations.'[99] The Labour MP Horace King was one of several politicians who called for US comics to be banned outright, complaining that they portrayed love as 'sadistic lust and not even comparatively decent pagan pornography'.[100] *Picture Post* argued, 'It is not only American comics that should be banned, but also many of the other false practices that have been imported into this country. The sooner we return to a sane

British way of life (built on traditional lines) the better for this great nation.'[101] After agitation from organizations ranging from the British Federation of Psychologists to the Women's Institute, in 1955, Parliament passed the Children and Young Persons (Harmful Publications) Act.[102] The panic was unnecessary. The *Eagle*, a wholesome publication founded in 1950 by the Revd Marcus Morris, was the bestselling comic of the decade, with sales of 1 million a week. Its hero, Dan Dare 'Pilot of the Future', combined the thrill of space travel with the British derring-do of the *Boy's Own Paper* which had thrilled prewar generations.

Television remained the focus of anti-Americanism and here too US influence was grossly exaggerated. Opponents of commercial TV argued that US coverage of the Coronation highlighted the transatlantic horrors which ITV would import if it was allowed to go ahead. US coverage had been interspersed with advertisements. Thus, it was said, even the most sacred events in a nation's life could be degraded. Shortly before the crown was placed on Elizabeth II's head, NBC switched to an advert for Blake's shampoo which claimed that the product 'Makes Every Girl Look Queenly'. There was also a notorious interview during the Communion with a chimpanzee called J. Fred Muggs, which was asked by the show's presenter, H. V. Kaltenborn, 'Is this show put on by the British for a psychological boost to their somewhat shaky Empire?'[103] Pertinent as Kaltenborn's question was, America's coverage of the event only served to convince many people that Britain still held the cultural high ground. The comparison between insolent chimps and the reverential dignity of the BBC was not without irony. The production techniques which the corporation used to broadcast the Coronation were based on those employed by American networks during the inauguration of President Eisenhower (BBC producers had travelled to the US in 1952 to get tips from their professional cousins). That did not prevent opponents of ITV equating the BBC with the monarchy itself. According to Christopher Mayhew, broadcasting monopoly and hereditary privilege were guarantors of British democracy: 'The BBC has not in practice abused its great powers. Its monopoly is like the British monarchy – a potential dictatorship in theory and a bulwark of democracy in practice. It is a typically British institution – as typically British as commercial broadcasting is typically American.' He concluded, 'It is time we British asserted ourselves against the colossal cultural impact of America.'[104]

In the bitter Parliamentary debates on the subject which took place between November 1953 and June 1954, MPs and peers lined up to defend British traditions. Lord Reith's speech attracted the most attention. 'Hunched, mountainous and speaking with a kind of controlled ferocity', according to one observer, he compared commercial television to 'Smallpox, Bubonic Plague and the Black Death'. Audience research, the means by which broadcasters discovered what the people wanted, he described as 'subversive, a menace'. Only the 'brute force of monopoly' could maintain cultural standards and he accused those who voted for the Bill of doing 'moral hurt to Britain'. Resigning himself to what he saw as the disintegration of all that he had fought for since the 1920s, Reith concluded that 'the altar-cloth of one age . . . becomes the doormat of the next'.[105] The virulent snobbery with which the broadsheet press attacked commercial TV did the campaign even fewer favours than the self-righteous Scottish Presbyterianism which Reith brought to the debate. The *Economist* said, 'In that subtle way that is unique to this Island, it is . . . self-evident that only cads would want to have advertising on the air.'[106]

The government's initial reply to this onslaught was to reassure its opponents that commercial television would not debase popular taste. Advertisers would not be allowed any editorial control by sponsoring programmes as they were in America; there would be no adverts within two minutes of a reference to or an appearance of a member of the royal family; and an Independent Television Authority (ITA) was set up as a quality controller of the TV companies' output (a demand that 80 per cent of their programmes should be British was rejected as unworkable). Attempts were also made to remind people that, like it or not, the British owed America a great deal, not only for helping to win the war but also in helping Britain recover from it with financial aid. David Gammans accused the critics of American culture of biting the hand that fed the nation: 'Whatever may be said against the Americans . . . we might sometimes remember that American prosperity is the highest in the world and that it has produced an over-spill which has helped us and a great part of the free world to live.'[107] Gammans added that, as far as 'moral hurt' was concerned, it should be remembered that in America Christianity was as healthy as ever.

The thrust of the government's defence, however, was to accuse its opponents of elitism. In doing so, it launched the first major attack on the mid-twentieth century attempt to reform British culture.

The government claimed it was enhancing the freedom of the individual by providing Britons with more choice. The opponents of commercial television were a paternalistic clerisy, intent on foisting an
elitist vision of British culture on an unwilling nation in order to
preserve their own power and status. In the House of Commons the
ITA Director-General, Sir Ian Fraser, declared:

> What they are saying is exactly what the priests and educationalists
> said hundreds of years ago when printing presses first came into
> existence. They said, 'Do not let this get out of our hands, because
> so long as we are a select and limited few who are cultured and
> educated, so long we can keep this power for us.'[108]

It was they, and not the opposition, who were upholding British
traditions because they were defending the principle of free speech.
Britain did not have one newspaper, so why should it have only one
TV channel? Employing the best Cold War rhetoric, they made a
tacit link between the Labour Party and Soviet totalitarianism. In
the Lords, Woolton accused Beveridge of 'a peculiar strain of dictatorship', while in the Commons Gammans rounded on Herbert
Morrison.

> The critics do not trust their fellow human beings with the freedom
> of a television knob . . . one of the worst changes [in recent years]
> is the way in which governments all over the world are arrogating
> to themselves the right to decide what their subjects shall read, see,
> believe and think . . . perhaps it is well that we got freedom of the
> press when we did because there are many people who would put
> up arguments against it now.[109]

The government was not alone. Just as the Opposition included
One-Nation Tories who were concerned about the fabric of national
culture, so the government's supporters included radicals who
loathed the paternalism of 'compulsory uplift'. A Popular Television
Association was formed in July 1953, funded by Tory Central Office,
the Advertising Association and the British Chamber of Commerce.
Its members included the historian A. J. P. Taylor, the President of
CND, Canon Collins, and the father of the documentary film movement, John Grierson. Grierson, who had championed state support
for the British cinema in the 1940s, lambasted Violet Bonham
Carter for going too far. 'Let us', he said, 'prefer the competitive
spoon of the Devil to the milk-and-water handouts of this Episcopal
clinic.'[110]

Some of this support was based on self-interest – namely, the greater employment prospects which expansion of the media offered; but support for ITV also came from a new generation of artists and intellectuals which emerged in the mid-1950s, men and women who had a more pluralistic approach to British culture. One of them was Kenneth Tynan, the drama critic who heralded the arrival of the 'Angry Young Men' in 1956 and who went on to become a key figure in the cultural revolution of the 1960s. In July 1953, shortly before joining the *Observer*, where he made his name, Tynan wrote to the *Manchester Guardian*, protesting at 'the untenably pompous position you have adopted'.

I should point out to you that many of the producers at present under contract to the BBC pray, nightly, for the quick introduction of sponsorship to jog the corporation out of its apathy ... You have really been badly misled. There is no feeling against commercial TV in this country except a) among those who have a political axe to grind and b) those who have never seen and rather dislike television anyway ... Even the Puritans gave the English theatre seventy years in which to prove itself a hotbed of vice and frivolity before they closed it down in 1642. Why condemn sponsorship *unseen?*[111]

Tynan's first column for the *Observer* condemned Britain as a country 'fearful of bad taste, obsessed by the monarchy and the past'.[112] After a year of intense debate and the tabling of 206 amendments by the opposition, the Television Act was passed by Parliament on 31 July 1954 by 291 to 265 votes, thanks to a three-line Tory Whip. Clement Attlee promised that Labour would repeal the Act if it won the general election of 1955.

In March 1955, Earl De La Warr announced that Sir Kenneth Clark would be the first Chairman of the ITA. The appointment was an inspired one. Both men had helped to found the Arts Council in 1939. Unusually among his generation, Clark straddled the two socially connected but ideologically hostile wings of the Establishment which had locked horns over commercial television. His lifelong patronage of British artists, his commitment to improving popular taste, and his exhaustive, often pioneering, work for a range of national institutions to achieve both those aims made him a respected figure in the arts world. At the same time, he was a member of the landowning classes with high-society connections and conservative political convictions that were as impeccably tailored as his many suits. Consequently, he was also admired by those who remained suspicious of the arts world as a bastion of unpatriotic liberals and amoral bohemians. This rare ability to embrace both sets while retaining his personal integrity had helped him to become the most significant cultural figurehead of mid-twentieth century Britain. What made him different from most people in the arts and business worlds was that he genuinely believed television (both public and commercial) was the medium through which popular taste could be improved. Here, gathered around a flickering screen, was the mass audience which, during the war, Britain's poets, painters and composers had reached on the Home Service. He regarded the ITA as an Arts Council of the air, monitoring but not controlling the output of the new companies. If anyone could repair the fractured consensus about the direction national culture in Britain should take, it seemed to be Kenneth Mackenzie Clark.

Yet he was doomed to failure precisely because so few shared his belief in the educative potential of ITV. Its opponents regarded him as a traitor to the cause of cultural reform and their prejudice was confirmed by his inability to check the power of the TV companies or temper their profit motive. Soon after his appointment, Clark was booed as he entered the Athenaeum by the club's normally reserved members. Convinced of what he called television's 'powers for good', he pressed on with the organization of a lavish banquet to launch ITV at the Guildhall in the City of London, an event televised live before the first night's programmes. Clark was determined to bring together the two warring sides of the British elite. He managed to persuade Sir Ian Jacob and the Chairman of the BBC, Sir Alexander Cadogan, to attend after they had initially refused. They were joined by 500 politicians, businessmen and luminaries from the world of arts and entertainment.

Everything about the event was designed to reassure. ITV began broadcasting at 7.15 p.m. on 22 September 1955, opening with a shot of the capital and the former BBC announcer Leslie Mitchell saying, 'This is London,' just as he had announced the start of BBC TV in 1936. The cameras switched to the white-tied throng inside the Guildhall. Clark had chosen it as a venue because he thought it would 'link the traditional commercial centre of the Empire with this new commercial enterprise'.[113] At 7.30 p.m. Sir John Barbirolli conducted the Hallé Orchestra in a rendition of Elgar's *Cockaigne Overture*. Clark then rose to address his guests and the millions watching at home. In his steady patrician voice, he described ITV as a typically British compromise in much the same way J. M. Keynes had announced the arrival of the Arts Council nine years earlier:

> This is an historic occasion. Here is a means of communication which enters the homes of millions of our countrymen, and has an unrivalled power to persuade . . . it's a terrifying power for good or evil and hitherto it has been in the control of a single institution. Ten minutes ago it was placed in the hands of four companies . . . And what is the ITA for? The ITA is an experiment in the art of government – an attempt to solve one of the chief problems of democracy; how to combine a maximum of freedom with an ultimate direction . . . [But] free television like a free Press will not be controlled by any council or committee, but by two factors – the television companies' sense of responsibility and the fundamental good sense and right feeling of the British people.[114]

The guests then stood for the national anthem. The first adverts followed to loud cheers at 8.12 p.m., starting with SR toothpaste embedded in a block of ice, with a crisp Home Counties voice describing it as 'tingling fresh'; it was followed by adverts for chocolate and margarine.

A few months earlier, BBC executives had decided that the only way to steal ITV's thunder and prove that radio was still a force to reckoned with was 'death of a violent kind in *The Archers*'. Thus, while Sir Ian Jacob sat through Clark's launch with gritted teeth, Grace Archer was meeting a grisly end running into a burning barn to save a horse. The plan was a partial success. As if to demonstrate the 'terrifying power' of broadcasting, the press treated Grace's demise as a personal loss for all Britons, she and her kith standing as an idealized version of the wider British family. A *Manchester Guardian* headline simply said 'DEATH IN THE FAMILY'. But there was no ignoring the fact that outside the cosy world of *The Archers* a revolution in British life had taken place.

In the first two years of ITV's existence, Clark worked hard to persuade the new companies to broadcast educative programmes. At the same time, TV moguls were keen to prove that businessmen were not necessarily philistines, as indeed was the case. Clark believed that the Television Act was 'as ambiguous as the Elizabethan prayer-book'[115] and saw 'a number of ways in which the Authority could intervene and prevent the vulgarity of commercialism from having things all its own way'.[116] One was for Clark himself to present a series of programmes about the history of art on Lew Grade's ATV.

A. J. P. Taylor delivered mesmeric lectures on European history without notes; John Betjeman did a series, *Around Britain*, travelling through the countryside in a Morris Minor describing the joys of churches and manor houses in what became an equally inimitable style. All these programmes attracted millions of viewers. Clark told ATV executives:

> I am . . . touched by the wide response to my programmes. It is extraordinary that in the same day Covent Garden porters and waiters at the Ritz hotel as well as the more highbrow members of society like chemists and booksellers, should all speak approvingly of my programmes . . . we must see what else we can do to extend the medium and bridge the gap between the brows.[117]

ITV also brought a fresh approach to news and current affairs by having newsreaders on camera and encouraging a more relaxed, friendly manner than the starched voices Britons were used to hearing. One of the recruits was the combative, bow-tied interviewer Robin Day, the first of a new generation who refused to defer to politicians in his attempt to get the truth out of them. He recalled, 'ITN set new standards of rigour, enterprise and pace . . . making the BBC version look stiff and stuffy, which it was. Ludicrous taboos were swept away by the post-1955 wind of change.'[118] In 1957, the American journalist Vance Packard called advertisers the 'Hidden Persuaders'. As a result of commercial television, they became rather more visible. Between 1950 and 1960, the amount spent on advertising in the UK almost trebled, from £162 million a year to £454 million.[119] But adverts in the Isles retained their national character. The industry took note of the British dislike of showiness and intrusion, as a result of which the 'in your face' selling style of the US was tempered by the gentle, ironic sense of humour which the British prided themselves on. According to the *News Chronicle*, adverts were 'muffled, as if making their entrance like well-mannered tradesmen at the side door'.[120] All of which caused a few words to be eaten. Even Reith swallowed his gargantuan pride and paid Clark a visit to ask for a post at the ITA (Clark wisely refused).

The honeymoon did not last. The enormous start-up costs of the television companies meant they were making huge losses in the first year and the first programmes to suffer were educational since with a few exceptions they received the smallest audiences. ITV bosses pressured the Eden government to be allowed more leeway, and by the autumn of 1956 the time devoted to serious features each week (excluding the news) had nearly halved, from four hours fifty minutes to two hours thirty minutes. 'The Tory gang moved in,' noted Clark, and despite requests to stay he resigned his post in October 1957. He continued to believe that TV 'was the most potent instrument of diffusion yet to appear ... bringing the fine arts home to millions who have hitherto enjoyed a marginal acquaintance with them ... Through television we are all one.'[121] But the experiment was effectively over. Roland Gillet, the Controller of Associated Rediffusion, wrote: 'Let's face it once and for all. The public likes girls, wrestling, bright musicals, quiz shows and real-life drama. We gave them the Hallé orchestra ... and visits to the local fire station. Well, we've learned. From now on, what the public wants, it's going to get.'[122] People still turned to the BBC during great state occasions and when there was a national or international crisis. But commercial TV took off. Its overall audience share was already 58 per cent in the spring of 1956 and by the end of 1957 it had risen to a staggering 72 per cent. The haemorrhaging of the BBC's audience was exacerbated by the fact that ITV poached many of the corporation's leading technicians, producers and performers.

Of more concern to the guardians of Britishness was the fact that ITV imported many American shows such as *Bonanza*, which had Britons glued to their new sets. Programmes made domestically also showed the influence of America which the BBC had held in check since the 1920s. The quiz show *Double your Money* was typical. Based on the US show *The $64,000 Question*, it ran from 1955 to 1968 and was hosted by Hughie Green, a Canadian born to Scottish émigrés in 1920 who had been a child star of stage and screen before the war. Green also hosted *Opportunity Knocks*, which combined music-hall variety with the talent competitions popular in working-men's clubs and Butlin's holiday camps. He glued these components together with glitzy US production techniques. The show had been rejected by the BBC in the early 1950s and under the aegis of ATV it went on to attract 25 million viewers. Green auditioned 10,000 acts each year, of which 175 were chosen, among them future stars like Peters and Lee, Freddie Starr and Les Dawson. Its most innovative feature was the 'clapometer', the first device designed to measure audience reactions so that they decided who won rather than the usual panel of worthies. Green's unctuous catchphrase, delivered in his mid-Atlantic drawl, 'Isn't that wonderful? I mean that most sincerely, folks!' came to epitomize everything which Britain's cultural elites loathed about ITV. Another influential Canadian with

Scottish origins was Roy Thomson, owner of the *Scotsman* and Scottish TV (STV). Thomson more than doubled the money he had invested in STV. His gleeful observation that commercial broadcasting was 'a licence to print money' provoked outrage among those already livid at the vulgarity of commercial broadcasting.[123]

What effect did the media revolution of the 1950s have on national identity? The answer is a great deal, and it was entirely positive. Until satellite broadcasting fragmented the audience of both terrestrial stations in the 1990s, ITV augmented the BBC's fostering of Britishness. It did this in two ways. First, contracts were awarded on a national and regional basis. Scotland had STV, Wales TWW (later Harlech TV) and Northern Ireland Ulster TV. From the start, their programming made an effort to reflect the cultures of each and were popular for doing so, especially in Ireland where Ulster TV was seen as a recognition of the statelet's right to exist. The Prime Minister, Brookeborough, welcomed it as 'a vote of confidence in the stability of the Northern Ireland government'; the *Belfast Telegraph* saw it as 'the symbol ... of Ulster's prestige, intelligence and culture.'[124] Compared to ITV, the BBC had been reluctant to accommodate other parts of the UK. Studios were opened in Edinburgh and Cardiff in 1952 and, after nationalist pressure, Broadcasting Councils were set up for each country a year later. The *Glasgow Herald* commented, 'It should be clearly understood that the occasion heralds television in Scotland, not Scottish television. For an indefinite time, most of the programmes viewed will come from the south.'[125] The paper was right. The new BBC studios were not autonomous units with any degree of editorial freedom. Consequently, non-English viewers saw few home-made programmes which expressed their way of life. Separate news bulletins for each country were not broadcast until 1957 and the amount of air time given to them became a bone of contention between nationalists and unionists for the rest of the century. Such was the success of ITV in countering southern dominance that in 1956 Parliament launched an official inquiry into TWW, accusing it of deliberately fostering nationalism in Wales. The company was cleared, despite its frank admission that one of its aims was to heighten Welsh consciousness.

Second, by making programmes that were universally popular across the UK, the ITV network brought millions more Britons together in a shared experience around the TV set, adding to the programmes they discussed at work or in the pub the next day. Most of its output was not from the US. Variety shows are a case in point.

Over 100 music halls closed down between 1945 and 1958 and by the early 1960s they had virtually disappeared. News of the death of Victorian culture was premature, however, because the format was simply transferred to TV in shows like *Saturday Night at the Palladium*. Many programmes that were American in origin became distinctively British as they were remodelled for native audiences. One was *This is Your Life*, in which the genial Irish host, Eamon Andrews, interviewed a range of home-grown celebrities, bringing on their family, friends and colleagues to offer anecdote and tribute (the cricketer C. B. Fry, the comedian Tommy Trinder and the actors Dame Flora Robson and Richard Todd were among those who appeared in early shows). It started in 1955 and was still running at the century's end, with average audiences of 13 million.

In 1955, Eamon Andrews commented, 'There is nothing that brings you closer to eternity than making an advertisement for television'.[126] This might appear to be a contradiction of Geoffrey Fisher's comment that the Coronation placed the nation on the threshold of Heaven. Not entirely. *This is Your Life* was a two-dimensional *Dictionary of National Biography* for the age of mass democracy. It helped to memorialize national heroes, imprinting their personality and achievements on the national mind and thereby contributing to a popular sense of Britishness. The *Dictionary*, whose aims these had been when first compiled in 1905, never reached out to a mass audience – partly because its subjects were politicians, intellectuals and civil servants, and partly because it was unaffordable to most people.

This is Your Life was also significant because it was one of the first programmes produced by the BBC in an effort to compete with its new rival. The success of ITV forced the corporation to rethink its historic mission to foster national culture. In 1957, after relentless criticism of the Third Programme's pathetic audience figures, the BBC cut its schedule by 40 per cent. A year later, expenditure on TV exceeded that for sound broadcasting for the first time. The great and the good lined up to condemn the social, psychological and physical effects of a nation slumped in its armchairs, mesmerized by a new visual opiate. 1957 saw the launch of the Third Programme Defence Society, which included Laurence Olivier, Ralph Vaughan Williams and T. S. Eliot, the last of whom wrote to *The Times* protesting that the corporation was 'lowering the standards of culture at home and lowering the prestige of Britain abroad' by pandering 'to the more moronic elements in our society'.[127] The reappraisal was clearly going to be a long and painful one. But the BBC had at least made a start.

The novelty of television did wear off after a while (audience research showed that it took the average family five years after purchase to break away from their sets and restore some traditional family activities). But the change in habits was still massive. The number of TV licences rose from 45,000 in 1947 to 7.5 million in 1957. In 1947, two-thirds of the population had never even seen a TV set. A decade later half the adult population watched it regularly. Within a few years of the Coronation, television went from being the whimsical distraction of a few wealthy people to the main leisure pursuit of the nation. The experience was, wrote one social historian of the time, 'the most extraordinary example of sustained "togetherness" in our national history'.[128]

6. We were the world

In a family sports guide published in 1947, the former cricket and tennis champion Lord Aberdare wrote: 'throughout our history one of the great strengths of our national character has been a capacity for playing games ... after a long period of hardships and rationing, few factors are more likely to restore the country to [its] natural strength and vigour than a correct and wise use of leisure ... We must remain what we have long been, a nation of games players, and not merely a nation of spectators at the arena'.[129] British sport initially suffered as a result of television. TV coverage turned millions from spectators into armchair fans. The introduction of *Sportsview* (1954), *Grandstand* (1958), *Match of the Day* (1964) and *World of Sport* (1965) were the landmarks. Added to which, sport had to compete with the wider choice of recreation that became available as a result of affluence. Football was affected the most by these developments. From its peak in the season 1948–9, when 41.2 million people passed through Britain's turnstiles, the figure fell dramatically to 27.6 million in 1964–5. The decline pushed many smaller clubs into bankruptcy including one of the oldest, Accrington Stanley. However, while Parliament was furiously debating the future of TV during the 1953–4 season, an event occurred which began the transformation of British football from an ailing working-class pursuit into a mass obsession that dominated national identity in Britain.

On 25 November 1953, the Olympic gold-medal-winning Hungarian football team beat England at Wembley 6–3 in a dazzling display of fast, short-passing play led by their captain, Ferenc Puskas. It was the first time that England had been beaten at home by a foreign side in ninety years of Association Football. The defeat reminded the English that their fortunes had changed since the war and it stirred them into following their team more closely. Hungary's victory overshadowed the elation of Everest and Roger Bannister's breaking the four-minute mile in May 1954, both of which were the achievements of amateur pursuits with little mass appeal. Football, on the other hand, was the most popular sport in Britain, where it had been invented sometime in the twelfth century. However, it fostered contrasting allegiances in the UK which tell us much about national identities in the twentieth.

In Ulster, soccer was primarily the sport of the Protestant majority, while Catholics followed Gaelic football and hurling. After partition, the North's few Catholic soccer clubs waged a long struggle to join the Southern Irish league, until, in 1954, FIFA finally recognized the Northern Ireland FA and ordered them to play for it. But with the noble exception of Derry City, clubs in Ulster did not develop cross-sectarian management or support. As a result, football never had the power to foster a common Northern Irish identity. In Wales, rugby union became the most popular sport in the 1870s and remained a focal point of Welshness thereafter. Wales had its own Football Association, but most clubs played in the English league and they, together with the national team, were poorly supported. The main reason for the supremacy of rugby in the principality was that (unofficially at least) it was professional, whereas in most other parts of the Isles it was an amateur activity followed by the middle classes. Miners and mineowners, labourers and landowners (and even a few ministers from the chapels) not only played and watched rugby together, they also supported it financially by contributing to players' wages and facilities. The opposition of the English-dominated Rugby Football Union to this practice simply hardened attitudes and reinforced the Welsh sense of difference at a time when the people of the principality were trying to re-establish their unique nationality. Because Welsh rugby utilized the talents of all social classes, by the 1930s the national team had become the best in the Isles. Its many

victories, particularly those over England, added to the fierce patriotism which the sport generated.

In Scotland, football fostered national identity more than anywhere else in the UK. Club loyalties could be intense (especially in
the bitter sectarian rivalries of Celtic v. Rangers and Hibernians v.
Hearts). But most Scots were intensely patriotic about their national
team because it provided a rare opportunity to express their uniqueness outside the traditional institutions of Church, law and education. The annual 'Home International' between England and
Scotland was the focus of soccer patriotism north of the border.
Inaugurated in 1872, it was the first international match to be played
in the world and from 1924 onwards it was staged alternately at
Glasgow's Hampden Park and London's Wembley Stadium. By the
1930s, the biannual trek of 60,000 Scots to Wembley had become a
huge patriotic jamboree, funded among poorer fans by savings clubs
run in pubs and factories. Replete with bagpipes, drums and banners
commemorating military victories over the English, football's 'Tartan
Army' consciously echoed the southern march of Bonnie Prince
Charlie's 5,500 troops in 1745. Women would see their menfolk off
at railway stations, doing jigs on the platform known as 'war dances'.
The whole event was, remembers one player, 'a chance to knock the
lion off its pedestal'.[130] The event was also seen as evidence of the
tenacious Scottish character; that dogged determination to compete
equally with its larger neighbour (it succeeded, winning forty matches
compared to England's forty-three in the fixture's 118 year history).

In contrast, the English paid much less attention to their team and
were bemused by the Scots' attitude to the Home International. The
difference between the two countries was strikingly apparent at
Hampden Park in 1948. Field Marshal Montgomery stepped on to
the turf to a deafening roar from 135,000 people. He made a point
of chatting for an equal length of time to the captains Tom Finney
and Willie Thornton, both of whom had served under him in the
Eighth Army in North Africa. But to Monty's evident discomfort,
the Hampden roar was not a celebration of the Anglo-Scottish unity
fostered during the war and symbolized by Finney, Thornton and
himself. It was for the Scottish team, and what the thousands present
desperately hoped would be a thumping victory against the Auld
Enemy.

In the early postwar period, the English still regarded cricket as
the sport which most embodied their national character: patience,

modesty, and of course a love of fair play. In fact, the original eighteenth-century game was characterized by raucous, sometimes violent behaviour by players and spectators alike. No matter. The moral vocabulary of the sport, developed during the heyday of the gentleman amateur in the late nineteenth century, survived the rise of the professional in the interwar period. 'It is far more than a game,"' wrote Neville Cardus in 1945, 'it somehow holds a mirror up to English nature'.[131] In 1960 the Wolfenden Committee on Sport and the Community reported, 'It is easy to ridicule the "that's not cricket old boy" attitude, but . . . it still provides the foundations of an ethical standard which may not be highly intellectual but does have a considerable influence on the day-to-day behaviour of millions of people'.[132]

Star batsmen were especially valued. They became the first national heroes in England's history who were not military men or explorers and they were the first sports people in Britain to receive public honours. Denis Compton, the greatest batsman of the early postwar period, also played football for Arsenal. But it was cricket which Compton regarded as the national sport. 'Cricket is of England', he wrote, 'From the greatest downwards an interest in [it] unites the people'.[133] The sport was run by Britain's governing classes through one of the UK's most conservative institutions, the MCC (Tory minister Walter Monckton remarked that next to the MCC, the most right-wing members of Churchill's cabinet were 'a band of pinkos').[134] Despite this, cricket's ability to promote social harmony was widely celebrated. Although played in both town and country, its historic spirit was seen to reside in rural England; in the village cricket match during which squires, labourers and their wives forgot their differences over a square cut to long-on and cucumber sandwiches at tea. In 1947, Vita Sackville-West wrote, 'the young gentleman from Eton and the son of the village blacksmith meet on equal terms . . . It is a . . . sort of cement, welding our queer ramshackle nation together'.[135] As well as narrowing the class divide, cricket also maintained a sense of the imperial family. The annual summer test matches against Commonwealth teams were an integral part of the English calendar long after the British lost their enthusiasm for empire. The mass appeal of Test Series was augmented by the BBC's commentary team, the most famous of whom were seen to embody English virtues almost as much as the players themselves. The long partnership of John Arlott, a stolid former Hampshire police constable, and Brian Johnstone, a jaunty Old Etonian and former Guards Officer, symbolized for millions the social compact which the sport encouraged.

Football, however, was a predominantly urban working-class pursuit which in England fostered local and regional identities rather than a national one. During the Second World War the League's three divisions had been reduced to two, Northern and Southern. And in peacetime, from 1922 until 1959, the Third Division was permanently split into North and South sections. But it went deeper than that. Since the English game had become properly organized in the 1860s, it had been administratively split along north–south lines. Soccer was further undermined by the class conflicts that so often accompanied that geographical fissure. The sport's governing body – the Football Association – was based in London and, like the MCC, it was a bastion of public-school amateurism. Its executives treated even great players like Stanley Matthews as if they were unruly Dickensian urchins who ought to be patriotic enough not to take the field for England without being paid for it (Matthews called them 'the blazer brigade').[136] When the FA selected the national team, men were often chosen on the basis of long service to their clubs or because of the local loyalties of selection panel members. The Football League, based in Lancashire and run by self-made northern businessmen, did not help. The long, grinding seasons it administered wore out the nation's best players and they were given little opportunity to train together because clubs were reluctant to release them for national duty. When the England team competed, men wore their shirts with pride and Wembley was full. But for players and fans as much as for the sport's executives, club football was more important.

British soccer was also more insular than cricket, despite the fact that by the 1930s it had become the world's most popular sport. The Foreign Office was aware of its diplomatic potential (in 1938 it ordered the England team to give the Nazi salute before a match against Germany in Berlin).[137] But there was no imperial structure to the game, and the rest of the world's footballers were regarded as children requiring tuition from the game's inventors. The international federation of football associations, FIFA, was set up by the French in 1904. But the four British associations did not join on a permanent basis until 1947, having spent the first half of the century fighting a losing battle to take absolute control of the sport. Even then, the British regarded the rest of the world with condescension.

The Scottish FA expressed the hope that Europe would benefit from the four nations' membership:

> Some things are allowed in continental tactics which are alien to our British game, but in the main, these variations are caused by temperament and may in the course of time disappear as a result of more frequent contact with British teams and British style of play and standards of sportsmanship.[138]

For the first time ever, a united British soccer team took the field in 1947, playing at Hampden Park against a Rest of Europe side to celebrate joining FIFA. Great Britain won 6–1. The result seemed to confirm that the British were, in the words of the *Daily Express*, 'the bosses of soccer'.[139] This arrogance coloured attitudes to the World Cup. It was inaugurated in 1930, but UK teams did not compete until 1950, and it was not until the 1958 finals in Sweden that the World Cup began to be seen as a significant event by the British people. Interest in the competition owed a lot to the extensive TV coverage it got from 1958 onwards. But what fundamentally changed the cultural role of football in England was the defeat by Hungary five years earlier.

England had lost at cricket to Commonwealth teams since 1900. But cricket was played within the confines of the imperial family and defeat did not undermine national pride to the same extent because test matches were then regarded as little more than home internationals. This match was lost against a European team deemed to be wholly foreign. The fact that it was a communist country (Hungary's players were resplendent in a cherry-red strip) added to the sense of national humiliation. *The Times'* football correspondent, Geoffrey Green, wrote that captain Billy Wright and his men were 'strangers in a strange world . . . of flitting red spirits'. It was, he said, 'Agincourt in reverse'.

> England at last were beaten by the foreign invader on English soil . . . [The Hungarians] have won a most precious prize by their rich, overflowing, and to English patriots unbelievable victory . . . over an English side that was cut to ribbons for most of an astonishing afternoon. Here, indeed, did we attend, all 100,000 of us, the twilight of the Gods.[140]

The significance of the event has been vastly underestimated by historians. The ninety minutes of football which twenty-two men in baggy shorts played on a fog-shrouded piece of turf in a north-west suburb of London in November 1953 helped to alter the trajectory of Britishness.

From that day on, football began to replace cricket as the game seen by most social classes to embody the nation's character and the game upon which England's international sporting reputation rested. Stanley Matthews, who in 1965 became the first British footballer to be knighted, was never cautioned by a referee in his entire career. He was celebrated as much because he represented the English tradition of fair play as for his sporting prowess. This trend survived the rise of hooliganism off the pitch, with the England team regularly winning FIFA's Fair Play award at World Cup finals. There were three long-term consequences of soccer's supremacy. First, its rise at cricket's expense accelerated the waning of imperial loyalties and underpinned England's gradual re-engagement with the Continent, because the sport's governing body and most of its great teams were based there and not in South Africa or Pakistan. Second, as respect for the institutions of monarchy, Church and Parliament declined, football's new popularity enabled it to replace those institutions as *the* focal point of English national identity. All of which had a crucial impact on Anglo-Scottish relations. Because cricket was disregarded by the Scots, sport had not traditionally been a source of rivalry and antagonism between the two countries. But once football became an outlet for English patriotism in the same way that it was for the Scots, battle was joined, and the game was turned from a shared leisure pursuit into the crucible of national tensions within the Union.

The Hungarian victory was not the cause of that change but it was undoubtedly the catalyst for them. The sports historian Richard Holt has written:

> At heart the English felt football was their property and were disinclined to co-operate with foreigners. Admiration for the originators of the game tempered Continental irritation with this variant of 'splendid isolation' . . . But by the time England started to take the rest of the world seriously, the rest of the world no longer had anything to learn from us. [After 1953] it was no longer possible to look down on these faintly ludicrous foreigners trying to play our game. It was the chauvinistic condescension of the English themselves that now seemed foolish.[141]

The English did not like to be made to look foolish. Hungary's 'flitting red spirits' made them realize the true state of international football and, stung by that realization, they began to take it much more seriously.

The post-mortem continued for the rest of the decade. In 1954, *Picture Post*'s Denzil Batchelor wrote:

> I do not believe that in the foreseeable future, England will again dominate the world of football. She gave the game to the world, as she gave in the past lawn tennis and Rugby, cricket and boxing . . . In the beginning we were not the champions of the world – we were the world. Then we became, with the passage of time, not the whole class, but at least the top of the class. And now, let us face the truth, we are nowhere near the top.

'What', he asked, 'were the lessons to be learned from the crushing defeat that brought about the end of an era?' Like most commentators, Batchelor blamed the insularity of the English for the defeat. 'We do not regard the foreign challenge as paramount,' he concluded; 'it is not an outlook which will win a World cup . . . it is not a soil from which a strong plant, a glorious flower, and a rich crop are likely to greet the sun.'[142] Little over a decade later a glorious flower did greet the sun. Its roots were laid by a thirty-three-year-old Spurs right-back who played his last match for England on that fateful night against the Hungarians: Alfred Ernest Ramsey.

Meanwhile, for the Scots who ignored the portents of Wembley, the moment of truth came in Switzerland in 1954 at their first appearance in the World Cup finals. While SFA officials argued about whether they should be there at all, Scotland lost to Uruguay 7–1. Despite the SFA's reluctance to take foreigners seriously, the Scottish team was already a focus for national identity, so a firmer basis for the game's renewal existed north of the border.

Several underlying trends helped to change attitudes to soccer in England. To begin with, the number of municipal cricket fields fell sharply. Unlike soccer, which could be played effectively in back streets and parks, cricket required large grass pitches which were expensive to maintain. From 1918 onwards, much of this valuable urban land was sold to property developers and working-class cricket clubs (particularly those in the north) were forced to disband. The Duke of Edinburgh's patronage of the National Playing Fields Association failed to halt the decline. Crowds still flocked to see the big Test Matches but little else. By 1977, more than half of all cricket spectators were over forty-five and two-thirds belonged to social classes I and II.[143] Because the majority of Englishmen were denied the facilities enjoyed by their forebears, they played cricket less and less (only 1.5 per cent of the adult population by 1983, compared to 20 per cent for football).[144] The long-term result of this was that the MCC had to rely more on the public schools, which in turn meant that the quality of the England team declined. This coincided with a dramatic improvement in the quality of West Indian and Asian national teams. Consequently by the end of the century England had fallen to the bottom of the world rankings, apart from some brief revivals, and cricket's ability to generate patriotism had been seriously damaged.

While cricket lost much of its working-class following, football began to gain a middle-class one. There were three reasons for this. First, the decline of Sabbatarianism in England led the FA to sanction Sunday Leagues in 1960 after decades of opposition from the Churches. In 1948, there were 17,973 amateur clubs affiliated to the FA; by 1985 this had risen to 41,069, many of which were based in affluent suburban areas.[145] By the end of the century football had replaced cricket as the main amateur sport in England and had become far and away the most popular physical recreation of the adult male (and a good few women too). Second, the massive growth of TV coverage, and the commercialism it brought with it, enabled professional football to reach a wider audience – not least because people who did not care to rub shoulders with the masses on windswept terraces could now enjoy the sport in the comfort of their living rooms (the MCC and its successor, the TCCB, resisted commercial sponsorship until the 1970s). Third, after England's defeat in 1953, the media as a whole took a much closer interest in the team's fortunes and whipped up patriotic fervour whenever it played. In the space of a few years, football moved from the back page to the front page, in broadsheets as well as tabloids.

Although the expansion of the grass-roots game evidenced a growing interest in the sport, the continuation of the amateur spirit at FA headquarters was less productive. The institutional inertia of the FA meant that improvements in the management and coaching of the England team were slow to come. The resulting combination of raised expectations and the failure to quite live up to them made for a febrile atmosphere which lent itself to xenophobia. In all sports, the modest, cheerful patriotism of the early postwar years began to be replaced by a more self-conscious, aggressive nationalism, as

Britons sought solace in sporting achievements for the UK's declining world power. However, the old affinity with empire was not initially replaced by a new affinity with Europe, and this ideological vacuum was especially apparent in football.

Soccer's governing bodies remained hostile to the Continent throughout the 1950s, a fact highlighted by their response to the creation of the European Cup in 1955. On 2 April of that year, the French newspaper *L'Equipe* convened a meeting of European football clubs at the Ambassador Hotel in Paris which set up the European Cup, a knockout competition for the champions of every country. Executives of the English League issued an edict from their headquarters at Lytham St Anne's in Lancashire preventing Chelsea from participating in the first competition held in the 1955–6 season. The Scots did not stand on their pride and entered straight away. It was a Scot, Matt Busby, who defied the League and took Manchester United to the Continent in 1956–7. It was therefore fitting that a Scottish club, Celtic, became the first British club to win the competition, in 1967. When Manchester United lost most of its players in a plane crash on an icy Munich runway in 1958, to many people it demonstrated that foreign competition was not worth it. The anti-European mood in sport reflected that which prevailed in British politics.

In the same summer that the European Cup was founded, talks were taking place at Messina in Sicily between the six countries of the Iron and Steel Community. Despite a few hiccups along the way, Messina led directly to the signing of the Treaty of Rome on 25 March 1957, which marked the effective birth of the European Union. Anthony Eden had always been a sceptic. Since the war, he had curbed the qualified enthusiasm of Churchill and ministerial colleagues like Harold Macmillan. After becoming Prime Minister in April 1955, he ensured that Britain played little part in the Messina talks. He sent an obscure under-secretary at the Board of Trade, Russell Bretherton, as an observer (it is significant that until 1960 European integration was resolutely discussed by the British Cabinet under the heading 'Commercial Policy'). Things got off to a bad start. When a senior French official rang London to invite the British to attend, he was told that Messina was 'a devilishly awkward place to expect a minister to get to'.[146] One of the architects of the European Economic Community, the Belgian Paul-Henri Spaak, met Rab Butler in London in an attempt to alter British policy. He implored Butler to imagine a different future for the nation state, but this did not appeal to Butler's empirical Anglo-Saxon mind. Spaak remembered, 'I don't think I could have shocked him more, when I appealed to his imagination, than if I had taken my trousers off.'[147]

Even Europhiles like the British Ambassador to France, Gladwyn Jebb, thought Messina was unimportant. In June he wired London, saying, 'No very spectacular developments are to be expected . . . progress towards European integration in the next few months will be purely verbal.'[148] At Messina in November, the moustachioed Bretherton observed the proceedings with an icy silence. Towards the end of the conference, he rose and addressed it:

> The future treaty which you are discussing has no chance of being agreed; if it was agreed, it would have no chance of being ratified; and if it were ratified, it would have no chance of being applied. And if it was applied, it would be totally unacceptable to Britain. You speak of agriculture which we don't like, of power over customs, which we take exception to, and institutions, which frighten us. Monsieur le president, messieurs, au revoir et bonne chance.[149]

With that, Bretherton picked up his briefcase, left the room and did not return. The cold shoulder which Britain turned to the Continent in 1955 was a broad one which encompassed most of Britain's elite, left and right.

There were three reasons for their scepticism. First, they felt a sentimental attachment to the Special Relationship with America which, for all the resentment about America's growing influence on Britain, still counted in the mid-1950s. Second, there was a disdainful attitude to Continentals which the war had exacerbated. Even the more sympathetic officials thought the EEC would collapse under the weight of the historic tensions between its member states. Third, the Empire still mattered to Britain's elites. Economically, it was vital. Until 1960, 67 per cent of Britain's exports and 92 per cent of her foreign investment went outside Europe. Out of this, the Empire made up by far the biggest proportion, accounting for 51 and 60 per cent respectively. Similarly, most of Britain's essential imports still came from the Empire: 66 per cent of her wool and 50 per cent of her butter from Australasia; 50 per cent of non-ferrous metals from South Africa and Canada and, crucially, 82 per cent of her oil from the Middle East.

Politically, Britain's elites were still committed to the imperial mission and they were attached to the status which the Empire brought them. As Eden put it, 'These are our family ties. That is our life; without it we should be no more than some millions of people living on an island off the coast of Europe, in which nobody wants to take any particular interest.'[150] Although the jingoism of the late Victorian era had waned, the idea of 'trusteeship' forged in the interwar period was still prevalent in Whitehall; it underpinned the British attempt to cling on to the vestiges of imperial power by turning the Empire into a more democratic Commonwealth of nations. Trusteeship was essentially a development of Kipling's idea of the white man's burden: British imperialism, it argued, was a gentlemanly, Christian and above all democratic form of rule. From the abolition of slavery to decolonization, it selflessly sought to civilize native peoples, bringing them the freedom and prosperity which Britons enjoyed. During the rise of fascism and communism in the 1930s and again during the Cold War in the 1950s, it was also presented as a more effective United Nations. The Commonwealth, went the argument, was a protective umbrella in a dangerous world under which smaller, poorer nations might shelter. They were tutored in the ways of British democracy not in order to take their chances in the rain but so they could help the British to hold on to the umbrella.

The Commonwealth was an attempt to return to the more informal Empire of the eighteenth century, to maintain Britain's international prestige and prosperity but replacing gunboat diplomacy with the economic and political development of former colonies. The return to an informal Empire seemed to have two advantages. First, policy-makers hoped it would contain colonial nationalism by appealing to moderate native leaders. Second, it would be cheaper to run, a major consideration since Britain could no longer afford the extensive network of military garrisons and civil servants which had kept the maps pink before the war. The Coronation had been a display of traditional British might. But behind the scenes a skirmish took place about the title with which Elizabeth should be proclaimed Queen; a skirmish that revealed how much had changed since the war.

Churchill wanted the Proclamation of 1937 to be issued unaltered, with its references to 'the Imperial Crown of Great Britain, Ireland and the British dominions beyond the seas'. These terms did not take account of India's independence in 1947 nor of Éire's departure from the Commonwealth in 1948 following the declaration of the Repub-

lic, never mind the growing number of colonial nationalist movements. In an attempt to be diplomatic, Churchill circulated a
personally prepared historical note to the Cabinet, in which he
attempted to show that the term 'Imperial Crown' was a product not
of high Victorian imperialism but of sixteenth-century English
nationalism, in which Henry VIII merely used the term to obtain
independence from the Papacy. The Cabinet were not convinced that
such historical niceties would be accepted either by Britons or by
foreigners. With Ministers unable to confront the great man, the task
fell to the Cabinet Secretary, Sir Norman Brook, who respectfully
but firmly explained the political realities which lay behind the pomp
and circumstance being staged by the Duke of Norfolk:

> We cannot restore the Empire of the 19th century by talking as
> though it still existed ... In 1949 we had to choose between an
> Imperial club, restricted to the nations of British blood, and a
> wider association in which there was room for coloured peoples
> who had won their way, under British tutelage, to independence.
> The first course would have been more comfortable for a time; but
> in the long run it meant suicide – for the Empire would have
> dwindled away as, one by one, the colonies achieved independence.
> The second at least gave us hope of holding by sentiment, in a free
> association of independent peoples, all that we once held by
> empire.[151]

Churchill gave way and the Proclamation was altered to 'Elizabeth
II, by the Grace of God Queen of this Realm and Territories, Head
of the Commonwealth'. On paper at least, the End of Empire was
now official. However, as Norman Brook's comment showed, the
British had not fully relinquished the idea that Britain was still a
superpower. Concluding his meditation on 'Coronation blues', J. H.
Huizinga wrote: 'There were many who were ... fully aware that
underneath all the rousing pomp of a Coronation ... there lay the
reality of Britain's vastly diminished status and power. But, it seemed
to me, there was a great difference between intellectual recognition
and emotional acceptance of the fact that the country had gone down
in the world.'[152] It needed a seismic humiliation to translate that
intellectual recognition into emotional acceptance and in twelve
months from 1955 to 1956 the British got it.

Two separate incidents woke them up: the Burgess and Maclean
spy scandal and the Suez crisis. Guy Burgess and Donald Maclean,
two public-school, Cambridge-educated senior Foreign Office offi-

cials disappeared to the Soviet Union in June 1951. After persistent rumours that they had been Soviet spies, the government admitted as much on 18 September 1955 when it published a White Paper detailing the case. A national outcry followed. It was fuelled by speculation about a 'Third Man'. His identity was eventually confirmed in 1963 as Kim Philby. The former First Secretary at the British Embassy in Washington and an undergraduate friend of the other two, he fled to Moscow in January of that year. The last major spy scandal in Britain had been Sir Roger Casement's work for the IRA during the First World War. But this betrayal went much further. In a furious speech to the House of Lords in 1955, Viscount Astor said: 'For the first time since the reign of the first Queen Elizabeth we have a Fifth Column in this country that has penetrated the highest ranks of the civil service and apparently scientists – even the Church.'[153]

Sometimes, the historic parallel between the communists of New Elizabethan Britain and the Catholics of Elizabethan England was made in an effort to convince the public that spies were patriots too. Catholic novelist Graham Greene was a good friend of Kim Philby. Introducing the spy's bestselling memoirs, *My Silent War*, he concluded that patriotism was a movable feast and that everyone was guilty of moving it to suit their personal ideals at some point in life: ' "He betrayed his country" – yes perhaps he did, but who among us has not committed treason to something or someone more important than a country? In Philby's own eyes he was working for a shape of things to come from which his country would benefit.'[154] The British had no wish to embark on the witch-hunt of communists carried out in the US by Senator McCarthy, on the oft-expressed grounds that it would be against the principles of British democracy to do so. But they were unconvinced by the arguments offered in mitigation of the spies' betrayal of their country. Most Britons did not believe patriotism was a movable feast. However dissatisfied you were with your country, you did not betray it. The Oxford historian Hugh Trevor-Roper dismissed Greene's argument as 'an engaging historical fantasy'.[155]

The great spy scandal did not breed complacency. Quite the opposite. The British were made to look fools. The Americans, though not without their own security problems, were able to assert their moral superiority as leaders of the Western world. Richard Dimbleby's Coronation claim that the Americans were 'so lacking in tradition' now seemed horribly complacent. What price tradition when Britain's national security had been so badly compromised? The affair prompted widespread accusations that the public-school-educated ruling caste was responsible for the amateurish bungling of the affair and for the wider conspiracy of silence which had protected the spies for so long. The MI5 officer Peter Wright confirmed these suspicions. His vetting in 1954 consisted, he said, of 'a Masonic handshake, a brief chat about politics, and the embarrassed question "Ever been queer by any chance?" '[156]

The affair also led directly to the coining of the term 'Establishment'. The man who coined it was a maverick thirty-one-year-old Scottish journalist, Henry Fairlie. Writing in the *Spectator* in September 1955, he argued that the 'matrix of official and social relations' which had protected Burgess and Maclean included not only political, military and religious leaders but also 'such lesser mortals as the Chairman of the Arts Council, the Director-General of the BBC and even the editor of the *Times* Literary Supplement'. These were the same people who opposed the media revolution and generally failed to utilize the talents of the working and lower-middle classes. The Establishment claimed to be serving the public but in fact, concluded Fairlie, 'it responds to no deep-seated national instinct'.[157] The popular press was equally dismissive. The *Daily Herald* said: 'WRONG MEN, RIGHT TIES – We want a little fresh air in the place, fresh minds, men who don't know, and what is more, don't care, what school anyone went to.'[158] The *Sunday Express* agreed: 'It is time we made these official mistake-makers realise that this isn't an old-school-tie society. That they are the servants of the nation, not its masters.'[159] Insiders admitted the truth of these accusations. Robert Cecil was Maclean's assistant at the Washington Embassy. He was also a descendant of William Cecil, the man who had set up the secret service during Elizabeth I's reign in order to protect England from Catholic subversion. Looking back on the 1950s, Robert Cecil wrote:

The Diplomatic Service, which had withstood the brute impact of war, had not yet adjusted itself to the more insidious pressures of the Cold War. The virtues of sportsmanship, plain speaking and fair play, for which Englishmen had been famous in an earlier and happier epoch, did not equip them to meet the subtler challenges of ideology and deception. It was the case of Burgess and Maclean that taught the necessary lesson and, for this reason, deserves to be remembered.[160]

Embarrassing and unsettling though the affair was, it was not sufficiently humiliating to force the British Establishment to take full stock of itself. That task fell to an Egyptian nationalist, General Gamal Abdel Nasser. In the autumn of 1956, just as Manchester United's pioneers were taking on the football teams of Europe, a crisis began to escalate in the Middle East. It dealt the Empire a fatal blow and forced Britain's political leaders to follow football stars to the Continent. Three years after Puskas found the net at Wembley, Nasser blew the whistle on British supremacy.

PART 4

SHOPPERS

I . . . cannot understand why the younger generation, instead of knocking at the door, should bash the fuck out of it.

Noël Coward, 1957

Britain is insular, bound up by its trade, its markets . . . with the most varied and often the most distant countries. Her activity is essentially industrial, commercial, not agricultural. She has, in all her work, very special, very original habits and traditions. In short, the nature, structure, circumstances, peculiar to Britain are different from those of the other continentals . . . How can Britain, being what she is, come into our system?

Charles de Gaulle, 1963

1. Holding by sentiment

The Suez Canal was built in 1859–69 to open up European trade routes to the east. In 1954 the Anglo-Egyptian Treaty was signed, under which the 80,000 British troops stationed there were withdrawn but the Canal itself remained under the ownership of Western shareholders. On 26 July 1956, Nasser broke the Treaty and nationalized the Canal. The British and French were apoplectic. After several months of mostly phoney negotiating, on 22 October their Foreign Ministers met with the Israelis at Sèvres outside Paris where they hatched a plot to invade Egypt and retake the Canal. The comically transparent plan went as follows: the Israelis would invade; the British and French would then demand a ceasefire; when that didn't happen, they would follow the Israelis in to 'keep the peace'. The first invasion took place on 29 October, the second on 5 November. Eden claimed he was facing down a dictator who threatened world civilization and he compared Nasser to Hitler. He expected Britons to respond with the sort of patriotism which had so united the nation during the Second World War. They didn't. Three ministers resigned. Amid tempestuous scenes not seen in the House of Commons since Chamberlain's fall in 1940, the Opposition Leader, Hugh Gaitskell, denounced Eden's misadventure. Furious Tory efforts to prevent him repeating this on TV failed. Live on the BBC, he called for the Prime Minister's resignation, saying 'we have betrayed all that Britain has stood for in world affairs'.[1] Half the population agreed and over the next few weeks there were demonstrations across the country, some of them violent.

More importantly, the Americans, who had not been told about the Sèvres Protocol, did not support the action – essentially because Arab oil was more important to them than the imperial pretensions of their NATO allies and they did not want their supplies cut off by a Middle East conflict. In addition to this the Soviet Union had taken advantage of the situation to invade Hungary and made threats towards the West as a whole which provoked fears of a Third World War. There was a run on the pound; $300 million of Britain's reserves were spent trying in vain to prop it up; the Americans refused to bail the British out unless they withdrew their forces. Economic disaster loomed and on 30 November the Cabinet decided to withdraw. On 20 December, the Prime Minister lied to the House of Commons, denying that there had been foreknowledge of the Israeli invasion. Amid continuing uproar, which prompted Eden's wife to say that she felt the Canal was flowing through her drawing room, Eden resigned on 9 January 1957 and was replaced by Harold Macmillan.

The Commonwealth experiment which ended with Suez was doomed to fail because the informal Empire which the British hoped to restore required the sort of power which only the Americans now had. Eden was one of those who thought it could be done. As Foreign Secretary he had negotiated the Anglo-Egyptian Treaty against the wishes of Churchill; two years later he had come to realize that modern colonial nationalism meant that gunboat diplomacy *was* required to protect Britain's interests even more than it had been in Palmerston's day. What he failed to realize was that such action now depended on the approval of the United States.

What was the long-term effect of Suez on national identity in Britain? Without doubt it was the most pivotal event in Britain between the Battle of Britain in 1940 and Britain's entry into the European Community in 1973. British casualties were small – twenty-two dead and ninety-seven wounded – but much worse damage was done to Britain's reputation. By highlighting its decline as a world power, it undermined the national confidence created by Britain's victory in the Second World War, confirmed American hegemony and began the long and tortuous process by which the British attempted to find a new role in Europe. Anthony Nutting, a Foreign Office minister who resigned over the issue, believed that 'it undoubtedly helped to speed up the pace of European integration'.[2]

A measure of the shock caused by the failure of Britain's imperial adventure was that Eden himself came round to the idea of Europe, though he warned that the British had been doubters for so long that they were now distrusted on the Continent – a comment which turned out to be richly prophetic. One of the last memos which he wrote as Prime Minister said, 'We have to try to assess the lessons of Suez.' The main lesson was:

We must review our world position and our domestic capacity more searchingly in the light of the Suez experience, which has not so much changed our fortunes as revealed realities. While the consequences of this may be to determine us to work more closely with Europe, carrying with us, we hope, our closest friends in the Commonwealth in such development, here too we must be under no illusion. Europe will not simply welcome us simply because at the moment it may appear to suit us to look at them. The timing and the conviction of our approach may be decisive in their influence on those with whom we plan to work.[3]

Edward Heath was then Chief Whip of the Conservative Party. On reading these words, he remembered feeling 'delight mixed with sadness at all it had taken to bring about Anthony's change of heart on the subject'.[4]

Had the European question rested on the Damascene conversion of Prime Ministers it might have been settled by the end of the twentieth century. But, as Edward Heath and like-minded politicians came to realize, it would take more than Suez to bring about a change of heart in the British people. The French, in contrast, rode out the debacle because their involvement in it proved that despite the humiliation of the Second World War they were still a player on the world stage; and because they were unequivocal about their new role in a united Europe. Sir Guy Millard, Eden's Private Secretary, said, 'The French simply wrote it off as a failure . . . and got on with life. They went on very soon after Suez to more than 30 years of national self-confidence and national success.'[5]

Nonetheless, Suez did convert a substantial proportion of the British elite to the European cause. Harold Macmillan repaired the damage to Anglo-American diplomatic relations at a summit with Eisenhower in Bermuda in March 1957; and the Queen made a successful visit to the US later that year ('She buried George III for good and all,' commented the British Ambassador).[6] But Eisenhower's 'betrayal' destroyed some of the sentimentality about the Special Relationship which had previously hampered attempts by Europeanists to convince sceptics that Britain's future lay in Europe. It even briefly revived the popular anti-Americanism of the war. Many shopkeepers erected signs saying NO AMERICANS SERVED HERE. More importantly, the debacle in Egypt forced most people to see that, whatever form the Empire took, it was no longer politically possible nor morally tenable.

In broader social terms, Eden's bungling dishonesty undermined what was left of popular deference towards Britain's political elite after the spy scandals. Nigel Nicolson was one of eight Conservative MPs who abstained in the vote of confidence held in the House of

Commons on 8 November. His father, Harold, wrote: 'it will take us years to regain our moral authority' after a 'squalid and most humiliating episode' in which a Prime Minister had 'told his country a series of shameful lies ... It was a disappointment that my countrymen, in whose political good sense I had firmly believed, could prove as gullible and emotional as the Germans.'[7] Many certainly did believe Eden's claim that Nasser was an evil dictator who had to be faced down. One such was Noël Coward, who visited the Edens at their country house after the crisis. Coward thought: 'The Americans really behaved vilely and stabbed us well and truly in the back ... Eisenhower was weak and silly. It is so horrible about appeasers.' On 3 February 1957 he wrote in his diary:

> Poor Anthony has resigned ... a tragic figure who had been cast in a star part well above his capacities ... It was obviously dotty of him to embark on the Suez adventure in complete secrecy. The petulant gesture of a weak and stubborn man, but it at least *was* a gesture and more in the tradition of English courage than the milksop compromises of his colleagues. If he had been allowed by world pressure and by English pressure to finish the job, we should at least have knocked Nasser off his perch and controlled the Canal. The, to me, saddest part of this garbled, untidy story is the split that occurred in England itself. All that silly demonstrating and arguing could only have been motivated by fear, as it was during Munich ... This is indeed a sad moment in English history.[8]

The British were not as gullible as Nicolson thought. Even those who supported the invasion on principle were shocked when it became clear that deception had been involved in order to carry it out. Quite simply, it offended the nation's sense of fair play.

2. The Red Dragon banned again

By accelerating imperial withdrawal, Suez played a part in undermining the Union. As Union Jacks were lowered around the world, the Scots and Welsh saw that the state into which they had merged their national sovereignty could no longer offer the professional opportunities and material rewards or the international status which had once justified that merger. Fintan O'Toole writes, 'It is not the foreigner's might that fuels a sense of national grievance, but the foreigner's current weakness ... rather than virgins and rapists, the more appropriate image for Scotland is of a contemptuous woman married to a husband who has gone to seed. England, shrivelled and pot-bellied, is no longer good company to step out with on the world stage'.[9]

The last of the many Empire Exhibitions staged between 1851 and 1940 was held in Glasgow in 1938. The Exhibition focused on Scottish imperial achievements and Scots thronged to see it (12 million Britons visited in all). One of the displays they saw told the life story of the Presbyterian missionary and explorer, David Livingstone. Attitudes to him are a paradigm of attitudes to the Empire as a whole. In the Union's heyday, Livingstone was a symbol of Scotland's sense of Britishness. He was feted by the Victorian public, particularly after a Welsh journalist, H. M. Stanley, rediscovered him deep in the African interior (Stanley attended the opening of the Suez Canal en route to locating him). Livingstone died in 1873 and to the immense pride of the Scots he was buried the following year in Westminster Abbey as a Briton, his coffin draped in the Union Jack. During the early twentieth century, more emphasis was placed on his Scottishness. In 1925, the slum house he was born in at Blantyre was rescued from dereliction and turned into an elaborate memorial, financed by public subscription. Most of the money raised consisted of small donations from working-class Sunday Schools and Bible classes of the kind that Livingstone had sprung from. It was opened by the Duchess of York (later Queen Elizabeth the Queen Mother) in front of 10,000 people. Leading Scots missionaries of the day returned from abroad to attend, delivering speeches in which they testified to the continuation of Livingstone's work among the Godless tribes of Africa. Blantyre soon attracted 90,000 visitors a year, most of whom were ordinary Scots on cheap excursions. The numbers dipped after the Second World War and from the early 1960s they went into steep decline. What had been one of the biggest imperial cults, and the most overtly Protestant of them all – spread by pulpit, pocket biography and the cinema – had virtually disappeared by the centenary of his death in 1973. Ironically, his name lived on among the descendants of those he had converted to Christianity. The only countries to celebrate the centenary were African, six of which issued special stamps for the occasion.[10]

The most telling evidence for the decline of Scottish imperialism is the changing pattern of emigration. Livingstone was one of millions of Scots who left their country to work in the Empire or elsewhere in the UK. During its peak between the 1820s and 1920s, when over 2 million left for non-European destinations, Scotland's net exodus was the largest of any European country except Ireland. But, unlike the Irish, most Scots who left their homeland were urban artisans and professionals whose motive was ambition rather than despair. Consequently there was a stronger pride in the creation of a Scottish diaspora, something evidenced by the network of Orange Lodges in colonial territories. In the 1960s, emigration rose to its highest level since the 1920s. The sharpest increase was in those going abroad, which rose to 157,000 in the decade 1961–71, up from 60,000 in the 1920s. Those who went to England and Wales fell from 330,000 to 169,000.[11]

This trend was partly due to the fact that England had its own economic problems and was therefore a less attractive proposition than before. Although research on the subject is still sketchy, it seems likely that the decline of internal migration helped to undermine Britishness because social interaction between the Scots and the English was significantly reduced. Meanwhile, the choice of foreign destinations shrank as a result of colonial wars and independence. The United States – traditionally the destination of the Irish – took most of the overspill. The sense of a common Britishness once fostered among Scottish and English expatriates amid the strange and seemingly less civilized natives of Asia and Africa was not felt as strongly in America. Nor was it reproduced among those who worked for large corporations in developing countries like the oil-rich states of the Persian Gulf. Lacking a sense of imperial mission, the expatriates of the late twentieth century were bound by a more private and less self-conscious national identity than their forebears.

The attitudes of those who remained at home also changed. Scots who left the UK were increasingly unskilled or semi-skilled workers trying to escape unemployment rather than entrepreneurs seeking to mould the world in their own image. Emigration was seen as a drain of Scotland's limited resources, forced upon its people by economic decline; an object of shame rather than a source of pride. The popular view of emigration, as well as the destination of those leaving the country, therefore came to resemble that of the Irish. During the same period, English leaders opposed what they called the 'brain drain' to America. But, as the term implies, it was an exodus of the most senior professionals and it did not become a source of popular concern in the south. Altogether, the most telling difference between the two countries in this period was that while the Scots became alarmed about emigration to more prosperous countries, the English became alarmed about immigration from less prosperous countries.

The Welsh had never embraced the Empire with quite the fervour that the Scots did. The few who did venture abroad in the eighteenth and nineteenth centuries went to the United States or South America. One group survived, the Patagonians of Chubut Valley in Argentina. But the aim of Welsh émigrés was to preserve their culture in foreign climes rather than aggrandizing Wales through association with the British Empire. In any case, most of the principality's émigrés continued to go to England rather than abroad. Decolonization was not, therefore, as big an issue in Wales as it was elsewhere in the UK. One issue did affect all the UK's member nations: the nuclear arms race. The onset of the Cold War in 1947 reinforced the need for collective national security. The thought of Scotland, Wales and Northern Ireland developing their own nuclear deterrents seemed absurd to most Britons. Most felt a warped pride in the UK having its own bomb and agreed with Ernest Bevin's bullish dictum 'we've got to have the bloody Union Jack on top of it'.[12] But at the same time, nuclear war made the conventional defence of the Isles pretty much irrelevant. If the Russians bombed London, the mushroom cloud would not stop at Shrewsbury or Carlisle, whether or not the British peoples were united against their enemy and whatever flag flew atop their own weapon of mass destruction. Therefore, the military raison d'être of the Union, which had been so apparent when pillboxes ringed Britain's shores from 1940 to 1945, began to wither.

Welsh discontent grew apace during the second half of the 1950s. One of the first decisions which the Macmillan government made when it came to power in January 1957 was to reject a report by the Council of Wales for a Welsh Office to be set up. While it was deciding how best to announce the decision, the government shot itself in the foot. On 31 July 1957 Parliament voted to give the Tryweryn Valley in Merioneth to the Corporation of Liverpool so that it could be flooded and serve as a reservoir for the people of Merseyside. The decision caused an uproar and proved that North Wales did not feel itself to be a branch of Lancashire (whatever Nye Bevan thought). The Home Office Minister responsible for the principality, Henry Brooke, warned the Prime Minister:

Feeling is running high in Wales just now, and therefore Welsh affairs need particularly sensitive handling if we are not to stir up trouble there. The Welsh Nationalists are a relatively small but vigorous and dedicated body. It is imperative to avoid creating . . . the feeling that Wales is merely being used by the English for their own convenience, and not treated as a nation of its own.[13]

The letter which the Prime Minister wrote to Huw Edwards explaining the decision not to establish a Welsh Office captured the English view of the two nations' relationship. Macmillan was sympathetic to the principality. But his vision was clouded by the cataracts of a long and peaceful coexistence, which made it difficult to appreciate the depth of Welsh discontent in the mid-twentieth century:

I believe that the vast majority of the Welsh nation are in agreement that their interests can best be furthered in association with England and the English people; at the same time Wales has not only her language but her distinctive needs and culture [she] has her own history, her own geography, her own hopes, her own life . . . Yet what Wales needs is not isolation from the rest of Britain, but wise understanding of Welsh problems . . . Wales, unlike Scotland, has the same system of law and of local government and of land tenure as England; there is no division or need for division there. The geographic and economic links with England are very strong. I am convinced by my study that here and now the main weakness which needs to be made good . . . lies essentially in the economic sphere. In economic development Wales is on the move . . . The Government's cardinal purpose is to put beyond all doubt that Wales as a nation has a place of its own in the counsels of Britain.[14]

A furious Edwards and four other members of the Council of Wales resigned in protest and their failure to influence the government lost the Council what little credibility it had ever had.

In an attempt to improve relations, the government staged the Festival of Wales between May and October 1958. It was conceived in 1955 by Edwards as 'a kind of Festival of Britain in miniature', to make up for the fact, so he claimed, that Wales had been neglected by the jamboree staged four years earlier.[15] On the eve of the Suez crisis, the Eden government refused to provide any funds for it. But with discontent growing Macmillan showed more enthusiasm for the event. He marshalled the Queen to act as patron and he dispatched Henry Brooke to open the Festival with the following speech:

Argument is silenced at the birth of the Festival; differences are dissolved, and it is peace: peace and rejoicing with gracious Royal blessing in which the Welsh nation proudly invites her visitors and her homecoming people from all round the whole wide world . . . When the Festival summer closes in fulfilment, let all eyes be to the future still and may God's blessing be renewed year in year out upon this loved and lovely land of Wales.[16]

The well-attended events which followed included a season of Welsh music at Llandaff Cathedral, a presentation of *Under Milk Wood* at Laugharne and a sheep-shearing festival at Capel Cruig. The Festival's centrepiece was more international: Cardiff staged the Empire Games for the first time, a deliberate attempt to accord Wales the status of imperial partner. In the souvenir programme, Huw Edwards emphasized that Wales and not Scotland had been England's original partner: 'We . . . want to remind ourselves of our own heritage because it is sometimes overlooked that our language and culture are among the oldest in Europe and that we are England's original partner in the great Commonwealth experiment of living together.'[17] But, like the Scots, the Welsh no longer saw the point of Empire. What they wanted was greater autonomy.

A flag and a capital city are prerequisites of a nation's existence. Until the second half of the 1950s Wales officially had neither. Several grandiose buildings had been laid out in Cathays Park in the early twentieth century, notably a startling white Civic Centre; the Marquess of Bute had spent some of the fortune he made from coal on tarting up the city's rather dull castle in an attempt to compete with Edinburgh; and in 1907 Cardiff had been designated a city. But half a century later it was still regarded by most Britons as a provincial one with the same status as Bristol, Manchester or Glasgow. The Welsh flag, meanwhile, had simply ceased to exist. The red dragon on a green and white background was the standard of Henry Tudor, adapted from those used by medieval Welsh princes. On taking the English throne, Henry had introduced the dragon into the royal standard of England. However, when the Stuarts succeeded the Tudors, they replaced it with the Scottish unicorn. Worse still, James VI did not include the Welsh flag in the first Union Jack designed in 1606 to mark the Union with Scotland; nor was it included by George III in 1801 when the flag was redesigned to mark the union with Ireland (in a sense, therefore, it was the Scots and Germans, and not the English, who erased the Welsh from the British mind).

On 1 June 1955, Cardiff was declared to be the capital city of

Wales after a two-year contest with Caernarfon in the north and Aberystwyth on the mid-west coast. To some extent the contest highlighted the divisions within Wales, but the good-natured acceptance of the decision indicated that the postwar heightening of Welsh consciousness was at last beginning to unite the principality. The old, petty adage of the north – better no capital at all than Cardiff – had disappeared. The decision was a popular one, but there was little pageantry to mark the occasion, few dignitaries visited Cardiff from outside Wales and it went unnoticed by most Britons. Four years later, the Prime Minister decided that he and the Queen had better pay a visit to the new capital of what had become an increasingly troublesome part of the United Kingdom.

Macmillan went on ahead to soften the Welsh up for the Queen. The vehicle he chose for his visit was the unveiling of a statue of the man who more than any other symbolized the successful marrying of Welshness and Britishness: Lloyd George. Macmillan's speech must rank as one of his most wily. He was the quintessential English gentleman. His grandfather had founded the London-based publisher responsible for this book; he had married the daughter of an English aristocrat; but he prided himself on having a popular touch, which he said he owed to his family's humble Scottish origins. It was as a Scot that he addressed the substantial crowd which gathered to hear him in the centre of Cardiff on 8 July 1960:

> David Lloyd George was a Welshman. I am a Scot . . . Our characters, and our attitudes to life were formed by the courage, dignity and faith of simple religious country people. David Lloyd George was brought up in a bootmaker's cottage in North Wales. I am descended from a crofter in the Scottish highlands.[18]

Having thus established his Celtic credentials, the Prime Minister then addressed a large gathering at the City Hall. There he acknowledged that Wales had serious economic problems; but he used this to emphasize the increasing necessity of the Union now that Britain was no longer the world's most powerful nation. The speech was pitched in a deliberately Churchillian way in an attempt to rekindle the British patriotism which had so united the country during the war:

> This new look has not been achieved by accident . . . It has been worked for by English, Scots and Welsh, collaborating together; a supreme example of co-operation. Our survival on this small island depends on our being able to compete in the markets of the world . . . All the talents of our people must be harnessed for the battle

of economic survival in a technological age. . . . Wales, as part of the United Kingdom, like Scotland and England, is playing its part nobly.[19]

The Queen and the Duke of Edinburgh followed a month later in a two-day spectacular which celebrated Cardiff's new status. The visit culminated with an embarrassed-looking Duke being made a Gorsedd member in front of 9,000 people. The Gorsedd was an assembly of 'bards' invented in London in 1790 by a homesick stonemason from Glamorgan. Claiming to be descended from the druidic priests of the ancient Britons, its members first met on Primrose Hill, dressed in white robes and pointed hoods, and they ran the national Eisteddfod from 1819. Despite the centrality of this Celtic flummery to Welsh national culture, the name which the Gorsedd gave the Duke, Philip Meironydd, did not catch on.

The struggle to gain recognition for the Welsh flag lasted longer because it directly involved the monarchy and therefore attacked the spinal cord of the Union. Much as they would have liked to alter the Union Jack, Welsh leaders knew it was a non-starter since a redesign would have opened a can of constitutional worms – not least over Ireland, whose red cross of St Patrick still haunted the flag despite the creation of the Irish Republic. In 1897, 1901, 1910, 1935 and 1945 the Welsh had instead petitioned the government to have the dragon incorporated once more into the Royal Arms. This pressure had borne some fruit in 1901 when the dragon was assigned to the Prince of Wales; but it depended for its existence on there being a Prince. The petition of 1945 was prompted partly by the fact that, with the heir to the throne being a nineteen-year-old single female, the office was effectively defunct for the foreseeable future and with it the official status of the flag.

It got nowhere. The reason given for the refusal was that Wales had never been a kingdom so could not therefore be part of any emblem of the United Kingdom. The Garter King of Arms, Sir Algar Howard, likened the principality to the ancient Anglo-Saxon kingdoms. He told the Home Office, 'There is no more reason to add Wales to the King's style than there would be to add Mercia, Wessex or Northumbria or any other parts of England.'[20] In other words, Wales was regarded as a dud English region. In 1953, Buckingham Palace again came under pressure for reform from politicians who were by now more edgy about nationalism and were looking for ways to deal with it. At a series of special meetings of the Privy

Council called to discuss the issue, David Maxwell Fyfe told the Earl Marshal that the status of Wales was at least comparable to that of Northern Ireland. Though it was not a kingdom, he said: 'One could not get away from the fact that Wales [is] a national entity comprising one race with its own language. The political problem facing [me is] to placate national feeling with the avoidance of agitation for a separate government.'[21] The Palace gave way and acknowledged the irregular nature of the office of Prince of Wales by designing a new royal badge for use at other times, consisting of a dragon with a crown above it, bearing the insipid motto 'Y Ddraig Goch Ddyry Cychwyn' ('The Red Dragon lends impetus'). Maxwell Fyfe needn't have bothered.

The new flag was flown on public buildings by command of the Queen but was roundly rejected by the Welsh. On one level, the people simply ignored the pettifogging concerns of the British Establishment and continued to fly their old flag whenever they liked. The most visible example of this was the sea of green, white and red which regularly greeted the nation's rugby team at Cardiff Arms Park. But at the same time, the fact that their flag was not given the same official recognition as the Scottish one caused deep resentment, especially because official permission had to be sought to fly it even on St David's Day. When permission was refused, as it was in 1958 during the Festival of Wales, the Western Mail thundered, 'THE RED DRAGON BANNED AGAIN'. The Royal College of Arms justified its decision on the ground that 'There is no such thing as a Welsh national flag.'[22] It was one of the less tactful official statements of the postwar era and a touching reminder of what British politics was like in an age when spin-doctors were interns and not consultants.

The Queen herself then stepped into the fray, telling Macmillan that she wanted to declare Charles Prince of Wales at the opening of the Festival so that the Welsh could have their flag back and with it a royal embodiment of their aspirations. The Prime Minister persuaded her that Charles was too young to endure the strain of an Investiture; but he liked the idea, believing that a change to Charles' title might appease public opinion. Henry Brooke told Macmillan that it 'would be tremendously popular throughout Wales . . . To possess a Prince of Wales has a meaning and a value for Welshmen which it is easy for us in England to under-estimate.'[23] In fact, they overestimated it. Pleased though many people were to have a new Prince, what they wanted was recognition of their flag. On 12 June 1958, the Gorsedd launched a campaign which won support right across Wales regardless of political allegiance, class or region and was given official support by the Council of Wales. The statement which the Gorsedd issued to the national press was a glorious mixture of romantic patriotism given a truculent edge by years of patronizing dismissal.

> We proclaim that the Red Dragon banner, as borne by Henry Tudor on Bosworth Field and as flown by Prince Cadwalador centuries earlier, is the only banner adopted by the Welsh people themselves over many years now as our national flag and that there is therefore no need to seek permission from any heraldic authority outside the Principality for the continuance of this usage. We entirely reject the badge granted in 1952–3 [as] too puny to signify anything.[24]

Eight months later, in February 1959, Brooke was forced to tell the Prime Minister that the badge of 1953 'has not taken on, and the old unadorned Red Dragon on a green and white background continues to be the popular flag in Wales'.[25] The result was that on 1 January 1960 the Queen conceded that the Red Dragon was officially the Welsh flag, regardless of the monarchy's dynastic affairs, and that permission to fly it did not have to be sought from the Crown. Within a short time it was fluttering on public buildings throughout the country, from government offices to banks and shops as well as at Cardiff Arms Park and other venues.

The Welsh had got their flag back and with it a substantial chunk of their nationality. The victory was important because, in a fundamental way, the Welsh had succeeded in publicly detaching their nationality from the monarchy – not through an upsurge of republicanism but by making a clear distinction between the House of Windsor and their own distinctive, though defunct, royal heritage. Many others cared little about heraldic history and saw it as a straightforward break with the monarchy. In the long run, the fact that the Welsh flag was not and never had been a part of the Union Jack gave it more credibility than the Scottish saltire as a symbol of self-determination.

3. Sir, there's a traffic light at red. Do we stop?

One should not overestimate the impact of Suez on the decline of popular imperialism. The Empire was no longer central to national identity in Britain by the time Suez occurred. To begin with, there were high levels of ignorance about it. Even in 1947, shortly after Britain surrendered the jewel in its crown by granting Indian independence, a poll revealed that the drama of the event had not impinged much on the British consciousness. Despite more than half a century of imperial propaganda in schools, youth movements and the mass media, three-quarters of the population did not know the difference between a dominion and a colony, half couldn't name a single British possession and 3 per cent thought the United States was still a colony.[26] Of course ignorance does not necessarily indicate indifference. Most Britons could not name their MP but that does not mean they would be happy to see democracy overthrown. But other evidence does suggest that by the mid-1950s the British did not care much about the Empire.

One indicator is the declining use of Empire by the British advertising industry. From the 1870s to the 1930s, domestic and colonial products had been successfully marketed on patriotic grounds, a belief in Britain's superior craftsmanship and husbandry linked to a pride in the nation's world supremacy. From the 1940s to the 1960s there was a steady fall in the number of adverts doing so, and a concerted attempt to develop post-imperial brand images. Tea is the best example. The leading brands – Brooke Bond, Lipton, Ty-Phoo and Lyons – began to sell their tea in a more neutral way, emphasizing its medicinal properties rather than its imperial origins. There were exceptions. Cusson's Imperial Leather soap still depicted its trademark piccaninnies bearing bars of the soap aloft until the 1960s. The greater emphasis on domestic culture did not prevent the market share of British goods declining in the face of foreign competition. Nevertheless, a definite change had taken place in the UK's material culture which reflected the decline of popular imperialism.

The most striking evidence that Britons rejected their imperial identity well before Suez was the declining observance of Empire

Day. The Empire Day Movement was founded in 1903 by the Earl of Meath, a Scottish aristocrat involved in most of the patriotic organizations of the Edwardian era. After a lengthy campaign, Empire Day was officially celebrated in the UK for the first time in 1916 on Queen Victoria's birthday, 24 May. During the interwar period it became a major part of the British calendar, with school parades, BBC broadcasts and huge, stage-managed rallies presided over by Church and Crown. It reached a peak of popularity in 1924–5 when Wembley Stadium was built as the centrepiece of the Empire Exhibition (90,000 people attended an Empire Day thanks-giving service there in 1925). George VI became patron of the movement in 1941; his daughter continued the patronage, with Churchill as vice-patron. In the early years of New Elizabethan optimism it enjoyed a brief Indian summer (new initiatives included the presentation of Empire programmes at children's Saturday cinema clubs). However, by the time the Poet Laureate John Masefield wrote a poem to mark the event in 1955, observance had begun to peter out. The BBC was reluctant to celebrate it and the public simply indifferent. The Scouting movement, which had provided cohorts of young Britons for prewar Empire rallies, also began to shed the imperial fervour with which Baden-Powell had imbued it. His death in 1941 did not affect Scouting's popularity. It remained the largest youth organization in the world and its UK membership rose from 343,000 in 1940 to 588,396 in 1960 (Girl Guide numbers went up from 400,236 to 594,491). But during this period, the movement's culture of God, King and Empire gave way to God, Queen and Country. From 1960 membership went into decline as young Britons discovered that pop music was more exciting (and often safer) than bivouacking in national parks with middle-aged men calling themselves Akela.[27]

Even those who served in the various colonial wars of the 1950s did not consider themselves to be part of the 'thin red line' of Victorian legend. The word 'wog' was still bandied about with ease in the armed forces and some were guilty of appalling brutality, in particular during the Mau-Mau revolt in Kenya. But by 1956 few British soldiers had the sense of imperial mission which had motivated earlier generations. When, during Suez itself, the part-time volunteers of the Territorial Army were sent emergency call-up papers, many were returned with the simple message *'Bollocks!'* written on them. Senior military officials were equally unenthusiastic. Frank Cooper, the Assistant Secretary at the Air Secretariat, described being summoned to a meeting by the Chief of Air Staff, just after Eden had decided to invade. The Chief began the meeting by saying, 'The Prime Minister has gone stark, raving mad.'[28] The oral testimony of the troops who did go reveals at best a professional desire to 'get the job done' – 'Let's get on with it and get it over with' as Don Hayward of the Paras recalled.[29] For most there was also a prevailing sense of the absurdity of it all and an embarrassed feeling that they were in someone else's country without permission. One story in particular captures that feeling. Derek Oakley of the Royal Marines, who commanded a tank during the ground assault into Port Said, recalls:

> As we trundled through ... suddenly the driver ... tugged my trousers and said, 'Sir, do you know if they drive on the right hand or the left hand in this country?' We hadn't gone very much further when he gave another tug; I said, 'What on earth's the matter now?' and he said, 'Sir, there's a traffic light at red. Do we stop?'[30]

The debacle certainly accelerated the decline of popular imperialism. But, to paraphrase Eden, Suez did not so much change fortunes as reveal realities about British national identity in the postwar era.

If Enoch Powell was ever right about anything, it was that ordinary Britons recovered from the shock of Suez more easily than those who ran the country. He observed 'the morale of the country was lowered' temporarily but it 'produced a cure for the British people. They recovered from their loss of Empire much more quickly than their leaders.'[31] Those that decolonization traumatized most were the middle and upper classes who had made a direct living out of the Empire – in particular, the proconsuls charged with imparting the British way of life to natives, men like Sir Richard Turnbull, one of the last Governors of Aden. Mourning the loss of imperial influence, Turnbull told the Labour politician Dennis Healey that 'when the British Empire finally sank beneath the waves of history, it would leave behind it only two monuments: one was the game of Association Football, the other was the expression "Fuck off".'[32]

Among the younger middle classes, however, there was a growing revulsion from imperialism. One focus of that revulsion was the ongoing colonial wars in Malaya (1948–58), Cyprus (1954–9) and Kenya (1952–60). Another was nuclear weapons. A Defence Review was undertaken in the wake of Suez, and Duncan Sandys' White Paper, published in April 1957, concluded that in the nuclear age large conventional forces were costly and unnecessary – 'Big Bang,

Small Army', as the papers said, was the way for Britain to maintain her world role. Defence expenditure was to be reduced from 10 to 7 per cent of GDP over the next five years and the armed forces cut from 690,000 to 375,000. Eisenhower agreed to supply Britain with missiles, and on 15 May 1957 Britain exploded its first H-bomb. All of which provoked the formation of the Campaign for Nuclear Disarmament (CND) in London on 17 February 1958, its leaders J. B. Priestley, Bertrand Russell, A. J. P. Taylor, the pacifist cleric Canon Collins and the military strategist Sir Stephen King-Hall.

Looking back on the period, Harold Macmillan recalled 'the general anxiety about nuclear arms, amounting almost to hysteria'.[33] Extravagant claims have been made about CND's historical importance by scholars of the movement. Worthy though its aims were, the organization's membership was mostly confined to the radical middle classes and there is no evidence that it had any effect on either British public opinion or on the world leaders whose fingers were on the button. The prewar peace movement, led by the League of Nations Union, had attracted nearly 407,000 members at its height in 1931; at its height in 1986, CND could muster only 110,000. It was also more pacifistic than the LNU, many of whose members had been patriotic Britons who simply wanted to avoid fighting another war. The pacifist tendency of CND put off many potential supporters: so too did its evident inability to do anything about the arms race. An account by the activist Marion Davies of a sit-in in Manchester's Princess Street in 1961 captures the almost comical ineffectiveness of the organization even after its adoption of a policy of civil disobedience in 1959. To Davies' delight, the police made sure that female protestors had chairs. During her subsequent imprisonment, she surveyed graffiti in her cell such as 'Dirty rotten coppers'. 'I had my pen and ink. Should I add a Ban the Bomb sign? But no, one doesn't write on walls, one is too well brought up.'[34] Ineffective though it was, CND is historically significant because it highlighted the questioning of 'Pax Britannica' among middle-class Britons who a generation or two before were either committed to Empire or at least tolerant of it.

To add insult to injury, a new generation of British intellectuals, hyped in the media as the 'Angry Young Men', were questioning the assumptions upon which Britishness had been based since the war. John Osborne – playwright and early member of CND – was the nation's leading tormentor. In 'A Letter To My Countrymen', published in the left-wing journal *Tribune* in 1961, he wrote:

This is a letter of hate. It is for you, my countrymen. I mean those
men of my country who have defiled it. The men with manic
fingers leading the sightless, feeble, betrayed body of my country
to its death . . . You are MY hatred. That is my final identity . . . I
think it may sustain me in the last few months. Till then, damn
you, England. You're rotting now, and quite soon you'll disappear.[35]

His play *The Entertainer* (1957) used the decline of the music hall
as a metaphor for the decline of the Empire. Its hero, Archie Rice, a
fading comedian whose son is killed in Egypt, sings:

The Army, the Navy and the Air Force,
Are all we need to make the blighters see
It still belongs to you, the old red, white and blue.
Those bits of red still on the map
We won't give up without a scrap.[36]

The Lord Chamberlain's office, which was then responsible for
censorship, was not amused. The man who adjudicated on the play,
Lieutenant-Colonel Sir St Vincent Troubridge, was a descendant of
one of Nelson's admirals. As well as the words 'shagged', 'rogered'
and 'turds', Troubridge objected to the line 'those playing fields of
Eton have really got us beaten'. He took particular exception to a
scene in which a woman playing Britannia appeared on stage carrying a trident and wearing nothing but a helmet. After intense
lobbying from the Royal Court Theatre, she was allowed to appear,
on the grounds that she sat motionless, and side-on to the audience
thereby 'concealing the pudendum'. But the fact remained that the
Empress no longer had any clothes, and Britons were increasingly
willing to say so.[37]

The decline of Britain's imperial identity in the mid- to late 1950s
was so pronounced that the government became seriously agitated
about it. Only five months after Suez, the Minister of Education,
Quintin Hogg, wrote to Macmillan lamenting that Empire Day was
'dead beat' and rapidly giving way in Britain's schools to the celebration of United Nations Day. Hogg suggested that the name
should be changed to Commonwealth Day and then vigorously
publicized.[38] Ministers agreed. Charles Hill wrote: 'Knowledge of,
and real interest in, the Commonwealth in this country is unsatisfac-
tory . . . We have missed a generation and there is danger of missing
another.'[39] The Colonial Secretary, Alan Lennox-Boyd, argued that a
revival of the event would show that British power had not withered

away. During this 'very difficult phase', he told the Prime Minister, 'when some [colonies] are getting their latch keys and others are clamouring for them . . . our task in dealing with them will be much eased if we can rely on a fairly solid basis of understanding in this country of what Colonial problems are'.[40] The decline of imperialism in Scotland and Wales was a particular source of concern to ministers. Henry Brooke wrote, 'Wales being at the moment . . . a predominantly Socialist country, the word "Commonwealth" is more acceptable . . . than the word "Empire" which, alas, rouses suspicions of misused power'.[41]

The Prime Minister was initially reluctant to put out more flags in the immediate aftermath of Suez. But once the furore had died down, in May 1958 he told his colleagues that 'really something ought to be done urgently'.[42] His decision was probably influenced by a number of things: the Queen's enthusiasm for the Commonwealth; a pragmatic desire to appease the right of the Tory Party; and the fact that a month earlier the first large CND march had taken place, from London to Aldermaston in Berkshire. Whatever the reason, the Cabinet agreed that Britain would benefit from a renewed sense of its mission to the world, so in December 1958 it decided to launch 'Commonwealth Week'. For seven days every year an exhibition would tour fifteen British cities. The first was opened by Princess Margaret in Liverpool in 1959. In the three years of its short life, Commonwealth Week was a dismal failure. In March 1962, a report by Duncan Sandys concluded, with typically British understatement, that it had not 'attracted continuous and enthusiastic support'. Part of the reason, he said, was 'a lack of enthusiasm for and appreciation of the Commonwealth ideal amongst many teachers'.[43]

The story of Empire and Commonwealth continued to be taught until the late 1960s. The history of each country was entirely bound up with Britain's – syllabuses began on the date a country was colonized and ended on the date they gained independence. However, imperial history was taught with decreasing enthusiasm after the Second World War and by the late 1950s it had became one of the least popular courses chosen by candidates for the General Certificate of Education. As for the flag-waving parades which had once been an annual event in schools, they now seemed as absurd as the map with the UK's possessions in pink which still hung at the back of some classrooms. A key problem imperialists faced was that, unlike Continental nations, the education system was decentralized. There was no national curriculum, created and policed by ministers and officials at the Department of Education. Following Napoleon's lead in the early nineteenth century, most European states had used such curricula to nurture, and in some cases invent, national identities. In Britain, education was run by a middle stratum of professional educationalists, their power based in myriad training colleges, examining boards and local education authorities. This unusual system had not previously hampered the British political elite because until the 1950s the teaching profession had been a conservative one, drawn mostly from the middle classes and keen to instil imperial patriotism in the young. From the early 1960s, it became a predominantly left/liberal profession and there was not a lot that government could do about it.

Yet Macmillan recognized that the decline of imperial Britishness went far beyond the classroom. The Sandys Report found that the adult population as a whole (even those who had been brought up on imperial propaganda) were either confused about or indifferent to the Commonwealth. 'The older age groups', said Sandys, found it

> a rather bewildering successor to the Empire, regarding Britain's membership of it as good and necessary without always understanding why . . . The younger generation, brought up in an era of international organisations, regional pacts and ever decreasing 'imperial' responsibility, approach the subject in a receptive but more critical attitude looking for more concrete evidence of the benefits of the association and Britain's part in it.[44]

With Cabinet agreement, Commonwealth Week was abandoned that year. Later in 1962, the Empire Day Movement accepted that a revival was impossible and formally dissolved itself after fifty-nine years of activity.

Half the population supported Eden's misadventure in 1956, and as late as 1965, 55 per cent of the population still thought Britain should have a world role. It was not until later that decade that the figure began to drop substantially, down to 30 per cent by 1975.[45] By then, little remained of the Empire and Britain had entered Europe, presenting imperial diehards with no option but to accept reality. However, the value which many Britons still placed on a world role between the 1940s and the 1960s was not a serious desire to retain imperial power, hence the fact that the League of Empire Loyalists never attracted support except on the far-right fringes of the Conservative Party. What these figures illustrate is a desire to maintain some influence on the international scene born out of a nostalgia for the status which Britain had once enjoyed. The trouble was that, given their scepticism about Europe, Britons weren't sure exactly how that could be achieved. In a private note written in December 1957, Macmillan confessed that he was 'anxious' about the isolationism of the British, a mood which he blamed on their increasing tendency to live on past glories:

> There are three main troubles; first, the anti-Americanism of many of our supporters, which of course reached its culminating point at Suez but has not yet died down. It is partly based on real apprehensions and partly, I am afraid, represents the English form of the great disease from which the French are suffering more than any other people – that is, looking backwards to the nineteenth century instead of looking forwards ... The second form of this isolationism is directed against Europe ... so we are reaching a position in which the English people of 50 million, who in material terms are quite unequal to the new giants, will move neither towards Europe nor towards America. It is a stultifying policy. The third problem, not I think so much in the Party but in the country, is all about the H-bomb, the American bases, the fatigue and worry of the long drawn out struggle against Russia.[46]

It is in the light of this confused, nostalgic stasis that we should view the famous observation of Dean Acheson that 'Britain has lost an Empire but has yet to find a role.'[47]

4. Our good name for tolerance

Britain's failure to find a new role was made startlingly apparent by the nation's attitude to black immigrants. Like bad breath produced by an undigested meal, racism continued to linger in British national identity after the death of imperialism. Conservative governments put even more effort than Labour ones into keeping Britain white. Churchill thought it 'the most important subject facing this country', fearing the creation of what he called a 'Magpie society'.[48] After all, as he told his doctor in 1952, 'Once you learn to think of a people as inferior it is very hard to get rid of that way of thinking.'[49] In 1953, he set up a working party to investigate ways of halting the unforeseen invasion of the UK. Altogether, between 1948 and 1962,

Cabinets of both parties ordered a total of twenty detailed investi-
gations into how Britain could close the legal door which Attlee had
inadvertently opened.

What prevented them from taking any action until the early
1960s was concern about the Commonwealth reaction to any
nakedly racist legislation. British governments watched in horror as
the French became embroiled in bloody conflicts in Algeria and Indo-
China, while the Mau-Mau revolt in Kenya served warning that it
could all too easily happen to the British. In order for decolonization
to be relatively peaceful, it was imperative that coloured nations
believed they were now regarded as equals. As Churchill's one-time
Private Secretary, Sir David Hunt, later remarked, 'The minute we
said we've got to keep these black chaps out, the whole Commonwealth lark would have blown up.'[50] However, as Britain's leaders
moved towards joining Europe, Commonwealth opinion became less
important.

In 1961, 136,400 coloured Britons entered the UK, compared to
42,400 in the year that Macmillan became Prime Minister.[51] As the
numbers of immigrants rose, so did the level of popular hostility
towards them. Small-scale disturbances took place in Liverpool and
Birmingham in 1948, Deptford in 1949 and Camden in 1954. Four
years later, the Notting Hill riots confirmed what every black Briton
had painfully discovered since arriving in the country: that the
national identity which they had imbued for most of their lives had
no place for them other than to help define what a Briton was not.
The riots erupted on the August Bank Holiday weekend of 1958.
Crowds 400–500 strong were in hysterics, screaming, 'Let's lynch
the niggers! Let's burn their homes!' before going on a rampage
through the streets. Hearing of the violence, thousands travelled to
Notting Hill to watch, as crowds had once travelled to watch
executions at Tower Hill. One local witness remembers the area
being full of 'English people coming to see the Nigger run'.[52] For the
first time, the black population organized themselves and fought
back. On Monday 1 September a group gathered in the Calypso
Club, where a new, charismatic black leader, Michael de Freitas, told
them to arm themselves. Friends and relatives came from Brixton to
help and that night 300 black men and women assembled in the
darkness above a café in Blenheim Crescent. A white crowd gathered
outside and just as they were preparing to torch the cafe, up shot the
third-floor windows and out flew the Molotov cocktails. The terrified
crowd scattered as glass crashed and flame erupted around them.

The riots had two immediate effects. The first was that three weeks later hundreds of black Britons gathered at Victoria Station bound for the West Indies. The exodus began almost exactly a decade after the *Empire Windrush* had docked at Tilbury, although this time faces were drawn with bitterness rather than animated with expectation. In a normal year, 150 returned to the place of their birth. In 1959, the number rose to 4,500. The other result was that in 1959 the Notting Hill Carnival was established by de Freitas and other community leaders. Held on the August Bank Holiday, by the 1970s it had become a national institution, a focal point for black British culture and eventually a symbol of racial harmony as white residents, tourists and the police began to participate. The only comparable event in the British calendar was the Last Night of the Proms, which remained a rumbustious celebration of Edwardian patriotism. However, the long-term effect of the riots was not dancing in the streets but the erosion of black Britons' dual national identity.

This manifested itself in three ways. First, a greater devotion to the cultural traditions of the Caribbean and a more intense desire (rarely fulfilled) to return there. Second, an increasing loyalty to the West Indies as a whole, rather than to individual islands, something which had always been discouraged by colonial administrators in order to divide and rule.[53] The fanatical support for the West Indies cricket team is a case in point. Since the birth of organized test series after the First World War, cricket had become one of the key bonds of Commonwealth. From the early 1960s, the competition became more pointedly competitive as coloured teams became focal points for black and Asian patriotism. For West Indians, this happily coincided with the complete dominance by their team of world cricket, and the regular humiliation of England by bat and ball offered especial respite from their troubles (their first victory in Britain took place in 1950). The third change, and one which was particularly true of the younger generation who had been born in Britain, was a greater affinity with black Americans. To the relief of politicians, this did not manifest itself politically in an American-style Civil Rights Movement. Culturally, however, the United States began to have a strong influence: in dialect, fashion and above all in music. Soul, funk, and later rap overtook calypso and ska in popularity (Jamaican reggae was the one important exception to the rule). In cinema, too, Hollywood offered a more accurate portrayal of black culture than its British counterpart. Two films were made by British studios about the race problem: *Sapphire* (1959) and *Flame in the Streets* (1961). They were an advance on the noble savage portrayed by Paul Robeson in the 1930s, but they dealt primarily with white anxieties about a multiracial society. Hollywood, on the other hand, began to address black culture, eventually producing black stars and film-makers. By the late 1960s African America had replaced the multiracial Commonwealth as the vehicle for black diasporic identity. Therefore the connection which racist commentators made in the 1950s between American and black culture when analysing the supposed degeneration of Britain was a connection which black Britons came to make as a result of that racism.

The moral bankruptcy of Britishness was not so apparent to the country's white population. Some felt deeply about the way in which the riots undermined what they saw as a national tradition of fair play. The *Daily Sketch* described them unequivocally as 'a blot on our national good name for tolerance'.[54] Colin MacInnes – one of the few British intellectuals after Orwell to take popular culture seriously and the first to assess the impact of black immigration on it – thought how un-English the whole event seemed. In the novel *Absolute Beginners*, published a year after the riots, he wrote:

> Inside Napoli [Notting Hill] there was blood and thunder but just outside it – only across one single road like some national frontier – you were back in the world of Mrs Dale and What's My Line? and England's Green and Pleasant Land. Napoli was like a prison or concentration camp: inside blue murder, outside, buses and evening papers and hurrying home to sausages and mash and tea.[55]

MacInnes' view was poignant because his mother was a cousin of both Stanley Baldwin and Rudyard Kipling, two men who between them had done more to define Englishness and its relationship to Empire than any other figures in the first half of the twentieth century.

The Prime Minister saw a chance to do what every government had wanted to do since 1948: reverse the legislation which had allowed black people to come to the UK and test a century of rhetoric about the inclusive nature of Britishness. Was there an alternative? Yes, there was. Academic surveys carried out at this time showed that between 65 and 75 per cent of white people were receptive to information about black culture.[56] Race education programmes were introduced by Dutch governments in this period with extremely successful results. A British one might have pointed out that there were black people in Britain 500 years before the Anglo-Saxons arrived from Continental Europe to form the English nation (African units of the Roman army were stationed on the island from 253 onwards; and they were among the troops who defended Hadrian's Wall in an effort to keep the Scots at bay!). But Macmillan did not give the UK's white population the history lesson it so badly needed.

Instead, three months after the Notting Hill riots, the government spent thousands of pounds on a campaign designed, as we have seen, to revive enthusiasm for the British Empire/Commonwealth. Macmillan promised to tackle what he saw as a public order problem stemming from the presence of alien races. Therefore, at a crucial moment which offered the country's leaders a chance to redefine British national identity in accordance with the law, they chose instead to reinforce the country's extant identity by portraying black Britons as aliens and changing the law accordingly.

Numerous commentators contributed to this poisonous climate in the late 1950s and early 1960s. In 1958 the journalist Phillip Gibbs published a survey of national life in which he dubbed Britain 'The Invaded Island'. 'Theoretically, one detests racial intolerance', he wrote. 'Our sympathy as a nation is with the victims of Apartheid in South Africa, and with the Negro children barred out of American schools.'[57] However, the Notting Hill riots (for which 'coloured men of bad character' were partly to blame) showed that Britain was in 'grave peril'. Like most theorists of the subject, Gibbs emphasized that the English were not of pure Anglo-Saxon stock; he welcomed a cosmopolitan invasion of Celts (especially 'the Scots – God bless them!') and Continentals. But if 'this invasion becomes a tidal wave from the countries of the coloured folk, all claiming the right of entry . . . we [will] gradually lose our English character and blood by too much mixture of foreign strains'.[58] Others stressed the social effects of immigration, revealing the extent to which racism was fuelled by a wider panic about the moral decay of Britain. One example of this was Lord Elton's book *The Unarmed Invasion*. Elton was Vice-President of the ailing Empire Day Movement. He was also a militant Tory Anglican, and so felt more animus towards Asians than Afro-Caribbeans who, he felt, were at least co-religionists. After cataloguing the 'Dickensian squalor' of Asian communities in the Midlands, he described immigration as 'the gravest social crisis since the industrial revolution'.[59] It could not have come at a worse time, when 'the intellectual, moral and cultural life of the nation is already in a state of flux, and accepted attitudes to crime and punishment, to sexual moralities, and to the arts have been altered out of recognition within a couple of decades'.[60]

In 1958 Colin MacInnes condemned the 'malignant rubbish' written daily in the press and wrote that coloured immigrants 'represent the New English of the last half of our century: the modern infusion of that new blood which, according to our history-books, has perpetually re-created England in the past and is the very reason for her mongrel glory.'[61] In an article for the *Spectator* in 1963, he challenged the British to redefine themselves:

> Whatever their origins of place and race, they are now Britons in every sense that we are. The alternative is a continuing, nagging misery and pretence: the fatal weakness of not seeing what our country *is*. History is unkind to pretension that is not sustained by power ... The choice is to be terrified and be; or cling to safe hatreds, and destroy ourselves as no bomb ever will.[62]

'Mongrel glory' did not become a popular slogan of the era because it was easier to cling to safe hatreds. The Cabinet took the decision to legislate on 10 October 1961, emboldened by polls showing between 75 and 90 per cent of the population in favour of immigration controls.

It approved a scheme in which most immigrants had to obtain a work permit before entering the country, thus establishing the sort of modus vivendi which officials had envisaged when making their appeal for black labour fifteen years earlier. Butler, the Home Secretary, was uneasy and warned his colleagues that the divisive nature of the solution might prove to be worse than the 'problem' itself.

> On the whole, the West Indian population is law-abiding, but pressure on housing, jealousy and other factors create a dangerous situation ... Such legislation would clearly have to apply to the whole Commonwealth and the Irish Republic, though in practice it would be necessary to use it only against coloured immigrants ... Legislation of this sort would be controversial, and would require a considerable breach in the doctrine that the United Kingdom is the mother country to which all citizens of the Commonwealth have free access.[63]

When the Cabinet pondered the race issue, the British view of Ireland came into play, just as it had in the 1940s. The Irish were initially included in the Commonwealth Immigrants Bill to give it the appearance of neutrality; indeed, Ministers agreed that the 'great merit' of their scheme was that it could be presented to the world as non-discriminatory when in fact 'its restrictive effect is intended to, and would in fact, operate on coloured people almost exclusively'. But the plan was dropped for three reasons: first, the practical difficulty of closing the border between the south and the north of Ireland to prevent Irish migration into mainland Britain via Ulster; and second because Macmillan didn't want to upset the Taoiseach, Sean Lemass, who was then helping Britain crush the remnants of the IRA through a joint policy of internment. But above all, the Irish were excluded from the Bill because despite being foreigners in international law, they were still considered to be more British than West Indians, Africans and Asians – simply by virtue of their skin colour.

The Commonwealth Immigrants Bill received its second reading in Parliament on 16 November 1961. To cries of 'Humbug!', Butler paid tribute to the 'contribution which the immigrants have made to our national life'.[64] He said the matter was not one of race but of numbers – which Britain, as an overcrowded little island, could not absorb. This was to become a familiar theme of racist apologias in subsequent years. It was a lie for two reasons: because the largest group of immigrants – the Irish – had been excluded from the new restrictions; and because throughout the postwar era, far more Britons left the country than entered it.[65] The Labour Party changed its policy and opposed the Bill, largely because (unlike Attlee) Hugh Gaitskell had a personal hatred of racism. He called it a 'miserable, shameful, shabby Bill' and demanded three counter-measures: a state-directed improvement of black social conditions, the re-education of white Britons, and legislation outlawing the incitement of racial hatred.[66] The government won by 283 votes to 200. William Haley's *Times* editorials were relentlessly critical. 'The damage, emotional, economic and political, which it is likely to do the already fragile fabric of Commonwealth can hardly be exaggerated,' said one, leading Macmillan to curse the man he called 'Halier-than-Thou'.[67] But these predictions were confirmed within a day of the debate. The Jamaican Prime Minister, Norman Manley, telegraphed Macmillan to say that the Act was a 'flagrant disregard of every liberal principle on which Britain has based its customs and traditions'.[68]

What Macmillan's legislation decisively demonstrated was that even people who cared passionately about the Commonwealth preferred to undermine its political unity than countenance any erosion of the Isles' whiteness, or even admit that Britain was already irrevocably a multiracial society. In other words, most white Britons felt it was more important to preserve a mono-racial definition of Britishness than it was to save the remnants of the imperial polity which gave birth to that national identity. The Act received Royal Assent as Acker Bilk's 'Stranger on the Shore' reached no. 2 in the Hit Parade.

5. Bash the fuck out of it

Black people could be prevented from entering the UK, but those already in the country could not be prevented from having children. And women of all colours could not be stopped having children who became teenagers. Here was the second problem confronting those who wanted to preserve traditional Britishness: youth. By the late 1950s there was widespread concern at the lack of patriotism among young Britons. There were three reasons for adolescent restlessness. First, the social dislocation caused by the Second World War spawned a generation of boys and girls who had lacked parental guidance at a crucial stage in their development. Second, Suez helped to undermine deference towards the governing classes. In 1959 the critic Kenneth Allsop said, 'The collapse of our old image of imperial splendour did give a spur to the idea that our national vigour and imaginativeness no longer lay in the field of panoply and splendour. Suez *was* a spur: a very palpable spur. Suddenly there was a violent swing to the culture of the great, gritty, youthful *lumpenproletariat* . . . Every generation of kids since has been swayed by the sort of scepticism and derision that produces Carnaby Street knickers with Union Jacks on them.'[69] Conservatives agreed. In *The Neophiliacs*, the journalist Christopher Booker noted: 'England's fundamental view of herself – a whole complex of sentiments and assumptions that had been built up over hundreds of years – had been irreparably undermined. The dam had burst.'[70] Some relished it bursting. The Tory MP Bob Boothby, who was then sleeping with Harold Macmillan's wife, Dorothy, observed: 'In 1935 we were on top of the world: by 1956 it had all gone. It took the Roman Empire three hundred years of most enjoyable decadence to achieve that end: all we can do is seek a fraction of that decadence in what we call our permissive society.'[71]

Third, and most importantly, the UK's 6 million teenagers had more money. By 1956, their incomes were 50 per cent higher than before the war. Moral panics about adolescents had been common since the late Victorian era. For example, the word 'hooligan' came into common usage in 1898 following August Bank Holiday mayhem by drunken working-class boys in London – an Irish term, its adoption highlighted the fact that indiscipline was thought at first to be un-British and, literally, beyond the Pale; in the twentieth century, several cults like the Teddy Boys and Skinheads originated in poor areas of the English capital. But, on the whole, modern youth culture blossomed because spending power gave teenagers independence on a scale they had never enjoyed before. At first, it was welcomed by Conservative leaders.

Harold Macmillan saw popular capitalism as the key to restoring national unity and mass education as the means by which Britons could make the most of the spoils on offer. Throughout the twentieth century, the Conservative Party led the way in providing mass education. David Eccles, the man who had staged the Coronation celebrations, was now the minister responsible for Britain's schools and universities. In 1959 he told Macmillan: 'A half-educated electorate is fodder for the class war and a menace to free institutions . . . Education is Conservative in spirit [because] it began with the Church and its purpose is to fit men to take opportunities and lead balanced lives'.[72] A svelte man, Eccles had been a contemporary of Kenneth Clark and Hugh Gaitskell at Winchester and was known to his Cabinet colleagues as 'Smarty-Boots'. Macmillan thought him 'very vain [and] frightfully bumptious' but recognized the value of 'bringing the Butler Act to life'.[73] In a memorable phrase, the Prime Minister told his Cabinet that universal access to good tuition would make the working classes 'feel that they play as full members of the team'.[74]

Among the government's achievements were the provision of free university tuition and the building of new universities and technical colleges, a trend accelerated by the Robbins Report on Higher Education, published in 1963. The report emphasized the need for more vocational training in order to compete with Germany, Japan and the US, something that became a common refrain as Britain's growth rate continued to slip behind those of other Western countries. But it also emphasized the cultural benefits to be had. 'The aim should be to produce not mere specialists but rather cultivated men and women.' A university's purpose was 'the trans-

mission of a common culture and common standards of citizenship
... by providing, in the atmosphere of the institutions in which
the students live and work, influences that in some measure compensate for any inequalities of home background.'[75] Until bitter
disputes erupted in the 1970s over the relative merits of grammar
schools and comprehensives, Robbins' commitment to building a
common culture formed the basis for a consensus in British education
policy.

The consumer and education boom brought unprecedented affluence and opportunity to the country. Between 1951 and 1974 the
cost of living went up by three times while wages increased by just
over six times, meaning that real incomes doubled in the period.
Women's pay remained on average 30 per cent lower than men's but
they too felt the benefit of fatter wage packets. Politicians fretted
constantly about the decline of Britain in relation to its competitors.
The UK's share of world manufacturing exports fell from 25.5 per
cent in 1950 to 9.3 per cent in 1975, mostly thanks to competition
from Germany and Japan, while that of France and other Western
European nations remained stable. Like the loss of political power
which followed the war and decolonization, this *relative* economic
decline became the subject of morbid fascination among historians.
But it didn't bother most Britons. They cared little about whether the
Japanese were taking over, say, the motorbike industry, as long as
they still had well-paid jobs to go to in another sector. Until the
1970s they did. Bearing in mind that Beveridge's definition of full
employment was 3 per cent of the workforce signing on, from 1945
to 1965 the figure was 1.8 per cent. Even in 1972, it was only 3.8
per cent. As Eric Hopkins has commented, 'Figures warning of the
country's relative decline were of little interest to the average working
man and woman who understandably enough were more concerned
with job prospects, conditions at work and standards of living.'[76] It
was only later, when unemployment began to rise, that the long-term
consequences of the nation's position began to impinge on the consciousness of ordinary Britons.

Despite concern about growing trade union militancy, Conservatives rejoiced in the three successive General Election victories they
won from 1951 to 1959. When Nye Bevan died in 1960, one
obituary observed 'the sound of class war is drowned by the hum of
the spin-dryer', a comment that must have had Bevan spinning.[77] In
1962, five years after saying 'most of our people have never had it so
good', Macmillan told the Cabinet:

We have, as a whole, raised the general standard of our people to a point never materially reached before with opportunities for educational and spiritual development that no country I know of has ever had in the world.[78]

However, throughout the island there was a refusal to keep postwar affluence within a prewar moral straitjacket. As elsewhere in the West, Britain's elites were discovering that popular capitalism brought with it new social problems as people applied the libertarian tenets of the free market to their private lives. Although 'immorality' was not confined to the under-thirties, it was the youth revolt and the vibrant popular culture which sprang from it that most worried conservatives.

The 'Angry Young Men' were blamed for rabble-rousing. Unlike previous generations of British intellectuals, most came from working- and lower-middle-class backgrounds. They were products of free secondary education, their radicalism nurtured on the very real frustrations of Britain's still class-bound society, rather than on well-meaning membership of the Left Book Club. Their work was shot through with a then shockingly realistic approach to sex and class, and the subjects they dealt with included abortion, delinquency and homosexuality. Noël Coward was the quintessence of the dramatists whose drawing-room view of British life social realists attempted to overthrow. Early in 1957, he had this to say about them:

I have just read *Look Back in Anger* by John Osborne and it is full of talent and fairly well constructed, but I wish I knew why the hero is so dreadfully cross and what about? ... I expect my bewilderment is because I am very old indeed and cannot understand why the younger generation, instead of knocking at the door, should bash the fuck out of it.[79]

The work of the 'Angries' was brought to a wider audience through press hype and popular film adaptations of their books and plays. A marker of the time was Ealing Studios' rejection of 'New Wave' scripts. They were offered to Sir Michael Balcon through Ken Tynan, then a young script editor at the studios, who tried hard to refresh a British institution that was showing signs of creative torpor. One of the ideas that made Balcon's jaw drop was a treatment of Colin MacInnes' novel *City of Spades*, which he rejected on the grounds that 'it contained references to prostitution and drug taking, not to mention a black man kissing a white girl'. Tynan resigned in frustration and he was scathing about Ealing's failure to modify the cosy 1940s vision of consensual Britain in which it was wilfully trapped. 'The no-man's land between Establishment and Outsider never began to be trodden,' he told Balcon, 'Good taste intervened to prevent action.'[80] Unwilling to move with the times, the studio which had made its name 'projecting Britain and the British character' folded in 1955. Fittingly, its studios were sold to the organization where Balcon's outlook still predominated: the BBC.

Black Britons were also blamed for the teenage revolution, partly because they were associated with promiscuity and drug-dealing and partly because of the influence of black music on rock 'n' roll (an ironic view, given that so many Teddy boys were self-proclaimed racists). Rock 'n' roll was thought to be a subtle form of revenge by colonial subjects on their former masters. The primitive beat of the African jungle, argued its opponents, was filtered through black American society, then transmitted to Britain by an unscrupulous US entertainment industry, run largely by Jews who were intent on the destruction of national cultures. In 1956, the *Daily Mail* published a front-page editorial, 'ROCK 'N' ROLL BABIES', describing the music as follows: 'It is deplorable. It is tribal. And it is from America. It follows ragtime, blues, dixie, jazz, hot cha-cha and the boogie-woogie, which surely originated in the jungle. We sometimes wonder whether this is the Negro's revenge.'[81] The music's intense sexuality was singled out to show the danger which black immigrants posed to British sexual mores. The *Mail* said, 'Rock 'n' roll . . . is sexy music. It can make the blood race. It has something of the African tom-tom and voodoo dance.'[82]

The popular press were not the only organs who took this view. Government officials blamed juvenile delinquency on unlicensed black dancing clubs and the supposedly voracious sexual appetites of the coloured men who frequented them. Women were thought to be particularly vulnerable, with drugs seen as a way of overcoming their 'natural' resistance to other races. This had been a feature of racist discourse since moral panics of the late Victorian period about young white women, known as 'Dope Girls', visiting Chinese opium dens in Britain's seaports. The alarm became more intense in this period. A London County Council Report submitted to the Home Secretary at his request in September 1964 observed that at the Flamingo Club in Wardour Street 'there is traffic in "pep pills" and . . . there is a great deal of "necking" especially with coloured people. In this atmosphere any young person is obviously in serious moral danger.'

The worst clubs were those further west in Notting Hill where 'heroin and hemp were said to be available and coloured men were associating with white girls'. The report concluded, 'It requires a strong character and a secure home background with understanding parents to avoid contamination once the young person has entered the "club world".'[83]

The main fear was that rock 'n' roll, together with the dizzying succession of cults and fashions it spawned, was accelerating America's erosion of British culture. Both right and left saw teenage affluence as a sort of ideological air-conditioning system. It cooled brains that were once febrile with poverty. But at the same time it spread the virus of transatlantic cultural degeneracy more quickly than it had ever been spread before. Attacks on the influence of America reached a peak in the late 1950s and early 1960s. The cinema disturbances by rockers which accompanied the release of *Blackboard Jungle* in 1956 (featuring Bill Haley's 'Rock Around the Clock') caused alarm. But most of all, it sprang from left-wing resentment of Conservative electoral successes and a failure to understand the sociological change behind them.

As Marks became more popular than Marx, the Labour Party panicked, claiming that British society was fragmenting under a wave of individualism. Hugh Gaitskell wrote: 'people nowadays are more family and less community conscious than they used to be'.[84] Advertisers were pilloried for exploiting the people, just as factory and mine owners had once been. The trouble was that this time the people seemed to be rather enjoying it and any criticism of their exploiters necessarily involved a criticism of them. It was a dilemma which had faced left/liberal cultural reformers throughout the century, but it became more acute during this period. In 1957 J. B. Priestley coined the term 'Admass' to describe a Britain in which 'people would cheerfully exchange their last glimpse of freedom for a new car, a refrigerator and a TV screen.'[85] In the same year, Richard Hoggart's *The Uses of Literacy* was published. Like Priestley, he was a grammar-school educated Yorkshireman who lamented the decline of Edwardian working-class culture. This, he believed had been alert, virile and open to improvement. In its place was a new 'candy-floss' world of passivity and ignorance. Hoggart reserved his bitterest prose for the 'American slouch' of the Teddy boys:

> The young men waggle one shoulder or stare, as desperately as Humphrey Bogart, across the tubular chairs. Compared with even

the pub around the corner, this is all a peculiar thin and pallid form of dissipation, a sort of spiritual dry-rot amid the odour of boiled milk. Many of the customers – their clothes, their hairstyles, their facial expressions – are living . . . in a myth world . . . which they take to be those of American life.

'This increasing diet . . . of sensation without commitment' was turning the young Briton into a 'hedonistic but passive barbarian'.[86] Over the next decade, the book became a Bible for the left, much as Robert Tressell's *Ragged Trousered Philanthropists* had been for previous generations of socialists. Language was also policed. The British Communist Party leader, Harry Pollit, rebuked younger comrades for using American slang: 'In these days when we are fighting for our national identity, why use the Yankee expression "gotten"?'[87]

The novelist and left-wing activist Doris Lessing condemned the 'deeply puritan, pleasure hating' strand in British socialism.[88] Some radicals – notably Anthony Crosland, Raymond Postgate, and Michael Young – tried to do something about it by putting forward the idea of the 'citizen consumer'. This was a Briton who combined material desires and professional aspirations with community-mindedness. The successful outcome of their fresh approach was Young's Consumers Association, founded in 1958, and Postgate's *Good Food Guide*, first published in 1951. By the early 1960s the *Good Food Guide* had become a national institution used by lorry drivers and MPs alike. A landmark in the history of British gastronomy, its success dispelled the myth that the British neither knew nor cared about food.[89] But radicals like Postgate had little effect on attitudes until the 1960s. In 1959, the Labour Party set up a Youth Commission which included the footballer Jimmy Hill, the jazz trumpeter Humphrey Lyttleton and the star of the cult teen-film *Expresso Bongo*, Sylvia Syms. But Labour Youth pamphlets like *Take It from Here* relentlessly ticked off teenagers, making it worse by explaining why: 'This doesn't mean that socialists don't have their fun . . . of course they do. But they keep these things in proportion. They enjoy life at deeper levels too – and they enjoy it the more intensely because "enjoyment" is not their main object.'[90] It was not surprising, therefore, that Labour's heaviest loss of support at the 1959 election was among the under-thirties. As well as heaping verbiage on the young there was also a concrete attempt to shore up the British way of life by restoring discipline among them.

The new Kingston Bypass at Tolworth in Surrey, flanked by semi-detached houses and their gardens, 1939. '[I saw] the England of arterial and by-pass roads, of filling stations and factories that look like exhibition buildings, of giant cinemas and dance halls and cafes, bungalows with tiny garages, cocktail bars, Woolworths, motor-coaches, wireless, hiking, factory girls looking like actresses, greyhound racing and dirt tracks, swimming pools and everything given away with cigarette coupons.' J. B. Priestley, *English Journey*, 1934.

Surviving riveters at work in the empty shipyards of Clydebank, c. 1935. 'Scotland is losing its industries as it lost a hundred years ago a great deal of its agriculture and most of its indigenous literature. The waste glens of Sutherlandshire and the literary depopulation of Edinburgh and Glasgow were not obvious blows at Scotland's existence, and so they were accepted without serious protest, for the general absorption in industrial progress and money blinded everybody to them. Now Scotland's industry, like its intelligence before it, is gravitating to England, but its population is sitting where it did before, in the company of disused coal-pits and silent shipyards.' Edwin Muir, *Scottish Journey*, 1935.

1914: The people of 'England' go to war against Germany. OPPOSITE 1939: The people of 'Britain' go to war against Germany. '[During the Second World War] there was a new spirit of independence and hope in Scotland's national life. You could sense it everywhere . . . We met England now without any inferiority complex. We were a nation once again.' Tom Johnston, Secretary of State for Scotland, 1941–45.

RAF Spitfires race to meet a Luftwaffe attack over the south coast of England during the Battle of Britain. 'Yesterday we were directed into a raid coming towards Beachy Head, and had an absolutely superb scrap about fifteen miles out at sea . . . Boy! This certainly is the life!' Nigel Rose, a twenty-one-year-old pilot in a Scottish squadron writing home to his parents, September 1940.

St Paul's Cathedral survives another German bombing raid in the autumn of 1940, thanks to the efforts of clergy, firemen and local volunteers. 'We fight to drive back from our Island the paganism overthrown by King Oswy in the last English battle for Christianity . . . We fight to save Europe from the foul spectacle of virtue dethroned and Hitler set up as the god of vice; and for ourselves we fight to save from destruction all that is noblest in our way of life.' Arthur Mee, bestselling author of *Nineteen Forty: Our Finest Hour*, 1941.

A Watford woman learns how to kill German invaders from a member of the Home Guard, 1941. 'It made me feel very English indeed, when one after the other stood up and announced herself not by her own name but by the name of the county she represented – "Norfolk! Devon! Warwick!" I felt how much, how very much, I liked the English; how much, how very much, how painfully much I loved England. Vita Sackville-West, after watching Women's Land Army recruits on parade, c. 1943.

America helps to win the war: GIs take pot shots at a caricature of Adolf Hitler in an amusement arcade, Piccadilly Circus, London, 1945. 'A noticeably more intelligent attitude towards the Americans exists among the people of this country than when they arrived, and an unmistakeable interest in America has been aroused among the young.' Sir Godfrey Haggard, Head of American Forces Liaison at the Ministry of Information, September 1945.

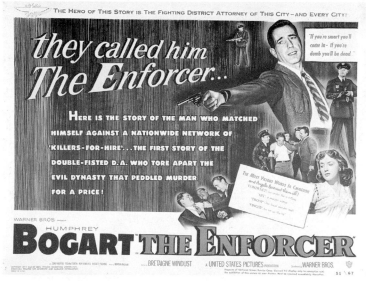

Humphrey Bogart enforces the American influence on British life, 1951. 'Speaking as an ordinary cinema-goer, I should like to see more films which genuinely show our way of life. I am tired of the sadistic gangster films made by diseased minds which occupy so much of our screen time. I should also like the screen writers to go up to the North of England, Scotland and Wales and the rest of the country and to all the parts of London which are not so frequently portrayed in our films.' Harold Wilson, creator of the National Film Finance Corporation, addressing Parliament, January 1949.

Jamaican ex-servicemen on board the *Empire Windrush* are welcomed to Britain by RAF officers after landing at Tilbury to start a new life, 22 June 1948. 'An influx of coloured people is likely to impair the harmony, strength and cohesion of our public life and to bring discord and unhappiness among all concerned.' Labour MPs, writing to the Prime Minister, summer 1948.

The Queen lays the foundation stone of the National Theatre on 13 July 1951, twenty-five years before it opened. To the right, the Archbishop of Canterbury, Geoffrey Fisher, looks on approvingly. 'I have an optimistic view of the future. This country has had a great loss of military power and wealth. These things have passed to those two remote monsters who live to the east and west of Europe. Their way of life, though very different, has no real appeal to us. But I am convinced that Shakespeare's countrymen are about to enjoy an Athenian summer of great interest and charm.' Lord Esher, leader of the campaign to create a National Theatre, addressing Parliament in February 1949.

The Festival of Britain, South Bank Exhibition. The Dome of Discovery and Skylon face a scaffolded Palace of Westminster, 15 May 1951. 'If we British do not deserve to show off and enjoy ourselves, then who in the name of thunder in this mad world does deserve it? We have fought the two worst wars in history from beginning to end: we have been burned, blasted and battered: we have pawned, scraped and queued up patiently for all manner of scrag-ends: we have set the world an example of public spirit, tolerance, self-discipline and patience; so – by Jupiter! – either there must be no enjoyment in this world, which is ridiculous, or we British are now entitled to our own slice of it. So – on with the Festival!' J. B. Priestley, May 1951.

Elizabeth I of Scotland sits above the Stone of Destiny after being crowned Elizabeth II by the Archbishop of Canterbury, 2 June 1953 (to her right stands Michael Ramsey, Archbishop of York and, later, of Canterbury). 'The Country and the Commonwealth last Tuesday were not far from the Kingdom of Heaven.' Archbishop Fisher, broadcasting to the British people shortly after the Coronation.

A Welsh family settle down to an evening's entertainment on 'the box' in the 1950s. 'This is an historic occasion. Here is a means of communication which enters the homes of millions of our countrymen, and has an unrivalled power to persuade . . . Free television like a free Press will not be controlled by any council or committee, but by two factors – the television companies' sense of responsibility and the fundamental good sense and right feeling of the British people.' Sir Kenneth Clark announcing the start of commercial TV in Britain, 22 September 1955.

A young Scot dreams of a Scottish parliament in January 1951, soon after the Stone of Destiny is taken from Westminster Abbey. 'During the war years party politics were in abeyance and the patriotic sentiment was concentrated on the war effort . . . Now there is a widespread feeling that Scotland is held to be of no account by British governments. The matter is of some urgency. There is a powerful upsurge of Scottish spirit at the moment . . . It is a kind of smouldering pile that might suddenly break through the party loyalties and become a formidable national movement.' Arthur Woodburn, Secretary of State for Scotland, warning the Cabinet to take his country seriously, Downing Street, 6 December 1947.

Robert MacIntyre, the first Scottish Nationalist MP, addresses a Home Rule rally in Trafalgar Square, 19 April 1953. 'I believe the English are finished as a world power and must be forced back on their own "right little, tight little" island, or rather that part of which is their own. Surely there is no need to slobber kisses on the feet that are trampling us down. We have nothing to be grateful for to the English.' Hugh MacDiarmid, co-founder of the SNP, 1949.

The Archdruid of Wales, Edgar Phillips, initiates the Duke of Edinburgh into the Gorsedd of Bards as 'Philip Meironydd', Cardiff, 5 August 1960. 'We want to remind ourselves of our own heritage because it is sometimes overlooked that our language and culture are among the oldest in Europe and that we are England's original partner in the great Commonwealth experiment of living together.' The Plaid Cymru leader, Huw T. Edwards, announcing the start of the 1958 Festival of Wales.

6. There is nothing debasing about discipline

Concern focused on the decision, taken in 1957, to phase out National Service by 1960. It had been introduced by the Attlee Government with cross-party support in 1947, and the armed services had begun taking the new conscripts from 1949. The annual intake was 160,000 men with approximately 2.5 million serving over its sixteen-year existence. Most were between the ages of eighteen and twenty-one and served 730 days. Politicians and service chiefs had been conscious that they were overturning a long-standing British tradition of not having a conscript army. What made them change their mind?

First, a lingering desire to retain a world role. Britain's armed forces had to police a continent threatened by the Soviet Union, as well as an increasingly rebellious Empire, and they were chronically overstretched as a result of postwar demobilization. Field Marshal Montgomery, promoted Chief of the Imperial General Staff in 1946, pressed Attlee on those grounds. In his memoirs he wrote, 'The whole idea of conscription in peacetime [was] repugnant to British traditions . . . [But] by September 1946, it had become clear that drastic measures would be necessary.'[91] The second reason was guilt over appeasement and the country's unpreparedness for war in 1939. Agreeing with the move, Churchill told the Commons:

> The only way to make us a nation in time of war is by national service in time of peace. As all our habits in the past have been to live in a peaceful manner, we have entered all our wars unprepared, and the delay before we are able to place an army in the field at the side of our allies has been a very serious weakness, not only in the physical but in the moral sphere.[92]

Churchill also argued that Britain could learn something from the Continent. 'It [has] been defended and practised by all the most advanced democratic countries in Europe since the French Revolution'.[93]

The third reason for its introduction was growing concern about the youth problem. National service was seen as a means of instilling discipline and patriotism in young Britons in order to check the rising levels of juvenile delinquency. In the long term, it was hoped that mass experience of military life would forge national unity by fostering more contact between different classes, as the Second World War had done.[94] The physical as well as the moral health of the nation was seen to be at stake. Since the Boer War, Britain's leaders had fretted that the working classes were not fit enough to defend the UK if called upon to do so. Although far fewer Britons were malnourished in the 1950s than in the 1900s, their physical fitness was still a source of concern. In 1953 the Minister for Labour and National Service, Walter Monckton, drew these themes together, telling Parliament that conscripts 'experience as good a comradeship as they are likely to get anywhere. They generally benefit a great deal in health and physique and put on weight. They have an opportunity of travel certainly in Britain and possibly overseas.'[95]

National service was a victim of the defence cuts which followed the Sandys White Paper in 1957. Growing acceptance that the Empire was no longer a viable concern and that nuclear power was the best way to defend Britain undermined the arguments advanced by Monty immediately after the war. A less publicized reason for abolition was the armed forces' concern that large numbers of blacks and Asians would be liable for the call-up as a result of immigration. They had served with distinction in the British armed forces for two centuries, but most had done so in native rather than UK regiments. The enlistment of black Britons into the professional army could be controlled by prejudicial selection, but statutory national service was another matter. Instead of restoring the patriotism of young Britons who were thought to have been corrupted by pop music, national service threatened to bring the source of the 'problem' into the heart of Britain's defence. An Army Council report concluded that the loyalty of black and Asian soldiers could not be relied on in wartime: 'To sum up, the enlistment of coloured men into the Army, and *a fortiori*, the grant of commissions in the British Army to them, constitutes, in the view of the Army Council, a threat to the discipline and well-being of the Army which might be a very serious matter in time of war.'[96] Service chiefs recommended that only men 'of pure European descent' should be allowed into the armed forces.[97] But racial affinity with other Europeans did not produce a concomitant desire to adopt their methods of defence.

Abolitionists were also motivated by persistent worries that conscription was an alien European measure for defending the nation-state. They believed it impinged on the freedom of the individual and undermined the voluntary tradition in both civil and military life upon which the British prided themselves. This was apparent in the official literature produced for the information of young conscripts. *A Guide For the National Service Man in the Army*, published in 1953, said:

> We are not strictly speaking a military nation. We are prepared to fight when we have to, but as soon as war is over we rush to disband our forces. We have not, like some Continental countries, a love of uniform, parades and displays . . . The net result of all this is that, whereas the Continental youth looks forward with pride . . . to his period of military service, and accepts it as the natural order of things, in this country it is still regarded as an innovation and an interruption to the normal course of life. [However] it is in truth an education in itself – the finest in the world: quite apart from the training and instruction the National Service man will receive, he will meet and live with men drawn from all classes of society, of all trades, of all standards of education, and of various religious and political faiths . . . Discipline is the foundation of the army . . . without [it] we should get nowhere. Discipline starts with the individual and there is nothing debasing about it; in fact the very reverse.[98]

Such apologias failed to change British attitudes. By the mid-1950s, national service had become unpopular among those who had to endure it and among the public as a whole. It was lampooned in literature and drama, notably David Lodge's *Ginger, You're Barmy*, Arnold Wesker's *Chips With Everything* (both 1962) and Leslie Thomas' *Virgin Soldiers* (1966). All three authors had been conscripted and they portrayed a generation of young Britons who were either irreverent towards military authority or dehumanized by it (suicides were not uncommon, a subject that Lodge's novel dealt with). Films dealing with the subject rejected the mores of the archetypal British war film, in which the classes were shown to be pulling together harmoniously. The first Carry On production, *Carry on Sergeant* (1958), lacked the sexual innuendo which the genre later became famous for, directing its slapstick wit at military authority. 'Your rank?' 'That's a matter of opinion!' was a typical exchange between officers and men. In the Boulting Brothers' *Private's Progress* (1956) officers were shown to be nice but ineffectual twits – Stanley Windrush, played by Ian Carmichael – or they were pompous rogues with a disdain for the men under their command – Major Hitchcock, played by the brilliant Terry-Thomas. Terry-Thomas' put-down 'You're an absolute shower!' (pronounced 'shar') became a national catchphrase, denoting the hapless fury with which Britain's officer class tried to maintain some discipline over the lower orders. In 1955, a committee of inquiry chaired by Sir John Wolfenden interviewed hundreds of conscripts. The report concluded: 'Our overwhelming impression is that, with few exceptions, the National Service man regards his . . . period of service as an infliction to be undergone rather than a duty to the nation.'[99] From July 1956 opinion polls showed that a majority of Britons wanted to see it ended and the numbers rose steadily after Suez.

However, as concern about Britain's youth turned into a full-blown moral panic in the late 1950s, national service recovered some of its popularity, particularly among those aged forty and over. By the time the last conscript was demobbed in 1963, regret over abolition had became a mantra of those who wanted a simple explanation for social change. Conservatives realized that restoring it would alienate younger voters. But for the rest of the century they mourned its loss. Abolition was widely seen as a decision taken in haste and an opportunity missed to shore up traditional British patriotism at a pivotal moment in the Isles' history. Harold Macmillan himself regretted the decision. 'We made a mistake,' he said towards the end of his life, 'we should have kept it for six months, something like the Swiss, just to teach soldiers the simple things.'[100]

Could the retention of national service have altered the trajectory of national identity in postwar Britain? Evidence suggests not. Certainly, some men benefited from the experience. Lance Corporal Griffith Roberts from north Wales, who served in the Royal Corps of Signals, remembered:

> My service gave me self-confidence, taught me comradeship, understanding of my fellow men, discipline and appreciation of my home and parents. I returned to Caernarvon a very responsible adult. I had come across quite a few hoodlums from the bigger cities, but the Army soon knocked them into shape and they left their National Service far better citizens than when they entered it.[101]

Another Welshman remembers 'most of us *did* feel proud to be part of an army which had only recently won the war.'[102] There was also a grudging acceptance that military service was a patriotic duty. 'We were a generation of war children, really, so [it] didn't strike us as strange ... We were the sort of kids that had picked up bits of shrapnel ... so it was a continuation of ... maybe we'll need to be the next defence line'.[103] There was also pressure from parents to go willingly. 'I don't think you could look 'em in the face if you didn't do it ... You had a feeling that you had to do your bit after your father and uncles had actually had to fight.'[104]

However, most accounts bear out Wolfenden's conclusion that it was an 'infliction to be undergone'. Iain Colquhoun, a Glaswegian corporal in the Royal Engineers, wrote: 'A young man is going to grow up at a given age no matter whether he's in an office, a factory, the army, or on a boat ... I worked for two years in the pits in Scotland ... Compared to the Army, the Scottish coal mines were a warm, profoundly moving and satisfying way to live.'[105] Others observed that the hard-drinking, womanizing culture of the barrack room did not exactly lend itself to moral reform. Just as prison could teach old cons new tricks, so the army could teach young squaddies old tricks. This tendency was accentuated if men did not see active service, as many did not.

More importantly, there is no concrete evidence that military standards of discipline were continued by men after they were demobbed. It is true that crime in Britain soared after National Service was abolished, up from 846,330 notifiable offences in 1960 to 1,735,600 in 1970, but the upward trend was already apparent in the second half of the 1950s. In the eight years before National Service ended, violent crime trebled and sexual crime rose almost as fast. By the mid-1950s, however much young, male Britons regarded themselves as patriots, they no longer saw military service as a criterion of that patriotism. Nor did they see it as a life experience which taught codes of behaviour that ought, for the good of the nation, to be carried over into civilian life. Indeed, the majority resented the interruption to their social and love lives, lives that were just getting under way when they were plucked from their homes. Supporters of national service were right to argue that abolition gave a boost to British youth culture, because it kept affluent, testosterone-fuelled young men on the streets at a crucial age in their development (the first thing Iain Colquhoun did after being demobbed was to go and see *Blackboard Jungle*). Abolition also widened the generation gap. Correlli Barnett has noted, 'The army and the nation began to drift apart, as the army became a closed "family"'. One does not have to lament that fact, as Barnett does, to see that the bond of military service between father and son was destroyed by abolition and with it a patriotic continuum in British life.[106]

In the early 1960s, Macmillan looked enviously across the Atlantic at John F. Kennedy, that 'young, cocky Irishman' who was inspiring a vigorous patriotism among a new generation of American voters. Such was the concern about British youth in this period that the Conservative Party became interested again in the idea that state patronage of the arts might create better Britons. Macmillan was at first dubious about the idea, given the abject failure of the experiment conducted in the 1940s. On one occasion when Sir Kenneth Clark went to see him to ask for more money for the Arts Council, the Prime Minister disconcertingly opened the discussion with, 'Good evening, Clark, now what's this trouble with your Arts Society?'[107] There was also an abiding feeling in the Conservative Party that the Council was incorrigibly left-wing. But when David Eccles approached the Prime Minister with a comprehensive plan which included state investment in British sport, Macmillan did respond. Replying to Eccles, he declared (somewhat tongue in cheek), 'I am all for tempting the Teddy Boys into the Geological Museum'.[108]

The Party set up an Arts and Amenities Committee, chaired by Keith Joseph to see how best to tempt them. Joseph, who became one of Mrs Thatcher's ideologues in the 1980s, defined the Committee's aim as follows:

There are two main reasons why the use of leisure has become a question of national importance since the war. The first of these is the emancipation of the adolescent, happening so suddenly that it has taken everyone by surprise. Young people nowadays have more spare time, more money and more surplus energy than they have ever had before. What all too many of them lack, however, is a corresponding sense of purpose and of personal responsibility. The second is the scientific revolution with its promise of increasingly more leisure. Rising productivity and growing 'automation' (in the home as well as in the factory and office) have already made for shorter working hours and higher living standards, and this welcome process will accelerate. The leisured class, it might be said, has made way for the age of leisure. We expect the end of 'call up' and the 'bulge' emerging from the schools to make this a compelling issue in the early 60s. The time is therefore ripe for the Conservative Party to formulate a comprehensive policy embracing . . . sport, recreation and the arts . . . It is government's clear duty to encourage the true leisure of the subject, as it has for long been to ensure his liberty. For leisure, wrongly used, constitutes a real threat to society.[109]

Over the following year, a range of figures attended the Committee's meetings, from the athlete and Tory MP Christopher Chataway to David Sheppard, cricketer and Bishop of Liverpool. Suggestions included replacing national service with a three-month youth service involving plenty of games and travel; and, rather less appealingly, the introduction of work camps. The result of these deliberations was that spending on arts and sports facilities increased slightly but little of note was achieved.

The Home Office fared no better. In 1959, Rab Butler convened a national conference on juvenile delinquency attended by thirty-four bodies ranging from the Church of England to the TUC. Sex was the main topic of conversation. One delegate complained that 'our young people know far more about sex than we did at their age'; he added that out of 301 girls admitted that year to the approved school he administered, 80 per cent needed treatment for venereal disease and that 'only one . . . was sexually intact.'[110] The conference agreed that better moral instruction was the answer. Other solutions offered by delegates included an appeal to Britons not to buy their *Radio Times* from newsagents selling pornographic magazines. Where boys were concerned, delegates thought corporal punishment was necessary and some regretted the abolition of the birch by the Attlee government. The Minister of Education, Geoffrey Lloyd, gave a vivid account of his rebellious youth at Harrow and the character-forming solution which one of his masters came up with:

> I went through a phase when I did not brush my hair in quite the way that was thought desirable, and my form master made me turn up at his lodgings at a quarter past seven every morning with my hair properly brushed and sing a tune for him [after which] he did not hesitate to administer mild corporal punishment to me, and I cannot myself feel that anything else but very great benefit resulted to me.[111]

Butler agreed that caning was 'a normal thing which has gone on throughout English educational history' and was most effective when used on 'naughty small boys'.[112] As a former headmaster of Repton, the Archbishop of Canterbury was no stranger to the cane (he had been known as 'Flog 'Em Fisher' by staff and pupils). The Archbishop quoted with dismay a social worker who had recently said the problem of delinquency would not be solved 'until these young people have somebody who loves them'. Fisher's answer was not love but leadership; leadership which, he said, the British intelligentsia was now failing to provide:

> I was shocked more than I can say to read that in the Festival Hall, which was built to bear witness to the fine spirit of England, there is to be a concert . . . at which ribald songs of the seventeenth and eighteenth century are to be performed . . . If the intelligentsia like to listen to ribald songs unfit for publication, why should we ask young people to ignore their own natural instincts in the way of sex?[113]

Butler, the Home Secretary, concluded: 'We may think we can win by moral leadership or religious inspiration, but human nature is very much helped if people have enough to do to keep them busy.'[114]

Keeping youth busy had been the motive behind the creation of a state youth service in 1939, when the Chamberlain government empowered local authorities to spend money on setting up youth clubs. It now became a priority. In 1960, the Albemarle Report on the Youth Service was published. Chaired by the philanthropist Diana, Countess of Albemarle, the Committee members included Richard Hoggart, his appointment prompted by Lady Albemarle's reading of *The Uses of Literacy*. What Hoggart described as her 'patrician decisiveness' led to a massive expansion in the youth service and, to the horror of the clergy, the abolition of prayers before meetings.[115] Central government authorized 1,200 projects worth £11.5 million up to 1964, while local authority spending doubled to £5.6 million. It was a worthy attempt to avert boredom and provide leadership, but there remained only one professional youth leader to every 5,000 teenagers.

More importantly, the outlook of those running the service did not change much. In 1959, the leader of the Everest expedition, Sir John Hunt, organized a National Youth Club Week in which a parchment section of 'Domesday Book' was relayed from Coventry to London by young athletes. As one journalist drily remarked, 'This daring gesture must have deeply impressed the leather boys trying their motorbikes on the brand-new M1 motorway.'[116] In 1960, a number of youth leaders were sacked for allowing their flock to play rock 'n' roll, billiards and darts. A report of one incident in Huddersfield recommended instead a diet of 'handicrafts, classical music . . . and drama festivals'. The failure was as much to do with naivety as authoritarianism. In 1962, the London Union of Youth Clubs, 'seek-

ing to mould the citizens of tomorrow', sent 100 teenage girls to sea
on an 'initiative' test in which they ended up spending the night on a
vessel full of merchant seamen. Tommy Hicks, from Bermondsey in
south-east London, began his working life as a steward in the
merchant navy. As Tommy Steele, he became the first major home-
grown rock 'n' roll star, with seven top-ten hits between 1956 and
1960. In an interview with the *Observer* Steele recalled his experience
of his local youth club. 'I always felt that it wasn't *my* club. What
we did was all right, but it was *all* arranged – handed down by
grown-ups. Fashions change and there are fashions in fun. Only the
young people know what they want at any given time.'[117]

The BBC attempted to find out what Britain's youth wanted. As
part of the corporation's attempt to compete with ITV, it produced
the first proper youth programme. *Six-Five Special* brought pop
music to the nation at Saturday tea-times in 1957–8. Because of the
non-existence of other such shows, it got an audience of between 9
and 12 million. But the programme revealed how little the BBC had
learnt from the whipping it was getting in the ratings and how little
it understood youth culture. Like many people at the time, Light
Entertainment executives thought rock 'n' roll was a passing fad and
after a tune from, say, Cliff Richard it would be off to Wales for a
report on the benefits of hill-climbing. The BBC proudly declared
that *Six-Five Special* had become 'a national institution equally
enjoyed by the parents'.[118] But audience research showed that teenagers were not satisfied with it. They particularly disliked the fact that
the presenters – Pete Murray and Josephine Douglas – were squeaky
clean, middle class and in their late thirties. The opening exchange
between the two captured the whole tone of the show:

PETE: Hi there, welcome aboard the Six-Five Special. We've got
    almost a hundred cats jumping here, some real cool characters
    to give us the gas, so just get with it and have a ball.
JO: Well, I'm just a square it seems, but for all the other squares
    with us, roughly translated what Peter Murray just said was,
    we've got some lively musicians and personalities mingling with
    us here, so just relax and catch the mood from us.[119]

The twenty-six-year-old producer of *Six-Five Special*, Jack Good,
was responsible for shaving off Cliff Richard's sideburns to make
him more respectable (a process which ended with a knighthood for
the singer in 1995). But it was not long before Good grew tired of
fighting for the right to party at the BBC and left for ITV. There,

shows devoted to pop and hosted by younger people such as *Oh Boy!* (1958–9) and *Ready, Steady, Go!* (1963–6) all trounced the BBC until in 1964 it introduced *Top of the Pops*. First broadcast from a disused church in Manchester, it became the most watched and longest-running of all music programmes.

7. You see, I am English and like to ply my hobby in privacy

The opponents of commercial TV fought a rearguard action which demonstrated once and for all how out of touch they were with the British people. On 15 September 1960, shortly before the fifth anniversary of ITV's birth, the government established a committee to examine the state of British broadcasting under the chairmanship of the Lancashire glass manufacturer and Director of the Bank of England, Sir Harry Pilkington. With the exception of the former England football captain Billy Wright, the majority of the committee's members were academics, Richard Hoggart among them. The debate was even more impassioned than it had been in the early 1950s because of the growing uncertainty about the future of Britishness.

In a leading article called 'The Uses of Television', the *Observer* explained: 'The morale and temper of the country in the next few years, which are likely to be the roughest in our history, will be formed as much by television as by any other factor'. TV bosses should try to refine taste rather than 'feeding the undoubted public appetite for trivialities and narcotics'.[120] At a speech in Manchester, the Chairman of the ITA, Sir Robert Fraser, defended the system.

> If you decide to have a system of people's television, then people's television you must expect it to be. It will reflect their likes and dislikes, their tastes and aversions, what they can comprehend and what is beyond them. Every person of common sense knows that people of superior mental constitution are bound to find much of television intellectually beneath them. If such innately fortunate people cannot realise this gently and considerately and with good manners, if in their hearts they despise popular pleasures and

interests, then of course they will be angrily dissatisfied with television. But it is not really television with which they are dissatisfied. It is with people.[121]

He was pretty much alone: 636 memoranda were submitted by various organizations, nearly all of them attacking ITV. The most damaging criticism came from Fraser's disillusioned predecessor, Sir Kenneth Clark, who told the Committee, 'More control will be needed to prevent a Gadarene descent.'[122] More control was exactly what Pilkington recommended. In a lengthy adjudication, published in June 1962, commercial broadcasting was condemned as 'trivial', the uplifting work of the BBC was warmly praised and the government was advised to improve the situation by allowing the ITA to take over programme planning and the selling of advertising time from the companies. Peter Cadbury, the Chairman of Westward Television, held a bonfire party at which copies of the report were burnt.

Though its response was less dramatic, the government also rejected the report. Macmillan had mixed feelings about TV. He was the first British Prime Minister to manipulate the medium. Like all those who do so successfully, he mistrusted it. But the Prime Minister also regarded TV as an antidote to the press barons whom he loathed; and neither he nor the Cabinet saw any advantage in interfering with a system that was both profitable and popular. The Postmaster-General, Reg Bevins, was equally unimpressed. A sharp-suited, working-class Liverpudlian, he was a fierce patriot who had supported the Suez invasion and despised liberal intellectuals 'whose public sport it is to throw mud at their own country'.[123] He told Macmillan, 'The committee has been swayed unduly by the evidence of prejudiced but articulate organisations and has largely ignored the inarticulate man on the street.'[124] The press agreed. The *Daily Mirror* headline 'PILKINGTON TELLS THE PUBLIC TO GO TO HELL' partly reflected the fact that the Mirror Group had shares in ATV. But for once corporate self-interest did reflect the national mood. The Committee's outlook and the public response to it was deftly summed up by Woodrow Wyatt in the *Sunday Pictorial*: 'You trivial people will have to brush up your culture.'[125] Pilkington was a minor but significant point in the history of postwar national identity. It refuelled the long debate on British culture which then dragged on for the rest of the century. Liberal reformers became more tactful as time went on. They spoke less about Britons improving their taste and more about the media 'dumbing down'. But their fundamental assumptions about what should constitute national culture remained just as narrow.

The emergence of the so-called 'New Left' in the late 1950s seemed to mark an intellectual break with the high-minded Victorian outlook of mid-twentieth-century reformers. Critics like Raymond Williams dismissed the attempt to improve British culture as a strategy for maintaining bourgeois power (which, in the tortured argot of the time, was now called 'hegemony'). But, like the Continental theories which influenced it, the British critique of liberalism sailed close to philistinism at times. Moreover, its leading figures often loathed popular culture even more than liberals did. In an effort to explain why capitalism still had such a hold on Western society, Marxists produced a flood of jargon-ridden, scholastic theories on how the media duped people. Raymond Williams' *Communications* (1962) is sadly typical: 'We find little that is genuinely popular, developed from the life of communities. We find instead a synthetic culture, or anti-culture, which is alien to almost everybody, persistently hostile to art and intellectual activity ... and given over to exploiting indifference, lack of feeling, frustration and hatred.'[126] Consequently, what began as an attempt to move away from the elitist vision of men like John Maynard Keynes ended in a more sterile intellectual climate which gave academic employment to thousands of people but did little to refresh British society. Like the Third Programme, few listened to the New Left outside the senior common rooms of the Isles' universities. The debate on Britons' bad habits went largely unnoticed by the people themselves. Most simply got on with trying to create and consume the sort of national culture they wanted. And they found the end result neither synthetic, alien or exploitative. Britons were certainly influenced by the 'Hidden Persuaders' of modern capitalism, but they were never their dupes. The few reservations that people had about the media revolution of the 1950s were based on more traditional moral considerations about sex and violence than the question of taste which obsessed their left/liberal critics.

The monarchy played a role in maintaining traditional notions of patriotism in this period and it met with the most success. The Crown's prospects did not look good in 1957. By then, New Elizabethanism was on the wane. A lame BBC TV programme in which British inventors explained their discoveries to the accompaniment of madrigals did not last, despite the fact that A. L. Rowse acted as historical adviser. The magazine *Young Elizabethan* fared little better. Launched in 1948 by Collins, it was aimed at boys aged ten to sixteen, offering adventure stories and advice on outdoor pursuits in an effort to nurture young Edmund Hillarys. The magazine reassured its readers, 'You need not have climbed Everest. A holiday in Torquay can be as adventurous as a journey through Tibet,' a thought which did not appeal to the millions dazzled by Elvis Presley.[127] Nine years after it began, *Young Elizabethan* folded. The Elizabethan Party was also short-lived, its attempt to affiliate to the Conservatives in 1955 stymied when Central Office decided that 'Their outlook is Fascist and anti-American.'[128] Jock Colville pronounced, 'The optimistic prophecies of a splendid New Elizabethan Age have not been fulfilled', a view confirmed by Lord Harewood: 'We felt we were on the crest of everything going right, with a young Queen looking to the future, not looking back. The feel of it was very real. But in the end it lacked substance.'[129]

Why did the movement fail? Although it was ideologically coherent, it lacked substance, since its mascot could not tie herself too closely to the idea of enterprise without being seen to compromise her neutral constitutional position. It was also overtaken by the social changes of the 1950s. The Queen was partly to blame for this. In 1955 she failed to back Princess Margaret's love match with a dashing but divorced Battle of Britain veteran, Peter Townsend. Margaret gave up Townsend and was forced to issue the following statement: 'Mindful of the Church's teaching that Christian marriage is indissoluble, and conscious of my duty to the Commonwealth, I have decided to put these considerations before any others'. The event signalled that the more conservative, religious elements of New Elizabethanism had prevailed. In August 1957 a young peer, Lord Altrincham (John Grigg), launched the first public attack on a sovereign since the nineteenth century. He condemned the 'tweedy entourage' of a court still made up of the landed aristocracy; of the Queen herself, he said, 'The personality conveyed by the utterances put in her mouth is that of a priggish schoolgirl, captain of the hockey team, a prefect, and a recent candidate for Confirmation.'[130] The TV presenter Malcolm Muggeridge wrote that she was 'dowdy, frumpish and banal' and described the monarchy as a soap opera.[131] Both were condemned by the broadsheet press and Altrincham got a punch in the face from the Deputy Chairman of the League of Empire Loyalists as he was leaving the ITV buildings after an interview. Together, they had broken a spell which the Windsors had successfully cast on the British since 1937.

Though the Queen was shocked, Prince Philip agreed with the criticism and did something about it. In 1957 he ended the presentation of debutantes at Buckingham Palace, and shortly after the abolition of national service was announced he set up the Duke of Edinburgh's Award scheme (Sir John Hunt was its first Director). This was an attempt to motivate and discipline Britain's youth through wholesome, outdoor activity and social work. Its inspiration owed something to Baden-Powell and something to the Spartan methods of the German educationalist Kurt Hahn, who ran the Prince's old school, Gordonstoun. Philip's generous attempt to make Hahn's methods available to those who could not afford a place at his alma mater was a success because the Prince was still a role model for young Britons. Until the mid-1960s he repeatedly topped popularity polls, beating pop stars and politicians alike. However much the Queen tried to appear modern, opening Britain's first nuclear reactor in 1957 and London's new airport at Heathrow in 1959, until the mid-1960s she was widely seen as the remote, uptight woman described by Altrincham. In 1960, Mass Observation reported that it was Philip who 'is felt . . . to signify a *continuation of the Coronation* trend: that is, to be *seen* to exist and *felt* to belong'; it cited comments like '[he's] not so snobby as some of the others.'[132] In May 1962, the *Daily Mirror* reported 'The Verdict of Youth' on the monarchy. The Queen's Consort was 'TOP OF THE ROYAL POPS'. Most respondents agreed with seventeen-year-old Wendy Ash, a hairdresser from London, that 'Prince Philip seems really interested in people, and he sponsors that award scheme'.[133]

Furthermore, the survey showed that, much as they disliked the Queen's personality, they still respected the institution of monarchy and did not want a republic. John Osborne's pithy remark that royalty was 'the gold filling in a mouthful of decay' did not wash with Britain's teenagers. Seven out of ten agreed with twenty-one-year-old Shirley Smith, an ice-cream seller, that 'having a Queen makes it seem as if we're all part of a family'.[134] It was a revealing expression which showed not only how much the family was still valued as a social unit, but also how much the idea of the British nation as an extended family, so prevalent in the 1940s, survived into the following decades. In December 1961 the Queen addressed 'the problem of youth' in her Christmas broadcast, almost certainly written by Palace officials in conjunction with Downing Street. It is one of the most significant speeches she made in the first half of her reign, because it implicitly acknowledged that New Elizabethanism had failed to capture the imagination of young Britons.

> We can only dispel the clouds of anxiety by the patient and determined efforts of all. It cannot be done by condemning the past or by contracting out of the present. Angry words and accusations certainly don't do any good, however justified they may be. It is natural that the younger generation should lose patience with their elders for their seeming failure to bring some order and security to the world. But things will not get any better if young people merely express themselves by indifference or by revulsion against what they regard as an out-of-date order of things. The world desperately needs their vigour and determination and their service to their fellow men.[135]

The speech did not prevent youth culture becoming even more strident in the years ahead, and it certainly did not revive New Elizabethanism.

Yet the monarchy did remain the central pillar of Britishness during the upheavals of the 1950s and continued to do so until the late 1980s, outlasting most other aspects of prewar national identity. After pressure from the BBC, the Queen allowed her Christmas message to be broadcast on TV in 1958. Hopes that this would appease the insatiable desire for royal tittle-tattle were dashed. In 1962, the editor of the *New Statesman*, Kingsley Martin, wrote: 'A glorified, religious view of the monarchy is the vogue. The Queen is not allowed to wear a crown; nothing less than a halo will suffice. But the halo is neon-lighted.'[136] This did not happen overnight. For another quarter of a century the Windsors skilfully manipulated the media, maintaining their halo while other sources of Britishness lost theirs. As a result of being televised, the Queen's message to the nation became an even more integral part of the British Christmas than the radio broadcasts begun by her grandfather in 1932. It illustrates once again how the Windsors maintained their popular appeal by presenting two faces to the British. On the one hand, by emphasizing the importance of duty and the value of the family, the Queen's annual message gave a sense of stability to those who were disorientated by social change. At the same time, by openly discussing change, and doing so through a thoroughly modern medium, the Queen reached a new generation of Britons with different beliefs and aspirations.

It would therefore be wrong to give the impression of a nation lurching from one crisis to another between 1957 and 1964 with ever increasing social conflicts. A lot of the population felt they had never had it so good *and* they retained a clear sense of what being British meant. Affluence, coupled with a gradual acceptance of the UK's declining power, relieved much of the anxiety in British society as the nation shed some of its foreign responsibilities. It was the release of that anxiety, as much as the radical demands for a new order, which laid the foundations for Britain's cultural renaissance in the 1960s. Cold War paranoia was far less marked in the UK than it was in America, where the burden of empire began to be felt by a nation unused to giving much consideration to the outside world beyond the immigration desks on Staten Island. This contrast between the UK and the US was apparent in the fact that the witch-hunt of communists in British public life was less extensive and less pathological than it was across the Atlantic. The British didn't much like the idea of communism and they knew that the Soviet Union was a totalitarian state every bit as oppressive as Nazi Germany had been. But neither did they believe Reds were under their beds or at their front door.

Science fiction, which in the US was dominated by a fear of alien invasion, in the UK concerned itself more with a suspicion of scientists, fear and craving of female sexuality and, like most British culture of the time, class tensions.[137] Real science also demonstrated the relative quiescence of the British. On 4 October 1957 the Russians won the first round of the space race by launching Sputnik 1. When Macmillan visited the US in October that year he found a country gripped by paranoia. Sputnik's impact, he wrote, 'has been something equivalent to Pearl Harbour. The American cocksure-ness is shaken.'[138] Wall Street slumped and Eisenhower appeared on TV to rally the nation. In Britain, it was seen as less of a defeat because Britain now had less to lose. 'FLYING SAUCERS – OFFICIAL' said the *Daily Mirror*. But the only sign of public anxiety came when the Russians launched Sputnik 2 a month later, this one carrying a dog called Laika. The Prime Minister noted in his diary that 'the English, with characteristic frivolity, are much more alarmed about the "little dawg" than about the terrifying nature of these new developments in "rocketry". Letters and telegrams were pouring in tonight to No.10 protesting about the cruelty to the dog.'[139] A mile away from Downing Street, the Canine Defence League held a demonstration outside the Soviet Embassy to protest on Laika's behalf, her heartbeat audible on BBC transmitters as she hurtled off into the stratosphere.

Domesticity characterized British life just as much as rebellion against it. The proportion of pet-owners rose from a quarter of the UK population to half between 1950 and 1970. The number of privately owned cars rose from 2.26 million to 11.5 in the same period. Car ownership was seen as a particular symbol of change, speeding as it did the transition from a rooted community-based lifestyle to a more mobile, individual and family based one. But the most telling example of national self-containment in this respect was the growth of gardening and DIY. The rambling style of British gardens, compared to the more formal style of Continental ones, had been taken as a symbol of British pragmatism since the eighteenth century by domestic and foreign observers alike. But during the 1950s, the mass enthusiasm for gardening, far more than the style it produced, came to be seen as a key component of Britishness.

Shorter working hours and the establishment of British Summer Time in 1916 enabled people to spend more time outdoors on summer evenings, a trend which in 1939 led *The Nurseryman and Seedsman* to claim 'we have been called a nation of shopkeepers; we might with equal justice be called a nation of gardeners'.[140] In the second half of the century, this could be said with even more conviction. From the 1880s to the 1950s, allotments predominated. They reached their peak in 1950 with 1.03 million plots – a point that marks the zenith of that Victorian culture that based itself in civic communality. By 1970, the number had halved while the number of gardens more than doubled to 14 million. Four-fifths of British homes had one (in all, they covered 620,000 acres, an area equal in size to the county of Dorset). An estimated 29 million Britons were active gardeners. *Gardeners' Question Time*, first broadcast in 1947 by BBC Radio Manchester, became one of the few radio programmes which retained a mass audience after the advent of TV.

The main cause of the garden explosion was house building: 5.63 million new homes were erected between 1950 and 1970, most of them in new towns and suburbs. Home ownership almost doubled, from 27 per cent of the population in 1947 to 50 per cent in 1970 (although it remained considerably lower in Scotland, a factor which limited the spread of gardening there). Affluence also enabled people to spend more money on their hobby, the main result of which was the growth of garden centres. In the same way that supermarkets made cooking easier by supplying processed foods, garden centres allowed people too busy or impatient for cultivation to create an instant Arcadia by purchasing fully grown plants.

The Macmillan government was well pleased. In a 1963 Cabinet report on recreational trends, the Minister without Portfolio, Bill Deedes, rebutted the idea that Britons had become passive citizens of the 'television age': 'Gardening is still the greatest British hobby'. He also observed: 'leisure occupations may permanently shape [the people's] character, determine their contentment or otherwise with everyday life, and perhaps, in total, mould the image of the nation'.[141] A similar government survey carried out in 1969 confirmed gardening to be the most popular leisure activity after television, occupying four times as many hours as drinking or watching sport. How did it, as Deedes suggested, mould the image of the nation?

As we noted earlier, gardening was not a symptom of rural romanticism. Its real significance was that, like car ownership, it marked a shift in emphasis from the public to the private sphere in British life during the 1950s, and more importantly, a shift in emphasis from an international arena to a national one. The garden was a bastion of privacy and one of the means by which Britons defined themselves as a nation that minded its own business. The privet hedge was a latter-day moat, shielding the home from the public gaze just as the sea shielded Britain from invasion. In 1950 one of the country's leading experts, Harry Roberts, explained why he had planted trees to block the view of passing trains. 'You see, I am English and like to ply my hobby in privacy. For I hold that a garden is a place whither one should be able to retire from the *profanum vulgus* – like a private study, like even silence itself, in that we may thence defy the outside world. This is an aim which the true gardener should bear ever in mind.'[142] When the US carried out a nuclear explosion on Bikini Atoll in March 1954, Giles of the *Express* drew the British Everyman out in the garden determined 'to get his plants in' regardless of the headline 'BIGGEST EVER H-BOMB'.[143]

Ross McKibbin has argued that one of the reasons why revolutionary Marxism never developed in England was that most people were simply too caught up with their hobbies and did not have time for it. Instead, they 'bred dogs and pigeons, grew flowers, raised canaries, founded angling clubs and cycling societies, put the local football team together, preached in church and chapel'.[144] Of all those activities, gardening was seen as *the* symbol of the evolutionary conservatism which lay at the heart of the British character. In Noël

Coward's film *This Happy Breed* (1944), Frank Gibbons is a staunchly patriotic lower-middle-class Englishman who personifies moderation and stability. His son Reg, who is drawn to radical politics, is told, 'We don't like doing things quickly in this country. It's like gardening. Someone once said we was a nation of gardeners, and they weren't far out. We're used to planting things and watching them grow and looking out for changes in the weather.'[145] In 1947, Sir Ernest Barker wrote, 'Not only the temper of compromise but also the habit of "muddling through", is a part and parcel of the English habitat [because] those who farmed the land, from early days, had to tack and turn under shifting skies and changing weather'.[146]

Although the craze for instant gardens meant that horticulture was no longer the painstaking process it had once been, the ideological link between horticulture and democracy proliferated in the 1950s. At the height of the Cold War in 1957, one gardening expert told his readers:

One of the surest ways to make our country safe from Communism or other 'isms' is to encourage our people to become gardeners. Can't you just imagine one of these warmed-over rabble-rousers harranging a mob of people and working them into a frenzy of violence and then walking calmly to take up the pleasant task of gardening? The soil gives too much comfort to a man's mind and soul to permit him the heat and excitement required to be a radical.[147]

It was not uncommon in this period for Britons to plant patriotic borders of red, white and blue geraniums to celebrate national occasions like royal weddings, just as the Loyalists of Northern Ireland painted the borders of their pavements during the marching season in the province.

Attitudes to the police are also a reminder that Britishness was not falling apart at the seams in this period. Although charged with containing the rising level of juvenile crime, the police force was still respected among all ages and classes. Since the mid-nineteenth century it had been seen as one of the institutions which distinguished the British from Europeans and Americans. Unarmed and (with the exception of the Metropolitan Police) administered by local rather than central government, they were not paramilitary agents of the state as in most Continental countries. Nor were they as politically compromised as they were in the US, where police chiefs and judges were elected. In the 1950s, UK forces were still regarded as the embodiment of Britain's impartial legal systems and a reflection of the nation's sense of fair play. Geoffrey Gorer's 1955 study of the national character concluded: 'The extent of enthusiastic appreciation of the police is peculiarly English and a most important component of the contemporary English character. To a great extent, the police represent an ideal model of behaviour.'[148] A 1962 Royal Commission on the police found 'an overwhelming vote of confidence' for them among the public. It also found that support was actually growing as more and more Britons became property owners and therefore acquired a vested interest in an institution the resources of which were mainly geared to the protection of property.[149] The nation's longest-running TV police series, *Dixon of Dock Green*, was based on an Ealing film, *The Blue Lamp* (1949). When the BBC first broadcast it in 1955 the show was already a rosy picture of British life and by the time it was pulled in 1976 it had become a cliché of conservative nostalgia for a gentler, more homogenous society. Nonetheless, in the first ten years of its life its huge popularity rested on the fact that the avuncular PC (later Sergeant) George Dixon and his colleagues accurately reflected how the British saw the police service and how a good many actually experienced it.

Taken as a whole, therefore, this era was marked by strong rumblings of discontent about nation, race and class which political, religious and cultural leaders were unable to contain or even, in many cases, understand. But these rumblings had yet to destabilize the Britishness forged during the Second World War. The culminating event of the mid-twentieth century demonstrated how reluctant most of the UK's inhabitants were to change their national identity: from 1961 to 1963, Harold Macmillan attempted to lead the British into Europe and discovered that they didn't want to go.

8. That blasted Common Market

It was fitting that the Empire to which the Scots had contributed so extensively should be wound up by a Prime Minister of Scottish descent and three Scottish Ministers: Macmillan; Iain Macleod, whom he appointed Colonial Secretary in October 1959; the Earl of

Perth, Minister of State for Colonial Affairs; and Sir Hugh Fraser, Perth's Parliamentary Under-Secretary. All were Highlanders. Macmillan and Macleod came from relatively humble crofting families. In fact their parents had grown up during the Hebridean land disputes of the 1880s which had prompted Lord Salisbury to set up the Scottish Office in an effort to contain nationalist discontent. Macleod's origins were central to his identity and close observers were in no doubt that the rapport between him and the Prime Minister was based on it. 'Both . . . had a sense of the outsider about them. They had at least some understanding from their family's collective memory of what it was like to live under the yoke of English rule. This set them apart from most other senior Conservatives'.[150] Whatever the truth of that observation, the fact is that decolonization began in earnest once the Macmillan–Macleod political partnership was forged.

In the half-century between the independence of India on 14 August 1947 and the ceding of Hong Kong to China on 30 June 1997, a total of sixty-four nations and approximately 500 million people, covering a quarter of the Earth's surface, ceased to be ruled by the British. The majority – thirty-seven nations – won their independence between Macmillan's decision to scuttle in 1960 and Britain's entry to the Common Market in 1973. Of the fifty-one countries who decided to maintain a diplomatic association with the UK through membership of the Commonwealth, twenty-nine eventually became republics. Broadly speaking, Macmillan got public backing for his decision. However, it was one thing to lower the Union Jack in one place and quite another to haul it up again somewhere else, particularly when that somewhere else was the Continent against which Britons had defined themselves since the late eighteenth century.

Macmillan's initial European venture was to create a trading block outside the Six. Established in November 1959, EFTA comprised Britain, Denmark, Norway, Sweden, Austria, Switzerland and Portugal. But it proved to be no match for the EEC. Eventually, at a Cabinet Meeting on 27 July 1961, the British government decided to apply for entry to the Common Market. Aside from decolonization, three things had changed since Messina. First, despite being initially wary about the economic threat of a united Europe, the Americans were now in favour because it would enhance Western unity. Sentimental attachment to the Special Relationship had not disappeared, but both isolationists and latter-day imperialists in the US broadly supported the Common Market, the former because they hoped it would avoid their having to intervene in another European war and the latter because they believed it would lighten the burden of policing the world. In Britain, this turnaround made championing the Special Relationship as an alternative post-imperial power bloc much more difficult than before. Second, the British economy was looking increasingly shaky after the boom of the 1950s. Third, the Common Market was proving to be a resounding economic success.

Macmillan called the decision to go in 'perhaps the most fateful and forward looking decision in all our peacetime history'.[151] He and his government knew just how fateful and forward looking it was. In December 1960, the Foreign Minister, Edward Heath, asked the Lord Chancellor, David Maxwell Fyfe, what effect joining the Common Market would have on British national sovereignty. Maxwell Fyfe responded with foreboding. Though not opposed to joining, he warned Heath that it would be an utterly different ball game to membership of NATO or the UN. 'I must emphasise', he wrote, 'that in my view the surrenders of sovereignty involved are serious ones and I think that, as a matter of practical politics, it will not be easy to persuade Parliament or the public to accept them.'[152] So it proved.

The British intelligentsia was generally in favour of entry. The pages of *Encounter* bristled with opinion and invective from three generations of thinkers. Most, from Leonard Woolf and E. M. Forster, through to W. H. Auden and Kenneth Clark, and on to Freddie Ayer and Ken Tynan, asserted their sense of a wider European civilization to which Britain belonged. Notes of caution were sounded. Most had reservations about the power which the Common Market would give to 'big business'. Arnold Toynbee, a veteran of the British federalist movement, hoped that it was only a step to world government. A few, like the novelist Iris Murdoch, did not want to see the Commonwealth rejected out of hand. But only John Osborne made an impassioned plea for Britain going alone:

There is much jeering talk of Little Englanders. Many clever, sophisticated people seem to imagine we are being called upon to make a choice about the Good Life, between Chateau Yquem [sic] and cocoa. As for the 'challenge of the technological age' and all the other forward-looking Common Market jargon and high-minded greed, I for one am sick to death of its ugly, chromium pretence, and am prepared to settle for a modest, shabby, poor-but-proud Little England any day.[153]

Artists and intellectuals had not lost the renewed sense of nationhood which war and the welfare state had given them. But nor had they ever lost their sense of the cultural unity of European civilization and they were deeply worried that popular hostility to the Continent had still not abated more than a decade since the end of the war. Their mood was summed up by William Plomer, the poet and critic who wrote the libretto to Benjamin Britten's Coronation opera, *Gloriana*: 'British virtues have done and still could do a lot of good in the world, but if Britain grows less insular, it would be pleasing to see a lessening of British smugness, ignorance, xenophobia and want of imagination. These attributes are not aids to survival.'[154] A number of intellectuals, together with captains of industry and military chiefs, lent their support to Gladwyn Jebb's cross-party Common Market Campaign.

So too did the British Churches. The new Archbishop of Canterbury, Michael Ramsey, had many things in common with William Temple, but a belief in European federalism was not one of them. Nevertheless, as an ecumenicist he welcomed greater dialogue with the Continental Churches and he was particularly committed to Anglo-German reconciliation. His opportunity to further that cause came with the Consecration of Coventry Cathedral on 25 May 1962. Though now largely forgotten, the event was seen as a landmark of the postwar era. Optimists believed not only that it demonstrated the enduring health of British Christianity but also that it bore testimony to a decline of the rampant Germanophobia which had characterized popular Britishness for nearly a century. Coventry's fourteenth-century cathedral was the only Anglican cathedral in the world to be destroyed during the war. Like the survival of St Paul's, its destruction initially symbolized the nation's bullish resistance to Nazi Germany, thanks partly to the Bishop of Coventry's call for swift and bloody retribution by the RAF. But within a few years Coventry Cathedral became instead *the* symbol of international reconciliation in the UK. In 1947, Sir Basil Spence was appointed architect and a modern concrete and steel building arose next to the Gothic ruins of the old one. Appropriately, the foundation stone was laid shortly before the Suez Crisis and the building was completed during negotiations for membership of the European Community.

In some respects, the project was the high point of that postwar reconstruction which self-consciously celebrated Britishness. Born in India in 1907, Spence was a Scot who, after training with Sir Edwin Lutyens, made his name designing the 'Britain Can Make It' exhibition of 1947 and then the Sea and Ships pavilion for the Festival of Britain. He was presented to the public as an amalgam of the different national characteristics which had made Britain great. The souvenir booklet produced for the occasion said, 'He combines to a quite unusual degree Celtic romanticism and Saxon shrewdness.' Benjamin Britten composed a *War Requiem* for the occasion; Graham Sutherland designed the altar tapestry, and John Piper the stained-glass windows, which one critic described as 'probably the greatest piece of stained glass since the Reformation'. All four men were stalwarts of the postwar attempt to reform national culture. The Consecration itself was also a very British affair despite the fact that the cathedral was an Anglican one, with representatives of all the British Churches in attendance.

Yet the thrust of the project was decidedly international. It was designed to show that Britain did have a sense of Europeanness. Spence had formed an ambition to build a cathedral when he was dug in in Normandy shortly after D-Day. He was deeply moved one afternoon by the British artillery's destruction of two Norman churches in order to remove German snipers positioned in their towers. The churches were little different to those the Normans had built in England, and Spence was reminded of Britain's historic links with the Continent. And when, ten years later, he got the chance to build his cathedral he was assisted by hundreds of German students who came to Britain to help with the building work on a scheme organized by the Foreign Office. At the Consecration, the royal family and British Church leaders were joined by representatives of sixty nations, with pride of place given to the German contingent. Afterwards, a special Chapel of Unity sponsored by the Church of Sweden was formally handed over to the Cathedral Provost by the Swedish Ambassador. In an interview, the Provost said: 'Somehow or other we have got to discover a way in which people of goodwill, without any sort of political tags tied to them, can form an over-arching bond above race, above nationality, above colour', and he hoped a start would be made 'at the toughest point, the long breach between Britain and Germany'.[155] Bishop Bardsley (the first in British history to see a cathedral started and finished) wrote, 'The very fact of this Cathedral becoming a great international centre of reconciliation is making us more conscious of our dependence upon the world ... The people of Coventry and of this diocese are, I hope, beginning to think more deeply in terms of the world than they have hitherto.'[156]

Like most British architecture of the 1950s, it was not a revolutionary design. But set next to the Gothic ruins of the old cathedral its modernity was shocking enough to attract hostility from the public and from the architectural establishment. The fact that it was a church building caused particular consternation. Spence himself received hundreds of abusive letters. 'Some did not even have stamps', said the architect, 'which shocked me as a Scot.' He defended himself on the ground that he was working in a spirit of progressiveness which he believed lay at the heart of the British character: 'Architecture . . . should not be a copy of past styles, and must be a clear expression of belief in contemporary thought. This I saw as our heritage, for we are an inventive nation and it is a denial of our national characteristic to limit our architectural vocabulary to past forms'.[157] The Provost declared that 'as many as ninety per cent of the critics have become admirers'.[158] It is not possible to test the accuracy of this statement, but it is true that, given the stamp of approval by the Queen and the Churches, the cathedral was eventually a success. Huge queues of local people, together with visitors from around Britain and the Continent, formed outside the building in its first year and it rapidly became an object of regional and national pride *and* a symbol of reconciliation with the Continent.

Britten's *War Requiem*, first performed in the cathedral five days after the Consecration, contributed greatly to that spirit of reconciliation. Britten set his music to Wilfred Owen's poem 'Strange Meeting', about a dream in which the poet meets a German soldier he has killed. The great German tenor Dietrich Fischer-Dieskau sang the lead and was so moved by the occasion that Britten's lover, Peter Pears, could not prise him out of the choir stalls after the performance. In his memoirs, Fischer-Dieskau wrote: 'I was completely undone; I did not know where to hide my face. Dead friends and past suffering arose in my mind.'[159] Similar emotions were aroused when the work was performed in Berlin a year later on the anniversary of the Armistice. The event was a far cry from the Festival of Britain buses which had parked in Berlin and played 'Land of Hope and Glory' to entice Germans to an exhibition about the glories of British civilization.

Back in the UK, the work won huge critical acclaim. The response to it demonstrated how much the British outlook had changed since Britten's critical portrayal of Elizabeth I in *Gloriana* had scandalized the country during the Coronation celebrations. For a contemporary classical work, it was also extraordinarily popular with the general public. Decca's recording of it, conducted by the composer, sold 200,000 copies in the first five months, prompting *The Times*' music critic, William Mann, to remark, 'The *War Requiem* has caught the public imagination to an almost unheard-of degree.'[160] This provoked envy among foreign composers struggling to achieve a similar audience for their works. Igor Stravinsky tartly observed that to criticize the work in Britain would be 'as if one had failed to stand up for *God Save the Queen*'.[161] The reason for the success of the *War Requiem* was not only that it captured a growing desire for reconciliation with Germany. It also became identified with the peace movement of the time, and was soon something of an anthem for supporters of CND. Writing to his sister just after the première at Coventry, Britten exclaimed, 'How one thinks of that bloody 1914–18 war especially – I hope it'll make people think a bit.'[162]

But the aesthetic and religious support which the European movement got from intellectuals and Church leaders was not enough to make the British think that their future lay in the Common Market. And the Prime Minister knew it. He had a fight on his hands just to convince the Conservative Party. On 20 July 1961, Harold Macmillan met the executive of the party's backbench 1922 Committee in his room at the House of Commons. He did not mince his words. He warned them, 'This question could break the Tory Party as Sir Robert Peel [broke] it in 1847' over the question of free trade.[163] So determined was Macmillan to get Britain into Europe that he was quite prepared to split the Conservatives over it. 'It never hurt the Party to split over something that was really in the national interest,' he told *The Times*' editor, William Haley, at one of their regular private meetings.[164] Publicly, however, he expressed caution, reassuring the 1922 Committee that any final decision would await the outcome of negotiations. He made similar reassurances on 31 July when he formally announced the government's decision to apply for entry. The *Manchester Guardian* commented: 'The plunge is to be taken but, on yesterday's evidence, by a shivering Government.'[165] Negotiations opened optimistically enough on 11 November, and the following August, Commonwealth leaders met in London. There were some heated accusations of betrayal, but most knew that Britain's star was waning and accepted her right to negotiate a slice of the Continent's booming economy.

But by that time disquiet had grown among the British both in Parliament and in the country. In successive debates on the issue over a period of eighteen months, the government was pressed by MPs on all sides to state whether or not the Common Market was destined to become a federal union. Peter Walker, a Conservative MP, said:

[The] government have avoided facing the reality that much of Europe wants political federation and a European Parliament. If that is so, it would be a tragedy from the point of view of Europe for this government, if they do not wish to see such a federation. On the other hand, if the government are enthusiastic for the cause of European federation [they should] state it perfectly clearly so that the country can understand what is being offered to it is, over a period of years, joining a federation of Europe – not becoming an offshore island, but becoming an offshore province of the European federation.[166]

Sir Derek Walker-Smith was one of many MPs who were in no doubt that federation would be the eventual outcome, and flatly opposed entry as a result. He argued that although national sovereignty was hard to define, it was a part of every Briton's birthright which they would miss when it was gone: '[It is] a difficult thing to discuss [but it includes] real things, deeply felt, instinctively understood and traditionally cherished by the British people ... little noticed in their presence but valued beyond price in the event of their deprivation.'[167]

As Macmillan acknowledged in his memoirs, by the summer of 1961 he could no longer deal with the question of federalism 'by the recognised parliamentary evasions'.[168] But still the answer given was never a clear one. Macmillan, together with Heath and other ministers, repeatedly told Parliament that nothing had been decided by the Treaty of Rome. The Common Market, they said, was a young organization and as a member Britain could shape its destiny as surely as if the nation had joined in 1950. On one occasion, the Prime Minister flatly denied that federalism was its objective, averring that what most European countries wanted was a confederal association. But more often than not the government simply told its critics that the Treaty of Rome was, if not a blank page, then at least a document whose aims were written in pencil, which the eraser of British pragmatism could amend at will. In the last major Parliamentary debate on the issue, on 7 and 8 November 1962, Heath told the House that there was no hidden blueprint for a federal Europe.

Increasingly, the Labour Party led the outcry against the government's dissembling. In 1961, Hugh Gaitskell told the House of Commons, 'The whole idea of the Six is a movement towards political integration. That is a fine aspiration, but we must recognise that for us to sign the Treaty of Rome would be to accept as the ultimate goal political federation in Europe, including ourselves.'[169] A year later, he was less charitable about this 'fine aspiration'. At the Labour Party Conference in the autumn of 1962, he made the most explosive speech of his career, warning Britons that they were throwing away 1,000 years of history: 'We must be clear about this: it does mean ... the end of Britain as an independent European state. I make no apology for repeating it. It means the end of a thousand years of history ... And it does mean the end of the Commonwealth.'[170] Despite the customary tendency to assume that the 1,000-year history of the English Parliament was also that of Scotland, Gaitskell's speech was one of principle. Like Attlee before him, he believed in Britain's civilizing mission to the world. A recent biographer has written of his 'deep patriotism'. 'The values that Britain represented to him were universal values from which the whole world could benefit. In his view Britain deserved a world role because British culture had much to offer.'[171] At the Conservative Party Conference a week later, delegates cheered when Rab Butler said, 'For them a thousand years of history. For us the future!'[172]

But behind the doors of No. 10, public opinion worried the government. In September 1962, as the second round of talks were about to begin in Brussels, Iain Macleod, by now Chancellor of the Duchy of Lancaster, prepared a report for the Cabinet on the nation's attitude to Europe. Based on a series of national opinion polls and soundings taken by Party agents in constituencies across Britain, it was supposed to help shape government strategy for selling membership to the British once the country had joined. Instead, it revealed the true depths of the nation's scepticism. Only 40 per cent were in favour of joining and then only 'if the government decided it was in Britain's interest'; moreover, this figure was declining as the negotiations dragged on (by December, it had slipped to 29 per cent). Age and class were major factors. Encouragingly, a small majority of those under forty-five in every social group were in favour of entry. But overall, supporters were professional and white-collar workers while skilled and unskilled manual workers, who still made up the bulk of the population, were against.[173]

The government faced another problem. Although supporters were receptive to economic arguments, the vast majority of opponents gave 'emotional', patriotic reasons which were harder to overcome. Edward Heath's unstinting attention to commodity prices at the negotiations in Brussels was impressing Continental ministers but it was not inspiring the British public. *Private Eye* dubbed Heath 'the Grocer'. There was more than an element of snobbery in this, a residual disdain among the upper classes for those in 'trade'. But the wider public reaction showed that while the British had happily become a nation of shoppers in the 1950s, when it came to altering the political trajectory of their country after two and a half centuries of relative independence they would not be bought off with cheaper food.

There were widespread fears that the (to some, significantly titled) Treaty of Rome was a Catholic plot designed to erect a new Holy Roman Empire. As we have seen, Britain remained a firmly Protestant nation in the 1950s and this affected the early debates on Europe. It had coloured Bevin's attitude to the Schuman Plan in 1950 and that of his assistant, Kenneth Younger, who wrote in his diary: '[Schuman is] a bachelor and a very devout Catholic who is said to be very much under the influence of priests. [His plan] may be just a step in the consolidation of the Catholic "black international", which I have always thought to be a big driving force behind the Council of Europe.'[174] A decade later, de Gaulle was seen as a cross between Louis XIV and Napoleon; and this time, critics argued, there would be no Blücher riding to Britain's rescue, since Chancellor Adenauer was a devout Catholic Rhinelander. Macmillan considered the religious issue of such importance that he decided to make the first visit by a British Prime Minister to the Pope in order to convince the Six of the good faith of his government's application (it eventually took place on 4 February 1963). On the left, the continuing prevalence of Nonconformists in the Labour Party, particularly among MPs from Scotland, Wales and the north of England, contributed to their scepticism. The fact that the Vatican and the Christian Democrat parties it tacitly sponsored were anti-socialist did not endear the European idea to Labour MPs either. In a party political broadcast of May 1962, Hugh Gaitskell felt compelled to reassure Britons that the Common Market wasn't 'a Catholic conspiracy'.[175] Intellectuals were not immune to these fears. Kingsley Amis listed it among his concerns; so too did Harold Laski, who said that 'any Jew must hesitate' to support the Common Market because the historic 'liberalising . . . Protestant influence' of Britain would be nullified by so many Catholic States.[176] The fact that conservative Anglo-Catholics like T. S. Eliot and the Mitford sisters were keen on a United States of Europe only confirmed these opinions.

Diana Mitford's husband, Oswald Mosley, was a consistent champion of European integration. In fact, he was arguably the only major twentieth-century British politician to be as keen on it as Edward Heath. Mosley saw the nascent EU as the means by which the fascist dream of a united Europe would finally be realized. After his internment during the Second World War as a potential traitor, he returned to active politics in 1948, formed the Union Movement (UM), and gave it the slogan 'Europe A Nation'. He wanted the reunification of Germany as an essential step towards that goal and he advocated a directly elected European Parliament to ensure that this time integration would be carried out consensually. Mosley's Europe was one in which the former colonial powers would be reborn as a self-contained, monoracial unit. It was dissatisfaction with Mosley's Europeanism that provoked many supporters to desert him and form the National Front in 1967, a year after he retired from active politics. At the peak of its popularity in the early 1960s, the UM could count only 15,000 supporters. In contrast, the NF, which campaigned on an anti-European platform, grew to be the fourth biggest political party in Britain a decade after its formation.

Although most Britons did not support extreme nationalist or fascist parties, there was a strong racial element in the popular hostility to Common Market membership in this period. Although the imperial identity of the British had been dissipated by the Second World War, Suez and decolonization, there was an enduring belief that Britain should somehow count in the world and, therefore, that membership of the Common Market symbolized national decline. In January 1963, *The Times* put its finger on the matter: 'Britain has so far faced only half the truth about her position. That she is no longer a great world power in the American–Russian class is accepted. That there is no divine right whereby she will, without exertion, automatically stay a leading second-class power has not yet sunk in.'[177] A specific racial affinity with the people of the Commonwealth ran alongside this sense of self-importance. The Macleod Report found that a majority did not want the Commonwealth 'harmed' because they felt 'bound by personal or family ties' to it.[178] As Macleod observed, what they meant by this was not an attachment to the whole Commonwealth as a sub-imperial political ideal but rather a cultural attachment to the *white* Commonwealth. To some extent, this affection was perfectly natural. Just as black and Asian Britons remained attached to the people they had left behind in coming to Britain, so white Britons were naturally fond of friends and relatives who had emigrated to countries like Australia and Canada. However, the extent of that loyalty was out of all proportion to those who had personal links there.

What this demonstrated was that most Britons still defined their national identity in racial terms. The centrality of race to the European debate in this period was apparent in the pronouncements of some of the leading sceptics. One was the man who had led the British army to victory in North Africa and Europe: Field Marshal Viscount Montgomery of Alamein. Monty was a vocal supporter of apartheid in the late 1950s and early 1960s, visiting South Africa and writing articles in the British press justifying racial segregation. He carried these views over into his hostile attitude to the EEC. Writing in the *Daily Mirror* in June 1962, he explained why 'We must not join Europe':

> I stand for the British Commonwealth with the Queen at its head ... There is only one race under Heaven which could stand between the Western world and utter destruction [in a Third World War]. That is the British race to which we belong – united by close ties of blood, speech and religion the world over ... Let the Mother of Nations gather her children about her to the call of common kindred; do not let her cast away the affection of her offspring. Let her grasp the hand of her children and draw them closer to her – rather than desert them. Thus will the ancient heart be warmed and inspired – a heart which is beating today just as firmly as ever it did in the days of Trafalgar and Alamein.[179]

Opposition to Europe in this period was sorely exacerbated by racial tension. It is important to remember that in the same year that the Macmillan government was wooing Europe, the government was busy legislating against black immigration. The 'ties of blood, speech and religion' celebrated by Monty appealed to a nation that was bitterly unwilling to accept that it was now multiracial. Although countries like Canada, Australia and New Zealand had never actually been monoracial, Britons looked towards them with a myopic mixture of nostalgia and envy as bastions of a Britishness which they felt the UK was losing.

This was a far more important reason for residual empathy towards the Commonwealth than any belief in it as a viable alternative to the Common Market. The failure to revive Empire Day and the willingness to undermine Commonwealth unity by limiting black immigration demonstrated that racism was a product of *post-*

imperial anxiety about what being British meant and not a revival of imperialism. Racial affinity with the white Commonwealth was part of a wider attempt to produce a new national identity from the ruins of the old one. Therefore, rather than seeing the European Question in terms of popular imperialism acting as a brake on the development of a new British/European identity, it would be more accurate to see it in terms of a conflict between competing forms of post-imperial Britishness.

The Common Market was essentially a club for Europe's former colonial powers. And yet Britons felt little or no racial bond with white Europeans which Macmillan could exploit in order to boost the case for entry. The reason for this was that in the final analysis, British scepticism about Common Market membership had more to do with attitudes towards Europe than it did with attitudes towards the Empire. The Queen's enthusiasm for the Commonwealth meant that support for it was associated in many people's minds with loyalty to the sovereign. But much more importantly, the monarchy was one of the ways in which the British defined themselves as un-European. The Crown was the most European of all the island's institutions. Since 1688, the British throne had been occupied by Dutch and German individuals and their dynastic marriages had linked the Crown to virtually every Continental nation from the Atlantic to the Urals. In a landmark speech in 1958 during a visit to Britain by the German president, the Queen spoke fondly of the Windsors' Teutonic origins; and in an address to the Anglo-German Association two years later, the Duke of Edinburgh condemned Britons who were still fighting the war and 'stoking the fires of hatred and suspicion'.[180] However, two speeches could not undo the efforts of George V and VI to distance the British monarchy from the Continent.

Which leads us on to our main point. What primarily made Britons hostile towards the Common Market was their view of Continental countries as inherently unstable, undemocratic and therefore too dangerous to be closely involved with. That feeling was the product of the hubris created by Britain's military and moral victory in World War Two. Macleod concluded his findings on British opinion thus: 'Agents report increasing distrust of foreign political connections and indeed of foreigners, and report fears that we are going to be "taken over", "pushed around", "outvoted", "forced into the Common Market to serve American interests" or "to surrender our independence to 'Frogs and Wogs.' "'

These were not the nice constitutional concerns which MPs had aired in Parliament over the previous two years. These were reactions that went deep into the bedrock of Britishness. Macleod warned the Cabinet, 'by far the main reason for opposition ... both amongst the working class and amongst those of the middle-class who are opposed, is a sort of patriotism (or its negative counterpart, xenophobia) ... these instinctive reactions outweigh the more thoughtful anxieties about the extent to which British sovereignty, traditional institutions and forms of government would be eroded.'[181]

The Second World War had persuaded Britons that a united Europe was necessary to maintain the peace. But it had also increased their distrust of the Continent and, above all, their dislike of the Germans. The French veto of Britain's application has distracted historians from the fact that *popular* opposition to membership of the Common Market was underpinned more by Germanophobia than Francophobia. This was apparent in the campaign mounted to oppose Britain's membership of the Common Market. Lord Beaverbrook, whose *Express* newspapers led the campaign, told the Prime Minister: 'That blasted Common Market ... is an American device to put us alongside Germany. As our power was broken and lost by two German wars, it is very hard on us now to be asked to align ourselves with those villains.'[182]

The German Question vexed Montgomery too. Monty was a keen supporter of NATO, having been instrumental in setting it up. But he believed the surrender of sovereignty involved in joining the Common Market was on a quite different and unacceptable scale. He also believed that although Germany was a junior partner in NATO under the aegis of Britain and America, in a united Europe it could and would flex its muscles. Monty knew exactly what buttons he was pressing on the British psyche when, in a full-page advert paid for by Beaverbrook, he claimed that membership of the Common Market would mean a German general giving orders to a British one. Germany, he said, 'has disturbed the peace of the world twice during the past 48 years, in 1914 and 1940. Are we to put up with all this again? Never!'[183]

The Prime Minister was also prone to this animosity. Macmillan had been an officer in the Grenadier Guards in the First World War and was wounded three times. Like most Britons who had experienced either or both world wars, he regarded the Germans as an innately militaristic people. At a Downing Street dinner held during the EEC negotiations, he told the Duke of Edinburgh, 'the Huns are always the same. When they are down they crawl under your feet, and when they are up they use their feet to stamp on your face'.[184] The private fears expressed by the Prime Minister are telling. But the depth of British Germanophobia only becomes fully apparent if one examines the public culture of the time.

9. Take that, you dirty Huns!

It has been argued that state commemoration of the Second World War was muted in comparison to that of the First World War. In his history of the subject, Adrian Gregory writes: 'The disillusionment that had begun during the last years of the 1930s had come to fruition. There was a new silence in 1945, the silence after Auschwitz and the silence after Hiroshima, the silence in which nothing meaningful could be said.'[185] Far from it. The silence was soon extinguished by a cacophony of nationalistic chest-beating, in which all classes, young and old, male and female, participated. The victory of 1945 led to a xenophobia which, in its range and intensity, matched that of the early twentieth century and had much the same effect on British national identity.

In 1946, the government, the Churches and the British Legion discussed how to commemorate the 1939–45 conflict. VE Day (8 May), VJ Day (15 August), Battle of Britain Day (15 September) and even 14 August (the signing of Magna Carta) were all suggested. Finally, the Cabinet decided to incorporate remembrance of the two wars in one Cenotaph service on the second Sunday of each November.

By merging these two ideologically different conflicts into one, the British emphasized that the human cost of all wars was terrible. But the overriding effect was to envelop the war against Nazism in a general commemoration of British–German conflict. Also, the ceremony was less contemplative than before. Armistice Day from 1919 to 1939 had focused on the bereavement of women in order to bridge the gulf between civilian and military experience; and the two-minute silence during the service in Whitehall was observed by tens of millions throughout the UK. After 1946, mass observance of the silence lapsed, despite attempts by the British Legion to revive it. The new service also placed veterans centre stage; their Whitehall march accompanied by patriotic songs from both wars, like 'It's A Long Way To Tipperary' and 'There'll Always Be An England'. It did so for two reasons. First, because the civilian–military gulf had been considerably narrower in the conflict of 1939–45; and second, because the conflict had been a more popular cause with a less traumatic outcome, as a result of which a little light militarism was seen to be acceptable.

The story of sculpted memorials, around which local services of remembrance were conducted, reveals a similar trend. In most places, the dead of the Second World War were commemorated by simply adding their names to the statues, panels and crucifixes which had been erected between 1919 and 1939. Separate memorials to the Battle of Britain were the exception. A commemorative chapel in Westminster Abbey containing an illustrative stained-glass window was opened by George VI in 1947, and thereafter an annual Service of Thanksgiving took place at the Abbey or at St Paul's. Almost a hundred panels in town halls were unveiled by military and civic leaders, as well as fourteen statues in open-air sites. All Battle of Britain memorials were in England and most were unveiled in the 1950s (the last and largest was a statue of an airman looking out to the English Channel, at Capel-le-Ferne on the Kent coast, in 1993). From 1945 onwards, selected RAF stations had popular annual 'At Home' days which allowed the public to visit the places from which The Few had kept Nazi Germany at bay. On the twentieth anniversary of the event in 1960, George Ward, the Secretary of State for Air, submitted a memorandum to Cabinet suggesting that a new memorial should be erected by order of Parliament as the focus of commemoration:

> There has so far been no falling off in public interest and it seems clear that the Battle of Britain is still regarded by the general public as a major victory and deliverance . . . As time goes on it will naturally become less a matter of recollection and more a matter of history . . . I do however believe that the Battle . . . has come to occupy a firm position in the minds of the public, possibly because it was a fight against the odds, in our own skies; it averted invasion; and it was the first decisive reverse to German arms.[186]

Ward's suggestion was not taken up on grounds of cost. Still, it reveals how much the Battle remained central to the idea of British-ness. This was in stark contrast to the public indifference towards Commonwealth Day around the same time.

British popular culture was laden with Germanophobia from the 1940s right through to the 1970s. Tabloid newspapers frequently portrayed German Chancellor Konrad Adenauer as Hitler, adding a little moustache to his image in photos and cartoons. A pioneering study by Professor John Ramsden has shown how the fiction and non-fiction market of this period was dominated by war books, most of them cheap editions affordable to all but the poorest Britons. Paul Brickhill's *The Dam Busters* was especially popular, selling over 1 million copies and appearing in both the *Reader's Digest* and a special 'Young People's' edition. Memoirs of war heroes like General Montgomery were best-sellers and their authors were made into even bigger celebrities by appearing on TV and radio to recount their stories. Others made it on to the big screen, like Brickhill's romantic account of air ace Douglas Bader's life, *Reach For The Sky* (1954), which coined the ironic phrase 'For you, the war is over!' The biggest seller of all was Churchill's six-volume *The Second World War*, published between 1948 and 1954, each volume of which sold 200,000 copies. Until the late 1960s the production of Churchill memorabilia amounted to a small national industry, churning out books and records of his famous speeches and quotations. His image adorned everything from Toby jugs to teatowels and biscuit tins – all of which constituted a personality cult of Maoist proportions.

The revival of the Victorian idea that war is an exciting game was already apparent in 1940–45. A decade later, it was a prominent theme in boy's comics. For example, in 1958, the *Eagle* ran a cartoon life of Churchill called 'The Happy Warrior'. The editor told its young readers, 'nowhere could you find an adventure story more thrilling'. In one section, as German paratroopers descend over Crete in 1941, a soldier exclaims, 'For Pete's sake, just look at those mushrooms!', to which his mate replies, 'Let's have 'em for breakfast!' before mowing them down.[187] As football became a greater source of patriotism in Scotland and England, it became the sport most commonly associated with wartime heroism. Comics offered a staple diet of soccer and war stories, often contriving to combine the two. Children were encouraged to see beating Germany on the battlefield and on the soccer pitch as complementary national achievements.

Far from declining in the early 1960s, war comics grew in number and increased their sales. The Dundee publishing firm, D. C. Thompson, led the field with *The Victor* (1961–92), *Commando* (1961–

present) and *Warlord* (1974–86). The London firm IPC ran *Valiant* (1963–76) and *Battle Picture Weekly* (1975–90). All commanded sales of approximately 500,000 per week (*Warlord* was still selling over 235,000 in the late 1970s). Most stories (often based on true events) were about ordinary soldiers' heroism against Germans who were shown to be doltish or insane. Typical of these was the cover story of *The Victor* in February 1964, which told how Corporal Sidney 'Basher' Bates of the Royal Norfolk Regiment won a VC for his part in the Battle of the Falaise Gap in 1944. After a comrade is shot, Basher exclaims, 'They've killed him! Those dirty Jerries have killed my mate. I'll show them'; which he does, running at a machine-gun nest shouting, 'Take that, you dirty Huns!' before being gunned down by astonished Germans saying, 'The mad Britisher!'[188] The development of plastics in the 1950s led to the mass production of pre-moulded construction kits by Airfix and other companies. Several generations of British boys spent hours building and painting tanks, planes and ships of the Second World War. Airfix's two best-sellers were the Spitfire and the Lancaster bomber.

The most influential form of the genre was the war film. During this period, the custom of standing to attention while the national anthem was played at the end of a film died out. Yet what people enjoyed on the screen was thoroughly patriotic. The heroic exploits of British forces were transferred on to celluloid with gusto and for thirty years they won a huge audience. Fact and fiction soon became blurred. Some of the genre's stars were war heroes themselves, notably Richard Todd, who played himself in *The Longest Day* (1962). State archives lent the studios film clips of real Second World War battles for action sequences; and the Ministry of Defence lent equipment from jeeps to destroyers (in 1956 manoeuvres of the entire Mediterranean fleet were organized around the filming of Michael Powell's *Battle of the River Plate*). Military chiefs joined the royal family at premières and recruiting desks were installed in cinema foyers to take advantage of the patriotism which the films encouraged while it was still fresh in the minds of young moviegoers. About 100 such films were made in the UK between 1945 and 1965, making the Second World War by far the largest cinematic genre of the postwar era – far bigger than the more critically acclaimed Ealing comedies which celebrated the peaceful nature of the British. Fewer were produced after 1965, but the shelf life of classics was considerably extended by television, which showed them regularly until the end of the century. Between 1955 and 1960, films such as *The Cruel Sea*

(1955) were the top box-office grossers. Their wry, stiff-upper-lipped leading men – notably Jack Hawkins, Richard Todd, John Mills and Kenneth More – were consistently the most popular stars among men and women in polls taken by the film industry. POW films were a major sub-genre, their dramas of endurance and escape acting as metaphors for the whole nation's narrow escape in 1940–41. Features such as *The Wooden Horse* (1959) were popular even in the most radical households. One afternoon in 1963, the left-wing Labour MP Tony Benn noticed his children had disappeared underground:

> The boys are frantically tunnelling in the garden, following a film they saw about POWs escaping during the war. They are way under the concrete path and will be in the next garden unless stopped. It is a beautifully concealed tunnel with a wooden top covered with mud and can already hold two full-sized people.[189]

Peter Hennessy recalls, 'We spent the fifties in cinemas absorbing an endless diet of war films in which Richard Todd and Kenneth More convinced us that there is a singular mixture of insouciance, bravery and flair that we British could bring to the conduct of international affairs'.[190] But the films did more than bolster the patriotism of schoolboys like Peter Hennessy and me. By characterizing Germans as innately cruel, aggressive and humourless people they perpetuated the Teutonic stereotypes forged in the first half of the century.

Liberal commentators berated the people who glorified the Second World War. They did not simply view the material as cliché-ridden second-rate pap. Even the artistically worthy films (of which there were many) were condemned as irresponsible because they whipped up anti-German British nationalism at a time when Europe was attempting to bury old enmities. In 1955, the BFI officially criticized 'the present obsession of British film-makers with the exploits of the armed services during the last war ... the whole thing is really an exciting game, it seems'.[191] The editor of *Films and Filming* wrote, 'It is to be hoped that the cinema, having shown how the last war was won, will now give us a little enlightenment on how to prevent the next.'[192] These criticisms became more frequent in the 1960s as European integration accelerated and the peace movement grew. War culture was thought to encourage a backward-looking Britishness that was stymieing social progress and might ultimately lead to Armageddon.

The censure of the liberal intelligentsia did nothing to curtail the public's enthusiasm for war stories any more than the opposition to spiv films in the 1940s had curtailed their love of gangsters. Sometimes the popular reply was blunt. The biggest CND demonstration of this period was deliberately scheduled on Battle of Britain Day, a decision that went down with the British people about as well as a burning Spitfire over the Channel. The theme music for *The Dam Busters* was composed by Eric Coates (who also wrote *Workers Playtime*) and played by the Billy Cotton Band. It was a best-selling record and became an unofficial anthem of the RAF. At CND demonstrations the tune was often sung by members of the public to counter the chanting of disarmers and on some occasions it was relayed by Ministry of Defence loudspeakers outside military bases. It also became a popular tune on the terraces of Hampden and Wembley during international football matches, along with tunes from other war films like *The Great Escape* and *The Bridge on the River Kwai*. It is worth noting that the anti-war films of the 1960s like Richard Attenborough's *Oh! What a Lovely War* (1969) and Joseph Losey's *King and Country* (1964) were not commercial successes. Moreover, they were set in 1914–18 rather than 1939–45. This was because the Second World War had become such a sacred and untouchable part of the nation's identity that in order to remobilize pacifist sentiment during the Vietnam era radical filmmakers had to turn back to a conflict that could more easily be presented as a bloody and pointless fiasco.

What were the roots of British war culture? First, it satisfied the perennial hunger for action and adventure among young men, offering them a vicarious escape from the drab routine of their lives by dispensing with the violent and authoritarian realities of national service. Unlike the films produced during the war itself, women were largely absent from those produced in the 1950s. When female characters did appear, it was to provide romantic interest for heroic British men. Overalls and uniforms were replaced by sensible dresses, and a woman's opinions were seen to be less important than a comforting hand placed on the furrowed brow of her husband. In this respect, war films can be seen as British westerns: a frontier male fantasy for an urban, domesticated society. Second, war culture was a symptom of anxiety about the decline of British power, providing nostalgia and inspiration for those who could not accept the end of empire. Until British studios were forced to rely on US finance in the second half of the 1960s, the American contribution to the Allied victory was played down; indeed, an alien observer watching a

British war film of this period might easily conclude that the UK had won the conflict single-handedly. Lewis Gilbert, who directed several successful features in the genre, described them as 'a kind of ego boost, a nostalgia for a time when Britain was great'.[193] Taking the point further, John Osborne equated them with the country's obsessive monarchism. In 1957, he wrote: 'the Royalty symbol is the gold filling in a mouthful of decay ... To a nation that finds her most significant myths in the idiot heroes of *Reach for the Sky* and *Battle of the River Plate* and longs for self-aggrandisement ... it is about the only wholly satisfying thing left.'[194] He was right. But above all, war culture was symptomatic of a viewpoint Osborne himself shared: opposition to European integration. Producers of books, comics and films did not overtly attack the Common Market in their work. But the message was clear: the fight against Continental tyranny could not be forgotten because it was not yet over. Germany's postwar resurgence caused the most anger.

Throughout the 1950s, the question of West German rearmament was a source of public concern, even though it was in the interests of Western security during the Cold War. Nye Bevan's 'No Guns for the Huns' was a popular cry, and 40 per cent of Britons thought as late as 1954 that there was a serious prospect of the Nazis returning to power. Even more vexing was West Germany's amazing economic recovery. Macmillan might point to the greater prosperity of Common Market members, but for most people that was simply a reminder that the UK had won the war and lost the peace. Instead of trying to learn from the Germans, the British mocked the ruthlessly efficient Teutonic character: industrial productivity, they convinced themselves, was only a step away from military aggression; demanding bosses were simply 'Little Hitlers'; time-and-motion studies merely a shop-floor version of the methods used in Hitler's factories of death. Hence, the stop-go stagnation of the British economy was not a symptom of complacent mismanagement but of Britain's democratic spirit; muddling through was a testament to the jolly character which had saved Western civilization. The Allied Occupation of West Germany may have ended in 1949, but as far as the British were concerned, it was still a pupil at the school of British democracy, and other Europeans still needed to be saved from their supine, collaborative leaders.

Patriotic cinema and literature in the 1930s had been dominated by tales of dashing gentlemen quelling the revolts of ungrateful natives in Africa and Asia. A generation later, it was dominated by tales of the Hun getting his just deserts from Dunkirk to D-Day at the hands of ordinary Tommies like Basher Bates. The White Man's Burden met the People's War and the Germans became the wogs of the twentieth century. The mad dictators and automaton followers of the master race were as richly deserving of being beaten into civilization as the primitive savages of the lesser races. Or so thought a generation stuck in a cultural bunker. War stories mimicked colonial epics in style. But the similarity ends there. Like the racist narratives of anti-immigration demagogues, war stories were a product of Britain's stunted post-imperial identity. They were the heroic self-image of a people caught between a rejection of their past and a fear of their future. The British hoped that as long as they clung to the patriotic certainties of the 1940s – of a united kingdom standing alone as the moral leader of the world – then the present, more complex, world might stop turning.

Germanophobia was also present in more elevated circles. A. J. P. Taylor was the greatest and most popular British historian since Macaulay. He was a radical man with an abiding love of the Continent, but he was also opposed to Common Market membership and he had a lifelong dislike of the Germans. From the 1940s until the 1970s, in books, newspaper articles and TV broadcasts, he argued that Germany could not be trusted, particularly if the reunification of West and East was ever allowed to take place. In 1961 he published *The Origins of the Second World War*, which concluded: 'Hitler was a sounding board for the German nation. Thousands, many hundred thousand Germans, carried out his orders without qualm or question ... [Hitler] gave orders, which Germans executed, of a wickedness without parallel in civilised history ... In international affairs there was nothing wrong with Hitler except that he was a German.'[195] Taylor summed up its argument in a letter to Kingsley Martin: 'Cause of World War 1: Germany. Cause of World War II: Germany. Now no Germany, so no war!'[196] *Origins* was an international best-seller and caused an international furore, angering those who wanted to rehabilitate Germany. But Taylor did not revise his views. In a letter to his Hungarian lover, Eva Haraszti, in 1969, he said: 'I doubt whether German wickedness explains the whole of modern history, though it no doubt explains quite a lot'.[197] As a young man, he had been opposed to appeasement. By demonstrating how popular it had been, *Origins* was a seminal attempt to show that the legend of the Finest Hour was not as simple as the British pretended. But Taylor did not cure British amnesia because the thrust of the book was his celebration of their heroism when the UK eventually went to war, and his demonization of the Germans. Intentionally or not, Taylor reinforced Germanophobia on the eve of the UK's application to join the Common Market.

One aspect of mid-twentieth-century British culture where European influence was celebrated was in the work of Jewish émigrés. But here too the effect was to promote a self-congratulatory mentality rather than to build bridges with the Continent. German and Eastern European Jews had been escaping to the UK from Continental pogroms since the nineteenth century. From 1933 to 1945, the government of the UK gave refuge to 63,000, most of them assisted with funds raised by Simon Marks, son of the co-founder of Marks and Spencer. Among them were some of the best artists, architects, scientists, writers, publishers and composers in the world. They were indifferent to the rest of the UK. Most either arrived as passionate Anglophiles or became so after being domiciled. They saw England not only as the country that saved Western civilization but as the country which had saved their own lives, and so celebrated it with all the force of their prodigious intellects. Their influence on British culture deserves a book in its own right, but a quartet of exemplars will have to suffice.

The political philosopher Isaiah Berlin invigorated British liberal thought at a time when it was under increasing attack from Marxists. He was born in Latvia in 1909, survived the Bolshevik Revolution and moved to Britain shortly after. He became an Oxford professor, was knighted in 1957, and in old age he counted Margaret Thatcher among his admirers. His most notable theory was 'negative tolerance'. He argued that it is not necessary to love one's neighbour and that merely accepting his or her right to privacy was a better guarantor of individual freedom. This was a philosophical vindication of gardener Harry Roberts' advice for Englishmen to grow trees so they could shield themselves from the outside world. His biographer writes:

> Isaiah more or less accepted everything the English liked to believe
> about themselves: that they were practical, untidy, eccentric, fair-
> minded, empirical, common-sensical and that ubiquitous word,
> decent. His was a version of Englishness frozen in the moment
> when he first encountered it in the 1920s: the England of Kipling,
> King George, the Gold Standard, empire and victory . . . Narrow-
> minded provincialism, philistinism and insularity played no part in

his idea of England. If the English took to him it was because he offered them back their most self-approving myths.[198]

The same could be said of most émigrés, not least the historian Lewis Namier. Namier was born in Poland in 1888, came to Britain as a young man to study then stayed on, becoming Professor of History at Manchester University. Like many arrivals from Eastern Europe, he was an ardent Zionist who believed that English democracy was the model on which the Jewish state should be built. But his first loyalty was to his adopted country. He took British nationality in 1913, changed his name from Bernstein and converted to the Anglican faith in 1947. Namier's greatest achievement was his stewardship of the History of Parliament (in England), in 1951–60. This huge research project had been established with public funds by Act of Parliament in 1934. Though still not complete in the year 2000, Namier's Anglomania reinvigorated the project, driving it on at a time when the Scots and Welsh were beginning to question the validity of Westminster and when the English were starting to doubt the rectitude of their governing classes.

The writer George Mikes reached a wider audience with his humorous studies of the national character. Mikes was born in Hungary in 1912 and came to Britain in 1938. His books were published by another Hungarian émigré, Andre Deutsch: beginning with *How To Be An Alien* (1946) and ending with *How To Be Decadent* (1977) they ran to thirty editions. Similar studies by foreign writers had been popular since the nineteenth century, flattering Britons while feeding the conceit that they, unlike other nations, were able to laugh at themselves. Mikes trod a well-worn path through the everglades of Englishness. But by persistently emphasizing how different the English were from other Europeans, by celebrating the superiority of Anglo-Saxon democracy, and by warning that membership of the Common Market would make the UK a 'suburb of Brussels', Mikes struck a very contemporary chord with the millions who bought his books. In the late 1950s, the Central Office of Information thought they were such an accurate guide to the nation's outlook that it distributed copies to new immigrants in order to speed up their assimilation into British society.

The most influential of all émigrés was the architectural critic Nikolaus Pevsner. A tall, slim, bespectacled man with owlish features, he was born in Leipzig in 1902, the son of a Jewish fur-trader. Like Namier, he was a convert to Protestantism. Pevsner emigrated to Britain in 1933 and found academic employment with the help of William Beveridge, eventually becoming Professor of the History of Art at Birkbeck College, London. In 1969, he was simultaneously honoured in Britain and Germany – knighted by the Queen and given the Grand Cross of Merit by the Federal Republic. Pevsner could be scathing about British insularity. In the 1955 Reith Lectures, published as *The Englishness of English Art*, he said that the nation's dislike for revolution 'is a forte in political development, but a weakness in art . . . what English character gained of tolerance and fair play, she lost of that fanaticism or at least that intensity which alone can bring forth great art.'[199] But he too spent most of his life celebrating his adopted country, especially in his monumental *Buildings of England* series. It was published by Penguin in affordable paperbacks and funded by ABC Television, on which he appeared, playing to a T the dotty German professor by which the British and Americans love to caricature intellectuals.

Pevsner conceived the project as an English version of the classic 1906 architectural guidebook to Germany, the *Handbuch der Deutschen Kunstdenkmaler*. It had been copied in most European countries except the UK, where topography veered between inaccessible academic tomes and impressionistic patriotic essays. Pevsner decided that England must have its *Handbuch*. From 1945 until the forty-sixth and last volume appeared in 1974 he drove round the country in a 1933 Wolseley Hornet observing, listing and analysing every single building of note. At first, Pevsner's Germanically systematic methods and his liking for modern architecture made him unpopular. But by the early 1960s *Buildings of England* was regarded as a major contribution not only to the public's architectural knowledge but also to their national identity, especially the awareness of England as a distinct country within the Isles (separate projects for Scotland, Wales and Ireland were not begun until 1978–9). The series never went out of print, and when Pevsner died *The Times* paid him tribute:

> The Teutonic method went to work on the vernacular of the rambling English countryside, an ominous collision . . . [But] a way of looking is Pevsner's gift to his adopted country. Hitler's bombs destroyed many buildings England would like to still have. But Hitler's Jew-baiters gave England a man who taught us to read those that remain and those that have sprung up since with a fresh and accurate eye. Sir Nikolaus Pevsner was one of those great spirits and an indebted beneficiary of German Jewry.[200]

The Times' verdict would have delighted its subject. In *The Englishness of English Art* he wrote: 'The question might well be asked why
I should have set myself up as a judge of English qualities . . . being
neither English born or English bred . . . [But] the very fact of having
come into a country with fresh eyes may constitute a great advantage
. . . England has profited from the un-Englishness of the immigrants
as they have profited from the Englishing they underwent.'[201]

It has sometimes been said that the arrival of large numbers of
black immigrants in the 1950s deflected hostility away from the
Jewish population. How true is this? The creation of Israel in 1948
did not solve the 'Jewish Question' as Zionists had hoped; and its
valiant struggle to survive provoked as much hostility in the UK as it
did sympathy. Furthermore, some racists even saw the multicultural
society as the latest Jewish plot to undermine the British nation.
However, it is hard to escape the conclusion that Jews, like the Irish,
were shielded from the full force of racial prejudice by the presence
of people considered to be more alien than themselves. It is surely no
coincidence that the last British anti-Semitic riots took place in 1947,
just ten months before the arrival of the *Empire Windrush*.[202]

What is less remarked upon is the unwitting role that Anglophile
Jewish intellectuals played in that restructuring of British racism.
Valuable though their work was, both in artistic terms and in
encouraging the British to define themselves less racially, in the end
the most prominent Jewish émigrés contributed to the stagnation of
English national identity. The English turned away from the fresh
eyes which looked at them from coloured faces. But they met the
gaze of Berlin, Namier, Mikes and Pevsner because such men
reinforced the nation's belief in its innate liberalism, while blacks
and Asians challenged that belief. Few émigrés lost their sense of
Europeanness; some implored the English to acquire one. And, in
any case, it would be trite to equate Isaiah Berlin's *Two Concepts of
Liberty* (1958) with Basher Bates' determination to take out as many
'dirty Huns' as he could. But the effect of their work was not entirely
removed from the publishers of *The Victor* or the producers of *Reach
For The Sky*. All contributed to a cultural climate in which the British
looked down on the Continent as a volatile place best kept at arm's
length. All, in their different ways, deceived by flattering.

10. The next great adventure
of our country's history

Despite the overwhelming evidence of popular scepticism towards the Common Market which the Macmillan government gathered, Iain Macleod optimistically concluded that it was possible to make Europeans out of the British. He argued that if the government used more imaginative propaganda which incorporated Common Market membership into the traditional 'island story', then the xenophobic tendencies of the British could be reined in and their patriotism made to incorporate a sense of Europeanness:

> The picture that emerges is that the country's head is convinced, the country's heart is opposed . . . It seems to follow that we need more than a logically convincing case for British entry; we need also the pull of idealism and sentiment. The fact that young people and those who form opinion are with us surely provides the key. We must I believe present this issue 'with trumpets' as the next great adventure of our country's history.[203]

The Cabinet agreed that it was at least worth a try. Macmillan thought an appeal should be made 'to the idealistic elements in British thinking'.[204] Among the welter of publicity which emerged from this decision was a pamphlet written by the Prime Minister himself.

Britain, the Commonwealth and Europe argued that the British had always been a part of the Continent and that its isolationist mentality had been responsible for two world wars just as much as the megalomania of foreigners:

> We in Britain are Europeans. That has always been true, but it has now become a reality which we cannot ignore. In the past, as a great maritime Empire, we might give way to insular feelings of superiority over foreign breeds and suspicion of our neighbours across the Channel . . . [But] we have to consider the state of the world as it is today . . . It is sometimes alleged that we would lose all our national identity by joining the European Community . . . It is true, of course, that political unity is the central aim of these European countries and we would naturally accept that ultimate

goal ... I myself believe that the bulk of public opinion in this
country ... is firmly against the extinction of separate national
identities and would choose a Europe which preserved and har-
monised all that is best in our different national traditions.

'This is no time', concluded Macmillan, 'to bury our heads in the
sands of the past and take the kind of parochial view which regards
Europe with distrust and suspicion.'[205] It was a laudable attempt to
nudge British national identity forwards from the Empire and wars
which had shaped it for so long. But such pronouncements were rare
and the question of political union was never fully confronted. Unlike
Heath, Macmillan was not a federalist. His government's dissembling
response to the federal question gave the impression that it was being
less than honest about what joining the Common Market would
eventually entail. Over the following quarter of a century, the
deliberate evasiveness of Britain's leaders on the European question
continued as they ran ever more scared of public opinion. This in
turn hardened popular suspicion of British Europhiles and of Europe
itself.

But even if the attempt to sell British membership had been more
frank, neither big set-piece state propaganda campaigns nor cathedral
consecrations could instil a sense of Europeanness in the population
as effectively as a long-term programme of education in Britain's
schools. There were two reasons why this proved to be difficult. The
first was the decline of British youth movements. Late-Victorian
Protestant imperialists had relied on organizations like the Boy Scouts
to augment the work of schools in fostering a sense of empire in
young Britons, and they had done so with a fair degree of success.
But the network of youth movements created between the 1890s and
1930s had been weakened by the war and by the youth revolt that
followed it. And as we have seen, government attempts to regain
some control over young Britons through youth clubs and the
criminal justice system failed miserably. The promoters of European
union therefore depended to a larger extent than their imperial
predecessors on the formal education system.

Here too Europhiles faced a problem, ironically the same one that
diehard imperialists faced in the 1950s: the lack of a national
curriculum. During the 1950s, Western European states not only
used school curricula to nurture the national identities of their
citizens, they also promoted a complementary European identity in
order to increase popular support for the Treaty of Rome. From the

Netherlands to Italy, children were taught about the Continent's bitter saga of conflict, the more recent story of European Union, and the benefits – political, material and cultural – which it brought its members. In the UK, it was much harder to do this because of the relative lack of control which the British state had over the nation's schools. Athena Syriatou's pioneering study of English and Welsh schools between 1945 and 1975 has shown that hubristic, insular attitudes towards Europe continued to be imparted through syllabuses and textbooks, despite the decline of imperial history.[206] The history of Europe was still taught only as it directly affected Britain and even then its scope was limited, with southern and Eastern Europe regarded as peripheral. Moreover, the Continent was usually presented as a volatile arena of war and revolution. There were only a few separate textbooks on Europe; among them was Richards' *Illustrated History of Modern Europe*. In print until the mid-1960s, it was illustrated with *Punch* cartoons depicting Europeans as a shifty, dangerous lot. Add to this the works of A. J. P. Taylor, which soon found their way onto school and university reading lists, and it is hard to disagree with Syriatou's conclusion, 'European history in Britain was presented with a great degree of professional conscientiousness, but was unable to escape completely the national tendency to see Britain as the centre of the world.'[207]

Faced with scepticism from virtually every quarter of the nation, Macmillan tried hard to reassure people that the course of European integration would be an evolutionary one that reflected Britain's political traditions. 'We would', he said, 'favour a more gradual approach worked out by experience, instead of a leap in the dark.'[208] A leap in the dark proved to be unnecessary because, shortly afterwards, the French President shone a harsh light on the gulf between Britain and the Continent. On 14 January 1963, after eighteen months of negotiations, de Gaulle said 'Non!' to the British application at a press conference in Paris.

Why was Britain's application vetoed? After all, de Gaulle was no more of a federalist than Macmillan. The rebuff was motivated partly by the Nassau Treaty of December 1962, in which Kennedy had agreed to share Polaris missiles with Britain. The Americans were keen for Britain to join the Community in the interests of Western unity. But to de Gaulle, the Nassau Treaty proved that the Special Relationship was more important to the British than Europe. Its membership, he believed, would be a Trojan horse for American influence. More than any other European country of the time, France was obsessed with Americanization; the cultural protectionism of the French state in cinema, for example, far outstripped that which the British attempted in the 1940s. De Gaulle was also motivated by a desire to remain the biggest fish in the sea, something he knew would be difficult once the British were swimming in it. And though he admired the British, he also disliked them. What Macmillan called 'his inherited hatred of England' was partly a historical sense of Anglo-French conflict which stretched back to the Middle Ages. The General's dislike of the British had intensified during the war, when he felt slighted by Churchill's refusal to take him seriously in the course of his exile in London as leader of the Free French. And, like most Continentals of the time, he still felt the wartime humiliation of his nation's occupation, a humiliation which the British were always keen to remind him of. In his diary, Macmillan wrote, 'Things would have been easier if Southern England had been occupied by the Nazis . . . that's why he found Adenauer, who'd also been occupied, an easier ally than me . . . I may be cynical, but I fear it's true – if Hitler had danced in London we'd have had no trouble with De Gaulle.'[209]

Historians have spent thousands of words and many more hours examining the ifs and buts of the Macmillan application in an attempt to understand what provoked the veto. Was it poor strategy by British negotiators or would de Gaulle have said no anyway because of his personal Anglophobia? What they usually ignore is the public reason that de Gaulle gave for the veto: the national identity of the British people. The French President genuinely thought that Britishness had not fundamentally changed since the war. Consequently, he believed that the UK would be an uncooperative partner and in the long term a threat to European unity. On all three counts he was absolutely right. On 14 January 1963 he told the 500 members of the world's press gathered at the Élysée that Britain had an island mentality:

> Britain is insular, bound up by its trade, its markets, its food supplies, with the most varied and often the most distant countries. Her activity is essentially industrial, commercial, not agricultural. She has, in all her work, very special, very original habits and traditions. In short, the nature, structure, circumstances, peculiar to Britain are different from those of the other continentals. How can Britain, in the way that she lives, produces, trades, be incorporated in the Common Market as it has been conceived and as it functions?[210]

In his memoirs, he wrote, 'Having failed from without to prevent the birth of the Community, they [the British] now planned to paralyse it from within.'[211]

When the formal veto was lodged on 29 January, the *Daily Express* rejoiced. 'Glory, glory, Hallelujah! It's all over; Britain's Europe bid is dead', trumpeted its front page. 'This is not a day of misery at all. It is a day of rejoicing, a day when Britain has failed to cut her throat . . . The [bid] was rejected by a majority of the people of Britain long before it was turned down by Europe. It went against the instinctive wisdom of the nation . . . against their passionate desire to remain British.'[212] In Brussels, a devastated Heath made a moving speech, re-emphasizing the nation's essential Europeanness:

> We are part of Europe by geography, history, culture, tradition and civilisation . . . There have been times in the history of Europe when it has been only too plain how European we are; and there are many millions of people who have been grateful for it. I say to my colleagues: they should have no fear. We in Britain are not going to turn our backs on the mainland of Europe.[213]

On the 28th, the Prime Minister noted in his diary, 'Our whole policy, external and internal, is destroyed. French domination in Europe is now a new, alarming fact.' In a letter to his confidante, Ava Waverley, he wrote: 'I do not remember going through a worse time since Suez.'[214] What neither he nor Heath fully addressed was that despite the barrage of speeches, pamphlets and broadcasts by a dazzling array of the UK's elites, the British had not come to think of themselves as European. Indeed, many positively loathed Continentals, a feeling which the French veto exacerbated. British pride had been hurt and the rest of 1963 was marked by a popular Francophobia not seen since the French had capitulated to Hitler in 1940. 'There is the return of the old feeling "the French always betray you in the end"', Macmillan observed a month after the veto.[215] Roy Hattersley has since remarked, 'The British took the opposite view of Groucho Marx's first rule of social conduct: they did not want to belong to a club which would not allow them to join.'[216]

Ultimately, however, hurt pride was not the problem. Had it been so, the UK's entry eight years later would have rectified it. No, the real problem was the deep and abiding scepticism of European integration at all levels of British society. The decision to leave Britain's application on the conference table of Brussels marked the opening of a fundamental divide between Britain's leaders and her people which had still not been resolved at the end of the century. Essentially, the situation was this: a substantial section of the Establishment had been profoundly shocked by the loss of empire and had turned, reluctantly but sincerely, to Europe as an alternative power base. Most Britons cared little about the Empire and did not mourn its passing, but neither did they have much wish to become European. They were happy being Little Britons. The divide would not become fully apparent until Edward Heath returned to the Continent in 1971 and was given a smiling 'Oui!' by de Gaulle's successor.

In the meantime, the European issue ceased to be of major public concern. In 1962, Harold Pinter wrote, 'I have no interest in the matter and do not care what happens.'[216] Like most of his plays, Pinter's remark was ahead of its time. But as the 1960s progressed, it became a gloriously accurate expression of British public opinion. There were two reasons for this. The first was common sense. It was clear to all those who did not possess Harold Wilson's vanity that any further application to join the Community would fail as long as de Gaulle was in power. The second reason was both more simple and more complex. The British had better things to do. Three days after de Gaulle's veto, on 17 January 1963, the Beatles shot to No. 2 in the Hit Parade with 'Please Please Me'. A cultural renaissance was under way which to many Britons proved they did not need Europe, America, the Commonwealth or anyone else for that matter. In the end it was more than a renaissance. It was a revolution. The period 1963 to 1973 proved that the forces which had started to rock Britishness in the 1950s could not all be gently absorbed within the country's evolutionary political tradition. With or without Europe, Britain and the national identity of its peoples were about to change for ever.

PART 5

SWINGERS

The reason for the notoriety [of the sixties is that] for the first time in British history, the young working class stood up for themselves and said, 'We are here, this is our society and we are not going away. Join us, stay away, like us, hate us – do as you like. We don't care about your opinion any more.'

Michael Caine, 1992

Did the Beatles deserve to be honoured by the Queen? The answer must be irrevocably and unquestioningly – Yeah! Yeah! Yeah! . . . Where the Beatles deserve their awards is in the field of prestige. Their efforts to keep the Union Jack fluttering proudly have been far more successful than a regiment of diplomats and statesmen. We may be regarded as a second class power in politics, but at any rate we now lead the world in pop music!

New Musical Express, 1965

1. The go-ahead people

The 1960s have a mythological status in the Western world. And nowhere more so than in the UK, where the period revealed the magnitude of the tensions which had built up within British society since the Second World War. The icons of the decade still loom over the scarred landscape of Britishness in the twenty-first century: the Mini (skirt and car), the Beatles, Michael Caine, England's World Cup victory, marijuana and the Pill are but a few. Jonathon Green, who worked on the radical magazine *Oz*, wrote in his history of the period:

> We live in the shadow of the Sixties. Of all the artificial constructs by which we delineate our immediate past, 'the Sixties' have the greatest purchase on the mass imagination. They stand, rightly or not, as the dominant myth of the modern era. That one might have been too old or too young to enjoy them, indeed, that one might not even have been born, is of marginal importance . . . The Sixties are as much a state of mind as a chronological concept. And like all states of mind they are open to many interpretations . . . Utopian, over-optimistic, naïve they may have been, but they offered hope. However inchoate their theories they looked forward to a possible future, rather than back to a long dead past . . . [A good deal of it] was simply psychedelic pipe-dreams, but much too was achieved.[1]

It was, without question, a transformative period of British history in which the promise of mass democracy came closer than ever to being realized. How did it happen, why did it happen at this time and what were the consequences for national identity in Britain?

Thanks to the steady growth of affluence, moral codes and the class structure became less rigid, creating a more meritocratic society which at last bore some resemblance to that of the United States. These developments came to a head during the 1960s because the generation in the 1940s which had benefited from free education became young adults in this period. It is one of the ironies of British history that Harold Macmillan pumped money into state education in order to make the lower classes feel that they played as 'part of the team'. They rewarded his party by evicting it from the pavilion on 16 October 1964.

The second reason for this transformation was the lead given by the government which presided over most of the period. Harold Wilson and the Labour government of 1964–70 have been much maligned. Yet they soldered together the various strands of mass democracy into a cohesive and highly patriotic definition of what it meant to be British. The Labour manifesto for 1964, *Let's GO with Labour for the NEW BRITAIN*, declared:

> The Labour Party is offering Britain a new way of life that will stir our hearts, re-kindle an authentic patriotic faith in our future, and enable our country to re-establish itself as a stable force in the world today for progress, peace and justice. It is within the personal power of every man and woman with a vote to guarantee that the British again become THE GO-AHEAD PEOPLE WITH A SENSE OF NATIONAL PURPOSE.[2]

It is easy now to mock this rhetoric. To some extent it was a flabby reprisal of the liberal patriotism of the early postwar period. Like Attlee before him, Wilson presented change as an amplification of British traditions rather than a betrayal of them. Where Wilsonian rhetoric differed was in its more overt use of science and technology to convey the idea that the British still had the potential to be world leaders.

The concept of a technological revolution was not as vacuous as it was later made out to be. It sprang from two very weighty strands of British political thought: the Victorian idea of progress, in which science was thought to profit the whole nation, to which Wilson added the mid-twentieth-century thought of left-wing British scientists, who argued that science was intrinsically classless and that if it was harnessed by a socialist state it would help to create economic prosperity within a just society. During the Cold War these scientists had been discredited in government circles for being communists and reviled by the literary intelligentsia for being philistines. One who survived, Patrick Blackett, became Wilson's Special Adviser on the subject, while the rest found their ideas once more in vogue. Wilson brought his twin themes of progress and equality together in an electioneering speech at Birmingham Town Hall on 19 January 1964, claiming, 'We are living in the jet-age but we are governed by an Edwardian Establishment mentality.'[3] What he famously called 'the white heat' of the 'scientific revolution' helped him to present Labour as a modernizing force and secure its narrow victory at the general election in October of that year.

The serious flaws in Wilson's plan soon became apparent. The first was simply ironic. Conservative and Labour governments had sponsored scientific endeavour since 1945 and the person who had done most to implant the importance of science in the public mind was not a classless technocrat but the Duke of Edinburgh, who had made it the most popular and enduring aspect of New Elizabethan patriotism. What Wilson did was to exploit the growing perception that Britons were being held back by the class system. What he failed to do was to attack the institutions – primarily the public schools – which perpetuated that class system and prevented the potential of Britons from being fully tapped. What he also failed to do was to address the underlying structural problems of the British economy – primarily a lack of investment in industry – without which technological advances could not deliver prosperity, however many state-educated and -funded professionals filled the nation's laboratories. Consequently, his revolution was still-born. Those who were not already aware of the fact were awoken to it by the devaluation of sterling in November 1967. Devaluation was regarded as a national humiliation and it confirmed the fragility of the British economy.

And yet that is not how the British think of the 1960s, because in other important respects the country did change for the better. According to a Gallup survey carried out in 1986, 70 per cent of people across all age groups believed the 1960s to have been the best decade of the century in Britain.[4] Why? Living standards continued to rise and the British rid themselves of the worst aspects of the old social order. The Wilson government played an active part in helping them to do so by overseeing the biggest tranche of liberal legislation since the creation of the welfare state. So often dismissed as a footnote to a sorry tale of economic mismanagement, the extent of this legislation is here recorded in full:

- The 1965 Murder (Abolition of the Death Penalty) Act abolished hanging for all murders, making high treason the only offence for which a Briton could be executed.
- The 1965 Race Relations Act criminalized racial discrimination and set up the Race Relations Board to act as a watchdog and arbitrator in disputes (a further Act in 1968 extended the law to cover housing, employment, entertainment, travel and the provision of goods and services).

- The 1967 Family Planning Act empowered local authorities to set up family planning clinics which made no distinction between the married and unmarried and freely distributed the Pill for the first time since it came on the market in 1961.
- David Steel's 1967 Abortion Act made abortions up to twenty weeks legal, on psychological as well as medical grounds.
- Leo Abse's 1967 Sexual Offences Act legalized sex between consenting homosexuals over the age of twenty-one.
- The 1968 Family Law Reform and Representation of the People Acts lowered the age of majority and the voting age from twenty-one to eighteen.
- The 1969 Divorce Reform Act enabled consenting adults to divorce on any grounds after two years (after five years one party could obtain divorce without the consent of the other).
- The 1970 Matrimonial Property Act established that a wife's work, either as a wage-earner or as a housewife, was equal to that of a man, thereby entitling women to half an estate in the event of divorce.
- The 1970 Equal Pay Act established the principle of equal pay for women (it became legally binding on employers in 1975).
- The 1970 Chronic Sick and Disabled Persons Act gave specific rights to the disabled for the first time, making it compulsory for local authorities to provide basic amenities such as toilets for the disabled and ramps in public buildings.

The legislation on race, homosexuality and disability did not go nearly far enough to establish civic rights for those groups, and there were significant regional and national variations in attitudes towards reform. Demand for it came predominantly from the liberal middle classes of south-east England, and in particular from the pen of Anthony Crosland MP, Secretary of State for Education and Science from 1965 to 1967. Since the mid-1950s, Crosland had been arguing that in an age of affluence, gas and water socialism should be accompanied by a drive towards 'personal freedom, happiness and cultural endeavour'.[5] Or, as a more obscure Party theorist put it, the politics of full employment should give way to 'the politics of full enjoyment'.[6]

But patchy though the ideological support was for an all-out attack on Victorian values, the fruits of that attack were welcomed by the vast majority of Britons. Women benefited inestimably from the control they were given over their bodies and their property. Older adolescents were recognized as adults instead of simply being seen as youths who needed to be disciplined by Church and state. People of all ages were liberated by the ability to end failed marriages instead of being miserably trapped and/or forced to live a double life with illicit partners. The abolition of hanging requires no comment. Taking the legislation as a whole, historian Jeffrey Weeks summed up:

> There was no official endorsement of hedonism. There was in fact a strong element of negative utilitarianism in the legislation, more concerned with removing difficulties, and minimising suffering, than in positively enhancing happiness . . . [However] it was not a simple reform of outdated laws, but a major legislative restructuring, marking an historic shift in the . . . regulation of civil society. And at the heart of these changes were the great series of reforms of the laws relating to sexual behaviour, amounting to the most significant package of legislative changes on morality for over half a century.[7]

Social reform not only made Britain a freer and more civilized place in which to live. The cultural matrix of Britishness was fundamentally altered by the relaxation of national mores.

Football, pop music and fashion came to rival and in some cases replace traditional sources of patriotism like Church and Parliament. The whole way that national culture was perceived began to change. The artificial barriers between the arts and entertainment which the Victorians had erected were torn down as more and more Britons questioned the idea of a hierarchy of taste and realized they did not have to make a choice between Elgar and the Beatles in order to demonstrate either their intelligence or their patriotism. The celebrants of the 'Swinging Sixties' succeeded where mid-century reformers had failed. Both the left/liberals who sought to refine popular sensibilities through state patronage of the arts and the conservatives who used the monarchy to mobilize a more entrepreneurial renaissance failed because they both had a limited and hierarchical vision of what Britishness should consist of.

The sum total of the changes described above is that between approximately 1963 and 1973 a cultural renaissance took place which laid the foundations of post-imperial national identity in Britain. Through a combination of the people's confidence, hard work, protest, good luck and conscious desire to remake themselves, the UK briefly became the cultural capital of the West. The essence of this new Britishness was that national culture in *all* its forms could be a worthy substitute for the loss of political and economic supremacy. In his highly critical study of the period, Christopher Booker admitted, 'The English "revolution" ... has been a revolution in almost every conceivable field – social, political, economic, technological, moral, artistic.'[8]

The revolution slowed the decline of British national identity because being British had become exciting once again. Yet the excitement wore off more quickly in Scotland and Wales than it did in England. It was in this period that Celtic nationalism became, for the first time in its history, a sustained mass political movement. This happened not because the new Britishness was unpopular beyond its nerve centre in Swinging London. After all, the Scots and Welsh happily incorporated most of its precepts into the new identities which they began to forge for themselves. The remaking of Britishness failed because it did not and could not halt the continuing decline of the Scottish and Welsh economies. What the period demonstrated was that redesigning British national identity was not enough to save it. In the meantime, the lights went down, the music went up, clothes were ripped off, and the best party Britain had ever had swung into life.

2. I had a mind as well as a vagina

In April 1943, the British Ambassador to the Soviet Union, Sir Archibald Clark Kerr, wrote the following letter to Lord Pembroke at the Foreign Office in London:

My Dear Reggie, In these dark days men tend to look for little shafts of light that spill from Heaven. My days are probably darker than yours, and I need, my God I do, all the light I can get. But I am a decent fellow, and I do not want to be mean and selfish about what little brightness is shed upon me from time to time. So I propose to share with you a tiny flash that has illuminated my sombre life and tell you that God has given me a new Turkish colleague whose card tells me that he is called Mustapha Kunt. We all feel like that, Reggie, now and then, especially when Spring is

upon us, but few of us would care to put it on our cards. It takes
a Turk to do that.[9]

The idea that sex was not something which should be mentioned on
a calling card captured the prevailing British belief that only foreigners made a public display of their sexual desires.

During the war, millions lost their inhibitions as the threat of
death made the deferral or denial of pleasure seem absurd – a trend
which triggered government campaigns designed to warn men of the
dangers of VD from supposedly loose women. But even then, sex
was not a major part of public discourse. During the early postwar
period little changed. In 1946, the chapter on sex in George Mikes'
look at the English character, *How To Be An Alien*, simply read
'Continental people have [a] sex life; the English have hot-water
bottles.'[10] In the 1950s, Donald McGill's saucy seaside postcards had
been a feature of British life for thirty years. But they were still
regularly impounded and destroyed by local authorities and McGill
himself stood trial for obscenity at Lincoln in 1954, aged seventy-
eight.

The British thought themselves to be a reserved and inhibited,
even frigid people. This had more to do with probity than it did with
Puritanism. Sexual integrity was part of the Victorian cult of the
gentleman. It was one way that the British defined themselves as a
moderate people, not given to the passionate, revolutionary extremes
of Europeans. Nina Epton's 1960 best-seller *Love and the English*
argued that sex was not an integral part of the British character
because the male sex drive had been channelled into building democracy and empire:

> For the Englishman, adventure consists in encounters with foes or
> the elements . . . Respect for the individual, a love of justice and
> freedom – the English are rightly and sensibly convinced that none
> of these can be woven into an impermanent relationship. The
> average Englishman loves his home, garden and children. He is not
> attracted by strange bedrooms. Even when he frequents a pros-
> titute, he hardly spends more than twenty minutes over the
> operation . . .[11]

Epton noted the new teenage habit of 'snogging' in public (a native
term, coined in the 1950s). But she reassured her readers that the
British ideal continued to be 'a sensible, dull, vaguely asexual . . .
married life destined to lead to a Golden Wedding Anniversary notice
in the local paper'.[12]

In the 1960s sex became a part of public discourse in Britain, oozing from the pores of a society anxious to remove the constricting raiment of Victorian morality. If the *Lady Chatterley* trial of 1960 undid a few top buttons by making erotic novels available to the public, the Profumo scandal of 1963 ripped the bodice off British probity. It was not the first British sex scandal to be reported by the mass media; nor was it the first to have political implications (Parnell's affair with a married woman in the 1880s lost the Irish nationalist leader credibility in Britain and set back the cause of Home Rule for a generation). But Profumo was the first scandal of its kind to implicate the entire British ruling elite. Christine Keeler had been simultaneously sleeping with the Minister of War, John Profumo, and a Soviet naval attaché. Their social links with the Astors of Cliveden revived folk memories of the prewar 'Cliveden Set' and its reputation as a cabal of high-society appeasers.

But although the government fretted about a possible breach of security, that was not why the scandal fascinated ordinary Britons. Nor was it because they had a fit of morality, since the story was consumed with salacious gusto (especially the rumour that a Cabinet minister had attended parties dressed in bondage gear with a sign round his neck asking to be beaten). The real, long-term effect of the Profumo scandal was that it undermined conservative attempts to contain postwar affluence within a prewar moral framework. Defending the introduction of commercial TV in 1954, Profumo had told the House of Commons that the British were not a nation of intellectuals. True. But they were not stupid either. People resented members of the Establishment using their influence to get away with behaviour which ordinary citizens had been repeatedly told was partly responsible for the country's decline as a world power. And the fact that Keeler's patron, Stephen Ward, was scapegoated showed how ruthlessly the Establishment was prepared to protect its double standards. The Suez crisis had lost Britain's ruling elites much of their political authority. Profumo lost them the moral authority which had buttressed their privileges throughout Britain's transition to parliamentary democracy. Profumo did not start a revolution. But henceforth Britons would not care to be lectured about their sexual habits; nor would they welcome any attempt by the state to prevent those habits being freely enjoyed.

Lord Denning's best-selling report on the affair did little to change the nation's mind. Alfred Thompson Denning was a hanger and flogger whose sixty-year career at the top of the legal profession was guided by two things: his devout Christian faith (he kept a Bible close to hand when writing judgements) and his ardent patriotism. He found the Profumo affair 'vile and revolting' and quashed rumours that half the British Establishment were involved. Instead, he blamed the press:

> It has been thought by some that these rumours are a symptom of a decline in the integrity of public life in this country. I do not believe this to be true. There has been no lowering of standards. But there is this difference to-day. Public men are more vulnerable than they were: and it behoves them, even more than ever, to give no cause for scandal. For, if they do, they have to reckon with a growing hazard ... Scandalous information about well-known people has become a marketable commodity. True or false, actual or invented, it can be sold.[13]

In a sense, of course, Denning was right. There had been no lowering of standards because there was never a time when Britain's rulers did not indulge their sexual desires. What had changed was the power and the willingness of the mass media to expose them.

For the rest of the century, shooting the messenger became the popular sport for public figures with something to hide. The need for privacy – that celebrated characteristic of the British – was invoked in an attempt to gain the nation's sympathy and keep the press at bay. It failed because the Victorian idea that private conscience and public duty were inextricably linked had been exposed as a sham. Writing to a friend in October 1963, Nancy Mitford compared 1960s Britain to Venice in the seventeenth century: 'Perhaps', she suggested, 'masked naked men, orgies and unlimited spying are an accompaniment of maritime powers in decline. Certainly the whole Ward affair comes straight out of *Casanova*'.[14]

Venetian or not, British culture became much more sexually explicit. The sex manual became almost as common in British homes as gardening, DIY and cooking manuals. The most famous was written by Alex Comfort, a fifty-two-year-old pacifist poet from north London. As its title implies, *The Joy of Sex: A Gourmet Guide To Lovemaking* (1972) treated the human sexual appetite as some-thing quite as normal as the appetite for food, whether it took place inside or outside marriage. Illustrated chapters were headed 'Starters', 'Main Courses', 'Desserts' and 'Sauces and Pickles', the last of which recommended a little light bondage of the kind enjoyed by Cabinet ministers. *The Joy of Sex* sold 12 million copies worldwide and, more than any other book of the twentieth century, it helped the British to relax, pursue and enjoy the satisfaction of their physical desires. In addition, film, plays, pop lyrics, adverts and newspapers all referred to sex more often and more overtly. The celebrities of 1960s Britain revelled in the new openness and their excesses set an example for others to follow.

None more so than Michael Caine. The film *Alfie* (1966) stamped him in the public mind as the embodiment of the hedonistic young male Briton. The press dubbed him 'the Birdman of Grosvenor Square', a reference to his self-confessed love of 'birds' and the flat he shared in west London with fellow East End actor Terence Stamp.[15] According to Caine, the flat was known to the two men as the 'Airfield':

> All at once it seemed that every pretty girl with no tits was modelling clothes and every pretty girl with big tits was modelling those ... Brassieres were discarded as breasts jiggled under blouses, but panties were retained as skirts rose higher to prove it. Eyes shone, teeth flashed and thighs gleamed ... The Sixties were here at last – and the sun seemed to shine on London for the first time since the end of the war ... The succession of individual dolly birds turned into a flock and I was the flight controller. Getting them in and out of the very busy airfield that our flat had become, without collision, meant keeping them on a very narrow and definite flight path.[16]

Few young people could afford to live in west London, but a greater number than ever before were able to rent or buy flats before getting married, giving them a space in which to take advantage of the new morality away from the prying eyes of parents. Those who could not afford flats found relief in the chalets of Butlin's where, for a small amount of money, they could enjoy sexual adventures away from interfering relatives and the legendary censoriousness of the British seaside landlady.

Much has been written about the extent to which sexual freedom for women simply meant being taken advantage of on the 'airfields' of Britain like the one described above. Some dismissed the whole agenda of sexual liberation as trivial. The Labour Minister for Transport, Barbara Castle, said:

> I became increasingly impatient with [feminists'] obsession with sexuality ... I had a mind as well as a vagina and I did not see why the latter should dominate – there are so many more interest-

ing things in life [and] it is hard for anyone, male or female, to fulfil themselves if they are poor, ill-housed, ill-educated and struggling with ill-health. Women's special problems must be grafted on to the battle against injustice wherever it may occur.[17]

If they cared to think about it, most Britons were well aware that Barbara Castle had a mind as well as a vagina. Sexual liberation did not overshadow other political questions. It was quite rightly seen as integral to them. It was not until the twenty-first century that British women began to be seen as true equals by the male population. But the revolution in their lives which began during the Second World War took off in this period and eventually it changed the way that Britishness was perceived.

Diana Dors was the country's first sex symbol and in films like *Passport To Shame* (1959) she presented her sexuality as a challenge to the fetid national culture of Britain. She told the press, 'I am, by English standards, a fairly flamboyant character . . . Before me female stars were either pretty or matronly. Sex was just an incidental – best left to the Continentals.'[18] By the early 1960s she had been superseded by stars like Julie Christie, Vanessa Redgrave and Charlotte Rampling – women who were not only independent, intelligent, articulate but who also got roles to match. Sometimes, as in *Darling* (1967) starring Julie Christie, they were shown to be manipulative, destructive individuals. But overall the image was a more positive one. Interviewed in the 1980s, Julie Christie said: 'Darling wanted to have *everything* . . . There was an element of possibility for women, of a new way of living, which is why the film was such a success.'[19] Feminist film critics agree. Surveying the whole genre of 'Swinging London' films, Christine Geraghty wrote: 'The codes of stardom developed in the 60s associated female sexuality with honesty, independence and freedom, and could suggest, to young audiences at least, that young women were not "the problem" but offered possibilities for a solution.'[20] Woman power was also apparent off camera. Ken Russell remembers one British female star who was so sick of being gawped at she refused to do another nude scene until the male film crew stripped off as well. 'The gobsmacked technicians fell for it', he recounted, and the scene went ahead 'with the lighting cameraman wearing nothing but an exposure meter'.[21]

It was not just film stars who benefited. The novelist Angela Carter, then struggling to establish herself as a writer, was adamant that the period changed women's lives:

So where does all the Swinging London stuff, pop music, hemlines, where did it all fit in? I'd like to be able to dismiss it as superficial ... but I'm forced to admit there was a yeastiness in the air that was due to a great deal of unrestrained and irreverent frivolity ... I find it very odd that women who are otherwise perfectly sensible say that the 'sexual revolution' of the sixties only succeeded in putting more women on the sexual market for the pleasure of men ... Truly, it felt like Year One ... The introduction of more or less 100 per cent effective methods of birth control, combined with the relaxation of manners ... changed, well, everything. Sexual pleasure was suddenly divorced from not only reproduction but also status, security, all the foul traps men lay for women in order to trap them into permanent relationships.[22]

Magazines for adolescent girls reflected the new openness. While boys still consumed a diet of war stories and football, girls began to read about the biological and emotional start of adulthood, and by the 1970s they were being given advice on the best techniques for achieving orgasm. Sexual idolization of men from the pop world became common and Beatlemania prompted a flurry of patronizing comment on adolescent female sexuality. According to one psychologist in the *News of the World*, 'the girls are subconsciously preparing for motherhood. Their frenzied screams are a rehearsal for the moment.'[23] But girls' magazines did begin to treat their readers as independent young adults with minds of their own rather than as vessels for the greater glory of British manhood.

Of course, talking about sex does not mean people are doing it more often; usually quite the opposite. In a study of adolescent boys in the East End of London carried out in 1969, one eighteen-year-old commented, 'Some people with a big mouth say "I do this and that with my girl." But they go home and masturbate, the same as everybody else.'[24] Another survey found that only 17 per cent of young English men had had more than one partner a year.[25] It is therefore important not to exaggerate the extent to which Britain was swinging in the 1960s. Permissive legislation did not create a permissive society, any more than race relations legislation created racial harmony. The portrayal of sex in British cinema is also a salutary reminder that British attitudes still differed from those of the Continent. Despite the creation of the 'X' certificate in 1951, cinema remained tightly censored compared to Europe, and few British studios made movies with an explicit sexual theme, let alone specialist sex films. Even the display of pubic hair was forbidden (in

Germany it was thought indecent *not* to have it). Britons in search of erotica had to make do with Continental imports, shown in a small number of metropolitan cinemas. Viewing one in the mid-1950s, the Chairman of the British Board of Film Censors, Sir Sidney Harris, remarked, 'I suppose we shall have to pass it, but men and women don't go to bed together with no clothes on.'[26] John Trevelyan (brother of the historian G. M. Trevelyan) had a better grasp of British sexual practice and he did much to liberalize the cinema during his tenure as Secretary of the Board (1958–1971). Trevelyan ensured that productions like *A Kind of Loving* (1961) – the first mainstream movie to show nudity – reached the screen.

Specialist sex films also began to be made in greater numbers from the early 1960s onwards. Sadly, the genre was no more erotic than it had been under the more conservative regime of Harris. While European and American studios switched to hardcore porn in the 1960s and 1970s, the British developed their own unique genre, the softcore sex comedy. From *Mary Had A Little* (1961) to *Confessions of a Window Cleaner* (1974), the British sex comedy took the saucy slap and tickle of the seaside postcard and the Whitehall bedroom farce and transposed it to the screen. Its high point, of course, was the Carry On series, beginning with *Carry On Sergeant* (1958) and ending mercifully after thirty-one films with *Carry On Columbus* (1992). The series took sexual innuendo to new heights. Typical was this scene from *Carry On Regardless* (1961) in which the camp, weedy Charles Hawtrey mistakes a strip club for an aviary:

> MANAGER: What do you want?
> HAWTREY: Your birds. Oh, I can't wait! Tell me – what sort are they?
> MANAGER: What sort do you like?
> HAWTREY: Blue tits . . . got any?
> MANAGER: No. My place is centrally heated.[27]

Though Carry Ons had none of the stiff upper lip that was common in romantic films like *Brief Encounter*, the sexual desire of the protagonists was just as thwarted. Whether the brazen Sid James, the gauche Jim Dale or the prurient Kenneth Williams were in pursuit of women, their domineering wives or disapproving bosses usually intervened. Or the objects of the men's lust – usually Barbara Windsor – simply declined the offer of a quick one. The nation's favourite squeaky-voiced busty blonde was trained by the radical theatre director Joan Littlewood, who once said of her, 'She honours

England in all she does.'[28] Who could doubt it? Yet it said much about British attitudes to sex that while America had Monroe and France had Bardot, the UK's leading sex symbol of the postwar period was Babs Windsor, with Hattie Jacques a close second.

Attitudes towards homosexuality are also a reminder of the limits of British liberalism in this period. Of all the social reforms of the 1960s, the legalization of homosexuality touched the rawest nerve because it was the activity most widely associated with the decadence of nations. The British may have been happy playing Greece to America's Rome, but this was one aspect of Greek civilization they preferred not to adopt. Although Women's Lib was grudgingly accepted, British power and fortitude was still thought to reside in the moral health of the nation's men. The prosecution for sodomy of respected notables caused a shiver in the frames of traditional patriots across the land. The third Baron Montagu of Beaulieu was one of the first peers to open his country house to the public. Among his publicity stunts was to get down on all fours and scrub the floors alongside his servants; a picture of him doing so appeared in the press with the unfortunate caption 'It's enough to bring a peer to his knees'.[29] A year later, Montagu was in court, facing charges of buggering a Boy Scout, one of many he employed on his estate to act as tour guides. The fact that pederasty was equated with homosexuality was itself an indication of British attitudes to the issue. As more details of the Burgess and Maclean affair became known in the 1960s, homosexuality became closely linked in the public mind not simply with a vague sense of national decadence but with something much worse: communist treason.

Jack Wolfenden had to be careful for precisely that reason. He was a Nonconformist Yorkshireman and a firm believer in the sanctity of marriage. He only advocated the legalization of homosexuality because he wanted to stamp out the blackmail which the outlawing of sodomy in 1885 had unwittingly encouraged (he referred to homosexuals and prostitutes as 'Huntleys' and 'Palmers' because he could not bring himself to say the words).[30] During the preparation of his report, his son Jeremy admitted to being gay. Jeremy Wolfenden was Moscow correspondent of the *Daily Telegraph*. He knew the exiled Guy Burgess well and while in Moscow he had been recruited by MI6, the CIA *and* the KGB. Wolfenden senior had already authored the 1953 report which advocated the controversial abolition of national service. If the press found out that his son was a homosexual spy, there would be hell to pay. Father wrote to son warning of the danger and giving this advice: 'Dear Jeremy, I have only two requests to make of you at the moment. 1) That we stay out of each other's way for the time being; 2) That you wear rather less make-up.'[31] Jeremy acceded to the requests. An alcoholic, he died, aged thirty-one, in mysterious circumstances two years before his father's recommendations were put on to the statute book.

Illiberal British attitudes to homosexuality were openly encouraged by press and politicians. When the Wolfenden Report was published on 3 September 1957, the *Sunday Express* called it 'The Pansies' Charter'.[32] In 1963, the *Sunday Mirror* helpfully published a two-page guide for its readers on 'How to Spot a Homo'. Telling signs were 'shifty glances', 'dropped eyes' and, the one that clinched it, 'a fondness for the theatre'.[33] A particular source of public anger was the argument, often made by reformers, that Britain should adopt Continental mores. When the House of Commons debated the matter in 1966, one Labour MP said:

> I am not concerned with what happens on the Continent. I know what happens on the Continent. But once we start, by legislation, to debase our minimum standards we are heading for trouble . . . It hits at the very roots of our society . . . I only know, coming from the class of society that I do, that our experience of sexual life was gained in a way which is still applicable to about 99 per cent of the population – at the local cinema, the ballroom, taking an occasional girl home. That is the way most of us learned. It is the natural way, and most of us enjoyed it.[34]

Lord Arran, who supported Leo Abse's Bill, offered this warning when it received royal assent on 27 July 1967:

> This is no occasion for jubilation; certainly not for celebration. Any form of ostentatious behaviour; now or in the future, any form of public flaunting, would be utterly distasteful . . . Homosexuals must continue to remember that while there may be nothing bad in being homosexual, there is certainly nothing good . . . no amount of legislation will prevent homosexuals from being the subject of dislike and derision, or at best of pity.[35]

How right the noble Lord was. A study by Geoffrey Gorer published in 1973 found that only 12 per cent of English people felt a 'tolerant' attitude towards homosexuality; 24 per cent felt 'revulsion' and 22 per cent 'pity'.[36] Not until the final decade of the century did a

majority accept gay people as normal human beings who posed no
threat to national security and the British way of life.[37]

Harold Wilson worried that legislation would cost the party 6
million votes, particularly those of the industrial working classes in
Scotland, Wales, the Midlands and the north where traditional
British masculinity, and with it homophobia, was most entrenched.
In Burnley, Lancashire, attempts to set up a gay club by Labour
activists in Co-op premises was thwarted by Party officials, one of
whom reassured local people that there would be 'no buggers club in
Burnley'.[38] In Scotland the opposition to reform reached hysterical
proportions. The Churches launched a campaign for state funds to
give homosexuals medical and psychiatric help. 'The sin of Sodom',
they told the government, 'must inevitably result in the judgement of
Sodom [on Britain]'.[39] The *Scotsman* declared that all homosexuals
were potential traitors to the nation because 'by the nature of their
disability [they] owe their primary allegiance to the homosexual
group before any other authority or loyalty in their lives. Hence the
connection between perversion and subversion'.[40] Civic leaders saw
legalization as a sign of English decadence and feared that even if
Scotland were exempted from it, England would still corrupt the
nation by becoming 'a Gretna Green for homosexuals'. In March
1966, the Secretary of State, Willie Ross, told the Home Secretary,
Roy Jenkins, that public opposition was 'substantially stronger' north
of the border. As a result, the government backed down and homosexuality remained a crime in Scotland until 1980 (in Northern
Ireland, it was not legalized until 1982). More than any other social
issue of the time, this one demonstrated that the divisions between
the British nations were not simply a matter of economics. And it
showed once again that although the cultural revolution of the 1960s
can be described as a British one, it was more muted in the north
and west of the island.

Still, the distinction between the British attitude to sex and that of
other Europeans became more blurred in this period. Sex was no
longer seen as something which, in the words of Diana Dors, was
'best left to the Continentals'. The criteria by which the British
considered themselves to be a liberal people had changed. Before the
1960s, sexual *restraint* was seen as emblematic of Britain's moderate
national character. From this period onwards, tolerance of individual
desires and activities became a benchmark of that same liberalism.
The institution of marriage remained popular, but being single lost
the stigma it once had. 'An unmarried person in this country is a

social misfit, and is suspect', the *Sunday Pictorial* opined shortly after the Coronation.[41] Twenty years later, most Britons regarded such prejudice with suspicion. Sex before marriage, and with successive partners, was now accepted – celebrated, even – as a person's right. Those who believed that premarital sex was immoral fell from 66 per cent of the population in 1963 to 10 per cent in 1973. The side-effects were rapid. Illegitimacy rose from 5 per cent of all births to 38 per cent by the end of the century; the abortion rate rose sixfold. Divorce soared, up from one in ten marriages in 1950 to one in three by 1970, by which time the UK had the highest rate of any European country.[42] A large part of that rise was attributable to women. From 1950 to 1977, the proportion of divorce petitions filed by them rose from 45 per cent to 73 per cent of the annual total. Marriage was still a relatively popular institution. The proportion of re-marriages rose from 20 per cent to 36 per cent in the same period. Overall, however, these figures show that female Britons had gained more power and were excercising it. The emotional, mental and sexual satisfaction which they had always craved but rarely achieved in their relationships with men became more attainable. In professional terms, British women were still second-class citizens. On average, they were paid less than men and obtained a significantly lower proportion of managerial positions. But outside work, they no longer had to tolerate men who didn't know what a washing machine, conversation or the clitoris were. Therefore, however much conservatives continued to say these changes evidenced Britain's moral decline, in truth they were a product of people's reluctance to be trapped in unsatisfying relationships when it was no longer legally, socially or (for women) economically necessary to do so. Most Britons revelled in their new freedom. And though they still stigmatized prostitution more than other Europeans, that was largely because paying for sex was seen as unnecessary in a sexually free society, and not because it was seen as morally wrong.

Sexual tolerance did not yet extend to public life, as erring politicians and clergy found to their cost. Most people believed that sexual freedom was a private right, best exercised discreetly within the home. In 1973, for example, polls showed that 75 per cent of British adults believed that pornography should be freely available as long as it was not on public display.[43] That same year, the musical *Hair* opened in London. Replete with nudity and swearing, the producers were able to stage it because the government abolished state censorship of the British theatre in 1968. Cynthia Jebb, wife of the diplomat Gladwyn Jebb and a hostess renowned for her Continental sensibilities, took her friend Gerald Wellesley, the seventh Duke of Wellington, to see *Hair*. Her diary records:

> It was ghastly. To begin with, the noise was deafening, as Gerry would sit in the front row, thinking he would not hear otherwise and wanting to see all the nudity. Then it was altogether so squalid and filthy, everybody in the cast looking unwashed and drugged, wearing grubby, trendy clothes. The very first thing that happened was that one of the men on the stage made a bee-line for me, removed his blue jeans and said 'Lady, hold these for me' . . . But the worst was when tiny white paper pellets, supposed to be snow, were showered down on to the stage and the first row of the stalls, so that we were covered in confetti which stuck in our hair and went down our necks. We arrived at the Savoy, to the acute embarrassment of Gerry, looking as if we had just got married.[44]

Cynthia and Gerald's response to *Hair* highlights the fact that many Britons continued to think that what is acceptable in the bedroom is not always acceptable in public, however alluring it might at first seem. In a sense, therefore, little had changed since Sir Archibald Clerk Kerr poked fun at the Turks forty years earlier. Foreign observers were right to observe that hypocrisy was still a British trait. Nonetheless, sexual freedom had become a fundamental part of the nation's identity and this marked a decisive break with the mores which had prevailed since the Victorian era.

Part of the reason why that change took place is that sex became closely allied with social mobility, intercourse with those from other classes being one way in which men and women felt they could transcend the barriers imposed by British tradition. The fascination of *Lady Chatterley* and Profumo owed much to this trend. It was also a dominant theme in the nation's cinema, from the contemporary social realism of *Room at the Top* to costume drama like *The Go-Between* (1967) in which Julie Christie played an Edwardian aristocrat having an affair with a tenant farmer. The British were as obsessed with class in this period as they were with sex. In both cases their obsession demonstrated both how liberated Britain had become and how much it remained a nation ill at ease with itself.

3. We don't care about your opinion any more

Class was not simply a source of difference in Britain, it was a fundamental part of the nation's identity. A study of British life published in 1956 concluded that Britain was 'still a profoundly class-ridden country, a snob's Elysium ... this snobbery, complex, subtle, guilty and enjoyable, is part of the English heritage'.[45] Class therefore functioned in a paradoxical way. On the one hand, class divisions undermined elite notions of what ought to constitute British culture. On the other hand, the idea of a social hierarchy was something that most people associated with being British in the first place. Questioning of the established order became widespread by the 1960s and it fundamentally altered the popular perception of Britain. In his study of the subject, David Cannadine concluded: 'By the mid-1970s, "the collapse of deference" was a phrase that seemed to be on everyone's lips, sometimes with regret, often with relish. Either way, it seems clear that perceptions of Britain as a divinely ordained and successfully functioning hierarchy were much diminished.'[46] Most Britons had a tripartite view of society; that is to say, they believed it was broadly divided into the upper, middle and working classes. Class barriers had never been rigid, but from the mid-1950s onwards they became more fluid, thanks to affluence, better access to education and the expansion of the service sector of the British economy.

Several important qualifications need to be made at this point. First, affluence did not significantly erode the cultural differences between the classes. This was mainly because a great many working-class Britons saw no reason to reject their roots when they passed through the doorway of an estate agent or a car showroom. Sociologists who investigated the subject found little evidence of what they called 'embourgeoisement'. They concluded that rather than becoming middle class, people were by and large simply discovering new, more enjoyable ways of being working class. Second, severe inequality remained as a result of the continued existence of the public schools. The Attlee government had ducked the issue in the 1940s and Wilson did the same. A Public Schools Commission, appointed in 1965, reported on 22 July 1968. Using the accumulated statistical research of twenty years, it demonstrated beyond any doubt that whether or not segregation was the intention it was certainly the result. The report concluded:

> The public schools are not divisive because they are exclusive. An exclusive institution becomes divisive when it arbitrarily confers upon its members advantages and powers over the rest of society. The public schools confer such advantages on an arbitrarily selected membership, which already starts with an advantageous position in life. There is no sign that these divisions will disappear if the schools are left alone.[47]

It recommended that local authorities take over the running of public schools – in effect municipal nationalization. The Commissioners were roundly condemned in the national press and an embarrassed and hostile Cabinet decided to ignore the report.

A bad decision was turned into a catastrophic one by the government's abolition of grammar schools in favour of comprehensive education. Tony Crosland told his wife, 'If it's the last thing I do, I'm going to destroy every fucking grammar school in England. And Wales. And Northern Ireland.'[48] Ministerial Circular 10/65 conveyed Crosland's intention to local authorities with rather more tact, but the effect was much the same. The abolition of a two-tier state system, and with it the injustice of deciding a child's fate at the tender age of eleven, was an easy egalitarianism which pleased the left. But it kicked away the only effective ladder for working-class advancement. The simultaneous introduction of mixed-ability classes and non-pedagogical teaching techniques, which mainly affected pupils with little or no recourse to instruction in the home, did not help. From 1963 to 1971, the number of students in full time higher education doubled to reach 443,000, but the number of working class Britons attending university was only a 2 per cent rise on the previous decade. Moreover, the proportion of university students from ordinary backgrounds actually fell in the 1970s, from 29 per cent to 20 per cent.[49] In her memoir of the period, Angela Carter (herself a beneficiary of grammar school education) commented:

> By the sixties, the 1944 Education Act had more or less percolated through the entire system, and the grammar schools were on the point of turning into training camps for the class war since they were run by and for the children of the lower classes, by that time.

That was why [Labour] put a stop to them, of course; [it] couldn't stomach a situation like that.[50]

There is no evidence that the motive for abolition was quite so premeditated. But there was a warped logic and a cruel irony to it. In a period in which Britain was enjoying a cultural renaissance which modernized its national identity, the institution which had done most to make that change possible was abolished. At the same time, the public school – the institution which had perpetuated the social system on which Victorian Britishness was based – was allowed to survive and thrive.

Therefore, those seeking to explain why the radical promise of the 1960s was never properly fulfilled should not look in the empty syringes and full ashtrays of partied-out rock stars. The answer is to be found in Circular 10/65 and the Cabinet minutes for 18 July 1968.[51] Despite all the promises made by Britain's leaders following the Butler Act, in the end the struggle for equal opportunity was not won on the playing fields of Britain because the playing fields were still not level even in 2000. The postwar expansion of state education led to the goalposts being repainted and the turf replanted, but the vast majority of Britons were still stuck at one end of the pitch playing uphill into a biting wind with no changeover at half-time.

However, attitudes to class changed even if its fundamental structure did not. The British upper and middle classes became less snobbish and more willing to accept that someone who ate 'tea' instead of 'dinner' in the evening might actually be intelligent, talented and have something valuable to say. In fact, the influence of the working- and lower-middle classes grew to such an extent during the 1960s that the way the British saw and experienced their national culture was radically altered. Social commentators rushed to proclaim the arrival of a new meritocratic Britain: in 1967, David Frost and Antony Jay's bestselling study of the national character, *To England with Love*, proclaimed:

Carnaby Street usurps Savile Row; Liverpudlian pop stars weekend at ducal castles; dukes go out to work; ancient universities welcome upstart sons of hobnailed workmen. The bad system is smashed. The archaic pyramid, upper-middle-lower, an unholy trinity of jealousy, malevolence and frustration, cracks and crumbles and those at the top – the people who said looking-glass for mirror, writing paper for notepaper, chimney piece for mantelpiece; the people who never said 'Cheers' when they drank; the peers and

courtiers and country squires – no longer signify. The three great
classes melt and mingle. And a new Britain is born.[52]

The decline of received pronunciation was one manifestation of that
new Britain.

Since the turn of the twentieth century, national and regional
accents in the UK had become less acceptable among Britain's
propertied classes. The BBC played a major role in defining lingual
codes. Reith believed 'you cannot raise social standards without
raising speech standards' and in 1926 he set up the Committee on
Spoken English to advise announcers and performers (Kenneth Clark
and Julian Huxley were among its members).[53] The result was that
by the 1930s the term 'Queen's English' gave way to 'BBC English'
to denote the ideal way for Britons to speak. In the 1960s, those
codes were rejected. The upper classes adopted the less plummy
accents and speech patterns of the middle classes, who in turn
adopted those of the working classes. Phonetician Dr J. C. Wells
explained: 'Working class culture has come to be admired in many
ways . . . People are a bit embarrassed to be seen imitating upper-
class behaviour. It has become smart to go down-market'.[54] One of
the bright young things who thought so was Kevin MacDonald,
nephew of press magnate Lord Northcliffe and co-owner of the
nightclub Sybilla's. In 1965, he told the *Evening Standard*, 'We're
completely classless. We're completely integrated. We dig the spades
man . . . We've married up the hairy brigade – that's the East End
kids like photographers and artists – with the smooth brigade, the
debs, the aristos, the Guards officers . . . It's the greatest, happiest,
most swinging ball of the century'.[55] Not happy enough, it seemed.
A few months later, MacDonald committed suicide.

One who survived and prospered was Michael Caine. More than
any other national figurehead, he personified the era, how Britain got
there and where it led to. He was born Maurice Micklewhite in
Rotherhithe in 1933, shortly after Hitler came to power. His mother
was a cleaner and his father a porter at Billingsgate fish market. They
brought him up in Camberwell, south-east London, in a hardy local
world dominated by spivs. Having survived the Blitz and early
postwar austerity, in 1951 he was called up for National Service and
served in Germany and Korea, an experience he hated. After demob,
he briefly followed his father into Billingsgate before answering an
advert in *The Stage*. He began his acting career in Surrey during
Coronation year, plunging into the fading world of rep. He escaped

because his talent and rare ability to provide a convincing Cockney accent made him an asset to the radical playwrights whose work burst onto the British stage in the late 1950s. In 1960 he went to the Royal Court in London, where he appeared in *The Room*, a debut play written by an East End boy made good, Harold Pinter. In 1962 he got his first leading role, in a BBC Play – *The Compartment* – written by Johnny Speight, another East Ender, who went on to create the anti-hero Alf Garnett. Soon after, Caine broke into film playing an aristocratic Victorian officer fighting African tribesmen, in the last of the British cinema's imperial epics *Zulu* (1963). His cult status was based on two rather different characters: the eponymous Cockney lothario Alfie (1966) and the cool, insolent MI6 agent, Sergeant Harry Palmer of *The Ipcress File* (1967). Created by Len Deighton, Palmer came to epitomize the decline of deference, whether rooting out spies among the officer class or advising his bowler-hatted boss on the best sort of mushrooms to buy for a cordon bleu meal. In his memoirs, Caine wrote:

> The reason for [the] notoriety [of the 1960s is that] for the first time in British history, the young working class stood up for themselves and said, 'We are here, this is our society and we are not going away. Join us, stay away, like us, hate us – do as you like. We don't care about your opinion anymore'.[56]

By the time he appeared in the supreme British gangster film *Get Carter* in 1971, he had become an international star, hailed in the US as part of a 'British invasion'. The *New York Daily News* said, 'First it was the Beatles and then it was miniskirts, and now see what the British have sent us in the flicks – a Cockney lad who's sure to be just our cup of tea.'[57] Caine was England's answer to Clint Eastwood. He was a man about town who never cultivated the persona of the brooding, existential frontiersman as Eastwood did; but, like the American, he became an icon who represented a key element of the nation's identity. Both on screen and off, Caine was a tough, self-contained individual; intensely patriotic, yet dismissive of Establishments wherever he found them. Of the 300 films he has made to date, he has only played Cockneys in a fraction of them. But Caine is, and will be remembered for, his Cockney persona because he represents for millions of Britons (and particularly the English) the point in their history at which the working classes began to take an equal place in the canons of Britishness.

Although London was the epicentre of Swinging Britain, the north

of England more than held its own. Hailed during the war as a centre
of military production and good-humoured stoicism, from approximately 1955 to 1970 it was celebrated as a cradle of reconstruction
and modernity. Heavily bombed industrial cities provided an opportunity for civic leaders and architects to make their mark on the
clean sheet provided by the Luftwaffe. In 1962, Britain's first shopping centre arose a few hundred yards away from Coventry's new
cathedral; in the north-east a local Labour politician, T. Dan Smith,
promised to make Newcastle 'the Brasilia of the North',[58] and the
Economist produced a plan to transfer the capital from London to
a new city in the north, to be called 'Elizabetha'. Northern vitality
was not only apparent in the gleam of mayoral jewellery. Britain's
cultural renaissance owed much to a so-called New Wave that sprang
from the region.

As well as the Merseybeat scene from which the Beatles emerged,
the north produced the Manchester School of composers, led by
Harrison Birtwistle, and a group of Yorkshire artists led by David
Hockney. The region's literati had the greatest impact. Most of the
writers known to the media as Angry Young Men came from the
North – 'Movement' poets Donald Davie and Philip Larkin and later
the 'Mersey Poets' Adrian Henri and Roger McGough; novelists Alan
Sillitoe, Stan Barstow, Shelagh Delaney and Keith Waterhouse. They
came from working- and lower-middle-class backgrounds and their
writing encouraged the franker approach to class and sex in this
period. They were unsentimental about the north but were strongly
attached to it. Donald Davie declared: '[Our] sociological importance
is very great, and it consists in this – that for the first time a challenge
is thrown down ... by a more or less coherent group, to the
monopoly of British culture sustained for generations by the London
haut-bourgeois.'[59] The southern literary Establishment fought back,
attacking the young upstarts as Little Englanders, often with snobbery that seemed to justify the original complaint. Edith Sitwell, for
example, compared the 'lifeless quatrains' of Movement poets to 'the
cramped dimensions of prefabricated houses'.[60] In 1963, John Gross
condemned their 'phoney regionalism' which, he thought, was typical
of the 'ridiculously parochial' nature of English life since the war.[61]

Was the regionalism of the New Wave phoney? Its leading figures
relied on the London media machine for publicity and their anger
was aspirational rather than subversive. But the growl of their
characters struck a chord with younger Britons – from Joe Lambton's

'[it's] old-fashioned, all that class stuff. Things have changed since the war . . . I'm as good as the next man' in *Room at the Top* (1959) to Arthur Seaton's more anarchic advice, 'Don't let the bastards grind you down. What I'm out for is a good time. All the rest is propaganda' in *Saturday Night and Sunday Morning* (1960). In the House of Commons, the Conservative MP for Nottingham, Lieutenant-Colonel John Cordeaux, protested that '*Saturday Night and Sunday Morning* creates an impression that the young men of our industrial towns are a lot of ill-behaved, immoral, drunken Teddy Boys.'[62] It did and, as a result, the north came to be associated in the national mind not only with industrial enterprise but also with social mobility and sexual liberation.

Television helped, particularly the commercial sector. As well as giving Scotland, Wales and Northern Ireland editorial autonomy, the ITA wanted its franchises, as far as possible, to 'give real creative power to the regions.'[63] The most powerful was Sidney Bernstein's Granada, whose studios in Manchester were designed by Ralph Tubbs, architect of the Dome of Discovery at the Festival of Britain. Bernstein was determined, he said, 'to start a new creative industry away from the metropolitan atmosphere of London.'[64] The most famous product of the Granada operation was commissioned as a direct result of the success of 'kitchen sink' cinema: *Coronation Street*. First transmitted in December 1960 and networked in May 1961, it became the longest-running and most successful soap opera in Britain, attracting an average 18 million viewers each episode. It was devised by a working-class homosexual Lancastrian, Tony Warren, and centred around a trio of women: upright publican Annie Walker, backyard gossip Ena Sharples and chain-smoking hussy Elsie Tanner. They reflected Lancashire's matriarchal society, a result of the high numbers of women employed in the region's textile trade and one of the characteristics which had set Lancashire apart from the rest of the north since the industrial revolution. The *Street* pictured a northern community with its traditions intact yet also influenced by postwar social change. Its longest-surviving character was Ken Barlow, a local grammar-school-educated graduate who returns to his home town to work (as Joe Lambton initially did) in local government.

When the Beatles were given MBEs by Harold Wilson, a cultural trend reached its zenith. The late historian Raphael Samuel summed up the importance of northernness in this period:

[The North] offered itself as an idiom for the degentrification of British public life. In place of an effete Establishment it promised a new vitality, sweeping the dead wood from the boardrooms, and replacing hidebound administrators with ambitious young go-getters . . . The Northern voice, as cultivated by the TV compere, was a classless one, an indigenous alternative to the starched accents of the Pathé newsreader and the BBC announcer. As projected by the Prime Minister, a professional Yorkshireman, it was also a gauge of authenticity.[65]

Wilson was among those who appeared on *The Morecambe and Wise Show*, which ran from 1961 to 1983. Eric Morecambe was from Lancashire and Ernie Wise was from Yorkshire. They combined music-hall slapstick with surreal wit and a gift for poking fun at intellectual pretension without being philistines. As Morecambe once said, 'We've always considered ourselves sophisticated Northerners.'[66] Viewers included the Queen, and participants included Laurence Olivier and Glenda Jackson. The great and the good queued up to be sent up, welcoming as they did Eric's invitation to 'Sit down and take the weight off your manifestoes'.[67] On 25 December 1977, 28.8 million Britons – half the UK population – watched the BBC's *Morecambe and Wise Christmas Special*, the largest ever audience for a light entertainment programme. That night arguably marked the end of the North's esteemed position within the cultural matrix of Britishness. Within a few years, the region was seen as a sorry locus of economic and social stagnation. In the meantime, Eric and Ernie's flirtation with figureheads from the arts world captured a key trend of the time: a desire to bridge the gap between elite and popular culture in a way that prejudiced neither.

Sixties Britain was not characterized by the embourgeoisement of the lower classes, nor by the proletarianization of the upper classes, nor even an alliance between the two groups. What took place was an unprecedented *dialogue* between the classes. For the first time since the nineteenth century, there was a serious attempt to take a more pluralistic view of what constituted British culture. In 1959 the critic Lawrence Alloway published an article called 'The Long Front of Culture'. In direct contrast to William Haley's 1948 concept of a pyramid up which every Briton worked their way through diligent self-improvement, Alloway posited the notion of a non-hierarchical culture in which all forms 'can be placed within a continuum rather than frozen in layers in a pyramid'. Individuals could range across this long front making choices according to their needs, desires and tastes. Arguing that 'mass' meant exactly the opposite of uniform, Alloway concluded, 'Acceptance of the mass media entails a shift in our notion of what culture is.'[68] A decade later, the Long Front was apparent in every endeavour from art to poetry. But it was in broadcasting and pop music where its influence was felt most.

4. Anti-patriotism, pro-dirt

Television was finally recognized as a medium in which entertainment and education could meet and prosper. In 1966, Keith Waterhouse observed 'the ghastly word "telly", which once conjured up a whitish flickering vision of awful drab families in Dagenham munching Mars bars and neglecting bingo, has entered the mock-cockney vocabulary of Kensington Mums who no longer pretend that they have got it for the au pair girl'.[69] This change owed a lot to the greatest Director-General the BBC ever had, Hugh Carleton Greene. Greene, who had served with the RAF during the Battle of Britain, ran the corporation from 1960 to 1969. In that short space of time, he dragged it into the century which had technologically given birth to it. He was a tall, bald, bespectacled man with a warm, cheeky smile who looked like a class swot playing truant and loving every minute of it. Greene had always disliked the corporation's high-minded self-satisfaction. When, shortly after his appointment, he returned from the Pilkington enquiry to be applauded by senior staff, he told them, 'you're behaving like Russians, clapping yourselves'.[70]

Greene was the first DG to take popular culture seriously. He understood that its role in national life was as important as that of the arts and that the two were complementary. He also relaxed the moral outlook which had underpinned the BBC's policy of cultural uplift. He gave programme-makers greater freedom to address contemporary social issues and he relaxed the guidelines on nudity and swearing. Assisted by visionary producers such as Stuart Hood, the BBC began to broadcast quality programmes with mass appeal, many of which became defining points of British life: *Dad's Army* (1968–77), *Z Cars* (1964–74) and *Steptoe and Son* (1965–73), to name a few. The BBC also sponsored the satire boom of the time, which reached a surreal apogee with *Monty Python's Flying Circus*

(1967–75). Radio One was started after the government closed down offshore pirate radio stations in 1967. Many disc jockeys, like Tony Blackburn, who made the first Radio One broadcast, were former employees on the illegal commercial networks. The *NME* thought the new station was 'youthful, fast-moving, pop-laden and a complete reversal of Auntie BBC's former image'.[71]

Drama was reformed by Sydney Newman, a Canadian inspired by John Osborne, discovered by John Grierson and poached from ITV. He commissioned people who took TV seriously and wanted to work for it, primarily *The Wednesday Play* (1965–1970) and its successor *Play For Today*. These programmes became the showcase for writers like Harold Pinter and Dennis Potter, directors like Ken Loach and actors like Michael Caine. With regular audiences of 10 million, *The Wednesday Play* proved that drama could reach a large audience given the right treatment. Newman later wrote, 'I am proud that I played some part in the recognition that the working man was a fit subject for drama, and not just a comic foil in a play on middle class manners.'[72] Greene said, 'I was like a Beefeater tampering with the Crown jewels'. Reith certainly believed so. He told Hugh's wife, Elaine, what he thought of her husband. His diary records:

> The dignity of the BBC has utterly departed ... I made my point of view absolutely clear – that Hugh and I were fundamentally in complete opposition of outlook and attitude. I lead; he follows the crowd in all the disgusting manifestations of the age ... Without any reservation he gives the public what it wants; I would not, did not and said I wouldn't.[73]

At the inaugural meeting of her 'Clean Up TV' campaign in May 1964, Mary Whitehouse described the new BBC as 'quite subversive of our whole way of life ... anti-authority, anti-religious, anti-patriotism [and] pro-dirt.'[74]

Another of Greene's achievements was helping to set up the Open University. It was Harold Wilson's idea, sketched out one day after church while on holiday in the Scilly Isles in 1963 and regarded by him as a worthy successor to the NHS. The Prime Minister's idea – for higher education based on broadcast lectures and coursework done by correspondence – had been pioneered in the USA and Soviet Union in the 1950s. The OU's Lectures were shown on the new BBC2, which started broadcasting in April 1964. From the start, the OU's founders saw it as one feature in a mixed economy of national culture rather than as the summit of self-improvement. Hence the reaction to it. *The Times* was amazed at Wilson's suggestion 'that there [are] even housewives who might like to secure qualifications in English literature, geography or history'. The eyebrows of the *TES* arched at the prospect of television's involvement: 'A university is not a mode of mass communication, it is a community'.[75] Approved by the Cabinet in 1966 and based in the New Town of Milton Keynes, the OU admitted its first students in 1971. At the first degree ceremony on 23 June 1973, Hugh Greene was honoured, and as he and the other graduands processed, Copland's *Fanfare for the Common Man* was played. There were also many common women present because the institution did become a springboard for housewives to enter or re-enter the workplace (women constituted around 40 per cent of the intake). The OU succeeded in demystifying further education in Britain and did much to atone for Labour's abolition of grammar schools. By the end of the century it was admitting 100,000 students a year, with a broader social intake than most conventional universities, and it was ranked seventh in the UK for the quality of its teaching and research.

If there was a Reithian presence in the 1960s, it was to be found in the office of Britain's first ever Minister of Arts, Jennie Lee – a dynamic Scotswoman who oversaw a late flowering of the nineteenth-century cultural reform movement. Lee was the daughter of a Cowdenbeath mining family. She had become Labour MP for North Lanark in 1929 before she was even old enough to vote, but she was most famous for being Nye Bevan's widow. She shared her late husband's belief in the social importance of the arts, seeing them as the most effective replacement for Protestantism. On one ministerial trip, Lee told a group of artists: 'Religion is a sham, the churches are dead; you the artists are now priests.'[76] Her White Paper on the State and the Arts, published in February 1965, echoed John Maynard Keynes' declaration of intent in 1945:

> In any civilised community the arts and associated amenities must occupy a central place ... More and more people begin to appreciated that the exclusion of so many for so long from the best of our cultural heritage can become as damaging to the privileged minority as to the under-privileged majority.[77]

State patronage, she concluded, would make Britain 'a gayer and more cultivated country'.[78] She was supported by the Arts Council Chairman, Arnold Goodman, a good friend and one of the Prime Minister's close advisers. Goodman feared that 'the pop groups are

winning the battle' for the minds of young Britons. In 1967, he told
the House of Lords: 'There is a crucial state in this country at this
moment. I believe that young people lack values, lack certainties,
lack guidance; that they need something to turn to; and need it more
desperately than at any time in our history . . . I believe that once
young people have been captured for the arts they are redeemed from
many of the dangers which confront them at the moment.'[79]

Arnold Goodman's pompous outbursts did not endear the Arts
Council to the British public. But a great deal was achieved. Council
funding trebled between 1964 and 1970, enabling it to meet a rising
demand fuelled by mass education. Attendances at exhibitions and
concerts rose, as did the number of Britons using public libraries.
Book sales shot up from 45.6 million in 1960 to 77.2 million in
1969, the biggest rise since the golden age of 1940–45. Lee also
revived the jewel in the crown of the Attlee era: the National Theatre
project. Thanks to her, Denys Lasdun's magnificent building finally
began to rise on the South Bank of the Thames a generation after
Princess Elizabeth had laid the foundation stone. And Jennie Lee
played a major role in the creation of the Open University. Like
Hugh Greene, she succeeded where others had failed because she
gave Reithianism the human face it so badly needed. A hugely sensual
woman, she knew that self-improvement need not involve self-denial.
When she criticized the rock cakes in the coffee shop at the National
Gallery, curatorial staff thought it showed her ignorance of art. They
would learn. Britons would not be drawn to places like the National
Gallery unless they were given a modicum of comfort, refreshment
and, ultimately, gaiety. Lee also sent her civil servants out in jeans
and T-shirts to attend rock concerts, so that they could keep in touch
with what was happening beyond the official world. The thought of
faded denims secretly hanging in Whitehall cupboards is an amusing
one, like that of Hugh Greene cautiously tapping his foot to Tony
Blackburn in his office at White City. But both those images convey
something of the new dialogue between rulers and ruled which
emerged in this era.

Nowhere was that dialogue more apparent than in the meteoric
explosion of British pop music between 1963 and 1973. Jonathon
Green explains:

The Sixties, for the vast majority of people, means essentially
music. The counter culture, while noisy, embraced relatively few
people; neither dope, sex, nor revolution impinged, other than

through the pages of the tabloid press, on the great majority of lives ... For most people it is songs, not LSD, that promote the most vivid flashbacks.[80]

What made the music of the period so special was not simply that it was dominated by the working- and lower-middle classes. Its significance lies in the fact that it was predominantly home-grown and succeeded in checking American influence. Almost entirely ignored by historians, the recreation of a recognizably British popular music in the 1960s was one of the most important developments of the century.

5. I was just that little bit more Union Jack conscious

British music became more British in the 1960s and was loved for it. Liverpool was the crucible of that change, and for good reason. When John Lennon and Paul McCartney were growing up there in the 1950s, it was still the UK's largest port after London and it was also the nation's transatlantic terminus. Like the Lutheran pamphlets which sailors brought to the east coast of England in the early sixteenth century, sailors from the US brought rare American records into Liverpool in the twentieth. Among the dealers who snapped them up was Brian Epstein. A uniquely British reformation was built upon these foreign foundations. Led by the Beatles, artists absorbed American music, naturalized it and eventually transformed it into a lyrically and stylistically distinctive idiom which in less than a decade came to dominate Western popular music. American music (especially black genres) continued to influence British songwriters, who frequently acknowledged its importance. But the pastiche of American rock 'n' roll which Cliff Richard, Tommy Steele and others had served up before 1963 gave way to songs about British life, often sung in native accents instead of the phoney American one with which their predecessors had mimicked rock 'n' roll. Several key songwriters, Lennon and McCartney among them, were directly influenced by Edwardian music-hall songs, which critics had long celebrated as a lost national tradition.

Many examples of the Britishness of 1960s pop could be cited but the best remains, in my opinion, the Kinks', whose album titles speak for themselves: *Kinkdom* (1965), *The Village Green Preservation Society* (1968) and *Arthur, Or The Decline and Fall of the British Empire* (1969). The single 'Waterloo Sunset' reached No. 2 in 1967 and celebrated London life more poetically than any piece of music since Elgar's *Cockaigne Overture* or Vaughan Williams' Second Symphony:

> Terry and Julie pass over the river
> Where they feel safe and sound
> And they don't need no friends
> As long as they gaze on Waterloo Sunset
> They are in paradise.[81]

The man confident enough to see paradise in a Waterloo Sunset – songwriter Ray Davies – summed up the native inspiration of his generation: 'Some people pick up their guitars and take Route 66. I took the M1.'[82] By 1968, 72 per cent of records in the UK charts were British. Before 1963, the figure had never risen above 53 per cent and rarely came close to that.[83] Long after the hits dried up and the groups split up, the leading songwriters of the 1960s influenced subsequent generations, including the doyens of Britpop at the century's end.

The Kinks, the Small Faces and The Who formed the musical nucleus of the largest and most cohesive youth cult of the 1960s, the Mods. According to one estimate, they numbered around 500,000 dedicated followers, with many more on the periphery who were into the music and fashion of the cult. Most lived in the south of England where the infamous seafront battles with rockers took place in 1964. But they could be found everywhere, as letters to *The Mod*, complaining of its London bias, show. The magazine was forced to recant: 'We're always inclined to think that the girls and guys up there walk about in kilts saying "haggis" or "och" with every other word. It's not true. Seeing the photographs that they have been sending . . . I'd say that in some parts they are in fact just as much fashion mad go-ahead as we are in London.'[84] The Who turned the RAF roundel and the Union Jack into fashion accessories, plastering their equipment with both symbols and donning red, white and blue jackets. The trend spread from the Mods to the rest of British society. Critics saw it as an ironic poke at patriotism. George Melly wrote: 'From shopping bags and china mugs it soon graduated to bikinis and knickers. Americans, for whom the flag in their century of Imperialism has a great deal more significance, were amazed by our casual acceptance of our flag as a giggle. They might burn their flag in protest but they'd never wear it to cover their genitalia.'[85] The fact that the British were able to ironize their national flag was symptomatic of a people who were easing their way towards a post-imperial identity. However, this was not a renunciation of Britishness but a democratization of it. The promiscuous use of the Union Jack was the most visible sign that the British were reclaiming patriotism from its traditional loci in monarchy, Church, Parliament and the armed forces. It was the expression of a people whose culture led the Western world, knew it and liked to celebrate the fact. Ironic it may have been, but there was nothing trivial or unpatriotic about it.

The international success of British Beat was a source of pride for fans and groups alike. President de Gaulle may have vetoed Britain's entry to the Common Market but he couldn't stop British pop sweeping the Continent. 'LES BEATLES IN PAREE!', screamed the *New Musical Express* in the summer of 1965: 'the Queen herself would have been proud of the Beatles ... if she could have seen these thousands of happy French folk stamping, cheering and shouting for the four little Englishmen'.[86] The French press agreed. *L'Express* said: 'England rules over international pop music. [Britain] is the country where the wind of today blows most strongly'.[87] Despite communist suspicion that pop was the advance guard of capitalism, Eastern Europe also gave way to the British. In the winter of 1965, Manfred Mann made the first foray by a Western group behind the Iron Curtain. On his return to the UK from Czechoslovakia, Manfred told the press: 'I came back thinking England was a good scene – and I was just that little bit more Union Jack conscious'.[88] After a tour of America, Pete Townshend of *The Who* said, 'what made us first want to go to America and conquer it was being English. We didn't care a monkey's about the American dream or about the American drug situation or about the dollars ... It was 'cos we were English and we wanted to go to America and be English'.[89]

The Beatles, of course, led the way across the Atlantic. On 7 February 1964 they were seen off at Heathrow on their first American tour by 1,000 screaming fans. The American Press dubbed it 'the British Invasion', a tag gleefully adopted in the UK. Although no one else matched their success, the appetite for British pop and rock did not abate. Between 1960 and 1963 only ten records by British artists got into the US Top 30; from 1964 to 1967, there were 173, of which 25 were by the Beatles. Overall, the proportion of British records in the US charts rose to 25 per cent, up from an average of 5 per cent before 1963.[90] By 1967, the *New Musical Express* was the world's largest-selling music paper, and it was notching up sales of 2.5 million in the US, having not been sold there at all until 1964. *The Times*' music critic, William Mann, wrote a famous appreciation of the Beatles in which he praised their 'chains of pandiatonic clusters' and compared their work to that of Mahler and Maxwell Davies. What is never quoted was the main point of Mann's article – the recreation of a native popular music:

> For several decades, in fact since the decline of the music hall, England has taken her popular songs from the United States, either directly or by mimicry. But the songs of Lennon and McCartney are distinctly indigenous in character, the most imaginative and inventive examples of a style that has been developing on Merseyside during the past few years. And there is a nice, rather flattering irony in the news that the Beatles have now become prime favourites in America too.[91]

With the exception of The Beach Boys, The Doors and a few Motown acts, the US could not compete. The British invasion provoked a rare bout of American cultural protectionism, as groups began to have trouble getting visas to tour the States. In July 1965, the government retaliated by announcing that US stars coming to Britain would be restricted to one TV appearance per month. The Americans backed down. It was sweet revenge for Wilson, who had been forced as a young minister to lift the embargo on Hollywood films during the 1940s when British culture was in poorer health.

John Winston Lennon was born in 1940 during a German air raid and owed his middle name to Britain's war leader. When the Beatles received MBEs a week after Churchill's death in 1965, several past recipients of the award returned theirs, including a Second World War veteran who said that 'decorating the Beatles has made a mockery of everything this country stands for'.[92] Some on the left attacked it as a stunt designed to make the monarchy look hip. Most Britons, however, saw it as justified recognition of the fact that pop had put the UK back on the map. Derek Johnson, feature writer of the *New Musical Express*, wrote:

> Did the Beatles genuinely deserve to be honoured by the Queen? The answer must be irrevocably and unquestioningly – Yeah!

Yeah! Yeah! . . . Where the Beatles deserve their awards is in the field of prestige. Their efforts to keep the Union Jack fluttering proudly have been far more successful than a regiment of diplomats and statesmen. We may be regarded as a second class power in politics, but at any rate we now lead the world in pop music! . . . What is even more relevant is the recognition which has been conferred upon the acting, ballet and 'serious' music professions. Some will argue that Alec Guinness, Margot Fonteyn and Malcolm Sargent were honoured because of their contribution to culture. But who could prove that the Beatles' music will not be regarded as culture by generations to come?

Readers agreed. 'In three years they have done more than a stuffy Civil Servant could hope to achieve in 100 years', wrote one.[93]

Drugs was the issue over which the British Establishment drew a line. Cocaine and opium had been widely used in the UK until the Dangerous Drugs Act of 1920 outlawed them on the grounds that they were undermining the British race. In the postwar period the number of proscribed narcotics rose steadily, from 33 in 1950 to 106 in 1970, thanks largely to two Acts passed in 1964 and 1966. Increasingly draconian penalties did not significantly reduce consumption. Cannabis in particular went from being a minority taste to a national pastime, indulged in at one time or another by most of the population. When Mick Jagger was prosecuted for possession in 1967, *The Times* famously asked, 'WHO BREAKS A BUTTERFLY ON A WHEEL?' 'If we are going to make any case a symbol of the conflict between the sound traditional values of Britain and the new hedonism, then we must be sure that the sound traditional values include those of tolerance and equity'.[94] 'KEEP SWINGING!', *Melody Maker* advised.[95] Soon after Jagger's release, a young producer on London Weekend Television called John Birt flew the rock star by helicopter into the garden of the Lord Lieutenant of Essex, Sir John Buggles-Rise. In one of the more bizarre scenes of the period, Jagger sat down to explain himself on TV to the Home Secretary, Frank Soskice, the Bishop of Woolwich and *The Times*' editor, William Rees-Mogg. 'Our parents went through two world wars and a depression', said Jagger, 'We've had none of that . . . I can't see it's anymore a crime against society than jumping out of a window. People should be punished for crimes not for the *fears* of society'.[96] Unfortunately that was the end of a sensible debate on the subject and not the beginning of one. Thereafter, drugs were demonized by successive British governments as a cause or at best a symptom of declining moral values.

Yet the same year Jagger spoke out, a record appeared which had been largely inspired and produced under the influence of LSD, one of the substances banned in 1966. The Beatles' *Sgt. Pepper's Lonely Hearts Club Band*, released on 21 June 1967, was an amalgam of whimsical British psychedelia, music-hall kitsch and the brass-band sound of northern England and Wales. Peter Blake's album cover – a collage which included figures from Lawrence of Arabia to Diana Dors – was a testament to the 'long front of culture'. Furrowing her brow, the Queen told the Chairman of EMI, Sir Joseph Lockwood, 'The Beatles are turning awfully *funny*, aren't they?'[97] But perhaps even she realized that the record stood alongside Britain's greatest achievements. Ken Tynan described it as 'a decisive moment in the history of Western civilisation'. The *Times Literary Supplement* called the group 'a barometer of our times', while in the US, *Newsweek* compared the lyrics with T. S. Eliot, concluding that 'A Day In the Life' was the group's *Waste Land*.[98] On 25 June 1967, a fortnight after the Arab–Israeli war began, the Beatles gathered in a BBC studio with other members of Britain's pop aristocracy and sang 'All You Need Is Love' live before a world audience of 400 million.

The song's sentiments may sound naive to a twenty-first-century ear. But the corporation's motto 'Nation shall speak unto nation' had never been so fully nor so movingly realized as it was in those five minutes. The event confirmed that Britain had found a post-imperial role as the cultural epicentre of the Western world. The 400 million people who watched the broadcast can have been left in no doubt that here was a nation which had successfully reinvented itself. Britain, once seen as a stuffy, class-ridden and prurient place, had become an incarnation of open-minded liberal democracy and, consequently, a cradle of inventiveness. This was not an anti-technological or anti-industrial sentiment by any means. But it did privilege cultural activity, for it was this at which the UK now appeared to excel. During this period, a belief grew that Britain was a peculiarly creative nation; no longer the workshop of the world, perhaps, but its recording studio and catwalk instead.

Pop stars did not engender the muscular patriotism of Nelson, Kitchener or Churchill, but they were feted almost as widely. British Embassies hosted receptions at which touring groups were the star attraction in order to sell the UK to the world. Addressing the City of London Young Conservatives in the spring of 1964, the Minister of Information, Bill Deedes, said, '[The Beatles] herald a cultural movement among the young which may become part of the history of our time ... for those with eyes to see it, something important and heartening is happening here'.[99] Churchill's former Private Secretary, Jock Colville, saw pop as a late flowering of New Elizabethanism:

It ... has risen straight and naturally from the heart, if not the very bowels of the people. The upsurge began with the Beatles ... while hundreds of other groups sang and twanged their way to the hearts of ecstatic and frequently hysterical teenagers. It is a genuine folk movement and even if people over forty may be partially deaf to its message, none would deny the wistful beauty of the best pop songs, nor would many dispute the quality of the music or the skill of the performance ... The music they have produced and the pleasure they have given are justly praised, and whatever their intrinsic merits relative to DNA and pulsars, Henry Moore and Francis Bacon, Osborne and Pinter, there can be no doubt that pop stars and pop music are the most widely-known British export in the world to-day.[100]

While the British were accepting, even celebrating, the loss of empire, far away in South-East Asia the Americans were discovering what a burden it could be. Despite US pressure, Wilson refused to embroil the UK in the Vietnam War. Decolonization was not officially completed until 12 January 1968 when the Cabinet agreed to withdraw troops from positions East of Suez, and problems remained in Rhodesia. But there was no getting away from the fact that the British Empire was as dead as Monty Python's parrot.

Some saw the cultural revolution as a direct consequence of decolonization. In 1965, a year before *Vanity Fair* published its famous article celebrating 'Swinging London', a US journalist, John Crosby, wrote:

Talent is getting to be Britain's greatest export commodity ... This explosion of creative vitality, a sort of English renaissance, has occurred on the very highest levels, as well as the more frivolous ones ... England, shorn of its world-wide responsibilities for keeping the peace, has turned its energies, previously dissipated in running the colonies, inward towards personal self-expression.[101]

Whatever the truth of that comment (it's impossible to prove) the fact is that the resurgence of British popular culture in the 1960s virtually eradicated the anti-Americanism of the nation's governing classes. In 1953, conservatives had protested that the sale of Union Jack knickers brought the country into disrepute. When Union Jack hotpants went on sale a decade later few complaints were heard. The idea that British culture was a worthy substitute for empire not only gained ground during the 1960s, it also lost the disgruntled smugness that Richard Dimbleby had expressed when he mocked Americans for their lack of tradition during the Coronation. Now, at last, Britain was successfully competing with the US in contemporary terms and not in a parody of its Victorian past.

Only the Marxist left still attacked the US with any vigour, championing the cause of Vietnam as it had championed the cause of Republican Spain in the 1930s. Aspirant revolutionaries like Tariq Ali and Vanessa Redgrave railed against Uncle Sam as the most evil of Western powers, its economic and military hegemony cemented by the cultural imperialism of Coca-Cola and Marlboro. Angry demonstrations and university sit-ins made good newspaper copy and the Rolling Stones paid tribute to them with the song 'Streetfighting Man'. But, like the CND activists of the 1950s, the Marxist left was in a minority. Most Britons would have agreed with Noël Coward's remark to Michael Caine while the two men were dining at the Savoy in 1968. 'Vanessa should keep on demonstrating', sniffed Coward, 'She's a very tall girl and it will give her lots of opportunities to sit down'.[102]

One of Coward's neighbours at his sunny retreat in Jamaica was Ian Fleming, author of the James Bond novels. Written between 1955 and 1963, the film adaptations of them produced between 1962 and the present day best illustrate how the British regarded their world role in the late twentieth century. On the one hand, the stories allowed the British to fantasize that they were still a power to be reckoned with. They constructed an imaginary world in which the UK is in the vanguard of the defence of Western civilization. American CIA agents play second fiddle to 007 as he dispatches a motley assortment of Slavic, Oriental and Asiatic villains with wit, ingenuity and courage. It is a world in which you only have to scratch a foreigner to find a villain; but, more importantly, it is a world in which Burgess and Maclean never defected and the Suez crisis never happened. Fleming's stories were the direct descendant of the prewar imperial spy thriller and Bond was the last of a long line of British gentleman heroes which stretched from John Buchan's 'Richard Hannay' to Edward Mason's 'Dick Barton'. However, the immense popularity of Bond in the UK rested, as it did internationally, not on quasi-imperial nostalgia but on something more contemporary.

James Bond's adventures portrayed a world of conspicuous material and sexual consumption which many people felt was now within their reach. Whereas Richard Hannay had leapt over bleak Scottish moors in pursuit of his quarry, Bond's jet-setting adventures took him to the best hotels, restaurants and beaches in the world. In an era when foreign travel was just becoming affordable to ordinary Britons, the films were a two-dimensional version of the relatively classless world of the colour supplement. Bond's use of technological gadgetry to thwart villains also appealed to millions eagerly consuming the latest labour-saving devices. 'Q' – the MI6 Quartermaster who designed Bond's gadgets – combined the homely eccentricity of the archetypal British inventor with the no-nonsense approach of the technocrats celebrated by Harold Wilson. As played by the Scottish nationalist Sean Connery, Bond was a patriot, but a freewheeling, cosmopolitan one, whose wry contempt for the British Establishment mirrored that of the working-class Harry Palmer. Then there were the Bond Girls. In 1964, shortly before he died of a heart attack, Fleming wrote, 'I am not an angry young man, or even middle-aged man. I am not "involved". My books are not "engaged" . . . They are written for warm-blooded heterosexuals in railway trains, airplanes or beds.'[103] Bond was rarely without a beautiful woman for the night, and this naturally appealed to men enjoying or fantasizing about the new opportunities for sexual fulfilment in the 1960s. But, as Bond Girls like Honor Blackman testify, 007's lovers were archetypes of the more independent female of the time. Versed in the martial arts as well as the older art of seduction, they kicked and punched their way to gratification. This, as much as Bond's suave machismo, explains the genre's appeal to women. The films were condemned by the Vatican and (just as predictably) by the British left for being immoral. The *New Statesman* opined, 'They are thoroughly English: the sadism of a schoolboy bully, the mechanical two-dimensional sex-longings of a frustrated adolescent and the crude snob-cravings of a suburban adult'.[104] Bond was a conscious break with social realism (the first, *Dr. No*, was released a year before the last of the British kitchen sink films, *This Sporting Life*, which flopped). 'People were getting tired of all those abortions', observed Terence Young, *Dr. No*'s director.[105] If there was a hollowness to the genre, it was that Bond's world of conspicuous consumption proved, in the end, to be out of reach for a good many people.

Herein lay the essential weakness of 'Swinging Britain'. Despite the massive growth of the so-called creative industries, the contribution they made to the UK's GDP did not compensate for the decline of other sectors. The same free market which powered music, fashion and the media was also responsible for the lack of investment in the industries of Scotland, Wales and the north of England. By the time the Beatles got their MBEs for exports, the group were about the only thing Liverpool was exporting. Commentators began to talk about a growing north–south divide, in which 'formerly stimulating differences . . . are now becoming inequalities'.[106] In 1959, the *Manchester Guardian*, a pillar of the northern liberal conscience since the 1870s, dropped 'Manchester' from its title and in 1964 moved its editorial operation to London, an event widely seen as a sign that the southern drift had not abated. In 1965, the *Daily Worker* proclaimed: 'the Mersey Sound is the voice of 80,000 crumbling houses and 30,000 people on the dole.'[107]

Even if one allows for the perennial joylessness of the British communist movement, the *Daily Worker* had a point. In the end, a copy of *Sgt. Pepper* and a pair of Union Jack pants were little consolation for a redundant factory worker stuck at home in a jerry-built tower block in Glasgow or Swansea. Furthermore, like New Elizabethanism, Swinging Britain was too flimsy a concept to hold the Union together. The former at least had an ancient institution as its ideological core. The latter had four young men unable to cope with fame and who, unlike the monarchy, had no real heirs. It was certainly ironic that the region where the Beatles came from was fast becoming one of the most depressed in the country. But the most important effect economic decline had on Britishness took place not on Merseyside but in Scotland and Wales.

PART 6

NATIONALISTS

Scotland is a more complete satellite of England than Hungary is of the USSR.

Winnie Ewing, 1967

Wales's greatest tragedy is that she is so far from God and so near England.

North Wales Free Church Council, 1968

1. Things are very bad in Scotland

In 1967, five typists from Surbiton started one of Britain's shortest-lived patriotic movements: 'I'm Backing Britain'. In order to restore national prosperity, the women offered to work an extra half-hour every day for no wages and invited the rest of the country to do the same. Pensioners were asked to collect silver paper, though what for was never explained. For a few months, it was headline news and several thousand Britons sported little Union Jack badges with *I'm Backing Britain* printed on them. By 1968 the campaign had fizzled out. The call to the colours from the offices of Surrey fell on particularly deaf ears in Scotland and Wales.

By the early 1960s it was apparent that the economies of Scotland and Wales were only in remission and that the affluence of the period masked long-term problems which early postwar growth had failed to address: namely, a failure to modernize industrial equipment and to properly market technological innovations. The three mainland nations might have united in adversity but for the fact that Scotland and Wales continued to suffer disproportionately from Britain's economic restructuring. The heavy industries on which they relied began to collapse in 1958–9 under the relentless pressure of foreign competition from Germany, Japan and the United States, a situation exacerbated by the steady reduction of imperial markets as decolonization gathered pace. In the space of one year from 1958, unemployment doubled in Scotland and Wales. Two examples stand out. Between 1960 and 1970 the number of collieries in Wales fell from 164 to 52. During the same period the number of miners fell from 106,000 to 60,000; and by 1979 there were only 30,000 left. A national way of life was coming to end – a fact cruelly symbolized by the Aberfan disaster of 21 October 1966, in which 111 children were killed when a slag heap collapsed on their school.[1] Scotland fared no better. In 1954, it built 12 per cent of the world's ships; by 1968, it could manage only 1 per cent.[2] Little wonder. Equipment in Scottish shipyards was depreciating by £9 million per annum while the money spent on research and development came to only £250,000.[3] The net result of these catastrophic trends was that by

1960 unemployment in Scotland and Wales was twice the level of England's and, despite a few blips, it remained that way for the rest of the century. For those in work, living standards didn't rise as fast in Scotland and Wales as they did in England and it was this disparity which led to the decline of Britishness. By the late 1960s it was so glaring that the economic crisis provoked an already sharp sense of cultural uniqueness into a demand for greater political autonomy.

The answer British governments came up with was an old one: regional aid – a strategy launched during the Depression, in which business was bribed by the Exchequer to relocate to its nineteenth-century heartlands. At first, there was a reluctance to see Scotland and Wales as special cases. When Harold Macmillan met Scottish MPs and trade unionists in May 1960, he told them the economy was a strictly British problem, shared by many parts of England. In other words, Scotland was still regarded as a region rather than as a nation and like everyone else it had to take what it was given by the Treasury. Macmillan added insult to injury by telling the Scots that they would attract more investment if they talked up their country instead of forever complaining that it was getting a raw deal. This perennial view of the Scots as whingers was still apparent three years later when the President of the Board of Trade, Freddie Erroll, told Macmillan that the Scots should do more to help themselves. They were, he said, prone to boasting that they had 'all the initiative and expertise in the world' but expected investment to 'come from outside Scotland'.[4] He actually had a point, because Scotland's twentieth-century commercial and financial leaders were as guilty as anyone of preferring fast profits in the south of Britain to long-term investment in the north.

However, by the time Erroll wrote that memorandum, Macmillan's government was in deep trouble and knew it. In the summer of 1962, Macmillan wrote, 'Things are very bad [in Scotland]; there is a gradual decay.'[5] The Scottish Development Council was set up to attract investment. But in January 1963 the Scottish Secretary, Michael Noble, was in a state of near desperation about the time it was taking for recovery to start. He complained that economic decisions were still being made using the traditional criteria of whether a project was feasible or not. He told Macmillan that 'rational economic enquiry' had to be completely dispensed with. 'The time has come to reach decisions . . . on a political basis . . .

otherwise there will be major trouble in Scotland for the government now, and for the Party at the next election.'[6] Macmillan agreed.

This was a defining moment in Anglo-Scottish relations and, indeed, of the UK as a whole. Since the 1930s the motives behind regional aid had been political. But it was not until the early 1960s that the fear of nationalism made political considerations paramount when economic aid was considered. Over the next fifteen years, successive governments tried to maintain Scottish and Welsh loyalism using a make-do-and-mend corporatism, hoping that the seeds of Treasury money would germinate and restore national unity. By the end of the 1960s, per capita public spending on Scotland was 22 per cent above the UK average, 5 per cent in Wales and a whopping 35 per cent in Northern Ireland. This system became entrenched after 1978 thanks to the Barnett Formula. Devised by Joel Barnett, Chief Secretary to the Treasury, it was intended to prevent squabbling between Scottish and Welsh Secretaries and Chancellors by fixing the greater levels of subsidy that England's partners enjoyed. Estimates vary but the overall disparity is indisputable.[7] For example, Labour Party figures show that by 1997 Scotland accounted for 10.1 per cent of British revenue while raising 8.8 per cent of it, a shortfall which required an annual subsidy of £6.6 billion.[8] The English remained blithely unaware of this until devolution took place at the century's end.

What effect did it have on Scottish and Welsh identification with the Union? It shored up popular belief in the necessity of partnership with England. Whether or not Scottish and Welsh citizens were aware of the extent to which they were subsidized (and a good many were as ignorant of the fact as the English), they enjoyed the benefits of those subsidies. It could be argued that propping up ailing industries in north and west Britain delayed their day of reckoning with global capitalism. Yet, had money not been directed there, economic hardship would almost certainly have taken place sooner and with greater ferocity. Regional aid did not halt the decline of Britishness. What it did was to blunt the appeal of Home Rule and independence by convincing the Scots and Welsh that, whether or not they liked the English, they could not afford to do without them.

Regional aid also buttressed Britishness by intensifying the rivalry between Scotland and Wales. Even after the Barnett Formula was established, the struggle between Scottish and Welsh secretaries to win Treasury funding was fierce. It would be an exaggeration to say that the English used the situation to divide and rule. But it is true to say that from 1957 to 1997, Labour and Conservative Cabinets, most of them opposed to devolution, were able to play on traditional rivalries and contemporary desperation by setting the Scots and Welsh against each other in regular bidding wars for state largesse. The result was that, however inclined Scottish and Welsh Secretaries were towards Home Rule they rarely united to press their claims on the rest of the Cabinet. This was also true of nationalist leaders, who cooperated informally but never consistently established a pan-nationalist front.

Rivalry between the two countries affected cultural and political as well as fiscal matters. Welsh leaders were acutely aware that their country was smaller and possessed fewer autonomous institutions. Consequently, when concessions were made to the Scots the Welsh demanded parity. Writing to Harold Macmillan in 1957, the minister responsible for Wales, Henry Brooke, observed: 'The ordinary Welshman is jealous because Scotland has a Secretary of State and Wales has not (it may sound absurd, but this passion to be on a nominal equality with Scotland goes very deep)'. 'The Joneses', he concluded, 'want so much to keep up with the Macs'.[9] That attitude was still apparent forty years later. In response, Scots claimed that Wales was not an equal and demanded that devolutionary differentials between the two countries be maintained. To some extent, this pattern produced a ratchet effect in which concessions to one resulted in concessions to the other. But on the whole, the effect was to maintain the rivalry between the two and thereby contain discontent.

The pattern became more apparent in the second half of the 1960s when Wales finally got a Welsh Office and the added clout that went with it. In 1964, Harold Wilson fulfilled a pledge made by Hugh Gaitskell and appointed Huw Griffiths as the first Secretary of State for the principality, seventy-nine years after the Marquis of Salisbury appointed the Duke of Richmond to be Scotland's first Secretary. Wilson believed it to be 'of great importance to over two and a half million people'.[10] Dick Crossman described it as 'an idiotic creation . . . all the result of a silly election pledge' and as pointless as the new Ministry of Technology.[11] The truth lies somewhere between the two. In 1965, the Royal Mint and its 1,400 jobs were moved from London to Llantrisant in the Rhondda Valley instead of to Cumbernauld, Fife. Two years later, the Welsh won their own economic plan. Like most of the fiscal schemes designed to prop up the Union, *Wales: The Way Ahead*[12] was more of a road-widening scheme than a new motorway. In 1969–70, the principality received an unprecedented £66,900,000 in various kinds of aid. The result, recorded Crossman, was despair in the Scottish camp:

> Poor Willie Ross, who sits next to me in Cabinet, was very depressed. Harold Wilson tells me he's talking of resignation because he's so miserably unhappy at the 10 per cent unemployment rate in Scotland and his failure to achieve any effective regional policy. What makes matters worse is that recently all the dispersal decisions have favoured Wales.[13]

Poor Willie Ross soldiered on, returning as Scottish Secretary in the third Wilson government of 1974–6. But none of these initiatives was able to prevent the relative decline of the Scottish and Welsh economies and with it the erosion of Britishness in each country.

Before moving on to the electoral consequences of all this, mention must be made of tourism. Like many declining industrial societies, Scotland and Wales found some economic respite by developing their heritage industries. Since the late eighteenth century, tourism worldwide has relied on selling national identity. What the Scots and Welsh mostly sold was a folkish rural arcadia set in the Highlands and Brecons that was little different to that sold by the English in the Lakes and Cotswolds. Scottish and Welsh Tourist Boards had been set up through local initiatives in 1946 and 1948 respectively, but the infrastructure which the industry required was not properly put in place until the creation in 1965 of the Highlands and Islands Development Board, and the 1969 Development of Tourism Act which gave state assistance to all the UK's potential holiday spots.

Tourism served another, more ideological, purpose than selling holidays. From the mid-1950s UK governments promoted the cultural distinctiveness of Scotland and Wales in order to reassure their inhabitants that they were seen as historic nations in their own right. Official guidebooks produced by the COI with Whitehall's assistance became crafted definitions of Scottish, Welsh and Northern Irish identity and their relationship to England (references to demands for Home Rule were ruthlessly cut from drafts). The senior civil servant responsible for official guide books argued that nationalism could be contained by encouraging 'a reasonable manifestation of patriotism', and that the British could learn something from the way the Soviet Union placated the different nations under its aegis:

> No one could fail to recognise the significance of the emphasis in Russian propaganda on the cultural traditions of the many varying

components of the Communist bloc . . . Government spokesmen by adopting a tone of mild regret that the Scottish, Irish and Welsh traditions were different from some 'standard' British tradition [are] throwing away an opportunity of illustrating their tolerance. If ignored these differences [are] inevitably exploited by extremists.[14]

Heritage was not, therefore, primarily an English obsession in the late twentieth century. In fact it was far more central to Welsh and Scottish culture, partly because it was actively encouraged in Whitehall for political purposes and partly because it reflected the intense pride that the people of Scotland and Wales felt for their traditions.

What tourism could not do was to return either country to economic parity with England. Indeed, it was sometimes a painful reminder of their plight. In Wales, the purchase of holiday homes by affluent English people caused bitter resentment because it pushed up house prices without bringing a regular income into rural areas. Nationalists condemned 'these conveniences for [the] dirty weekends of Birmingham businessmen' and mounted a guerrilla campaign in which hundreds of properties were burnt to the ground at dead of night.[15] Neither trend was repeated in Scotland, but the economic limitations of tourism were felt just the same. Chris Harvie has made the point brilliantly: 'In the 1950s families toured the Highlands in Morris Oxfords and complained about Japanese knick-knacks. In the 1970s they could buy quality pottery and handweaves to take home in their Datsuns.'[16]

Writing shortly after he had repatriated the Stone of Destiny in 1950, Ian Hamilton warned: 'If we do not solve the problem of Scottish government, people less moderate than we are will sweep us aside and make of Scotland another Ireland.'[17] Violence did not erupt north of the border. But by the mid-1960s, Hamilton's prophecy was coming true in other respects. From 1959 to 1974, Plaid Cymru's share of the vote rose from 0.2 per cent to 20 per cent, while the SNP's share rose from 0.1 per cent to 30.4 per cent. Their support came mainly from those under forty-five and it ranged across all social groups. In Wilson's second general election victory of March 1966, the Labour Party enjoyed its biggest triumph ever in Scotland and Wales, taking forty-six of seventy-one seats and thirty-two of thirty-six seats respectively. To moderate devolutionists, the result proved that nationalism could be halted if concessions were made; to sceptics it proved that devolution was simply unnecessary. Within a year, both were proved terribly wrong. The SNP breakthrough came on 2 November 1967 at a by-election in the safe Labour seat of Hamilton. Winnie Ewing, a thirty-eight-year-old Glasgow solicitor, took the seat with a majority of 1,779 on a swing of 16.6 per cent. Magnus Magnusson – then a journalist for the *Scotsman* – was ecstatic: 'The Hamilton electorate swept thunderously and unequivocally through the tired, monotonous dialogue of contemporary party politics and voted resoundingly for Scotland: Scotland as a whole, Scotland as a nation, Scotland as a people not yet shorn of their identity like sacrificial sheep.'[18] The Labour government dismissed the result as a protest vote. Even pundits in broadcasting and academia thought it was merely evidence of a wider trend towards regionalism in the UK. The *Scotsman* had the measure of the situation: there was, it said, not merely 'temporary discontent' north of the border but 'a loss of faith' in the Union. This loss of faith was founded on 'many years of cultural nationalism' which, having never been properly addressed, had grown to such a level that it was possible even economic recovery would not now halt the nationalist advance.[19]

The depth of discontent with the Union cannot be simply measured in terms of support for the SNP or Plaid Cymru. There was a much larger underlying swell of nationalist fervour which was provoked by the continuing myopia of Britain's leaders and upon which nationalists were able to build a broader consensus for devolution. Examples of Westminster's thoughtlessness abound. But the most notorious occurred when the Government decided that the seven hundredth anniversary of the English parliament in 1965 and the nine hundredth anniversary of the Norman Conquest in 1966 would be celebrated as British events. On 22 June 1965 the entire Royal Family processed into Westminster Hall to the tune of 'Greensleeves'. After paying tribute to 'the customs and traditions that Scotland and Ireland have so fruitfully contributed', the Queen said that the liberties protected by the English parliament for 700 years were the UK's 'greatest glory', a testament to the 'idealism and self-sacrifice that is interwoven in the normally sober and pragmatic character of our peoples'.[20] The SNP wrote to Scottish MPs, demanding that they absent themselves from the event. 'At no time in its history', said the party, 'has our homeland been faced with such a determined onslaught on our national identity as it does at the present time'.[21]

Scottish backs were up, and they rose further still when the Ministry of Education sent a Memorandum to every Local Education Authority in the UK suggesting that a school holiday should be granted on 14 October 1966. Arguing that the Conquest had led directly to Magna Carta and the rule of law, it said, 'There is no doubt that the coming together of the Norman and Anglo-Saxon culture in the period following the Battle of Hastings was an event of first importance in the history of the British people.'[22] The Scottish Office agreed. 'One does not have to subscribe to the Whig view of history to take the view that [the event is] of great symbolic significance throughout the English-speaking world.'[23] But Scottish opinion was outraged, not only because the event being commemorated was an English one but because education was one of the three areas where the Scots had retained some control over the running of their country under the Treaty of Union. A letter to the *Scotsman* (one of many) put the case well:

> Up until now we have assumed that our education system was one of the three great institutional pillars of our nationhood by which our national identity was to be preserved and transmitted, since we had given up existence as a political entity in 1707. It is now clear that this is not so. The teaching profession is to be used as an agent of assimilation, instilling respect for English events which have no relevance whatsoever to Scotland ... Mr. Ross should have the grace to withdraw his circular and apologise to the Scottish people, with whom he has broken trust.[24]

Scottish MPs received hundreds of letters from constituents protesting about the decision and nineteen out of the thirty-four local education authorities in Scotland refused to declare a holiday, among them Glasgow and Edinburgh. A number also served notice that they would instead commemorate the six hundred and fiftieth anniversary of the Declaration of Arbroath in 1970. The government failed to pass off the story of English democracy as an achievement from which the whole island had benefited. That failure highlighted how much Westminster had come to be seen as an English institution with concomitant priorities.

We have already observed the decline of Scottish imperial identity. By the 1960s it formed the basis of a much more serious problem. Had imperialism on the so-called 'Celtic fringe' simply disappeared more quickly than it did in England, the nationalist advance might eventually have stalled as the four countries of the United Kingdom jointly forged a new identity. But instead of disappearing, the Scottish and Welsh sense of empire was stood on its head. More and more people saw themselves not as former partners in a British Empire but

as perennial victims of an English one; the first to be colonized by
the English and the last to be given their freedom. For all the
injustices which Scotland and Wales had endured over the centuries,
this rewriting of their history was an audacious attempt to re-invent
national identity. The culture of victimhood did not take root for
another decade. But Winnie Ewing's 1967 campaign statement that
Scotland was 'a more complete satellite of England' than Hungary
was of the USSR highlighted the serious contortions that Scottish
national identity began to undergo in this period.[25]

The Scottish view of political economy changed too. Since the
nineteenth century, periodic complaints about the economic iniquity
of the Union fostered a caricature of the Scot as a parsimonious
creature. The Scots accepted this caricature, not in order to humour
the English, but in order to transform it into a more positive aspect
of Scottishness. What they did was to present their supposed parsimony as evidence of an astute, prudent, businesslike character which
underpinned their astounding commercial success within and beyond
the Union. It was, of course, largely a middle-class image, but like
many such images it was promoted so pervasively that it became part
of the accepted national character. However, by the late 1960s
prudence appeared to be a worthless attribute. Increasingly, the Scots
saw themselves as an non-commercial people, or at least a people
who, unlike the English, had not lost their sense of community and
social responsibility. It closely resembled the identity which the Welsh
had created for themselves a century earlier; that sense of being the
moral conscience of Britain. The difference was that the Scots and
Welsh were now more concerned to save themselves from England
than they were to save England from itself.

2. All your seats are marginal now

In Wales the decline of Britishness was just as apparent. On 14 July
1966 Plaid Cymru won its first seat in Parliament in a by-election at
Carmarthen, prompted by the death of the veteran campaigner for
devolution, Lady Megan Lloyd George. The Party's leader, Gwynfor
Evans, turned a Labour majority of 9,233 into a nationalist one of
2,436. When he arrived at Paddington Station to take up his seat in

the House of Commons, 500 jubilant supporters greeted him on the platform singing 'Land of My Fathers'. Evans was not allowed by the Speaker to recite his oath in Welsh, a decision which did not soothe tempers.

The victory at Carmarthen was not a flash in the pan: 79 per cent of the town's population were Welsh speakers but two further by-elections over the next two years showed that Plaid was starting to make an appeal in Labour's more Anglicized, southern industrial strongholds. At Rhondda West in March 1967, where only 28 per cent were Welsh speakers and where all other parties had lost their deposits at the general election the previous year, Labour's majority was cut from 17,000 to 2,306. In July 1968 at Caerphilly (Welsh speakers 12 per cent) a majority of 21,000 collapsed to 1,874 on a swing of 40 per cent. One miners' leader told James Griffiths, 'You had better realise that all your seats are marginal now.'[26]

Fewer people were in favour of home rule (59 per cent) or independence (17.5 per cent) than in Scotland but those numbers were much higher than they had ever been before. Moreover, those in favour of some form of devolution matched the levels in Scotland: around three-quarters of the population. Perhaps most significantly of all, a major study by Strathclyde University found a similar number (69 per cent) now thought of themselves as Welsh rather than British, a figure which never dipped below 55 per cent in any social group or region and which almost matched the shift in Scottish national identity during the same period.[27]

It is generally assumed that Welsh nationalism is merely a cultural phenomenon, lacking the bite of its Scottish counterpart. Certainly, Plaid Cymru has never achieved quite the level of support that the SNP has enjoyed. However, two things should be remembered. First, Welsh nationalism gained political support in times of economic recession, just as it did in Scotland. Second, the Welsh focused on their culture more than the Scots not because they were averse to devolution but because they lacked separate legal, educational and religious institutions. Consequently, they were forced to alight on traditions which, however arcane and manufactured, marked them out from the English. This movement itself became more politicized during the 1960s, partly because the Welsh had to shout louder to get noticed, but also because cultural discontent was part of a wider protest against the constitutional status quo. Only this can explain a campaign for autonomy which, in its more violent moments, had more in common with Northern Ireland than Scotland.

If Welsh nationalism had a weakness, it was that the demand for economic development was accompanied by a schizophrenic fear that capitalism was destroying 'ancient' Welsh culture. The battle that ensued between modernists and traditionalists sapped the strength of Welsh nationalism for most of the twentieth century. In 1963 the *Sunday Times* sent a team of photographers and journalists to find an answer to the question 'How Welsh Is Wales?' They concluded: 'Inquisitive, eloquent, melodious, passionate, gifted and tricky, the half-legendary Welshman is gradually disappearing as the television sets, the neat bungalows, the Ford Cortinas and the Age of Affluence advance into the valleys . . . [But] it seems to be beyond dispute that the Welsh are different'. They remained, it said, an idealistic people – their purpose in British life, 'the necessity of thoughtful derision'.[28] A 1968 report on British tastes confirmed this. 'Beneath the pall of homogeneousness imposed by a modern, mass consumption economy . . . Britain is a highly varied country and is going to remain so' was its general conclusion.[29] Researchers found that in Scotland, and especially in Wales, lower levels of consumption of household goods and luxuries were the result of moral hostility towards materialism as well as lower living standards. Wales, said the report, was 'A Number Nine nation . . . parading for life in Number Eight shoes'.[30] The desire to be recognized as a distinct *gwerin* (folk) manifested itself partly in a folk music revival, the star of which was Dafydd Iwan. Unlike the traditional male voice choirs of the chapels his songs were strongly anti-English. But Iwan was no match for Tom Jones. A former miner turned transatlantic crooner who never lost sight of his roots, Jones became a national hero by straddling the Wales of the Ford Cortina and the Wales of the pithead.

The foundation of the new identity which the Welsh carved out for themselves in the 1960s was language. Welsh had been in decline since industrialization linked the principality more closely to England and the wider world. In 1700, around 90 per cent of the population spoke it; by 1891 the figure was down to 54 per cent. However, this was not a colonial strategy by the English but a choice made by the Welsh. Like Gaelic in Scotland, the language had never been proscribed; indeed, strenuous attempts were made to revive it at the Board of Education in the first half of the twentieth century. But they had little effect, and the figures continued to drop – down to 23 per cent in 1961. Tim Williams has observed:

The Welsh people had no wish to be a Folk. Disadvantaged by social class, they had no desire to compound this evil by being deprived of the language of the state. That is, a utilitarian people ... showed a sensible awareness of necessary change, and sought to exchange the language of the museum for the language of modernity and power.[31]

During the 1960s the Welsh did the opposite and as a result the decline was halted in a generation (Welsh speakers stood at 19 per cent and rising in 1991). In Scotland, Gaelic never played more than a symbolic role in Scottish identity, for two reasons. First, a much smaller number of Scots spoke it (bilingualism fell by 67 per cent between the 1930s and the 1950s, leaving only 3 per cent of the population in command of the language by 1961). Second, the few remaining Gaelic speakers were located almost entirely in the Highlands. Scottish Nationalists were wary of making it an issue of self-determination because it was seen to be a lost cause and a potentially divisive one that would alienate Lowland voters. In Wales, on the other hand, a majority came to see it as one of the defining elements of their national identity.

The catalyst for the revival was the founder of Plaid Cymru, Saunders Lewis, who came out of retirement in 1962 to deliver a lecture on BBC radio calling for the language to be saved. Lewis blamed its decline on a national inferiority complex made worse by the indifference of the English. He attacked Plaid Cymru for wasting money on 'purposeless parliamentary elections', concluding that 'success is only possible through revolutionary methods'. That year, he became President of a new Welsh Language Society (Cymdeithas yr Iaith Gymraeg) which attracted a younger generation of student activists and became the main protest movement in Wales at a time when elsewhere in the West such movements were internationalist in outlook. In 1963 it began a campaign which involved traffic blockades, sit-ins at television stations and government buildings and, most famously of all, the defacing of English road signs. Like other protest movements, the core membership of the society (which by 1970 numbered 1,500) were students. This prompted Ted Heath to describe Welsh nationalism as 'flower politics for flower people', a comment that was also a reference to the fact that the daffodil replaced the less dignified leek as the national symbol of Wales in this period.[32] However, it is worth noting that the University of Wales had the highest proportion of working-class students (40 per cent) of any university in Britain – a testament to a Welsh tradition of self-help. Also, the remainder of the Welsh-speaking population were in the areas (north, mid- and west Wales) which at that time were the worst hit by economic decline. Nationalism was therefore both literally and metaphorically a far from academic question.

What is more significant is that the society's well-publicized activities began to gain support among a wider section of the population, including English speakers, for many of whom the existence of the language became an object of national pride even though they had no wish to learn it. A poll carried out for the *Western Mail* in 1968 showed that 46.5 per cent of the population thought it should be taught in every school while 30 per cent thought it should be up to parents in each area to decide. Only 10.5 per cent were actively opposed. Attendance at the annual national Eisteddfod also shot up to unprecedented levels – from 60,000 in 1960 to 200,000 in 1970, figures which remained steady even when it was held in heavily Anglicized counties like Flintshire.

Some people resented being classed as second-class Welsh because they were not bilingual, and unionist politicians attempted to capitalize on that resentment. In 1960 Harold Macmillan said, 'I do not accept that a Welshman is less a patriot because he does not speak Welsh.' Eight years later, Eirene White, Minister of State at the Welsh Office, condemned the 'self-righteousness' of Welsh-speakers who 'elevated a proper pride in their language to idolatry'.[33] Nationalists began to take note. In 1951, the Eisteddfod had become a monolingual event for the first time but in 1966 the President of the event, Aneirin Talfan Davies, attacked the ruling. Davies, the man who had commissioned Dylan Thomas and who had since become Head of Programmes at BBC Wales, told a large crowd: 'You can't preserve the Welsh language by hedging around it and pushing it into a cultural ghetto . . . If Wales is to continue as a nation and not as an unequal yoking of two nations, then we shall have to act in a creative way in order to keep the non-Welsh speaking people within the range of the fire on the Welsh hearth.'[34] He was backed up by the Chairman of the Arts Council in Wales, who called on people to show 'that the Eisteddfod really belonged to the Swinging Sixties and not to the last century'.[35] Davies' call was rejected, but the Eisteddfod did begin to include more pop music in subsequent years.

Other nationalists were less compromising and decided that the fire on the Welsh hearth would best be kept alight by dropping burning coals on the nation's carpet. During the mid-1960s, there was a short-lived Free Wales Army (FWA), which modelled itself on

the IRA, something which even the Scots shied away from, and
which not surprisingly Plaid Cymru condemned. The FWA began by
using secret radio transmitters to broadcast calls to the Welsh to
shake off the English yoke. Less comically, they used the sort of
violence which soon became common in Northern Ireland. It threatened the Secretary of State with assassination at the Aberavon
Eisteddfod in 1966. It blew up the Temple of Peace in Cardiff and
damaged the police station there. It also sent parcel bombs to public
officials, seriously injuring an RAF officer and on another occasion
blowing the hands off a small girl. Before the FWA's leaders were
rounded up and imprisoned, the Welsh kept the bombing in perspective, displaying a sense of humour which sometimes escaped the
English as they struggled to understand why the Welsh found their
400-year-old Union with England objectionable. On one occasion,
the police removed a set of large spherical black candles with 'BOMB'
stencilled on them from an Aberystwyth crafts centre 'on the grounds
that they are not funny'.[36] A more representative expression of Welsh
nationalism in this period was the formation of a breakaway movement of the Women's Institute, calling itself Merched y Wawr
(literally, Daughters of the Dawn).

The formation of a Welsh Women's Institute did not send Ministers scurrying to No. 10 for late-night Cabinet meetings. But the
language campaign, the bombings and the disastrous by-election
results, together with the simultaneous rise of nationalism in Scotland, did shock the Wilson government into action. At stake was not
simply Labour's majority in its old 'Celtic' heartlands and therefore
its ability to form a majority government in England. The very future
of the Union – with Wales as well as with Scotland – seemed to be
in doubt. The Home Secretary, Merlyn Rees, declared that 'Welsh
Nationalism shows many of the traits of fascism', which did little to
curry favour with the Welsh.[37] The government's more considered
and sensible response was twofold. First, Wilson took some of the
sting out of cultural discontent by giving Welsh the same legal status
as English, in the Welsh Language Act of 1967. In the same year, the
Welsh Arts Council, along with its Scottish counterpart, achieved
executive independence from London. But what did more than
anything to shore up Britishness in the principality was the Investiture
of Charles Philip Arthur George Windsor as Prince of Wales in 1969.

3. A prince is born

The Investiture was the biggest royal event in Britain between the Coronation of 1953 and the marriage of Charles and Diana in 1981. The modern title 'Prince of Wales' was originally designed to crown England's domination of its western neighbour. It had first been given to the heir to the English throne by Edward I in 1301, in order to legitimize his annexation of the principality. Charles was the twenty-first Prince. Few had been formally invested and of those only two had been the subject of major state occasions. The first took place in 1483 when the regicide Richard III attempted to secure his teetering dynasty by investing his son Edward, but the boy died a year later just before the Tudors won the English throne. The second was in 1911, when George V invested his seventeen-year-old son – the future Edward VIII. Although Elizabeth II owed her throne to that abdication, she told Harold Macmillan during one of his audiences with her in 1958, 'Neither of them are really very good auguries.'[38] In view of the troubles which later beset her reign and the role which Charles played in them, the Queen's remark must count as one of the most prophetic she ever made.

After returning to Downing Street, having advised the Queen to delay the Investiture until Charles was older, Macmillan wrote, 'The whole ceremony of Investiture seems to have been invented by Lloyd George for political reasons in 1910 – or so the Queen believes.'[39] The Queen was quite right. It had been staged by the Prime Minister first to cement his position as the de facto leader of the Welsh people, and more generally to halt the march of socialism, which was then beginning to threaten the Liberal dominance of the principality. Lloyd George had skilfully used the monarchy to bring together the old Welsh aristocracy, the Anglican Church and the Nonconformist middle and working classes in a ceremony which fused the sham antiquity of the druidic bards with the industrial culture of massed choirs.[40] Caernarfon Castle was chosen over Cardiff to emphasize that the soul of Wales was to be found in the mountains.

The purpose of the 1969 Investiture was no less political: it was staged primarily in order to blunt the appeal of Welsh nationalism. Harold Wilson's government worked closely with Buckingham Palace and Welsh leaders with that aim clearly in mind, and they

succeeded. The campaign effectively began when Charles was sent to
the University College at Aberystwyth for a crash course in the Welsh
language and the history of Welsh nationalism. In an interview
beforehand, he was asked what sort of reception he thought would
get. His reply revealed the sensitive, endearingly artless man who
became the despair of successive public relations experts employed
to improve his image:

> It would be unnatural, I think, if one didn't feel any apprehension
> about it . . . as long as I don't get covered in too much egg and
> tomato I'll be all right. But I don't blame people demonstrating
> like that. I've hardly been to Wales, and you can't expect people
> to be over-zealous about the fact of having a so-called English
> Prince to come amongst them.[41]

Despite peaceful protests from some of the students, Edward Mill-
ward, a member of Plaid Cymru and its prospective candidate for
Montgomeryshire, agreed to be his tutor. Charles came away
impressed, writing to a friend at Cambridge, 'I'm sure speaking to
these people sympathetically is the best thing one can do. So many
people in the government seem to dismiss them as bogeymen and I
feel that is fatal.'[42] Charles spoke at the Eisteddfod of 1969 in Welsh,
a gesture which was much appreciated at the time.

Meanwhile, preparations for the event were under way. Three
significant changes were made to the ceremonial of 1911. The first
was that Anglicanism had little to do with it. Since the disestablishment of the Church of Wales in 1920, relations between it and
Nonconformism had been frayed. Moreover, Nonconformity was
still regarded as an important part of Welshness even though Wales
had become a more secular country. The Prime Minister and religious
leaders therefore decided that the Church in Wales would take a
back seat. The Archbishops of Canterbury and York were not be
invited at all on the grounds that 'there would be resentment in
Welsh religious and . . . wider circles' if they were (although the
Roman Catholic Archbishop of Cardiff was present).[43] It was also
thought 'highly desirable that the Prince should visit a Nonconformist Chapel', which he did.[44] The second change was that the military
presence was vastly scaled down in order not to provoke nationalists
with a display of Anglo-Welsh military might and so as to make the
ceremony appear more in tune with a decade in which the young had
taken against military service. 12,000 troops of various kinds had
been present in 1911. George Thomas thought the Edwardian event

had been 'a militaristic, pompous and essentially alien ceremony', cut the number of troops to 3,000 and stationed them around the periphery of the castle.[45]

The Investiture was also part of a wider attempt to relaunch the monarchy in the late 1960s; to cast off its tweedy image and regain some of the excitement which had greeted the New Elizabethan Age. The modernity which the royal couple had successfully projected in the mid-1950s had faded for two reasons. First, the Duke of Edinburgh's championing of British science and technology was hijacked by Harold Wilson. The link which the Labour leader made during the 1960s between technological development and the creation of a meritocratic society politicized the subject, making it harder for royalty to be associated with it. At the same time, Labour's failure to deliver a meritocracy reduced the popular allure of science because it became associated with economic mismanagement and political vacuity. As the Duke commented in an interview in 1968:

> The monarchy is part of the fabric of the country and as the fabric alters, so the monarchy and the people's relations to it alters. In 1953 . . . we were a good deal younger. And I think young people, a young Queen and young family are infinitely more amusing and newsworthy. You know we're getting on for middle age and I dare say when we're really ancient there might be bit more reverence again.[46]

In the meantime, the twenty-one-year-old Prince of Wales was enlisted to freshen the monarchy up.

The man behind the relaunch was the Queen's new Press Secretary, William Heseltine. He masterminded the 1969 TV documentary *Royal Family*, which showed the family going about its business in a faux–informal 'behind the scenes' way. Heseltine put the Earl of Snowdon, Anthony Armstrong-Jones, in charge of designing the Investiture ceremony. As well as having Welsh ancestry, Snowdon was Princess Margaret's photographer husband of relatively humble origins and, as such, a consort for the 1960s if ever there was one. He was made Constable of Caernarfon Castle in order to carry out his duties but was fondly referred to in the press as 'Tony the Constable'. The old guard were not happy but gave way. The Duke of Norfolk, who had staged the Coronation, gruffly told him, 'You know about art, you get on with it.'[47]

Charles' great-uncle had been invested inside a mock Crusader tent. The set Snowdon produced was stark and modern: a plain dais in the courtyard of the Castle with three plain thrones to match, each made of Welsh slate. Above the dais was a transparent canopy supported by steel shafts, designed to let the cameras observe every moment without obstruction. Snowdon played down its significance, commenting that it was merely what 'Henry V would have done . . . if he'd had perspex'.[48] In fact, it was deeply symbolic. This time there were no arguments about which part of the ceremony would be televised and much less cant about its religious significance. In 1953, the velvet curtains of custom had been partially drawn in order to let some proverbial daylight in on the magic of monarchy. In 1969 they were swept back for good and repeated attempts to close them again were to fail. The Investiture was the staging post between the Court Circular of *The Times* and topless photos of royalty in the *Sun*.

In the meantime, the British political Establishment got to work. At a meeting of the Investiture Committee in October 1968, George Thomas said there was 'growing evidence . . . that the Investiture was popular with the overwhelming majority of the Welsh people'. In reply, the Lord Mayor of Cardiff warned that 'opposition in Wales should not be underestimated'.[49] He was right. Opinion polls showed that enthusiasm was greater in England than in the principality, where half the population thought it 'a waste of time'.[50] The Free Wales Army threatened to disrupt the event in order to 'throw off the rusty chains of England'. In an effort to reassure the Prince, Harry Secombe, his friend, former Goon and professional Welshman, wrote to him promising to throw his considerable girth in front of any bullet that came Charles' way. The demonstrations ranged from bombings before the Investiture to booing during it, and on the morning of the ceremony two men were killed trying to attack the Royal Train on its way to Caernarfon. But these incidents lost nationalists a lot of support among the moderate majority.

On 5 July 1969 Charles recorded in his diary, 'Last week has been an incredible one in my life . . . I now seem to have a great deal to live up to and I hope I can be of some assistance to Wales in constructive ways. To know that somebody is interested in them is the very least I can do.'[51] The British press made a predictable dig at the Welsh he spoke; the *Daily Mirror* remarking, 'To this Space Age Prince, those words must come like verbal crustaceans on the Rock of Ages.' But under the headline 'POMP AND PERSPEX' it continued: 'It is a brave non-Taffy who would presume to speak for Wales while imported English coppers look for gelignite in public lavs . . . Yet [we] say that Charles has triumphantly and spectacularly draped his ermine-trimmed mantle around the shoulders of a nation and received more than an affectionate hug in return.'[52]

The *Western Mail*, which like the *Scotsman* was in favour of moderate devolution, agreed. Charles made a triumphant tour around the principality in the following week, with Wales' national newspaper providing lavish coverage. It noted the excitement of young girls everywhere but reserved its most emotive commentary for the reception which the Prince got in the nationalist heartlands of the north: 'The gaiety in each village, the flag-waving, the singing and the tears on some well-worn faces showed beyond doubt that all Wales was prepared to accept her newly-invested Prince with open arms.'[53] In 1911 the monarchy was used by a Liberal government to promote Welshness to curtail socialism; in 1969 it was used by a Labour government to curtail nationalism. The event was therefore a testament to the political journey which the Welsh made in the twentieth century.

More importantly, it revealed the quiet depths of unionist feeling in Wales. The Welsh did not become ardent monarchists in 1969. Having never had a monarchy of their own or even a royal holiday home like Balmoral, they did not have the same sentimental attachment to the institution which the Scots had; and people remembered how the monarchy had been forced to recognize the Welsh flag only a decade earlier. Nor was the Crown Celticized by the event; much as some people appreciated Charles' attempt to learn the language, no one thought he was truly Welsh any more than the Scots thought the Duke of Edinburgh was truly Scottish. In Wales, the Crown was essentially a convenient institution around which the people could unite and simultaneously express their Welshness and their Britishness, and this they did at Caernarfon.

The event generated considerable pride in the fact that Welsh culture had been honoured in front of an international TV audience. But whatever discontent had arisen about the Union, Britain was still seen as the only feasible vehicle in which Wales could function as a distinctive nation on the world stage.

4. The Irish story is a queer one

In 1962, Harold Macmillan wrote in his diary: 'The Irish story is a queer one ... Hundreds of years of bitter quarrels ... civil war among the natives following the complete surrender of the British – and now, peace – perfect peace.' Ireland, he concluded, was 'the last happy country in Europe'.[54] And so it seemed to most Britons. During the Suez crisis a new IRA campaign had been launched in the North which continued until February 1962. It caused £1 million worth of damage, cost the Treasury £10 million in extra security and left six RUC constables and eight IRA men dead. But the campaign failed to stir up the Irish, North or South. By the early 1960s, it did seem that the Irish Question was finally going away and that the five nations of the Isles were settling into a relatively harmonious coexistence. In 1961, UK government officials concluded that 'the spirit of 1916 and 1922 is on the wane'.[55] The IRA agreed. After its defeat, the organization issued a statement acknowledging that 'the attitude of the general public' was not supportive of its struggle.[56]

In the North, a new liberal regime under Terence O'Neill (1963–9) attempted to reform the province in order to win the allegiance of Catholics and create a non-sectarian society. O'Neill also started a dialogue with the Republic. He met the Taoiseach, Sean Lemass (a veteran of the Easter Rising), in Belfast and Dublin in 1965, the first face-to-face contact between Irish government leaders since Partition. Meanwhile in the South, economic growth after years of stagnation was creating a new, urban middle class which the British hoped would be more willing to bury the hatchet. Shortly before Britain signed a Free Trade Agreement with the Republic in December 1965, the Secretary of State for Commonwealth Relations told the Cabinet:

> The disappearance of old leaders in the Republic and the increasing prosperity there have introduced a new realism into Irish politics. There is a readiness to put less emphasis on the issue of Partition and, particularly among the growing middle class and the business leaders, to accept the economic interdependence of the Republic and Britain ... An Agreement could place our political relationship with the Republic on a better footing than ever in the past.[57]

To cement the relationship, in April 1966, on the fiftieth anniversary of the Easter Rising, the British returned the tricolour which de Valéra and his comrades had hoisted on the flagpole of Dublin's Post Office (it had been taken back to Britain and displayed in the Imperial War Museum as a trophy of British power).

Later that year, during a royal visit to Northern Ireland, a beer bottle was thrown at the Queen. On returning home, she told Harold Wilson that it was an 'unpleasant experience'. The Prime Minister made discreet enquiries and was reassured by the security services that the culprit was a mad woman from Salford who 'is greatly exercised by the illegality of the Hanoverian succession.'[58] There is something wonderfully Shakespearean about the incident. Like a crone from *Macbeth* prophesying doom, the woman was a sign of things to come. Two years later, in the summer of 1968, after several rather more rational warnings from diplomats, Northern Ireland erupted into civil war. This time, the bottles were filled with paraffin and the cause was both more ancient and more contemporary than the Hanoverian succession.

Like most reform programmes brought in after generations of political oppression, O'Neill's pleased no one. The better access to housing, jobs and education which he provided was based on his belief that 'If you treat Roman Catholics with due consideration and kindness they will live like Protestants despite the authoritarian nature of their church.'[59] Kindness was not enough, even for moderate nationalists. On 1 February 1967 they formed the Northern Ireland Civil Rights Association (NICRA) to press for a thorough political reform of the province. At the same time, O'Neill's concessions outraged Unionists. They regarded NICRA (with some justification) as a front for those seeking a united Ireland. Over the next two years, Unionist gangs violently attacked civil rights marchers and then moved into Catholic areas to attack anyone they could find. In response, the Provisional IRA was set up on 22 September 1969, led by Sean MacStiofain. Splitting from the 'Official' IRA, which had renounced violence after the failure of its 1956–62 campaign, the 'Provos' renewed the armed struggle for a united Ireland. They also upheld the policy of 'abstentionism', a republican article of faith, which forbade any of its members from taking up seats they won in the Belfast, Dublin or Westminster parliaments. It was to be another seventeen years before the Provisional IRA, under the influence of Gerry Adams, began to accept that political negotiation was the only way to end British rule in Ireland. Meanwhile the 'Provos' saw a chance to renew the armed struggle for a united Ireland while posing as the protector of Catholic communities. It was more determined, more organized and undoubtedly more popular than previous incarnations of the IRA. Old Loyalist paramilitary groups like the UDA were re-formed and new ones like the UVF formed in order to counter the insurrection. The war had begun. On 14 August 1969, Harold Wilson belatedly sent British troops to the province to keep order. His Press Secretary, Joe Haines, told him, 'The troops will have to be there for months,' to which Wilson replied, 'They're going to be there for seven years at least.' As the twenty-first century got under way they had still not left.[60]

The full impact of the Troubles on the United Kingdom were not felt until the 1970s. But already, the image of Northern Ireland as a peaceful and prosperous outpost of the realm had been dented. Within five years the North was stamped on the cortex of the mainland as an alien, un-British place which was part of the Irish problem not a victim of it. With some justification, Terence O'Neill believed that a major reason for this change was the gradually fading memory of the Second World War. In 1968 he said, 'Our wartime conduct won us many friends, as compared with the neutrality of the South – but we must accept, I fear, that as these events fade from the memory so also does the sentiment of gratitude . . . Post-war loyalty count[s] for much less than [it] did, especially amongst the young.'[61] Two weeks later, on 9 December, he broadcast to the people of Northern Ireland: 'Ulster stands at the crossroads . . . What kind of Ulster do you want? A happy and respected province in good standing with the rest of the United Kingdom? Or a place continually torn apart by riots and demonstrations and regarded by the rest of Britain as a political outcast?'[62] They chose the latter. But the rest of the UK was also at a crossroads in the late 1960s. Ulster was only the most extreme expression of nationalist discontent with the Union, discontent which stretched from the north of Scotland to south Wales and even into the heart of England itself.

When the British Cabinet decided to set up a Royal Commission on the Constitution on 29 October 1968, it was clear in ministers' minds that it would have to cover all 'the countries, nations and regions of the United Kingdom', including Northern Ireland. Yet there remained a deep-seated complacency in Westminster about the health of the British state and the national identities of the British people. The Welsh Secretary had warned Wilson that however many subsidies it got, Wales might go the way of Ireland if it was not given some form of elected representation: 'To ignore the problem of Welsh nationalism would be a short-sighted and perilous course, for it would alienate moderate opinion, increase sympathy for the extremists and risk repeating some of the mistakes made in Ireland and elsewhere.'[63] Another Welsh minister wrote to the Prime Minister: 'It would be a grave error to suppose that present problems are transient. Our aspirations certainly manifest themselves with different force at different periods. But they continue to recur after 500 years.'[64] But, like previous governments, Wilson's was opposed to devolution on ideological grounds, regarding it as a can of worms best left unopened. In reaching its decision to set up a Commission, the Cabinet agreed that radical change was out of the question:

> A written constitution would destroy the sovereignty of Parliament and put obstacles in the way of rapid action by a government desiring to introduce change; it would tend towards the preservation of individual rights and privileges and against the community as a whole. Critics of the government might also suggest ... that the way would be open for an attack on the monarchy and the advocacy of republican government.[65]

Richard Crossman had pressed the Prime Minister to support devolution and he chaired the Cabinet Committee on the subject. But in 1968 he concluded, 'We were not prepared to undermine or compromise the sound structure of the United Kingdom constitution simply to placate a sudden movement of public opinion.'[66] The growth of nationalism was not a sudden movement of public opinion. It had been building up for a generation and it was not about to go away. In England, it took a different form: racism. Crossman observed that opposition to black immigration was the English 'counterpart' of Scottish and Welsh nationalism.[67] He was right. But dealing with it proved to be far more difficult than analysing it.

5. Those whom the gods
wish to destroy

Race was never absent from British politics after 1945. But from the
mid-1960s until the early 1980s, it was regarded as the most important issue facing the country apart from the economy and Europe. It
engaged more English people more passionately than any other
political subject and threw their national identity into sharp relief.
Like Scottish and Welsh nationalism, race became a more prominent
issue in this period because of economic stagnation. Since the 1950s,
politicians had warned that once the postwar boom ended, blacks
and Asians would make an easy scapegoat. What had been a problem
in a period of full employment turned into a crisis when unemployment and inflation rose. But whereas in the north and west of Britain
the reaction to economic stagnation was a declining sense of Britishness, in England stagnation combined with a fear of black people to
produce a racially based nationalism.

That nationalism was articulated as British but it was almost
entirely English in impulse, for two reasons. First, most blacks and
Asians settled in the Midlands and the south (90 per cent of the UK's
coloured population resided in England, and Greater London alone
accounted for 50 per cent). Second, most immigrants thought of
themselves as Anglo-British when they arrived. British citizenship
facilitated their passage to the UK and it provided the legal and
political framework for their struggle to remain and be accepted. But
the dominant culture of colonial rule, from schools to street names,
had been English, particularly in the West Indies, where most immigrants came from. It was therefore English culture with which and
latterly against which they primarily defined themselves.

From the outset, the Labour government's policy on race was a
continuation of the Conservatives': the appeasement of racism. Wilson knew that most of the country was opposed to black immigration
and that the moral stand Gaitskell had taken a few years earlier was
costing Labour votes. Lest Labour were in any doubt about the
strength of public feeling, they got a swift reminder at the general
election when the Shadow Foreign Secretary, Patrick Gordon Walker,
was unseated in his Smethwick constituency in the Midlands by a

Conservative campaign based on the unofficial slogan, 'If you want a nigger neighbour, vote Labour.'[68] The swing to the Conservatives in Smethwick was 7.5 per cent against a national swing of 3.2 per cent to Labour. The government's worries were confounded by the fact that the 1962 Immigration Act had not significantly reduced immigration. This was partly because, like drinkers faced with last orders at 11 p.m., many people rushed to beat the new restrictions; and partly because the dependants of those already in Britain still had the right to enter the country and did so in large numbers.[69] In 1965 the White Paper *Immigration from the Commonwealth* outlined a series of measures to further reduce the inflow, primarily a proposal to limit the rights of dependants.

Blacks who remained in their country of origin and accepted their traditional place on the imperial margins of Britishness continued to be seen as an asset and not as a threat. Many West Indians, particularly middle-class ones, remained ardent monarchists, partly out of sentiment and partly because they saw the Crown as a bulwark against Third World communism. Royal visits were used to encourage this loyalty. One such was the Queen's visit to Trinidad and Tobago in February 1966. Before she arrived, the Prime Minister of Trinidad, Dr Eric Williams, had condemned Britain as 'bankrupt and racialist', but as a shrewd politician he used the visit to shine in the Queen's reflected glory. The High Commissioner's report to the Commonwealth Relations Secretary, Arthur Bottomley, summed up a mutually advantageous visit. A garden party for 5,000 multiracial guests at Government House in Port of Spain allowed the cream of Trinidadian society 'to see at first hand the grace and charm of Her Majesty, and to experience the lively wit of His Royal Highness the Duke of Edinburgh'.[70] After watching 'Her Majesty sail away from Trinidad in the moonlight', the Commissioner concluded:

> The abiding impression of the last few days is of the magic of the Monarchy. The Royal visit has encouraged much healthy pride in Trinidad and Tobago; and the stability of this sophisticated community has been further enhanced. The four days when Her Majesty visibly reigned in Trinidad and Tobago will long remain in the minds of her loyal subjects in the land of the calypso.[71]

The Commissioner's moonlit report from the land of the calypso and others like it from elsewhere in the black Commonwealth reveal how much the inclusivity of Britishness depended on the remoteness of the Queen's coloured subjects from the UK. Put simply, it is hard to imagine Elizabeth II visibly reigning with as much enthusiasm nor with as much success had she visited some of her Trinidadian subjects at the popular Calypso Club in London's Notting Hill.

What made Labour governments from Wilson onwards different was that, while limiting immigration, they also attempted to protect ethnic minorities by enforcing tolerance in law. The first Race Relations Act, in 1965, outlawed the incitement of racial hatred and racial discrimination in places of public resort and it set up the Race Relations Board (later the Commission for Racial Equality) to monitor the situation. Far from protecting Britain's 'unrivalled tradition of tolerance' as the Home Secretary claimed, Conservatives argued that the Act was intolerant of people's legitimate views and infringed the ancient English right of free speech. For example, Peter Thorneycroft, speaking for the Opposition, told the House:

> Let anybody go to Speaker's Corner . . . on any Sunday, and he will find blacks saying things about whites and whites saying things about blacks . . . very rough things are said all round. However, on balance, we in this country think it right that . . . [unless] they are likely to cause a breach of the peace, people should be allowed to say what they want to say.[72]

He added that the Bill was a 'taint of criminality against the kindly, just and wise British people'.[73] At the same time, he made it clear that he did not consider blacks to be British, telling MPs, 'These are important matters, which affect millions of our fellow countrymen and thousands of coloured immigrants.' A further Race Relations Act followed in 1976, and the Labour government gave a lead by making the cricketer Learie Constantine the first black life peer, in 1969, a fitting reward for a man who during the Second World War had exposed British hypocrisy by challenging the country's informal colour bar in the High Court. However, in the end no government could either legislate away racial prejudice or reduce it with gestures like that made to Constantine.

British popular culture in the 1960s and 1970s reflected a country which had not accepted the physical presence of black people, never mind come to terms with the need to alter its national identity. While teenagers enjoyed black American singers like Otis Redding and Stevie Wonder performing on *Ready, Steady, Go!* and bought their records, many more tuned in to the *Black and White Minstrel Show*, in which George Mitchell and his singers blacked up to perform old

Mississippi melodies. First screened in 1958, it remained one of the BBC's flagship Saturday night light entertainment shows until 1978. Even more revealing was television comedy. Media historian Andy Medhurst has written, 'If you want to understand the preconceptions and power structures of a society or social group, there are few better ways than by studying what it laughs at.'[74] The situation comedy was an American invention of the 1950s which, like pop music, was incorporated into the national culture in this period. It is a particularly accurate barometer of Britishness.

The most popular sitcom of the 1960s was the BBC's *Till Death Us Do Part*, written by Johnny Speight and screened between 1966 and 1968. Set in the East End of London, it centred upon Alf Garnett, a working-class, Tory-voting, God-fearing, monarchist, sexist, racist bigot who worked in the docks and lived with his long-suffering wife, daughter and son-in-law in a small Victorian terraced house. His diatribes ranged across every area of English life, charting the decline of a once great nation from its zenith during the Finest Hour to a nadir of socialist permissiveness in the 1960s. But it was black people for whom he reserved the angriest utterance of his catchphrase, 'Blaady marvellous, innit?'

The foundation of Alf's patriotism was a belief in the glory of England's Empire. Its history, he argued, stretched back to the Henrician Reformation when 'God told Henry to ignore the Pope and to build His . . . Kingdom on earth here in England'. From then on, England started 'to win the world and rule it for its own good'. Alf's patriotism was stirred by a fear of 'blaady coons'. His explanation for the multiracial society was simple: 'They loved us so much that when we left their countries, they followed us home.'[75] Alf believed that this display of native affection had undermined the purity of the English race and would eventually destroy the country. Since the purity of 'blood' was such a preoccupation, one episode was set in a blood donor clinic to pinpoint the absurdity of Alf's views. Alf complained that black people's blood might be given to white people, thereby turning them into 'coons'. The solution, he argued, was to establish separate transfusion services for the races.

Keen to avoid accusations that he was being negative, Alf's complaints were usually followed by what he saw as rational, constructive solutions to England's decline. The following monologue, in which he offered a simultaneous answer to the problems of immigration and feminism, was typical:

Before the war started we was experimenting . . . trying to solve the black question . . . trying to breed 'em smaller. Ideal for chimney sweeping – even have five of 'em sitting under the bonnet of your car pedalling it. An' that's what we was doing, experimenting, like they do with your dogs. You see, your big dogs breed down to little miniature dogs, an' we was trying to breed your coloureds down to little miniature blacks. But of course, the war put a stop to all that and they went on breeding any old how, an' have grown to all sorts of awkward sizes. Miniature blacks would have been a very handy size to have about the house. I mean, you'd only need a dog kennel or a little shed to put 'em in, and they'd have been very handy nipping about the house cleaning out the ashtrays, peeling potatoes, and all them sort of little woman's jobs. It would have put an end to this question of woman's lib too, wouldn't it? Not too late – could breed 'em fast [if someone] put up a four-year plan.[76]

Within little over a month, the programme was watched regularly by half of Britain's adult population (18 million viewers), knocking *Coronation Street* off its spot as the most popular British television programme of the era.

However, the satirical Swiftian intent behind modest proposals such as the one above was lost on many Britons. Many actively identified with Alf and enjoyed his ability to air reactionary attitudes in an age when it was becoming officially unacceptable to do so. He provided a voice for people who felt that their right to free speech had been curtailed by the state in order to appease a foreign minority. When the first series ended, Milton Shulman, television critic of the *Evening Standard*, argued that the fascination of *Till Death Us Do Part*

lay in its ability to act as a distorting mirror in which we could watch our meanest attributes reflected large and ugly. Like some boil on the back of the neck that one cannot resist stroking or touching [he] demanded the nation's attention. Alf's views . . . can be seen and heard most days in most pubs, factories and boardrooms in the land . . . Fortunately, there are few of us who possess all of Alf's bulging portmanteau of hates and prejudices. But it is only the saint among us who does not share at least one.[77]

The programme deserves to be reassessed. Race was not its only preoccupation. It was a brilliantly funny satire on the mores of the prewar generation which discussed sex, politics and religion with a frankness rare in any television genre and which incurred the wrath of conservatives for doing so. In a sense, Alf Garnett was the successor to Colonel Blimp: a lovable rogue whose absurdly reactionary views helped the English to locate their liberalism during a period of immense social change. However, the devil had all the best lines in the script, in addition to which there was no central black character to challenge Alf's prejudice. A BBC audience survey carried out in 1968 in London found that 95 per cent did *not* think that the show provoked racial prejudice. But oral evidence suggests that the country's black population felt at best uneasy about the comic treatment of attitudes which had seriously damaged their lives.[78]

The series stood at a juncture in the history of English national identity. Coming soon after the passage of the Race Relations Act, it was a brave attempt to confront a controversial aspect of Englishness which many people would have preferred to ignore. But the unreflective approval with which it was met by a substantial proportion of the population confirmed that the racial character of national identity in Britain had not substantially changed since the war. Further, devastating proof of this stasis came just two months after *Till Death Us Do Part* was dropped by the BBC, when Enoch Powell rose to address the West Midlands Conservative Political Centre at the Midland Hotel in Birmingham at 2.30 p.m. on Saturday, 20 April 1968.

Enoch Powell was a racist. His sins (on earth at least) were absolved when he died in 1998. To the disgust of black Britons, politicians of left and right proclaimed him to have been a great intellectual and parliamentarian. His major flaw, they argued, was that he simply took the logic of his arguments too far. Yet, by his own admission, Powell believed that black people, even those born in the UK, were not English and that their presence would lead to the nation's downfall. In a BBC interview towards the end of his life, he asked, 'What's wrong with racism? Racism is the basis of a nationality . . . Nations are, upon the whole, united by identity with one another . . . and that's normally due to similarities which we regard as racial similarities.'[79]

Until the 1950s, Powell was a committed imperialist of a High Victorian kind. Born in 1912 to middle-class Birmingham schoolteachers, his belief in the Empire – like that of many Englishmen of his generation and background – was based on three things: a love of classical Greece as a model of civilization; a belief in the destiny of the English race, based on a romantic view of the Anglo-Saxon era; and an equally romantic view of colonial India, which he gained

while stationed there in the army. Unlike many politicians of the
time, Powell accepted that the Empire was effectively over after the
war and it was foolish to believe that the Commonwealth was
anything other than a chimeric substitute for vanished glories. He
argued that instead of being obsessed with the end of empire the
English should see it as an opportunity to rediscover their national
identity. But unlike others who disavowed the Empire in the mid-
twentieth century, Powell did not see the European Union as a
vehicle for this change. Nor, much as he admired the Greeks, did he
share Macmillan's enthusiasm for playing Greece to America's Rome.
This was partly because he had an especial loathing for the United
States.

Powell sought instead to take English nationalism back to racial
basics. To do this, he first asked people to make contact with their
Anglo-Saxon ancestors. Taking up a theme which had run through
militant English nationalism since the seventeenth century, Powell
portrayed the English as latter-day Israelites, God's chosen people in
the modern world. But unlike either Cromwellian or Victorian
Protestant theorists who used this idea to justify the conquering of
foreign lands, Powell saw the English as a diaspora who had returned
home from the far corners of the world to realize their nationhood
once again. In a speech to the Royal Society of St George in 1961,
he said:

> Our generation is like one which comes home again from years of
> distant wandering. We discover affinities with earlier generations
> of English, generations before the 'expansion of England', who felt
> no country but this to be their own. We look upon the traces
> which they left with a new curiosity, the curiosity of finding our-
> selves once more akin with the old English. Backward travels our
> gaze, beyond the grenadiers and the philosophers of the eighteenth
> century, beyond the pikemen and the preachers of the seventeenth,
> back through the brash adventurous days of the first Elizabeth and
> the hard materialism of the Tudors, and there at last we find them,
> or seem to find them, in many a village church, beneath the tall
> tracery of a Perpendicular East window and the coffered ceiling of
> the chantry chapel. From brass and stone, from line and effigy,
> their eyes look out at us, and we gaze into them, as if we would
> win some answer from their inscrutable silence. 'Tell us what it is
> that binds us together; show us the clue that leads through a
> thousand years; whisper to us the secret of this charmed life of
> England that we in our time may know how to hold it fast.'

The answer which they whispered to Powell was, apparently, 'the unlimited supremacy of Crown in Parliament', an institution which he emphasized was thoroughly English despite 'all the leeks and thistles and shamrocks ... grafted upon it'.[80] However, simply stripping away imperial sentiment from English national identity by making a connection with racial ancestors and the institutions they had bequeathed would not turn the clock back, because the Empire had pitched up on England's doorstep. Powell argued that for the nation to be reborn, its homogeneity had to be restored by halting coloured immigration and repatriating as many people as could be induced to go. In short, what Powell did was to take the puckered thumb of imperialism out of the English mouth. But instead of encouraging the child to talk properly he replaced the thumb with a badly soiled dummy.

Powell had pressed his party to take action since 1956. But it was his 'Rivers of Blood' speech in April 1968 that made immigration one of the central issues in British politics. The speech is now a familiar one, but it has to be quoted again to remind us of the ferocity with which Powell, in his words, showed his 'cloven hoof' and invited the nation to do the same. He began: 'Those whom the gods wish to destroy, they first make mad. We must be mad, literally mad, as a nation to be permitting the annual inflow of some 50,000 dependants ... It is like watching a nation busily engaged in heaping up its own funeral pyre.' The thrust of his argument was that the country was in danger not only from a continuing 'invasion' but from those already in the country who constituted an enemy within. He acknowledged that some coloured people had made an effort to integrate but most, he argued, had not. Citing a letter received from a constituent, he portrayed blacks as inherently anti-social: 'She is becoming afraid to go out. Windows are broken. She finds excreta pushed through her letterbox. When she goes to the shops, she is followed by children, charming, wide-grinning piccaninnies'. Powell also attacked the new state-sponsored race relations organizations as the means by which immigrants were pursuing 'actual domination'. He predicted, 'In this country in fifteen or twenty years' time the black man will have the whip hand over the white man.' And he predicted all-out race war, with the famous words, 'As I look ahead, I am filled with much foreboding. Like the Roman, I seem to see "the River Tiber foaming with much blood".'

These views were no different to those expressed by many respected figures in Whitehall and Parliament since the 1940s. What

made Powell's speech political dynamite was that he accused Britain's
political elite of betraying the English people by not acting decisively:

> For reasons which they could not comprehend, and in pursuance
> of a decision by default on which they were not consulted, [the
> English] found themselves made strangers in their own country . . .
> the sense of being a persecuted minority which is growing among
> ordinary English people in the areas of the country which are
> affected is something that those without direct experience can
> hardly imagine.[81]

The rhetoric of victimhood appealed directly to the white working
classes whose racism was to some extent the product of economic
deprivation. By scapegoating black immigrants for what were the
failures of capitalism Powell hoped to remobilize the English working
classes to the Tory cause in a way that Heath's pompous manageri-
alism never could.

He was swiftly condemned. Speaking at a May Day rally at
Birmingham Town Hall in Powell's heartland, the Prime Minister,
Harold Wilson, reminded Britons of the contribution ethnic minorities had made to national life. He also commended the Race Relations Bill as a 'political breathalyser' into which the country must
now breathe in order to demonstrate its faith 'in a society of
tolerance, of kindliness, and of fair play, qualities for which the
British people are admired throughout the world'.[82] Heath did not
hesitate to sack Powell, partly because he posed a threat to his
leadership of the Conservative Party but also because he was genuinely disgusted at what he had said. The press was against Powell
too, *The Times* calling his speech a 'disgraceful', 'racialist' outburst.[83]

Rivulets if not rivers of blood flowed as a direct result of the
speech. Verbal and physical attacks on ethnic minorities increased in
the days and months after it. Paul Boateng, one of the first black
Britons to enter Parliament, recalled, 'I was one of those wide-eyed
grinning piccaninnies that he saw fit to quote in a letter and that was
hurtful of course. For the first time in the country of my birth and
the country of which I'm proud to say I belong, I was shouted at and
spat at and abused in the street for the first time ever, the day after
that.'[84] Asian Britons suffered an intensification of 'Paki-bashing',
with particularly serious outbreaks in Luton, Leicester and Bradford.
The Beatles, who like much of Western youth in the 1960s were
influenced by Asian music and philosophy, responded by recording
'Get Back'. At first entitled 'Commonwealth Song', its central lyric

was 'Don't dig no Pakistani taking all the people's jobs/Get back to where you once belonged.' The situation was so volatile that the group changed the lyrics, fearing that the song might be misconstrued and used by racists to make their point. (The revised version dealt instead with transsexuals.)[85]

On St George's Day 1968, as the Race Relations Bill was due to be discussed in Parliament, 1,000 real-life Alf Garnetts walked out of London's docks and marched to Westminster in support of Powell. By early May, he had personally received 40,000 letters, only 800 of which disagreed with him. Conservative Party Headquarters received nearly 100,000, approximately 90 per cent of which supported him. This one was typical:

> We don't want them here, we don't like them, their attitude is insolent and before long they will be taking over more and more. I say send the lot packing and let this country get back to some decent standards. We had no drug addiction problem till they came. And their veneer of civilisation is thinner than a sheet of plastic. We are loaded down with a bunch of nasty primitives and are fast becoming the laughing stock of the world.[86]

In a poll of Conservative constituency associations taken a year later, 327 out of 412 wanted all black immigration stopped immediately. The left was horrified. Richard Crossman wrote in his diary that Powell 'has successfully appealed to the mass of the people for the first time since Oswald Mosley, and in doing so he's stirred up the nearest thing to a mass movement since the 1930s . . . He isn't a fascist but a fanatic, a bizarre conservative extremist with violent views on this subject. However he has changed the whole shape of politics overnight . . . It has been the real Labour core, the illiterate industrial proletariat, who have turned up in strength and revolted against the literate.'[87] As a consequence of both popular and elite prejudice, the race card was played by British governments for the rest of the century, resulting in successive Acts of Parliament which tightened the restrictions on immigration. Discussing one such Act in 1971, the Cabinet even considered limiting the voting rights of black Britons.

Yet confrontation is not what really characterized this period. There was actually a toning down of racist rhetoric and, to a lesser extent, an amelioration of discriminatory behaviour. This had little to do with the sanctions imposed by race relations legislation: rather it sprang from a more informal, collective attempt by the British to maintain the idea that they were a liberal people, without actually changing their racial definition of Britishness. In other words, they learnt to couch their views in more egalitarian terms and to moderate their behaviour accordingly. The main strategy employed was to state that black immigrants were merely different – or, to give the strategy its social scientific term, ethnocentrism. Paul Gilroy has written, 'Contemporary British racism deals in cultural difference rather than crude biological hierarchy. It asserts not that blacks are inferior but that we are different, so different that our distinctive mode of being is at odds with residence in this country.'[88] A common expression of ethnocentrism was the cliché that 'Some of my best friends are black', numerous variations of which entered popular discourse in the 1960s as a means by which Britons claimed that their hostility to immigration was not motivated by racism. This cliché was dismissed by anti-racist campaigners as hypocrisy, one example of the failure of Britons to establish a moral link between the private and public spheres of their lives. 'SOME OF MY BEST FRIENDS ARE FOREIGN SCUM' read one banner in a demo of the time.

Hypocrisy does not explain it; ideological schizophrenia does. Ethnocentrism was the expression of people bewildered and afraid of black immigration but who also knew that discrimination was wrong and that it contradicted the democratic principles of Britishness. It is for this reason that the Gallup Poll taken at the end of April 1968 showed 74 per cent agreeing with Powell and a comparable figure – 65 per cent – believing that Wilson's anti-discrimination legislation was right and proper. It also explains why historian Arthur Bryant could, in all sincerity, write an article in the *Illustrated London News* called 'This Sunburnt Face'. It supported repatriation yet insisted, 'What really appeals to [immigrants] is our libertarian form of life and rule ... with a touching and pathetic enthusiasm they clamour to be let in and to count themselves and their progeny among the heirs of Hampden, Russell and Sydney.'[89] Academic and official surveys repeatedly showed that at least two-thirds of the population were, by any rational criteria, racist. One, carried out for Gallup in 1964, showed that only 5 per cent would be pleased to have a black person as a colleague, neighbour, friend or relative.[90] Yet most did not believe themselves to be prejudiced in any way. A report by the Race Relations Board in 1969 concluded that seven out of ten Britons described themselves as tolerant (they singled out the pub as the main arena of harmony). The *Daily Mirror* remarked:

There is little cause for self-righteous congratulation about this verdict ... the immigrant population – especially the second generation immigrants – don't want simply to be tolerated. They want to be accepted ... they are NOT economic units. They are human beings. They are citizens of this country here to build a new life for themselves and their families. It is as fellow citizens and fellow human beings that they are entitled to be accepted. And Britain must show the way in the decisive years ahead.[91]

Ethnocentrism sprang from an historic contradiction within the nation's identity which we touched on in earlier chapters. Since the eighteenth century, British liberal thought had accommodated the Empire by developing the idea that its main purpose was to civilize rather than to exploit the world. Thus did the British define themselves against other European colonial powers. The reason why whiteness remained a criterion of British national identity for so long was not because the British clung on to dreams of world domination, it was because they failed to address the ideological legacy of empire, namely a schizophrenic adherence to both racism and liberalism. Black immigration challenged that contradiction but could not easily overcome it because in the twentieth century liberalism had become the central tenet of Britishness. From the 1960s onwards, Britons were repeatedly confronted with evidence that proved beyond doubt that the tolerance they took such pride in had been tested and found badly wanting. More often than not their reaction was a defensive denial of any wrongdoing and a passionate restatement of national traditions. To understand that reaction, one has to appreciate that for the indigenous population to admit intolerance of black Britons meant that they had to unpick the entire fabric of their national identity. It was an unpalatable task that required a depth of honesty few Britons were yet capable of.

Race also exacerbated the national divide between England and the rest of the UK. Opponents of immigration often looked enviously at the relatively homogeneous societies of Scotland, Wales and Northern Ireland. For example, Sir Cyril Osborne told the House of Commons in 1968: 'The Scots are a better educated, a prouder and more independent people than the English. It is high time that we learned to do for ourselves what the Scots do for themselves and not rely on immigrant labour ... This is a white man's country and I want it to remain so.'[92] But England's partners did not reciprocate this admiration. Increasingly, they saw and condemned racism as an English trait. This was partly because Enoch Powell was that rare thing: a self-confessed English nationalist. But it was also because the Scots and the Welsh came to view themselves as a more tolerant people. This was a by-product of the nationalist attempt to develop a post-imperial identity based on the idea that their former partner in conquest had in fact been their imperial oppressor all along. Nationalists did not make common cause with black and Asian Britons. But they did favourably contrast their race relations with those of England's in order to demonstrate the superiority of their national cultures.

Asian migration presented Scotland with its first significant coloured population. Their numbers rose from approximately 600 in 1950 to around 45,000 in 1990, making up 85 per cent of Scotland's total coloured population. This migration was attributable partly to the fact that the Scots had played a major role in governing India, not least establishing the medical schools from which many NHS doctors were recruited. But many also chose Scotland to avoid racism in England, happy to ignore the fact that the standard of living was lower there. This included many who had originally settled in England. A little-known effect of the Notting Hill race riots is that they prompted thousands of black Britons to move north. From 1960 to 1990, internal migration from England accounted for 40 per cent of Scotland's Asian and Afro-Caribbean population. Bashir Man, one of the country's Asian leaders, wrote: 'Scottish people in general are more tolerant and accommodating than their English cousins.' The reason, he claimed, was that they sympathize with underdogs because 'they themselves have been underdogs to the English for a long time'.[93]

Claims that the English were intrinsically more racist than the Scots or Welsh should be treated with caution. There is no evidence that ethnic minorities fared substantially worse in England because of a difference in the national identity of the three countries. Certainly, neither Scotland nor Wales produced the organized political movements which England did – support for the National Front was concentrated in the south – but this was mostly due to the fact that Scottish and Welsh tolerance was never put to the test. Ethnic minorities never accounted for more than 1 per cent of their population compared to around 15 per cent of England's, and they were more evenly spread around, instead of being concentrated in a few urban conurbations. They therefore presented less of a challenge to established notions of what constituted Scottishness and Welshness.

But whatever the difference between perception and reality, black immigration unwittingly drove a wedge between the British nations. Whether people congratulated the Scots, Welsh and Irish on remaining predominantly white or whether they congratulated them for being more tolerant of blacks than the English, the idea of Britishness as a common culture of whiteness took a knock. Because of the disproportionate settlement of ethnic minorities in the south, racial homogeneity was no longer something which bound the four nations of the UK together. Like it or not, England was different.

6. We're more popular than Jesus now

In 1963, W. H. Auden observed, 'I have the suspicion that the English man-in-the-street still nourishes, though probably unconsciously, strong anti-popery feelings. He may not admit it but, in his heart of hearts, he thinks that Roman Catholics are idolaters, immoral and physically dirty, that only a Protestant can be respectable.'[94] A decade later that could not be said with the same assurance. If, broadly speaking, the 1950s saw the death throes of empire as a mainstay of British national identity, then the 1960s marked the end of Protestantism's role in uniting the Scots, Welsh and English. The decline, already apparent during the Second World War but temporarily halted in the 1950s, accelerated rapidly in the 1960s and did not recover thereafter.

In 1960 Geoffrey Fisher stood down after fifteen years as Archbishop of Canterbury, remarking that he had left the Church 'in good heart'. On 27 June 1961 his successor, Michael Ramsey, was enthroned as the hundredth Archbishop of Canterbury since St Augustine in 601. He began his term of office with less optimism than Fisher, warning, 'It may be the will of God that our Church should have its heart broken'.[95] Whether or not it was God's intention, Ramsey's prediction came to pass. The total active membership of British Protestant Churches fell from approximately 8 million in 1945 to approximately 4 million in 1995. Between 1960 and 1970 it fell by a staggering 19 per cent, the biggest drop in any single decade. Participation in religious rites of passage also fell sharply. The number of baptisms declined from two-thirds of the population to less than a third; confirmations also fell by half. Another striking change was the British way of death. The Romano-British practice of burning the dead was replaced by burial in the third century AD, mainly as a result of the Christian Church's belief in the sanctity of the body. Cremation was only legalized again in 1885 and it remained unpopular until the second half of the twentieth century. The Church of England officially accepted the practice in 1944 and, following the Cremation Act of 1952, local authorities invested heavily in crematoria in order to save valuable land space. By 1967, 50 per cent of the population were choosing to be cremated and by 1998 the figure had risen to 72 per cent (up from only 4 per cent in 1939). Most funeral services were still conducted by the clergy. But because crematoria were run by local authorities or private companies and were denominationally neutral, the religious element of British death rites became less pronounced. Moreover, because crematoria covered wide areas – sometimes encompassing hundreds of thousands of people – the intimate connection between Britons and their parish of origin was greatly diminished. The public acceptance of a custom once seen as barbarically heathen reflected the fact that Britain had become a more secular and more mobile society. The public was well aware of the fact. In 1963, 64 per cent of the population believed that the influence of religion on British life was declining.[96]

Why were Protestant hearts broken? Primarily because they felt the full effects of affluence, moral relativism and medical advances, all of which combined to make the lives of ordinary Britons more enjoyable and their fear of death less intense. As a consequence, their need for spiritual comfort diminished. From 1945 to 1960 the Churches had benefited from the fear of social change. The Protestant faith had provided an ideological framework for opposition to everything from sexual freedom to black and Asian immigration. Thereafter, the reformation of British life became so widespread and so deep-rooted that it had the opposite effect, overwhelming the religious impulse of millions – particularly the young, who increasingly saw Christianity as the expression of an outdated social system.

The haemorrhaging of Church membership among the young was quickened by the decline of religious instruction in the UK. In 1947, the BBC ended the strict limits on air time given to atheists, agnostics, Catholics and other religious minorities which Reith had established in 1928 to protect the established faith. During the 1950s, direct attacks on Protestantism were still rare due to the policing of schedules by the corporation's powerful Central Religious Advisory Committee (CRAC) – a pan-Protestant front consisting of broadcasters and clergy from the main denominations. But when Reithians lost control of the BBC during the 1960s, religious programming became less didactic, more discursive and more concerned with general moral principles than the claims of any particular Church. An even more important development in this respect was the contraction of Protestant schooling.

The Butler Education Act of 1944 was as responsible for the decline of British Protestantism as it was for the rise of a meritocracy. Rab Butler had offered the Churches a choice: give up their schools to the state or retain their independence but pay for 50 per cent of running costs. Scottish, Welsh and English divines decided that they could not afford the latter. The result was stark, especially in England. In 1940 there were 9,000 Church schools; by 1970 only 2,000 still existed. Moreover, the religious instruction in most state schools was negligible because teachers became as reluctant to impart Protestantism to children as they were reluctant to teach them about the Empire. Later in life, Butler regretted the trust he had placed in the teaching profession, saying that their irreligious attitudes had begun 'to imperil the Christian basis of our society'. It is a view endorsed by Church historians; Adrian Hastings writes: 'The quickly advancing secular consensus of middle England in the Sixties owed a great deal to the educational choices made in the 1940s.'[97]

The Church of England also contributed to that consensus by pursuing liberal theology and politics. In 1963 the Bishop of Woolwich, John Robinson, published *Honest to God*. UK sales totalled 300,000 copies, making it the biggest selling British religious book since William Temple's *Christianity and Social Order* twenty years earlier. Robinson had already caused a stir by appearing as a defence witness in the *Lady Chatterley* trial, arguing that sex was a sacred act. *Honest to God* went further. It claimed that God was love and not a bearded gentleman in the sky, still less a bearded British gentleman. Michael Ramsey permitted such unorthodox views and himself caused uproar by saying 'I expect to see atheists in heaven'. He was a gentle man but with radical opinions firmly held: theologically a moderate Anglo-Catholic; politically a left/liberal. Geoffrey Fisher had been Ramsey's headmaster at Repton in the 1920s and opposed the succession of his former pupil on the grounds that he was a troublemaker. When told of this, the Prime Minister said

'[Fisher's] not going to be *my* headmaster' and went ahead. Like Churchill's absent-minded appointment of Temple in 1942, Macmillan's bloody-mindedness had ironic consequences. For, if it can be said that Temple blessed the welfare state, then Ramsey blessed the permissive society (when he died in 1987 he was buried, at his own request, next to Temple).

Ramsey and his bishops gave valuable and often vital support to Labour's reforming legislation on divorce, abortion, homosexuality and capital punishment as it passed through the House of Lords. While giving a lead on the ideal way of life which he thought Britons should lead, Ramsey was a genuinely tolerant man who understood why they could not always do so. He once read a letter from a member of the public and calmly put it to one side with a smile, telling his secretary, 'I don't think that is of *much* value as it begins "You lying bastard"'.[98] He also softened the Church's approach to the youth question, making statements like this one in the *Daily Mirror* in 1963: "what I like most about modern youth is its uninhibited frankness. You know exactly where you are with them".[99] It was a refreshing contrast to Flog 'em Fisher's flat condemnation of teenage mores. Attitudes to women also changed. In 1975, the Synod agreed that it had no fundamental objections to women priests and eventually, on 11 November 1992, it voted to ordain them. The Church's change of direction reflected the political outlook of its clergy. By the late 1960s, a majority of Anglican vicars voted Liberal or Labour, and by 1992, 76 per cent of the General Synod's House of Clergy were so inclined. The largest Church in the UK was no longer 'the Tory Party at prayer'.

Many practising Anglicans were horrified by the liberalization of the Church of England and this contributed to the decline of Church membership. The more conservative Protestant denominations took some of the malcontents. They were not numerous enough to start a Nonconformist revival but they found a potent figurehead in Mary Whitehouse. Born to Scottish parents in 1910, Whitehouse was a Nonconformist schoolteacher in Shropshire who saw the media revolution as the main source of Britain's degradation. In January 1964 she launched the Clean-Up TV Campaign (later the National Viewers and Listeners Association) at a rally in Birmingham, calling on the 'women of Britain' to 'restore God to the heart of our national life'. 'Men, women and children', she said, 'listen and view at the risk of serious damage to their morals, their patriotism, their discipline and their family life'.[100] Within a few months, 365,000 people signed her Manifesto.

The Catholic Church benefited most from the dissatisfaction with modern Anglicanism. A reform programme begun by the Second Vatican Council in 1962 dragged Roman Catholicism out of the seventeenth century. Rome did not quite make it into the twentieth, keeping its opposition to abortion, contraception and divorce and, therefore, its conservative appeal. But enough reforms took place to reinvigorate the Church and so make the most of that appeal. The biggest change was that priests were allowed to conduct services in the vernacular rather than Latin, as a result of which the Catholic Church appeared more democratic, less foreign and therefore more appealing to wavering Protestants. Between 1946 and 1970, the UK's Catholic population rose by 61 per cent to 4.97 million, of which 2.71 million were Church members. The largest rise occurred during the 1960s. Irish immigration was partly responsible of course (a desire to escape the Troubles compounding the traditional desire to escape poverty). But native Protestant converts formed a sizeable part of the figure. Annual conversions were just over 14,000 in 1961 and continued steadily thereafter. The strength of Catholic education was a key factor in the revival. While Protestant Churches naively withdrew from the classroom, their historic adversary did the opposite, assisted by a 1967 Act of Parliament which provided grants of 80 per cent of running costs. Already by that year, 9.3 per cent of children were in state-assisted Catholic schools, almost as many as the 11.8 per cent in Anglican ones (compared to 5.4 per cent and 40.2 per cent in 1900). Changes were also afoot in the upper echelons of British public life. By the late 1960s, the Director-General of the BBC, the editor of *The Times* and the General Secretary of the TUC were all Catholics, a situation that would not have been countenanced a few years earlier. By 1980, the unthinkable had happened: there were more active Catholics in England than Anglicans. But these figures can be deceptive and here we must pause to qualify the decline of British Protestantism.

In the UK as a whole, Catholics were still outnumbered by two to one and remained so for the rest of the century. Moreover, anti-Catholic prejudice did not disappear until the 1980s. Two of Mary Whitehouse's allies were the Catholic activists Lord Longford and Malcolm Muggeridge. But they were exceptions which proved the rule that the battle for Britain's soul was still fought along denominational lines. In 1958 the lay leader of British Catholics, the Duke of Norfolk, wrote to the Prime Minister suggesting the appointment of a Papal Nuncio to the UK and a British Ambassador to the Vatican. Norfolk argued that Britons appreciated 'the role which the Vatican plays . . . in checking the spread of atheistic communism.'[101] Apparently not. The Cabinet rejected the proposal on the grounds that 'it might relight the flames of religious controversy' and 'would offend some Protestants in the United Kingdom. In Ulster, it might have a serious political effect for a time.'[102] A further attempt was made in 1965, but Michael Ramsey objected, paying a visit to Downing Street to make his views clear. Like most postwar archbishops, he was a keen ecumenicist in principle, but he saw the Catholic Church as reactionary on social issues and he was determined not to compromise the liberalization of British society in pursuit of theological rapprochement. When Harold Wilson visited Rome in 1965, he reassured the Pope that 'religious intolerance in Britain' had greatly diminished. Back home, the Cabinet decided that the establishment of diplomatic relations with the Vatican would arouse serious opposition and it dropped the plan.[103]

Other incidents prove the point. Liverpool was a paradox. Though it was the second city of the cultural revolution, it was also a city riven with religious sectarianism. When a new Catholic cathedral was built there in 1966 (nicknamed 'Paddy's wigwam' by local Protestants after its striking modern design) the Archbishop of Canterbury and the Moderator of the General Assembly of the Church of Scotland advised the Queen not to attend the opening. Roy Jenkins told the Prime Minister, 'there remains a good deal of antagonism to the Roman Catholic church, particularly in Liverpool.' The Queen's presence would represent a 'significant change of policy' and 'might produce a reaction which would do great harm to the cause of unity'.[104] Tentative plans for the Pope to make a historic visit to Britain in 1967 also came unstuck. Cardinal Heenan told the *Daily Mirror*, 'who knows – he might be a bigger attraction than the Beatles'.[105] Liverpool City Councillors responded with this statement:

> We, Citizens of Liverpool, being loyal Protestant subjects of her Majesty, and believing that the preservation of the Protestant Reformed faith in our beloved land is essential to the preservation of truth and liberty throughout the world, protest most earnestly against permission being given to the Pope to visit the land of Great Britain, believing that such a visit would imperil our Protestant national heritage . . . bringing nearer the day when our

national liberties and Protestant faith would be brought under the sway of the Bishop of Rome with his false and blasphemous claim to be the supreme arbiter of conscience, faith and morals throughout the world.[106]

The proposal was given careful consideration by ministers, who consulted Britain's police chiefs. The Met's Chief Constable promised that the Pope would get a warm welcome in the capital. But his counterpart in Liverpool warned: 'we should expect deployment of police resources on a considerable scale . . . We would expect "anti-Pope" demonstrations by Liverpool Orange Lodges who would no doubt be reinforced from Glasgow and Belfast'.[107] Militants were not the only headache. The Cabinet Secretary, Sir Burke Trend, felt bound to remind the Prime Minister that the Queen 'as Head of the Established Church is technically a heretic in the Pope's eyes'.[108] She would therefore have to receive him as a head of state somewhere like Windsor in a private, non-religious setting. In the end, both the government and the Vatican decided that it would be too embarrassing for everyone. The plan was dropped, and it was not until 1982 that a pope first set foot in Britain.

In short, the sea of Protestant faith was receding fast but it left a tidemark which the British were reluctant to clean up. Anglicanism, Scottish Presbyterianism and the Welsh Free Churches had what sociologists call a huge 'latent membership' of approximately 30 million people who retained a patriotic loyalty to their national Churches even though they had ceased to worship with them. Vicars and ministers continued to be seen as the most trusted members of British society. In England, Michael Ramsey was extremely popular among the public, who credited him with building a less censorious faith that was more in touch with modern Britain.[109] Moreover, this latent membership was predominantly theistic rather than agnostic. Faith survived the decline of Church attendance. A study carried out by Mass Observation in 1948 found that approximately three-quarters of Britons thought God existed, and only one in twenty were atheists. This figure held up across class and age groups and did not change significantly over the next fifty years. According to a European-wide study carried out in 1990, 71 per cent of Britons still believed in God (compared to a European average of 72 per cent).

It is also worth noting that there was little support for Disestablishment of the Scottish and English Churches, even during a period when the term 'Establishment' was used pejoratively to describe the

entrenched power of an elite to which the Church belonged. The
reason lay in attitudes to monarchy and race. We have seen that
support for the Commonwealth during the debates on Europe in the
early 1960s was based on the belief that because the Queen was
Head of the Commonwealth, going into Europe would undermine
her position. The same perceptions were true of religion. If they
thought about it (which admittedly was not often) most Britons
thought that Disestablishment would undermine the Queen's position
as the nation's figurehead. They also saw their Churches as bastions
of an immutable national culture. Whether or not they actually went
to church, describing Britain as a Christian country was one of the
ways in which opponents of immigration presented their racism in
cultural rather than biological terms. Anti-racists, on the other hand,
celebrated the fact that Britain had become a multi-faith society.

Both sides did (and still do) profoundly misjudge the relationship
between religion and multiculturalism. Black immigrants did not
undermine British Christianity. They reinvigorated it. Most were not
only Christians when they arrived. They were Protestants, and
Anglican to boot – living testaments to the success of Victorian
missionaries, as well as to the bravery of indigenous priests who had
maintained Christianity in Africa since the sixth century. Muslims,
Sikhs, Jews, Hindus and other non-Trinitarian religions made up
only 7 per cent of the UK population by the end of the century,
compared to 64 per cent who were Christians. The Afro-Caribbean
community was actually much more religious than indigenous Britons. This was a reflection of the societies from which its members
came (in the West Indies and Africa, 70 per cent of the population
still attended church in the 1960s). Dilip Hiro has observed: 'to their
utter bewilderment and confusion, they found the British, the very
people who brought Christianity to the West Indies, mostly indifferent to religion.'[110] White congregations did not generally welcome
their new brethren. Church leaders took an active stand against
racism, calling for the state to give a lead on the issue and regularly
turning up at Downing Street to prod the consciences of Prime
Ministers. But at parish level it was a different story. Watching a
white Christian move to another pew on one's arrival was a common
experience for black immigrants. This most painful of rejections
drove over 50 per cent of them to evangelical Nonconformist
Churches like the Seventh Day Adventists, where they were more
welcome. Some set up their own places of worship, the largest
network of which was the Pentecostal Church. By the end of the

1960s it had established itself as the only major black British institution that was not state-sponsored. Afro-Caribbean Protestantism therefore not only endured, it thrived, even though it did so partly because it offered black communities cultural solidarity and spiritual comfort in the face of white hostility.

The real impact of Protestant decline on British national identity is not to be found in the rise of Catholicism and non-Trinitarian faiths. It is to be found in the fact that Protestantism declined faster in England than elsewhere in the UK. Active Church membership in England peaked in 1927 but not until 1956 elsewhere. In 1975, 37.8 per cent of the Scottish population and 23.3 per cent of the Welsh population were Church members, compared to 14.3 per cent in England. In 1990, the disparity between Wales and England had narrowed slightly, with 16.5 per cent for the former and 11.1 per cent for the latter; but the numbers for Scotland remained three times as high as south of the border, with 30.1 per cent of Scots still being practising Christians. There were two reasons for this. First, the Presbyterian Churches of Scotland and Wales were a much greater focus of national identity than Anglicanism was in England. As discontent with the Union grew, the Churches of the two disputatious nations maintained support by presenting themselves as exemplars of the unique cultures of Scotland and Wales. Their clergy were also heavily involved in devolution campaigns and they formed a significant proportion of nationalist party membership. Second, the faster rate of economic growth in England made the spread of secular individualism more extensive there. This resulted in more of the tight-knit communities over which the church once presided breaking up, as people moved into suburbs and to other areas of the country altogether. Southern affluence also meant that the English felt themselves to be less in need of religious faith and of the practical support which the Church gave to the needy.

The difference was apparent in several ways. In cinema and TV, the Anglican Church was the object of affectionate ridicule. Vicars were portrayed as a well-meaning but comically ineffectual individuals who were out of touch with the modern world. The Boulting Brothers' film *Heavens Above!* (1963) starring Peter Sellers, the BBC sitcom *All Gas and Gaiters* (1967–71) starring Derek Nimmo, and the Reverend Timothy Farthing in *Dad's Army* are all examples of this tendency. In Scottish and Welsh drama, ministers were still shown to be the linchpin of the communities they served. The difference between the three countries primarily manifested itself in attitudes to the cultural revolution. The Scots' strong opposition to the legalization of homosexuality has already been discussed. In Wales, battle was met over Sunday licensing laws.

More than any other country in Britain, Welsh Protestantism had forged a separate national identity as much as it had maintained a bond with the rest of the UK. By the late nineteenth century, Nonconformism was the principality's dominant faith, yet the Established Church of Wales remained Anglican. The campaign for Disestablishment, begun in 1886 and finally victorious in 1920, was a campaign for national self-determination which mobilized almost every section of Welsh society. Welsh Protestantism was underpinned by Sabbatarianism. Stronger in the principality than elsewhere in Britain, it had been enshrined in another victory for self-determination, the 1881 Sunday Closing Act. In the late 1950s pressure mounted to abolish the law, particularly with regard to pubs. The Licensing Act of 1960 allowed each area of Wales to decide its own fate with a vote (this was designed to prevent the less populous rural areas of the north and west, where Sabbatarianism remained strongest, from being outvoted by the south). Opponents of change sent hundreds of letters to the government, claiming that Sunday opening would not only encourage immorality but that it would destroy the Welsh way of life. 'We resent any interference with the Act of 1881 which has recognised our national entity and safeguarded our spiritual heritage', wrote the United Churches of Clwyd.[111] Wrexham Baptists told the Prime Minister 'we are still a nation and we have our own way of life'.[112]

The Sunday Opening Council, led for obvious reasons by the breweries but supported by the trade unions, collected thousands of signatures saying otherwise; and it disputed the idea that Welshness was in peril, arguing that it had already changed.

> We know by our intimate contact with the people of Wales that they are greatly annoyed by the outcry of the teetotal faction . . . [Teetotallers] will not appreciate the change in the moral, social and fiscal influence which has altered the way of life and indeed the attitude of the people. The continuous reference by this minority to the Welsh way of life is a ludicrous red herring . . . The local licensee is in many cases a Father Confessor and he knows that the Welsh way of life lies in the heart, conscience and culture of the individual soul . . . restrictions on personal freedom are out of touch with the independent character of the Welshman.[113]

The breweries were right. In 1961, ten out of seventeen areas voted to end the ban. George Thomas, teetotaller, Cardiff MP and later Secretary of State for Wales, accepted defeat saying, 'The chapels have fought a good fight and they have reason to be proud.'[114] The good fight was taken up once more in 1968 when another vote was taken, but this time the figure in favour of opening rose to thirteen. By 1989 further votes on drinking whittled down opposition to one area, Dwyfor, which made up only 1 per cent of the population. All of which prompted the North Wales Free Church Council to declare: 'Wales's greatest tragedy is that she is so far from God and so near England'.[115] The rise of Welsh national consciousness in this period was therefore based as much on what the Welsh left behind of their historic culture as it was on what they rediscovered. Preachers might argue that Wales had lost its guiding star. But in the long run, the emptying of chapels and the filling of pubs made Welshness more attractive. It encouraged more permissive generations to embrace other aspects of Welsh culture, and thus was the nationalist momentum maintained.

But where British religiosity as a whole is concerned, the significance of the battle to preserve the traditional Welsh Sunday is that it showed England to be a more secular country. English Sunday observance had begun to decline in the early 1950s. What was a long-running and bitter dispute in the principality barely registered east of Cardiff and Wrexham and when it did it was the subject of perplexed mirth. England's greater indifference to the faith made it difficult for the Scots and Welsh to feel a confessional bond with them. The uneven pattern of secularization across the UK therefore exacerbated the tensions caused by the overall decline of Protestantism. Neither the liberal drift of the Church of England nor the reactionary campaigns of mavericks like Mary Whitehouse were able to halt that decline. Britons searching for a less dogmatic religion found succour in eastern religions like Buddhism and a host of cults ranging from Scientology to rearranging furniture. Those who wanted moral certainty usually joined the Catholic Church; and those who couldn't decide what they wanted worshipped the monarchy, sports teams, pop groups, the arts, horoscopes or the whole lot.

Of all those alternatives, sport was the most popular. As Peter Clarke says, 'in twentieth century Britain, organised mass sport filled some of the psychic space which was being vacated by organised mass Christianity'.[116] It was not an outcome which the cultural reformers of the century had foreseen when they set out to fill that space with a love of the arts. And they certainly did not foresee that soccer would be the most popular sport of all. Its quasi-religious role in British society was demonstrated when the Scots-born Liverpool manager Bill Shankly famously remarked, 'Some people think football is a matter of life and death. I can assure them it is much more serious than that.'[117] Shankly's rhetorical exaggeration conveyed an essential truth that most Britons recognized, and he was not accused of blasphemy as he might have been a generation earlier. At the end of the century, more people still went to church on Sunday than to football matches and the audience figures for *Songs of Praise* remained higher than those for *Match of the Day*. But football was a more popular source of patriotism than religion and this had serious consequences for British unity. Since the seventeenth century, the Scots and English had disagreed, often violently, about Protestant doctrine, but from the Civil War of the 1640s to the Bishops' Report of 1957, they had been united by an essentially common faith. In football, there was no underlying unity. In the end, you either supported Scotland or England.

Three other events which took place during the 1960s highlight the changes that British religiosity underwent in the late twentieth century. The first was John Lennon's remark that the Beatles were more popular than Jesus. The Beatle came from an Anglican background and as a child was a chorister in his local church. In March 1966, he gave an interview to Maureen Cleave of the *Evening Standard* in which he said, 'Christianity will go. It will vanish and shrink . . . I'm right and it will be proved right. We're more popular than Jesus now; I don't know which will go first, rock 'n' roll or Christianity.'[118] In the United States, his comment provoked outrage among America's huge Protestant fundamentalist population, leading to death threats and the public burning of Beatles records. Fifteen years later it cost him his life at the hands of an American lunatic seeking revenge on Jesus' behalf. In the meantime, he was forced to a make a public apology. He explained the more pluralistic religiosity of the 1960s in terms familiar to readers of John Robinson: 'I believe in God, but not as one thing, not as an old man in the sky. I believe that what people call god is something in all of us.'[119] In Britain most people accepted that he had made a rational and accurate observation about the extent to which pop culture had replaced traditional sources of faith among young Britons. Some Church leaders thought so too; one Anglican Bishop pointedly remarked, 'in the only popularity poll in Jesus' time, he came out second to Barrabas'.[120]

Second, in 1969, Pope Paul VI reformed the calendar of the Catholic Church. As a result, St George was placed on a list of 'doubtful saints' – those whose credentials owed more to myth than historical fact. 23 April was demoted from an obligatory holy day to an optional local festival. The English didn't take up the option. In fact, they didn't even notice what the Pope had done. Even during the 1940s, when the cult of St George was at a low ebb, such a decision would have provoked comment, both from the Church of England and from secular patriots. That it did not in 1969 was both a measure of England's muted nationality and the fact that religion now played little part in it.

Finally, we turn to Northern Ireland. Church membership in the province was consistently the highest in the UK: 82.3 per cent in 1975 and 67.7 per cent in 1990. When the Troubles broke out, most people saw it as a struggle between Protestant and Catholic – and hence the conflict of people from a bygone age. This reaction (of which more in Chapter 8) revealed how few people in Britain now defined themselves as Protestants and, as a consequence, how far apart Britain and Northern Ireland had drifted.

To sum up, then: the British were no longer consciously united by their faith. Like class, religion never disappeared. Just as embourgeoisement was often merely a different way of being working class, secularization was largely a process in which Britons found alternative ways of being religious. Because the head of state had a constitutional duty to uphold the Protestant faith *and* because most practising and latent Christians subscribed to it, Britain could still be unequivocally described in social terms as a Protestant nation. However, from the 1960s onwards Protestantism was no longer seen as one of the defining characteristics of the British. Opposition to papal visits or the building of mosques and temples was little more than the death throes of a national identity which had been diseased for half a century. Protestantism now had to compete with a variety of faiths, many of them well organized, well financed and growing in popularity. But the most important change was this: whatever people's religious faith, it was now a matter of the individual's conscience and rites of passage rather than a patriotic credo which defined and united the nation.

The sociologist Grace Davie has described the postwar religiosity of the nation perfectly. It was, she wrote, 'believing without belonging'. An academic survey carried out in Islington, London in 1965 (when it was still a predominantly working-class district) concluded that popular faith was essentially superstitious with little ideological coherence. The most telling response was the following:

> 'Do you believe in God?'
> 'Yes.'
> 'Do you believe in a God who can change the course of events on earth?'
> 'No, just the ordinary one.'[121]

The 'ordinary God' to which the respondent referred was the one who was present for the landmarks of human life – at baptisms, marriages and funerals. But He was not a God who could rally the nation in time of war; nor could He unite it with a common purpose in time of peace.

7. I fought the war for your sort

Some Britons regarded the cultural revolution as a travesty of the nation's struggle during the Second World War. This feeling was captured in *A Hard Day's Night*. When the Beatles enter a first-class train compartment, open the window and turn on their transistor radio, the City gent in the compartment indignantly tells them, 'I fought the war for your sort.' To which Ringo Starr replies, 'I bet you wish you hadn't.'[122] Many did wish they hadn't. Noël Coward regarded Beatlemania as 'a mass masturbation orgy' in which Britain was 'whirling more swiftly into extinction than we know'.[123] In September 1963 Coward attended the annual dinner for Battle of Britain veterans. Believing the veterans were now forgotten and despised, he was overwhelmed by sadness and anger, as his diary records at some length:

> The Battle of Britain was twenty-three years ago and the world has forgotten it. Those young men, so many of whom I knew, flew up into the air and died for us and all we believed in ... What did they die for? I suppose for themselves and what they believed was England. It *was* England then – just for a few brave months ...

The peace we are enduring is not worth their deaths. England has become a third-rate power, economically and morally. We are vulgarised by American values. America, which didn't even know war on its own ground, is now dictating our policies and patronising our values.

I came away from that gentle, touching, tatty little party with a heavy and sad heart. The England those boys died for has disappeared. Our history, except for stupid, squalid social scandals, is over . . . But oh, oh, oh! What was it I minded about twenty-three years ago? An ideal? An abstract patriotism? What? I wanted to stand up and shout 'Shut up! Stop it. What's the use of this calculated nostalgia? . . .'

We are now beset by the 'clever ones', all the cheap frightened people who can see nothing but defeat and who have no pride, no knowledge of the past, no reverence for our lovely heritage . . . Perhaps, just perhaps – someone will rise up and say, 'That isn't good enough.' There is still the basic English character to hold on to. But *is* there? I am old now . . . I despise the young, who see no quality in our great past and who spit, with phoney, left-wing disdain, on all that we, as a race, have contributed to the living world . . . I say a grateful goodbye to those foolish, gallant young men who made it possible for me to be alive today to write these sentimental words.[124]

Coward should not have been so hard on his younger compatriots: the Second World War remained a fulcrum of Britishness for them too.

However much the generations disagreed about *why* the war had been fought, few thought it had been a waste of time. Nor did people lose their respect for those who had fought. The generally accepted dichotomy between, on the one hand, the patriotism of the Second World War and the homogeneous national culture it celebrated and, on the other hand, the freewheeling, relativistic world of affluent permissiveness did not exist in the minds of most Britons. At the extremes of British society – Mary Whitehouse's Christian moralists and Richard Neville's hippy anarchists – there was open warfare. Most people inhabited an ideological world somewhere in between. Britishness remained a pluralistic national identity. It successfully incorporated pride in the martial spirit of the Second World War, pride in the institutions of social democracy *and* pride in the post-imperial culture of pop music, fashion and football.

The public response to Churchill's death in January 1965 demonstrated how central the Second World War still was to British national identity. The conventional view of the send-off of this reconstructed imperialist is that it was the reluctant funeral of British imperialism, an attempt to end the Empire with a bang instead of the whimper uttered in 1956. David Cannadine has written that Churchill's state funeral 'was not only the last rites of the great man himself, but was also self-consciously recognised as a requiem for Britain as a great power'.[125]

Certainly, there were moments when it recalled the fragile imperial pageantry of the Coronation: 'Rule, Britannia' was played by a military band, and leaders from 110 countries attended. The *Observer* said: 'This was the last time that London would be the capital of the world. This was an act of mourning for the Imperial past. This marked the final act in Britain's greatness. This was a great gesture of self-pity and after this the coldness of reality and the status of Scandinavia.'[126] The Minister of Housing, Richard Crossman, took a novel to read during the funeral service, but found himself moved by the 'ashen magnificence' of the occasion. Crossman compared it to Tennyson's 'Passing of [King] Arthur' and felt for 'poor Anthony Eden, literally ashen grey, looking as old as Clement Attlee' while shakily bearing the coffin as the trumpets sounded the Last Post. Looking round at the 3,000 people seated in their pews, Crossman concluded: 'Oh, what a faded, declining establishment surrounded me. Aged marshals, dreary ladies, decadent Marlboroughs and Churchills. It was a dying congregation gathered there and I am afraid the Labour Cabinet didn't look too distinguished either. It felt like the end of an epoch, possibly even the end of a nation.'[127] Richard Dimbleby, already dying of cancer, made his last great commentary on a state occasion, a fitting climax for a man who had ushered in the late imperial hopes of a New Elizabethan age in 1953.

The meaning of the event for most Britons was not imperial in any sense. What it did was to memorialize another narrative of national greatness: the Finest Hour over which Churchill had presided. His funeral richly symbolized the fact that Britishness was underpinned by the legends of the Second World War and the idea of Britain as a defiant, self-contained island rather than the motherland of an imperial diaspora. The event did not mark the transition from Empire to Europe so much as formalize the shift from one form of British nationalism to another, which, as we have seen, took place over thirty years before. 'Never will the name of Winston Churchill be separable from the "finest hour", from the pride and heroism of

1940', said *The Times*.[128] Henry Fairlie, who coined the term 'Establishment', wrote that it was 'a vision of England which people discovered in themselves, and for themselves in 1940, and then found voiced for them in one man'.[129] Dimbleby's lushest commentary recalled the 'People's War'. Watching people file past the catafalque in Westminster Hall, he said: 'I have stood for half an hour ... watching this silent flow of people, imagining who they were and where they came from, and realising that this is simply the nation, with its bare heads, and its scarves, and its plastic hoods, and its shopping bags, and its little puzzled children'.[130] The gun carriage bearing Churchill's body from Westminster to St Paul's Cathedral was escorted by RAF men and in pride of place in the procession behind it were twelve pilots, now group captains, who had fought in the Battle of Britain; the service was held in the building which symbolized the nation's defiance during the Blitz. There were also many young people in the crowd. John Gale saw 'a girl in strange, purple thigh-length boots; lots of boys with hair longer than the Beatles; there seemed more young than old'.[131] 'Not since the war has there been such a shared emotion,' concluded Laurie Lee.[132]

After the service, a boat took Churchill to Waterloo (he was the first Briton since Nelson to be borne along the river in death). From there, a train ('Battle of Britain' Class) took him to Bladon in Oxfordshire to be buried. All along the route, people turned out to watch it go past. Sir Leslie Rowan, Churchill's wartime Private Secretary, was on the train. He recalled:

> Two single figures whom I saw from the carriage window epitomised for me what Churchill really meant to ordinary people: first on the flat roof of a small house a man standing at attention in his RAF uniform, saluting; and then in a field, some hundred yards away from the track, a simple farmer stopping work and standing, head bowed and cap in hand.[133]

Churchill was the first non-royal personage to be given a state funeral since the Duke of Wellington in 1852. Richard Dimbleby concluded, 'There has not I think been in the whole history of our land a state funeral or an occasion which has touched the hearts of people quite as much as this one is doing today.'[134]

The 321,360 people who saw Churchill lie in state (16,000 more than for George VI); the many more who lined streets, riverbanks and railway lines; the shoppers and football crowds who observed two minutes' silence across Britain on that cold Saturday afternoon;

the 30 million who watched it all on TV; these were not all members of 'a faded declining establishment' which Crossman observed in St Paul's. These were ordinary Britons remembering the war, the national unity it fostered and the freedom it secured. It was, observed the *Daily Telegraph*, 'VE Day recollected in tranquillity'.[135] Moreover, there was a feeling (even in conservative quarters) that the event should not be an exercise in nostalgia. The *Sunday Times* said, 'He would not be an imperialist in a country without Empire . . . He would have wanted to create the new Europe . . . He would have wanted us to use the powerful emotional impetus of his funeral to look only a little back and chiefly forward.'[136] The *Sunday Telegraph* told its readers not to 'relapse into nostalgia'.[137] In the same newspaper, Colin MacInnes hoped: 'His death may finally liberate us from our obsession with "the war"; from our stupid hatred of Germany, our futile jealousy of America, our daft illusion that the Commonwealth is the Empire he admired and sought, impossibly, to sustain.'[138]

After Churchill's death, a serious attempt was made to liberate the British from their obsession in order to prepare them for a second application to join the EEC. This time, the Germans were courted because the government thought that they might pressure the French into rethinking their veto on British membership.

Four months after Churchill's funeral, in May 1965, the Queen visited Germany to mark the twentieth anniversary of the cessation of hostilities. It was the first visit by a British sovereign to Germany since George V attended the wedding of Princess Victoria of Prussia in 1913. The Germans had suggested a visit as far back as 1958 but the Cabinet had repeatedly turned down the idea, on the grounds that British public opinion was not ready. In terms of diplomatic relations with Germany, the visit was a success. The Queen was greeted by jubilant crowds in Berlin and elsewhere, although the Foreign Secretary, Michael Stewart, said that she found the rhythmic chanting of 'Elizabeth, Elizabeth' disturbing. 'I think she thought this was . . . too reminiscent of ritual Nazi shouting,' he suggested.[139] The visit made the French even more uneasy. In one speech, the Queen cited the help which the Prussian general Blücher had given the Duke of Wellington at Waterloo as an example of Anglo-German cooperation. The French press erupted, *Le Figaro* demanding that the celebration of all European battles should be abolished in the interests of European unity. Britain's Ambassador to France wired London, describing it as 'typical French touchiness'.[140] In Hanover, the Queen was taken to the state archives where she was shown the letter written in 1714 by Whig grandees to her ancestor George, Elector of Hanover inviting him to assume the British throne.[141]

Back home, neither the symbolism of eighteenth-century Anglo-German Protestant unity nor that of nineteenth-century military alliances struck a chord with the British public. Although the sight of the Queen being fêted in Berlin stirred some patriotic emotions, most Britons were uneasy about such an overt display of reconciliation only twenty years after the war. In August 1965 Michael Stewart concluded that the British were still anti-German. He told the Cabinet that this had to be urgently countered not only to assist Britain's Common Market application but also because there might be a revival of German nationalism if the Germans continued to feel rebuffed:

> Two world wars and the horrors of Nazism have left such a legacy of bitterness that we cannot be sure that Anglo-German reconciliation will last unless we for our part make it do so . . . We ought to develop Ministerial contacts, technological collaboration and cultural and youth exchanges . . . If we try to encourage the British people to think of contemporary Germany in a more friendly way, all the indications are that the Germans will be happy to come more than half way to meet us and that this, in turn, will be the best possible insurance against a return to atavism. They feel a particular need for reconciliation with the British people and this is an asset which we can turn to good account. Anglo-German friendship is all the more desirable because political stability in Germany is a tender growth . . . If we rebuff the Germans they are that much the more likely to conclude that striking independent nationalistic attitudes may be the best way of seeking their objectives.[142]

The Cabinet agreed. What it did not foresee was that less than a year later an event would take place which cemented, at least in the English mind, the popular view of Germany as an opponent rather than a partner; an event which would come to dominate English national identity in the late twentieth century: the World Cup Final of 30 July 1966.

8. They think it's all over

The 1966 World Cup was the largest sporting festival ever held in the British Isles, and it was one of the most intensely patriotic events of the postwar period. Many still see it as part of the Golden Age of the 1960s – all the ebullient, meritocratic optimism of the decade compressed into nineteen days of footballing action. The tournament was certainly a testament to how much the country had changed since the war.

Football had become a part of the cultural revolution. The minimum wage for players and the restrictions on them transferring to other clubs were abolished in 1961 after a long campaign by Jimmy Hill. With money in their pockets, they enjoyed lifestyles to match those in the pop and film worlds. By the mid-1960s, top footballers were worshipped by young Britons like the stars of vinyl and screen, none more so than Belfast-born George Best. This was also the period in which football songs, made up by fans and chanted in unison, replaced the spoken invective which had traditionally punctuated cheering. Welsh rugby fans had adapted hymns to support their teams in song since the nineteenth century and one – 'Guide Me, O Thou Great Redeemer' – became popular among soccer fans too, but most football songs were adapted from British pop music of the day. The lyrics which fans made up to tunes by the Beatles and the Kinks often lacked the wit of spoken invective, but traditional British folk music had the same shortcomings, so the sounds which arose from the terraces in the 1960s can, with some justice, claim to be its modern equivalent.

Alf Ramsey was not part of the cultural revolution. He was born in Dagenham, Essex in 1920, the son of a hay dealer. After a spell running a grocery shop, he became a successful player for club and country, winning thirty-two caps for England, the last in the 1953 defeat by Hungary. Ten years later, he replaced Walter Winterbottom as England manager. Ramsey believed in the stiff upper lip of the English gentleman and he had an urge to self-improvement which included taking elocution lessons. His strangulated vowels and emotional reserve were the subject of amusement in the press, but he was a deeply patriotic man. The FA believed that he could administer 'an injection of Celtic or Gaelic fervour' into the players, making them as conscious of their Englishness as the Scots were of their Scottishness. Ramsey obliged, telling the press, 'I have three loves in my life. My wife, my country and football',[143] and on another occasion, 'I believe in England and Englishmen, as well as English football'.[144] His patriotism drove him to revolutionize the management of the national team. The lessons of 1953 had been slowly learnt by the Football Association: scientific coaching techniques had been introduced, but the squad had continued to be picked by a panel of FA executives. Ramsey was the first England manager who picked the team himself, having insisted on it as a condition of his appointment. In time, this responsibility would help to make it an impossible job because the buck stopped on the bench and not in the boardroom. In the short term, it helped Ramsey to win the World Cup.

England's progression to the 1966 Final against West Germany was a tempestuous one. But the Final had an extra edge because of recent history. On the morning of 30 July, the *Daily Mail* was among several papers which explicitly portrayed it as a rerun of two world wars: 'If Germany beat us at Wembley this afternoon at our national sport, we can always point out to them that we have recently beaten them twice at theirs.'[145] Hugh McIlvanney of the *Observer* thought the event 'deserved to be chronicled by Rudyard Kipling'. The Germans, he reported, were 'bewildered and appalled by the militaristic nationalism of the English'[146] (though even he compared the German manager, Helmut Schön, to Rommel after one press conference). Werner Schneider, Germany's top football commentator, said that the English had yet to learn the lessons of nationalism: 'They want to fly flags and beat drums because they are winning at football . . . Tin soldiers I call them. It is said that the Germans are the most militaristic people in the world but it is not so. The British are. Even winning at football is treated like victory in a battle.'[147] Schneider's opposite number at the BBC, Kenneth Wolstenholme, had a more nuanced recollection of the event. 'There was a little animosity towards the Germans,' he wrote, 'but it was shown mainly by those people from countries which had been occupied during the war . . . In fact, some of the European commentators draped a Union Flag from the front of my position and added, "You mustn't lose this one." '[148] It is impossible to say how many Europeans out of the 40 million worldwide who watched the event shared that sentiment. But the story is a telling reminder that the English were not the only people with anti-German tendencies and that Continentals still

sentimentally regarded Britain as the country they could depend on
to check German power. Only the French press refused to wish
England good luck (perhaps reflecting the jealous suspicion of Britain
which had led to de Gaulle's veto, as well as the fact that France had
lost to Ramsey's men in the first round).

The techniques of the two finalists were seen to reflect their
national characters. Despite the new professionalism which had got
Ramsey's men to the final, the English emphasized that they had not
become Teutonic machines. Geoffrey Green of *The Times*, for
example, observed that the Germans were 'coldly efficient' while
Ramsey's men were 'burningly resolute'.[149] The players' determination to win was fuelled by an aggression borne out of recent history.
Jack Charlton recalled, 'For six years we had waged a war against
Germany; now we were preparing to do battle on the football field.
A strange thought just before a vital match. But that's how it was'.[150]
As they gathered in the centre circle to prepare for extra time, the
diminutive, gap-toothed midfielder Nobby Stiles said, 'We can fuck
them!' and with a few minutes to go, a Geoff Hurst shot bounced off
the crossbar onto the goal line.[151] The Germans surrounded the
Russian linesman, Tofik Bakhramov, as the Swiss referee walked
over to consult him. The goal was allowed, making it 3–2 to
England. Bakhramov, a former Red Army private from the Azerbai-
jan region, had fought the Wehrmacht on the Eastern Front. The
Germans claimed this influenced his decision but only he knows.

What we do know is that the crowd burst into a deafening chorus
of 'Rule, Britannia'; some people, famously, ran on to the pitch;
Hurst scored another goal to make it 4–2 and England were champions of the world. Jack Charlton fell to his knees with his face in
his hands trying to grasp the magnitude of the moment amidst the
pandemonium; his brother Bobby burst into tears. Ramsey sat
impassively on the bench. A decade later he observed: 'Since [1966]
Englishmen have become more emotional and if it happened today
I might jump for joy'.[152] The most symbolic moment came when
Bobby Moore stepped up to receive the Jules Rimet trophy. Like
Ramsey, the England captain was a Cockney. As Elizabeth II handed
him the trophy, she looked the East End in the eye as surely as her
mother had when touring bomb sites during the Blitz. Before accepting the trophy, Moore paused to wipe the sweat from his hands onto
his shirt – in order, he said later, to avoid soiling the Queen's white
gloves. That small, deferential gesture revealed that despite the social

changes which were sweeping Britain in the 1960s, there yet remained a popular reverence for the monarchy. One fan, Dave Hill, remembered 'the moment was seen as decisive evidence of a kind of Wembley Stadium of the national spirit, with chivalry and deference its twin towers, with the monarch as its blameless guardian and Moore representing the dauntless decency of the English working class.'[153] That night, the gardens, streets and squares of England's towns, cities and villages were filled with millions of jubilant people.

What was the significance of the 1966 World Cup? First, it showed the extent to which cultural achievements had come to act as a compensation for Britain's political decline since the war. Second, it showed how important the Second World War still was to national identity in Britain. There were also faint echoes of empire. In the run-up to the tournament, the FA had spoken publicly of 'England's Duty to the Past', urging the team to win the Cup in memory of the Victorian Britons who had invented the modern game.[154] A policeman on duty at Piccadilly Circus remarked, 'This is Mafeking night and VE night all rolled into one.'[155] For some, the victory was what the conquest of Everest had been for a previous generation; it seemed to prove that England was still a country with clout. The FA Secretary, Denis Follows, declared, 'Everyone now looks again to England to lead the world.'[156] The *Sun* said the trophy had come home to 'the Motherland of football'; and it compared the victory celebrations to Coronation Day (in this context, it was fitting that the FA Chairman was the same Lord Harewood who had instigated Britten's disastrous Coronation opera in 1953).[157]

But the most frequent comparison that observers made was with VE night. The victory mutually reinforced war and football in the English mind. By the early 1970s, Kenneth Wolstenholme's fourteen words as Geoff Hurst scored the final goal, 'Some people are on the pitch . . . They think it's all over . . . It is now!' had become a patriotic mantra for all seasons, as well known as Churchill's most famous speeches. The victory was a peacetime version of the Finest Hour. A battle of freedom against the Continent was played out with eleven men instead of millions; balletic headers replaced aerial dog-fights and sliding tackles replaced carpet bombing. Football had become 'war minus the shooting', as Orwell once observed.[158] There was another resonance: to many, the event proved that despite her superior standard of living, Germany had not entirely won the peace. The *Sunday Express* said:

A blaze of union Jacks waved, as people unashamedly gripped by emotion and patriotism danced, wept and hugged each other . . . What they will tell their grandchildren in the years to come is that it was English nerve and English heart and English stamina which finally overcame the tenacious resistance of [the Germans] . . . No one who saw this historic World Cup Final can deny England their 'finest hour'.[159]

It was, therefore, a dramatic coda to Churchill's funeral, stamping the Second World War on the national cortex but doing so in a more dynamic way than funeral pomp ever could.

Third, the intense patriotism which the victory generated speeded up the process by which football become the focus of national identity in Britain. In 1950, *The Times* had reported the fortunes of British teams with a discreet item under the by-line 'Some Interesting Games'. After 1966 it was front-page news on broadsheets as well as tabloids. Politicians and diplomats courted national football heroes like they courted pop stars and England's defence of the World Cup in June 1970 affected the date Wilson set for the general election of that year. But as with the pop world, there was a serious intent behind all the flim-flam. The belief that Britain's moral health could be measured by the success of its national soccer teams, and that it could even be determined by them, first emerged after the Hungarian defeat of 1953. Thirteen years later it was taken as read (not for nothing was Ferenc Puskas sought out by the British press for comment). What is extraordinary about the reaction to England's World Cup victory is how much it was seen as a spur to Britain's recovery. This view would not have been expressed a decade or two earlier. Reviewing England's victory, the Football Association made a thinly veiled attack on militant trades unionists and students who had forgotten their patriotism:

[The victory] raised our prestige throughout the world . . . [it] is indeed one of the few bright spots in the sombre economic situation which faces the country this Summer. We feel sure that many of our export industries will derive . . . a welcome boost from this success. The players who have made it possible worked hard and made many sacrifices. They have set an example of devotion and loyalty to the country which many others would do well to follow.[160]

Harold Wilson immediately recognized the importance of the event and he became the first Prime Minister to exploit the fortunes of

Britain's national football teams for political ends. He had just returned from seeing President Johnson in Washington where they had discussed, among other things, the growing economic crisis in Britain. Wilson needed a good photo-opportunity as never before.

His request to be interviewed at half-time to comment on the progress of the match was refused by the BBC. But that evening he joined Alf Ramsey and the team on the balcony of the Royal Garden Hotel in Kensington High Street. After milking the adulation of the crowd as surely as Churchill had done on the balcony of Buckingham Palace in 1945, Wilson and several ministers attended a victory banquet at the hotel. Sitting next to Jim Callaghan, a heartily drunk George Brown (a West Ham fan) sang several tuneless renditions of 'I'm Forever Blowing Bubbles'. The Sports Minister, Denis Howell, said, 'This has been the best half-million pounds the government has ever spent.'[161] Even Wilson's critics acknowledged the importance of the event. The day after, Dick Crossman wrote in his diary:

> I must record a big change in Harold's personal position. Luck was running against him till the end of the week; now it seems suddenly to have turned. I would guess he has had . . . a real success with President Johnson. But it is also a tremendous help for him that we won the World Cup on Saturday . . . When I told Anne [his wife] over lunch today that the World Cup could be a decisive factor in strengthening sterling, she couldn't believe it. But I am sure it is. It was a tremendous, gallant fight that England won. Our men showed real guts and the bankers, I suspect, will be influenced by this, and the position of the government correspondingly strengthened.[162]

Anne Crossman's incredulity had something to do with the fact that football was still largely a male pursuit, a fact confirmed by the victory banquet in Kensington. To their disgust, women, including the players' wives and girlfriends, were not allowed into the main banquet but dined in a separate room. Even the *Sun* was horrified, comparing their treatment to that of 'slave girls in an Arab bazaar'.[163] Despite this, the players ended up in good hands. Jack Charlton woke up the next morning in a garden in Walthamstow. Blinking in the July sunshine, he was greeted by a woman next door leaning over the garden fence exclaiming, 'You're Jack Charlton! I know you. I knew your mother.'[164] Tea was served.

Although the victory had a long-term impact on English national identity, the City was not impressed. Fifteen months later, on 18

November 1967, Wilson was forced to devalue the pound. The technological revolution he had promised had failed to improve the economy. He knew how important sterling was to Britons' sense of prestige, telling his Cabinet 'it would be necessary to emphasise that devaluation would mean that we should be more in control of our own destiny and less at the mercy of foreign opinion.'[165] Devaluation gave a brief boost to the economy, but it did not get the support Wilson had hoped for. The British saw it as further proof that their country was now the sick man of Europe.

The 1966 World Cup event also highlighted the extent to which the English remained oblivious of Scottish nationalism. Virtually all the fans at Wembley and the millions who partied in the streets afterwards waved Union Jacks. Wolstenholme regretted this lack of self-awareness among his compatriots. His memoirs record: 'Sooner or later I hope it will dawn on all English fans that the Union flag is the flag of the United Kingdom and that the flag of England is the St George's Cross.'[166] The Scottish Football Association sent a note of congratulation to the FA, claiming it as a great *British* achievement.[167] But most Scots did not see it as such and, what is more, they bitterly resented England's success. The Scottish international Denis Law refused to watch the match and remembers it as 'the blackest day of my life'.[168] In the *Observer*, Glasgow-born Hugh McIlvanney wondered if God was English after all. The 'Auld Alliance' was evident in the fact that Scots joined the French in refusing to celebrate. 'Scottish supporters sat in a smouldering sulk in corners of the Press centre . . . and insisted that they did not know what all the fuss was about.' Any Scot like him who enthused about England's achievement was accused of 'betray[ing] their birthright'.[169] Their attitude was reflected in the Scottish press, which barely covered the event. The English were unaware of the pervasive meanness of spirit north of the border, content as they were in their Anglo-British world and its complacent assumptions. In any case, the four nations of the United Kingdom still agreed wholeheartedly on one thing. They were not European.

9. The self-preservation society

Towards the end of 1966, Wilson dragged a reluctant Labour government into a second application for membership of the Common Market. Like Macmillan's earlier attempt, it showed how stuck British national identity still was in a no man's land between America and Europe. As a young man in the 1940s, Wilson had been a member of Federal Union. But this had always conflicted with his sentimental attachment to the Commonwealth and in the 1950s he had ditched his federalist beliefs and followed Gaitskell in defending 'a thousand years of history'. However, with the economy failing he desperately needed a big idea to rescue the government's reputation.

Even Europhiles like Roy Jenkins acknowledged that Britain would only start to benefit economically from membership after several years. But the benefits still appeared to be there for the taking, so long-term economic considerations buttressed the short-term political motives for joining. Opinion polls also led Wilson to believe the British were ready to join. In the summer of 1966, more people (approximately three to one) were in favour than at any time since 1961. The intense patriotism generated in England by the World Cup had not turned the country against Europe. On 22 October Wilson got the Cabinet's backing. Most sceptics lent their support – either, like Jim Callaghan, for the same reasons that had led Wilson to change his mind, or, like Denis Healey, because they didn't think de Gaulle would change his; thereby making the exercise pointless and not worth splitting the party over.

On 15 January 1967, the Prime Minister and his new Foreign Secretary, George Brown (a keen Europhile), set off on a Grand Tour of Western Europe's capital cities to drum up support. An inebriated Brown spent much of the time chatting up secretaries at the back of the plane. Although the rest of the Six were keen on Britain's entry, Brown had about as much success with de Gaulle as he had with the secretaries. On 24 and 25 January, he and Wilson met de Gaulle at the Élysée. They strove to convince the General that Britain had technology to share with the Community and that it was ready to join not as a bridge between America and Europe but as a committed member of a Union in which a Franco-British axis would form a third force between Europe and the US. 'The task of . . . France and

Britain was not to be mere messenger boys between the two powers,'
Wilson told him.[170]

De Gaulle made encouraging noises, telling Wilson he believed the
British were changing. The minutes record:

> He had the impression of an England which had evolved much
> from the position it used to take . . . he had the impression of an
> England which now really wished to moor itself alongside the
> Continent . . . he had the impression of an England which seemed
> disposed to detach itself to some extent from the special relation-
> ship which it had, or had had, with the United States, thus enabling
> it to be a European country.[171]

Blinded by vanity and desperation, the Prime Minister and Foreign
Secretary returned to Britain to tell the Cabinet that they had
convinced de Gaulle of Britain's sincerity, adding '[He was] discon-
certed by the determination and novelty of our approach.'[172] Dick
Crossman (a self-confessed Little Englander) wrote, 'Harold's illusions of grandeur in foreign policy scare me stiff [but] most of the
Cabinet now realize that that whether we like it or not we must
make a serious effort to get in as fast as possible.'[173] Barbara Castle
led the antis vigorously but after a two-day Cabinet meeting at
Chequers on 29 and 30 April the vote went thirteen to eight in
favour. When Parliament debated the matter on 2 May the vote was
488 to 62. It didn't matter.

After Wilson had announced the government's application in May,
he declared that a 'Great Debate' had begun. But Britons did not
rush to the dispatch box. Although most polls still showed a majority
in favour of joining, it faded fast as the economic situation worsened.
The prevailing attitude to Europe was now a mixture of cynicism
and apathy, with a high number of 'don't knows' and a significant
proportion of all viewpoints mistrusting Wilson's motives. In one of
its most devastating covers, *Private Eye* captured the country's mood.
Beneath the headline 'COMMON MARKET: GREAT DEBATE BEGINS',
the editor, Richard Ingrams, placed a picture of pensioners asleep in
deckchairs in a park.

This was not the picture presented to the Continent. In September
1967, Wilson's chief negotiator, Lord Chalfont, addressed the Council of Europe in Strasbourg in a final attempt to sway Europe's
leaders. Chalfont assured his audience that, having completed the
process of decolonization begun twenty years earlier, the British now
thought of themselves as European. 'New Britain', he said, 'is not

Little England.' He told the Council that youth was the vanguard of this 'New Britain':

> I commend a close look at the young people of Britain. I hope no one will be deceived by the trivialities of Carnaby Street and much of 'Swinging London'. Behind all this there is, rising in my country, a generation of young men and women, tired of humbug, angry with social inequality, sickened by war and resolved to do something about it. To these young people the future that lies within . . . the European idea is as exciting as anything that has happened in the long and vivid history of Britain.

Who were these serious young people who were eschewing Swinging London in favour of the exciting European idea? According to Chalfont, they were 'our bankers, our artists, our university lecturers, our doctors and other professional men'. Or they were students 'hitch-hiking across the continent and effacing in their new comradeship the bitter memories of war'.[174] Among these groups, the numbers in favour of entry were certainly high. But it was hardly a representative sample of the British people.

A more accurate picture of the British attitude to Europe was shown in *The Italian Job* (1969). Starring Michael Caine and Noël Coward, it tells the story of a group of criminals who mastermind a gold-bullion heist in Turin. The operation is financed from Wandsworth prison by a patriotic gentleman con, Mr Bridger (Coward, in his last film), who is persuaded by Charlie Croker (Caine) to do it because it will help the UK's balance of payments crisis. The film combined two British cinematic genres, the criminal comedy caper and the wartime escape film, updating both for a 1960s audience. The gang members come from every social class. But whereas officers plan and direct the escape in prisoner-of-war films, in *The Italian Job* the toffs are no longer in charge and they are the object of some derision. There is only a token woman, a King's Road swinger who is flown home before the heist begins. The gang includes a black man and a gay man, but it does not have any Scottish or Welsh members. The UK on display here is a male, English one. Yet the message is clear and of its time: if the talent of every Briton is pooled, the nation can be a world-beater once again, without Europe's help and preferably at its expense.

The film pokes fun at Continentals – in this case, the Italians – who are seen as comical idiots, or simply 'Bloody foreigners' as one gang member puts it. Caine's men enter the country disguised as football fans heading for an England v. Italy match, their van covered in Union Jacks and the slogan 'England Rule OK'. The Minis in which the gang escape are painted red, white and blue, symbolizing the patriotic ingenuity of a nation which, like the car itself, is small yet fast and versatile. Their escape is accompanied by 'The Self-Preservation Society', a pop tune sung in raucous Cockney accents, the title of which speaks for itself. When news reaches Mr Bridger of the gang's success, he gives a royal wave to Wandsworth's cheering inmates while 'Rule, Britannia' bursts onto the soundtrack. The film's ending is particularly symbolic. Having ditched the Minis, the gang head home in a coach through the Alps, take a bend too quickly, and come to a halt with half the vehicle hanging over the edge of the mountainside. The stolen gold is at the rear and it's about to tip them over when Caine says without any conviction, 'Er, hang on a minute, lads. I've got a great idea.'[175] The credits roll.

Like the British people, they are in limbo, suspended between an imperial identity and a European one, both of which they have rejected. Film historian Nick Cull has written: 'Identity has been acquired at the expense of others, but the weight of the ill-gotten gain leaves the country that refuses to acknowledge the nature of its identity in a place of great instability ... swaying on the precipice between oblivion and stability.'[176] It is also hard to resist the observation that it is the black gang member who, without meaning to, drives the coach over the edge, a moment that perhaps symbolizes the fact that black immigration unwittingly took Englishness off the road in this period. The most ironic thing about the film is something Caine himself pointed out. Austin Motors refused to lend any Minis to the film-makers, failing to see the publicity potential. Within a few years, the British car industry was dead. The film is therefore an example of the central theme of this chapter: real and transformative though the cultural revolution of the 1960s was, it failed to deliver the economic revival that was necessary to resuscitate Britishness fully. Whatever one might read into *The Italian Job*, what is beyond dispute is that it was one of the most popular British films of the twentieth century. And in England especially, its cheeky, swinging Europhobic patriotism continues to touch the national psyche like few other movies.

For the time being, British indifference to Europe didn't matter. At a press conference on 27 November 1967, de Gaulle vetoed Britain's application a second time. 'This great people', he said, 'so magnificently gifted with ability and courage, should on their own behalf

and for themselves achieve a profound economic and political transformation' before they could join. To let them in beforehand 'would
lead to the destruction of the European structure of which she is a
part'.[177] On the Continent, the veto caused even more dismay than
the first. The founding father of the European Economic Community,
Jean Monnet, called de Gaulle's action 'fundamentally anti-European'. He paid tribute to Wilson's decision not to withdraw the
application by recalling the bulldog spirit of the war. It was proof,
he said, 'of that determination in the face of difficulty which the
British people had shown in 1940 in the defence of freedom.'[178]

The British *were* unmoved, but more out of cynicism and apathy
than any bulldog spirit. The second veto produced less Francophobia
than the first because people had become more used to the diminu-
tion of Britain's power since the early 1960s. Furthermore, many
Britons had since found solace in a cultural revolution which side-
lined Europe and seemed to prove that the country didn't need the
Continent to maintain its international prestige. Therefore, although
Europe didn't give Wilson the second wind he had hoped for, de
Gaulle's rebuff didn't damage his reputation as much as it had
damaged Macmillan's. However, it did have a long-term impact on
public opinion. The 1967 veto reinforced the popular view that the
EEC was an essentially alien body, run by a typical, dictatorial
Continental leader. Support for membership, which had briefly
reached its highest level since Macmillan's application, plummeted to
its lowest level since just after the 1963 veto. Despite periodic blips,
support did not fully recover for any significant length of time until
the end of the century. Furthermore, the fact that Britain's leaders
were determined to join come what may, revealed a disregard for the
views of the majority that would become a running sore in British
society, souring the project and at times coming close to scuppering
it altogether.

10. A living land of violence, passion and change

Sir Kenneth Clark's thirteen-part television series *Civilisation*, screened on BBC2 from February to May 1969, was a brilliant defence of Europe's cultural heritage which conveyed a sense of its historic unity more than any government pamphlet. Clark was the most sophisticated, humane and popular of Britain's twentieth-century cultural reformers and the series was the culmination of a lifetime devoted to disseminating the arts in the belief that doing so had a liberalizing effect on society. It earned him a peerage and hundreds of letters of congratulation. Among them was a note from the aesthete James Lees-Milne, who reminded Clark that civilization was decaying all around his viewers, sometimes in the next room:

> I cannot refrain from telling you what sheer pleasure you have given Alvilde and me; nor how much you have edified us. I may say that first of all we carefully bolt and bar all doors and windows because you must be responsible for more country house burglaries than any man of letters on record. They, the burglars, do a roaring business raiding the homes of the intelligentsia every Sunday in these parts. From 8.15 to 9pm it is money for jam.[179]

Lees-Milne touched on an important point. So glued were they to the beautiful sounds and images on their TVs that many viewers failed to notice what Clark was actually saying.

He was pessimistic. He gloried in the spiritual certainties of medieval Christendom and in the artistic achievement of the Renaissance on which he was an expert. But from the Reformation to the industrial and technological revolutions, he saw European history as a tragic tale of cynicism and materialism, one interrupted only by the amelioration of the worst human suffering, like Britain's abolition of slavery. Clark ended the series in the peace of his home at Saltwood Castle, Kent. He quoted W. B. Yeats' 'The Second Coming' (1921): 'Things fall apart; the centre cannot hold; / Mere anarchy is loosed upon the world'. He then faced the camera and said with a poignant mixture of urbanity and passion, 'The trouble is that there is still no centre. The moral and intellectual failure of Marxism has left us with no alternative to heroic materialism and that isn't enough. One may be optimistic but one can't exactly be joyful at the prospect before us.' With that, as he wrote in his autobiography, 'I walked into my library, patted a wooden figure by Henry More, as if to imply that there was still hope, and it was all over.'[180]

What was the impact of this tumultuous period on national identity in Britain? In 1950, a study of the middle classes concluded, 'The English middle classes perform the same function as their American counterparts: they provide the nation's brains, leadership and organising ability, and they are the main vehicle for the transmission of the essential national culture.'[181] Little over a decade later, the middle classes – English, Scottish and Welsh – still provided the bulk of Britain's governing elite. But it could no longer be said that they were the main vehicles for the transmission of the essential national culture. In a definitive study of the Beatles, Ian Macdonald made the point well:

> Fast-moving and devolved, the pop culture of the Sixties was intrinsically democratic . . . It represented an upsurge of working-class expression into a medium mostly handed down to the common man by middle-class professionals with little empathy for street culture. The true revolution of the Sixties was an inner one of feeling and assumption: a revolution in the head . . . It was a revolution of *and in* the common man.[182]

The long nineteenth century finally came to an end as the people of the United Kingdom rejected the values of the Victorian era. Future attempts to resuscitate those values would have only partial and sporadic success. During the 1960s, the British emerged from a protracted adolescence in which the acne of empire, the squeaky voice of class deference, the wet dreams of sexual repression and the tantrums of isolationism started to become things of the past; occasionally recalled but only with acute embarrassment or uncontrolled laughter.

However, the revolution of the common man came too late to save Britishness. In fact, by intensifying public disdain for the UK's rulers, it hampered the best efforts to re-unite the country in the remaining years of the twentieth century. In June 1970, the British elected a Conservative government led by Edward Heath that was committed to taking the UK into Europe. Relieved that civilization was not after all coming to an end, Kenneth Clark wrote to congratulate the new Prime Minister. But membership of the EEC did not solve the nation's problems. With millions of other despairing voters, Clark watched the conflict between the UK's classes, nations and races become more ferocious than ever during the 1970s. The Isles' belated entry into Europe added another source of tension to an already strained society as British nationalists blamed the country's misfortunes on its apparent betrayal to foreigners across the sea.

'Look, you British bastards', wrote Ray Gosling in 1962, 'this isn't a land of red pillar boxes and straight faces, it's a living land of violence, passion and change.'[183] British national identity had begun at last to be remade. But violence, passion and change would eventually destroy it altogether.

PART 7

SCEPTICS

Britain will not lose its identity if we enter the Common Market. The Common Market is 13 years old. Yet France remains as French as ever she was, Germany as German, Italy as Italian . . . Nor would Britain have to change its Parliamentary system, law courts or social institutions. The British way of life – based on our constitutional Monarchy – would continue unchanged. National identities are safeguarded by the way the Common Market operates.

Europe and You (Conservative Party Pamphlet), 1971

Jerusalem may yet be built in this pleasant land, but never in the typists' pools and conference rooms of Brussels.

John Osborne, 1974

1. Cheaper holidays in sunny Spain

The period 1972–82 has come to be seen in Britain as the most dreadful of the postwar era, a litany of racial conflict in England, nationalist discontent in Scotland and Wales, war in Ireland and perpetual strikes everywhere. According to Francis Wheen, 'If the Sixties were a wild weekend and the eighties were a hectic day at the office, the Seventies were one long Sunday evening, heavy with gloom and torpor.'[1] It is hard not to agree. But this was the last period of the twentieth century when Britishness was a genuinely popular and viable national identity. Bruised and confused though they were by the changes of the postwar era, most of the population were still committed to the Union and felt that being British still mattered to them. Moreover, they appeared to be collectively prepared to adopt a third, European identity by joining the EEC. Domestic and foreign observers thought that the British had at last found the courage to fill the ideological vacuum left by the Empire. On the eve of the UK's third application to the EEC, A. J. P. Taylor described it as 'the most decisive moment in British history since the Norman conquest or the loss of America'.[2]

Diplomatically, the prospects for changing the course of British history looked good when Edward Heath came to power on 18 June 1970. More than any other British politician of the twentieth century, Heath was a federalist, committed since the 1940s to taking Britain into a Union which he hoped would become a United States of Europe. His childhood was rich in symbolism. He was born during a Zeppelin raid in 1916, in Broadstairs on the north Kent coast, the son of a builder and a maid. Heath did more than walk to the end of the pier. Unusually for a boy of his class and generation he visited Paris, flying there on a school trip. He also became a competent pianist and a highly cultivated young man. The arts helped him get accepted into Oxford University as an organ scholar. More importantly, the arts gave him a heartfelt sense of the unity of European culture and Britain's natural place in it. During the war he read the federalist tracts of the day and his experience of battle confirmed his belief in the necessity of European integration. He entered Parliament in 1950, and from the time of his maiden speech, in which he praised the Schuman Plan, to his leadership of the team negotiating UK entry in 1962–3, Heath showed that he was determined to make his dream become reality.

The trust and goodwill that Britain's new Prime Minister enjoyed on the Continent was augmented by the fact that General de Gaulle had been replaced by Georges Pompidou, a man less hostile to the British. On 19–20 May, Heath met the new French President in Paris. At the end of the talks, they held a press conference in the same room in which de Gaulle had announced the first veto eight years earlier. Pompidou said: 'There were many people who believed that Great Britain was not European and did not want to become European, and that Britain wanted to enter the Community only to destroy it . . . Well, Ladies and Gentlemen, you see before you two men who are convinced to the contrary.'[3] In fact, neither the French nor the other members of the Community were under any illusions that British national identity had changed. But they reached the conclusion that if the UK was continually excluded it would do more damage to the Community than if it was allowed to enter. Emile Van Lennep, a senior Dutch politician who knew Pompidou well, remembered, 'I found out very early that there was not to be another veto . . . Not because Britain had changed, but because the application couldn't be resisted any more. British membership became a political necessity not just for the British but for the others as well.'[4]

On 24 May the Cabinet agreed to go ahead with detailed negotiations. Seven months later, they resulted in a deal being done. It was not a particularly good deal but it was the best that any British Prime Minister could have got at that time and, as Lord Crowther told the House of Lords, 'You do not haggle over the subscription when you are invited to climb aboard a lifeboat. You scramble aboard while there is still a seat for you.'[5] However, dragging the British people on board was another matter altogether. Shortly before the 1970 election, Heath had said that the Community could not be expanded 'except with the full-hearted consent of the parliaments and peoples of the new member countries'.[6] Those words were a rod for his back during the rest of his life. In early 1971, with the negotiations successfully completed, the White Paper on entry being drawn up by officials, and the entire British political Establishment gearing up to do battle, the inner circle of the Heath government turned to the question of how to gain the 'full-hearted consent' of

Britain's Parliament and people. A report by the government Chief Whip, Francis Pym, on the opinion of Conservative MPs concluded that approximately two-thirds were in favour of entry. Of those who were opposed, many did not have ideological objections to entry, but they did feel that the British people were against joining and that therefore a referendum should be held to secure a clear mandate. Pym concluded that without the offer of a referendum there were considerable risks of parliamentary failure.

Tory MPs had good reason to fear public opinion. Support for Europe was at rock bottom. By April 1970, polls showed that only 19 per cent favoured entry, while 57 per cent thought Britain's application should be dropped altogether before talks even began (by the time the talks did begin in June, the figure had risen to 60 per cent). This was a complete reversal of opinion from 1966, when Britons had favoured entry by three to one. The Cabinet, realizing the extent of British scepticism, approved the launch of a pro-Europe campaign and set up a Cabinet Committee to coordinate it. From 1971 to 1973 the biggest state publicity campaign since the war took place, with nearly 300 ministerial speeches made outside Parliament. These were aided by a glittering array of the great and the good drawn from across the political spectrum. Labour MP Arthur Morris complained that taxpayers' money was being used for propaganda. He told the Commons, 'They are as frenetic in their enthusiasm to convert public opinion as the Chinese Christian who decided to baptise his troops with a hosepipe. I warn the Prime Minister and his colleagues that the British people are in no mood to be hosepiped on this issue.'[7]

Yet there were signs that the British people were open to persuasion. In January 1971 the Director of the Conservative Research Department, Sir Michael Fraser, submitted a report to the Prime Minister on attitudes to Europe. As a snapshot of how Britons saw the Continent, it mirrored the report submitted by Iain Macleod to Harold Macmillan in 1962. But its findings were rather different. Support for entry still consisted of a vague feeling that there would be economic benefits and most of this support still came from the business and professional classes (although the gap had narrowed a little since Wilson had modified Labour Party policy). What had changed significantly were the reasons given by those who were opposed to entry.

There was still considerable anxiety in the Tory Party about betraying the Commonwealth, particularly among grass-roots activists in the shires where right-wingery was strongest. But Britons as a whole were even less bothered about the Commonwealth in the 1970s than they had been in the 1960s. Nor were they so bothered about Britain ceding some of its sovereignty to Europe. The over-whelming obstacle in people's minds was now prices and the belief that they would rise further as a result of entry. Wilson's devaluation of the pound and the growing industrial unrest of the late 1960s, together with rising inflation and unemployment, had all sunk into the popular consciousness. In other words, awareness of Britain's relative economic decline had overtaken awareness of the decline in its political power. Moreover, the report found that no direct link was being made between the two so that money worries were not exacerbating wounded national pride. The fact that the standard of living of the Six was nearly three times higher than Britain's was at last sinking in, with the result that the promise of a share in the Continent's wealth was making membership more attractive to the British. All these findings were good news for the government. The emphasis on economic issues made it easier to present a straight-forward case based on Britain's standard of living and to avoid what Iain Macleod had called the 'emotional' questions of national iden-tity. Fraser concluded that the British were more confused than hostile to Europe and he advised Heath to play up the material advantages of joining, especially the more fun aspects such as 'cheaper holidays in sunny Spain and cheaper German beer'.[8]

Heath could not afford to ignore the more emotive issues. When Britons were asked in July 1971 whether they would lose their national identity if the UK joined the Common Market, 27 per cent thought 'a lot', 62 per cent 'some' and 35 per cent 'a little'. Only 27 per cent thought they would lose none of their Britishness at all.[9] But, in any case, Heath did not want to ignore the issue. His special advisor, Michael Wolff, told him that Europe 'is an appeal that can be based on high ideals and national destiny and should be particu-larly aimed at youth'.[10] One widely distributed pamphlet, *Europe and You*, said that Britishness was safe in Brussels' hands:

Britain will not lose its identity if we enter the Common Market. The Common Market is 13 years old. Yet France remains as French as ever she was, Germany as German, Italy as Italian . . . Nor would Britain have to change its Parliamentary system, law courts or social institutions. The British way of life – based on our constitutional Monarchy – would continue unchanged. National identities are safeguarded by the way the Common Market operates.[11]

Europe and You offered stock reassurances about the way the West worked: decisions of the Council of Ministers had to be unanimous, so no one could boss Britain around; like NATO and the UN, sovereignty was shared not surrendered; yet, as those organizations proved, the freedom to act completely independently of other nations was a luxury that Britain could not afford in the modern world. The government's White Paper on Europe, published in July 1971, also looked at the broader picture, arguing that Britain could have no effective post-imperial role outside the Continent. If Britain said no, 'in a single generation we should have renounced an Imperial past and rejected a European future'.[12]

The British intelligentsia lent vociferous support to the campaign, as they had during the 1960s, and they again argued the case for Europe on first principles. *Encounter* repeated the straw poll which it carried out in 1962. Some were still opposed. Kingsley Amis and Anthony Burgess argued that national differences would be eroded; A. J. P. Taylor and John Osborne saw it as a gravy train for the British political elite, the latter writing, 'Jerusalem may yet be built in this pleasant land, but never in the typists' pools and conference rooms of Brussels'.[13] Ken Tynan condemned it as a bankers' club – 'the most blatant historical vulgarity since the Thousand Year Reich', which would succeed where Hitler had failed.[14] But they remained a minority in the intellectual community. Forty-six of *Encounter*'s respondents were in favour, with only seventeen against and four undecided, a pattern that repeated itself in other journals. The Marxist critic Raymond Williams overcame his suspicion of the EEC as a bankers' club, arguing, 'There would be a better basis ... for breaking some of the locks in English culture on which the present political hegemony depends.' Sir Hugh Casson implored people to lie back and think of Europe. 'Stifling an inborn mistrust of foreigners ... I opt without flippancy for "Going In" because a national shake up of this scale is likely to be healthy ... so why not lie back and enjoy it?'[15] Colin Wilson also attacked British insularity:

> There is something peculiarly unlikeable about the British temperament, and I think that a closer liaison with Europe might improve it. There is something naturally closed and narrow-minded about us ... due to the geographical accident of our being separated from Europe by a body of water ... We are patient, plodding, and

empirical; we are like blinkered cart-horses; we put up with a lot. But the trouble with patient, stupid people is that once they begin to build up a grudge, nothing will dislodge them. Over the past twenty-five years, the English have built up a national grudge perhaps due to disappointed expectations after winning the War – and now it is so firmly established that the country resembles one of those Strindbergian households where everybody nags and tries to make everybody else miserable. On the other hand, the Germans at the end of the War had the same advantage as Britain at the beginning – of facing a crisis situation that left no room for resentment or petulance. The result was the German economic recovery. Meanwhile, like spoilt children, the English sit around scowling and quarrelling, and hoping for better times.[16]

Important though the British intelligentsia were in mobilizing middle-class opinion in favour of Europe, it was to the monarchy that the government looked to give the project a patriotic blessing.

The Queen's support for the Common Market was as important as her father's support had been for the abortive Franco-British Union in 1940. Apart from the obvious need for the head of state to endorse such a fundamental change in Britain's political trajectory, Heath also had to reassure the country that entry would not undermine the Crown, as this was still a feature of British scepticism. Reassurance from the horse's mouth was worth a hundred pamphlets. Elizabeth II dutifully did her bit in her Christmas broadcast of 1971:

> Britain is about to join her neighbours in the European Community and you may well ask how this will affect the Commonwealth. The new links with Europe ... cannot alter our historical and personal attachments with kinsmen and friends overseas. Old friends will *not* be lost; Britain will take her Commonwealth links into Europe with her. Britain and these other European countries see in the Community a new opportunity for the future ... We are trying to create a wider family of nations.[17]

What were the Queen's real views on Europe? Between 1961 and 1971, she had been persuaded by her Prime Ministers of the economic and geopolitical advantages of joining. Martin Charteris, her Private Secretary from 1972 to 1977, was keen on entry and helped to secure her acceptance in subsequent years.

But acceptance was all it was. In her heart, Elizabeth II was not enthusiastic about the European idea. Her focus on the Commonwealth in the Christmas broadcast is revealing. Since few Britons cared about it, we may conclude that if the Queen was reassuring anyone it was herself. Emotionally trapped in the late-imperial sunset of the 1950s, the Commonwealth was the only vehicle with which she could maintain some of the aura of Empress bestowed by Disraeli on her great-great-grandmother. It gave her a political role in the world which she did not have in countries where she was simply sent to drum up trade, however glittering the receptions and however obsequious the hosts. Her Prime Ministers indulged her love of the Commonwealth with decreasing enthusiasm as her long reign wore on and her whole political outlook came to seem ever more moribund. Europe, in contrast, gave her no formal role, since its highest regular contacts were Prime Ministerial. In addition, despite friendly relations with the other royal families of member states, the Windsors' twentieth-century withdrawal from close dynastic involvement with the Continent meant that monarchical links were not strong enough to provide the foundations for a sense of Europeanness based around the Crown. At a function in 1977, Tony Benn heard her say, 'We had the heads of the Common Market here to dinner the other night . . . they were all so cynical and disillusioned and [Helmut Schmidt] was so rude and unfriendly.' In his diary, Benn noted: 'That confirmed what I have long suspected: that the royal family loathe the Common Market because they have no role in it. There is no European Presidents' Council in which Queen Juliana can meet the Grand Duchess of Luxembourg: they have no forum and therefore are driven back into a quaint tourist role.'[18] All these forays into the cultural and political implications of membership were an important part of the debate. However, the attempt to convince the British they were European was more muted in the campaign of 1971–3 than it had been in 1961–3.

Sir Michael Fraser's view that government propaganda should concentrate on bread-and-butter issues prevailed. The leisure opportunities that membership would bring were loudly trumpeted. In the summer of 1971, women clad in T-shirts bearing the logo 'SAY YES TO EUROPE!' were sent out to distribute copies of an official rag called the *British European*. These jolly government girls were most in evidence on the nation's beaches. It was a clever stunt for two reasons. First, because Britain's windswept strips of soiled sand and rusty piers were the most iconic part of the island geography which Churchill had said Britons would defend to the last. Here was the nation's frontier, the point where the British had to be convinced they were no longer an island people. The stunt was also designed to persuade those sheltering behind stripy windbreaks with cups of tea that foreign travel had more to offer than diarrhoea and strange languages. The front cover of the *British European* displayed a page-three girl clad in a skimpy Union Jack bikini, next to the headline 'EUROPE IS FUN! More Work But More Play Too!'

Inside, it assured readers that national heroes were in favour of joining; among them were the actor Kenneth More, veteran of British war films, and Bobby Moore, England's triumphant football captain. But, on the whole, persuasion took the form of simple economic graphs showing the EEC's faster growth rate since 1945, with accompanying promises that membership would bring everyone a higher standard of living.

Were the UK's leaders honest with the British people about Europe? The 1971 White Paper claimed 'There is no question of any erosion of essential national sovereignty'.[19] This was not the case in 1971 and Europhiles knew full well that it would not be the case in years to come when integration accelerated. Propaganda produced by the EEC for UK audiences could be laudably frank. One leaflet declared 'The European Community is moving towards full economic union and eventually to political union.'[20] But such pronouncements were rare, and in British propaganda they were virtually non-existent. When national identity was discussed, it was usually placed in the misty realms of 'Britain's destiny'. Such rhetoric conveyed 'high ideals' in a manner suggesting the inevitability of the UK's date with Europe while at the same time avoiding any serious discussion of the political implications of joining. Or, as in *Europe and You*, national identity was mentioned in a defensive way in order to reassure people that their essential Britishness was not threatened.

Heath was also a shrewd tactician when it came to forcing through his dream. Like his compatriots in Brussels, he knew that neither the British people nor their Parliament would approve entry on principle alone. They did not want to see themselves as Europeans. And if they were made aware of the full federal implications of the Treaty of Rome – that Europe would move 'towards ever closer union' – the enterprise would have collapsed. Some of his sympathizers admitted this. Denis Healey said: 'If Heath had laid it on the line what he thought it would lead to he wouldn't have got it through. He thought it was more important to get it through, even if it was ignorant and misunderstanding acquiescence rather than support, than to let it go. And I suspect he was right about that.'[21]

It was only later in life, when Europe was the only success Heath could celebrate in an otherwise dismal premiership, that he presented the case for membership in unrelentingly absolutist terms. He claimed to have done so from the start. 'It wasn't disguised in the least,' he said, 'it was all there.'[22] Sarah Morrison, Vice-Chairman of the Conservative Party at the time and a close friend of Heath's, agreed: 'Those who argue that nobody levelled with the British public . . . [are] slightly unfair because I believe that they did level. But the British public now has decided that it didn't at that time hear.'[23]

A proper scrutiny of the historical evidence does not bear this view out. People didn't hear for the simple reason that no one in the pro-Europe camp was shouting *Federalism, here we come!* from the rooftops. At the same time, sceptics who argue that noble Britons were brazenly lied to by their unscrupulous leaders ignore the extent to which the country was receptive to a pragmatic appeal based on material self-interest. Britons were not duped. They were told what they wanted to hear by a political elite well aware of what the reaction to the Common Market's ultimate agenda would be. The questions were there to be asked but Britons supinely accepted what they were told. It was essentially a compact between a disingenuous governing class and a people too preoccupied with the economic problems of the day to pick a fight over a constitutional issue which even the most politically astute knew would not begin to affect their lives for many years to come. The ferocity of the national debate on Europe later in the century sprang from the fact that both sides chose to blame each other rather than admitting their mutual culpability in the matter.

In the meantime, another problem which the Heath government faced was the opposition of the Labour Party. Labour was still the more sceptical of the parties and its scepticism was shared by the trade union movement. As well as Barbara Castle, the leading figures of this wing were Peter Shore, Tony Benn and Jim Callaghan. Callaghan believed that entry would 'mean a complete rupture of our identity' amid 'an aroma of continental claustrophobia'. Pompidou's brief attempt to make French the official language of the EEC gave sceptics a stick to beat opponents with. In a speech in May 1971, Callaghan promised that 'the language of Chaucer, Shakespeare and Milton' would be defended by the Labour Party: 'If we are to prove our Europeanism by accepting that French is the dominant language in the Community, then the answer is quite clear and I will say it in French to prevent any misunderstanding: "Non, merci beaucoup." '[24] This was more than cod-Churchillian rhetoric.

Callaghan convinced Wilson to take a more sceptical line than the one he had adopted when scuttling ingratiatingly around the capitals of Europe in 1967. Together they cooked up a policy of opposing entry on the terms negotiated by Heath. They hoped it would unite the left and right of the party, but it failed to do so, just as it had in Gaitskell's time, and revealed instead how much Europe was becoming a cross-party issue.

The House of Commons debate on entry matched the government campaign in scale, lasting for six days between 21 and 28 October 1971 and including over 100 speeches. There was a palpable sense that history was being made and that much of the world was watching. One of the Commons' old attendants told an observer, 'See the Ambassador's Gallery over there? Haven't seen it so full since we used to matter in the world.'[25] If ever there was a moment for the Grocer to raise the debate above the level of food prices this was it, and for once his earnest gravity matched the occasion. Heath rose from his seat and declared, 'No Prime Minister has stood at this Box in time of peace and asked the House to take a positive decision of such importance.' He ended with an emotional appeal for the British to forge a new, post-imperial identity; and he did so by referring to words spoken to him by an Indian diplomat after the veto of Britain's first application to the Common Market:

> When you left India, some people wept. And when you leave Europe tonight, some will weep. There is no other people in the world of whom these things could be said . . . Tonight when this House endorses this Motion many millions of people right across the world will rejoice that we have taken our rightful place in a truly united Europe.[26]

Despite the three-line whip imposed by Wilson, sixty-seven Labour MPs, led by Roy Jenkins, voted with the government. This gave it a majority of 112, with 356 votes for and 244 against. After pressure from his advisers, Heath had allowed a free vote among Conservative MPs. Thirty-seven followed their consciences and voted against entry. It was the biggest Tory backbench rebellion since the vote of confidence against Neville Chamberlain in 1940. As the result was announced by the tellers pandemonium broke out, during which the rebels were jostled and someone shouted 'fascist bastard' at Jenkins. Jenkins was sustained by the knowledge that he had helped to change the course of British history.

I did not find this unsettling because I was convinced that it was one of the decisive votes of the century and had no intention of spending the rest of my life answering the question of what did I do in the great division by saying 'I abstained'. I saw it in the context of the first reform bill, the repeal of the Corn Laws, Gladstone's home rule bills, the Lloyd George budget, the Parliament bill, the Munich Agreement, and the May 1940 votes and was consequently fortified by my amateur historical interest.[27]

If the parliamentary debate on entry matched the greatest in British history, then the signing of Britain's Accession to the Treaty of Rome matched the greatest peace conferences in Europe's. The difference was that, unlike the Congress of Vienna, the Conference of Versailles or the Yalta Summit, there appeared to be no losers. On 22 January 1972, Britain's political leaders processed into the great hall of the Château Egmont in Belgium to watch Edward Heath sign the Treaty. Among them was the frail but sparky Harold Macmillan, there to witness the victory which his protégé had wrested out of the jaws of their defeat in 1963. Hugo Young has summed up the moment:

> As a late entrant to the club, Britain paid a price that had gone up. The Last Europeans had played no part in making the rules. The captains and the kings gathered to salute the end of a journey from snooty detachment through humiliating rejection to rather desperate supplicancy and success. But what about the people? The deed was done, the compact signed, the governing class was all agreed. The political argument about a Treaty that changed Britain for ever had barely begun.[28]

What about the people?

Young describes their attitude as 'changeable, ignorant and half-hearted'.[29] There is some truth in that. A Conservative Party official sent to Liverpool on a fact-finding mission in the early 1970s, stopped a woman in the street to ask her views on the Common Market. 'Where are they building it, luv?' came the reply.[30] But her comment does not tell the whole story of this period.

2. Games without frontiers

The British were stirred by the debate on Europe more than ever before. When the White Paper went on sale there were queues outside bookshops which had not been seen since the publication of the Beveridge Report in 1943. A shortened version of the White Paper sold over 1 million copies, making it the bestselling government document of all time. At its peak in July, 100,000 copies a week were passing over the counter. For a while, it seemed that the government's publicity campaign had managed to 'hosepipe' the British. From the end of 1971 to the following spring, support for entry rose slightly. Opinion polls were not the only indicators of popular feeling. Throughout the 1970s, a softening of attitudes towards the Continent was apparent in British cultural and social life, of which four examples stand out.

The first was the successful introduction of decimal currency in 1971. The system of pounds, shillings and pence had prevailed on the island since the sixteenth century. Following a revolutionary French and American lead in the 1780s and 1790s, most nations of the world switched to decimal currencies in the nineteenth century, and nations which emerged since then had also adopted it. But Britain had stuck doggedly to its archaic system despite several attempts, both domestic and foreign, to get it to change. In 1961, a combination of pressure from British business and the government's approach to Europe persuaded Harold Macmillan to set the ball rolling and he appointed an inquiry under the chairmanship of John Giffard, third Earl of Halsbury. Halsbury was a cross-bench peer whose grandfather was three times Tory Lord Chancellor and author of *The Laws of England* (1885), a reference work still in use today. Halsbury shared his grandfather's belief in the superiority of the British constitution and to it he added his personal conviction that Europe was an immoral, sordid place. Since 1949, he had led the unsuccessful attempt to develop a British computer industry. What little time he had left from sponsoring British inventors he spent campaigning against the Continental pornography which flooded Britain after the 1960s. The finest hour in his fight to save the nation from foreign mores came in 1986, when he introduced a Private Member's Bill to stop homosexuality being discussed in British schools. This passed into law as the notorious 'Section 28'. Halsbury was no more enthusiastic about decimalization than he was about homosexuality. He admitted that currency reform would have practical benefits in the everyday life of the British people, but he also believed that it was the first stage in the eventual abolition of the pound. Although he argued his case vigorously, the Committee voted four to two in favour of decimalization and he reluctantly went along with the majority.

In 1966, three years after the Halsbury Committee had recommended change, James Callaghan announced that it was government policy.[31] Five years of further prevarication ensued before decimalization was finally introduced on 15 February 1971 with cross-party support.[32] It was initially greeted by nationwide whingeing, particularly among the elderly. However, the opposition to it was not based on patriotic resistance to the Continent but on the more prosaic fear that British shopkeepers would use the transitional period to short-change confused customers and put prices up. But there was little of the hysteria which a decade later greeted moves towards a single European currency. The vast majority of Britons were more concerned about the declining value of the pound as a result of inflation (together with perennial anxiety about simply not having enough money) than they were about the arithmetical structure of their currency. Moreover, because the Queen's head and assorted national heroes were still emblazoned on notes and coins, it was easy for the government to reassure Britons that sterling was still sterling and that, as a consequence, Britain remained an independent nation. Within a year, this key harmonization with Europe had been accepted as a rational modernization of British life.

The second example of changing attitudes was a TV phenomenon of the 1970s: *It's A Knockout*. The programme was launched in Britain by the BBC on 7 August 1966, a week after Bobby Moore held aloft the Jules Rimet trophy. It began life as an initiative of the European Broadcasting Union. Local teams of men and women from around the UK competed in comical games to represent Britain in the Continental competition staged by Eurovision, *Jeux sans Frontières*. The programme ran until 1982 and at the peak of its popularity in the 1970s it attracted 18 million viewers, encompassing all age and class groups. It combined the badly timed slapstick of a provincial circus, the eccentricity of a Butlin's poolside competition and the homely athleticism of a school sports day. Its host, Stuart Hall, recalled that it also thrived on patriotism. Each Saturday night, the

nation urged 'postmen, café owners, office clerks and engineers . . .
to do battle for Queen and country on a giant record player while
over-fat policemen squirted water at [them] from a high-powered
hose'.[33] *Jeux sans Frontières* – literally 'Games without Frontiers' –
encouraged a positive awareness of Europe. It showed that Britishness, even at its most patriotic, need not conflict with a wider
European identity. More than any other TV programme in the era
when the British were being coaxed into Europe, *Jeux sans Frontières*
brought ordinary Continentals into the nation's homes and showed
that they too could laugh at themselves. As during the World Cup,
anti-German feeling on the Continent helped to promote an uneasy
form of unity. Stuart Hall said, 'Every country wanted to beat the
Germans,' and this ensured that competition between the others
never got out of hand. Above all, the show proved that 'Europe is
Fun!', just as the propagandists said.

One change much commented on at the time was the increase in
au pairs coming to Britain, on average 24,000 per annum by the
early 1970s. The middle classes discovered that they could fill the
worst gaps left by the withdrawal of the British working classes from
domestic service at a low cost, by merely feeding and accommodating
young Continentals in return for housework and child-minding. Most
came from Germany, followed by France, Switzerland and Denmark.
It was a particularly British phenomenon because a majority of
European girls (60 per cent) chose the UK, eager as they were to
learn the lingua franca. The practice declined in the 1980s when the
middle classes discovered that illegal immigrants from Eastern
Europe and South-East Asia made even cheaper servants. In the
meantime, most girls enjoyed the experience (around 70 per cent
according to one survey). Affairs between au pairs and their employers were not uncommon. Throughout the 1970s, this exchange of
European bodily fluids provided the tabloid press with salacious
material. Like the Minister for War and the call girl, the popularity
of stories about the bank manager and the au pair rested more on
the jealous fantasies of the working classes than they did on moral
opprobrium. But the au-pair trend did help to foster some sense of
Europe among all sections of British society.

A more sober form of exchange was the practice of town twinning.
The first twinning was made in 1920, between the town of Poix-du-
Nord in France and Keighley in West Yorkshire. Only one other was
established before the Second World War. From the 1940s to the

1960s, Coventry led the way after Alderman George Hodgkinson persuaded city councillors to twin the city with Volgograd in 1944. But the real surge took place after the UK joined the Common Market. Between 1973 and 2000 the number of European towns twinned with British ones increased from 175 to 1683. The vast majority were in France (900) and Germany (463). Non-European towns twinned with British ones were far fewer – 77 in the United States and 69 in the Commonwealth. The practice forged unprecedented links between British and Continental civic elites.[34] With assistance from the European Commission, a link was usually established on the basis of geographical similarities between the towns and/or because there was a direct historical relationship between them. The practice appealed to local worthies precisely because it was not regional. Small in scale, it corresponded to the British system of local government established by the Victorians and it allowed the most inconsequential villages to be twinned as effectively as the biggest cities.

Twinning was also responsible for an increase in the number of British schools organizing visits to the Continent for their pupils. It was on a school trip that Edward Heath's sense of Europeanness had been confirmed. An experience which in his youth had been a rarity for young Britons started to become a common one from the time of his premiership onwards. The development was assisted by subsidies which the UK government and the EU gave schools. School trips appealed to Common Marketeers because they had a more cultural slant than the average package holiday. As such, they were an opportunity for the state to inculcate a loftier sense of Europe than that which children got with their parents on the beaches of Torremolinos. My own experience is that boys and girls often disappeared to shops and bars as soon as the teacher's back was turned during a museum visit. In any case, British children felt that the trips were beneficial, and where an official link existed they got a friendlier reception than the glower of low-budget hoteliers which usually greeted them on unofficial trips. It is difficult to assess accurately the impact of town-twinning on the British national consciousness, since official EU literature on the subject is little more than propaganda. But one indication of its beneficial effect may be found in the story of British road signs. Where a village, town or city was twinned with a Continental one, it was proudly displayed on signs welcoming visitors to the area, sometimes in several Continental languages. They had a particularly symbolic value in Britain because during the war road signs had been removed to make it harder for German invaders to find their way around.

If it was no longer the case that all roads led to London, then the Channel Tunnel created a physical link with the Continent which had far greater implications for British national identity. The story of the Tunnel reflects that of the island's relationship with the Continent over the last 200 years. The idea for a link was first mooted in 1751 by the French engineer Nicolas Desmarest, and then in 1802 by his compatriot Albert Mathieu. Mathieu's proposal was supported by the British radical politician Charles James Fox and by Napoleon before the Napoleonic Wars put the French dictator's enthusiasm into perspective. From then until 1984, a total of 138 attempts were made to revive the project (including proposals to build a bridge instead). Enthusiasm reached a new peak following the successful opening of the Suez Canal in 1867. A railway promoter, Sir Edward Watkin, began tunnelling inside the cliffs at Dover in 1880, held champagne parties inside, and got a mile and a quarter to France before the Board of Trade stopped him. Like all previous attempts, Watkins' heroically silly one failed because of fears that a tunnel would be used by hostile European powers to invade Britain. In 1936, Winston Churchill (who supported the idea) lamented, 'There are few projects against which there exists a deeper and more enduring prejudice than the construction of a railway tunnel between Dover and Calais.'[35] The Second World War did not allay British fears. In 1949, the Chancellor, Stafford Cripps, believed that the war 'had diminished the attractions rather than increased them!'. His Treasury adviser, Alec Cairncross, wrote, 'The idea has about as much relevance to current economic policy as a project to re-erect the pyramids in the Scottish Highlands.'[36] When Churchill returned to power, the Chiefs of Staff vetoed it on the usual security grounds.

What changed Whitehall minds was the Suez Crisis. In 1956, shortly after the Suez Canal Company had seen its property nationalized by Egypt, the company supported fresh proposals for a Channel tunnel put forward by a French aristocratic entrepreneur, Baron Leo d'Erlanger. The *Economist* attacked it as 'pie under the sea', but times had changed. Britain's approach towards the European Economic Community in the wake of the Suez crisis placed the tunnel firmly on the political agenda. By 1960, the Foreign Secretary, Selwyn Lloyd, was arguing that its construction would demonstrate 'our realisation that the days of "splendid isolation" are over'.[37] Crucial support also came from Britain's military chiefs, who between 1957 and 1959 changed their minds about the military implications. They argued that, far from being a threat, a tunnel would enable Britain to send forces to Europe quickly in the event of a ground war against the Eastern Bloc, while at the same time it could be easily destroyed with modern explosives if Britain was attacked. The formal decision to support the project was made by Alec Douglas-Home's Cabinet in January 1964.

After extensive Anglo-French discussions over the next decade, in March 1973 Edward Heath finally took the plunge and announced plans to build a tunnel by 1980. The government White Paper talked up the benefits for trade and tourism. It also emphatically declared that 'Britain is no longer economically or socially an island'.[38] Meeting a few weeks later, Heath and Pompidou agreed that the tunnel was essentially a political project, the financial cost of which was unimportant. The tunnel, said Pompidou, would be an umbilical cord, between the UK and the Continent, which would finally quell British hostility towards the EEC.[39] There were serious Cabinet fears that the government might lose the parliamentary vote. After heavy whipping and high emotion, the Bill passed its second reading in December 1973 by eighteen votes. Sadly, the project got no further than the division room of the House of Commons. It was abandoned by the second Wilson government in January 1975 partly on grounds of cost, partly because the Labour left was still hostile to the EEC and partly because the British people were not keen on being physically rejoined to the Continent. As Barbara Castle noted in her diary, it offended the first principle of their national identity: 'This is not only anti-Common Market prejudice. It is a kind of earthy feeling that an island is an island and should not be violated. Certainly I am convinced that the building of a tunnel would do something profound to the national attitude – and certainly not for the better.'[40] Though Britons had overcome their fear of subterranean invasion they did not shed any tears when Wilson abandoned the tunnel before a single skip had been filled. Their indifference to this most visionary of projects symbolized how much work the politicians boring into the rock of Britishness had yet to do before they saw a chink of Continental daylight at the other end.

3. The Euro-baby that couldn't care less

The British remained deeply sceptical about Europe for three reasons which, until the 1990s, completely overshadowed the little signs that they were warming to their new partners. First, the isolationism which two world wars had bred had not dissipated. Second, the Community was based on an elitist conception of European civilization and this severely restricted its popular appeal. Third, the apparent failure of EEC membership to improve Britain's standard of living undermined the pragmatic attempt to sell membership on material grounds, and this extinguished what little appeal the Community did enjoy.

The folk memory of the Second World War continued to grip the British imagination. It was unfortunate that the mammoth twenty-six-part ITV documentary *World at War* was broadcast throughout most of Britain's first year in Europe. Narrated by Laurence Olivier, with music by Carl Davis, the story was told in a mournful tone as a moral lesson of the price of nationalism. And it had a global perspective which emphasized that Britain did not win the war alone. But *World at War* inadvertently succeeded in reaffirming the idea that the Continent meant trouble and it helped to memorialize the Finest Hour at a moment when the legend would have been better left alone. *Colditz* (1972–4), a drama about British POWs trying to escape from their German captors, attracted a regular audience of 10 million, while new series of *Dad's Army* attracted nearly twice that. And although the production of war films declined considerably, they were given an extended shelf life by repeated and much watched TV screenings.

The press helped to whip up isolationism, emphasizing how different the British were from their new partners and reminding politicians that they had not given the people an opportunity to decide their fate. At best, the press smugly emphasized the contribution which the British tradition of political stability and business acumen would make to the Community. Despite relative economic decline and mounting industrial conflict, Britons, it seemed, still regarded themselves as more enterprising and more moderate than

Continentals. On its front page, the *Daily Express* splashed a picture of Debbie Bushby, the first child to be born in the UK on 1 January 1973. Next to the caption 'The Euro-baby who couldn't care less', it said, 'Debbie has hardly opened her eyes yet . . . but when she does, she'll have to accept the fact that she's joined the . . . Euro-babies'. The paper warned that in twenty years' time children could be registered as European citizens. Meanwhile, it reassured readers that Debbie's nineteen-year-old mother, Sylvia, regarded her child as British. A front-page editorial said:

> [Our entry] DOES NOT carry the approval of the majority of the British people . . . But now that we are in, the Express believes it would be fatal to hang back, that there can be no purpose in pining for the past . . . Britain has a powerful role to play. Her tradition of political stability, her skills in finance and business are what Europe needs. Let there be no doubt: If it becomes clear that there is no place for Britain in the developing European Community, Parliament has a way out. So watch out, Europe – Here we come![41]

The idea that Britain was doing Europe a favour by being in the Community sprang from a belief that Britain was not so much abandoning its imperial past as renewing its civilizing mission to the world by giving Europe the wisdom it had formerly bestowed on Africa and Asia. Britain did have something to contribute other than the contents of its Treasury, and this was readily acknowledged by Continental leaders. They did so partly in order to soothe patriotic pride; to make the British feel that their distinctive national culture was valued and was therefore safe in Brussels' hands. They were particularly ready to acknowledge the country's lone defence of democracy during the war. Commenting on the UK's accession, Maurice Schumann said, 'I am deeply happy, as a life-long friend of Britain and as a man who remembers that, had it not been for England [sic], there would have been no Europe after 1940.'[42]

But the idea that Britain's contribution was a superior one was less politic. It was an attitude which might have been tolerated had Britain joined the Community in the 1950s at the height of her moral authority in the West. But it was not one that endeared the British to their partners by the time they finally joined. The most popular *Express* columnist, Jean Rook, wrote a typically rumbustious account of what the Community should expect:

Since Boadicea, we British have slammed our seas in the faces of invading frogs and wops, who start at Calais. Today, we're slipping our bolts. And, of all that we have to offer Europe, what finer than contact with our short-tongued, stiff-necked, straight-backed, brave, bloody-minded and absolutely beautiful selves? To know the British (it takes about 15 years to get on nodding terms) will be Europe's privilege.[43]

In vain, *The Times* reminded Britons that the EEC was a Community and not a club of which the British had just become secretary. In a leader entitled 'A GREAT DAY FOR EUROPE', it said, 'They have solved many of the problems of adaptation to the postwar world better than we have. The European nations are certainly not waiting for Britain as though we were the good fairy in the pantomime.'

However, the second reason why the EEC did not capture the British imagination cannot be blamed on the rabble-rousing of sceptics in Parliament and the press. It was the failure of British Europhiles, through blindness, ineptitude and downright snobbery, to establish a sense of Europe's common culture among ordinary Britons. This is an issue of class and not of nationalism and as such it does not fit easily into the settled historical view that British scepticism was the product of a peculiarly insular people. It is a sign of the appalling myopia on this subject that while Britons are regularly chastised for not adopting a European identity, few scholars stop to examine what the European identity they are being offered actually consists of.

Ever since the idea of European Union was first mooted in the 1930s it was based on a vision of Western civilization which disdained popular and minority cultures. The Continent's genesis was seen to be Ancient Greece. From this flowed a Whiggish narrative of progress that would have made Macaulay blush. It proceeded from the Roman Empire through medieval Christendom, the Renaissance, the Enlightenment and on to the Romantics. The violent conflicts of these eras were not ignored by polemicists – especially the liberal revolutions of the nineteenth century which brought some degree of democracy to Europe. But the first half of the twentieth century was seen to be a catastrophic period during which this rich civilization came close to extinction as a result of revolution and war caused by the extreme right and left. From 1950, so the story went, the European Union arose to rescue its members, bringing them unprecedented peace, prosperity and cultural enlightenment. A Community pamphlet, published in 1970 for a British audience, explained:

It was Europe that gave birth to modern civilisation ... Building on Greek and Roman civilisation and the Judeo-Christian religion, Europe developed the idea of individual freedom and dignity; parliamentary democracy ... ; the rule of law to which all, high and low, are subject; music and the arts; social welfare, with society accepting responsibility for those who are ill-equipped for its strains and stresses. From Europe these ideas have been carried to the farthest corners of the earth. Some features of Europe's past – intolerance, violence, the struggle of nations to dominate other nations, and even continents – are today a source of shame. But, by and large, Europe's achievements call forth pride and wonder. For out of tyranny and misery they are fashioning freedom, humanity, and prosperity.[44]

The ideology of European unionism was essentially a liberal reworking of nineteenth-century imperialist discourse about the superiority of Europe as the cradle and driving force of world civilization. For all the rhetoric of democracy and welfare, the Community was essentially a club for imperial powers whose rivalry had come close to destroying each other and whose leaders now sought to bury their differences. European unionism provided an antidote to nationalism by offering its members a new pan-European nationalism, rather than a genuinely international outlook.

It was for this reason that European Union appealed not only to disgruntled imperialists but also to many fascists. It also goes a long way towards explaining why the idea consistently failed to excite ethnic minorities in the Community's member states. True, they were spared further holocausts on the scale of the 1940s. But ethnic minorities regarded the whole European story in a more critical light. For them, it was not 'by and large a story of pride and wonder', but a story of the exploitation of their ancestors by colonial powers. Moreover, the large degree of racism in modern Britain and (even more so) on the Continent did little to endear this post-imperial alliance to them. Even those who were well disposed towards the EEC had little time for it, being far too busy asserting their right to be British to bother about adding an additional tier to their national identity.

Most Britons were not put off entry because they disliked the thought of belonging to European civilization per se. But they were alienated by the way in which the *structure* of European civilization was defined because it took little account of the way that most of them lived their lives and viewed the world. Were they a more philistine people than other members of the Common Market? Certainly, there was an anti-intellectual tradition in Britain. But this should not be taken at face value. There is no evidence that farmers from Languedoc read Victor Hugo any more than their counterparts in, say, the Yorkshire Dales read Dickens.

The British were different for two reasons. First, they had a less traumatic, humbling memory of the war and were less bound together by a fear of it happening again. Therefore, because European union seemed less of a geopolitical necessity for the British, more than any other member of the EEC they had to be convinced that they had a cultural bond with their new partners. Second, Britons already had a far greater cultural bond with America than other Europeans did. Long after Britain's entry to the Common Market, the Atlantic was a narrower stretch of water in the British mind than the Channel. Of all the comments made about Britain's postwar involvement in Europe, that of W. H. Auden was one of the most perceptive. Writing in *Encounter* in 1963, he observed:

> One will never understand the current debate about England joining the Common market if one thinks of it as merely a clash between various economic interests. Beneath the arguments Pro and Con lie passionate prejudices and the eternal feud between the High-Brow and the Low-Brow ... Instinctively, I am Pro. I know Europe first hand, and as a writer I cannot conceive of my life without the influence of its literature, music and art.

On the other hand, he said, America and the Commonwealth appealed to the Low-Brows:

> [They] are inhabited by their relatives and people like themselves, speaking English, eating English food, wearing English clothes and playing English games, whereas 'abroad' is inhabited by immoral strangers ... and ... an Englishman who goes there often, still worse, decides to live there, is probably up to no good.[45]

By the time Britain entered the Common Market, shortly before Auden's death in 1974, the differences were less stark. The expansion of education had created a new elite whose cultural revolution blurred the boundaries between popular and high culture. But there was still a gulf between the taste of Britain's nascent meritocracy and the majority of the population, and this undermined the creation of a European identity in Britain.

Edward Heath personified that gulf. Though he envied Wilson's common touch, he set himself against any flirtation with Britain's 'pop aristocracy', parading his musical good taste before the nation as a sign of his integrity. Harold Wilson gave MBEs to the Beatles but Heath's went to the composer William Walton. While Wilson loved football, Heath's passion was for yachting. Neither choice could be deemed unpatriotic. Walton was one of Britain's great composers, who had scored the music for the Coronations of George VI and Elizabeth II. Similarly, yachting had echoes of the British seafaring tradition around which the Prime Minister had grown up. The reason why neither of these choices endeared him to the British public was not that they revealed a lack of patriotism in the man but the fact that both pursuits were alien to the experience of most Britons. Relatively few people listened to classical music and yachting was a sport enjoyed by a wealthy few.

The cultural renaissance had peaked by the time Heath came to power. But although Britain was no longer the driving force behind Western popular culture, she was still a force to be reckoned with and great store was set by that fact. In an era when pop music and football had become such focal points of national identity and benchmarks of Britain's standing in the world, not to have (or at least not to demonstrate) much interest in either was fatal. In 1971, Heath told the Royal Society of Arts: 'The artists, writers, and the musicians have shown the economists and the politicians the way. We have to bring to the creation of European economic unity the same interplay of ideas and aspiration . . . that enabled them to make a reality of European cultural unity'. It was a noble aim. But the British people were not minded to follow the artists, writers and musicians of the Continent, any more than they had wanted to follow British artists when urged to do so by the more nationalistic reformers of the mid-twentieth century. The different cultural outlook of rulers and ruled became chillingly apparent during the festival which Heath staged to celebrate the UK's entry to the Common Market on 1 January 1973: the 'Fanfare for Europe'.[46]

4. Fanfare for Europe

Fanfare for Europe was organized by a government-appointed committee, chaired by the Chairman of the Arts Council, Arnold Goodman. As well as old war horses of the national culture like C. P. Snow, three relatively young, charismatic products of the 1960s sat on the Committee: Roy Strong, Director of the Victoria and Albert Museum; Peter Hall, Director of the National Theatre; and David Attenborough, recently appointed Director of Programmes at the BBC. With a modest budget of £350,000, a range of events were staged across the country from 4 to 13 January 1973.

The Fanfare received the usual criticism which attends all state festivals – namely, that it was government propaganda the country could ill afford. On the left, Dennis Skinner asked the Prime Minister 'how the British people can celebrate a national disaster in the middle of a wages freeze'. Denying that it was 'a propaganda exercise', Heath replied, 'They will celebrate the opportunities of improving their real living standards.'[47] Heath was supported by Margaret Thatcher, the Minister for Education, who promised MPs that the celebrations would cater for 'a wide variety of tastes'.[48] Given the historic nature of the event it was marking, the Fanfare should have been one of the largest national events in twentieth-century Britain. But it completely failed to capture the public imagination, and three out of four Britons opposed its taking place at all. Why?

One reason was that the organizers played down the significance of the event for fear of alienating the country, knowing that once the subject moved from economics to culture the question of national identity would raise its awkward head again. The day before Fanfare began, Lord Goodman wrote in *The Times*:

> Europe is now accepted by most people with resignation, if not enthusiasm. The issues are too complicated for mass enthusiasm. People will dance through the streets when relieved of a mortal threat – by victory in a war; they will mourn for the death or assassination of a beloved monarch or friendly ruler; but to expect them to dress themselves up in woad or plait a maypole because we have successfully negotiated an elaborate customs treaty is to underrate their sense of proportion. Hence, I believe that the festivities of Fanfare for Europe . . . have been pitched at quite the

right note. They do not call for delirium, alcoholic frenzy or public screams of joy or defiance. They enable as many people as wish to do so to enjoy a splendid programme of musical and other events, with an emphasis on the reflective quality.

He went on to reassure Britons that this 'customs treaty' was not a threat to Britishness:

This country is embarking into trade adventures which enable us to graduate from a nation of shopkeepers ... into a nation of industrialists, financiers and scientific and efficient agriculturalists. With due regard to the proportion of this historic event, I hope that it does not overshadow Crecy and Agincourt, or make Waterloo irrelevant, or diminish the Battle of Britain.... This country will not lose its national identity. In 10, 20 or 30 years' time we shall not be speaking French, Italian or Dutch instead of English ... Neither will our culture be synthesised with those of the Continent. It is almost illiterate to believe that national cultures can be merged for economic reasons. What I hope will happen is ... an increased taste for British music, drama and painting and vice versa ... The European Community is a splendid adventure relating to trade ... It does not, I believe, touch the essential spirit of the individual and national character but it stimulates the best in it for the better deployment of national resources and the greater prosperity of the people.[49]

Official reticence manifested itself in the fact that there was no major exhibition telling the story of the British in Europe, as the Festival of Britain had told the more insular, self-reliant 'island story' (although, with deference to Scottish and Welsh nationalism, small exhibitions were mounted in Cardiff and Edinburgh which illustrated their historic links with the Continent). It was difficult for local authorities to make good the deficit with their own events. In 1951 civic leaders had enhanced a sense of national identity by using local patriotism to celebrate the diversity of British life. But in 1973 they struggled to present themselves as part of a much larger, more distant Continental culture. Town-twinning ceremonies were held across the island, but these failed to spark the popular imagination. Nor did the many local arts festivals staged with the assistance of the Arts Council. For example, the people of Hull were treated to a show at their Arts Centre by local poets and actors based on the less than plausible theme 'Hull is the Gateway to Europe'. Even the idea of Hull *becoming* a gateway to Europe soon acquired a terrible irony when the city's fishing industry, like others around Britain, was ravaged by

the opening of British waters to foreign fleets under the terms of the
Accession Treaty.

Many towns staged more traditional celebrations. The people of
Ivybridge in Devon lined streets decorated with the flags of every
Common Market member to watch a parade led by the Mayor, a
marching band and a teenager dressed as Britannia. Afterwards,
they gathered in the town hall for a big party. The Mayor, John
Congdon, later recalled, 'My thoughts on it was, let's become friends;
better friends than enemies. And that's why I was pleased to lead
Ivybridge into the Common Market.' His citizens were less idealistic.
Ivor Martin, the local odd-job man who put out the flags along the
parade route, said, 'When we went into the Market . . . people didn't
know what they were doing; they didn't know what was going on.
It was a big con-job. [The Fanfare] wasn't a celebration of going
in; it was literally a good excuse for a booze-up on someone else's
expense.'[50]

The main reason why the Fanfare failed to be more than an
excuse for a booze-up was that, to a far greater extent than the
Festival of Britain, it reflected the cultural outlook of the nation's
governing classes. Appropriately, it was launched with an ecumenical
service at Coventry Cathedral. The full programme began a day later
with an evening of music and readings at the Royal Opera House in
Covent Garden. Dodging a demonstration by supporters of Enoch
Powell, Heath arrived to welcome the Queen and the Archbishop of
Canterbury into a hall bedecked with artificial pink roses. Two
figures from the TV series World at War were involved. Carl Davis
conducted a concert of Britten's Spring Symphony and Beethoven's
Ninth, following which Sir Laurence Olivier read from Wordsworth.[51] The evening ended with Davis' modern reworking of the
national anthem, during which the Queen was reported to look
distinctly uneasy.

The overriding tone of the Fanfare was captured in the official
programme published for it. There were essays by J. H. Plumb on
the Grand Tour, C. P. Snow on Continental literature, Lord Montagu
of Beaulieu on vintage car motoring and Martin Du Pré on classical
music. An essay by the Times wine critic, Pamela Van-Dyke Pryce,
told of her struggle to make the British accept the European way of
life:

> I wonder if anything we do will affect those who . . . chill white
> wines to iced lolly texture, who serve young wines after old ones

... who dry their wine glasses with the cloth used for wiping greasy dishes, don't rinse the detergents from their decanters, and consider that two randomly selected half bottles will do to refresh a dinner party of eight. One goes on trying.[52]

Indeed. It is fair to note that some of the essays in the programme were lively and humorous and there was an attempt to incorporate popular taste into the festivities themselves. A football match was staged at Wembley with a team made up of players from the EEC's existing six members and players from the new arrivals, Ireland, Denmark and the UK. It was poorly attended. Although football was something all Europeans enjoyed, national teams generated nationalism. A joint British team, still less one that played alongside Irishmen and Danes could not therefore be a vehicle for European harmony.

A series of pop concerts were also staged. But pop was even more incapable than football of being a vehicle for rapprochement. European pop music was unremittingly awful: a formulaic pastiche of middle-of-the-road Anglo-American pop, laced with national folk tunes, which was both musically and stylistically inferior to that of Britain and America. This fact was rammed home on an annual basis by the Eurovision Song Contest. The contest was started in 1958 by the European Broadcasting Union as part of its attempt to use TV to bring the peoples of Europe closer together. But unlike *Jeux sans Frontières*, what it did was to reveal their differences. Occasionally, a Continental group like Sweden's Abba had an impact. After Abba won in 1974 (appropriately with a song called 'Waterloo') they went on to become one of the most popular groups in Britain, without whose music no Christmas office party was complete. But they were an exception which proved the rule.

For politicians this was an ephemeral sideshow to the debate about Europe. In fact, popular music formed a major cultural barrier between Britain and the Continent. It reinforced Britons' sense of superiority and it did so among precisely the age groups which Europhiles had to win over for their project to be a success. Surely pop was and is a global phenomenon that brought people together, regardless of their language and customs? Only up to a point. In *The New Europeans*, Anthony Sampson argued that pop, like sex, drugs and travel was a force for internationalism: 'the throbs and wails of pop music are about the nearest we have to a common European language.'[53] Sampson told how he had given a lift to a young Scottish apprentice when driving around Germany. The man, he noted with approval, 'had spent a hectic international month moving from pad to pad'. The author concluded:

> The young European may not take the idea of 'making Europe' as seriously as their elders; with no memories of war, the talk of reconciliation is just boring. But they are able to live in Europe much more casually . . . Beatniks, flower people or drug-takers are hardly distinguishable across the frontiers; since they talk very little, language hardly matters . . . English pop groups wander from town to town, as English jig-dancers did in the sixteenth century. The Beatles were first discovered on the Reeperbahn in Hamburg.[54]

So they were. But what Sampson did not mention was far more important: no *German* groups were discovered on the Reeperbahn who achieved even modest international success.

Since the birth of the gramophone in the 1890s, British and American music had been successfully exported to the Continent. By the 1970s, a pan-Western lexicon of rebellious hedonism had been established; a lexicon which in theory enabled a steelworker from Durham to play air guitar to 'Pinball Wizard' with an accountant from Dortmund, just as easily the same two might enjoy the skills of Bobby Charlton and Franz Beckenbauer. But, unlike football, this cultural traffic was virtually all one way. There was no musical equivalent of Beckenbauer for the British to admire. And as a result, there was no real cultural exchange in pop music of the kind that was needed to create a distinctly European youth culture with the power to affect British national identity.

The *New Musical Express* encouraged its readers to get into European music in the early 1970s. The editor, Richard Williams, contributed to the Fanfare for Europe programme with an essay called 'Can Eurorock replace the Mersey Beat?'. Criticizing 'the unconscious xenophobia of the British pop audience', Williams said, 'We're just beginning to realise what a wrong-headed attitude it is that no Europeans have anything whatsoever to contribute in the sphere of pop music.'[55] But the pop and rock concerts staged during the Fanfare for Europe highlighted the gulf. The groups which the government booked for the Rainbow and the Palladium were Slade, Wishbone Ash, Status Quo, The Kinks, Eric Clapton and Steeleye Span. There was even a hint of defiance. The Kinks ended with their hymn to London life, 'Waterloo Sunset'. Introducing the song, Ray Davies told the audience, 'I'm really going to enjoy doing this one tonight.'[56] The *NME*'s own review of the concerts was caustic:

Exactly what it had to do with going into Europe, few knew and
less seemed to care. Slade played just one encore, 'Mama We're All
Crazee Now'. That pretty well summed up what was going on
around the auditorium. Suddenly the lush Palladium curtains fell
and 'God Save The Queen' was put out over the P.A. Christ, it
seemed out of place.[57]

The clearest sign that attitudes to Europe were not changing fast
enough was the xenophobic reaction of the British to Continentals
when they met them on holiday. Cheaper holidays in sunny Spain
may have been one of the Common Market's selling points but
popular travel in this period did not appear to foster a sense of Europeanness.

5. There is some corner of a foreign beach that is for ever Britain

The growth of foreign travel in the 1970s was one of the most
important transformations in British life of the twentieth century.
For the first time in history, the masses could go to foreign countries
without being asked by their employers and rulers to exploit or kill
people when they got there. The number of holidays that Britons
took abroad began to grow steadily during the 1950s. In 1951 the
Association of British Travel Agents estimated that the figure was 1.5
million. By 1971 it had risen to 4.2 million, while the number of
passports issued each year went up from 470,000 to just over a
million during the same period.[58] However, the biggest jump took
place over the following quarter of a century. By 1981, 13.13 million
holidays were taken abroad, and by 1997 it was 29.14 million, a
sevenfold increase on the number taken at the start of the 1970s.[59]
In 1971 only a third of the British people had ever been abroad on
holiday. By the 1980s only a third had not.[60] This cultural explosion
was experienced by the entire developed world. By the 1980s,
tourism accounted for 12 per cent of the global economy, twice as
much as the international arms trade.[61] But Britain was arguably
more affected by it than most.

The immediate result was the decline of the British holiday camp and of seaside resorts in general. Of course, Britons continued to enjoy their own country. In 1997, they took 30 million holidays in the UK, mostly short breaks to complement foreign travel.[62] The seaside continued to account for three-quarters of that figure; and Blackpool – the mecca of the working classes since the Victorian age – remained the most popular domestic holiday destination.[63] But there was no escaping the fact that the nation had changed. Many of the beaches which had been defended with such gusto in the 1940s fell empty in the 1970s; the amusement arcades and souvenir shops were boarded up; and the hotels were kept in business by the state, which filled them with people on Social Security. Even pensioners began to desert traditional resorts, their passage assisted by the creation of SAGA Holidays, a firm that catered especially for the over-fifties (it was quickly dubbed Send All Grannies Away).

Most Britons went to the Continent, and above all to Spain. The song 'Y Viva España', which reached No. 4 in the pop charts in August 1974, captured the ebullience of the early years of mass foreign travel. Mediterranean resorts provided what British ones could not: consistently hot, sunny weather. Putting up with goose-flesh was not considered to be a patriotic duty, and people headed off to sunnier climes as soon as they were able to. They did not need the dolly birds of the *British European* to encourage them to do so. Safe, efficient jet travel was established towards the end of the 1950s. But it was not until the early 1970s that living standards rose sufficiently for people to take full advantage of aviational developments. By the time Britain entered the Common Market, the foreign package holiday, which had been pioneered by Thomas Cook in the mid-nineteenth century for the middle classes, finally became available to most people. Cook's, which had been nationalized in 1948, expanded its operation to cope with demand. Seeing the trend emerge, new companies like Horizon, Cosmos and Thomson's successfully challenged its dominance of the market. Cook's self-proclaimed reluctance to adopt 'a Majorca with chips' image was its undoing and led to its privatizion in 1972.[64] Competition in the travel industry was good for the consumer; it led to a price war which made foreign holidays even more affordable. Several other developments kept the momentum going. In 1970, travel allowances (imposed by Wilson) were lifted by Heath, enabling people to take more cash abroad. Second, restrictions on charter flights were relaxed. Third, a new generation of fast short-distance planes were introduced, notably the Boeing 727–200 in 1971.

Initially, hopes were high that tourism would lead to greater international understanding. The UN designated 1967 International Tourist Year, its General Assembly passing a resolution that it was 'a basic and desirable human activity, deserving the praise and encouragement of all peoples and all governments'. Announcing the start of the Fanfare for Europe celebrations, the Prime Minister emphasized the importance of travel in bringing Europeans closer together: 'Many more of us in Britain, in particular young people, travel to other European countries than a decade ago. Irrespective of our formal position under Treaties we have become steadily more "European" in terms of our knowledge and contacts.'[65] In the souvenir Fanfare programme, the historian Sir Jack Plumb applauded the 'masses' for 'finding excitement, delight [and] inspiration in European travel' just as the aristocracy had done in the eighteenth century and the middle classes in the nineteenth. 'Our history', he concluded, 'proclaims that we are a European people.'[66]

The optimism did not last. The middle classes continued the Grand Tour tradition by combining the quest for sensual pleasure with a search for cultural enlightenment, but it soon became apparent that most Britons went abroad purely for the former. Places like the Costa del Sol replicated the light-hearted orgy of sex, drinking and fair-ground fun perfected by the British seaside resort. Airports that once resounded with the clipped echo of handmade shoes, leather valises and the measured tones of the self-satisfied gave way to the squeak of trainers, plastic hold-alls and a cacophony of drunken, scantily clad, sunburnt adults and screaming children. Once abroad, most Britons disdained foreign food. Ruby Webster, a devotee of Majorca, remembers: 'I loved the Spanish people, they were so friendly, but I didn't go much on the food. So I said to the waiter "have you ever heard of rice pudding?" he said "no, no, no, not rice in the pudding?" and I said "yes, yes, yes". So he took me into the kitchens and I told them how to make it. We had rice pudding every day after that and the English people loved it . . . because in Majorca they didn't know a lot about English cooking in those days.'[67] In case they were forced to eat foreign food, Britons brought their own toilet roll abroad with them, as well as a supply of medicines that would have kept a Victorian expedition to the African interior going. They also refused to speak foreign languages, preferring instead to talk loudly and slowly in English in the hope of making themselves understood. Thomas Cook employees regaled the press with stories about the ignorance of those who did make an effort, such as the woman who asked one air hostess, 'What's French for à la carte?' And the souvenirs they brought home – sombreros, miniature toreadors and castanets – were seen as tacky proof of the working classes' failure to improve themselves through foreign travel. But worst of all was the growing number of reports that Britons were inflicting their xenophobic views both verbally and physically on the locals and also on tourists from other countries.

David Frost's study of the British character, published during International Tourism Year, humorously commented that the British definition of Hell was still as follows: a place where the Germans are the police, the Swedish are the comedians, the Italians are the defence force, Frenchmen dig the roads, the Belgians are the pop singers, the Spanish run the railways, the Turks cook the food, the Irish are the waiters, the Greeks run the government and the common language is Dutch. In the *New Statesman* Malcolm Muggeridge wrote, 'Thomas Cook and the American Express, not the *Internationale*, unite the human race'. But, for Muggeridge, travel – like communism – was a debased form of unity. 'Travel narrows the mind', he concluded in disgust.[68] A study of the phenomenon published in 1975, *The Golden Hordes*, described tourists as 'the barbarians of our age of leisure'. They were, it said, engaged in a 'new form of colonialism' which had no respect for indigenous peoples; at worst inflicting loutish behaviour on them and at best treating them like amusing animals in a game reserve.[69] Liberal disappointment was made more acute by the fact that Spain, where most Britons went for their holiday, was not then a member of the EEC. Indeed, it was still a fascist dictatorship, ruled until 1975 by General Franco – an irony which the ageing Oswald Mosley must have appreciated.

The outlook and behaviour of young Britons was a particular source of concern. University students were praised for backpacking around the Continent, a practice which grew thanks to the introduction of InterRail in 1971. But while student travel was regarded as a way of bringing Europeans closer together, the package holidays which most people went on were seen to have quite the opposite effect. There were two reasons why youth tourism took off in the 1970s. One was the economic independence which young Britons had been steadily gaining in the postwar period. The second reason was more specific: in 1968, Butlin's stopped taking group bookings from single teenagers. This followed public criticism that holiday camps had become 'a glorified knocking shop without money changing hands'. Since the late 1950s, Billy Butlin had successfully sought the teenage pound. Tony Peers was sixteen when he went to Butlin's at Pwllheli in the early 1960s:

> It was utopia for us teenagers. There were thousands of us and we walked around without our parents for the first time, and we felt really grown up. Butlin's was glamorous. There were live bands and the place was crawling with girls. We sat in the coffee bar during the day playing the jukebox and chatting up the crumpet. At night we packed into the rock 'n' roll ballroom. It was a struggle to get to the bar and we got brainless every night ... The wonderful thing about Butlin's was that for the first time for all of us, there was booze, girls and somewhere to take them.[70]

Following the change of policy, millions like Tony Peers transferred their activities to the Mediterranean. British youths found that they had even more freedom to indulge themselves abroad, and the mounting disapproval of their activities did nothing to reverse the trend.

Foreign travel had a particularly liberating effect on women because it temporarily freed them from the drudgery of domestic life. Pat Mancini and her husband went to Benidorm, Spain, in the early 1970s. She remembers: 'We made love more on holiday ... I mean you never had sex in the afternoon at home because you were baking or frying chips or something; but on holiday – bang, crash, wallop – you've got time for it. When you'd arrived abroad with the heat, the wine, the atmosphere, it was like the first time all over again. You were more sensual lying there with no sheets and nothing on.'[71] Women were stigmatized less for sexual promiscuity when they were abroad, and many exploited their new freedom in liaisons with foreigners; in fact, studies showed that they did so considerably more than men, and as a result tended to be more open-minded than men about the European Economic Community and more likely to engage with its culture. Cassie McConachy, another Benidorm regular, remembers: 'If you went with your mates you wouldn't mind having one night stands ... The drink helped you lose your inhibitions. It didn't matter if it was a Spaniard, an American, or a German. You probably wouldn't have been seen dead with them at home because everyone would talk about you, but on holiday abroad nobody cared. You would sort of step out of bed in the morning and say "thanks very much, bye".'[72] During this period, stories about British women falling for smooth-talking, sun-tanned Mediterranean

Romeos littered the popular press. The lascivious approval that accompanied reports of men seducing their au pairs did not extend to the female population. Reports of broken-hearted holidaymakers were presented as a moral warning of what happened if women went with foreigners. Like the gum-chewing GIs of wartime Britain, the martini-sipping Mediterranean of the 1970s was seen as a threat to British society. This double standard also mirrored older, imperial attitudes towards Africa, Asia and the Orient. Then a blind eye was turned to colonials who had sex (consensually or not) with native women, while native men who had any kind of relationship with 'Britannia's daughters' faced imprisonment and death. Women weathered the prejudice. Independent access to foreign holidays became an important stage in their emancipation during the twentieth century, challenging as it did their given role as guardian of the home and bearer of the race.

Despite popular fears about the sexual threat of European men, disdain for mass tourism was predominantly a middle- and upper-class prejudice. It sprang from resentment that the masses were spoiling places which the few had previously enjoyed in peace. This was a logical extension of the fears expressed earlier in the century that domestic tourism was desecrating rural Britain. As such, the issue was as much about ancient class snobberies as it was about contemporary enthusiasm for European union. Educated Britons sought out ever more remote places in order to avoid the hordes and to experience what they saw as authentic foreign cultures. Some went to the poorest, most dangerous parts of the world. Others bought luxury holidays like sea cruises, which were marketed as a glimpse of the 'golden age' of prewar travel. Whether trekking on camels or dining under chandeliers, these Britons thought of themselves as travellers rather than tourists. As well as eating foreign food, attempting to speak foreign languages and even dressing in foreign clothes, they consumed travel writing in a self-conscious effort to understand the places they were visiting. British travel writing emerged as a literary genre in the 1920s, but it was during the 1970s that it became firmly established, adopting a more elegiac tone that reflected the sense of loss that the middle classes felt about the exotic becoming the everyday.[73]

Disdain for popular tourism was also caused by a specific disappointment that it had failed to make Britons more aware of their Europeanness. Richard Hoggart continued his lifelong lament about the quality of twentieth-century British working-class culture by saying that Europe was simply seen as 'a source of cheap drink and easy sex'.[74] There was a reluctance among British commentators of all political outlooks to accept that cheap drink and easy sex were valid enough reasons to go abroad. And they failed to see that such simple, fundamental pleasures might eventually foster a sense of Europe as effective as the Graeco-Roman–Judaeo-Christian cultural heritage. It is ironic that ancients like Epicurus would have understood perfectly what it was that drew millions of Britons to Mediterranean beaches every year. The reluctance of critics to see beyond their refined mental parameters, or even to understand what those parameters contained, sprang from the puritanical strain within British culture as well as from the elevated view of Western civilization which prevailed within the European movement.

There was also a large element of hypocrisy about the criticism of popular travel. First, globalization actually did much more to erase the distinctiveness of European countries than popular tourism and in that sense the lower classes were made a scapegoat for corporate capitalism. Second, tourists who clutched their Michelin Guides while visiting cathedrals and museums were often no less xenophobic than working-class Britons slumped in beach bars. British gentleman travellers in the eighteenth century had not always been cosmopolitans. Their interest in classical civilization usually involved stealing bits of it or buying it cheap and taking it back to country houses – or, if they were really public spirited, the British Museum. Moreover, the admiration of the gentleman traveller for the beauty of a classical statue was often matched by his disgust at the modern inhabitants of the places he visited. It is also a myth that, in the twentieth century, xenophobia was solely a disease of the working-class tourist. In the 1950s, when foreign travel was the luxury of a few, the middle and upper classes of Britain were often hostile to the Germans they encountered while on holiday abroad. The Foreign Office saw travel as a way of overcoming the enmities generated by the Second World War. But, in 1954, it noted that the newly formed Federal Republic, and the wealth it was rapidly generating, had 'reactivated the aggressive and tactless characteristics of many Germans'. 'It is hardly surprising', one official concluded, 'that the vast hordes [of Germans] pouring into foreign countries [on holiday] should cause some ill-feeling, particularly in those countries which were occupied by Germany'.[75] Therefore, the idea that aggressive 'Krauts' always get to the pool chairs first may have emerged in the 1970s. But it was merely an extension of prejudices already felt and voiced by the educated classes twenty years before. And, as the Foreign Office noted in the 1950s, those prejudices were shared by millions of other European people. More than any other cultural trend, the visceral reaction to popular travel from the 1960s to the 1980s handicapped the European cause.

The only real attempt to promote Europe in a more populist way was to sell it as a lifeboat for Britain's sinking economy. But as we've seen, this was predominantly a way of avoiding the issue of national identity, rather than confronting it in order to forge a new kind of Britishness. Of all the broadsheet newspapers, the strongly pro-EEC *Times* was the most alert to the necessity of creating a popular European identity. In 1973, it commented: 'Europe needs an idea, and it needs to have more appeal to human nature than mere geographic propinquity or economic interest provide. The people of Europe should be able to see themselves as a European nation with a particular character and aims.'[76] But here was the rub, the dilemma which Europhiles continued to face for the remainder of the century. Concentrate on economic matters and the issue of national identity could be ducked, at least for a time. But Britishness would remain more or less unaltered as a result. Attempt to confront national identity and there was a long-term chance of establishing a sense of Europeanness. But in the short term, this strategy risked provoking British nationalism.

The economy was also a highly dangerous way of selling the European dream in the 1970s, because it was so unstable. Surveying British opinion in the spring of 1972, Heath looked with some confidence at the opinion polls, which showed a slight revival of enthusiasm for the Common Market and at the favourable response to decimalization. He told an American diplomat that Britons were a little more excited by the prospect of joining Europe. It was a false dawn. Amidst spiralling inflation and unemployment, the economic priorities which the Fraser Report had identified, and on which Europhiles had dominated the public debate, turned decisively against them. The economic benefits of Common Market member-ship were a long way away. And they depended on the economy being healthy enough to benefit from entry, which it was not. Despite a brief, imprudent credit-fuelled boom, the British economy was collapsing under the weight of long-term structural weaknesses. The situation was made worse by a dramatic rise in world oil prices in October 1973. Paradoxically, this actually benefited the European cause for a time. The social conflict which the economic crisis provoked was so severe that Britons were temporarily distracted from the 'enemy' across the Channel.

Edward Heath had wanted to modernize Britain in order to fit it for membership of the European Union. But Britain did not want to be modernized. The connected stories of Common Market entry and social unrest in this period point to a paradox within British national identity which Heath failed to resolve. On the one hand, the centrality of the Second World War to Britishness continued to prejudice attitudes to the European Community. But at the same time, the dissipation of wartime social unity prevented the country's leaders making the economic changes necessary for the UK to benefit from EEC membership. Because the British were unable to share in the Continental standard of living, popular Euroscepticism remained as strong as it had been in 1970.

6. The trumpet gave an uncertain sound

The story of the UK's early years in Europe was not a happy one. On the first official day of membership, the Union Jack was mistakenly but ominously flown upside down next to the flags of its new partners outside the Community's Brussels headquarters.[77] The *Guardian* forecast trouble ahead:

> If the trumpet gave an uncertain sound, who shall prepare himself for the battle? Well, it's a pity that the Fanfare for Europe is not more harmonious; but in politics as in music dissonance has always been inevitable if the Second Fiddles play a different tune. In this case it must be acknowledged that a large part of the country is not ecstatic about the score. The journey in Europe will be bumpy and discordant . . . The transition period will not be all beaujolais and boules. Change is always painful and, although the change arising from membership will not be as sudden or all pervasive as either its zealots or its most fiery critics believe, there will be enough change to cause trouble if people are determined . . . We enter Europe with the reputation of being a nation of shopkeepers; we would be unwise to present ourselves as a nation of second-

hand car dealers. Above all, we should avoid creating a new, semi-permanent rift in British society between pro and anti-Europeans.[78]

On returning to power, Harold Wilson insisted on renegotiating the terms of Britain's entry. He won a small rebate in Britain's budgetary contribution in March 1975 which did not justify the irritation it caused abroad.

Three months later, on Thursday, 5 June 1975, the British finally got a referendum on the European Question. Asked whether they wanted to stay in the EEC, 67.2 per cent said yes and 32.8 per cent said no. The turnout was a respectable 64.5 per cent. The regional voting pattern showed that scepticism in this period was strongest in Scotland and Northern Ireland (Wales voted with England despite predictions that the principality would register a no vote). People on the northern periphery of the UK felt that their distance from the Continent would give them even less power than they had at Westminster, a view encouraged by the SNP and Plaid Cymru in this period. The Ulster Unionist parties were also against. Smarting from the imposition of direct rule on the province in 1972, they regarded Brussels as a further erosion of the absolute power which they had wielded for half a century. The fear of Continental Catholicism (no longer a factor on the mainland) added to concern about the marginalization of Northern Ireland. William Craig warned that Britain would be run by 'a collection of polyglot nations, people who speak strange languages, have foreign cultures and in so many cases a different national religion'. In his inimitable style, Ian Paisley declared 'the Virgin Mary is the Madonna of the Common Market.'[79]

It was the first time that a referendum had ever been held in Britain and it was fitting that a form of plebiscite which originated on the Continent should have been the instrument by which the British decided to be members of the EEC. Why did Britain vote yes? The *Sunday Times* believed that national identity in Britain had fundamentally changed: '[It was] the most exhilarating event in British politics since the war. By a clear majority, uncomplicated by a bad electoral system, the British people have declared themselves to be Europeans.'[80] They had done no such thing. In his study of the referendum, the nation's leading psephologist, David Butler, argued that the vote reflected British fear of radical change. Had it been held *before* entry the result might well have been no; by 1975, membership seemed the safest option – hardly a ringing endorsement of a new national identity.

There was a more positive aspect to the 'Yes' vote but it rested on surviving hopes that the EEC would deliver a better standard of living. 'No' campaigners like Labour minister Peter Shore tried to convince the British that their way of life was coming to an end: 'What the advocates of membership are saying . . . is that we are finished as a country; that the long and famous story of the British nation and people has ended; that we are now so weak and powerless that we must accept terms and conditions, penalties and limitations almost as though we had suffered defeat in war.'[81] Early in the campaign, the government-sponsored 'Britain In Europe' group met this challenge head on with two posters about the war. The second of these was issued on the thirtieth anniversary of VE Day and read: 'Thirty years ago today, the war in Europe ended . . . Millions had suffered and died in the most terrible war Europe had ever seen. On VE Day, we celebrated the beginnings of peace. Vote Yes to make sure we keep it.'[82] But, it was soon decided that mentioning the war was likely to have the opposite effect, and that economic benefit was still the safest ground on which to fight (thirteen of the seventeen subsequent campaign posters concentrated on jobs and prices). As in 1971, political caution made some strategic sense. Polls showed that for 58 per cent of Britons, the cost of living was their main concern, while only 9 per cent saw national sovereignty as an issue.[83] However, with the luxury of hindsight, an opportunity was missed to adjust British national identity to the geopolitical realities of the late twentieth century. Although even the most lavish Fanfare would not have achieved that adjustment on its own, this was a time when the British were relatively open-minded about Europe and a more courageous 'Yes' campaign might have prevented the rampant nationalism which characterized British attitudes to Europe in subsequent years.

The best that could be said about the result of the 1975 referendum was that the British, like their Queen, accepted membership of the Common Market as a practical necessity. According to Harold Wilson, the referendum settled the matter. Maybe, but not for long. David Butler concluded:

> When the Referendum was over, the issue ceased to divide the country. The decision to stay in the EEC was accepted . . . yet the verdict of the referendum must be kept in perspective. It was unequivocal but it was also unenthusiastic. Support for membership was wide but it did not run deep . . . So far from reflecting high-minded idealism about European fraternity most electors

seemed to have voted Yes in the spirit caught by Sir Christopher Soames, 'This is no time for Britain to consider leaving a Christmas club, let alone the Common Market.'[84]

The British outlook was highlighted by the apathy and hostility with which the European Parliament was viewed. Its creation in 1978 was primarily an attempt to foster a popular sense of Europe, but in the world's first direct elections to a multinational Parliament, on 7 June 1979, the UK turnout was a pathetic 32.7 per cent of the electorate, little more than that for local authorities and less than half the number who voted in General Elections. Over the next twenty years, the average turnout was 30 per cent, compared to 60 per cent in other member states.

The continuing lack of emotional commitment to the European idea meant that it was easy for sceptics to continue the fight to get Britain out. It was also easy for unprincipled politicians, whatever their real views on the subject, to manipulate Europhobia in order to prove their patriotism to electors. When scapegoating black Britons for the UK's problems became less morally acceptable, the EEC made a useful substitute. In short, Brussels replaced Brixton as the whipping boy of British nationalists. Metrication offered a particularly tempting buttock in the early years of membership. Although Britain's currency was not a major source of scepticism, weights and measures were. In 1971, Heath's advisers warned him that metrication aroused strong emotional opposition which could be exploited by opponents of the Common Market. But he had pressed ahead with plans to introduce it.[85] Metrication was as sensible as decimalization, but reason did not prevail because imperial measurements were linked in the public imagination with specific goods, some of which (like beer) were icons of Britishness. And for a few, 'imperial' meant just that: one last dugout in the retreat from empire. Returning from a summit in Paris three months after the referendum, with the country sinking deeper into debt, Harold Wilson proudly announced that he had saved Britain from the horrors of the 'Euroloaf' and 'Eurobeer'. 'An imperial pint is good enough for me and for the British people, and we want it to stay that way', he told the press.[86]

Over the next thirty years, politicians and the press were repeatedly blamed for fostering the 'semi-permanent rift in British society' over Europe which the *Guardian* had predicted. Roy Denman, the senior civil servant involved in Britain's entry negotiations, observed of the period 1973–96:

[Wilson's] role was that of a principal boy in a pantomime, wrapped in the Union Jack, crowned by the helmet of St. George, and standing up to foreign dragons. The pantomime has continued for more than 20 years; periodically the cast has changed, but not the script. Britain's European partners have received it at first with disillusion, then with irritation and finally with growing indifference.[87]

The European cause was hampered by British hypocrisy. However mistaken was the expectation of a European quick fix, Britons had come to believe that economic recovery depended on their joining the Common Market rather than on their own enterprise and hard work. When a quick fix did not take place it was easier to blame the Common Market than their own failings. Europe, they believed, was still bent on their destruction and it had been given the chance to succeed by a small, unrepresentative group of appeasers within their political elite. Over the following quarter of a century, the parallel myths of 1940 and 1973 reinforced each other until they reached a point where they were virtually indivisible.

Although anti-European politicians and press made the problem worse, the truth is that Britons' scepticism was there to be manipulated. The European Parliament failed miserably to make the EEC's governing Commission more accountable. As a result, what began as a laudable attempt to make ordinary people feel that they had a stake in the Community ended with Britons, at least, viewing the whole European enterprise as an irredeemably undemocratic imposition on their way of life. Moreover, even if the Common Market had delivered instant prosperity, it could never have been sold to the public on purely material grounds. However prominent economic concerns had become in the 1970s, they had not erased the more fundamental questions of national identity. Most historians focus on 'missed chances' in the conference rooms of Europe, arguing that if Attlee or Eden had signed up to the nascent EU, all would have been well. If the UK had joined in the 1950s, Britons would have had more time to get used to the idea of being European. But it is also likely that at the point of entry the public's reaction would have been more hostile than it was later on. In any case, historians of the missed chance theory are themselves completely missing the point. For European Union to be a reality, the British had to be convinced that they had a cultural bond with the Continent, because it is upon such bonds that federations, no less than nations, are built. Without them, the most exquisitely drafted constitution has little more durability than the piece of paper that flapped in Neville Chamberlain's hand at Croydon Aerodrome in 1938. Economic self-interest may hold nations together for a time. But, as Scotland's declining allegiance to England and Wales proved, it is not enough.

Therefore, British Euroscepticism in the late twentieth century cannot simply be blamed on an ignorant, xenophobic population. Scepticism sprang just as much from the failure of Europeanists to define and promote a European identity which had some relevance to the lives of ordinary Britons. Edward Heath was an extraordinary man to whom the nation owes a great deal. He was arguably as destined to take the British into the European Union as Churchill was destined to marshal them in the war which gave birth to that Union. But Heath was the wrong man to *lead* the British into Europe. When he won the parliamentary vote taking the UK into Europe, he returned to Downing Street, and there, alone at his grand piano, he played Bach's forty-eight preludes and fugues. In 1974, the symbol of Heath's downfall which resonated most in the public mind was the sight of his grand piano being hoisted into a removal lorry outside No. 10. When he left Downing Street, the man who took Britain into Europe was visibly seen to be taking its culture with him. And, with the likes of Pamela Van-Dyke Pryce promoting the Common Market by chastising Britons for overchilling white wine, politicians found it ridiculously easy to muster British nationalism by defending the pint of beer. Consequently, Britain's accession to the EEC was not the end of the 'Great Debate' but merely the start of a new and more ferocious stage of it. Accession did not put Britain at the heart of Europe but it did put Europe at the heart of Britain.

PART 8

STRIKERS

I have been expecting the collapse of capitalism all my life, but now that it comes I am rather annoyed. There is no future for this country and not much for anywhere else . . . Revolution is knocking at the door.

A. J. P. Taylor, 1974

I loathe and detest the miserable bastards . . . savage murderous thugs. May the Irish, all of them, rot in hell.

Lord Arran, 1974

1. Play 'The Red Flag' for Jack

Was civilization all over, as Kenneth Clark claimed in his epic TV series? Many Britons believed that their country was sliding into anarchy and even revolution during the 1970s. Orwell's observation that gentleness was the main characteristic of Britain, 'a land where the bus conductors are good-tempered and the policemen carry no revolvers', now seemed hopelessly dated.[1] Postwar industrial unrest did not begin in 1970; it had been a serious concern since the 1950s, though successive governments had backed away from tackling it legislatively. In 1947 the former General Secretary of the TUC, Sir Walter Citrine, concluded his history of the movement by reassuring readers that unions were patriotic, democratic organizations:

> The British Trade Union movement . . . recognises that power finally rests with Parliament as the ultimate custodian of the liberties of the people . . . [And] it realises that the destiny of labour is inseparably bound up with the welfare of the community as a whole . . . at no period in British history has the contribution which the organised workers have made to the success of their country been more widely or readily recognised.[2]

Union membership continued to grow until 1979, thanks to the increasing number of white-collar workers (membership reached a peak of 13.29 million, about half the workforce). But twenty years after Walter Citrine wrote those words, no union leader could have extolled the patriotism of trades unions without inviting derision. The number of days lost through strike action rose from 2.84 million in 1945 to 6.85 in 1969; the number of people involved rose from 531,000 to 1.66 million. Long before Edward Heath came to power, the British worker was satirized in cartoons and films as an idle, obstreperous and unpatriotic individual, willing to be led by left-wing trade unionists to achieve his or her material aims. The most notable example of postwar anti-union satire is the Boulting Brothers' film *I'm All Right, Jack* (1959), written and produced by the same team who had satirized national service in *Private's Progress* (1956). Terry-Thomas reprised his role as Major Hitchcock, the officer unable to control his men. He has become managing director of an armaments firm, and his tormentor (played by Peter Sellers) is Fred Kite, a Leninist shop-steward able to withdraw his members' labour at the slightest infringement of union regulations and liable to turn an even deeper shade of red at the mention of the word 'productivity'. 'Kite', says Hitchcock in one scene, 'is a real shocker, the kind of chap who sleeps in his vest!' *Tribune* thought the film 'as brilliant as it is contemptible', a criticism which did not prevent it becoming the most commercially successful film in Britain in the year that Harold Macmillan was elected Prime Minister.[3]

By 1970, the union movement was full of high-flying Kites. Heath's relationship with them looked promising at first. He had been on good terms with Vic Feather, the General Secretary of the TUC, since his brief stint at the Ministry of Labour ten years earlier. And he had known the most powerful union leader, Jack Jones, since the 1930s after they met in Spain lending support to the International Brigade during the Civil War. As Opposition leader in the 1960s, Heath courted them both. Jones remembers one extraordinary meeting which took place in 1969 at Heath's flat in Piccadilly when the leader of the Conservative Party led his guests in a rendition of 'The Red Flag'.

> There is no doubting Ted Heath's sympathy for people and we quickly established a feeling of camaraderie. It was a pleasant evening with Heath talking of his yacht and musical interests. At one stage he showed us a new piano he had bought and at our invitation played one or two short pieces. Then Vic Feather called out, 'Play "The Red Flag" for Jack', and the leader of the Tory Party cheerfully played Labour's national anthem. It put the seal on a jolly evening. [4]

There were to be no more jolly evenings together. Within a year of their sing-song, the men gathered around the piano in Piccadilly were facing each other across the conference tables of Whitehall in a bitter struggle for control of the country.

It began with a dock strike in June 1970, only a fortnight after the Conservative election victory, prompting the Prime Minister to declare a state of emergency under the Emergency Powers Act of 1920. Among other things, this allowed the armed services to carry out essential public tasks. During the three and a half years of his blighted premiership, Heath implemented this legislation no less than five times. By the end of 1972, the number of working days lost to strikes was 23.9 million, four times higher than the number in 1969, and 13.5 times higher than the early 1950s. It was a dramatic change. Unrest peppered most Western societies in this period but only Canada, Australia and Italy had a worse record. The situation was exacerbated by the government's attempt to clamp down on militancy with the Industrial Relations Act of 1971. This was a laudable attempt to secure industrial peace through a corporatist compact between government, employers and workers which set out the legal rights and duties of each. But it only provoked an already febrile union movement into further action.

The unions had never had such a political influence before and the effect of it on British life was enormous. Transport was often reduced to a skeleton service or paralysed altogether. Food shortages occurred periodically (though often caused as much by panic hoarding as by supply problems). During the miners' strikes in the winters of 1972–4 power cuts were frequent, plunging homes into periods of darkness not experienced since the Blitz and forcing offices and factories to conduct their business using torches and candlelight in an almost pre-industrial atmosphere. Even broadcasting was brought to a halt, something which had been carefully avoided during the General Strike. Announcements were posted on TV screens saying '—Television regrets the loss of your programmes. This is due to an industrial dispute.' TV had been the staple of popular leisure since the 1950s and these eerie, flickering messages did more than anything to convey the feeling that national life was being undermined.

At the start of the decade, Gallup had asked the British to describe their expectations of the 1970s. Optimistically predicting a more leisurely, affluent lifestyle, 43 per cent thought the nation would only have to work a three-day week. On 13 December 1973 they got their wish, though in rather different circumstances to those they had imagined during the optimistic after-glow of the 1960s.[5] Declaring a state of emergency in a televised address to the nation, the Prime Minister announced that in order to save fuel the working week would be cut to three days. Looking ashen-faced from strain, he called for national unity:

> At times like these there is deep in all of us an instinct which tells us we must abandon disputes among ourselves. We must close our ranks so that we can deal together with the difficulties which come to us from within or from beyond our own shores. That has been our way in the past, and it is a good way.[6]

Most of the press repeated Heath's call, condemning strikers for their lack of patriotism and evoking the memory of wartime unity in an attempt to rekindle it. Hughie Green did his bit, ending each edition of *Opportunity Knocks* with patriotic songs of his own invention such as this:

> We are still the nation
> That bred a generation
> Who in 1940 dark
> Made a torch of one last spark
> Fanned it into life to mark
> Freedom! Freedom in victory!

After repeated warnings from ITV (and falling viewing figures), one of Britain's longest-running shows was taken off the air in 1978. Green was convinced it was a left-wing plot. 'TV's been taken over by anti-patriots,' he said. 'The Reds aren't under the beds, they're right in there running programming. Why else did they stop me praising our heritage, and giving viewers good old rousing patriotic stuff to get the country back on its feet?'[7]

A certain amount of Blitz spirit was apparent during the worst periods of disruption. Productivity levels during the Three-Day Week almost matched those in normal working time, proving that when they had to be the British could be efficient and hard-working. But on the whole, Heath's appeal to 'close ranks' had about as much effect as Eden's call for national unity during the Suez crisis. As in 1956, the country was not simply divided over an important political issue. The very nature of British patriotism was being contested. Conservative Britons resented being asked to make sacrifices when the enemy was not a foreign one. After one power cut in 1972, Virginia Graham wrote to her friend, the entertainer Joyce Grenfell:

> Turned on the tele and the cut came. So off we went & filled bottles & climbed into our beds! I must say it's mighty drear, reading by torchlight, innit? Indeed the whole business which we are facing with such stoicism, makes one wonder whether democracy is quite the answer! When we were suffering for the nation's survival during the war the task was easy, but now we seem to be silently suffering, as we watch the country brought to its knees. It's ridiculous that a quarter of a million men should be allowed to paralyse the country, with all that there coal just sitting behind gates which nobody dares open.[8]

On the left, the challenge to wartime patriotism was even more pronounced. In February 1971, 150,000 trade unionists from around Britain marched through London to protest against the Industrial Relations Bill. In Trafalgar Square, Vic Feather addressed the crowd from the plinth of Nelson's column and turned Churchillian rhetoric on its head. 'This', said Feather, 'is D-Day, 1971. D is for demonstration. D is for democracy . . . The lame ducks are in the Cabinet, limping about on thin ice and quacking away about uniting the nation.'[9]

The decline of tea-drinking in this period reflected the decline of national unity. Once seen as the national drink, whose refreshing qualities oiled the wheels of British society at work, at play and in battle, it now became associated with the ubiquitous tea-break. Strikes over the length and frequency of tea-breaks were common and by the late 1970s the national drink had become instead a symbol of the bloody-minded laziness of the British worker. Tea consumption in the UK fell heavily from the early 1960s onwards despite the introduction of the teabag. This was partly because of the competition from American soft drinks. But market researchers discovered that the decline also sprang from the fact that tea had lost the classless image it had acquired in the 1880s because of its association with working-class militancy and the blame attached to that militancy for Britain's perceived decline (the biggest fall in consumption took place between 1970 and 1980).[10]

Some workers wrote to *The Times* in an effort to explain that they were not subversives but that patriotism, like most things in life, did not come free. Describing himself as 'a working class engineering employee', Roderick Colyer said:

Why hit the workers' pay packets? Will that unite us? Will it hell! . . . I do not want Communism, but I do want a Britain where no man forces another to be his slave to earn a survival wage . . . If I sound bitter, it is because I am . . . I am bitter because I can no longer meet mortgage payments and other financial expenses. I am bitter because my marriage has broken under financial strain.

Colyer ended with a swipe at those who dared suggest that the present generation of Britons were not worthy of the sacrifice made by their parents in the Second World War.

I am bitter because pensioners like my Mum and Dad cannot get £480 a year, yet it was they that brought us through the last two world wars that the government and others keep referring to. Unite us, Heath? Not me – and not millions like me.[11]

Another man made the point that with the arrival of a global economy, patriotism was a commodity in short supply in the board-room as well as on the shop floor:

> We get lectured about our duty to the country through exports. Well, more and more we work for international firms. What country are they loyal to? Dividends and profits is the answer. I am not a communist or an anarchist. I believe there must be differentials. But the trouble is the differentials are all wrong . . . Where I work there are lavatories for bosses . . . you can only get in with a key, hot and cold air conditioning, nice soap, individual towels. Then there are lavatories for senior staff . . . hot and cold, not so good soap, a few individual towels, but good rollers. Then there is ours . . . no hot and cold, rough towels, cheesecake soap. And no splash plate in the urinals. How do you think we feel about things like that in the twentieth century? Waving Union Jacks doesn't help. And if, as my mate says, we want to try to have the bridge and the Beaujolais as well as beer and bingo, what's wrong with that?[12]

What indeed. It was upon such aspirations that Thatcherism played so cleverly a few years later. In the meantime, complaints about the lack of splash plates in the workers' urinals seemed to prove that the spirit of Fred Kite had indeed vanquished that of Winston Churchill.

What effect did the social unrest of this period have on national identity in Britain? Primarily, it gave the progressive remaking of Britishness a sharp jolt by showing how much class conflict remained a feature of national life. For all the advances made since the 1950s towards the creation of a more meritocratic society, institutionalized inequality of opportunity was still rife. When heightened popular expectations coincided with economic stagnation, a collision was inevitable. Like most class conflicts, it was not a straightforward fight between workers and bosses. Trade unionists were more con-cerned than employers to enforce the gaps in pay and conditions between skilled and unskilled workers. Their obsession with 'differ-entials' and 'relativities' reflected Britain's elaborate class structure just as much as the lavatorial hierarchy established by some employ-ers. And the militancy of the period was such that many normally quiescent white-collar unions took industrial action. But in the popular imagination the conflict was seen to be between the working and middle classes.

Contrary to most historical accounts, the real political revolt of the postwar era did not take place in Grosvenor Square but at Saltley Coke Depot. It was initiated by people clad in donkey jackets on the freezing picket lines of grim industrial sites, not by those draped in paisley in the warm haze of marijuana-filled sitting rooms. Unlike the more fashionable middle-class revolutionaries of the 1960s, most strikers had no wish to turn British society upside down. Even those who would have liked to do so could not afford to. Lacking the cushion of inherited and/or salaried wealth which so many revolutionaries enjoyed, their priority was to improve their basic standard of living here and now. Yet, the strike action of these millions of ordinary, hard-up Britons affected society on a far greater scale than any campus sit-in or anti-Vietnam demo. And their actions provoked real fears that the established order was collapsing. To many people, 'D' did not, as Vic Feather claimed, stand for demonstration but for dictatorship. Some union leaders were eager to confirm those fears, publicly stating that their aim was to bring down the Heath government. When the miners went on strike, the Cabinet agreed that the entire authority of the government was at stake. They lost it, forced into a humiliating capitulation on 18 February 1972, and never fully recovered. 'Here was living proof that the working class had only to flex its muscles and it could bring governments, employers and society to a complete standstill', said a young miners' leader called Arthur Scargill.[13]

2. I do not believe that they are like the Scots or the Welsh

While Britain was rent by class conflict, another part of the United Kingdom descended into a very real civil war which directly challenged the authority of the state. During the 1970s, the constitutional settlement which had created Northern Ireland in 1922 unravelled spectacularly, causing the deaths of over 3,400 people and billions of pounds' worth of material damage. At their height, between 1969 and 1976, the Troubles were the greatest British political crisis since Suez, dominating the governance of the UK and highlighting the extent to which Britishness was being contested by more and more of its citizens. The press drew parallels with America's war in South-East Asia, and privately the government agreed. Early in 1972, for example, Douglas Hurd warned the Prime Minister that unless he ended the conflict soon, the British public would turn as sour over Ireland as the American public had done over Vietnam.[14]

The policy of internal reform of the province pursued during the 1960s had failed. At the same time, military chiefs were beginning to accept that the IRA could not be permanently beaten. The internment without trial of terrorist suspects introduced in August 1971 did little except increase international condemnation of Britain. The search for an alternative solution was also prompted by the fact that Northern Ireland was no longer of any use to the British. Economically, it was worthless. Its linen industry had been in decline since 1953 and its shipbuilding (which had done so much for the British war effort against Germany) since 1960. As a result of the Troubles, decline turned into collapse and few financiers were inclined to invest in a war zone to restore the province's fortunes. Unemployment was twice the UK average and due to discrimination Catholic males were twice as likely to be out of work as Protestants, a trend which aggravated their opposition to British rule. All of which left the British taxpayer to pick up the bill in welfare payments and industrial subsidy – though, unlike Scotland and Wales, economic assistance to Northern Ireland was incapable of pacifying nationalism. The annual Treasury subvention rose from £73 million in 1969 to £3 billion in 1994, making Northern Ireland far and away the most costly part of the UK (by the 1980s, public spending accounted for 70 per cent of its GDP).[15]

Despite the covert help which the British army received from Protestant paramilitary groups, the spiralling cost of the armed resistance to nationalist insurgence also lost its appeal in Whitehall because the province ceased to have any global military significance. In the nuclear age, Northern Ireland, like Britain's bases east of Suez, was of much less use in a world war than it had been in the 1940s. Furthermore, the Irish Republic was no longer a threat to Britain's security. By the early 1970s, the republic was locked into the NATO alliance and it was preparing to join the European Economic Community with the UK. The prospect of the republic being used as a back door into Britain by a foreign enemy had therefore become negligible. European leaders were hopeful that the entry of Britain and Ireland into the Community would resolve this ancient conflict as it had resolved that between France and Germany. Until paramilitary leaders were welcomed at Brussels, however, this was a naive outlook; and it was shown to be so when, on the day the two countries joined the EEC, IRA leader Martin McGuinness was arrested on the Irish border in possession of explosives. It was not until the Downing Street Declaration of 1995 that Britain formally admitted that it had 'no selfish or strategic interest' in Northern Ireland. But a policy of unification by consent was actively pursued from the late 1960s onwards, with the long-term intention of ridding Britain of what most of its people regarded as a costly and tiresome conflict.

Minds were concentrated by the Bloody Sunday tragedy. On 30 January 1972, thirteen people were shot dead by a platoon of British troops in Derry City, during an illegal NICRA march in which they allegedly came under fire from IRA snipers. The incident, together with ongoing anger about internment, provoked large demonstrations in the South as well as rioting in the North. The Irish Ambassador to London was withdrawn. In Dublin, Sir John Peck evacuated the British Embassy and destroyed secret documents shortly before 20,000 people marched on the building and burnt it to the ground on 1 February. A special plane was put on standby to airlift Peck and his staff back to Britain (a scenario that eerily preceded the evacuation of American Embassy staff from Saigon in 1975). Peck believed that Ireland was closer to civil war than at any time since the 1920s. For all the balaclavaed mourning staged by Sinn Fein/IRA, an incident like Bloody Sunday was precisely what its leaders wanted in order to move the war into a more vicious phase, encouraging normally moderate Irish citizens to support the struggle against Britain. Conor Cruise O'Brien was a Member of the Dáil at the time, and in his memoirs he recalled the national mood:

> What swept the country . . . at the end of January and in early February was a great wave of emotion, compounded of grief, shock, and a sort of astonished, incredulous rage against an England which seemed to be acting in the way we often accused her of acting but of which we had not for decades really believed modern England capable. The scenario seemed to have slipped back to 1921, or even earlier. For a few days, people talked and wrote of a national change of mood like that which had set in after the executions of 1916 . . . Sinn-Fein–IRA, and its friends in the

press and media, set themselves both to exploit this mood and to convert it into one of settled hatred, appropriate to a war of Ireland against England.[16]

For three years, Heath consulted eminent historians and political scientists; ministers and civil servants offered reams of advice on constitutional minutiae, strategies and timetables for implementing change.

In the end it came down to four options, outlined in September 1971 by the Central Policy Review Staff, a Whitehall thinktank headed by Lord Rothschild.

1. Direct rule of the province.
2. A power-sharing executive leading to a pluralistic, self-governing Northern Ireland.
3. A deal with the republic leading eventually to a united Ireland.
4. Immediate withdrawal, with the problem handed over to the UN.

Rothschild saw it as an essentially colonial problem. He plumped for withdrawal and told the Prime Minister that mainlanders would support the abandonment of Ulster, just as they had supported decolonization elsewhere in the world. The Cabinet rejected this on the ground that, whatever their views on Empire were, the British would regard military withdrawal as a capitulation to terrorism. A negotiated tripartite settlement involving the republic was, ministers agreed, the only way forward. They briefly considered trade sanctions against the republic and the suspension of the dual citizenship to which the Irish were still entitled. But they also rejected this idea, for two reasons: because Ireland was too close to Britain, geographically and culturally, for severance to be practicable; and because it would anger the Irish government, making a lasting peace harder to secure.

On 14 March 1972 the British government suspended Stormont and imposed direct rule on the province as the first step towards a settlement. Unionists, led by Brian Faulkner, the Prime Minister of Northern Ireland, were bitterly opposed to the move. They knew it was not a recognition of Ulster's Britishness but the end of the absolute power they had enjoyed for half a century. The Queen's representative there was also none too pleased. The last Governor of Northern Ireland, Lord Grey of Naunton, was a committed Unionist. Originally from New Zealand, since the late 1950s he had been governor of a series of colonial trouble spots, from Nigeria to British Guiana. Grey took up the Ulster post in 1969, from where he observed, 'So far both sides have been extremely nice to me. I only wish they were a little nicer to each other.'[17] He was regarded by the Heath government as a genial political fossil and played no part in the peace process. His recall to London in 1972 symbolized that, whatever Northern Ireland's future, the political order had changed irrevocably.

On 20 March 1973 the government published a White Paper, *Northern Ireland Constitutional Proposals*, which formed the blueprint for British policy for the rest of the century. It upheld the province's right of self-determination. But it also recommended an eighty-member assembly elected by proportional representation and overseen by an executive made up of Unionists and Nationalists. From then, it was downhill most of the way. The Unionist movement was split in half. Elections to the Assembly were held on 28 June which resulted in a majority for those opposed to power-sharing. Tortuous negotiations were held at Sunningdale in Berkshire from 6 to 9 December 1973, the first conference since 1925 at which British and Irish heads of government were present. The main result of Sunningdale was an agreement to set up a Council of Ireland consisting of seven Irish and seven Northern Irish ministers to harmonize policy on transport, agriculture, power and tourism. This intensified Unionist opposition. In January 1974, fist fights broke out in the Assembly chamber, leading to the forced removal of several members. On 23 March the Ulster Workers' Council was formed in order to bring down the Assembly with a general strike. On 30 May its aim was achieved. The Assembly was prorogued and officially dissolved in March 1975.

What did the conflict reveal about British national identity in this period? On the one hand, it strengthened the traditional view that Britain was an innately rational, moderate nation in comparison to its western neighbour. Even the most militant trade unions and the most debauched hippies appeared to be ardent patriots next to Irish terrorists. The following letter to *The Times*, published shortly after Bloody Sunday, typified this outlook:

> Sir, The real tragedy of the Ulster problem is not, hard though it may be for the relatives and friends of those involved to understand, the dead and injured, but the real and deep division between the people of Great Britain and those of Ireland ... It is difficult for any Englishman, though probably less so for the Scots and Welsh, to understand the almost appalling depth of irrational feeling the Irish have about their country ... The English are no

great brooders on martyrdom. Ask any hundred people in London who was Nurse Cavell and it is doubtful 10 could answer . . . I am afraid that just as we are incapable of understanding this type of logic, there will be a backlash in Britain by people who will no longer be willing to see their soldiers shot or their policemen injured, in the interests of a turbulent and seemingly irrational people, who rely on us for their economic existence, whether in Ulster or Eire, whose citizens have free access to our country, and liberty of expression here.[18]

Shortly after the collapse of power-sharing, Lord Arran wrote in the *Evening Standard*, 'I loathe and detest the miserable bastards . . . savage murderous thugs. May the Irish, all of them, rot in hell.'[19] However, this was not conventional anti-Irish prejudice because it was directed at the North as well as the South. The real significance of the Troubles is that they fundamentally changed the British view of Ireland, a process which revealed how much Britishness itself had changed.

Until the mid-1960s, Britons regarded the Northern Irish as civilized compatriots under siege from an alien, backward country. By the mid-1970s they were regarded as part of the problem, and by the end of the decade the North was seen to be far more backward than the South. Meanwhile the British identity of the Protestant majority hardened as a result of the Troubles. In 1968, 20 per cent thought themselves Irish. By 1989 this had fallen to 3 per cent while those who saw themselves as British rose from 39 per cent to 68 per cent.[20] Inspired by the Scottish literary renaissance of the mid-twentieth century, radical Ulster intellectuals like the poet John Hewitt attempted to construct a more autonomous national identity for Northern Ireland. Some political activists even toyed with the idea of an independent state. But most Protestants clung on to their Britishness with ever more ferocity. This did not endear them to the rest of the UK. To the mainland ear, the cry of 'No Surrender' was not an echo of Churchill's wartime promise 'We shall never surrender', it was the cry of a people refusing to adapt their national identity to a radically different postwar society.

The Irish problem was originally created by British colonialism. But by the late twentieth century it had become a more subtle ethnic conflict between two firmly established but violently hostile communities – one Irish and one British/Irish. The influence of religion on their identities made the conflict more intense but does not entirely explain it. These nuances were lost on mainland Britons. Most saw the war in Northern Ireland as an archaic religious conflict between Protestant and Catholic. That they did so was partly because British governments failed to educate them about the historical complexities of the problem. Privately, Sir John Peck mused: 'Despite all our kindred and affinity with the Irish, the ignorance of Ireland among the English is even more profound than their ignorance of Europe, and the parish priest is a stranger and more sinister phenomenon than the frog's legs and the garlic.'[21] But it was also indicative of the very real ideological gulf which existed between Northern Irish Protestants and their former co-religionists in Britain. Church membership in the province was three times higher than in Scotland and Wales and six times higher than England. Overall, it stood at the 1900 level of the mainland. On one occasion when Jim Callaghan visited Belfast, as Home Secretary, he won over a group of angry Protestant housewives from the Shankhill Road by getting them to sing 'God Save the Queen' with him. But the gulf between them became evident when, later in the visit, he met the Revd Ian Paisley. Callaghan remarked, 'We are all the children of God,' to which Paisley replied, 'No, we are all the children of Wrath!'[22] Paisley frequently claimed he was no more sectarian than the Queen, who had promised at her Coronation to defend the Protestant faith. 'The British Constitution is founded on sectarianism', he said. Strictly speaking, he had a point;[23] but in fact he was living a fantasy. Few Britons still revered the Constitution because it upheld Protestantism: they saw that provision in the same way that they might an ancient by-law allowing them to drive sheep down a high street on the third Saturday of every month. It was so anachronistic that it troubled hardly anyone and was therefore not worth revoking. To the rest of the UK, the centrality of religion to loyalist national identity proved that they were ignorant fanaticists obsessed with the past. Former Prime Minister Terence O'Neill lamented his people's refusal to countenance a pluralistic society, writing: '[They] chose to put [their prosperity] at risk in the interest of maintaining a Protestant ascendancy that had ceased to have any meaning elsewhere in the United Kingdom.'[24]

The negative view of Northern Ireland was reinforced by the fact that the British cultural revolution was severely stunted there. The province had a youth culture which produced punk groups from both sides of the sectarian divide. The best groups crossed that divide and gained a large following throughout the UK, notably Derry's The Undertones and Belfast's Stiff Little Fingers. But while the latter sang hopefully in 1979 of an 'Alternative Ulster', the high point of each year for most young Protestants was not a Stiff Little Fingers concert but the July parades, when jeans and T-shirts gave way to uniforms, and air guitars were replaced by flutes. And when a Mod revival took place from 1978 to 1982, Protestant followers of the trend sported red, white and blue roundels on their Parkas while Catholics coloured theirs green, white and orange.[25] The difference between the province and the mainland was also apparent in its resistance to much of the social legislation of the time. Opposition to abolition of the death penalty was much higher in Northern Ireland than elsewhere in the UK and a successful campaign was fought to keep abortion and homosexual practices illegal (they were also illegal in the republic, a fact which showed that the two Irelands had more in common with each other than either cared to admit). Many main-land Britons would have preferred gay sex to remain illegal in their countries too. But homophobia was no basis for a revival of sym-pathy for Ulster.

Shortly after the Second World War, Herbert Morrison described the Britishness of the province as 'an aggressive loyalty'.[26] It was the intensity of Northern Irish patriotism as much as its archaic roots which alienated the mainland. Practices such as painting pavement kerbs red, white and blue and the annual Orange parades were once respected as British traditions, even promoted to attract tourists. Now they seemed to be an immodest, intolerant and therefore un-British form of patriotism. Between 1968 and 1973, the proportion of mainlanders who thought the Northern Irish were intolerant rose from 8 to 44 per cent; those who thought them hardworking fell from 34 to 20 per cent and those who thought them friendly fell from 35 to 14 per cent.[27] This view became more common after the collapse of power-sharing in 1974. The British public was against any treating with the IRA and when news periodically leaked out that secret talks had been held, cries of 'Appeasement!' went up. However, the intransigence of Loyalists towards moderate National-ists and to what seemed a fair and sensible solution to the conflict lost them what little support they had in the UK.

Loyalists could not even rely on the support of Scottish Protestants – the people from whom they were descended and who were tradi-tionally their closest allies on the mainland. In 1971, the Grand Secretary of the Orange Order of Scotland raised around 3,000 volunteers to help Loyalist paramilitaries. This was a poor showing compared to the 12,000 Scots who had promised to bear arms for

Ulster against the South when they signed the Ulster Covenant in 1914, and the 27,412 Ulster Volunteers (the Ulster Volunteer Force was accepted almost unchanged into the British army as the 36th (Ulster) Division). Some of the 1971 volunteers went to fight in Ulster, but they were a tiny minority and their limited influence was epitomized by the hopeless gun-running carried out by the volunteers who stayed behind. The largest consignment of arms they mustered (seventeen rifles) was transported ineptly around the west of Scotland before the gun-runners were arrested.

There were two specific reasons why the Scots didn't rally to the defence of Ulster. First, their sense of Britishness was waning rather than growing like that of Loyalists. England, not the Republic of Ireland, was regarded as the main threat to their nationhood. A majority of Scots wanted devolution; they did not want to keep the Union of 1920 intact. By 1974, the Orange Order was championing devolution and condemning any involvement in terrorist activities. Scottish paramilitary leaders thought Ulster should move with the times. Said one UDA man from Glasgow, 'Like we do here, they have got to accept that the Taigs are there. They're not going to go away. They've got to give them a say in things and get on with it. It can never go back to the way it was.'[28] Second, the geographical closeness of Scotland to Ulster made revulsion against the war greater than in the rest of Britain. Many Scots feared that the conflict would spill over into their country, destabilizing it at a crucial period in its history when national unity was needed to press the claims of Scottish autonomy. Historian Tom Gallagher explained: 'Scots who might have tolerated religious or pro-Irish zealots . . . because they suddenly remembered their own Catholic Irish ancestry or Calvinist childhood, emphatically refused to give them houseroom once the toll of death and destruction mounted just sixty miles from the Scottish coast.'[29] The Troubles also affected the way that the British political elite viewed the claims of Scotland and Wales. Until the 1960s, Northern Ireland was seen as a model of devolved government. Supporters of Home Rule campaigned explicitly for their own Stormont and whenever devolution was considered by British governments the Ulster polity was consistently seen as a possible solution. This ceased to happen in the 1970s, not only in Whitehall but also among Scottish and Welsh nationalists. The SNP began to win over Scotland's Catholic working classes (traditionally Labour voters) by reassuring them that neither Home Rule nor independence would create an entrenched Protestant Ascendancy such as existed in Northern Ireland.

What of the English? The IRA's renewal of mainland bombing in 1974 was concentrated in England and it provoked a wave of anti-Irish sentiment there. Some argued for the deportation of the entire Irish population of Britain; and there were louder calls for the return of the death penalty than at any time since its abolition. Anglo-Irish friendships ended overnight. One London resident told the press, 'Even mates that I've worked with for years, Eddie from Wales, I've seen him blank me. Mates in the pub, they come out with comments like "Bloody Irish murderers, they should all be shot." '[30] No one was shot, but there were arson attacks on Irish pubs, community centres and Catholic churches in a number of cities. One of them was Birmingham, where the worst IRA bombing of all took place in a crowded pub on 21 November 1974, killing 24 and injuring 200. The Labour Home Secretary, Roy Jenkins, visited the city the next day. He recalled:

> I was in the city for four hours. It seemed an eternity and was one of the most difficult, draining, and unpleasant visits that I have ever paid. It was a dry, still, misty, rather cold day . . . and the atmosphere in the unusually deserted city centre of the city hung heavy with some not wholly definable but unforgettable and oppressive ingredients . . . Partly no doubt it was the lingering scent of the explosions, but there was also a stench of death and carnage and fear. Maybe this was all in the imagination, but what was certainly physically present was a pervading atmosphere of stricken, hostile resentment such as I had never encountered any-where in the world.[31]

However, even at the height of anti-Irish feeling in the mid-1970s, Britons made little distinction between the nationalism of those fighting for a united Ireland and the patriotism of those defending Partition. Except in areas like Glasgow and Liverpool, outrage at IRA atrocities was not generally expressed as support for Unionism. It was a reaction to the invasion of British sovereignty; a patriotism in and for Britain *not* the United Kingdom. The 'stricken, hostile resentment' observed by Jenkins could not, therefore, form the basis of a renewed affinity for Northern Ireland.

Perhaps nothing demonstrated this more than the reaction to Enoch Powell's decision to leave the Conservative Party and serve as Official Unionist MP for South Down from 1974 to 1987. He saw the province as a last bastion of that unambiguously patriotic, racially pure Britain which he had hoped to restore on the mainland. Large sections of the population continued to share his views on race – so much so that in 1973 a secret Government report compared relations between black and white Britons with relations between Protestant and Catholic across the water. However, Powell's move to Northern Ireland turned out to be a political exile. None but the most right-wing members of the Conservative Party and neo-fascist groups supported his stance on Ulster. His exile demonstrated how the province had become virtually a foreign country in the British mind; in the words of the travel writer Dervla Murphy, it was 'a place apart'.[32] Against this background of profound alienation, the cost of maintaining Partition became the concern not just of White-hall but of the nation as a whole. During the general strike which destroyed the Sunningdale Agreement, Harold Wilson made a broad-cast to the nation in which he accused loyalists of 'sponging on British democracy'.[33] The speech hardened support for the strike in Ulster but it struck a chord with the British public.

In 1972, the Foreign Secretary (and former Prime Minister), Alec Douglas-Home, was the only government minister against direct rule. Douglas-Home thought a united Ireland was the only solution; not because of any nationalist sympathies but because he believed that the Northern Irish were completely different from the people of Great Britain. Writing to a friend, he said:

> I really dislike Direct Rule for Northern Ireland because I do not believe that they are like the Scots or the Welsh and doubt if they ever will be. The real British interest would best be served by pushing them towards a United Ireland rather than tying them closer to the United Kingdom. Our own parliamentary history is one long story of trouble with the Irish.[34]

Home was writing as a Scottish aristocrat from the Borders, brought up in the Scottish Episcopalian (Anglican) faith. He feared that if Northern Ireland was brought closer within the orbit of the mainland its volatility would have a knock-on effect, destabilizing a Union that was also showing signs of strain. Politicians, their advisers and the secret services also regarded the Troubles as the extreme manifesta-tion of a general trend towards subversive disorder in the Isles. Following the IRA bombing of army barracks at Aldershot in 1973, right-wing Tory Sir John Biggs-Davidson MP told the Royal United Services Institute: 'What happened at Aldershot reminds us that what happens in Londonderry is very relevant to what can happen in London, and if we lose in Belfast, we may have to fight in Brixton or Birmingham.'[35]

3. We are on the same course as the Weimar government

According to one senior Whitehall figure, in 1972, shortly after the miners' strike, the Cabinet formally discussed the possibility that it was facing not simply a series of conventional industrial disputes but a political challenge by organized labour to the whole structure of Parliamentary democracy.[36] The upsurge of violence in Northern Ireland during this period, and the serious threat it posed to the integrity of the United Kingdom, added to that fear. In the summer of 1972 the Cabinet agreed that emotions were running so high in Britain that unless there was clear popular consent for government measures to tackle economic problems, the support of the British people for the rule of law could not be relied upon in the event of further industrial action.[37] In other words, a limited form of civil war *on the mainland* was a possibility.

There were some who saw the struggle between British capital and labour in even more apocalyptic terms: those of the international struggle against communism. The United States did nothing to discourage this view. Richard Nixon regularly encouraged Heath to take on the unions as he himself had done in the US. Douglas Hurd recalled that during an Anglo-American conference outside Oxford in January 1974, 'the atmosphere was almost Chekhovian. We sat on sofas in front of great log fires and discussed first principles while the rain lashed against the windows.'[38] Heads of the home Civil Service are known for their icy calm, but such was the anxiety in Whitehall that Sir William Armstrong suffered a mental collapse at the 1974 summit. One minister remembers him being 'really quite mad in the end . . . lying on the floor and talking about moving the Red Army from here and the Blue Army from there'.[39] Even those who remained calm and in control of their faculties feared for Britain's future in the 1970s. At a dinner party in December 1973,

Geoffrey Rippon (the minister who had led the negotiations for Britain's entry to Europe) told friends, 'We [are] on the same course as the Weimar government, with runaway inflation and ultra-high unemployment at the end.'[40]

Rippon's comparison with Weimar Germany was not a flippant one. During the mid-1970s, sections of the military, secret services, industrialists and extremist political groups (such as the cutely titled National Association for Freedom) held discussions about the possibility of a coup to establish a military junta if civil disorder got any worse. There were rumours, circulating around the Commander of the National Defence College, that the movement was called PFP – (Prince) Philip for President. The respected military historian John Keegan remembers hearing a speech by Cecil King at Sandhurst, in which he urged the top brass to act soon. 'I had no doubt', said Keegan, 'that I was listening to a treasonable attempt to suborn the loyalty of the Queen's officers.'[41] Given the paucity of information available, it is difficult to say exactly how extensive contingency plans were and how many people were involved. Some of the plans are scarcely believable, such as the suggestion which one group of army officers made to the managing director of the Cunard shipping line that the *Queen Elizabeth II* could be used as a prison ship for the Cabinet in the event of a coup. But there can be little doubt that for the first and probably the only time in the postwar period, sections of the British Establishment gave serious consideration to suspending parliamentary democracy in Britain.

Not all right-wing activity went on behind closed doors. During the 1970s, British fascism was more successful than it had been during its original heyday in the 1930s. In 1967, the National Front was formed out of a motley assortment of groups, primarily veterans of Mosley's British Union of Fascists, A. K. Chesterton's League of Empire Loyalists, and the Greater Britain Movement led by John Tyndall and Martin Webster. The latter were the dominant force and they led the movement away from Chesterton's lost imperial cause and Mosley's advocacy of European Union, hoping to create a distinctively British nationalist party. The Front won a series of local elections and by 1977 it was the fourth largest political party in Britain. It owed its success mostly to the economic crisis of the 1970s, encouraging people to scapegoat black and Asian Britons, just as Mosley had scapegoated Jews before the war. It profited from the consensus over race relations policy at Westminster, in which immigration was controlled while those already in the country were (in theory) protected by race discrimination legislation.

Trevor Griffiths' play *Oi! For England* (1982) captured the despair which exacerbated old hatreds. It told the story of a group of young skinheads and the political activist who recruited them with the following speech:

> Doleboys like yourselves, school over years back, job not yet begun. English. Working class. White. Sicker bein' kicked around, ignored, shat on, pushed to the bottom of the midden, up to their necks in brown scum, the diarrhoea their rulers have seen fit to flood this England with. Their England. Made on the backs, made by the sweat of the white working class, generation after generation. This England, run BY foreigners, FOR foreigners. Jews, Arabs, coons, Pakis, wogs from all corners of the earth. Chocolate England.[42]

Attacks on ethnic minorities soared in this period, up from 2,700 cases per year in 1975 to over 7,000 in 1981 according to the most conservative official statistics.[43] Following the formation of the Anti-Nazi League in 1977 there were regular, violent clashes between it and the National Front. A TV interview given by Mrs Thatcher in January 1978, in which she expressed sympathy for people who 'are really rather afraid that this country might be rather swamped by people with a different culture', did nothing to diffuse tensions.[44] Nor did the Nationality Act of 1981. In order to prevent further 'swamping' it undid Labour's 1948 Nationality Act by establishing three tiers of British citizenship, only one of which offered the right to settle in the UK. Commending the Bill to the House of Commons, Willie Whitelaw, the Home Secretary, said 'it is time to dispose of the lingering notion that Britain is somehow a haven for all those whose countries we used to rule.'[45] Little wonder, then, that the Anglo-British identity of the black population declined still further. Recalling his West Indies childhood in the 1940s, Michael De Freitas wrote: ' "Land of Hope and Glory". We sang that song as little boys with the greatest fervour. I was thrilled with the prospect of seeing the Mother Country'.[46] During the 1970s and 1980s, the poet Linton Kwesi Johnson captured the angry disillusionment of England's black population. In his most famous poem he wrote,

> Inglan is a bitch
> dere's no escapin' it

Inglan is a bitch
y'u bettah face up to it.[47]

From mother to bitch in a generation. The white destruction of black patriotism made England's alienation of the Scots look like a lovers' tiff.

One of the lesser-known but most colourful founders of the National Front was Andrew Fountaine. Born in 1918, he was a Norfolk landowner who fought for Franco during the Spanish Civil War. After serving in the Royal Navy as a lieutenant commander during the Second World War, he became a Conservative parliamentary candidate and thrilled Tory Party conferences of the 1940s with rollicking speeches, such as the one which described the Labour Party as a group of 'semi-alien mongrels and hermaphrodite communists'. In 1950 he left the Tories and over the next decade or so set up a series of fascist groups, announcing, 'The man who can gain the allegiance of the Teddy boys can make himself ruler of England.' In 1962, he established an 'Aryan camp' on his estate near Swaffham where fellow travellers could enjoy physical exercise and political discussion. Some Teddy boys came. But he never achieved his ambition of ruling England; indeed, he never won over his beloved mother, who heckled him at public meetings. After helping to set up the NF, he became its first parliamentary candidate at a by-election in 1968. He polled 1,400 votes by claiming that immigrants lived 'one third off prostitution, one third off National Assistance, and one third off Red gold'. Over the next twenty-three years, Fountaine's life mirrored that of the fascist movement in Britain. He spent it either expelling rivals or being expelled himself in perpetual internecine feuds. He retired from the movement in 1981 to plant trees on his estate and died in 1997.[48]

Why did Fountaine retire in 1981? It is commonly argued that the reason for the collapse of the National Front after the general election of 1979 was that the rightward drift of the Conservative Party under Mrs Thatcher appealed to extremists who had previously been forced onto the political fringe by the postwar consensus. She did publicly welcome them 'back' to the party.[49] But the reason why the far right had so little success in Britain is more complex than Mrs Thatcher's critics will allow. Many on the far right thought Thatcher was no better than her predecessors or worse (Fountaine described Thatcherites as 'the greatest bunch of traitors in history'). British fascists, like those elsewhere in the world, believed in the corporatist state and despised laissez-faire economics as a vehicle of Jewish domination. The fact that many of Thatcher's advisers – from Sherman to Joseph and Saatchi – happened to be Jewish did not go unnoticed. More importantly, the Thatcher theory does not explain why, throughout the twentieth century, extremists in Britain had far less success than they did on the Continent.

There were in fact several reasons. First, at no point did the British economy experience the free-fall into which Continental countries plunged at various times. Even the severe recessions of 1929–35 and 1972–82 were not comparable to the chaos of, say, Germany and Russia in the 1920s and 1990s respectively. At key moments in the twentieth century, British governments contracted the economy. For all the misery this caused in poorer areas, it succeeded in preventing the hyperinflation which on the Continent hit the salaries and savings of the better off and helped to drive them into the arms of the far right. Even during the inflation of the 1970s, Britain's overall standard of living continued to improve. Relative economic stability shored up popular faith in the ability of parliamentary democracy to deal with the periodic crises of capitalism.

The stability of the political system itself was another factor. On the Continent, France went through four constitutions from 1940 to 2000, Germany three, Spain and Italy two. Proportional representation, and the more fragmented party system it led to, also caused regular paralysis (the most afflicted, Italy, went through sixty governments between the end of the Second World War and the end of the century). In Britain, on the other hand, the electoral system tended to give governments an overall majority; and it tended to concentrate power in the hands of the Prime Minister and Cabinet. The exception to this was the general election of February 1974, in which the UK's chronic instability led to a hung Parliament. But it is an exception which proves the rule. Generally, the British electoral system ensured that people who wanted it felt the smack of firm government. They were therefore less inclined to see the punch of authoritarian government as a solution to the nation's problems. Religion was a third factor. From the 1680s to the 1960s, Britons prided themselves on the supposed ideological link between Protestantism and democracy. In fact, it was the decline of organized religion – both Protestant and Catholic – which helped to immunize them from extremism in the twentieth century. Whereas the Continental far right, especially in Spain and France, was able to mobilize support by presenting itself as the defender of Catholicism against atheistic communism, the much steeper decline of popular religion in Britain made appeals to national faiths a non-starter. Furthermore, because the two main British Churches were established with a privileged position within the state, they were prevented from (and saw no need to) officially sponsor political parties of their own. Hence the Christian Democrat movement, rife and powerful on the Continent, had no equivalent in mainland Britain.

A fourth factor was that the UK was a victor in both world wars and was not invaded. However much some Britons felt their country had declined since 1945, the sense of national humiliation on which extremist movements played so effectively on the Continent was much weaker in Britain. Overall, the relative economic and political stability of Britain coupled with a fragile but enduring sense of national greatness made it difficult for extremist movements to win mass support and to scapegoat ethnic minorities for Britain's problems. In addition, a nation that had just fought a crippling world war – defined partly as a struggle to defeat the notion of racial supremacy – was highly sensitive to charges that it too was fundamentally racist. Ironically, part of the reason for that sensitivity was another facet of British nationalism: Germanophobia. To be linked with the Germans in any ideological way was simply anathema to most Britons, however much they themselves believed that non-white races were unqualified to be British.

That leads us on to the final reason why the British rejected extremist parties: the importance of liberalism to their understanding of Britishness. This is not a fashionable theory. Andrew Thorpe has suggested, 'to argue that extremism failed ... because the British were and remain "jolly good eggs" ... seems rather dated and hollow. Generalizations about "national character" are best left out of consideration when discussing the reasons for the failure of political extremism in ... Britain.'[50] Few would conclude from the history of industrial or race relations in this period that the British were 'jolly good eggs'. But the fact that they perceived themselves to be so has to be taken seriously. Despite the refusal of a large, influential minority to heed the appeal for national unity, social unrest ultimately reinforced the popular belief that the British were an innately moderate people who valued democracy. The sitcom *Citizen Smith* (1977–80) followed the misfortunes of Wolfie Smith, leader of the Tooting Popular Front, a tiny revolutionary cell in south London. Scripted by John Sullivan (who went on to write *Only Fools and Horses*) it poked fun at the naivety and hypocrisy of the

far left. But, like his right-wing counterpart, Alf Garnett, Wolfie
Smith was not simply a testament to the presence of immoderate
groups in British society. In a broader sense, laughing at Wolfie and
his gang of social misfits helped the British to locate their essential
liberalism in a period when they felt it to be under threat.

A final mention of Andrew Fountaine is instructive in this context.
The National Front founder made repeated attempts to contact
Harold Macmillan in the early 1960s, believing that the Conservative
leader could be persuaded to do more to keep out coloured immigrants. The Prime Minister ignored the advances. 'Used to ring him
up at his home', Fountaine recalled, '. . . he'd pick up the receiver,
and as soon as he heard it was me, pretend he was the butler.'[51]
Macmillan's ruse was not simply that of a man unwilling to confront
the racism in British society. Like most of the people he governed, he
believed that Fountaine's views were as profoundly un-British as
those of communists. In March 1971 he went to Chequers to offer
Heath some fatherly advice about how to deal with the unions. He
was in no doubt that the mood of the country had changed since he
left office. The British, he said, had been corrupted by the amoral
pragmatism of Harold Wilson; a mean spirit of envy had gripped the
country, which communists were manipulating. But he believed that
the reasonable national character would prevail.[52]

> The English people do not like power and fight it when it appears.
> It has always been so. They broke the power of the barons in the
> Middle Ages, they broke the power of the Crown under Charles I,
> then the landlords in the Reform Bill, then the press, then the
> middle class. Now it is the trade unions. It has all happened before,
> dear boy.[53]

Though born out of a dislike of extremism, the desire for order in
the mid-1970s did not signal a restoration of political consensus nor
a willingness to face up to Britain's problems. It merely showed how
weary the British were of their predicament. When Britons weren't
trying to laugh at their tormentors like Citizen Smith, they escaped
from them into the nostalgic world of a lost and sometimes entirely
mythical national past.

The appointment of John Betjeman as Poet Laureate on 10
October 1972, following the death of Cecil Day-Lewis, came at a
bad time for an overworked sixty-six-year-old man who had been
looking forward to semi-retirement. But it could not have come at a
better time for a deeply troubled country. Through his accessible yet

utterly brilliant verse, his newspaper columns and his TV programmes, Betjeman had become the most popular British poet since
Kipling. Indeed, when Day-Lewis succeeded Masefield as Laureate in
1967 Betjeman was already the unofficial holder of the post and
many Britons thought he should have got it instead. When the call
from Buckingham Palace finally came, he received nearly 6,000
letters, the vast majority from ordinary members of the public. In the
Sunday Telegraph, his great friend Philip Larkin celebrated the
appointment:

> In a sense Betjeman was Poet Laureate already: he outsells the rest
> (without being required reading in the Universities), and his audi-
> ence overflows the poetry reading public to take in the Housman-
> *Omar Khayyam* belt, people who, so to speak, like a rattling good
> poem. In this he is like Kipling . . . Lucky old England to have
> him.[54]

'Betj' was no crusty reactionary. But his religiosity, his campaigns
to preserve Victorian architecture and his melancholic yet passionate
celebration of British life – especially the homely petit-bourgeois
culture of England's suburbs – made him especially loved when
patriotism was being so mightily contested. One of his friends
lamented that as Laureate he would have to write 'odes "On Entering
the Common Market" '.[55] To their mutual relief, he did not. In fact,
his poetic powers were fading, and he composed little verse at all. It
didn't matter. His very existence in the post was a reassuring sign
that somehow the nation had weathered social unrest and would
continue to. One of his favourite TV programmes was *Upstairs
Downstairs* (1971–75). It was no coincidence that this was one of
the most popular drama series of the period. Set in an Edwardian
London household, the programme showed the interconnecting lives
of Lord and Lady Bellamy and their servants. The Bellamys' paternalism was buttressed by the discipline instilled in the junior servants
by the English cook, Mrs Bridges, and the Scottish butler, Mr
Hudson. Despite reading improving literature in his spare time, the
latter steadfastly regarded the Bellamys as his 'betters'. Together,
Bridges and Hudson represented the NCOs of Britain, who in the
contemporary world seemed to be taking over the house and destroying most of its contents. *Upstairs Downstairs'* depiction of social
harmony, based on a hierarchy in which everyone knew their place
but respected each other, summoned up a vision of a Britain which

had never existed. But it appealed to a nation fearful of where class antagonism was leading.[56]

Increasingly, the English country house became a focus of nostalgia, representing as it did the core of the myth of aristocratic paternalism which *Upstairs Downstairs* peddled. Despite assistance from the government since 1946, houses were still being destroyed by owners who could not afford to run them. 'The Destruction of the Country House', an exhibition staged by Roy Strong at the V&A in 1974, drew attention to the problem and it was instrumental in the rise of the so-called 'heritage industry' later in the century. Four years after the exhibition, Strong admitted that the potency of the whole concept of 'national heritage' rested on uncertainty about the present and a fear of the future:

> It is in times of danger, either from without or from within, that we become deeply conscious of our heritage . . . within this word there mingle varied and passionate streams of ancient pride and patriotism, of a heroism in times past, of a nostalgia too for what we think of as a happier world which we have lost. In the 1940s we felt all this deeply because of the danger from without. In the 1970s we sense it because of the dangers from within. We are all aware of problems and troubles, of changes within the structure of society, of the dissolution of old values and standards. For the lucky few this may be exhilarating, even exciting, but for the majority it is confusing, threatening and dispiriting. The heritage represents some form of security, a point of reference, a refuge perhaps, something visible and tangible which, within a topsy and turvy world, seems stable and unchanged. Our environmental heritage is therefore a deeply stabilising and unifying element within our society.[57]

With rather more hyperbole, Christopher Booker wrote, 'Never before in history had there been an age so distrustful of the present, so fearful of the future, so enamoured of the past. Therein lay the significance of the Seventies.'[58] One event in particular proved Booker's point: the national celebrations held to mark the twenty-fifth anniversary of the coronation of Elizabeth II.

4. A Queen of all hearts

The Silver Jubilee of 1977 reassured the British that the class, racial and generational conflict which had come to a head in recent years was an aberration; that Scottish and Welsh nationalism had not, after all, undermined the Union; that the Troubles in Northern Ireland were a peripheral problem with little relevance to the mainland; and that membership of the Common Market was not a threat to the British way of life. In short, the Jubilee wrapped a Union Jack around the battered body of Britishness and said, 'There, there.'

The pageantry was on a smaller scale than before and, with American supremacy now an accepted fact of life, there were fewer comments about how good the British were at pomp and circumstance. It was, suggested Philip Ziegler, 'the Coronation in miniature'.[59] The aloof dowdiness of the Queen, which had prompted the Palace to project Charles and Anne during the 1960s as representatives of a new Britain, was the monarchy's main selling point in the 1970s. More than at any other time in her reign, Elizabeth was a reassuring symbol of stability. John Grigg, who in 1955 had launched the first postwar attack on the monarchy, now praised the Queen for the same reason he had once damned her.

> She looks a Queen and obviously believes in her right to be one
> ... These outward graces reflect the exceptionally steady character which is her most important quality. Through a period of fluctuating fashion and considerable moral disintegration, she has lived up to her own high standards and, in doing so, has set an example which has been grudgingly admired even by those who have not followed it. In particular, she has shown how much family life means to her, and has stood rock-firm for all that it represents ... No breath of scandal has ever touched her ... She behaves decently because she *is* decent.[60]

The Jubilee was designed actively to reunite the British after a period of almost catastrophic social tension.

Tuesday 7 June 1977 was designated Jubilee Day and a Bank Holiday was granted. In the morning, the Queen and the Duke of Edinburgh drove in open carriages to a service in St Paul's, officially described as 'A thanksgiving to Almighty God commemorating the blessings granted to the Queen's most excellent Majesty during the 25 years of her reign'. The real theme of the event became clear during the address by the Archbishop of Canterbury, Dr Donald Coggan, who had succeeded Michael Ramsay in 1974. Preaching to a congregation of 2,700 and an international television audience of 500 million, he said: 'Many are seeing the supreme need for reconciliation and understanding at the heart of a people, where rivalry or suspicion could so easily lead to open conflict . . . Penitence, dedication and thanksgiving. This is what matters . . . We build again the foundations which have been broken down by our neglect.' He added, in a swipe at trade union wage demands, 'Jesus . . . taught that the only way to build a society worthy of sons of the Most High was to build on a willingness to give and not grab.'[61] In 1953 warnings had been sounded about the growth of class consciousness since the war. But the possibility of open conflict had not been countenanced. The emphasis on reconciliation in 1977 was an explicit acknowledgement that national unity had broken down. If her Coronation had invited the British to renew their spirit of enterprise and adventure, Elizabeth's Jubilee implored them to forget their differences.

How did the British respond? To some extent, popular opinion followed a familiar pattern: initial whingeing about the cost and a few token expressions of republicanism on the left, culminating in popular enthusiasm, commercially exploited, as the event drew nearer. Union Jack underwear, out of fashion since the 1960s, made a reappearance; Robert Lacey's book on the monarchy, *Majesty* (a chatty version of Richard Dimbleby's reverential *Elizabeth Our Queen*), sold 200,000 copies. By May, a poll showed that only 13.5 per cent of Britons thought the country could do without a queen, down from 16.4 per cent since February.[62]

On Jubilee Day itself the streets of London were lined with around 1 million people. Sporadic boos greeted the Prime Minister, James Callaghan, when he arrived at St Paul's. The Queen was met with unremitting cheers. She walked from St Paul's to the Guildhall talking to the crowd as she went. Thousands stretched out their hands towards her, a scene which recalled medieval peasants wanting a cure from the royal touch. At the same time, her walkabout was welcomed as a sign that the monarchy was adjusting to the democratic age by becoming more accessible. 'QUEEN OF ALL HEARTS', said the *Daily Express* the next day.[63] Nearly twenty years later, as the Queen's popularity crumbled, this accolade was transferred to

British soldiers celebrate capturing a British-made gun from Egyptian forces during the Suez Crisis, 21 November 1956. 'As we trundled through Port Said suddenly the driver tugged my trousers and said, "Sir, do you know if they drive on the right hand or the left hand in this country?" We hadn't gone very much further when he gave another tug; I said, "What on earth's the matter now?" and he said, "Sir, there's a traffic light at red. Do we stop?" ' Derek Oakley, Royal Marines tank commander, recalling the embarrassment his men felt at being in a foreign country without its permission.

A barefoot Teddy Boy and his girlfriend dance the night away at the Blue Heaven Club in Soho, London, July 1954. 'ROCK 'N' ROLL BABIES: It is deplorable. It is tribal. And it is from America. It follows ragtime, blues, Dixie, jazz, hot cha-cha and the boogie-woogie, which surely originated in the jungle. We sometimes wonder whether this is the negro's revenge.' *Daily Mail* editorial, 5 September 1956.

Police respond to the Notting Hill white riots, August 1958. 'On the whole the West Indian population is law abiding, but pressure on housing, jealousy and other factors create a dangerous situation . . . Legislation would clearly have to apply to the whole Commonwealth though in practice it would be necessary to use it only against coloured immigrants . . . Legislation of this sort would be controversial, and would require a considerable breach in the doctrine that the United Kingdom is the mother country to which all citizens of the Commonwealth have free access.' Rab Butler, the Home Secretary, explains to ministerial colleagues how the Commonwealth Immigrants Act will reduce the number of black Britons entering the UK, 19 July 1960.

Learie Constantine – cricketer, lawyer and Britain's first black peer – makes his way to the House of Lords as Baron Constantine, after a service in Westminster Abbey, 3 October 1966. 'Once you learn to think of a people as inferior it is very hard to get rid of that way of thinking.' Winston Churchill, in conversation with his doctor on the subject of black immigration, 1952.

A ploughman in the Cotswolds stops work to listen to the broadcast of Winston Churchill's funeral service, 29 January 1965. 'Two single figures whom I saw from the carriage window epitomised for me what Churchill really meant to ordinary people: first on the flat roof of a small house a man standing at attention in his RAF uniform, saluting; and then in a field, some hundred yards away from the track, a simple farmer stopping work and standing, head bowed and cap in hand.' Sir Leslie Rowan, recalling the train journey on which Churchill's coffin was taken from London to Oxfordshire for burial.

The *Victor* shows British boys how to win at war and football, 22 February 1964. 'Germany has disturbed the peace of the world twice during the past forty-eight years, in 1914 and 1940. Are we to put up with all this again? Never!' Field Marshal Viscount Montgomery of Alamein, opposing the British government's first attempt to join the European Community, *Daily Mirror*, 4 June 1962.

Michael Caine and his Minis see off angry Continentals in *The Italian Job* (1969). 'The journey in Europe will be bumpy and discordant . . . Change is always painful and, although the change arising from membership will not be as sudden or all pervasive as its most fiery critics believe, there will be enough change to cause trouble if people are determined . . . We enter Europe with the reputation of being a nation of shopkeepers; we would be unwise to present ourselves as a nation of second-hand car dealers. Above all, we should avoid creating a new, semi-permanent rift in British society between pro and anti-Europeans.' *Guardian* leader, 1 January 1973.

Supermodel Twiggy sells her own brand of tights in Selfridges, London, March 1970. 'I find it very odd that women who are otherwise perfectly sensible say that the "sexual revolution" of the sixties only succeeded in putting more women on the sexual market for the pleasure of men . . . Truly, it felt like Year One. The introduction of more or less 100 per cent effective methods of birth control, combined with the relaxation of manners, changed, well, everything.' Angela Carter, 1988.

"Come on, Sir—admit you hate me."

A train driver wages class war, the British way, during a rail strike in 1971 – as drawn by Giles of the *Daily Express*. 'The reason for the notoriety of the 1960s is that for the first time in British history, the young working class stood up for themselves and said, "We are here, this is our society and we are not going away. Join us, stay away, like us, hate us – do as you like. We don't care about your opinion any more." ' Michael Caine, 1992.

Soldiers arrest a Catholic youth for trying to overthrow the British state in Northern Ireland, Belfast, c. 1969. 'I am afraid there will be a backlash in Britain by people who will no longer be willing to see their soldiers shot or their policemen injured, in the interests of a turbulent and seemingly irrational people, who rely on us for their economic existence, whether in Ulster or Éire, whose citizens have free access to our country, and liberty of expression here.' Letter to *The Times*, February 1972.

Members of Scotland's Tartan Army invade the pitch at Wembley Stadium after beating England 2–0 during the Queen's Silver Jubilee, 4 June 1977. 'Give us an Assembly and we'll give you back your Wembley.' Chant by Scottish fans during the pitch invasion.

Pope John Paul II celebrates Mass in front of 70,000 Britons at Wembley Stadium, 29 May 1982. 'We, citizens of Liverpool, being loyal Protestant subjects of Her Majesty protest most earnestly against permission being given to the Pope to visit the land of Great Britain, believing that such a visit would imperil our Protestant heritage.' Petition by Liverpool City Councillors to the Prime Minister in response to a proposed visit by Pope Paul VI, October 1965.

**Men of 2 Para settle into a sheep pen for the night at Fitzroy in the Falklands, 1 June
1982.** 'I think we had to fight because they had invaded British territory. It's really all a
question of pride. I think Britain had to have pride in herself or, as a nation, where
would we be know? They had to do it. But the price my family paid . . . no one will ever
know exactly what price we paid. Perhaps it was worth it for Britain's sake.' Dorothy
Foulkes, Falklands widow, 1987.

A British family enjoy the sunshine and freedom of Benidorm in Spain, August 1986.
'Since Boadicea, we British have slammed our seas in the faces of invading frogs and wops, who start at Calais. Today, we're slipping our bolts. And, of all that we have to offer Europe, what finer than contact with our short-tongued, stiff-necked, straight-backed, brave, bloody-minded and absolutely beautiful selves? To know the British (it takes about fifteen years to get on nodding terms) will be Europe's privilege.' Jean Rook, commenting on the UK's accession to the European Community, *Daily Express*, 1 January 1973.

Father and daughter celebrate England's first win over Germany since 1966, Trafalgar Square, 1 September 2000. 'We're a nation too you know, not just a bunch of regions'. Linford Christie, speaking on the BBC's *Newsnight*, St George's Day, 1998.

her troublesome daughter-in-law, Diana. Meanwhile, with Diana a shy, unknown fifteen-year-old girl, Britain basked in the menopausal radiance of Elizabeth II.

The *Express* described 'The People's Joy' as the royal family appeared on the balcony of Buckingham Palace at the end of the day. For many, that moment recalled not only the Coronation but VE-Day. 'We had a community feeling', concluded the paper, 'that most adults have forgotten ever existed and most children should theoretically have learned of only in their history lessons.'[64] The *Daily Mirror* said: 'As Britain's worldwide power in the world has declined, the Queen's prestige has risen ... She is a worldwide symbol of GREAT Britain',[65] and on the day itself published a 'Singalonga-Jubilee' pull-out songsheet. As well as old favourites like 'There'll Always Be An England' and 'Land of Hope and Glory', it also contained the Beatles' 'Yellow Submarine' and Cliff Richard's 'Congratulations'.[66] Young people were much in evidence during the celebrations, making up 70 per cent of the crowd in London, according to one estimate. Their presence was felt in banners and badges with slogans like 'Liz Rules OK!' and 'Cool Rule Liz'; and in the adaptation of a popular football chant, 'Two, four, six, eight/ Who do we appreciate? LIZZIE!'

In the village of Shilton, Oxfordshire, sixty people gathered at their church under two huge flaming crosses, said prayers for the nation then processed to the village pond where they formed a circle and sang 'Land of Hope and Glory'. Few celebrations were that intense. But approximately 6,000 street parties were staged in the capital and around 2,000 in larger provincial cities. Cockneys again fulfilled the role allotted to them since the 1930s as the patriotic heart and soul of the British working classes. Louis Heren of the *Times* returned to the East End where he had been brought up. 'Nothing like a street party to keep people together,' said an unemployed docker.[67] Many parties were held in affluent areas where merchant bankers put on Union Jack hats and danced with anyone, perhaps sensing an opportunity to rekindle patriotic bonds between the classes. 'It was quite amazing,' said one forty-five-year-old Kensington woman. 'You found yourself talking to the most unlikely people and we ended up after midnight drinking brandy in the house of someone we'd never met before.'[68]

Many on the left also revelled in the atmosphere, drawn to the social harmony which the Crown seemed to inspire. At a street party in a working-class area of Worcester an electrician encountered a long-haired student enthusing about 'the real community spirit'. The electrician recalled: 'I made my noises about working-class culture and he seemed suitably impressed, saying "Great, man, great!" '[69] There were even signs of a lull in industrial disputes. The binmen of Hammersmith called off a strike over a claim for a £40 bonus to clear up the rubbish left by the celebrations, patriotically accepting the council's peace offer of an extra £10. It was noted with relief that a significant number of black and Asian Britons participated in the celebrations, despite the fact that the public display of so many Union Jacks brought uncomfortable reminders of National Front marches (fortunately, the flaming crosses of Shilton received little publicity).

The attempt to offset Celtic nationalism met with less success. The Queen had been privately concerned about it for some time. She had a Victorian fondness for picturesque Highland culture and its pater-nalistic world of gracious lairds and grateful tenants. As it was of Victoria herself, Elizabeth II's favourite residence was Balmoral where every summer, dressed in tartan, she and her family presided over the annual Highland Games. But however much she enjoyed Balmoral, she was astute enough to know that outside its peaceful walls Scotland was no longer the country it had been in the 1950s, never mind the 1850s. She feared that devolution might eventually lead to the break-up of her realm, leaving her in a vulnerable position as the symbolic link between two separate and antagonistic nations. Her concern was intensified by the economic crises and industrial strife of the period, not to mention the events in Northern Ireland. She was persuaded by successive Prime Ministers that some form of devolution must take place. Like European Union, it was sold to her as a practical necessity rather than as a desirable ideal. But she was reluctant to see the constitutional boat rocked more than was absol-utely necessary and in the second half of her reign, no less than in the first, she was a willing agent of government attempts to use the Crown to rekindle popular Britishness.

On 4 May 1977 the Queen made her private fears public in a controversial address to both Houses of Parliament: 'I cannot forget that I was crowned Queen of the United Kingdom of Great Britain and Northern Ireland. Perhaps this Jubilee is a time to remind ourselves of the benefits which union has conferred, at home and in our international dealings, on the inhabitants of all parts of this United Kingdom.'[70] She followed the speech with a tour of the United Kingdom more extensive than that which she made in 1953. In

Ulster, there was a brief lull in the violence. Fifty Catholic Boy Scouts joined a Jubilee march in Craigavon, an event optimistically described in the *Guardian* as 'togetherness in Northern Ireland'.[71] But the real significance of the Jubilee was that the Queen made her first visit to the Province since 1968 and used it to bolster the morale of loyalists. In a speech at Coleraine, she unequivocally described Northern Ireland as part of the UK and assured listeners that she and her subjects on the mainland cared deeply about the suffering 'taking place within our own country'.[72] The affection which Protestant crowds displayed on her visit gave the Queen huge pleasure and prompted Martin Charteris to comment (without any side), 'It felt wonderful sailing away from Londonderry.'[73] There were twenty further royal visits to the Province between 1977 and 1985, and the resumption of normal service was seen by many loyalists as proof that Westminster's attempt to disengage from Northern Ireland during the early seventies was over. In Wales, meanwhile, the monarchism encouraged by the Prince of Wales' Investiture in 1969 was again on display, much to the chagrin of nationalists.

Scotland was a rather different story. In Orange Glasgow the Queen received a rapturous welcome. But schoolchildren in Aberdeen (the author among them) who were made to watch her visit by their teachers did so with little enthusiasm. Straw polls showed a similar attitude among the general population. 'She knows we're slipping out of her clutches and she's panicking,' said a thirty-six-year-old man from Edinburgh. A Glaswegian, also in his thirties, remarked, 'In Scotland it seems to be confined to mainly middle-aged to elderly middle-class men and women of a conservative persuasion who feel themselves under attack and see the sovereign as a personification of their threatened standards.'[74] What made matters worse was that officials in Downing Street and Buckingham Palace seemed not to have learnt their lesson about the importance of symbolism, despite the cock-ups in that department during Coronation year. For example, the royal car took the Queen around the country bearing the English coat of arms, a mistake denounced in the letters pages of the Scottish press.

Most Scots were still monarchists and there was little sign as yet of republicanism becoming a major force in the country. However, monarchism was declining much more rapidly in Scotland than in England. A widespread indifference to the Crown had developed north of the border which left a dangerous vacuum at the heart of Scots' Britishness. Even conservative observers acknowledged the fact. In a study of popular attitudes to the Crown, published in 1978, Philip Ziegler concluded: 'It is possible to detect an indifference far more widespread than in England, a feeling that the monarch is an irrelevance, something alien to what matters in Scotland today: that Elizabeth is, in fact, Elizabeth II, Queen of England.'[75] But in England and Wales too there were signs that enthusiasm for the monarchy was waning, especially among the young. Nothing exemplified this more during Jubilee Year than punk music.

The Sex Pistols stuck a safety pin through the Queen's nose on the cover of their single 'God Save the Queen'. This, together with the song's less than respectful lyrics, resulted in it being banned. 'God Save the Queen / She ain't no human being / There ain't no future in England's dreaming.' The ban helped it to sell 200,000 copies in Jubilee week, propelling it to No. 2 in the charts. Derek Jarman's film *Jubilee* trashed the last vestiges of New Elizabethanism. It showed Elizabeth I transported to 1970s Britain where a civil war raged between punks and a fascist police force amid urban desolation. The *Gay Times* described it as 'a Seventies equivalent of an Ealing Comedy'.[76] Many other exaggerated claims were made for the punk movement during its brief life from 1976 to 1979. The cultural critic Dick Hebdige wrote: 'Punks were not only directly *responding* to increasing joblessness . . . they were *dramatising* what had come to be called "Britain's decline" . . . The Punks appropriated the rhetoric of crisis which had filled the airwaves and editorials throughout the period and translated it into tangible (and visible) terms.'[77] As Jarman himself recognized, it was nowhere near as radical. 'In reality the instigators of punk are the same petit bourgeois art students . . . who've read a little art history and adapted Dadaist typography and bad manners, and are now in the business of reproducing a fake street credibility.'[78] Yet punk was a sign of the times. Nihilism had replaced idealism at the heart of the nation's youth culture. It said much about the disillusionment of the 1970s that while the Beatles' MBEs had been welcomed in 1965 as a sign that British culture was resurgent, punk was condemned because it launched an all-out attack on the Establishment, successfully calling on British youth to gob on the tableaux of traditional Britishness paraded before them.

Assessing the overall impact of the Jubilee, the Queen's Press Secretary, Ronald Allison, declared, 'For a year which began with Britain borrowing £2,300 million from the International Monetary Fund and with well over a million people unemployed, to say nothing of . . . more deaths in Northern Ireland, 1977 did not turn out too badly in the end.'[79] At the other end of the social spectrum, a Liverpudlian housewife noted that several weeks after the Jubilee different classes and races, not to mention Protestants and Catholics, had been brought together by the event: 'People speak together who last Christmas would not have looked sideways at anyone. Young mothers are allowing their children to speak and play with one another – even of different religious backgrounds.'[80] Both their testimonies are representative. The Silver Jubilee of 1977 did succeed in uniting much of the nation and it captured the public's imagination to a far greater extent than the Fanfare for Europe had. But did it have any lasting effect on Britishness?

The answer must be no. Unlike the Coronation of 1953, the Jubilee offered no coherent vision of who the British were or what direction they should take. Aside from the Queen's desperate plea for unity between the four nations of the UK, the event was pure escapism. The ersatz wartime camaraderie which it briefly inspired did not last much beyond the summer of 1977. The event merely revealed how dangerously reliant the British now were on the monarchy to bind them together. *The Times* ruefully observed that the Queen was the only link 'with whatever pleasure [her subjects] take in the beauty, familiarity, antiquity and genius of their country'.[81] In 1977, Jock Colville assessed the first twenty-five years of Elizabeth II's reign in his book *The New Elizabethans*:

> There is no sign that the inveterate good sense of the people has deserted them, facing though they do the challenges of inflation, immigration and constant interference by the State in their private affairs. They look, as much as they ever did, for a comforting gauge of the permanence which all men desire. They look, too, for an emblem of their faith and temporal loyalty, an institution they can admire because it is above dispute and untarnished by corruption . . . It is not rash to prophesy that when, in 2002 AD, Queen Elizabeth celebrates her Golden Jubilee, the applauding crowds will be as great, and the cheers as loud as in 1977, and the people will sing, as fervently as they did at the Coronation and to-day, God Save the Queen.[82]

Looking back on the Jubilee, the *Daily Express* insisted, 'If anyone really believed the monarchy was on the slide in Britain, they can forget it. Some settlement has taken place, but in a humble rather than regal way yesterday the Queen made it good for generations.'[83]

In fact, the settlement held for little more than a decade. The fact that the monarchy was now the one and only weapon of unionists (and a fragile one at that) simply showed how weak the cultural nexus of Britishness had become. The problem which faced the Establishment was not simply that the Scots and a violent minority in Northern Ireland spurned the royal touch. In the kingdom as a whole, popular national identity was in a confused limbo. The British neither wished to return to the past nor were they willing to embrace the European future mapped out during the 1970s. Self-delusion prevailed; not the self-delusion that Britain was still a major force in the world, but the belief that somehow, if they stood still for long enough, the British people would sort out their problems. The search for stability was, in truth, a licence for stagnation. The British had not arisen. They had put their feet up by the fire and fallen asleep. The growing dependence on the monarchy to maintain the illusion of social stability was fatal because it relied on the royal family continuing to be seen to set a moral example to the nation. When they no longer did so, the drama acted out in the 1970s turned into a crisis, eventually forcing Britons to confront their bankrupt national identity.

David Cannadine has written, 'The jubilee was an expression of national and imperial decline, an attempt to persuade, by pomp and circumstance, that no such decline had taken place, or to argue that even if it had, it didn't matter.'[84] But of course it did matter. A few recognized the depth of the problem. After the bunting had been taken down, *The Times* mused gloomily on Britain's failure to adopt a new national identity since her entry into Europe:

> The jubilee is above all a popular festival, and the popular imagin-
> ation can no longer feed on the glories and wonders of empire or
> even on the evolutionary subtleties of the British Commonwealth
> of Nations ... Nor, it has to be admitted, does the Britain of
> 1977, relieved of almost all its imperial baggage, present the sort
> of spectacle to light in the mind the bonfires of national rejoicing
> ... Behind the better living standards Britain's decline in relative
> power, influence and wealth is universally perceived. The everyday
> symbol of that decline is the common note of exchange, the pound
> note, bearing the Queen's image, and now having one quarter of
> the value it had when the Queen came to the throne. What is
> more, the very integrity of the kingdom is under attack in Northern
> Ireland and is called in question in Scotland; and some of the old
> assurance with which these threats might have been repulsed is

lacking. We have put down roots in a continental European combination. However wise or inevitable the decision, and however
solid the electoral endorsement of it, it has not yet supplied a clear
context for national policy, or, at a popular level, supplied a new
focus for a sense of political identity and loyalty and ideals to super-
sede the national focus which was implicitly condemned by that
historic change of direction.[85]

The failure to forge a new Britishness at this crucial juncture cost the
Union dearly over the next quarter of a century.

5. Give us an Assembly and we'll give you back your Wembley

In 1971, Heath's Private Secretary, Douglas Hurd, co-wrote a political thriller called *Scotch on the Rocks*, in which an IRA-style Scottish
Liberation Army launches a major revolt against the English. The
army and Glasgow's Chief of Police (the prophetically named 'Mr
Blair') manage to quell the revolt, but the government is forced to
concede Home Rule. The leader of the SNP becomes Prime Minister
of Scotland, and as the King looks out onto a wet, windswept
Holyrood Palace shortly before the hand-over ceremony, he remarks
sadly to the Lord Chamberlain, 'I doubt if we'll survive.'[86] The two
countries remained very different, of course. There was absolutely no
threat of violence in Scotland and little non-violent protest aside
from a brief hunger strike by the veteran campaigner Wendy Wood.
But it was apparent that Scottish nationalism was growing to
alarming proportions and, as such, *Scotch on the Rocks* was indicative of the period in which it was written.

The discovery of North Sea oil in 1971 helped nationalists regain
the momentum of the late 1960s. At first, the oil bonanza seemed to
offer British governments a chance to claw their way out of economic
crisis and so reunite the UK. In fact, it only increased tensions. Most
of the capital and technology for developing the oil-fields around
Scotland came from American multinational corporations and the
tax revenue which the British Treasury received from their profits
was lavishly redistributed around the UK. However, in September

1972, the SNP launched a campaign which claimed that 'Scotland's oil' was being stolen by the English. It was a success, and by the time oil started to be pumped ashore in 1975, a political strategy had become a nationalist legend.

The Prime Minister soon became worried again about the situation north of the border, and in January 1972 he held a meeting in Downing Street to discuss it with Scottish Secretary, Michael Noble, the Minister for Trade and Industry, John Davies, and the Chairman of the Scottish Conservative Party, Sir William Younger. Although Heath was in favour of devolution, he was also exasperated at the failure of Scottish businessmen to invest in their own country and by the growing tendency of the electorate to regard oil as a quick fix. The Prime Minister told his colleagues that he despaired of the economic good sense of the Scots. But he also started to look at ways in which oil revenue could be labelled as Scottish, appointing the Scottish Office Minister, Lord Polwarth, 'Oil Supremo' in March 1973.[87] When the subject made it onto the agenda for the Prime Minister's weekly audience with the Queen in May, it was, revealingly, described as 'Scottish oil'.[88] What's in a name? Very little. The multinationals took the bulk of the profits (Britoil, a nationalized exploration company set up in 1975, was sold off in 1982).

Over the next twenty years, North Sea oil was not only instrumental in fuelling resentment about English domination, it also began to transform Scottish nationalism from a desire for Home Rule into a desire for independence. For, at a stroke, the discovery drastically reduced the traditional fear that Scotland could not go it alone economically. The fact that a number of the most oil-rich Middle East states were as small as Scotland added to the popular conviction that size did not matter when it came to growth. The Middle East oil crisis of 1973 also helped. Prices were quadrupled by OPEC in the wake of the Arab–Israeli War. The soaring price of crude undermined the already vulnerable British economy, making the UK look an even less attractive proposition to Scots. At the same time, the dizzying revenues oil now offered added to the belief that if Scotland could reclaim 'its oil', the country would be well placed to mount its own recovery. The Welsh, on the other hand, only had a declining coal industry. Even the most militant Welsh nationalists therefore found it hard to explain how they would survive without subsidies from Westminster, particularly given the damage that the burning of holiday cottages was doing to the Welsh tourist industry. Consequently, Plaid Cymru remained a Home Rule party and most of its support continued to come from that moderate standpoint.

Meanwhile, a statistical war raged between the SNP and Whitehall in which the latter tried to prove that North Sea oil changed nothing and that Scotland was still dependent on her southern paymaster for survival in the post-imperial world. Like many statistical contests, it ended in a draw. But such was the emotional power of nationalism by this stage that the fairy-tale allure of 'black gold' reached chambers of the Scottish heart that no amount of Treasury statistics ever could, and for the next few years the SNP had the edge over the mandarins. Growing confidence in the economic viability of a Scottish nation state did not restore the Scots' idea of themselves as a commercial people. What it did was to make them believe that they could afford the social-democratic state denied them, for different reasons, by the unionist parties.

The general elections of 1974 reflected the continuing nationalist momentum. In February, the SNP won seven seats (five of them in the oil-rich north-east), taking 21 per cent of the Scottish vote; in October the party won eleven with 30 per cent of the vote. The party took many votes from Labour but even more from the Conservatives. What remained of the Tories' Protestant working-class supporters after secularism had taken its toll mostly defected to the nationalists. The SNP was now a serious parliamentary party, and it only formed the tip of the iceberg. Polls consistently showed that around 75 per cent of Scots now thought themselves to be Scottish *rather than* British and a similar number wanted Home Rule. In other words, while many Scots still baulked at the idea of complete independence, a massive consensus had now emerged for major devolution which the unionist parties could no longer ignore. The holding operation of the previous quarter of a century had failed and the English began to notice.

The impact of nationalism on popular culture was striking. In the mid-1970s it became fashionable and lucrative for stars to make more of their Scottishness. Aside from Rod Stewart, the best exponents of transatlantic tartanry were the Bay City Rollers. Between 1974 and 1976, they had nine Top Ten hits, including the No. 1 song 'Bye Bye Baby' in the spring of 1975. The Rollers, a pretty male quintet from Edinburgh, sang catchy tunes in the style of Motown and the Beach Boys and had lyrics about teen angst to match. The group's clothes were more ethnic: their tank-tops, flared trousers and jumpsuits were covered in tartan trim, and, at the very moment when the British political Establishment was fretting most about the SNP, 'Rollermania' offered the curious sight of teenagers from Basildon innocently waving tartan scarves and saltires on *Top of the Pops*. To the nationalist folk movement, they represented the debasement of Scottish music by American mass culture, and their popularity in England damned them still further. To some extent, their southern fan-base was a clear example of how pop music and fashion brought young Britons together. But the Rollers were more popular north of the border and, like Douglas Hurd's thriller, that was indicative of a period in which Scottishness became more strident.

The event that really woke the English up was not the half-hearted waving of Union Jacks on the Queen's Scottish walkabouts, nor the furious waving of tartan at Bay City Rollers' concerts, but a football match. Although the Scots had traditionally supported their team more fervently in the annual Home International against England, the tone had remained one of friendly rivalry. This was symbolized by the two teams and their fans singing 'God Save The Queen' in unison before each match. In the late sixties, friendly rivalry began to be replaced by an edgy aggression on the Scottish side. In 1967, as the SNP bandwagon began to roll, 'God Save the Queen' was loudly booed before the match at Hampden Park in which the Scots beat Alf Ramsey's World Cup winning side. By 1976 the situation had become so embarrassing that the Football Associations of each country agreed, with government approval, to let the Scots sing 'Flower of Scotland' before play started. There were few more potent symbols of the changes wrought on national identity in postwar Britain than forlorn English teams haltingly singing the monarchist ditty which had once been the popular national anthem of the Union, while the Scots belted out their own anthem. In 1978, the SFA's annual report noted:

> Traditionally, Scots have tended to associate their worth as a nation with the exploits of their football team, and in these days when strong feelings of nationalism sweep the country and protests against repression, real or imaginary, are heard on all sides, this ... has produced a situation where a quite unprecedented volume of support for the team is exhibited.[89]

The Scots' rejection of Britain's national anthem did nothing to place the annual match against England on a more friendly footing.

In Jubilee year, the Tartan Army travelled south for the match at Wembley on 4 June. After beating England 2–0, a pitch invasion followed during which over a hundred clods of turf were dug up as souvenirs and the goalposts were broken by jubilant fans. 'It was sheer ecstasy ... one of the most brilliant moments in my life', remembers Alex Torrance, who later planted a piece of the turf in his Glasgow garden.[90] Three hundred people were arrested. It was painfully appropriate that the vandalism took place in a stadium built as the centrepiece of the 1924 Empire Exhibition in order to celebrate the power of the British Empire and the unity of its peoples. The Tartan Army left the English in no doubt that this was not merely a drunken orgy. As the pitch was invaded, thousands chanted 'Give us an Assembly, and we'll give you back your Wembley'.[91]

The Welsh followed their rugby team with as much patriotic fervour. Passions were heightened by two things: the completion of the Welsh National Stadium at Cardiff Arms Park in 1970 and the fact that the team dominated the sport more than ever. Between 1964 and 1979, it won the Triple Crown seven times, England failed to win a single match in the principality, and players like Barry John became national heroes. Most English people didn't care too much. Football was another matter altogether.

The national team was now followed with as much passion as it was in Scotland. Consequently, the reaction of the English public to the rampage at Wembley was as angry as their reaction was when the Stone of Scone had been taken from Westminster Abbey in 1950. This time, an ancient symbol of Church and state had not been touched, but in an age when football was becoming an equal source of patriotism, the incident had just as much resonance. In fact, it had rather more. Whereas the Stone had been taken by a small group of students who expressed their loyalty to the Union, Wembley's turf was taken by thousands of ordinary Scots who made no such declaration. Scottish papers condemned the act. But English editions of the British press had an additional edge to them which demonstrated a nascent reaction to the Scots. The *Daily Mirror* said:

> Scotland's football fans didn't celebrate their team's victory over England at Wembley ... they mutilated it ... there was nothing good-natured about the way they tore up the hallowed turf ... it was downright destructive ... There is only one consolation. It won't happen again. By the next time the Scottish hordes descend on Wembley the crowd will be caged in. In the long history of battles between the two countries the Wembley fences will be the football equivalent of Hadrian's Wall. And they will need to be

just as effective. Not so much to keep in the sods. But to keep the clods out.[92]

The event was a sharp and timely reminder that, however many obsequious smiles Scotland's civic worthies flashed at the Queen on her tours, it would take more than a Royal Jubilee to curtail Scottish nationalism.

At Westminster, politicians had been debating how to prevent the situation getting any worse. In 1973, the Royal Commission on the Constitution, set up by Harold Wilson as a holding exercise, finally reported. The Commission categorically stated that 'the basic economic problems of Scotland and Wales cannot fairly be attributed to the union with England.' But it did find that the English were ignorant of their fellow Britons.

> Although there is no ill-will or intended discourtesy in th[e] attitude of the English people, people in Scotland and Wales are irritated by it. It fails to recognise the special character of their separate identity, of which they themselves are keenly conscious and proud; and at the same time it implies that the resentment they feel arises only because they are living in the past and getting agitated about something which is no longer important.[93]

If its conclusion was depressingly similar to the Royal Commission of 1954, its recommendation was more radical. The Commission's original Chairman, Lord Crowther, had died during its lengthy deliberations and was replaced by a Scottish Liberal peer, Lord Kilbrandon. Kilbrandon was a lifelong believer in Home Rule and, emboldened by the continuing rise of Celtic nationalism, he steered the Commission towards recommending 'Home Rule all round', devolving power to what he called 'the historic nationalities in Britain'. The report was welcomed by the Liberal and Nationalist parties.

Only the Labour Party remained sceptical. After returning to power in March 1974, Wilson was opposed to it on the same grounds as before. So too were most of his Cabinet and his parliamentary party. This was thanks in part to the relentless agitation of the MP for West Lothian, Tam Dalyell. Dalyell, supported by a young Robin Cook, asked why Scottish MPs should continue to vote on English affairs at Westminster when English MPs would no longer be able to vote on Scottish affairs. What became known as the West Lothian Question was as relevant as it had been when A. V. Dicey asked it during the abortive passage of Gladstone's first Irish Home

Rule Bill in 1886 and when Hector McNeil had raised it with Attlee in 1950. The logical solution was also the same: to compensate the English for the constitutional imbalance left by devolution, Scottish representation at Westminster would have to be reduced, as Ulster's had been following the creation of Stormont.[94] Otherwise there was a risk that English nationalism would be provoked and turned into a cohesive political movement similar to those of England's disgruntled Celtic partners. In which case, a further wedge would be driven between the nations of the British Isles. Dalyell's solution worried Labour MPs because it threatened to eat further into Labour's Scottish heartlands without guaranteeing that the nationalist threat would recede. Given that by the end of 1974 only two out of six Labour governments had ever had an overall majority, taking devolution to its logical conclusion threatened to impede permanently Labour's chances of forming a majority government.[95]

However, Labour was forced to give way on devolution because after the October 1974 election the party only had a majority of three. It was therefore dependent on the support of the eleven SNP, three Plaid Cymru and thirteen Liberal MPs. In November 1975, the government published a White Paper, *Our Changing Democracy*.[96] It proposed a 142-member Assembly, directly elected on the first past the post system but with no power to raise taxes. The Secretary of State would have executive control over the Assembly with the power to hire and fire its leader, thus preventing a Scottish Prime Minister vying with his counterpart in Downing Street for control of the country in the event of a nationalist majority. This placed Scotland on a par not with Northern Ireland but with the prewar Raj, with the Secretary of State for Scotland effectively combining the old jobs of the Viceroy and Secretary of State for India (as the White Paper somewhat tactlessly pointed out). Jim Callaghan, who took over from Wilson three months later, was no more enthusiastic than his predecessor about devolution. According to his biographer, 'like most Englishmen' he viewed it as 'concessions to parochial nationalism, in conflict with the central power of Cabinet and parliament, as well as with socialist notions of planning'.[97] But like Wilson, he was forced to act – not least because the Liberal Leader, David Steel, made it one of the conditions of the Lib–Lab pact agreed with Callaghan in March 1977 to keep Labour in power.

Most Liberals and Nationalists accepted the White Paper on gradualist principles as the best they would get for the time being. The West Lothian Question was left unanswered by Callaghan in the hope it would go away. This did not make the passage of devolution any easier. Indeed, the issue tormented the Labour government of 1974–9 as it had Gladstone's, and the spectacle ended in ignominy for all concerned. Two crucial amendments were forced on the government by its own MPs and by Conservatives who, under their new leader, Mrs Thatcher, were being steered back towards an uncompromising defence of the Union after Heath's flirtation with devolution. The first amendment was that referenda would have to be held on the issue. The government accepted it, but this did not save the Devolution Bill of 1977, which, after a great deal of skirmishing, was killed on 22 February. When the Bill was reintroduced a year later, a second amendment, tabled by the Labour MP George Cunningham, was added to the effect that 40 per cent of the Scottish and Welsh electorate would have to vote yes in the referenda for devolution to go through. This time, the Bill passed, receiving Royal Assent in July 1978. But, as Kenneth Morgan has written, Cunningham's amendment 'doomed Welsh devolution at birth . . . and it made Scottish devolution far more difficult to achieve'.[98] The goalposts had been moved, a fact made all the more painful for nationalists by the knowledge that Cunningham was a Scot, born and bred in Dunfermline.

The campaigns in the run-up to the vote were a disaster. They took place in the middle of a winter bitter with cold and industrial strife. In Kenneth Morgan's words, they 'turned into a plebiscite on the government's record as a whole during the "winter of discontent". Overflowing dustbins, closed schools, and undug graves did not assist the cause of devolution, or make the voters of even staunchly Labour Wales and Scotland love their government.'[99] The campaigns were also hampered by the government's continuing apathy towards constitutional change, which reached new levels as the country imploded and it became increasingly apparent that the vote would be no. Helen Liddell of the Scottish Labour Party urged Callaghan to join the fray, but aside from a brief visit to Glasgow he kept away. On 1 March 1979, the people of Scotland and Wales voted directly for the first time on whether they were happy about their union with England. On a turnout of 58.3 per cent of the Welsh electorate, only 11.8 per cent were in favour of change, while 46.5 per cent were against. In Scotland it was much closer. On a turnout of 63.63 per cent, 32.85 per cent were for and 30.78 per cent were against. But this was still 7.15 per cent short of the 40 per cent required to alter the British constitution. The Union, it seemed, was safe. Over thirty years of constitutional debate had come to an end with the Scots and the Welsh deciding that they would quite like to remain British after all. Unionists everywhere breathed a collective sigh of relief.

A wave of recriminations began in Scotland. Some blamed the Cunningham Amendment. But many others blamed the Scottish national character. Perhaps, they said, we are a country of self-pitying, pessimistic whingers; well able to dislike the English and their works, but afraid to take control of our own affairs when given the chance to do so. The morning after the vote, Scotland's *Daily Herald* had a picture of a moth-eaten Scottish lion sucking one thumb and twiddling the digits of another. 'I'm feart', said the caption. Charges of empty tartan hubris were given added weight by the performance of the Scottish football team in Argentina in the World Cup of 1978. After a lot of nationalistic bluster in which manager Ally MacLeod predicted that Scotland would win the competition, the team lost to minnows Iran and Peru in the first round and flew home in disgrace. It was easy to mock the Scots after the referendum and the English lost no opportunity to do so. Enoch Powell's solution was exile. 'If you don't like your geographical position – being away from the dense population markets – get out of it . . . but don't ask people to give you handouts. That's the begging bowl mentality.'[100]

Wales offered unionists the most reassurance. Every one of the eight Welsh counties said no. The heady days of the 1960s when nearly 60 per cent of the population wanted full Home Rule landed with a dull thud. Unlike the SNP, Plaid MPs did not turn against Labour in the vote of confidence which brought the government down. With the Referendum result so overwhelmingly negative, it was difficult for them to scapegoat the British political Establishment. As the Secretary of State for Wales, John Morris, put it, 'When you see an elephant on your doorstep you know that it's there.'[101] There was even a minor Tory revival at the general election of 1979, as Liberal voters reacted to the industrial strife of the Winter of Discontent and hammered home the anti-devolution message by supporting a party now utterly opposed to constitutional reform. The Conservatives took eleven seats in the principality, their best showing since 1874 – enabling someone to travel from Holyhead to Chepstow without leaving a Conservative constituency.

The result and its aftermath was interpreted not simply as a judgement on constitutional reform but as a judgement on Welshness itself. Many claimed that a huge chapter of the nation's history had come to an end and that the Welsh were, after all, Britons first and foremost. Enoch Powell, who forty years earlier had drafted a Tory Charter declaring Wales to be a nation, now said the opposite.

> Whatever may be true of Scotland, at no time in the last thousand years – and maybe longer still – has it been possible to draw a line on the map along Offa's Dyke, and pointing to the west of it, to say 'that is Wales'. The whole history of England, so long as it has been a nation, has been penetrated and interfused with Wales and the Welsh . . . the heritage and achievement of the Welsh people is nothing less than the heritage of Britain itself.[102]

However, like the 1975 referendum on the European Union, the 1979 referenda on the British Union were not the end of the debate about the future of the UK but the start of a new and more ferocious stage of it.

6. Pray for the recovery of capitalism

At the close of Jubilee year, Roy Strong recorded these thoughts in his diary:

> This has been a strange year, one of problems and mirages, of pageantry and nostalgia, of the stirrings of radical sentiment. The middle and the professional classes have had their incomes and their values seemingly flung to the wall. The virtues of talent, hard work and reward are in disrespect . . . we end the year seemingly on an even keel, North Sea Oil promising untold millions and the stock market rising fast but we are still faced with unemployment, vast cuts and strikes. The Wealth Tax rides again, hitting anyone whose property or income exceeds £100,000, a figure easily reached by vast racks of the educated section of the community: a house, a cottage, some shares, a couple of pictures and you are there.[103]

The plight of those struggling to hang on to a second home and a few paintings is easily mocked. But it was politically significant. By the late 1970s, the middle classes were in open revolt against the postwar settlement. The revolt did not simply consist of angry conservatives. It also included disillusioned liberals, those who had sustained Keynesian Britain for more than thirty years. Paying higher taxes to improve the lot of the people was one thing. Suffering daily inconvenience while they disrupted essential services in pursuit of better pay was quite another.

When the miners won their first battle in 1972, A. J. P. Taylor wrote to *The Times* saying, 'Now the miners have avenged the defeats of 1921 and 1926 February 19 will be long remembered as a glorious day in the history of the British working class.' But as the strikes continued through the decade, he began to have doubts. 'I am all for the working classes asserting themselves but it is a great nuisance as well,' he wrote in 1973. A year later, he admitted to being 'terrified' at the prospect of revolution and civil war. 'I have been expecting the collapse of capitalism all my life,' he told his Hungarian lover, '[but] now that it comes I am rather annoyed.' Taylor asked her to 'pray for the recovery of capitalism' and went on: 'There is no future for this country . . . you can't realise how close we are to catastrophe. All our banks may close their doors in a few months' time . . . You are lucky to be living in a Communist country and safe from such things.' In 1976, he abandoned the idea of writing a new edition of *English History 1914–45*, fearing that to look back at the patriotic optimism of that work might 'destroy the spirit'. 'When I wrote [it] I still had great hopes for the future. Now I have none,' he explained.[104]

By the end of the decade the revolt was more widespread and the bitterness more severe. In 1974, Heath had called a general election based around the slogan 'Who Governs?'. The question summed up the mood of the time, as did the campaign fought around it, which pleaded for national unity. Unity was what the British wanted. But on 28 February 1974 and again on 10 October they voted for the Labour and Liberal parties to restore order. The consequent return of Harold Wilson to 10 Downing Street brought a brief cessation of hostilities, as the unions were bought off with more pay rises and capital was pumped into the public sector. But this did little to improve the British economy and inflation continued to soar. When Jim Callaghan succeeded Wilson as Prime Minister in April 1976, he brought fresh energy but no ideas to match. In November the government was forced to borrow £2.3 billion from the International Monetary Fund; the alternative, it said, was 'economic policies so savage that they would lead to rioting on the streets'.[105] Yet what followed was civil disruption on a scale not seen since the General Strike of 1926.

The Winter of Discontent of 1978–9 entered British folklore and became a direct counterpoint to the Finest Hour, creating a legend of resistance to enemies within just as the war had done the same for enemies without. The phrase, adapted from Shakespeare's account of Richard III's usurpation of the English throne, captured the popular belief that trade unions were no longer champions of the people but were instead abusing their power in order to undermine the British way of life. The number of working days lost to strikes in 1979 – 29.5 million – exceeded those during the Heath era. And the number of workers involved – 4.6 million – was nearly three times higher than in 1972, with many normally quiescent groups joining in. As well as the usual disruption to power, transport and manufacturing, the emergency services were hit, forcing the army to operate the ambulance service at one point. But the increasing number of people taking part in strike action could not hide the fact that most Britons were sick and tired of the disruption. The popularity of trade unions fell sharply. Between 1952 and 1972, an average 61 per cent of Britons thought them a good thing; by early 1979, this had fallen to 44 per cent, while a full 84 per cent thought they had become too powerful.[106]

A strike by refuse workers left rotting rubbish piled high in the streets and crawling with rats. Another by gravediggers left the dead unburied. The suffering it caused the bereaved came to symbolize the extent to which British values of decency appeared to have eroded. Even the left of the Labour Party was worried. Tony Benn noted in his diary in January 1979, 'The press is just full of crises, anarchy, chaos, disruption. I have never seen anything like it in my life.'[107] Jim Callaghan's most sympathetic biographer admits that 'Britain in the last phase of Labour corporatism seemed close to being ungovernable.'[108] By the late 1970s, a third of the British population (and half of the under-twenty-fives) said they would emigrate if they could afford to. Like the desertion of troops in the midst of battle, there can be no more damning indictment of a nation in peacetime than a desire to leave it for good.

The National Theatre Director Peter Hall watched in horror as strikes by technicians periodically closed down the theatre after its opening in 1976. Since its inception by Act of Parliament in 1949, the National's progress had been hampered by government parsimony. Now, it was not the state but the workers – those for whom it was originally intended – who were preventing the theatre from carrying out its mission to bring art to the people. Few things symbolized the rejection of that mission more than the National's closure over the pay and conditions of its staff. For Peter Hall, it was the last straw. In May 1979 he voted Conservative for the first time in his life. In his diary, he recorded why:

> Labour was the party of social justice . . . It's now the party of sectional interest; the party that protects pressure groups and bully boys . . . I fear for the Tories getting in because it could make the way easier for Tony Benn in five years' time; but I also fear if they don't, because our present decline into a land without opportunity will continue.[109]

The civil disputes of the 1970s provided a much starker counterpoint to the patriotic solidarity of the war than did the moral relativism of the 1960s. Right-wing commentators tried to argue that industrial chaos was the direct result of the liberalization of national mores during the 1960s. Britons did not agree. Much as they disliked union power and wanted it to be controlled by the state, they did not believe that strikes were linked to the fashion for hot pants. Britons continued to relish the benefits of the Pill, marijuana and pop music, as well as the freedoms granted by the relaxation of the divorce laws and the legalization of homosexuality. It is significant, for example, that when the Croydon madam, Cynthia Payne, was imprisoned in 1980 for running a brothel, she was not stigmatized as a symbol of national malaise but instead became something of a folk hero. Her customers included a peer, a Northern Irish MP and a former Battle of Britain squadron leader, as well as the usual array of vicars and bank managers. They paid her, in truly British fashion, in luncheon vouchers. Payne's claim that she and her girls '[gave] the elderly their confidence back' was accepted by the country if not by the courts.[110]

The 1979 referenda on devolution began a series of events which changed the course of British history and with it the nation's identity. Enraged that the Cunningham Amendment had done its wrecking work, the SNP withdrew its support form the embattled Callaghan government. On 23 March 1979, the government was defeated by one vote in the House of Commons in a vote of No Confidence. A general election followed on 3 May which put the Conservatives back in office with a majority of forty-three. It is one of the great ironies of British history that Mrs Thatcher came to power thanks in part to the votes of Scottish and Welsh nationalist MPs, for it was during her eleven-year rule that the tensions within the Union which had been building up since the end of the Second World War started to come to a head. She was an uncompromising Unionist, yet her economic policies and resolutely English personality provoked the Scots and Welsh into finding the courage they had so pitifully lacked in 1979. After nearly 300 years of productive union between the three nations of Great Britain, what had been one of the great political experiments of the world was about to come to an end on a tide of bitterness, resentment and paranoia.

PART 9

HUSTLERS

The working class has come a long way in recent years, all of it downhill ... There never used to be all these fat tattooed slobs, dressed for the track and built for the bar, leaning out of the window of their van – those rusty white vans – and screaming with rage, 'Yew *carnt*! Yew farking *carnt*!' as they cut you up and mow down a Lollipop lady. They are the reason you prefer to avoid Indian restaurants at closing time. You see them at the post office on Monday morning, at the football ground on Saturday afternoon, at every pub – those manly troughs – at any time. They belch and fart and threaten their way through life. They are the lager vomit on the Union Jack. They turn the city into a tattooed jungle.

Tony Parsons, 1989

Some part of our unpopularity must be attributed to the national question on which the Tories are seen as an English party and on which I myself was apparently seen as a quintessentially English figure ... The Tory Party is not, of course, an English party but a Unionist one. If it sometimes seems English to some Scots that is because the Union is inevitably dominated by England by reason of its greater population.

Margaret Thatcher, 1993

1. Lager vomit on the Union Jack

Like the shadow of Nosferatu on a bedroom wall, Margaret Thatcher still haunts Britain. The homogeneous national identity of the 1940s had been steadily eroded by the economic, social and cultural changes of the intervening thirty years. But Mrs Thatcher finished Britishness off as a meaningful cultural identity. Given that she was the most nationalistic Prime Minister of the postwar era, this was tragically ironic. It was not unlike Churchill presiding over the fatal undermining of the British Empire between 1940 and 1945. How did Mrs Thatcher achieve such a remarkable feat? Essentially, she destroyed what was left of the social compact fostered by the Second World War.

Describing her election as Conservative Party Leader in 1976, the Labour Party activist John O'Farrell has written: 'Her first act as leader was to appear before the cameras and do a V for victory sign the wrong way round. She was smiling and telling the British people to fuck off at the same time. It was something we would have to get used to.'[1] She was born in Grantham, Lincolnshire in 1925 and, like most people of her generation, her outlook was shaped by the Second World War. But whereas previous Conservative leaders took from it both the futility of appeasement *and* a desire to maintain the social compact of the People's War, she was prepared to learn only the first of these lessons. Consensus was achieved, she said in 1981, by 'abandoning all beliefs, principles and values ... Whoever won a battle under the banner "I stand for consensus?"' Those who raised that banner she regarded as 'Quislings, as traitors'.[2]

However fragile the social democratic consensus had been in practice, as an ideal it had helped to shape national identity in postwar Britain, giving the nation's legendary gift for moderation a more coherent ideological form and a popular legitimacy lacking since the creation of universal suffrage. If social democracy often failed as a blueprint for the remaking of Britain, it did at least act as a compass in the storms which buffeted the island, helping at crucial moments to steer the British away from extreme left- or right-wing solutions to their problems. By throwing away the compass, Mrs

Thatcher was not simply moving the Conservative Party to the right. She was challenging the basis upon which Britishness had been constructed for nearly half a century. What was her alternative?

A return to what she described as 'Victorian values'. With Victorian economic liberalism as her weapon, she sought to revive militant nineteenth-century British nationalism, presenting the self-reliant individual as the microcosm of a proud, self-reliant nation. True Britishness, she believed, rested on 'the acknowledgement of the Almighty, a sense of tolerance, an acknowledgement of moral absolutes and a positive view of work'.[3] To borrow the title of a contemporary sci-fi blockbuster, hers was a journey 'Back to the Future'. The native lineages of Thatcherism were complemented by a strong Gaullist element. One political scientist, David Marquand, has called her ideology 'British Gaullism'. Thatcher did not share the French leader's Colbertian faith in the ability of the state to turn peasants into patriots. But both had *une certaine idée* of what their country stood for which they believed they themselves personified. As a result, both claimed an intuitive sense of what their people wanted, an almost divine right to lead them, and a style of leadership which can best be described as authoritarian populism. They both offered their people an end to what was perceived to be a long period of decline, by reasserting key national traditions. Just as de Gaulle had led the French out of a paralysed Fourth Republic in 1958, she aimed to rid Britain of the collectivism of the 1940s, the moral relativism of the 1960s and the chaos which both had produced in the 1970s.[4]

Peter Hennessy has summed up the practical legacy of Conservative rule between 1979 and 1997:

1. The breaking of trade union power. The balance will never again tilt so far in favour of the labour movement as it had by the 1970s.
2. The public/private boundary will not return to the *status quo post* Herbert Morrison or *ante* Margaret Thatcher. The argument from now on will be more about regulation than about ownership.
3. With two-thirds of state assets sold off in her first ten years, the spread of shareholding from 3 million individuals in 1979 to 9 million in 1989 will have a significant, permanent place in British economic history.
4. That other significant form of public asset disposal – council house sales – saw a million homes transferred to private own-

ership on very favourable terms, a substantial shift by any standards towards that 'property-owning democracy' of which Conservatives have spoken since the nineteenth century.

5. ... Mrs Thatcher put the kind of mark on Britain's 'permanent government' that Gladstone left when he turned the Civil Service from a patronage society into the country's first meritocracy by establishing the principle of recruitment by competitive examination in the late nineteenth century.[5]

To use the Lady's own terms, was it all cost-effective? To some extent, yes. By 1991, the number of days lost annually to industrial disputes had fallen from 29.47 million to 761,000, and those involved from 4.6 million to 298,000; union membership was down by 30 per cent and output per worker rose slightly by 3.2 per cent over the same period. The island's ailing, cosseted economy was opened up properly to international competition, and the British lost their reputation as the laziest, bolshiest workers in Europe. It is a plain fact that most Britons were financially better off at the end of her rule; average incomes rose spectacularly by 37 per cent between 1979 and 1992. This trend was helped by the fact that inflation was cut from 29 per cent to 3 per cent. However, Britain's manufacturing base was cut by 25 per cent in 1979–81 and finished the period 40 per cent down. This helped to send unemployment past the 3 million mark for the first time since the 1930s (it peaked at 3.29 million – 11.8 per cent of the population – in 1986). Furthermore, the gap between rich and poor widened: the income of the richest 10 per cent of the population rose by 61 per cent while that of the poorest 10 per cent fell by 18 per cent. That growing division provoked the most serious civil disturbances of the postwar era: the Brixton riots of 1981, the miners' strike of 1984–5 and the poll tax riots of 1989.

There were two consequences of this. First, the reputation of the police was sullied by the heavy-handed way they were used to contain industrial action and civil protest. Once seen as an embodiment of British fair play, they were now widely seen as the enforcement agency of an authoritarian right-wing government (much to the despair of many officers who objected to the politicization of the force). The police reputation for neutrality had been in decline since the 1960s, but it was not until the 1980s that a clear majority of the nation lost faith in them and they ceased to be part of the pantheon of Britishness. Their exemption from race relations legislation and evidence of widespread racism within the force did not help matters.[6]

The second result of civil strife in this period was that the popular perception of Britain as a peculiarly class-bound society became even more entrenched. Indeed, most Britons believed class *struggle* to be a central feature of national life. On eighteen occasions between 1961 and 1996, Gallup asked whether there was a class struggle in the UK. The number who answered 'Yes' rose from 60 per cent in the 1960s to 80 per cent in the 1990s. And by the time Thatcher left office, 85 per cent subscribed to the existence of a new 'Underclass'.[7]

Although Mrs Thatcher disliked any talk of class, she was a grocer's daughter who viewed small businessmen like her father as the backbone of Britain. The upper classes she regarded as decadent and soft-headed paternalists; the professional middle classes were venal, self-interested hypocrites; and the working classes she saw as 'idle, deceitful, inferior and bloody-minded', according to one Cabinet Minister.[8] 'Those poor shopkeepers!' was her response to the news of rioting in the inner cities. In reality, global capitalism made life harder for small businesses than looters ever did and most aspirant Britons found themselves working for large corporations. But this only reinforced their idealization of the family firm. A lovingly polished counter and a carefully arranged window display remained as central to the British dream as the Wall Street deal did to the American one. In 1985, Gallup asked the British what sort of job they would most like to have: the majority of respondents said 'shop owner', followed closely by 'publican'.[9] The Thatcherite revolution was essentially a petit-bourgeois one. It was the revenge of Slough, in which unfriendly bombs were sent from suburban villas to rain down on citadels of middle-class power like the BBC as much as on pit-heads and factories. It was, to borrow Orwell's phrase of 1940, 'Shopkeepers at War', except that many shopkeepers had become pension salesmen and the enemy was not Germany but any Briton who stood in the way of their revolution.

Hence those who condemned Thatcherism did little more than dress up feral snobbery towards the lower-middle classes in the respectable clothes of liberal consensus. The writer and theatre producer Jonathan Miller said he found her 'loathsome, repulsive in almost every way'; he specified 'her odious suburban gentility and sentimental, saccharine patriotism, catering to the worst elements of commuter idiocy'.[10] The Prime Minister compounded her faults by having few cultural interests, believing instead that state patronage of the arts was merely a handout to the middle-classes which the nation could ill afford. In 1988, Sir Peter Hall, who had voted for her in 1979 to quell the unions, claimed (probably accurately) that 'well over 90 per cent of the people in the performing arts, education and the creative world are against her'.[11]

Not since the 1930s had the British intelligentsia been so at odds with the mood of the nation nor so reluctant to engage constructively with it. They retreated into an easy internationalism, affecting in some cases to being Eastern European underground recusants (*Samizdat* was one of the journals founded to oppose the Thatcher 'regime'). In 1983, the novelist Salman Rushdie told readers of the *New Statesman* that Thatcherism represented everything that was bad about the British:

> I find myself entertaining Spenglerian thoughts about how there can be times when all that is worst in a people rises to the surface and expresses itself in its government. There are, of course, many Britains, and many of them – the sceptical, questioning, radical, reformist, libertarian, non-conformist Britains – I have always admired greatly. But these Britains are presently in retreat, even in disarray; while nanny-Britain, strait-laced Victorian values Britain, thin-lipped jingoist Britain, is in charge. Dark goddesses rule; brightness falls from the air.[12]

The journalist Tony Parsons was at the forefront of the punk explosion of the late 1970s, cutting his intellectual teeth on the *New Musical Express*. To mark the tenth anniversary of Mrs Thatcher's election as Prime Minister, he published an article which concluded:

> The working class has come a long way in recent years, all of it downhill . . . There never used to be all these fat tattooed slobs, dressed for the track and built for the bar, leaning out of the window of their van – those rusty white vans – and screaming with rage, 'Yew *carnt*! Yew farking *carnt*!' as they cut you up and mow down a Lollipop lady. They are the reason you prefer to avoid Indian restaurants at closing time. You see them at the post office on Monday morning, at the football ground on Saturday afternoon, at every pub – those manly troughs – at any time. They belch and fart and threaten their way through life. They are the lager vomit on the Union Jack. They turn the city into a tattooed jungle.[13]

Who stood up for Thatcher and her vision of Britishness? One of the few who did was Parsons' ex-wife and former colleague on the *NME*, Julie Burchill. A working-class Bristolian, she lobbed her spittle onto the liberal stage throughout the decade. In her article to mark Mrs

Thatcher's tenth anniversary, she posited a direct link between Thatcherism and the punk movement:

> Punk was about a break with consensus. And we media brats, like our more sussed soulmates who would come up a few years later in the City, were McLaren *and* Thatcher's children . . . We were still non-U upstarts with names like Steve and Paul and Julie and Debbie. What we all shared was Attitude; short-haired, impatient, get-rich-filthy-quick, liberal baiting and hippy-hating.[14]

Anarchists all? She had a point. But for precisely that reason, this period did not mark such a radical break with the 1960s as hippy-baiters in Soho and Smith Square made out. The cultural revolution of the 1960s had also been a celebration of individualism, entrepreneurial zeal and hedonism, though its movers and shakers dressed up their aspirations in prettier clothes and nicer politics. It was no coincidence that several of the most fashionable young entrepreneurs of the 1960s such as Richard Branson became national role models during Thatcher's rule. Nor was it a coincidence that the Prime Minister's few supporters within Britain's artistic elite had been partly responsible for the cultural revolution. Several Angry Young Men of the 1950s became Angry Old Men in the 1980s, seeing in Mrs Thatcher the same anti-Establishment spirit which had motivated them years earlier. Kingsley Amis said 'she has replaced the Queen as my dream-girl'. In 1984, Amis became poetry editor of the *Daily Mirror*, picking a poem five days a week. He took the job, he explained, because of 'how cross it'll make them all [the literary Establishment]. Dosing the honest masses with stuff about patriotism and religion and the countryside and out-of-date ways of thought'.[15]

The significance of the 1980s trahison des clercs was not what it did but what it failed to do. During a period when the government was resurrecting a Britishness based on an unsustainable vision of the UK's power, there was an intellectual failure to offer an alternative vision; a realistic yet emotionally compelling identity that might have rescued the British from their cruel date with reality. Instead, the British intelligentsia launched a self-indulgent and misplaced attack on two paper dragons: the national curriculum and the heritage industry.

2. Geography is about maps and history is about chaps

All over the world since the nineteenth century, the battle for the past has been fought in the classroom and the museum. Britain in the 1980s was no exception. Since the decline of imperial history in the 1950s, American, European and Third World history had become more prominent on syllabuses. The teaching of British history also changed, with women, the working classes and ethnic minorities making a belated appearance on the historical stage. The catalyst for this development was a new methodological approach in which everyday lives were studied and less time given to national heroes and to the chronological structure with which previous generations had learnt their 'Island Story'.

In an echo of Tory protests thirty years before about the lack of imperial instruction in British schools, Thatcherites argued that the fragmentation of the island story was a socialist plot to undermine Britishness. In 1983, one of the Prime Minister's advisers, the historian Hugh Thomas, began a campaign to reverse the trends, in favour of a 'continuous national history' based on an agreed curriculum. In a speech to the Historical Association in the same year, the Minister for Education, Keith Joseph, urged teachers to develop a 'proper pride' in the institutions and 'shared values' of Britain – 'that commonality that defines us'.[16] Geoffrey Elton's 1983 inaugural address as Regius Professor of History at Cambridge University questioned 'that curious extra-terrestrial place, the Third World' and argued for 'long stretches of English history' to be taught in order to remind Britons that theirs was a 'country worth living in and coming to'.[17] Elton was one of the illustrious Anglophile Jewish émigrés who came to the UK from Europe in the 1930s. In his last book, published in 1992, he wrote: 'perhaps the English are about to emerge from their British phase . . . and will once again come to respect the rights of the individual; the rights not of Man but of English men and women'.[18] His parting words were ironic as well as prophetic, because his nephew was the left-wing comedian Ben Elton, whose TV tirades against 'Thatch' were a feature of the period.

The eventual result was the Education Act of 1988. Next to the poll tax, it was to be the flagship legislation of Mrs Thatcher's third term, though in the end it had about as much success. For the first time in Britain, it introduced a national curriculum which standardized what children learnt. This not only allowed central government instead of local authorities to decide what was taught; more importantly, it became easier to test children. This gave parents a more accurate understanding of their progress and it made the teaching profession more accountable. The study of maths and English were made compulsory (until then, only Religious Instruction had enjoyed that status). The Act also established guidelines for a minimum amount of British history to be taught. Kenneth Baker, who succeeded Keith Joseph as Education Minister in 1986, had a motto: 'Geography is about maps and history is about chaps'. He believed that the education system had lost its way since the 1960s and that history teaching was especially important 'because it conditions children's attitude to their own country'.[19] Touring schools, he noticed that they could distinguish between a brontosaurus and a tyrannosaurus better than they could between Charles I and Cromwell.[20] Mrs Thatcher believed strongly that 'There was insufficient weight given to British history'.[21] As an Education Secretary in the Heath government, the Prime Minister took the issue seriously enough to chair the Cabinet Committee on Education herself. The Act which it framed made a tortuous way through Parliament assailed by more than 5,000 amendments.

Though generally hostile to Thatcherism, university academics made a constructive attempt to refashion British history, to keep the best of new historiographical trends while maintaining the framework of the old island story. In particular, they took a less Anglocentric approach to British history, studying the distinctive but interlocking histories of Scotland, Wales and Ireland instead of regarding English and British history as virtually synonymous, as previous generations had done. They also made a more vigorous attempt to understand national identity itself. This book is a product of all those developments. The teaching profession was less enthusiastic. State school teachers fiercely resisted the national curriculum, partly because they saw it as a right-wing nationalist project and partly because, like the doctors who opposed the setting up of the NHS in 1948, they resented losing some of their power to the state. Above all, they had no wish to be accountable to parents. Despite making exams easier, the result was that numeracy and literacy rates in the UK remained among the lowest in Europe and that children continued to know more about the brontosaurus than they did about Nye Bevan. At the end of the century, the debate was still raging, as surveys showed how little youths knew about their history compared to older generations. One carried out by Gallup in 1996 showed that less than a quarter of sixteen-to-twenty-four-year-olds knew who designed St Paul's cathedral and only one in ten knew which English monarch signed Magna Carta. Thankfully, eight out of ten knew that Barbara Windsor ran the Queen Vic pub in *EastEnders*.[22]

The irony of the teachers' position was that the origins of the national curriculum were Continental. The government freely acknowledged the Continental inspiration for the Education Act. In the *Observer*, Hugh Thomas called for 'educational reform which ensures that everyone at school is given a real sense of the history of our nation at least as good as French children learn about their country'.[23] He might have added that on the Continent the teaching of national history had not prevented the development of a European consciousness. Christopher Hill replied that history worked on the Continent because most of its peoples had had successful democratic revolutions. Europeans therefore studied their past in a context where 'history is not just kings and battles, [but] is the people on the streets, taking command of their own destiny'.[24] Hill had a point, but to argue that national history should not be properly taught until Britain had had a revolution was an abnegation of responsibility. The other irony was that in Scottish schools (still regarded as the best in the UK) national history was taught with some vigour in order to nurture Scottishness. Since 1956, a debate had taken place about the Anglicization of the curriculum. In 1960, the *Scotsman* said that the country's children 'have to be bi-historical . . . and too often the Scottish history is scamped . . . History by reference to England is not enough'.[25] By 1979, the Scottish Office had established a national curriculum in all but name. While maintaining the country's tradition of broad, non-specialist teaching, Scottish history became an established subject.[26] The left's hostility to educational reform was matched by its hostility to how the national past was presented in Britain's museums.

What concerned critics was not just the indifference of the government to the arts but the fact that it had a different vision of national culture altogether. The Conservative approach was to restore the role of commerce in arts patronage and historic preservation in order to make them more accessible to the public, and therefore more profitable. Also, more emphasis was placed on Britain's heritage than on contemporary culture. In 1980, the Arts Minister, Norman St John-Stevas, announced that the Association for Business Sponsorship of the Arts would receive a direct grant from the Treasury. ABSA had been founded in 1976 to promote corporate patronage, which then stood at £600,000 a year. A decade later this had risen to approximately £30 million. Its director, Colin Tweedy, told the public sector to buck up its ideas: 'Arts organisations', he said, 'often fail to understand that they are selling a product to a potential customer and have to deliver benefits accordingly.'[27] The expansion of ABSA was followed by the privatization of the state's own antiquities. In 1983 English Heritage was set up to run the historic buildings and land which had been under the care of the Ministry of Works since 1882. Like most privatization schemes, government aid did not cease. The Land Fund, established by the Attlee government and suspended by Macmillan, was re-activated so that more property could be offered to the nation in lieu of death duties. Announcing the new National Heritage Memorial Fund in 1980, St John-Stevas said that the Fund, like its predecessor, was to be a memorial to those who had died saving Britain from destruction during the Second World War.

When Parliament passed the first Ancient Monuments Act in 1882, it listed 68 monuments deemed worthy of preservation. A century later the figure had risen to over 12,000. In addition there were 330,000 listed buildings and 5,000 conservation sites. The biggest rise took place during the 1970s and 1980s, as did the number of visits – up from 200 million to 330 million in the second half of Mrs Thatcher's premiership.[28] There was also a dramatic increase in the number of museums opened in the UK. Between 1971 and 1987 the number doubled to 2,131, over half of them in the private sector. By the end of the 1980s the Museums and Galleries Commission estimated that a new museum opened in the UK every fourteen days.[29] The Chairman of the NHMF was the Queen's former private secretary, Lord Charteris, who declared that heritage meant 'anything you want'.[30] Some took him at his word. Pruno Peek, whose name recalls a Victorian circus ringmaster, was a freelance heritage manager. In 1988, he told *The Times*, 'If you've got something to sell, then package it up and sell it, and what's history if you can't bend it a bit?'[31]

The British demonstrated a desire to escape from the rigours of the modern world in virtually every area of their life. There was a commodification of national culture in this period on a larger scale than at any time since the early twentieth century, when imperial patriotism had been used to sell colonial goods. The difference was that this time the past was being marketed more than the present. Among the many examples that could be cited are the following: the great British fry-up was offered by Berni Inns as a 'Heritage Platter'; Dulux offered a range of 'Heritage Colours' designed to turn the humblest home into a stately one; and a company in Watford even sold the share certificates of bankrupt British companies as 'Heritage Originals'.

In TV and cinema, romantic costume dramas proliferated. *Brideshead Revisited*, Evelyn Waugh's homoerotic lament for the decline of the aristocracy, was lavishly serialized for ITV in 1981. Costume dramas had been a staple of British cinema since the heyday of Gainsborough Studios in the 1930s and had never entirely died out. But they enjoyed a renaissance between 1980 and 1995, thanks largely to the Merchant Ivory team. Notable films in the genre included *Chariots of Fire* (1981), *Another Country* (1984), *Room with a View* (1986) and *Howards End* (1992). Reviewing *Howards End*, the *Mail on Sunday* said: 'It is an instant national treasure ... [This] is because historic insights into British character still ring as true as church bells ... The film is one to lift the spirits. That it should be an epic about class makes it an immediate part of the British heritage.'[32] 'Heritage cinema' was not entirely conservative. The best films asked the question 'Who shall inherit Britain?' and some answered that the working classes (*Howards End*) and ethnic/religious minorities (*Chariots of Fire*) should be among those who will. But the films were open to criticism. The stories were usually about English upper-class life shortly before and after the First World War. Using pretty photography, they celebrated the pathos of frustrated desire and the need to cross social barriers, but they did so at a safe distance from the modern world. Heritage films were, as *Sight and Sound* commented, 'the barricaded room of an English identity'.[33] The director Alan Parker simply described them as 'the Laura Ashley school of film-making.'[34]

In pop music and fashion, the angry, macho nihilism of punk gave way to the camp, hedonistic fancy-dress party that was New Romanticism. Retro-chic, pioneered by David Bowie and Roxy Music in the 1970s, reached a peak of colourful absurdity. The eighteenth-century dandy highwayman, Adam Ant, the Jacobite highlander look of Spandau Ballet, the Victorian/Ruritanian toy soldiers of Visage and Ultravox, and the ethnic mélange worn by pop drag queen Boy George, all encouraged British youth to choose an era or two and escape into them. Peter York remembered, 'Old was new, borrowing was a sweet psychosis, the dressing-up cupboard had been ripped open and its doors had been ripped off. This was British post-Modernism *for real*.'[35] One of the biggest new romantic parties (attended by hundreds from around Britain) was held on the Second World War battlecruiser HMS *Belfast*. Moored on the Thames as a floating monument to the British navy's last great conflict, its grey decks thronged with men in purple make-up as London's skyline glittered in the dark.

How are we to assess the heritage phenomenon? Sympathetic political philosophers located heritage within a wider Western trend they called post-modernism: a liberating pick-and-mix world where the barriers between past and present, private and public, high and low culture were dismantled and everything accorded the same value – a democratic free-for-all in which the 'long front of culture' dreamed of in the 1960s was finally constructed. Most, however, detested the selling of the British past, for two reasons. First, they argued that commerce debased culture, leading to a representation of the past that was vulgar in tone and reactionary in content. It was vulgar because it privileged the visual over the textual; for example, the use of interactive video screens and employment of people dressed in period costumes to animate exhibits and talk to visitors 'in character'. It was reactionary because it sanitized the past, giving little hint of the conditions in which people had actually lived or the political struggles they had fought to improve them. An irony frequently pointed out was that in a period when Britain's industrial base was being reduced, defunct factories and mines were turned into heritage sites, with the local unemployed acting the parts of their ancestors. In some cases, they even played themselves. At the Big Pit colliery in Gwent, miners bought the pit from the National Coal Board for £1, turned it into a museum and kept their mining gear on to show visitors round.

Second, critics argued that the heritage industry showed that in the midst of decline Britain could only wallow in nostalgia. Towards the end of 1987, following Mrs Thatcher's third general election victory in a row, the criticism became more vitriolic. In the *Observer*, the Scottish journalist Neal Ascherson explained why 'Heritage is Right Wing, Vulgar English Nationalism':

The heritage industry, like the proposed 'core curriculum' of history for English schools [sic], imposes one group's version of history on everyone and declares that it cannot be changed. One of the marks of the feudal *ancien regime* was that the dead governed the living. A mark of a decrepit political system must surely be that a fictitious past of theme parks and costume drama governs the present.[36]

In the same year, Robert Hewison, who coined the phrase 'heritage industry', argued that it was 'bogus history':

The heritage industry presents a history that stifles, but above all, a history that is *over*. The development of Britain has reached a finite state that must be preserved at all costs against the threat of change . . . Instead of the miasma of nostalgia we need the fierce spirit of renewal . . . we must live in the future tense not the past pluperfect [sic].[37]

Stirring words. But was the critique of the heritage industry justified? Had David Eccles' 1954 warning that Britain would become 'a nation of subsidised museum-keepers' come to pass?

To some extent it had. For the British, the past was not a foreign country but a dominion offering safe passage for anyone who preferred not to confront the nation's failure to discover a post-imperial identity. In particular, the heritage boom was a testament to a confused England; a country beset by troublesome Celts, blacks and Europeans, seeking solace in vanished glories which were 'bent a bit' to make them more appealing. The boom was also a response to the social unrest of the period 1965–85, from the apparent moral decline in private lives to the more threatening industrial strife which brought Britain's public life to a standstill. Foreigners relished the archaism which seemed to have engulfed a nation. By the end of the century, tourism in England was worth £30 billion and employed 1.7 million people, making it the largest employer of any industry.[38] But at this point our critique encounters an awkward obstacle: historical fact.

To begin with, the phenomenon was not a peculiarly English one. In fact, the most nationalistic forms of the heritage industry were found in Scotland, Wales and Ireland, just as the most national-minded school curricula were. We have already noted the growth of 'Celtic' tourism in the 1950s. Its growth accelerated in this period. Not only did attractions like the Loch Ness Monster Experience double in number, there was also a growing demand for state-sponsored museums to tell more exclusive national stories which downgraded the Union and in some cases rewrote history altogether.

The Welsh had established a National Museum in Cardiff in 1907 and a Folk Museum was added in 1946. In 1985, the Royal Museum of Scotland was created by Act of Parliament, amalgamating two antiquarian institutions founded in the eighteenth and nineteenth centuries by private benefactors. Four years later, the Royal Bank of Scotland sponsored an exhibition there called 'The Wealth of a Nation', covering 6,000 years of Scotland's history. One of the trustees was Magnus Magnusson. A veteran nationalist, he called for 'a new and visionary' institution which explicitly told the Scottish story.[39]

The idea had first been mooted in the late 1940s after the creation of the Welsh Folk Museum. Funding and fear of nationalism had hampered its progress, but finally, on 30 November 1998, at a cost of £52 million, Elizabeth II opened the splendid new Museum of Scotland in Edinburgh, which housed 10,000 artefacts. The first room displayed the Declaration of Arbroath and the last displayed video footage of Celtic winning the European Cup. Although its director was (controversially) an Englishman, he and his curators obliged nationalists by presenting the history of Scottish imperialism as a brief period in which the 'adventurous spirit' of the Celts was manifest. 'The museum doesn't define Scottishness in terms of England', said archaeologist David Clarke.[40] Which was precisely the problem. It is also worth noting that visitors were offered Gaelic commentary but not Gujarati, despite the fact that speakers of the latter far outnumber those of the former in Scotland. By 2000, England was the only nation in Britain with no permanent national exhibition of its own. For the time being, the English were content with the British Museum, that eighteenth-century cornucopia of imperial spoils. England was also the only nation not to have its own national library. Wales established hers in 1905; Scotland in 1925. Their partner had the British Library. Few things, apart from the flying of Union Jacks instead of St George's crosses, so symbolized the fact that England remained naively wedded to a Britishness which her compatriots were rejecting.

The second point is this: whatever the faults of the UK heritage industry, it was not a reactionary brake on British culture. There were three principal reasons for this. The first is that at no stage did it prevent the creation of contemporary works of art. The ICA was never filled with bouncy castles, pot-pourri baskets and resting actors dressed as Herbert Read; nor were artists forced to build visitor centres outside the studios of Hackney, or to re-enact fin-de-siècle

Parisian cafe discussions on the merits of Impressionism for the delight of coach parties from Bradford. The avant-garde went on being an avant-garde. Moreover, the heritage industry did not set national culture in aspic. One of the reasons why listing increased in this period was that English Heritage led the way in recognizing the value of twentieth-century architecture and ensuring that its finest examples were preserved. The listing of concrete high-rise flats such as Erno Goldfinger's Trellick Tower provoked outrage. But it demonstrated that the country house was not seen as the be all and end all of British civilization. Lord Charteris' comment that heritage meant 'anything you want' was a licence for a more imaginative view of what constituted the archaeology of Britishness.

Second, there was a major contradiction at the heart of liberal criticism of the heritage industry. The notion that commerce and culture do not mix was historical rubbish, as any scholar of the Renaissance would testify. Moreover, in the nineteenth century this spurious idea had underpinned the Victorian intellectual reaction to industrialization. It was that reaction which spawned the preservation movement in the first place. Not for nothing was Robert Hewison a devotee of John Ruskin, gripped like his hero by the idea that art should be an ersatz religion, seeking out national 'values' to improve the masses. And, though they talked up the creative possibilities of information technology in a plausibly modern way, critics of the heritage industry were really the immediate successors of the crabby Reithians who had railed against commercial TV in the 1950s. Armed with a moral certainty of what was best for the British people, they reprised the mid-century battle to defend national culture from the forces of mass-consumer society. At its most conservative, the attack on popular tourism was a continuation of the snobbery which the working and lower-middle classes had endured since they ventured en masse into Britain's coast and countryside in the 1930s and from there to the beaches of Spain in the 1970s. The people going to new 'visitor-friendly' monuments, beauty spots and museums were once again accused of invading and debasing potentially redemptive spaces, robbing the discriminating few of the opportunity for serious contemplation which only connoisseurship and tranquillity could provide.

The third and most important point to remember about the heritage industry is that it *was* educative; it was historical tourism first and nostalgic consumerism second. A national survey carried out by the Museum of London in 1985 found that most regular visitors likened museums, whether new or old, to libraries (40 per cent) and monuments to the dead (28 per cent). No one agreed that they were like department stores and most liked that fact.[41] But they also liked the more exciting, interactive way these library-monuments were telling the story of Britain. Thanks to the museological revolution, Britons learnt some of the national history that schools were failing to teach them. They did so partly because they enjoyed themselves instead of enduring it as a classroom chore; and partly because even the most commercial museums set out to inform.

Heritage managers angrily rejected the accusation that they were all cynical hustlers. Peter Lewis, Director of the Beamish Open Air Museum and (Orwell would have loved this) a former Piermaster of Wigan Pier, said:

> We try to be objective, avoiding the sin of 'romancing the grime'. Equally, however, we try to avoid the equally dangerous sin of portraying the past as a period of unremitting misery . . . I am not ashamed that my colleagues and I try to convey the spirit of people now past . . . They have passed on to us an essential Englishness, the dread of poverty, the fear of loss of face. We may no longer whitestone our doorsteps or preserve the sanctity of the parlour, but we still . . . urge our children to wear clean underwear 'in case of accident'. They were a generation who with courage and good humour resisted adversity. To their credit they insisted on a pattern of social changes and benefits that have revolutionised our society.[42]

From academia, the socialist historian Raphael Samuel fired this broadside at the grubby attack on 'Disneyland Britain':

> The denigration of 'heritage', though voiced in the name of radical politics, is pedagogically conservative . . . [Heritage] is accused of taking the mind out of history, offering a Cook's tour or package-holiday view of the past as a substitute for the real thing . . . The association with the world of entertainment is clearly a cause of great offence, inviting the scorn of the high-minded, mingling as it does the sacred and the profane, high culture and low . . . Heritage is also discredited . . . by its association with what used to be called, in the heyday of aristocratic snobbery, 'trade'; but which in post-1960 critical theory is more apt to be labelled 'consumerism'. Literary snobbery also comes into play; the belief that only books are serious; perhaps too a suspicion of the visual, rooted in a Puritan or Protestant distrust of graven images.[43]

As for the protests about British heritage cinema, it is worth remembering that the cult film of the decade was not a Merchant Ivory country-house idyll but Bruce Robinson's *Withnail And I* (1987). A rollicking, autobiographical tale of two drug-taking, drop-out actors in 1960s London, the film charts a disastrous weekend in the country where the two men encounter all manner of in-breds and bigots. The idea for the trip begins one day on a park bench in Kentish Town. 'You know what we should do . . . ?' says Marwood. 'Get out of it for a while. Get into the countryside and rejuvenate.' To which Withnail replies, 'Rejuvenate? I'm in a *park* and I'm practically dead. What good's the countryside?'[44]

To sum up: the obsession with the national past and the way in which the past was disseminated exposed the contradictions of Britain in the 1980s. The introduction of a national curriculum and the emphasis it placed on traditional British history highlighted a conservative determination to prop up Britishness at source by reaching the youngest in society; yet it drew the country educationally closer to the Continent. The heritage industry revealed the extent to which culture had become a substitute for world power and how much British patriotism still depended on a sentimental, conservative vision of that culture. Equally, the most bilious criticism of the industry highlighted the continuing failure of Britain's liberal elite to come to terms with mass democracy in the twentieth century. But, however much popular consumption of the island story gave people pleasure and enlightenment or provoked them to disgust and fury, both the national curriculum and the heritage industry were side-shows. Ultimately the decline of Britishness during the 1980s was not caused by the atrophying of national culture but by its resurgence in a new and more fissiparous form.

3. The Union is inevitably dominated by England

With the precision and good intent of a nurse, Mrs Thatcher unpeeled the fiscal bandages which British governments since the 1930s had placed on Scotland and Wales in an effort to heal the wounds of industrial decline. Thatcher thought that a splash of her moral iodine, together with some monetarist fresh air, would do the job instead. Her intention was to reinvigorate Scotland and Wales through laissez-faire capitalism; to help their people rediscover the material benefits of union with England. In fact, she succeeded only in reminding them why it was no longer paying them dividends.

In 1986, the Essex entrepreneur Peter de Savary bought Land's End and John O'Groats. The symbolism of the purchase was a hollow one, for the 'economic miracle' of the 1980s did not stretch from one end of Britain to the other. Many areas remained stagnant or continued to decline; and unlike the economic crisis of the 1970s which affected every part of the island, that caused by Thatcherism largely affected Scotland, Wales and the north of England. In the south it was party time. A *Times* cartoon in May 1987 depicted the Prime Minister as St George, with the caption 'CRY GOD FOR MAGGIE, SOUTH-EAST ENGLAND AND ST GEORGE'.[45]

During the 1980s, the relative economic decline of Scotland and Wales became starker than ever as monetarism scythed through economies which had been ailing since the 1960s. The southward drift of the British economy which had begun at the turn of the century reached a disastrous apogee, thanks to the deregulation of the City and other measures designed to free the movement of capital. Already reluctant to invest in Scotland and Wales, City financiers now had more freedom to put their capital where they wanted it: England and abroad. To make the disparity even worse, Thatcher slashed regional aid as part of her reduction of public spending. In 1985–6, £2.4 billion out of £4.7 billion of Scottish manufacturing capital was transferred to London. Unemployment rose from 5.7 per cent of the population in 1979 to 11.1 per cent in 1986.[46] North Sea Oil provoked even more nationalism than in the 1970s. During the first nine years of Thatcher's premiership, the Treasury received £62 billion in oil revenues, yet all this seemed to pay for north of the border was social security benefits.

In Wales unemployment rose from 5.5 per cent in 1979 to 13.2 per cent in 1986, the second highest in Britain after north-west England.[47] The principality lacked the oil with which Scots thought they could pay for Home Rule; moreover, the mining industry was destroyed by the recession, and with it one of the most cherished facets of Welsh national identity. Already making a loss of £2.5 million per week, it was finished off after the miners' strike of 1984–5 failed to prevent pit closures, the number of miners falling to 2,000 by 1992. The strike united Wales more than any other postwar event. North and south, rural and urban, English- and Welsh-speaking, all provided practical, financial or moral support to keep the strikers going. It demonstrated once and for all that Wales was more than a hotchpotch of warring regions.

Industrial decline had one positive effect in Wales: it curtailed the romanticization of the lantern-jawed man of the Valleys and gave women a more central place in Welsh culture. Welsh women, dressed in national costume, had repelled the only Napoleonic invasion of Britain before local men arrived, at Carregwastad Point in February 1797. Women of the principality had played an important part in industrial disputes in Wales since the nineteenth century, but, unlike the textile workers of northern England, they played little part in industry itself. Critic Deirdre Bedoe has written:

> Welsh women are culturally invisible. Wales, land of my fathers, is the land of coalminers, rugby players and male voice choirs . . . Not only are these groups exclusively male but they are *mass* groups. Think of Wales and you think of Welshmen in *large numbers*, at the rugby match, in the mines and in the concert hall. Besides their corporate ranks, the tiny, usually solitary figure of the Welsh woman in national costume pales further into insignificance.[48]

The condition of unemployed men forced to rely on their wives' wages, coupled with greater career opportunities for women in the principality, began a partial demasculinization of Welshness. But this was scant consolation for the Welsh and none whatsoever for the Scots.

Nationalism also regained its appeal because the Scots and the Welsh rejected Thatcherism while most of England embraced it. In three successive elections, they voted overwhelmingly for the Labour and Liberal parties, yet they were forced to endure Conservative rule because the English electoral majority voted Conservative. At the 1987 General Election, Scottish Young Conservatives sported T-shirts saying '*YCs do it with the woman on top*'. The woman in question was shoved off in an angry act of political interruptus. The Conservative Party lost half its Scottish seats, down from twenty-one to ten; its share of the vote, 24 per cent, was nearly half that in England. In Wales, fourteen seats were reduced to eight. A great deal of cant was talked about this subject. From 1945 to 2000, the English had a Labour government foisted on them three times because of the strong socialist vote on the Celtic fringe. In 1950, 1964 and 1974, Labour did not obtain a majority in England yet narrowly won power thanks to the Scots and Welsh. But what matters is that as far as the Scots and Welsh were concerned, British democracy was failing them. Protestantism and Empire had already gone. Now, in a sense, Democracy went too.

Following the 1987 election, pro-devolution sentiment revived dramatically. In the second half of the century, the Scottish Office had grown in size as it was given more responsibility by Westminster. In 1937, the Office's civil servants numbered 2,400; by 1992 there were 13,500.[49] But bureaucrats were powerless to protect Scotland from Thatcherism. On 30 March 1989, fifty years after John Macormick's Covenanters gathered in the Edinburgh Assembly Hall, a cross-party Constitutional Convention did the same, convened by Canon Kenyon Wright. A year later, it put forward its proposals in *Towards Scotland's Parliament*. Polls showed three out of four Scots were once more in favour of Home Rule; the SNP found a new, more aggressive leader in Alex Salmond; and in 1992, his colleague Jim Sillars accused the Scots of being 'ninety-minute patriots' – passionate about their football team but lacking the guts to translate that passion into political change. Sillars' phrase echoed down the next decade; it challenged many Scots to re-examine their patriotism, and almost certainly had a positive on effect on attitudes to devolution.

By June 1987, an opinion poll for HTV found 52 per cent of the Welsh population in favour of an Assembly, a higher level than at any time since the 1960s (the figure rose to 60 per cent when people were asked what their attitude would be if the Scots got one).[50] The Prime Minister cared little for the Welsh and was prepared to give them some leeway. While the IRA's Bobby Sands was allowed to starve himself to death in Ulster's H-block in 1981, Plaid Cymru's leader, Gwynfor Evans, was spared a similar fate. In 1980, he refused to eat until his country got a Welsh-language TV channel. S4C began broadcasting on 2 November 1982. Thatcher not only denied the principality its first martyr, she also allowed the Welsh Secretary, Peter Walker, and his 2,200 Cardiff civil servants to use the 80 per cent of public finance they controlled to create a high-spending, corporatist fiefdom which ameliorated the principality's decline. This, together with the limited devolution that took place in preceding years, had a discernible effect on Welsh society. By 1984 there were 466 organizations and institutions that were either wholly Welsh or were semi-autonomous branches of those based outside the country

– from the Welsh TUC to the Young Women's Christian Association. R. Merfyn Jones wrote: 'a social membrane of officials and advocates whose centre of gravity, at least in the first instance, is the Welsh "capital" of Cardiff, rather than London, now stretches across Wales . . . a matter of no small consequence in the process of state-building'.[51] In short, Welshness flourished.

The more the English revelled in the benefits of Conservative rule, the more the Scots and Welsh saw them as a nation of callous, selfish individuals. In contrast, they saw themselves as peoples with a unique sense of community and compassion; a belief which the nationalist parties encouraged. Plaid Cymru stated in 1989, 'Wales is home for a set of values – values that are poles apart from the repugnant ideology of Thatcherism'.[52] Neil Kinnock was the fifth Welshman to lead the Labour Party. He had been an opponent of devolution for most of his career; his patriotism, of a traditional Welsh-British kind, ran deep. But he played up to his roots in an attempt to convey the Gemeinschaft of Labour's vision by telling the viewers, 'I've always felt Welsh . . . particularly in the sense of the kind of community from which I came that gave you confidence and an identity'.[53] But Kinnock was mocked as a 'Welsh Windbag' and a 'Boyo' who lacked gravitas. However Herculean his attempts to modernize the Labour Party, he was a self-proclaimed scion of the Valleys and the radical-ism which the Valleys were associated with was now anathema to most of the English electorate.

The result was that Thatcherism, and Conservatism in general, came to be synonymous with English nationalism in north and west Britain. This belief fuelled the legends of Anglo-Saxon oppression on which Celtic nationalism thrives. Was Thatcher 'the first unashamed English nationalist ever to occupy Downing Street'?[54] Yes and no. She was certainly very conscious of her Englishness and in public she played up a certain kind of genteel, bossy matronliness which grated more on the Scots than on her own countrymen and women. She also regarded England as the greatest nation in Britain. But she did so only in the sense that it was the largest, as a consequence of which it made a greater contribution to the entrepreneurial and martial history of Britain. In her memoirs, she wrote:

Some part of [our] unpopularity must be attributed to the national question on which the Tories are seen as an English party and on which I myself was apparently seen as a quintessentially English figure. About the second point I could – and I can – do nothing.

I am what I am and I have no intention of wearing tartan camouflage. Nor do I think that most Scots would like me, or any English politician the better for doing so. The Tory Party is not, of course, an English party but a Unionist one. If it sometimes seems English to some Scots that is because the Union is inevitably dominated by England by reason of its greater population. The Scots, being an historic nation with a proud past, will inevitably resent some expressions of this fact from time to time ... It is understandable that when I come out with these kind of hard truths many Scots should resent it. But it has nothing whatever to do with my being English.[55]

This view was no different to that of any other English Prime Minister. She was just more tactless in expressing it. Much as Mrs Thatcher regarded the Scots as junior partners, they were partners towards whom she had no aggressive intentions. It will come as little comfort to the Scots, but she actually had a special respect for them, based on the achievements of the Protestant mercantile and industrial elites of the eighteenth and nineteenth centuries. And the philosophical father of monetarism was a Scot, as she never tired of reminding his successors. Her memoirs record: 'Scotland in the eighteenth century was the home of the very same Scottish Enlightenment which produced Adam Smith, the greatest exponent of free enterprise economics till Hayek and Friedman. It had been a country humming with science, invention and enterprise – a theme to which I used time and time again to return in my Scottish speeches'.[56] Her stern Methodist background added to the affinity she felt. Addressing the General Assembly of the Church of Scotland in May 1988, she used Biblical texts to claim that without the profits from hard work and thrift there could be no charity toward the poor. The Moderator responded by presenting her with a Church report called *Just Sharing*, while another minister who heard the speech described it as 'a disgraceful travesty of the Gospel'.[57] The introduction of the reviled poll tax in Scotland in April 1989 – twelve months before England and Wales – was seen as proof of Thatcher's contempt of the Scots. In fact, she thought the idea of local fiscal responsibility might appeal to their legendary prudence. Moreover, it was the Scottish Conservative Party which requested early implementation. 'Tory values are in tune with everything that is finest in the Scottish character', said Thatcher, 'Scottish values are Tory values – and vice versa'.[58]

Like most of her compatriots south of the border, Mrs Thatcher was a *British* nationalist, or patriot as she preferred to call herself.

Her Victorian sense of Britain's role as a free-trading, capitalist military power demanded that the Union on which that role had been built should be preserved. Hence her fierce opposition to any form of devolution. It was a matter of principle not realpolitik. Had she truly been an English nationalist, she would have let the Scots go their own way, enabling her to pursue her revolution with greater ease in her own, more accommodating country. In order to ease tensions, in 1989 she approved a decision by the Scottish and English Football Associations to suspend the annual Home International between the two countries. Once a source of friendly rivalry, since the late 1960s the fixture had become a source of mutual animosity and an embarrassing reminder of how much Anglo-Scottish relations had deteriorated. In the last match, England won 2–0 at Hampden Park. It was, of course, a pyrrhic victory. The Tartan Army would no longer throng the streets of London every alternate year singing patriotic songs. But less than ten years after the Home International was suspended, another, more sober and more powerful Tartan Army would have its say in the polling booths of Scotland.

Scottish national identity was already changing by the time Mrs Thatcher came to power. However, by not understanding that the spirit of Adam Smith had been replaced by the spirit of John Smith, and by failing to act accordingly, she accelerated the decline of Britishness. Looking back, she lamented that industrial decline had turned a mercantile nation into a socialist one. This explains, she said, why 'there was no Tartan Thatcherite revolution.'[59] Thatcher conveniently ignores her own contribution to Scotland's economic problems. But she was not solely responsible for them. In a sense, therefore, her continuing faith in the Union was as much her tragedy as it was that of the Scots.

4. He who dares wins, Rodney

The orgy of prosperity in southern England also created a stark 'north–south' divide in the 1980s which for the first time since the 1940s renewed hopes that English regionalism would become a political movement. By 1986, unemployment north of a boundary stretching from the Severn to the Wash was 60 per cent higher than

to the south.[60] Even the west Midlands suffered. It had weathered
the storm until the mid-1970s due to its more diverse economy and
in some periods had enjoyed incomes comparable to those in the
south-east. But its unemployment rate at 12.9 per cent of the
population was little short of the 13.8 per cent in the north-west.[61]
As for the general standard of living, by 1989 incomes in the south-
east were 20 per cent higher than the national average (30 per cent
in London) compared to just under 14 per cent in 1971.[62] All of this
was reflected in the poorer health and lower life expectancy of people
in the north. Some cities, like Leeds and Newcastle, found respite by
belatedly diversifying into the service sectors which had helped to
enrich the south-east. But these were exceptions.

As the southward drift became an avalanche the cultural balance
of power between north and south which had been maintained for
most of the twentieth century was upset. The north was no longer
seen as an example of the English gift for enterprise or even of
stoicism in the face of adversity. Instead, it came to be virtually
synonymous with an archaic working-class culture that was stuck in
the 1930s and truculently refused to rise to the challenges of post-
industrial society. Raphael Samuel is worth quoting at length again:

> In the 1980s, in the first shock of disindustrialisation, and with an
> electorate increasingly divided on regional lines, the North was
> turned from an avatar of modernisation into a byword for back-
> wardness. The very qualities which had recommended it to the
> 'new wave' writers and film-makers now served as talismans of
> narrowness. The rich associational life, such as that of the work-
> ingmen's club, was seen not as supportive but as excluding, a way
> in which the natives could keep newcomers at bay. Likewise pubs,
> though warm and friendly places to the regulars, took on a quite
> different character when viewed from the perspective of health
> food fanatics and associated with the horrors of beer gut. The
> solidarities of the workplace were reconceptualised as a species of
> male bonding, a licence for the subjection of women; while the
> smokestack industries which had been the pride of the north now
> appeared, retrospectively, as ecological nightmares. In another set
> of dialectical inversions, the modernisations of the 1960s were
> stigmatised as planning disasters, imprisoning the local population
> in no-go estates and tower blocks.[63]

Such disparagement was not simply a middle-class activity. At football matches between teams from north and south, it was common

for southern supporters to chant, 'You'll never get a job! Sign on, sign on!' while gleefully waving their wallets in the air.[64]

In popular culture, the Cockney became the dominant British stereotype in the 1980s, a lovable rogue whose aspirations embodied those of many ordinary people. The 'wide boy' was a sociological fact, examined and tabulated by academics as well as journalists.[65] He worked either as a trader in the East End markets or on the trading floor of the newly deregulated stock exchange in the City, applying the same money-making skills to each job and, where the latter was concerned, contributing directly to the north's decline. Since the nineteenth century, the Cockney had been seen as a seller rather than as a maker of things, with criminality never far behind. This image was strengthened in the 1960s as the Pearly movement declined into a sentimental tourist attraction and the East End became associated with the glamour gangster. The Cockney had therefore never lost his position in the national imagination. But in the deregulated world of the post-Big Bang City, he reached his zenith as the supreme emblem of what was perceived to be a revival of the English entrepreneurial spirit. In comedy and drama, the wide boy was personified by Arthur Daley, in the series *Minder* (1979–94)[66] and then in *Only Fools and Horses* (1981–97) by the street-trader Derek Trotter – 'Del Boy' – who lived in a Peckham tower block with his gormless brother Rodney and dreamt of becoming a big-time City businessman. Exceptions can always be found to cultural trends. The Yorkshireman Ted Hughes became Poet Laureate in 1984 and in popular culture one could point to the rave scene of the late 1980s which began in Manchester and swept over Britain as comprehensively as Merseybeat had done a quarter of a century earlier. Nonetheless, Del Boy's popular catchphrases, 'He who dares wins, Rodney' and 'This time next year, we'll be millionaires', entered the popular lexicon and captured a fundamental shift within Englishness.

In 1987, one mayor from the north-east warned that there would be a 'bloody uprising' if the situation continued.[67] The fact that the north's decline had the same root cause as Scotland's led left/liberals to argue that the region now had more in common with Scotland than it did with the south. In November 1987, MPs and groups from the labour movement in Scotland and the north-east met in Carlisle, where they agreed that each would support the other's campaign for a directly elected assembly. This was a significant move, since northern MPs had previously opposed devolution on the grounds that it would give the Scots and Welsh an unfair advantage in combating problems which they shared. As in the 1930s, social solidarity in the face of hardship provoked a more pronounced pan-northern identity that was some consolation for the loss of power and wealth to the south-east. But at no point did the north or any of its constituent regions produce an identity strong enough to create a demand for regional autonomy.

The Scottish historian Christopher Harvie has called English regionalism 'the dog that never barked'.[68] In fact, it barely even whimpered. There were five main reasons for this. The first was the paradoxical role which Anglo-Saxon history played in the shaping of English national identity. From the nineteenth century onwards the seven Anglo-Saxon kingdoms of Northumbria, Mercia, East Anglia, Essex, Kent, Sussex and Wessex were regarded as the cradle of the English nation. Schoolchildren were taught that the heptarchy provided both the biological source of their racial make-up and the practical source of their democratic traditions, the kingdoms' embryonic parliaments – the *witan* – being the forerunners of today's Westminster. However, the heptarchy was also seen as an example of national weakness. Even under the strong rule of Alfred in Wessex, the Anglo-Saxon kingdoms had been easily picked off by the Danes and other invaders between the ninth and eleventh centuries. The Normans' creation of a centralized, unitary state was regarded as the true making of England, despite the fact that it was the product of a humiliating invasion which destroyed much of Anglo-Saxon culture.[69] 1066 was *l'année un* in the English mind, as Sellar and Yeatman famously testified. The Anglo-Saxon period therefore functioned both as a romantic backdrop to the story of the English *and* as a warning of the destruction to which institutionalized political divisions led. Furthermore, because the sovereignty of Parliament was synonymous with the idea of liberty in the English mind, any attempt to split that sovereignty, even for practical or enlightened reasons, was seen as an infringement of the individual's liberty rather than as an extension of democracy.

What we might call regio-scepticism therefore sprang from the same nineteenth-century narrative of British history which damned Scottish, Welsh and Irish nationalism and European federalism. This outlook continued to inform English national identity long after it had been rejected elsewhere in Britain. The continuing resistance to regionalism was in effect a defiant last stand against the dissolution of the Anglo-British polity. But regio-scepticism also sprang from the fact that England was one of the first European territories to become a unitary nation state and one of those that survived intact the longest. Although France and Spain were recognizable entities in the fourteenth and fifteenth centuries respectively, the process of national unification began later on the Continent. It gathered pace in the early nineteenth century, and again following the dismemberment of the Austro-Hungarian Empire in 1918. But Nazi Germany and the Soviet Union extinguished the independence of many fledgeling countries; and not until the nationalist revival of the 1990s, after the collapse of the Soviet Union, was the process completed.

In England, the traces left by the heptarchy were so slight that no region had any of the building blocks of political autonomy, such as a separate Church or legal and education systems, which in different ways provided a focus for Scottish and Welsh discontent with the Union. Nor, with the exception of Cornwall, did any of them have their own ancient language, as Wales did; the territorial boundaries of the Anglo-Saxon kingdoms which had frequently changed even in the Middle Ages, barely corresponded to modern geographical ones. The periodic existence of clear territorial boundaries over several centuries is a vital element in the maintenance of an identity. Even Wales, despite its extensive integration with England, had achieved that feat. And, given how difficult it was for Welsh nationalists to create a popular interest in the fourteenth-century exploits of Prince Llwellyn, the chances of Offa of Mercia becoming a regional hero were pretty remote. Among the Anglo-Saxon kingdoms, only Wessex carried any resonance in modern England, and this was the result more of its association with Thomas Hardy than of its association with the greatest of the Anglo-Saxon kings. The concept of Wessex was assiduously marketed by the English Tourist Board from 1945 onwards. But politically it meant little more to the people of the area it encompassed than other regions of the Victorian literary imagination such as Wordsworth's Lakes or the Brontës' Dales. Such 'regions' were at worst marketing tools. At best they were, as Harvie argued, 'politically innocuous cultural divisions of the national community'.[70]

All of which helps to explain the second reason why our dog never barked. Each part of England was seen to be an exemplar of the national culture and not an alternative to it. As Harvie put it, English regionalism 'rejected particularism; it projected a national identity through a regional example',[71] whereas in most other European countries the opposite is the case. Often, traditions lost their local associations altogether once they became nationally popular. One example is fish and chips. The trade began in Lancashire in the 1860s as a cheap form of eating out for industrial workers. It combined a northern custom of frying potatoes with a London custom of frying fish, the latter introduced by Eastern European Jews who had settled in the metropolis a few years earlier. The new dish was promoted by fryers like Harry Ramsden and Sam Isaacs as a democratic food born of the nation's great seafaring tradition, and it led to the expansion of the British fishing industry. The frying trade won further government approval when it provided fast food for munitions workers during the First World War, and by the 1930s the dish was seen as an icon of Britishness, comparable in status to roast beef, which was traditionally associated with the well-being of bourgeois middle England. Other traditions which remained local, such as the annual burning of an effigy of the Pope in Lewes, did so because they did not appeal to enough people outside their place of origin. Yet they too signified Englishness. Why? Because the existence of these diverse little Englands was believed to demonstrate the tolerance of the English people – the virtue which supposedly formed the basis of their national character.

The arch-herald of Anglo-Saxon Englishness in the twentieth century, Enoch Powell, had no time for regionalism for precisely these reasons. In a speech made in 1964 he said:

> The homogeneity of England, so profound and embracing that counties and the regions make it a hobby to discover their differences and assert their peculiarities; the continuity of England, which has brought this unity and this homogeneity about by the slow alchemy of centuries . . . From this continuous life of a united people in their island home springs, as from the soil of England, all that is peculiar in the gifts and the achievements of the English nation, its laws, its literature, its freedom, its self-discipline.[72]

The third reason for regio-scepticism was apathy. As a historical force apathy is underestimated because it lacks the romance of opposition. Yet, by allowing other groups to take control of an event or an historical process, apathy can just as easily help to decide the course which they take. Consequently, history is frequently written not by the winners but by the engaged. In this case, the English had lost interest in local government. At the local elections of 1958, only 27 per cent of the electorate voted.[73] By 1999, it was only 20 per cent. The only part of the UK where local government still mattered was in Northern Ireland. There, Unionist gerrymandering made the local franchise a focal point of nationalist protest. Electoral reform came in 1972, but the imposition of Direct Rule in the same year meant that local government remained a political cauldron as Unionists and Nationalists fought to control the running of essential services.

Back in Britain, apathy was exacerbated by two factors. Corruption had always happened, even in the golden age of Victorian civic pride about which devolutionists got so excited. But from 1970 to 1990 it became more apparent after the exposure by the national press of a series of scandals, notably the Poulson affair of 1972, which brought down T. Dan Smith. Globalization was the other major factor. For those in affluent regions local government was simply an amusing irrelevance. To those in less affluent regions it was not so amusing but was equally irrelevant, since it was clear that, given the inability of national governments to control their economies in the face of globalization, even the strongest, most fiscally independent regional assembly would be helpless when the tectonic plates of the world economy moved periodically. Therefore, Mrs Thatcher's abolition of the metropolitan authorities may have left deprived areas 'bereft of institutions able to operate and plan at a regional, strategic level' but few outside town halls cared.[74] And later claims that devolution would revive local democracy and increase regional clout fell on deaf ears or were wearily dismissed as more 'jobs for the boys'.

Fourth, the European factor. The fact that directly elected assemblies were a more democratic form of regional government than the wartime areas controlled by unelected commissioners made little difference because the whole concept of regionalism was seen to be alien – just as the creation of an elected European Parliament in 1979 did little to alter England's perception of the European Union. The English did not feel as threatened by regionalism as they did by federalism. But the championing of a 'Europe of the regions' did spread alarm. Although designed to reassure people that they were not about to be subsumed by a super-state, it forged a link in the public mind between regionalism and European federalism, which intensified hostility to both. It was a mistake which opponents of devolution were quick to exploit. They claimed that the EU wanted to divide England up into regions to make it easier to digest, just as the heptarchy had been picked off by Continental invaders centuries before. An official EU map was published in 1995, on which Scotland

and Wales were marked, but the word 'England' omitted in favour of its regions. To make matters worse, regional enthusiasts had a tendency to cite the German *Länder* as an example of how devolution could bring practical benefits without hindering the expression of national identity. This was a perfectly rational argument which deserved to be heard. But considering how central Germanophobia remained to English national identity in the late twentieth century, parading Germany as a model of democracy displayed a sorry lack of tactical awareness, particularly since the *Länder* had been specifically designed by the Allies to contain German nationalism in the postwar era.[75]

Finally, however bitter they were about southern dominance, the north, west and east felt more English than they did Scottish or Welsh. As socialists they might sympathize with the economic plight of the Celtic nations. But they did not identify with them. They continued to vote Labour believing that a British Labour government based in Westminster and legislating nationally was the best solution to the uneven effect of economic decline. Ultimately they had stronger cultural bonds with the south than they did with Scotland or Wales, a fact demonstrated by the fervour with which they supported the England football team, and these bonds actually grew stronger in this period. Economic decline substantially reduced the number of people migrating between Scotland and the north in search of work. And although it took the English some time to appreciate the depth of Scottish discontent with the Union, Scottish nationalism did increase awareness in the north that Scotland was a distinct country with its own customs – one of which was a dislike of the English wherever they hailed from. The origins of the term 'Geordies' illuminates the historical continuity in the Scottish–north relationship. When Charles Stuart and his army marched into England in 1745 to reclaim the British throne for the Scottish dynasty, the north-east declared for George II and styled themselves 'Georgies', later adapting it to the name by which they are known today.

The exception that proves the rule about regional identity in England is Cornwall. By a natural process of trade and intermarriage, Cornwall was integrated with the rest of England by 1600.[76] It was the last English county to be reached by the railway network but this was due to engineering difficulties rather than a belief that it was a place apart from the rest of the nation. The development of tin-mining had made Cornwall a confident, outward-looking regional industrial culture – distinctive yet fully integrated with the rest of

Britain. It had its own food which became nationally popular: the Cornish pasty – developed, like fish and chips, as a cheap and convenient meal for industrial workers on long shifts. The central irony of Cornish identity is this: the Cornish do have much in common with the Welsh, but it is the industrialized, heavily Anglicized south Wales of the late nineteenth century rather than the rural society favoured by romantic nationalists. Migration between the mining communities of Cornwall and Wales led to the adoption of beliefs and pursuits that were common to both. By the 1900s, brass bands, male voice choirs, rugby union, Protestant Nonconformism and Liberalism had become the central pillars of Cornish culture.

The idea that the Cornish are a unique Celtic people has a long pedigree. But it did not conflict with Anglo-British national identity until the mid- to late twentieth century. Leading antiquarians, philologists and archaeologists began to study Cornwall's Celticity in the 1750s, but their purpose was to assert the Britishness of the county, not its separateness. By learning more about the civilization of the Ancient Britons, scholars hoped to establish a sound historical basis for the new British identity which Hanoverian polemicists were constructing. The popularization of the myth of King Arthur from the 1850s onwards heightened national interest in the county. Arthur, who was reputedly born at Tintagel on the north Cornish coast, was a story of ancient British kingship which provided the English, Scots and Welsh with a less controversial shared monarchical heritage than the one provided by their legal Unions (the fact that Arthur was one of the most popular British Christian names between 1850 and 1950 was a testament to this).[77] Cornish studies were also part of an attempt to vindicate Britain's Union with Ireland by liberal unionists who rejected the idea that the Irish were inferior beings. As an English county with Celtic origins, Cornwall was seen by these observers as an example of the plurality of the British race and of the shared history and folklore which bound the two islands together. In short, the county was a unique crucible of nineteenth-century Britishness: celebrated as a progressive, industrial Protestant society but also as a poetic and mystical place, home to the original Britons and relatively unstained by the bloody history of British–Irish conflict.

The romance of Celticism continued to attract a number of prominent English intellectuals in the twentieth century as well as a growing number of tourists and settlers. They were drawn by the vision of a common British–Irish civilization and the apparently pre-industrial romance of its rugged scenery. The Cornish-born Arthur

Quiller-Couch, a Cambridge poetry professor who promoted English literature as a source of English national consciousness, wrote extensively about the county until his death in 1944; the 'St Ives Group' of artists also found inspiration there in the 1950s. So too did the composer Arnold Bax, whose symphonic poem *Tintagel* (1917) established a reputation which enabled him to succeed the Welshman Walford Davies as Master of the King's Musick in 1942 (Bax was also heavily influenced by the poetry of W. B. Yeats and Irish Celtic culture; he spent much of his life in Ireland and died in Cork in 1953). In the second half of the century, John Betjeman and the popular historian A. L. Rowse also wrote lovingly about the area, as did Inglis Gundry, an Anglo-Cornish collector of folk songs who studied under Ralph Vaughan Williams.

However, while sympathetic outsiders continued to see Cornwall as a quaint part of a united Britain, the Cornish began to develop an altogether different identity. When the Cornish economy faltered in the 1900s, the Celticity of the county began to form the basis of a nationalist movement which, though electorally unsuccessful, achieved a significant influence on Cornish identity. As in other areas of the UK, relative economic decline made an existing sense of uniqueness more pointed: cultural traditions were invented and the history of the region's relationship to England was rewritten. The Cornish historian Bernard Deacon has written: 'Surrounded by the relics of a failed industrialism, they preferred to return to the pre-Reformation era when Cornwall was more indisputably 'Cornish' and non-English . . . They set to with a will to create and recreate all the symbols and paraphernalia of a Celtic nationality.'[78] By the 1950s, the basis of Cornish identity had become more racial: that is, many of its people saw themselves not only as Celtic, but fundamentally different to the English, whom they defined as Anglo-Saxon. Some saw Cornwall as a nation in its own right which, like Scotland, Wales and Ireland, was a victim of English imperialism. In 1951, a nationalist party, Mebyon Kernow (Sons of Cornwall), was formed.

The Cornish mimicked the Welsh by labelling pastimes they shared with other Britons as special to them. Thus, tin mining became a symbol of Cornish uniqueness instead of a local variant of the British mining industry, its decline symbolizing the rapacious plundering of the county's natural resources by foreigners (the flag which the Cornish made their own in the 1950s – a white cross on a black background – was that of St Pirrin, the patron saint of miners). Rugby union was transformed into a focus of nationality, even though the Cornish team still competed, like Ulster, in the County rather than the National Championships of the UK. The team was followed by a large army of men carrying Cornish flags, singing patriotic folk songs and wearing kilts (the tartan they invented for themselves was yellow and black). In 1991, the Chairman of Cornwall RUFC described the club as one of the focal points for 'a Celtic people striving to preserve an identity'.[79]

As in Wales, the most important factor in the transformation of Cornishness was the rescue and revival of its ancient language. In 1932, a pressure group was founded called Tyr ha Tavas (Land and Language). Based in Surrey, it was dedicated to 'the culture and idealism characteristic of our race'.[80] After repeated battles with the Ministry of Education over the next thirty years, the language movement finally achieved success in 1967 with the establishment of the Cornish Language Board and the subsequent introduction of an optional Certificate of Secondary Education in Cornish in the county's schools and colleges. The number of people who spoke the language remained tiny: in 1981, those studying it reached a peak of approximately 1,000, but only 93 sat the exam, and the numbers declined again thereafter, because the revivalist movement became split into three factions, each championing different versions of the language. By the end of the century, some 200 people spoke Cornish competently – only 0.04 per cent out of a population of 500,000. But, as in Wales, the language remained a powerful symbol of 'nationality', its very existence proof of Cornish distinctiveness and a source of pride to many who did not speak it.

Migration from England sharpened Cornish nationalism. Concentrated on the county's eastern borders, it consisted of middle-class English families and groups of hippies, all in search of Celtic authenticity and cheap property. In 1977, Mebyon Kernow proposed to tax holidaymakers and migrants as they crossed the county border. 'Cornwall', it declared, 'belongs to the Cornish ... unwelcome drifters and drop-outs will be a charge upon their own governments – at present we contribute heavily for the privilege of entertaining seasonal parasites and idlers from beyond our land. Holiday makers come as our guests and not by natural right.'[81] At the end of the century, one party member could explain his dislike of English Heritage signs thus: 'the worst thing is their symbol of the Tudor rose. For us, it's like a Swastika to the Jews'.[82] The Duchy of Cornwall, a semi-feudal relic from the fourteenth century, was a focal point for Cornish monarchism. It also provided a symbolic link with Wales, since the Duchy provided the modern Princes of Wales with their main source of income. Cornwall even had a Druidic Gorsedd modelled on that of Wales. The political precedent for a Cornish Parliament was the Stannary, a thirteenth-century legal assembly established to exercise the Crown's jurisdiction over tin-mining communities. It last sat in 1752 but nationalists revived it amid considerable publicity on 20 May 1974, and in the late 1980s and early 1990s it became a focal point for Cornish resistance to the poll tax. Stannary members claimed that 'tinners' were exempt because the tax had never been ratified by the Stannary.[83] Mebyon Kernow was electorally inconsequential, failing to make a dent in the Liberal and Conservative dominance of the county.

Nevertheless, a popular demand for devolution did emerge in the 1980s. Despite the income Cornwall earned from tourism, its economy continued to decline. The death of the tin-mining industry was compounded in the 1980s by the decline of its fishing industry, thanks to the strict quotas imposed by the European Union on its fleet. In 1991, nearly a century of hardship culminated with Cornwall being officially named the most economically deprived region in the whole of the United Kingdom and one of the most deprived in the EU. Graffiti daubed on the walls of Cornwall's last tin mine (South Crofty, closed in 1998) became part of Cornish iconography. It read:

> Cornish lads are fishermen
> And Cornish lads are miners, too.
> But when the fish and tin are gone
> What are the Cornish boys to do?

The answer, for most, was to have more control over the government of their county. From the 1960s onwards, polls consistently showed that although most people continued to doubt the efficacy of independence, around 70 per cent favoured a Cornish assembly with tax-raising powers. This was the same proportion as the Scots and by a long way – around 30 per cent – the highest figure of any English region.[84]

Given how long Cornwall had been integrated, this might seem extraordinary, until you remember three things. First economic decline was sharper in Cornwall and it began a quarter of a century before it did elsewhere in the UK. Second, it had a ready-made Victorian Celtic heritage on which to build a new identity; and third, British governments made few devolutionary concessions towards it, so that at no point in the twentieth century was Cornishness assuaged.

Exceptional though Cornwall was, its identity highlighted one of the weaknesses of English regionalism: the inability to define what exactly a region was. For most of the century, Cornwall had been administered in one way or another with Devon and Dorset as 'the West Country'. But other parts of the West Country were as alien to Cornish patriots as the Home Counties. And, despite the fact that the Cornish felt a racial affinity with the Bretons, they were not keen on the European Union because it had decimated their fishing fleet. Consequently, proposals to give the West Country some form of regional assembly aggravated discontent, because such plans were seen as colonialism in disguise.[85]

Cornishness was neither understood nor recognized by the rest of the UK. The Celts with whom they claimed an affinity were frankly indifferent to their cause, because the nuances of English culture were of little interest to people busy formulating their own cosmology of Anglo-Saxon oppression. Nor was Cornwall's claim recognized by the rest of England. Cornish 'national' identity was expressed in a more overtly racial way than elsewhere in the UK, where it became illegal and frowned upon to do so. Although the term Anglo-Saxon was still sometimes used to define the English, their sense of race was based more on a more generic concept of whiteness than the arcane racial categories of nineteenth-century romantic antiquaries which dominated the construction of Cornishness. Because the English could not see any fundamental difference between themselves and the Cornish, they too disregarded them.[86] And although the county remained a popular domestic tourist destination, English people in search of real Celticity began to look further afield, to the Republic of Ireland.

5. What a coup for the Paddys!

When, on 12 October 1984, the IRA blew up the hotel in Brighton where most of the government were staying, Alan Clark – maverick MP and son of the great Sir Kenneth – characteristically expressed admiration for the terrorists. 'What a coup for the Paddys!' he noted in his diary, 'The whole thing has the smell of a Tet Offensive. If they had just had the wit to press their advantage, a couple of chaps with guns in the crowd, they could have got the whole government as they blearily emerged.'[87] The whole nation blearily emerged from its view of the Troubles that morning and saw Ireland in an utterly different light.

The very word 'Troubles' is a classic example of British understatement. It implies a long-running and embarrassing family dispute about which its members would rather not talk. Refusing to acknowledge that it was a war, liberals talked incessantly about the immorality of covert operations by the British army and secret services. This not only enraged conservatives in the UK, it also played into the hands of Irish Republicans, who knew they were waging a bloody war and needed all the sympathy they could get. Liberal cant reached a peak of self-righteousness in 1988 after the SAS shot three IRA members in Gibraltar. Mrs Thatcher reminded everyone that Britain was fighting 'guerrilla warfare'. Realizing her 'mistake', she corrected herself, saying, 'They are thugs – that's all.'[88] But she knew better. A year after the Brighton bombing she had pushed through the Anglo-Irish Agreement, which gave the Republic a say in the affairs of the North for the first time. It was not a solution; its historical significance is that the British did not regard it as a betrayal of compatriots. By 1985 they were heartily sick of the Troubles and wanted Britain to pull out of the province.

Despite her Nonconformist background and strong belief in Unionism, the Prime Minister recoiled from the patriotism of Ulster, as this passage in her memoirs illustrates:

> I knew that these people shared many of my own attitudes, derived from my staunchly Methodist background . . . Their patriotism was real and fervent, even if too narrow. They had often been taken too much for granted . . . Any Conservative should in his bones be a Unionist too. Our Party, has always, throughout its history, been committed to the defence of the Union . . . But what British politician will ever fully understand Northern Ireland? I suspect that even the most passionate English supporters of Ulster do so less than they imagine . . . In the history of Ireland – both North and South – which I tried to read up on . . . reality and myth from the seventeenth century to the 1920s take on an almost Balkan immediacy. Distrust mounting to hatred and revenge is never far beneath the political surface. And those who step on it must do so gingerly.[89]

Apart from frustration at the continuing intransigence of the Protestant community, there were two reasons for the haemorrhaging of popular empathy with Ulster.

By the late 1980s, the one institution on which unionists had always relied to foster a sense of cross-Channel Britishness – the Crown – was failing them. In contrast to Northern Ireland, mainlanders were increasingly indifferent to the institution. On 28 August 1979 the IRA assassinated Lord Mountbatten while he was on holiday in the Republic. Mountbatten, a Second World War veteran who had negotiated the independence of India, was the first member of the royal family to be killed by the IRA, and this was the last moment when monarchism formed a really strong bond between Ulster and the rest of the UK. As news began to filter through in 1989 of royal scandal, interest in the monarchy returned but respect and affection for it did not. When eleven people were killed in the bombing of a Remembrance Day service at Enniskillen in 1987, the *Independent* headline read 'GLORIOUS DEAD DISHONOURED' while the *Star* led with 'SCUM: COWARDS STRIKE ON DAY WE HONOUR OUR DEAD'.[90] The use of the first person plural was telling. The bombing reminded people that Northern Ireland had fought alongside Britain in the Second World War while the South had not. But the sense of affinity with Ulster did not long survive the funerals of the victims.

In the 1980s the British finally gave up on the Union of 1801. They not only learned to see the Republic as a foreign country, they learned to love it. Like most of the Western world, the British were seduced by the Irish in the late twentieth century. A people once caricatured in Britain as lazy, superstitious drunks became the epitome of a spirituality the West felt it had lost. A romantic view of the Emerald Isle had never completely disappeared from British culture. But thanks to the Republic's assiduous marketing of itself from the 1980s onwards, that view came to predominate. More than any other tourist board of the Isles, the Irish Tourist Board sold the public a phoney, sanitized view of its subject. Its self-confessed aim was to provide 'interpretative gateways into our heritage . . . The end result will be . . . the creation of a strong brand image of Ireland as a quality heritage destination'.[91]

The image of Ireland which predominated was that of a Celtic nation full of beautiful colleens, poets, comedians and generally friendly people. The British view of Ireland therefore began to correspond for the first time with the American view of it. Even the

Irish joke declined in popularity. The supposedly innate conviviality of the Irish – their love of 'the craich' – centred around alcohol. By 1990, St Patrick's Day was celebrated by more Britons than St Andrew's, St David's or St George's Day. Moving with the trend, British breweries converted hundreds of their outlets into Irish theme pubs. In towns and cities across the Britain, the Crown and Anchor became Mary O'Milligan's. No other development so symbolized how much the British view of Southern Ireland had changed. In the mid-1970s, IRA pub bombings in England had provoked a wave of anti-Irish feeling. Now, the exact locus of IRA atrocity became places where the British could imagine they were sharing in the craich of a peaceful, kind-hearted people.

It was not all blarney. The modernization of Ireland had a positive effect on its image. The growth of the so-called 'Celtic Tiger' economy and the partial liberalization of Southern Irish society (in particular its attitude to women's rights) filed the edges off de Valéra's conservative Catholic Irishness, which had so alienated the British earlier in the century. So too did music and the cinema. On the rare occasions that Ireland featured in mid-century British cinema, it was shown to be synonymous with violence. Films like *Shake Hands with the Devil* (1959) portrayed IRA leaders as psychopaths who either renounced violence for the love of a good woman or were killed by the great British bobby. During the 1980s that changed. Funded partly by the Irish state, film-makers such as Neil Jordan presented the UK with a more sophisticated portrait of their country with films like *The Crying Game* (1992). Ireland's pop and rock groups did the same. Just as tartan-clad English teenagers danced to the Bay City Rollers during the devolution debates of the 1970s, so the 1980s witnessed the extraordinary sight of young Britons dancing to U2's 'Sunday, Bloody Sunday'. Another symbolic change worth noting occurred in 1997, when Liverpool was twinned with Dublin. Since the industrial revolution, Liverpool had been the most sectarian of England's cities – the place from where, in 1967, city councillors had opposed a papal visit on the grounds that it would 'imperil our Protestant heritage'. Thirty years later, their successors crossed the Irish sea with Catholic colleagues to sign a charter of civic amity with their counterparts in Ireland's capital.

The Northern Irish majority could not compete. Literally, in fact. Not only had empire, Protestantism and monarchy ceased to bind Ulster to the rest of the UK, in an age when football was the major focus of national identity in the world, the fact that Northern Ireland could not compete effectively in the sport helped to consign the province to the outer reaches of British consciousness. Tourism finished the job. Since Partition, commentators sympathetic to the South had urged the British to travel there and see for themselves that it was not populated by savages. H. V. Morton said in the introduction to his *In Search of Ireland* (1930):

> The most unhappy and regrettable chapter in the history of Great Britain has ended, and the two nations are at last free to make friends ... I would like to ... encourage people to spend their holidays in Ireland and make friends with its irresistible inhabitants. Friendship and sympathy between these two warm-hearted and kindly people would be a fitting end to centuries of political misunderstanding.[92]

And so it was. By 1981, the Republic of Ireland had become the sixth most popular holiday destination for Britons, after France, Spain, Greece, Italy and the US. In 1951, a guide book for visitors to the North told its readers: 'It's a land of long memories, strong loyalties and warm hospitality. There's a crisp Ulster saying ... "Y'r welcome!" '[93] Few now valued their loyalty or sought their welcome and Ulster's tourist industry collapsed as spectacularly as the South's grew. While the South was characterized in the British traveller's mind by a smile and a log fire, the North was characterized by a grimace and a firebomb.

Ireland was still regarded as Britain's pain; like an old bedsore, whichever way the patient turned it would not go away. There was still sympathy for the many innocents who were caught in the crossfire of the Troubles. But the source of the problem was no longer thought to be the South. For the first time, the British distinguished between the Republic of Ireland and the republican attempt to destroy a part of the United Kingdom. In less than half a century a British view of Ireland several hundred years old had been completely stood on its head. In 1949, Whitehall officials described the Southern Irish as 'an unpredictable and inconsequent people'. By 1989, mainland Britons took that view of the North. The reaction was bitter. One Ulsterman said, 'Thatcher sends my son and thousands of other squaddies to defend fifty sheep shaggers on the far side of the globe and then signs us away in the Anglo-Irish accord.'[94]

Which brings us to the next section. Having examined the part that Mrs Thatcher played in undermining Britishness, it is time to look at how she attempted to rekindle it and why she failed. In an interview in 1975, shortly after Mrs Thatcher became leader of the Conservative Party, A. J. P. Taylor was asked what he thought would reunite the UK. He replied:

> The best time we ever had, in my lifetime, when the country was best run, the most egalitarian society and the most efficient, was during the Second World War. We might consider having a war with somebody – but it would have to be someone just big enough to give us a fright, and yet not big enough to defeat us.

Seven years later Taylor got his wish when Britain went to war against Argentina over the Falkland Islands. For a brief period, it seemed as if Britishness was not only intact but had reverted to the simplistic, cocksure form of the early 1950s.

PART 10

TUNNELLERS

We have ceased to be a nation in retreat. We have instead a newfound confidence – born in the economic battles at home and tested and found true 8,000 miles away ... And so today we can rejoice at our success in the Falklands and take pride in the achievement of our task force. But we do so, not as at some flickering of a flame which must soon be dead. No – we rejoice that Britain has rekindled that spirit which has fired her for generations past and which today has begun to burn as brightly as before. Britain found herself again in the South Atlantic and will not look back from the victory she has won.

Margaret Thatcher, 1982

[The European Union] is all a German racket designed to take over the whole of Europe ... I'm not against giving up sovereignty in principle, but not to this lot. You might as well give it to Adolf Hitler, frankly ... I'm not sure I wouldn't rather have the shelters and the chance to fight back than simply being taken over by economics.

Nicholas Ridley, 1990

1. We are all Falklanders now

The Falkland Islands are situated 300 miles off the coast of Argentina. They were first landed by English sailors in 1690; they were named after Viscount Falkland, the Commissioner of the Navy. The islands have been continuously inhabited since 1833, mostly by émigré Scots and Welsh farmers. The only Englishmen involved were the absentee landlords and shareholders of the Falklands Islands Company, formed to run it as a profitable venture. A tiny windswept landmass with a population of only 1,800, the main activity the islands saw was farming 600,000 sheep. In 1770, Britain went to war with Spain over the islands. In a pamphlet written to condemn the action, Samuel Johnson described them as:

> An island thrown aside from human use, stormy in winter, barren in summer, an island which not even the southern savages have dignified with habitation, where a garrison must be kept in a state which contemplates with envy the exiles of Siberia.[1]

Shortly before his death in 1983, the exiled spy Donald Maclean said of the Falklands, 'I told them in 1951 to get rid of them!'[2] The Foreign Office didn't take his advice. But nor did it pay much heed to Argentina's repeated threat to capture the islands.

At dawn on 2 April 1982, a large invasion fleet approached. The Governor, Rex Hunt, summoned Majors Mike Norman and Gary Noot to the capital, Port Stanley. With classic British understatement, he told them, 'It looks as if the buggers mean it.' After a spirited but futile effort to repel the invasion, the two officers and their sixty-eight men surrendered at 8.30 a.m.[3] With the phone lines down, the Foreign Office was only able to confirm the surrender thanks, appropriately enough, to a radio ham in Wales who picked up a distress call from one of the islanders. The following day, a picture of British soldiers lying face down on a road were splashed on the front pages of newspapers around the world. A War Cabinet was immediately set up. On 5 April a 'Task Force' set sail for the South Atlantic, made up of forty-four ships and 10,000 troops, at an eventual cost of £2,000 million.

Referring to the conflict of 1770, Dr Johnson made his legendary comment 'Patriotism is the last refuge of a scoundrel.' Though often taken out of context, the quote perfectly describes Mrs Thatcher's manipulation of British national identity in 1982. Left/liberal commentators thought that her rush to defend the sovereignty of a group of islands 8,000 miles away in the Atlantic was an absurd imperial adventure and that the bellicose manner in which she prosecuted the war fostered a jingoism which had never entirely disappeared from British culture but which received a second heyday as a result of her misadventure. That view endures today. Even more conservative commentators like Max Hastings and Simon Jenkins, whose book on the conflict was the first serious study to be published, wrote in their foreword: 'This is the story of a freak of history, almost certainly the last colonial war that Britain will ever fight'.[4]

The Falklands conflict was certainly a freak of history. But it has been widely misunderstood. The operation was *not* imperial in intent. By the early 1980s, the Conservative Party had finally lost all interest in the Commonwealth and did little or nothing to promote it. Edward Heath had no time for it as a distraction from the European cause. His successor viewed it with even more disdain, as an assembly of corrupt regimes which sought to manipulate liberal guilt over the Empire to get financial aid to mop up the mess left by their own economic mismanagement. Alan Clark recalled that the annual Commonwealth Heads of Government Meeting (CHOGM) was known to Ministers in the 1980s as Compulsory Hand-Outs for Greedy Mendicants. The Queen was virtually the only person left in Britain who did care about it. Without Elizabeth II and the continuing need for Prime Ministers to court her, it is unlikely that the Commonwealth would have survived at all. As for the Falklands themselves, there was some talk of oil deposits in the area (they were never found), but unlike Suez the islands had no economic significance other than being a drain on the British taxpayer. Nor did they have any strategic importance. The only avowedly imperial comment Mrs Thatcher made during the conflict was one in which she compared herself not to Palmerston but to Napoleon: 'I had the winter at the back of my mind. *The winter*. What will the winter do? The wind, the cold. Down in South Georgia the ice, what will it do? It beat Napoleon at Moscow.'[5]

The patriotism which swept Britain in the spring and summer of 1982 was not predominantly imperialistic either. What the Falklands revealed was that roughly half of the British population still hankered after being an international power, having a seat in all the best security councils and enjoying the respect of their peers. As I have argued in previous chapters, that is not necessarily the same thing as wanting to rule the world. The other half (a figure which had been rising steadily since the 1960s) were content for Britain to be a modest, second-rank nation but one, naturally, which could defend itself and the few small overseas territories which had chosen to remain British.

Traces of imperialism were, undeniably, present during the conflict. Among the young, they were visible in a brisk trade in T-shirts bearing the *Star Wars* caption 'The Empire Strikes Back!' For older generations, the fact that the retaking of the Falklands was primarily a naval operation recalled Britain's imperial seafaring tradition which in the nuclear age had come to be virtually redundant. More importantly, the Falklands restored the martial pride which the British had lost at Suez, just as the Gulf War restored that which America had lost in different circumstances in Vietnam. Mrs Thatcher had learnt no end of a lesson from the Suez crisis: namely, that American support was now necessary for any operation of this kind. What little diplomatic effort she expended trying to resolve the conflict focused on making sure Ronald Reagan was on side. Thanks to the skill of the British Ambassadors to the US and the UN, Nicholas Henderson and Anthony Parsons, the Americans were persuaded to choose the Special Relationship over their normal policy of propping up anti-communist South American dictatorships. On 30 April the United States government declared its support for Britain.[6]

It also helped Thatcher's cause that the islanders were white and could be easily identified, according to the still prevailing definition of Britishness, as British citizens. In the Emergency Debate on the invasion (the first time the Commons had met on a Saturday since the Suez crisis), the Prime Minister tacitly emphasized Britons' racial affinity with the Falklanders: 'Like the people of the United Kingdom [they] are an island race . . . They are few in number, but they have the right to live in peace, to choose their own way of life and to determine their own allegiance. Their way of life is British: their allegiance to the Crown'.[7] Her Foreign Secretary, Lord Carrington (who resigned over the invasion), had 'a sympathetic understanding that the whole of the country felt angry and humiliated . . . Inhabitants of a British colony – men and women of British blood – had been taken over against their will.'[8] Even a renowned Tory 'wet' like Julian Critchley MP had visions of a patriotic continuum stretching back to the Middle Ages, a vision he shared with readers of the *Daily Telegraph*:

> Compare the shared emotion at home and the superb morale of our fighting men in the freezing Falklands with what we know of the spirit of Agincourt, of the Elizabethans' response to the Spanish Armada, of Trafalgar or Waterloo, the flood of volunteers at the start of the First World War, or the Battle of Britain in the Second. It is the same inherited, untaught devotion to one's homeland which has survived all the changes and chances of our national life, untouched by all the plans of the twentieth century to ensure peace and the proliferation of international organisations.[9]

Tony Benn recalled 'the House was in the grip of jingoism'; later adding 'Mrs Thatcher is an absolutely Victorian jingoist. I find it embarrassing to live in Britain at the moment.'[10]

But these were only distant echoes of the lion's roar. For most Britons, the pride which the adventure restored was a national one, lost in the morass of economic crisis and social disorder of the period 1972–82, not the one lost as a result of decolonization between 1947 and 1968. The historian of empire Bernard Porter made the point well:

> There was no imperial *rationale* to it. Britain did not fight the Argentines over the Falkland Islands for profit, or for the security of her sea-lanes, or for the material or spiritual good of anyone. She fought them for a principle (to resist aggression), to restore her *amour propre*, and possibly for electoral profit ... The jingoism released by the affair was, equally, not at all an imperial one; that is, one that revealed a particular imperial as against a merely national pride ... So far as the empire itself was concerned ... few Britons cared at all for what remained. They were, most of them, proud of defending the Falklands; but none was particularly proud of *having* them to defend.[11]

Like Churchill's funeral in 1965 – another event mistakenly seen as imperialesque – the national past which the Falklands conjured up was that of the Second World War. The patriotic rhetoric of Parliament, press and people focused on the British refusal to give in to appeasers. It was the lesson Mrs Thatcher claimed to have learnt from the war. And, as we have seen throughout this book, it provided the central litany of postwar national identity: the British were not an aggressively nationalistic people; they were peaceful, slow to anger, but when stirred by ruthless foreigners they rallied round, dug in and fought the good fight to save the world from tyranny. The international order was not threatened by the Argentine military junta as it was by the Third Reich, but the Prime Minister persistently claimed that if the British did not set an example by standing up to Argentina, the world would eventually pay a heavy price as tinpot dictators everywhere started to fancy their chances.

In an editorial shortly after the invasion entitled 'We are all Falklanders now', *The Times* presented a Churchillian vision of the struggle ahead:

> As in 1939, so today. The same principles apply to the Falklands. We have given our word, and we must, where we can, prevent the expansionist policies of a dictatorship affecting our interests. But there is a more important dimension now. The Poles were Poles; the Falklanders are our people. They are British citizens. The Falkland Islands are British territory. When British territory is invaded, it is not just an invasion of our land, but of our whole spirit. We are all Falklanders now.[12]

Among those who directly compared Thatcher to Churchill was Jean Rook in the *Daily Express*: 'Our Churchill's fire isn't out. She may not have the oratory or the platform presence or sheer bulk. But in the past, dark 48 hours, she's shown the metal.'[13] There was no question of a coalition government being formed. But Michael Foot, who replaced Callaghan as Labour Party leader in 1980, briefly assumed the role of Attlee. During the Emergency Debate he spoke in support of the task force, saying that it offered an opportunity to 'uphold the claim of our country to be a defender of people's freedom throughout the world'.[14] When he sat down, Edward Du Cann rose to congratulate him for speaking so patriotically: 'There are times in the affairs of our nation when the House should speak with a single, united voice ... The Leader of the Opposition spoke for us all'. Meanwhile, ninety-year-old Sir Arthur 'Bomber' Harris was wheeled out to give the men of the Task Force troops his seal of approval. 'They're the same breed of men I had,' he told the press, thus reassuring Britons that their national character had not changed over the last forty years.[15]

Important though this martial spirit was, oral evidence suggests that the redemptive power of Falklands patriotism rested more on the national unity which the war fostered. Coming at a time when the country was so divided, the echo of 1940–41 was a sweet sound to the British ear. The following response is typical of those given to a Mass Observation survey at the end of 1982:

> Remembering Dunkirk, and without in any way being jingoistic, only Britain could have done it . . . memories of another army flooded back; an army, dirty, torn, without equipment, scrambling back in little boats, in the 'Saucy Sal' and the 'Three Sisters' after Dunkirk . . . phrases slip into the mind: 'I counted them all out and I counted them all back', words which will pass into the history books with 'the lights are going out all over Europe'. Nothing could withstand the last flood of Rule Britannia.[16]

As well as class and generational unity, there were also signs of a renewed compact between the three nations of Britain, a trend helped by the fact that many of the Falklanders were of Scottish and Welsh origin. Speaking to Scottish Tories at Perth a week before the Task Force landed, Mrs Thatcher said she felt 'this ancient country rising as one nation . . . the springs of pride in Britain flow again'. Such was the Scottish response to the war that the organizers of the Edinburgh Festival cancelled a concert by the Geneva Opera Ballet, whose director was Argentinian. The company's performance of *Tango*, a celebration of Latin American music, was deemed 'inappropriate in present circumstances'. In Wales, too, Falklands patriotism was apparent. The only political party in Britain to oppose the war officially was Plaid Cymru, but this won it few plaudits among the Welsh people. As in Scotland, the war bolstered the dual identity of England's western partner: a pride in being simultaneously Welsh and British. At the same time, the contribution which both countries made to beating Argentina led, as it did after 1945, to a feeling that they should be rewarded with more recognition of their core nationality. A Glamorgan woman wrote to the *Times*:

> Sir, From Agincourt to the South Atlantic Welsh soldiers have fought with pride in the British Army. At Bluff Cove they suffered the worst casualties of the Falklands War. Is it not time for the Welsh national flag to be incorporated into the Union Flag?[17]

Subsequent conflicts in the twentieth century, like the Gulf War and Kosovo, united the British on only the most shallow of bases: that of having relatives in the armed forces and/or a generic belief that the action was a morally just one. One of the most significant things about the Falklands episode is that it was the first and last time between 1945 and 2000 that the Scots, Welsh and English were emotionally united by a war fought by the British state.

Analysing the war, Lucy Noakes has argued, 'The battle for the Falklands sometimes appeared to be less about regaining the islands than about "rediscovering" Britain's true nature, lost since 1945.'[18] The Falklands were presented as a vision of a lost Britain and their people a living lesson in how to be truly British. Not only were they white; they were also a hardy rural people, living a harmonious, peaceful life, replete with eccentrics but untouched by the unemployment and riots which beset the cities of the UK. It was claimed that the islanders read Hansard regularly, a sign that they possessed a keen sense of democracy which many Britons appeared to have lost in recent years. *The Times* concluded:

> They are more British than the British in many ways ... [the weather] is unpredictable ... typically British. Port Stanley ... is rather like a waterside village in the West Country. And there is that same easy going feeling about the place. The shops look as if out of the 1920s ... The island exists in a sense in a sort of timeless vacuum.[19]

Another people considered to be 'more British than the British' were the Protestant majority in Northern Ireland. But Northern Irish identity had come to be seen as neurotically aggressive. That of the Falklanders on the other hand, was seen as modest in a properly British way. This was especially ironic because, a year before the Argentine invasion, Parliament had refused to give the Falklanders full UK citizenship. Stranded on the periphery and of no apparent value, they had been fobbed off with Dependent Territory Status.

Falklands patriotism owed much to the careful projection of the war by the government and the media. If the Establishment had learnt from Suez that American permission was required for foreign military action, like the Americans it had also learnt a lesson from Vietnam: public support depended on making the fight seem a clean one. Indeed, press coverage was worse than it had been during the Crimean War. The Charge of the Light Brigade was reported in detail twenty days after the event. In 1982, some TV film took twenty-three days to get back to the UK, and when it did it was heavily censored. The photo-journalist Don McCullin, whose harrowing pictures of Vietnam and Biafra had done much to intensify opposition to those wars, was refused permission by Ministry of Defence chiefs to cover the Falklands. Said McCullin, they 'considered my experience in war coverage a threat to the image that they would find comfortable'.[20]

As in the Suez crisis, the BBC's verbal reporting was attacked by the right for being even-handed. The Editor of News and Current Affairs, John Wilson, sent a controversial memo to staff on 26 April called 'Not Our Troops' which said: 'We should try to avoid using "our" when we mean "British". When we say "our troops", "our ambassador" or "our ships" we sound like a mouthpiece of government. We are not Britain, we are the BBC.'[21] The *Sun* called the corporation 'General Galtieri's Fifth Column'; in the House of Commons, the Prime Minister weighed in, saying 'The Argentines are being treated almost as equals . . . it gives offence and causes great emotion among many people.' On 13 May, the Director-General, Alasdair Milne, a proud Scot and the last of the Reithians to run the corporation, attended a meeting of 125 angry Tory backbenchers at Westminster. Milne describes it in his memoirs as a 'very nasty meeting . . . a special form of Star Chamber'. He was accompanied by the Chairman of the Board of Governors, George Howard. 'You, sir, are a traitor,' one MP barked at Howard. The BBC's Chairman, whose normal manner was that of a landed aristocrat addressing his retainers, completely lost his reserve and snapped back, 'Stuff you!'[22]

As this exchange suggests, the patriotism of 1982, like the national identity it expressed, was not seamless. First, it is worth remembering that Falklanders were much mocked even among the most ardent armchair patriots during the war. The Governor of the Falklands, Rex Hunt, was widely seen as an absurd character. Pictures of him dressed in his plumed hat, driving around the islands in a black taxi, recalled an era of imperial pretension which few people related to any more. As for the general population, the term 'sheepshaggers' (denoting a simple, inbred, rural people and usually reserved for the Welsh) was a common appellation at the time, both among troops and among those back in Britain. It showed that not everyone fell for the South Atlantic rural idyll, any more than they fell for the British one from which it sprang.

More seriously, a significant minority of the country – 20 per cent – were completely opposed to the war. Many more viewed with distaste the jingoistic excesses (imperial and otherwise) which marred the whole episode. The distaste intensified as the death toll mounted; 255 British dead and 672 Argentinians by the end of the conflict. The sinking of the cruiser *Belgrano* with the loss of 386 Argentine lives was heralded by the *Sun*'s notorious comic-book headline 'GOTCHA!' over a picture of the stricken vessel. To this it added 'STICK IT UP YOUR JUNTA!'. And, after one engagement between the two sides, the sports page and the front page became indistinguishable: BRITAIN 6, ARGENTINA 0. The spoof *Private Eye* competition, 'KILL AN ARGIE AND WIN A METRO!' captured the unsavoury ideological forces let loose by the war.

Before replacing Foot as Labour leader in 1983, Neil Kinnock memorably silenced a heckler who shouted at him, 'Mrs Thatcher showed guts!' 'It's a pity', Kinnock replied, 'that others had to leave theirs on the ground at Goose Green to prove it.'[23] Not surprisingly, the British intelligentsia were almost entirely against the war. Alan Bennett described it as 'The Last Night of the Proms erected into a policy'.[24] Salman Rushdie said:

> [Mrs Thatcher's] are the politics of the Victorian nursery; if somebody pinches you, you take their trousers down and thrash them . . . This was fought to drown the noise of our own diplomatic chickens coming home to roost. It was a war to save Mrs Thatcher's face . . . It is not a face worth launching a thousand ships, or even a task force to rescue.[25]

Roald Dahl said: 'In 1939 we were all prepared to risk our skins to fight against aggression. Today, excessive Socialism seems to have nurtured a flabby idle breed of people who would rather compromise than fight. I would fight.'[26] Was he right? To some extent, yes. The Prime Minister's encouragement and exploitation of jingoism for her own political ends richly deserved to be criticized, and the willingness of the Left to do so was a refreshing example of British democracy at work.

But there did come a point when anti-war arguments were as crude as the jingoism they were attacking. Hatred of Thatcher and Thatcherism blinded many people to the central question at hand: the rule of international law. Like many on the left at this time, Tony Benn was a champion of British sovereignty when it came to the European Union's peaceful encroachment upon it, but he was unable to apply the same principles when the military aggression of a fascist dictatorship threatened that sovereignty. He also deluded himself that the war was not really popular. 'I'm certain', he wrote, 'that a majority of the British people are against the war . . . but the media are preventing that view becoming apparent.'[27]

Feminists, already apoplectic that Britain's first female Prime Minister was a Tory, were also furious. The magazine *Spare Rib* declared that the war was an expression of 'male power', and its prosecutor an example of how a woman who gains power in a man's world is perverted by masculine culture.[28] There was a gender bias in the reportage of the war which showed that women were still second-class citizens within the popularly imagined community of Britishness. Their portrayal as passive patriots whose duty it was to cheer on warrior-men reflected male insecurity about the growing number of successful career women in the 1980s. It was also, perhaps, a response to the fashionable bisexuality in pop culture which, from David Bowie to Boy George, had challenged traditional British notions of masculinity over the previous decade. While men in mascara danced the night away on HMS *Belfast* by the Thames, real men were said to be found on the *Ark Royal* risking their lives for Queen and Country in the South Atlantic.

The Prime Minister was portrayed by cartoonists as Britannia. Britannia had intermittently been a national symbol since the Roman occupation of the island in the first century AD, originally designed by the Romans to unite the Celtic tribes which they had conquered. She enjoyed a revival in the early seventeenth century after the union of the Scottish and English crowns and again in the nineteenth century when Queen Victoria assumed her guise in cartoons, engravings and statues. The symbolism of Britannia has changed little over the centuries. As one specialist on the subject has noted, 'From her very beginnings as a Romano-British deity she has been a syncretistic construct which linked Amazonian fertility goddesses with patriarchal assertions of imperial power.'[29] Her feminine yet martial image perfectly suited her for adoption by Britain's first woman Prime Minister and self-proclaimed 'Iron Lady'.

The ideal British woman was shown in the press as a devoted housewife and mother, waiting for her menfolk to return home from the war. Non-combatant servicewomen who sailed with the task force were apparently there to service the sexual needs of their male counterparts ('SEXY CAPERS ON THE OCEAN RAVE' was one *Sun* headline). It was all a long way from Rosie the Riveter. But if the war was an expression of male power, then it has to be said that many women found it to be an aphrodisiac. To the delight of troops, a few painted their breasts with Union Jacks and bared them from the quaysides as the Task Force set sail. During the conflict, thousands more wrote to servicemen in the South Atlantic offering them sex and marriage on their return, while a similar number gathered at Portsmouth to welcome home naval ships, many (not always wives and girlfriends) flinging their knickers onto the deck as the ships docked.

Overall, the reaction of the left to the patriotism of 1982 revealed far more about its own inadequacies than it did about those of the British people. The left's pleas for the problem to be solved by the UN echoed the naive belief during the 1930s that the League of Nations could sort out Hitler, Mussolini and Franco. Moreover, the hard lessons which socialists had learnt between 1940 and 1970 about the importance of *patria* to any sense of national community seemed to have been forgotten. Michael Foot's support for the government was widely condemned as the act of a traitor to social-ism. And because the Thatcher government was seen as a proto-fascist regime (and, therefore, the 'real' threat to the country), in a perverse twist Michael Foot was cast as an appeaser. The first charge was ironic because he presided over the Labour Party's suicidal lurch to the left in this period. The second charge was simply ignorant. As the author of *Guilty Men*, Foot had played a leading part in branding prewar Tories as appeasers. His support for the Falklands War was utterly consistent with his anti-fascist patriotism forty years before. What had changed was not the Labour leader but the left's attitude to patriotism.

Most now saw it as an opiate of the people in much the same way that the right regarded chemical opiates. Like cannabis, love of country was condemned as the first hit in an addiction which led inevitably to the crack cocaine of nationalism and on finally to the heroin abuse of fascism. Michael Foot was not entirely alone. In the *New Statesman*, a brave article by R. W. Johnson summoned the spirit of Orwell to denounce the cheap internationalism of the left:

> [The left] have always proclaimed their hatred of military aggression and of fascism so this ought to be an easy issue for them. But when it comes to the crunch they find they hate a right-wing Tory prime minister even more. They simply can't bear to find themselves on the same side as their old class enemy even if the old class enemy is doing the right thing for once. It is just easier, in the end, to parrot what the Russians are saying about an imperialist war in which British and Argentinian workers are going to get killed . . . [Orwell] would not have been surprised (though he would have been angry) at the way the left has undermined its own moral credentials . . . Most of all, Orwell would have under-stood the fact that workers, trade unionists, even the unemployed, are flocking to Thatcher in their droves. It would, no doubt, have stuck in his throat to say she deserves their votes. But Orwell did feel, to his very marrow, that socialist intellectuals and their parties

have no presumptive right to the workers' votes. He was after all, the man who wrote . . . in 1940 of 'the spiritual need for patriotism and the military virtues, for which, however little the boiled rabbits of the left may like them, no substitute has yet been found.'[30]

The boiled rabbits took no notice. Neil Kinnock once told the author that after becoming Labour leader in 1983, he tried and failed to get the NEC to read Orwell's essays on patriotism to dispel the party hierarchy's belief that it was synonymous with conservatism.[31]

If the war broke the heart of the left, then its immediate aftermath wound it up into a frenzy of moral opprobrium, and nowhere more so than in the victory parade which the government staged in the City of London on October 1982. A colourful extravaganza, televised live by the BBC, it was condemned for attempting to glorify the war. Like most Britons, Enoch Powell was unmoved by the imperial echoes of the conflict. But watching the parade, he was so stirred by the public expression of affinity for a white diaspora that he did feel his idea of the nation had been vindicated. He wrote: 'The England that tolerated the British Nationality Act of 1948, the England which had thought it could reoccupy the Suez Canal, was an England which had not recognised itself.' By defending the Falklanders, 'England had known itself'.[32] In vain, the Daily Mail pointed out that not all the British soldiers who had fought to liberate the islands were white. 'There were soldiers there with brown skins among the fallen as well as with white. Their sacrifice knew no discrimination,' it declared.[33]

Comparisons were made with the victory parade of 1946. A retired bank official, who attended both, wrote:

> Our forces exist to defend by force the kind of freedom that we in this country hold to be important . . . there is no doubt in my mind that the British people still have a tremendous sense of national pride . . . my friends and acquaintances are, like myself, still aware of the 1939–45 war. In a way we were re-living the Victory services and parades of 37 years ago.[34]

One difference between the two events was that whereas George VI had taken the salute in 1946 while Churchill and Attlee sat watching below, Elizabeth II was not present at the parade in 1982. Instead, Mrs Thatcher took centre stage, reviewing the troops from a balcony at the Guildhall with the Lord Mayor of London. To many, this confirmed that the Prime Minister was determined to make as much political capital as she could from the victory.

Among the government's sternest critics after the war were Church leaders. At a service of thanksgiving held a few months earlier in the quiet of St Paul's on 26 July, the Archbishop of Canterbury, Robert Runcie, clearly defined the boundaries of Christian patriotism in a sermon worthy of William Temple. Runcie praised the courage of British troops but he described war as a human failure and, calling for sympathy for Argentina's bereaved, he stressed the importance of a common humanity. He closed with the following statement: 'Those who interpret God's will must never claim him as an asset for one nation or group rather than another. War springs from the love and loyalty which should be offered to God being applied to some substitute, one of the most dangerous being nationalism.'[35] Runcie's mailbag was seven to one in favour; among the letters of praise was one from the Queen, expressing 'admiration' for the way he met the 'formidable challenge' of delivering such a crucial sermon (this may have had more to do with the Queen's fury at being usurped during the parade as it did with any desire for reconciliation with Argentina).[36] Mrs Thatcher was 'spitting blood' afterwards, according to her husband, and Conservative MPs lined up to condemn the 'cringing clergy'.[37]

2. Britain found herself again

What were the long-term effects of the Falklands conflict? First, Mrs Thatcher's personal popularity rating shot up, helping to re-elect the Conservatives, increasing their majority from 43 to 143 in 1983; Labour got its lowest share of the poll since 1931 – 27.6 per cent. The *Sun*'s advice was 'VOTE FOR MAGGIE ... More than any other leader since Churchill was baying defiance at the Nazis, she has captured the hearts, the minds and the imagination of the nation'.[38] In the years immediately after the war, the Conservatives recaptured patriotism as a uniquely Tory virtue almost as decisively as they had done a century earlier under Disraeli.

The electoral effect of victory in the South Atlantic has been exaggerated by socialists. So busy were they condemning the war that few on the left noticed that the circulation of the *Sun* actually *declined* in the six months between the invasion and the victory parade, its jingoistic coverage proving too much for a lot of the

working-class Tory patriots who made up its readership. Furthermore 81 per cent of the country supported the BBC's stance (Prince
Charles made it plain that he was one of them in a speech at the
Open University). It seemed clear that while people agreed that
the BBC was 'not Britain', there was a deeper sense in which the
corporation was still thought to represent what the nation stood for:
the principle of free speech; the democracy, in other words, that
Britain was fighting for in the South Atlantic.

Therefore, despite the state control of news coverage during the
war and after, it was not a capitalist media conspiracy which helped
the Tories to monopolize patriotism in this period but two quite
different factors. First, the left's failure to acknowledge the democratic principle at stake in the Falklands and to realize that that
principle had been at the core of national identity in Britain for
nearly half a century. Second, Britons' simple rejection of Labour's
left-wing election manifesto of 1983. Aside from the manifesto's
obvious economic drawbacks, Labour's commitment to unilateral
nuclear disarmament appeared to many to be a form of appeasement
which was precisely what the Falklands had been fought to avoid.

The war fostered an atmosphere of national self-confidence in
many parts of the island between 1983 and 1988 which helped Mrs
Thatcher to establish a revolution that before the war had been
looking distinctly shaky. She called this confidence the 'Falklands
Factor'. At a rally at Cheltenham race course on 3 July 1982, in
front of 5,000 people, the Prime Minister set out her postwar aims
in one of the defining speeches of the 1980s:

> There were those who thought we could no longer do the great
> things which we once did. Those who believed that our decline
> was irreversible . . . those [who feared] that Britain was no longer
> the nation that had built an Empire and ruled a quarter of the
> world. Well, they were wrong. The lesson of the Falklands is that
> Britain has not changed and that this nation still has those sterling
> qualities that shine through our history. This generation can match
> their fathers and grandfathers in ability, in courage and in resolu-
> tion . . . We have ceased to be a nation in retreat. We have instead
> a newfound confidence – born in the economic battles at home
> and tested and found true 8,000 miles away. That confidence
> comes with the rediscovery of ourselves and grows with the
> recovery of our self-respect. And so today we can rejoice at our
> success in the Falklands and take pride in the achievement of our
> task force. But we do so, not as at some flickering of a flame which

must soon be dead. No – we rejoice that Britain has rekindled that spirit which has fired her for generations past and which today has begun to burn as brightly as before. Britain found herself again in the South Atlantic and will not look back from the victory she has won.[39]

As an example of the nation's potential, Mrs Thatcher cited the wartime adaptations made by British Aerospace to the Nimrod freight aircraft in sixteen days which normally would have taken a year. In contrast, she pointed to the railway strike which had started on the previous Tuesday. The train drivers had misunderstood the 'new mood' of Britain and she called on every driver 'to put his family, his comrades and his country first'.

'Why', asked the Prime Minister, 'do we have to be invaded before we throw aside our selfish aims and begin to work together?' She concluded that 'the Falklands Factor' was 'to see that the spirit of the South Atlantic – the real spirit of Britain – can now be fired by peace.'[40] Most of the press agreed. Announcing FREEDOM'S DAY on 15 June, *The Times* reminded its readers that the previous day was the anniversary of Magna Carta and declared that people had found the essence of their Britishness once more:

> Modern man has come to be overawed by a sense of the big battalions . . . These assail individuals in their everyday lives and induce a feeling of puniness and impotence where life loses its meaning. The invasion of a small community in the South Atlantic by the mass forces of a dictatorship somehow exposed all those deep feelings which had been suppressed in Britain and perhaps explains the vigour with which the nation responded to an invasion of its spirit. Certainly that invasion and the war to recover the islands has stirred emotions which have been sunk deep within the spirit of Britain. That spirit has been rediscovered as people have rediscovered something about themselves and their country. It came to individuals not to the mass. There were no mass rallies, no shouting, no parades. But the strength and the resolution which the country showed was carried on a tide of millions of acts of individual rediscovery.[41]

Translating wartime patriotism into peacetime conditions had been a constant theme of British politics since 1945. With a victory behind her, Thatcher had more reason than most to hope that it might be achieved. In her memoirs, she recorded that the war changed foreign views of Britain: 'Everywhere I went after the war, Britain's name meant something more than it had.'[42] One of her inner circle, Lord Young, later commented, '[There] was a general feeling that . . . we could make it. If you went overseas, the way people regarded the United Kingdom in the late eighties was a way they hadn't regarded it since the war.'[43]

How true was this? There was much amusement in the European press about the Falklands despite the official support that European governments gave Britain during the war. Even the Americans found the affair laughable. Al Haig, the American Secretary of State, remembered, 'In the early hours of the crisis, most of the staff shared the amusement of the press and public over what was perceived as a Gilbert and Sullivan battle over a sheep pasture between a choleric John Bull and a comic dictator in gaudy uniform.'[44] Nonetheless, there was a grudging respect for the British stand throughout the world, a respect which Mrs Thatcher's bellicosity on her travels after the war encouraged. In 1985 the editor of the Italian daily *La Repubblica* wrote, 'She is regarded abroad as a crusader, in the powerful tradition of Churchill, De Gaulle and Queen Victoria. Even if Mr Kinnock should win the next General Election, he will not be able to get away from Mrs Thatcher's legacy of a patriotic and industrious Britain . . . Like Talleyrand, she has restored her country to its prewar mover-and-shaker status, not financially secure perhaps, but politically aggressive and influential.'[45]

More importantly, Mrs Thatcher got Britons to believe that they had won back the respect of the world. One concrete sign of this was the result of a study, carried out in 1985, of how British patriotism had changed since 1965. It found that a majority of Britons (62 per cent), believed that the country was getting less prosperous, compared to the reverse twenty years earlier. Another majority (55 per cent) thought that Britain should have no world role, not even a post-imperial one, wanting it instead to be more like Scandinavia or Switzerland. This too was a reverse of the figures in the 1960s. Yet *levels* of patriotism matched those during the 1960s, with 47 per cent proclaiming themselves to be very proud of being British and 33 per cent quite proud, with only 16 per cent not proud.[46]

What these figures indicate is that the Falklands victory did restore national pride after a nadir in the 1970s. But they also indicate that Britons were under no illusions that their country was economically healthy or that it was (or even *should* be) a political force in the world. The British had come to terms with their reduced situation. Post-Falklands patriotism therefore rested not on an inflated sense of national importance but on Britain's reputation abroad, an unstable foundation at the best of times. Returning to London from the US for a meeting at Chequers in May 1982, Sir Nicholas Henderson met his old friend the Irish historian Robert Kee for lunch at the Garrick. Kee commented, 'The British people are beginning to show again that spirit of bovine determination that we used to ridicule [in the 1930s] as insular complacency.' But later on, when Henderson paid a visit to the Foreign Office with his colleague Sir Anthony Parsons, he noticed signs of decay in the nation's capital. In his diary, he recorded:

> London, with holes in the road and piles of bricks and corrugated iron on many abandoned building sites, the warning lights half fused, has a Third World look about it. . . . As we moved back into the squalor of the Foreign Office – the lifts not working, half-empty milk bottles everywhere and a pervading air of dishevelment and decay . . . we shuddered at the thought of ever having to work there again . . . There is talk that the Falklands Islands crisis will awaken the British from their slumber. I wonder.[47]

He was right to wonder. Mrs Thatcher's call for national unity stirred hearts in Cheltenham. But in places like Caerphilly, Clydebank and Corby it acquired an almost obscene irony. Millions were unprepared for the brutal restructuring of the British economy which began in 1979. Monetarism may have countered inflation and improved productivity. But the curricula vitae produced by officers of the Department of Social Security for middle-aged ex-miners and steelworkers amid the plastic pot-plants and orange carpet of Britain's Job Centres had about as much value as a wheelbarrow of marks in Weimar Germany. As in the 1930s, what made the depression worse was that the south of England was so visibly prospering from the restructuring.

The south's affluence did not mean that all its inhabitants were happy with the growing divisions in Britain. Poll after poll in the 1980s and early 1990s showed that a majority of the population thought that Britain had become more divided under Thatcher and didn't like the fact. In short, many of those who had benefited from her 'economic miracle' were worried about its social effects. Some simply feared the wrath of the dispossessed or felt guilty about their growing wealth, but many others were genuinely concerned. When the economic miracle turned out to be little more than a huckster's trick performed from the back of a lorry and they too were hit by recession in 1990, reservations about Thatcher's revolution made her position untenable. It should also be remembered that even at the height of her popularity in 1983, only 42.4 per cent of the electorate voted for her, compared to 27.6 per cent for Labour and 25.4 per cent for the Liberal–SDP alliance; the split within the opposition caused by Labour's drift to the left played a crucial part in sustaining her in office for a decade.

The patriotism generated by the Falklands during the 1980s rested to a large extent on Mrs Thatcher's own reputation, because the Prime Minister had tied herself so closely to the conflict. It was always her war. In the short term this paid the Conservative Party huge political dividends. But in the long term, her growing unpopularity undermined Tory attempts to embed the Falklands Factor in British culture and to make it not simply a patriotic episode but – like the Second World War – a part of national identity itself. Churchill had tied his reputation to the war against Hitler and by neglecting the demand for social reform paid the price in 1945. The difference was that he had returned to lead a relatively popular government in old age. And whereas he left office convinced that his life was a failure, he did so in his own time and with some dignity, his wartime legacy intact. Thatcher left office convinced that she was the most successful Premier of the century but having been rejected by British public opinion and humiliatingly ousted by a party coup. Of course, the conflicts of 1939–45 and 1982 were vastly different in two obvious ways. Civilization was not at stake in the latter and Britain itself was not attacked. Consequently the British could not reasonably claim they had saved the world; nor was there much of a Home Front in 1982 which could foster a legend of national unity comparable to the Finest Hour. But the unpopularity of Mrs Thatcher and her policies prevented the Falklands from becoming an enduring feature of Britishness.

The failure was evident in two ways. Unlike the Second World War, few memorials were erected to the Falklands. In 1992, Mrs Thatcher unveiled a statue of 'The Yomper' outside the Royal Marines Museum in Eastney, Portsmouth. It was named after the 'Yomp', the long march which the Marines made from Goose Green to Port Stanley to liberate the islands. Unveiling it, Thatcher made an explicit link between 1940 and 1982:

They were impossible odds; if we were to assess the chances of victory by feeding in statistics to some computer, the outlook in the Falklands and in the Battle of Britain could have been very different. But great causes which stir men's souls are not decided by mere statistics but by what I call 'the British factor': the unbroken spirit of the British people and her armed forces. It is that which lives on.[48]

Second, the sentiments expressed by Lady Thatcher at the unveiling of the Yomper were challenged by Falklands veterans, many of whom resented the way in which they had been used for political ends, their trauma and the sacrifice of the dead tarred indelibly with the brush of Thatcherism in the public mind. On the fifth anniversary of the conflict, a number voiced their feelings in television interviews. Brigadier Julian Thompson RM, in command of land forces during the campaign, said: 'You don't mind dying for Queen and country, but you certainly don't want to die for politicians.' His attitude on the battlefield was: 'I'll win the war for these buggers, and then I shall go.'[49] Widows of Falklands soldiers also expressed an ambivalence that their grandmothers generally had not in 1945. Dorothy Foulkes from Lancashire, whose husband Frank was killed on the *Atlantic Conveyor*, said:

> I think we had to fight because they had invaded British territory. It's really all a question of pride. I think Britain had to have that pride in herself or, as a nation, where would we be now? They had to do it. But the price my family paid . . . no one will ever know exactly what price we paid. Perhaps it was worth it for Britain's sake.[50]

Perhaps. Mrs Foulkes went on to say how bitter she was about the way the Ministry of Defence had treated her 'as a third-rate citizen' after the war. 'Suddenly, if you're not an officer's wife, you're nothing . . . [Frank] was presented with a campaign medal that came through the post. It was in three pieces. There was a bit of ribbon, and you got a medal in another jiffy-bag. They are good with jiffy-bags, the Ministry of Defence.'

The conflict made a brief reappearance in the public arena when England played Argentina in the World Cup of 1986. The goal scored by Diego Maradona's hand-ball (which he later described as 'the Hand of God') seemed to confirm that the Argentinians were a people who did not play by the rules of the game. But by the time the teams met again in the World Cup of 1998, attempts by tabloid newspapers to stir up Falklands xenophobia failed, the passion of the match having more to do with the epic struggle on the pitch than memories of what had taken place 8,000 miles away sixteen years before.

In conclusion, the Falklands War did not mark a return to an imperial identity, nor did it make a lasting impact on Britishness as a whole. Its significance lay in the fact that it confirmed the extent to which national identity in Britain was shaped by the Second World War. In the process, 1982 did two things. For a brief moment it reunited the three nations of Britain in common cause. It also reinforced popular reservations about Europe, the success of unilateral military action helping to perpetuate British insularity by appearing to show that the nation could still go it alone. With that point in mind, it is now time to examine the policy for which Mrs Thatcher will be most remembered: her concerted attempt to defend the British way of life from what she saw as its destruction at the hands of the European Union.

3. The party's in Europe

Mrs Thatcher was the most Europhobic British Prime Minister since Anthony Eden, and during her time in office she encouraged Britons to share her views, through government policy and still more through her populist rhetoric. Enlarging upon the effect which the Second World War had on her, she wrote:

> I drew from the . . . War a lesson very different from the hostility towards the nation-state evinced by some post-war European statesmen. My view was – and is – that an effective internationalism can only be built by strong nations which are able to call upon the loyalty of their citizens to defend and enforce civilised rules of international conduct. An internationalism which seeks to supersede the nation-state, however, will founder quickly upon the reality that very few people are prepared to make genuine sacrifices for it. It is likely to degenerate, therefore, into a formula for endless discussion and hand-wringing.[51]

In contrast, her fondness for the Atlantic Alliance was unbounded. As it was for most Tory radicals since the war, America was as much of a model for her populist capitalism as Victorian Britain. And in the tax-cutting, Red-hating Ronald Reagan she found a soulmate, allowing him to park his cruise missiles in her silos in readiness for an attack on the free world.

But unlike Churchill's, Thatcher's Atlanticism and her defence of the nation state from European subjugation were not characterized by affectionate magnanimity towards the Continent. Privately, she loathed the Germans, seeing them as bullies for whom the European Union was merely the latest vehicle for Teutonic hegemony. At a dinner to mark forty years of Anglo-German friendship in March 1990, she told a former German Ambassador, 'You need another forty years before we can forget what you have done.'[52] Again and again in government discussions on Europe during the decade, the Prime Minister worried at the question 'Can we trust the Germans?', and she returned to the issue in her memoirs:

> There was – and still is – a tendency to regard the 'German problem' as something too delicate for well-brought-up politicians to discuss ... I do not believe in collective guilt: it is individuals who are morally accountable for their actions. But I do believe in national character, which is moulded by a range of complex factors: the fact that national caricatures are often absurd and inaccurate does not detract from that. Since the unification of Germany, under Bismarck – perhaps because national unification came so late – Germany has veered unpredictably between aggression and self-doubt ... It is economic expansion rather than territorial aggression which is the modern manifestation of this tendency. Germany is thus by its very nature a destabilising rather than a stabilising force in Europe.[53]

It was these doubts that lay behind her brief, futile attempt to prevent German reunification, which finally took place on 1 July 1990.

Such was the Prime Minister's obsession with the German problem that she organized a day-long conference at Chequers that year to discuss it. Among those who attended were two of her supporters in the historical profession, Professors Hugh Trevor-Roper and Norman Stone, both of whom told her that Germany had changed. She was unconvinced and a distorted account of the meeting was written by her adviser Sir Charles Powell and leaked to the press. It described the German national character as '*angst*, aggressiveness, assertiveness, bullying, egotism, inferiority complex, sentimentality ... [a] capacity for excess, to overdo things, to kick over the traces ... to overestimate their own strengths and weaknesses'. The document concluded that people should ask 'how a cultured and cultivated nation had allowed itself to be brain-washed into barbarism', and whether 'the way in which the Germans currently used their elbows and threw their weight about in the European Community suggested that a lot had still not changed'.[54]

If the Germans were, so to speak, taking liberties with Europe, the French were regarded as intellectually responsible for the whole project. Against their fondness for abstract ideas, Mrs Thatcher celebrated British empiricism, which she claimed to have imbibed as a research scientist before entering politics: 'You look at the facts and you deduce your conclusions.' This, she believed, was the guiding spirit of the British legal and constitutional tradition: 'you learn your law, so you learn the structures ... You judge the evidence, and then, when the laws are inadequate for present-day society, you create new laws.'[55] Thatcher was not content to claim that Britain was different. She had no doubt that it was superior, a conviction based on a Victorian view of Britain's relatively peaceful, evolutionary development. In Paris with other European leaders for the bicentenary of the French Revolution in 1989, she publicly challenged the view that the Revolution marked the beginning of Europe's long journey towards democracy. Its real legacy, she said, was the subsequent Terror from which all modern totalitarianism had sprung. She then told her hosts that democracy had begun in Britain with the Glorious Revolution of 1688, which she said had established constitutional monarchy and the sovereignty of Parliament. In one gloriously tactless moment, Mrs Thatcher had summed up the ideological gulf between Britain and the Continent around which Britishness had been substantially defined for 200 years.

Here again was a link with de Gaulle. Though the French leader had been a Europeanist, one of the conclusions which both he and Thatcher reached after their forays into the souls of their respective nations was that Britain's peculiar national identity was inimical to European union. Like most nationalists, they shared a dislike of foreign influences on their language. It said much about the nature of Franco-British divisions that while de Gaulle hated the colloquialisms of Anglo-American pop culture, Mrs Thatcher hated French socio-political terms. When one of her champions, Peregrine Worsthorne, described her philosophy as 'bourgeois triumphalism', she told an interviewer, 'Dear Peregrine, why does he talk about "boo-jhwha"? Boo-jhwha? Why can't he find a plain English word for the plain people of England, Scotland and Wales? The *boo-jhwha* live in France.'[56]

Thatcher was not the first postwar British Prime Minister to hold such views but she was the first to express them in such a strident way that they soured Britain's relations with the Continent. It did not help that she and several of her Cabinet Ministers regarded the French not only as naive idealists but as cowardly collaborators with the cynical and ruthless Germans, a demonology shot through with the ghosts of 1940. In July 1990, her Minister for the Environment and close confidant, Nicholas Ridley, was forced to resign after making the following comment in an interview with the *Spectator*: '[It's] all a German racket designed to take over the whole of Europe ... I'm not against giving up sovereignty in principle, but not to this lot. You might as well give it to Adolf Hitler, frankly ... I'm not sure I wouldn't rather have the shelters and the chance to fight back than simply being taken over by economics.'[57]

Left/liberals' loathing for the Prime Minister's attitude to Europe was as nothing compared to their loathing for their lower classes who shared her views on the subject. The focus of concern during the 1980s was the football hooligan. Like most moral scares about delinquent youth since the nineteenth century, the 1980s hooligan was a composite picture of how the lower classes had failed to live up to bourgeois expectations of social progress. In this case, he was an uneducated, drunken, xenophobic, racist and sexist lout; a man who, in the words of Tony Parsons, was 'lager vomit on the Union Jack'. The hooligan was also seen as a symbol of national decline, a violent relation of the boorish package holidaymaker who was sullying Britain's good name on the beaches of the Mediterranean.

Hooliganism did increase after the war. To take just one indicator, in 1946 the Home Office recommendation for policing ratios at matches stood at just one policeman per thousand spectators. By 1986, this had risen dramatically to one officer for every seventy-five spectators; and at particularly troublesome clubs like Millwall in south-east London, it was not unusual for 500 officers to watch over 7,000 fans (a ratio of one to fourteen).[58] There had always been violence at football matches, but it had been confined mostly to spontaneous pub-size brawls and had not been organized by large gangs. Moreover, though club loyalties were passionate in the first hundred years of Association Football, violence was not as tribal, it being just as likely to break out among people cheering for the same team. Did Britain's relative decline cause these changes?

On the whole, the answer is no. Modern football hooliganism began in the early 1960s during a period of economic buoyancy when the faults in the British economy had yet to materialize fully. And hooligans came as much from the more affluent south of the island as from the north, both then and later. Alan Clark's 1989 BBC drama *The Firm* (for which West Ham's 'Intercity Firm' were consultants) showed the ICF 'Generals' to be stockbrokers and solicitors with homes and families in respectable suburbs.

The phenomenon was more a product of social change than of national decline, for four reasons. First, growing tribalism among fans was a response to the loosening of family and community ties brought about by ill-conceived urban redevelopment in poorer areas and by the continued move of more affluent workers to the suburbs: the football club offered an alternative community to many young Britons who felt displaced. Second, hooliganism was a product of the link forged between football and pop culture in the 1960s; it was no coincidence that the problem was first detected in Liverpool during the height of the 'Merseybeat' craze. In the late 1980s, drugs like cocaine and ecstasy which fuelled the rave scene also became a staple diet on the terraces. To a great extent, both football and pop were merely the latest vehicles in the quest for excitement by youths whose daily routine at work and home was mind-numbing. Though the fusion of the two could be explosive, football was no more inherently given to violence than pop music was. The sports historian John Williams' analysis is that, 'Sustained by the self-confidence and greater autonomy provided by the new youth cultures and buoyed by the nationalistic excess inspired by the England World Cup success of 1966, the "lads" began to establish the Saturday afternoon rituals which quickly attracted aspiring "hard cases" from the city neighbourhoods.'[59]

Hooliganism was, thirdly, a product of anxiety about black immigration, and it provided an umbrella for organized racist attacks. The National Front and later Combat 18 were heavily represented in a number of gangs. A member of the Leeds 'Service Crew' told the *Yorkshire Post* in 1986 that when they went into battle with opposing fans 'we look for blacks and Pakis to do over'.[60] Whether racist or not, hooligans were motivated by an increasingly virulent nationalism directed largely against the Continent: as Cas Pennant, a West Ham footsoldier, observed in 1985, 'The party's in Europe.'[61] If the World Cup victory of 1966 provided the 'inspiration', then anxiety about European hegemony was the spur which time and again launched the firms into battle abroad. The first serious disturbances on the Continent occurred a year after Britain's accession to the EEC, in 1974, when Spurs fans rioted at a UEFA Cup Final tie against Feyenoord in Rotterdam. The trend culminated eleven years later with the Heysel Stadium disaster of 1985 when, shortly before the start of the European Cup Final, Liverpool fans charged Juventus fans, killing thirty-seven Italians. Three years later during the European Championships in Germany, England fans coined the chant 'Two World Wars, one World Cup, doo-dah, doo-dah', which quickly entered the vocabulary of English nationalism.

As that chant suggests, hooliganism was a symptom of Britain's declining power in the world; and it particularly expressed the fear and resentment of Germany's peacetime success, discussed in earlier chapters. Richard Holt has concluded:

> Chauvinism, local and national, lies at the heart of hooliganism, and England fans seem to find in foreigners a convenient target for a vague resentment of Britain's diminished place in the world. Football has become a substitute for patriotism amongst the disaffected, half-educated white working class youth of a nation which, only a generation ago, was respected and feared throughout the world.[62]

The English were more closely associated with the hooligan problem during the 1980s and 1990s for good reason: racism towards ethnic minorities was more of an issue in England, where most immigrants had settled, and the English were more anxious about the European Union than the Scots or the Welsh, who tended to see it as a check on English dominance.

Yet we must be careful. Hooliganism, motivated by racism and nationalism, was also present in Scotland, as the vicious activities of the Glasgow Rangers 'casuals' testify. Nor was it confined to Britain. A European Parliament inquiry into xenophobia in 1990 fingered the UK as the main source of the problem. But there is ample evidence that Continental youths looked up to and mimicked British hooligans, sometimes exceeding their levels of violence, while the more politicized members of British firms found inspiration in the activities of neo-fascist gangs on the Continent. Although they enjoyed fighting each other, most hooligans recognized that they had more in common with each other than they did with their law-abiding fellow-countrymen. Indeed there existed a tacit compact between national gangs which arguably promoted European unity, albeit of an illiberal kind. The extent to which football-fuelled nationalism was not solely a British phenomenon was demonstrated in September 1981 when Norway (which rejected membership of the EU in a referendum in 1994) beat England for the first time. As the final whistle went on a freezing night in Oslo, the Norwegian commentator slipped into English and jubilantly screamed this message into his microphone: 'England! Lord Nelson! Lord Beaverbrook! Sir Winston Churchill! Sir Anthony Eden! Clement Attlee! Henry Cooper! Lady Diana! . . . Maggie Thatcher, can you hear me? MAGGIE THATCHER, YOUR BOYS TOOK A HELL OF A BEATING!!'[63]

Finally, in any consideration of this subject, it must be remembered that most Britons were not hooligans, nor did they condone their activities. There was a good deal of hypocrisy in the tabloids' condemnation of violence when their xenophobic reporting of foreign affairs contributed to the narrow outlook of the violent minority in the first place. But they were a minority and the country supported the successful efforts by governments in the 1980s and 1990s to stamp out the problem. When the problem occasionally reappeared, as it did when England fans were involved in riots during the 1998 World Cup Finals in France, hysteria followed. Commentators across the political spectrum saw hooliganism as the inevitable result of English nationalism. They also contrasted English behaviour with the peaceful bonhomie of Scottish supporters. A dissenting voice came from Scottish novelist Irvine Welsh. He detected in the hysteria a profound animus towards the lower classes which said more about Britain's elites than it did about football fans: 'The reaction to the riots showed just how much the English working class, continually vilified and abused by the nation's liberal and conservative establishments, have been left to carry the can for the country's failure to establish an inclusive post-imperial identity.'[64] Welsh was absolutely right. Of all Britain's postwar leaders, Mrs Thatcher must take the blame for that failure. And nowhere did she fail more spectacularly than in her dealings with the European Community.

4. No! No! No!

Diplomatic relations with Europe in the 1980s were dominated initially by bellicose discussions over money, as Mrs Thatcher fought for a £1,000 million rebate on Britain's contribution to the Community's budget. Arriving in Dublin for a European Council meeting in November 1979, she said that she 'wanted her money back'. She got some of it after negotiations in 1980 and 1984. But her unremittingly hostile approach caused Europe's leaders to wonder if de Gaulle had not been right after all when he said that Britain would destroy the Community if it joined. In May 1982, at the height of the Falklands conflict, President François Mitterrand suggested that it would be better for everyone if Britain ceased to be a full member and negotiated instead a 'special status'. A diplomatic crisis was averted by the Foreign Office, which Mrs Thatcher came to loathe as the nursery of Europhilia.

When the European Community began a new phase of integration in 1985, the debate moved away from finance and firmly into the more emotive arena of national identity, from where it would not be dislodged for the rest of the century. At a meeting in Milan in June 1985, the European Council agreed to the creation of a Single European Market by 1992, a project close to free-trading Conservative hearts. But it also led to the Single European Act. Approved in Luxembourg in December 1985, the Act established majority voting (rather than national vetoes) over a wide range of issues and was a significant step towards integration. At the time, its implications were underestimated by the government, the press and the British people. Lord Cockfield, the British EC Commissioner, put this down to 'the fact that in the United Kingdom we do not have a written constitution and many of these matters appear strange if not incomprehensible to us'.[65] It was a Phoney Peace.

Four years later, in April 1989, a report by the Commission President, Jacques Delors (1985–95), proposed that the EU move towards monetary union in three stages and the European Question ignited once again. The first stage of the Delors Plan was membership of a European Exchange Rate Mechanism (ERM) designed to get European currencies working in tandem; the second was the creation of a European Central Bank; the third was the creation of a single currency – the ecu, or euro as it became known. The Delors Plan was an unashamed step towards a federal United States of Europe, a blueprint for a restructuring of the nation state by and in the continent which had given birth to it 1,000 years before. Born in 1925, its architect was a cultivated, intellectual socialist who had begun his career as a French civil servant in the late 1960s. Delors compounded these original sins by telling the TUC in October 1988 that federalism offered an unprecedented opportunity to create social justice throughout the Continent. Discredited by the militant excesses of the 1970s and stymied by Thatcher's anti-union legislation, TUC delegates grasped the prospect of renewal which Delors offered them and gave him a rapturous welcome. Added to which, in 1987 Neil Kinnock reversed the Labour Party's commitment to leave the Community (one of the policies on which Labour had fought the 1983 general election). After forty years of scepticism and prevarication, the British labour movement had finally embraced the European ideal.

Already opposed to any further encroachment on British sovereignty, Mrs Thatcher now saw Europe as a means by which socialism would be let in 'through the back door' and her revolution undone. She later wrote:

> The more I considered all this, the greater my frustration and the deeper my anger became. Were British democracy, parliamentary sovereignty, the common law, our traditional sense of fairness, our ability to run our own affairs in our own way, to be subordinated to the demands of a remote European bureaucracy, resting on very different traditions? I had by now heard about as much of the European 'ideal' as I could take.[66]

On 20 September 1988 she launched her most vehement counterattack yet, in a speech to the College of Europe in Bruges. She proposed an alternative 'wider, looser Europe' which would include former Warsaw Pact countries, anxious to realize their nationhood after years of oppression by a Soviet super-state. Her Europe would be a giant, democratic free-trade area which respected national identities.

> Europe will be stronger precisely because it has France as France, Spain as Spain, Britain as Britain, each with its own customs, traditions and identity. It would be folly to try to fit them into some sort of identikit European personality ... Let Europe be a family of nations, understanding each other better, appreciating each other more, doing more together, but relishing our national

identity no less than our common European endeavour. Let us have a Europe which plays its full part in the wider world, which looks outward not inward, and which preserves the Atlantic Community – that Europe on both sides of the Atlantic – which is our noblest inheritance and our greatest strength.[67]

This was not an isolationist speech; nor was it an overtly xenophobic one, though Thatcher's critics were quick to claim that it was.

As more and more Britons debated the European Question in pubs and sitting rooms across the country, the many moderate Eurosceptics among them complained that their opposition to federalism was unfairly caricatured as xenophobia. They were justified in feeling misrepresented, for many were sincere in their affection for the Continent despite not wanting further political ties with it. As for the more general charge of insularity, those who favoured free trade with the whole world instead of privileging a wasteful, bureaucratic and often corrupt Continental cartel could hardly be accused of navel-gazing. Quite rightly, moderate sceptics also resented being told that they were political dinosaurs. Federalism was the intended outcome of the Treaty of Rome. But it was not the inevitable outcome, any more than the First World War was the inevitable outcome of the Triple Entente between Britain, France and Russia. To argue that it was is like saying that the war had to go ahead in 1914 because the troop trains had started to move and their timetables could not be altered. The fact is that Europe was entering a radical new phase during the 1980s which had major implications for the British polity. It was a new phase because of Delors' acceleration of Western integration and because Europe as a whole was changing thanks to the end of the Cold War and the break-up of the Soviet Empire.

In order to convince the British that the EC was merely evolving along a clearly defined course, treaties and White Papers were dusted down which pointed to clauses stating that the EU's goal was 'ever-closer union'; Hansard, press and TV archives were rifled for proof that the British had long ago been told federalism was on the agenda. Strictly speaking, one could argue that the British had been notified. But a proper historical study of the way in which Europe was sold to the British between 1962 and 1992 would have shown them that federalism had not in fact been advertised by Britain's politicians. As we saw in Chapter 7, politicians had either gone out of their way to distract the British from the issue by playing up economic questions, or they had reassured them union would take place with their consent. The 1975 referendum did not grant that consent because Britons had merely been asked if they wished to remain in the European Community as it then stood as a trading bloc. This was rather like an unscrupulous pension salesman (of whom there were many in this period) telling people who had discovered they had been sold an inappropriate policy which left them out of pocket that they had not read the small print.

However, turning to the question of a threat to British traditions, we must suspend our respectful consideration of the Eurosceptic position. Even the most ardent of federalists had no wish to destroy the national identities of member states. They merely wanted to create a second tier of European identity on top of existing loyalties, just as those who forged the union between England, Wales and Scotland from the seventeenth to the nineteenth centuries had constructed Britishness with the aim of enriching its constituent parts. Would national identities in Britain be extinguished anyway? Some claimed that the pooling of sovereignty favoured the strongest, biggest nation in the union – in this case Germany – and the inevitable result would be to override Britain's self-determination and therefore its sense of self. This was absurd, just as it was absurd of some Europhiles to hope that they could foster a popular Europeanness by signing a piece of paper. Treaties cannot make or break national identities on their own. They require a long and complicated process of cultural direction which has the tacit consent of a majority of the people. Despite English dominance, Scottish and Welsh culture had thrived for three centuries in a far more centralized Union than the one proposed by Jacques Delors because the Scots and Welsh had wished to retain their distinctiveness. The drift towards nationalism in Britain since 1945 had occurred partly because the British state was over-centralized and partly because its economy was lopsided in a way that favoured the south of England. The threatened break-up of the island nation in the late twentieth century therefore had more to do with its own, long-standing internal contradictions than it did with recent moves towards European integration.

Why then did Mrs Thatcher and her supporters so fervently make the erroneous claim that the British way of life was threatened? The main reason was to play down the right-wing ideology which underpinned most scepticism. Defending the right to have the lowest wages, longest working hours, highest retail prices and worst cancer survival rates in the Community would not rally a people. Tell them, however, that the EC wanted to ban the sale of home-made jam at village fêtes (because it was thought unhygienic) and the British might believe that some essential national spirit was being extinguished as surely as if troops had landed at Dover. The other reason was that Europe seemed to offer a way of reuniting the three nations of Britain by whipping up resistance to a common foe. Unemployment in Scotland and Wales could be blamed on EC directives which improved the terms and conditions of workers to such an extent that employers were forced to cut their workforces in order to stay in business. And in any case what did it matter if factories stayed open if Britons' ancient way of life was destroyed?

The Prime Minister's Bruges speech had little immediate political effect. Unlike six years earlier, when she gave her post-Falklands address in Cheltenham, she was now on the back foot, both in the country and at Westminster. After pressure from several of her ministers, notably the Deputy Prime Minister, Geoffrey Howe, and the Chancellor of the Exchequer, John Major, she was persuaded against her will to take Britain into the ERM on 5 October 1990. It seemed as if the Lady was, after all, for turning. Until, that is, the European Council met in Rome three weeks later on 27 and 28 October. There, member states decided by eleven to one to move towards a single currency by 1994. Addressing Parliament on 30 October, the Prime Minister warned that a federal Europe was imminent in a manner which suggested that the Community was mustering its forces for a military invasion. Departing from the text prepared for her by the Foreign Office she said, in her most stentorian tones, 'No! No! No!' to the prospect.

From there it was downhill all the way. Two days later Geoffrey Howe resigned. On 13 November he attacked Mrs Thatcher in a speech of beautifully controlled ferocity in the House of Commons. She was, he said, confronting Britons with a 'bogus dilemma' between federalism and Britishness. Then he criticized the 'nightmare image conjured up by the Prime Minister, who sometimes seems to look out on a continent positively teeming with ill-intentioned people, scheming, in her words, to extinguish democracy, to dissolve our national identity'. A few weeks earlier, the Prime Minister had employed a cricketing metaphor to express her defiance of Delors: 'I am still at the crease, though the bowling has been pretty hostile of late. And in case anyone doubted it, can I assure you there will be no ducking bouncers, no stonewalling, no playing for time. The bowling's going to get hit all around the ground.' Howe turned the metaphor against her. Arguing that it was impossible for a British Foreign Secretary to conduct business on the Continent with a Prime Minister so hostile to the Community, he concluded: 'It is rather like sending your opening batsmen to the crease only for them to find, the moment the first balls are bowled, that their bats have been broken before the game by the team captain.'[68]

This rhetorical exchange highlighted yet again the importance of cricket to the English sense of fair play. But what followed afterwards was more of a rugby maul. The speech so damaged the Prime Minister's authority that it led to a leadership election which eventually removed her from office on 22 November and installed John Major in No. 10 six days after that.

Conventional wisdom has it that Europe led to Mrs Thatcher's downfall. In reality, she was removed because she had become an electoral liability as a result of unpopular domestic policies (notably the poll tax) and because of the onset of the second recession in a decade. Europe was no more the underlying cause of her downfall than the Norwegian campaign was the cause of Chamberlain's. Within the Conservative Party, all that her removal did was to begin a decade of bitter division over Europe which fulfilled the prophecy Harold Macmillan made to his backbenchers in 1957, that Europe would split the party in the twentieth century as free trade had split it in the nineteenth.

Moreover, popular though her removal was, it did not accurately reflect the British attitude to the European Union. Large sections of the population remained hostile or indifferent. Economically, the EU could not win. In the 1970s, it had failed to deliver the prosperity which Edward Heath promised would be the result of membership. A decade later, people in the north and west of Britain were still waiting for the goose to lay its golden egg, while those in the south put their new prosperity down to a revival of the British entrepreneurial spirit and not to the benefits of European trade. Britain had entered the EU when national confidence was at a low ebb. Mrs Thatcher's brief and patchy restoration of that confidence sharpened scepticism by leading some Britons to think that they could, after all, do without Europe.

A good deal of instinctive xenophobia also remained lodged in the British consciousness. Mrs Thatcher did not create that feeling any more than she created Britain's economic problems, but she was responsible for making it worse. By stating that federalism was a threat to Britishness, she deliberately cast the debate in the sort of fundamental cultural terms which made Euroscepticism a rallying point for British nationalism and not simply one valid position in an important constitutional debate. Unlike either the 1960s or the 1970s, there was no government-sponsored campaign to counteract Euroscepticism. The tabloid press did not help. In the late 1980s, Jacques Delors became as much of a comic-strip baddie as General Galtieri had been earlier in the decade. 'UP YOURS DELORS!' was the *Sun*'s famous response to monetary union in 1990.[69] Shortly afterwards, the paper carried a cut-out picture of Delors' face on its front page, suggesting that readers stick it on to their Guy Fawkes effigies before burning them on Bonfire Night. The *Sun*'s Fifth of November special was a chilling, if tongue-in-cheek, echo of an age when threats to the body politic carried worse penalties than vitriolic leader articles.

All of which seems to lead us to the conclusion that the British grew more hostile to Europe in this period. Indeed, such is the colossal influence of Mrs Thatcher that her term in office is seen as *the* period when the British revolted against the course they had been falteringly led along since 1962; a period when they sat down, unpacked their bags and refused to go any further in adjusting their national identity to meet the demands of European Union. Yet we too must stop and look around at this point of the story. Fascinating though they are, powerful individuals do not make history on their own. And sometimes, for all their pomp and circumstance, they do not make it at all. If we cast our eye away from the fetid atmosphere of Westminster, Whitehall and Fleet Street and carry out a broader examination of British society in the 1980s, another picture emerges. While Mrs Thatcher and her cohorts were raging themselves silly in Brussels and London, the British were quietly and steadily becoming more European.

5. Auld alliances

By the 1980s there were clear signs that British attitudes towards the Continent were softening. In Scotland and Wales, where disenchantment with the British state was strongest, the move towards Europe was an overtly political one. The decline of Britishness in parts of the island that were geographically furthest away from the Continent brought them mentally closest to it. The fear of German domination which so troubled the English was of less concern to nations who felt they had already laboured under English domination for centuries. Economically, the European Community offered substantial benefits. Despite the generous subsidies that Scotland and Wales received from the British Treasury, their weak economies made them eligible for EC development grants. Politically, Europe offered Scotland and Wales a way to regain a place on the world stage lost since the end of the British Empire.

Thus Europe came to be seen as a counterweight to England's natural dominance of the island, and for some it was an attractive alternative to the UK altogether. In 1973, Basil Skinner, from the Scottish Committee of Fanfare for Europe, predicted: 'This feeling of looking outward to Europe, has always been very much part of the Scottish creative background. Closer community with Europe for the Scots will not be strange; in a sense, it will be a coming home.'[70] A decade later, the sense of 'coming home' was widespread. For the Scots in particular, being at the heart of Europe was part of the rediscovery of their nationhood and not a threat to it. Membership of the European Community was seen as part of a long and noble history of independent links with the Continent and this strengthened the belief that union with England was merely an aberration. The geopolitical outlook of the Scots and Welsh in the late twentieth century had more in common with that of their ancestors in the sixteenth century than it did with their own only a few years before. The Scots and Welsh had lost an empire, but unlike the English they had at last found a role. This was not simply one more ideological difference between England and the rest of Britain but a seismic shift in national outlooks. Consequently, the Conservative strategy of presenting Europe as the common foe of all Britons backfired spectacularly. Because the Tories were now seen as an English nationalist party, the more they furiously attacked the EC, the more the Scots and Welsh warmed to it.

A key stage in this transition was the volte face of the Scottish and Welsh nationalist parties. They had been opposed to the Community since its inception, having no wish to jump out of a British frying pan into what they saw as a European fire. In common with the unionist left in Britain, they believed it to be a bankers' club which threatened the already vulnerable economies of their countries. They also feared that Scotland and Wales would lose even more sovereignty by being subsumed in a second super-state. From 1961 onwards, nationalist opposition to Europe was also based on sheer pique that the British state was negotiating the future of Scotland and Wales without proper reference to their people. During the 1975 Referendum on Europe, the SNP and Plaid Cymru had campaigned vigorously to get the UK out of the Community. The Scots in particular had responded, registering the lowest support for EEC membership of any British nation. In the early 1980s, however, the growing powerlessness which both countries felt about the imposition of Thatcherism prompted a complete change of direction.

The founder of Plaid Cymru, Saunders Lewis, was a European enthusiast. He was also a Catholic with a romantic view of medieval Christendom. He argued that Wales had been a distinct nation when the West was united by the Catholic Church and that consequently independence and European Union were wholly compatible. But in 1942 Lewis was replaced by a Nonconformist more acceptable to the Welsh electorate and from then until the 1980s, Plaid Cymru became the most sceptical of the nationalist parties, its outlook on Europe fired by the same religious fervour which had prompted its founder's enthusiasm. But from 1983 onwards, Lewis won a posthumous victory over his party as Plaid began to campaign enthusiastically in European elections, and after a lengthy internal debate on the subject, in 1989 formally came out in favour of the EC. It adopted a dual, two-stage policy of gaining independence for Wales within the existing European Community, after which it pledged to participate in the creation of a federal Europe. Once that was achieved, Wales would then accept her place as an autonomous national region within the new super-state. Absurd though this policy might seem to readers unversed in nationalist politics, it was actually a clever one because it successfully resolved a conflict which had plagued the party since its creation in 1925: Plaid's moderates had always argued that a completely independent Wales was impractical, and that such a policy would be disastrously unpopular in a nation whose sense of Britishness remained strong. The policy of independence followed by devolution in Europe satisfied both wings of the party. Moreover, by removing the bogey of isolationism, it made the electoral appeal of independence far more powerful. An expert on the subject, Peter Lynch, concluded in 1996:

> The party's position ... is actually much clearer now than in previous periods of [its] history. Vague talk of self-government and Home Rule has been replaced with something more concrete, and the party's constitutional goal has become inextricably linked with European integration ... Plaid has finally found a position that allows for maximum self-government whilst avoiding the negative aspects of nationalism ... that have been criticized by Plaid members since the 1920s.[71]

Plaid's new stance was secured after Dafydd Wigley assumed the leadership of the party in 1984. A lifelong Europhile, he had fought since the 1960s to persuade Welsh nationalists that the European Community was the only way out of their political dilemma.

Scottish nationalists had always been more sympathetic to Europe than their Welsh counterparts. The SNP felt that Scotland had less to fear from European integration because it was an older and more fully fledged nation with institutions that were capable of withstanding a supranational authority. In addition, Scottish nationalists could call on a rich history of alliance with Continental nations, especially France. Since the medieval period, the Auld Alliance had not only helped to check the power of the English; in the case of the later Stuarts, it had been used to resist the Hanoverian Union of 1707. Continental links were therefore more easily assimilated into Scottish nationalist legends.

From 1948 to 1954 the SNP supported the embryonic European movement, arguing that it offered Scotland a more beneficial association than the UK. Unfortunately, the party's love was unrequited because Continental powers had even less respect for Scotland than the English did. They were hopeful they could persuade the whole of the UK to join the nascent European Union and saw no reason to court Scotland and Wales separately when the nationalist parties were so tiny and electorally insignificant, and when doing so would only rile the British political elite and reduce the chance of getting the UK to join. As a result SNP interest in the European movement declined, and by the early 1960s it had hardened into outright opposition. Ironically, when the Macmillan negotiations on entry began, the party actually defended the Treaty of Union of 1707, claiming that British entry would contravene clauses in it which guaranteed the Scots the right to a say in any future alteration in the sovereignty of the British nations.

The success of Thatcherism changed the SNP as it did Plaid Cymru, prompting it to end the isolationism of the previous thirty years and return to its pro-European ideological roots. In 1983 the party's leader, Gordon Wilson, began to steer it towards Europe as part of his attempt to heal the wounds of the civil war which had split the party since its trouncing in 1979. In the teeth of fierce opposition, he pushed through a new policy: as soon as independence was won, Scots would get a referendum on whether or not to stay in Europe. Subject to the successful renegotiation of Scotland's membership, the SNP would then campaign in favour of staying in. It had echoes of the tortured policy which Harold Wilson had cooked up in the early 1970s to unite the Labour Party, but it worked rather better. Harold's namesake sold it to the SNP on the basis that Europe would fork out for the start-up costs of independence. He described it as 'a first class way of pushing the advantages of political independence without any threat of economic dislocation. Within the common trading umbrella the move to independence can take place smoothly and easily'.[72]

In the mid-1980s, Jim Sillars (a renegade from the Labour Party) upped the ante by arguing for an unreserved commitment to independence within Europe. In 1989, the party formally adopted this position within a few weeks of Plaid Cymru doing the same. Over the next few years, it had a significant effect on Scottish public opinion. In 1987, only 2 per cent of Scots favoured independence, with 50 per cent for devolution. Two years later, shortly after the SNP's historic decision, the Scots were asked for the first time what their attitude to independence in Europe was: 24 per cent said they were in favour. By 1992, after a fourth Conservative victory, the figure had risen to a staggering 50 per cent. Having once disdained the nationalist movements of each country, European leaders now took them very seriously. Frustrated by the obduracy of Britain's Prime Minister, they saw an opportunity to promote federalism behind her back and they became adept at flattering Britain's recidivist nations with promises of political influence and economic largesse.

A lot of rubbish was talked about the innate Europeanness of the Scots and the Welsh. Much of their new enthusiasm for the EC was based on a dislike of English power rather than an identification with the federal idea, or for that matter with the peoples of Europe. Far from being immune to xenophobia, they simply directed theirs towards their present partner rather than towards their future one. But however pragmatic support for the Community was in Scotland and Wales, the fact remained that in growing numbers the people of those nations were beginning to adopt Europeanness as their secondary national identity in place of Britishness.

What about the English? Of the three nations, they were by far the most sceptical, seeing Europe not as a rediscovery of their nationhood but as an abandonment of it. That does not mean that Euroscepticism was English nationalism in disguise. At least until the mid-1990s, it was an offshoot of *British* nationalism. But, like most postwar British nationalism, it was predominantly defined and expressed by the English. The irony of Euroscepticism was that, like the Thatcherite ideology which gave it coherence, it was a creed which no longer had any meaning. Defending Britain from Europe grew increasingly absurd as it became clear that England's partners had little wish to be defended. When the English eventually peered through the bushes at the century's end, they discovered that the cries they had mistaken for their partners' distress were actually the satisfied groans of Scotland and Wales enjoying a threesome with their bitterest enemy. The fact that their erstwhile partners liked to remind them that the EU was bigger and more satisfying provoked a bitter reaction. Increasingly, the English felt trapped in a pincer movement between Celtic nationalism to the north and west and European federalism to the south and east. The more the Scots and Welsh expressed enthusiasm for European Union, the more the English viewed it as an elaborate plot to break up Britain.

That was not the case. But here we come to one of the great ironies of postwar British history. The European Union was the main beneficiary of the rupturing of Britishness. Edward Heath had dragged the UK into the Common Market in the belief that it would help to modernize the British economy, returning prosperity to the poorest nations of the UK in order to hold the Union together. He failed. But his failure was the foundation for a greater success. Because Britain's relative economic decline continued after 1973, the Scots and the Welsh lost faith in the ability of Britain's leaders to do anything about it, and as a result they turned more wholeheartedly towards the Continent than the English did. Eventually, the English were persuaded to follow, if only because they had no viable alternative. Therefore the origin of Britain's acceptance that its future lay in Europe was not a new, post-imperial compact between the English, Scots, and Welsh, as Europhiles had originally hoped; instead, support for the EU sprang from the chronic disunity of the British peoples. It was a strange and paradoxical victory for Heath, not without disappointment. But it was a victory nonetheless.

However, just as one must not get carried away with the idea that the Scots and the Welsh fell in love with the Continent, it would be a gross distortion to argue that the English hated it. Although they had more reservations about federalism, their cultural bonds with the Continent were strong and getting stronger, and the postwar Europeanization of Britain got fully under way during the 1980s. By this I mean that the adoption of a range of Continental customs, which was first noticed in the Macmillan era, started to have an effect on national identity in Britain during the Thatcher era. It was a slow, osmotic process and no single event or individual can be pointed to which marked its beginning. But it was clearly discernible to sociologists and, eventually, to historians. Travel was largely responsible for a revolution in taste which affected the whole island. The English did not sit sulking in seafront shelters with flasks of tea and cheese sandwiches while the Scots and the Welsh travelled the Continent, urbanely sipping black coffee in elegant cafes. Nearly all Britons travelled abroad at one time or another and all of them discovered something they liked about Europe.

6. Lift up your eyes to the Continent and take an interest in exotic ingredients

As the number of Britons holidaying abroad continued to rise during the 1980s, criticism of their 'low' cultural outlook became more febrile, and the moral panic about football hooliganism exacerbated the tendency. Millions of people who peacefully enjoyed their lasagne, chips and lager by the beach were bracketed with the few psychotic xenophobes who roamed the streets of European cities starting riots. But those not blinded by class prejudice could detect a Europeanization of British taste taking place.

The greatest effect that Europe had on British life was a change in the national diet. In his history of the subject, first published in 1966, John Burnett stated, 'In nutritional terms we are better fed than at any previous recorded time.'[73] However, despite improvements, the British diet remained unimaginative and between 1945 and 1975 it varied very little. A Gallup enquiry for the *Daily Telegraph* in 1962 found that Britons' idea of a perfect meal was exactly the same as it had been at the height of austerity in 1947: tomato soup, followed by roast chicken, potatoes, peas and sprouts, finished off by trifle and cream. Burnett wrote, 'The dietary pattern has changed little since before the war: decontrol and a rising standard of living has only meant that people have attained or, in some cases, approached more nearly to what they previously regarded as an ideal diet.'[74] In 1968, the normally optimistic Anthony Sampson declared, 'In spite of a common agricultural policy, kitchens in the Common Market remain bastions of national character.'[75] In 1973, a *Daily Mirror* poll indicated a change in attitudes. Although the English breakfast remained hugely popular, Britons apparently relished eating Continental dishes, particularly in restaurants, could when they afford to. The *Mirror* exclaimed, 'any lingering idea that the British are a stuffy lot who believe that God created the English Channel to preserve them from foreigners and their funny ways gets ditched today'.[76]

The *Mirror* was a little premature. But a decade later, thanks to rising living standards, a quiet revolution was in motion. The development of a more exotic diet was initially the product not of Europe but of the Empire, when colonial civilians and servicemen who had not been starved to death in Japanese POW camps returned from the Far East and India with a taste for the food they had eaten there. Postwar immigration gave Britain a larger community with the know-how to cook the food. In 1948, there were only six Indian restaurants in Britain; half a century later, there were 5,300, with on average a new one opening each day. The Chinese takeaway grew just as quickly. It was invented by John Koon, a London restaurateur, with the help of Cliff Richard, in 1958. The idea was born when Cliff and other pop stars, rehearsing for ITV's *Oh Boy!* in a nearby church hall, asked for ready-cooked meals to take home. Koon obliged, and within a few years the Chinese takeaway had become a standard feature of Western life. American food arrived in Britain when Wimpy opened the first hamburger outlet in 1962, followed by KFC in 1965, Pizza Hut in 1973 and McDonald's in 1974. Thankfully, small Asian and Oriental food businesses survived the US corporate onslaught. However, the real revolution in taste was not driven by the empires of the English-speaking world, old or new. What truly changed British life was a mass, post-imperial discovery of Continental cuisine.

The cookery writer Elizabeth David began the dietary revolution

in the 1950s, imploring her millions of readers to 'Lift up your eyes
to the continent and take an interest in exotic ingredients.'[77] Among
those ingredients, olive oil, previously only available in chemists for
unblocking waxy ears, became a staple of the British kitchen. Born
in 1913, David came from a family of wealthy, landed Northumbrian
Tory politicians (her maternal grandfather had been Home Secretary
in the 1890s). After setting sail at the age of twenty-six in a yacht
with a pacifist lover, she lived in France and Greece and then on the
Mediterranean coast of Egypt, where she became part of the Alex-
andrine artistic and literary set that included Lawrence Durrell. She
returned to Britain in 1946, finding it even more dismal than when
she had left. Over the next forty years, she imported some of the
colour of the Mediterranean to Britain and brought a literary quality
to cookery writing unknown to a generation brought up on Mrs
Beeton. Her classic work, *French Provincial Cooking* (1965), offered
a nutritional and cultural manifesto of healthy but exotic good living.

By the 1980s, millions were able to take her advice because the
planes which flew tourists to and from the Mediterranean also
transported ingredients used by the new cookery writers. Refrigera-
tion techniques developed in the late 1970s made fresh foreign
produce more widely available much more cheaply. Technological
developments in the processed foods industry (that is, an array of
chemical flavourings and preservatives) enabled people who lacked
the confidence or the time to cook Continental dishes to eat them
without any bother, a development which gave rise to the ubiquitous
Chicken Kiev. Rubber chicken oozing garlic butter was not the only
culinary adventure which the British embarked upon. Between 1970
and 2000, the number of products which an average Sainsbury's
supermarket stocked rose from 4,000 to 23,000, a trend followed by
its competitors.[78] Also, it was during this period that supermarkets
stopped placing things like pasta in separate 'Foreign Food' aisles
and integrated them with traditional British produce. Remaining
dietary differences between the classes were due to income levels
rather than nationalism. Most Britons had not only heeded Elizabeth
David's call to lift up their eyes and take an interest in Continental
food. In their millions they had opened their mouths, tasted its
delights and, as it slipped down their throats, swallowed much of
their xenophobic pride. By the end of the century Terence Conran
could say with some justification: 'Elizabeth David opened British
eyes and tempted British palates to the tastes and flavours of France,
Italy and Spain and the traditional food of Great Britain. More than

that, she helped to educate a generation to enjoy food ... Her influence has revolutionised what we buy in supermarkets up and down the land.'[79] The consumption of Continental food was accompanied by a huge and unprecedented rise in the amount of wine drunk in Britain.

For centuries, wine was the preserve of the upper classes in Britain. With the growth of foreign trade in Tudor times, wealthier merchants, government officials and clerics drank it as a status symbol, while many poorer people consumed the cheaper sweet varieties like port and Madeira which became available thanks to England's alliance with Portugal. But despite the reduction of wine duties by Chancellors Gladstone and Cripps in the 1860s and 1940s respectively, much less wine was consumed than on the Continent, for two reasons. First, because the British middle classes tended to see it as a faintly sinful display of luxury, or as the lubricant for outright debauchery; and second, because wine was still beyond the purse of most working people.

In the late twentieth century, a dramatic change in taste took place. From 1960 to 1970, consumption doubled from 3.6 pints a head per year to 7 pints, the highest figure since the fourteenth century. It continued to climb thereafter, to 17.9 pints in 1980 and 32.1 in 1995, a ninefold increase on the 1960 figure. The rise in consumption was not because the middle classes were drinking themselves silly to celebrate their latest salary rise, it was because the habit had spread to all social groups. By 2000, an estimated 30.45 million Britons drank wine regularly. The supply of wine improved when supermarkets began to sell it cheaply on open shelves, accompanied by helpful labels, so that social stigmas could more easily be overcome. Sainsbury's was the first to do so, at its Bristol store, in 1962. The demand for wine was primarily stimulated by foreign travel, and in particular the growing popularity of restaurants. The restaurant as we know it today first came to Britain from France in the mid-nineteenth century and became established as a result of the 1860 Refreshment Houses Act which permitted wine to be sold with meals. Eating out became more popular during the Second World War thanks to Churchill's state-subsidized British Restaurants. But it was not until the 1960s that rising incomes, combined with the discovery of foreign food, served in pleasurable surroundings, that the restaurant became a truly democratic institution. Accurate figures do not exist for earlier periods, but by 1999, 69 per cent of British adults ate out regularly, a similar number to those who now drank wine.[80] Whatever the cause of this change, there can be no doubting its effect. John Burnett concluded: 'Wine has passed from a drink of privilege to one of mass consumption, and Britain has been at least partially converted to a Europeanisation of taste'.

British governments defied an EU ruling in 1984 that duties should be harmonized, as a result of which, wine, beer and tobacco continued to be more expensive in Britain than anywhere else in Europe. The British voted with their white vans. Millions travelled across the Channel to stock up in French supermarkets or they bought from the growing number of professional smugglers, plying their trade around the south coast of England. The smuggling of alcohol is a great British tradition (when wine was particularly heavily taxed in the eighteenth century, the wealthy filled their cellars with illicit cases). The tradition was revived in the late twentieth century as a direct result of the state's refusal to pass on to its citizens the most basic economic benefits of Community membership. Chastising Britain's intelligentsia for being unpatriotic, in 1941 George Orwell famously wrote, 'they take their cookery from Paris and their opinions from Moscow'. Half a century later, ordinary Britons had come to share intellectuals taste in food, if not their perpetual tendency to sneer at patriotism.[81]

The nation's favourite sport also took on a more Continental air. Although the Scotland, Wales and England teams became the main focus of fissiparous national identity in Britain, football also created a greater sense of Europe. European Cup victories by Celtic, Liverpool, Nottingham Forest and Manchester United from 1968 to 1999 confirmed that the British game had recovered from the nadir of the early postwar period and raised the value which Britons placed upon sporting participation in Europe. We noted earlier that nationalistic hooliganism never involved more than a highly visible minority who were roundly condemned as an embarrassment. The import of Continental players and managers from the 1980s onwards added to the sport's cosmopolitan character and the warm welcome they got from fans demonstrated that the British were not the rabid xenophobes they were thought to be. The biggest stars became popular heroes and some received the ultimate accolade of fans waving their heroes' national flag at matches (even, in Eric Cantona's case, humming the 'Marseillaise'). The EU's Bosman Ruling of 1994 which abolished the limit on the number of foreign players a club could employ led to a huge rise in numbers, most of them from Europe. In 1994, there were 33 foreign players in the English Premiership; by 2000 the figure was 200 and rising – a third of the total playing force and the highest proportion of any league in Europe apart from Italy's Serie A. On 26 December 1999, in a match against Southampton, Chelsea made history by becoming the first British club to field eleven foreign players at the same time. And in 2000, the English people warmly welcomed the appointment of a Swede as the first foreign manager of the England team.

In short, football began to create a rare bridge between British and Continental popular culture which did much to compensate for the fact that only a minority of Britons had a sense of Europe's musical, literary and artistic heritage. The fact that football was hardly played in the United States added to its influence in this respect. Nick Hornby's bestselling *Fever Pitch* (1992) epitomized the new, more cosmopolitan British football scene. There was a nice symbolism in the fact that the author's father, Sir Robert Hornby, was the Chief Executive of British and Continental Railways, the company that secured the contract to run trains in the Channel tunnel.

7. Tunnel of love

The tunnel was revived by Mrs Thatcher, who saw it as 'my tunnel'; a grand enterprise that would memorialize her rule.[82] In November 1984, the Prime Minister flew to Paris for a meeting with President Mitterrand, taking with her her Foreign Secretary, Howe, her Chancellor, Lawson, and her Transport Secretary, Ridley. She was then at the height of her power: the Falklands were won, the Labour Party was crushed, with the miners about to follow suit, and Jacques Delors' challenge to her supremacy had yet to emerge. Thatcher and her team swept in to the British Embassy in the French capital, a building purchased by the Duke of Wellington from Napoleon's sister as a base for his peace negotiations with the French in 1814. At 11 p.m. they sat down with the Ambassador, Sir John Fretwell, and discussed the project, lubricated by a large quantity of Fretwell's whisky. Initially, the Prime Minister was hostile. It would cost too much, she said, and the traffic would devastate Kent, the Garden of England. But, as the night wore on, Geoffrey Howe remembers her attitude changing. 'Something must have stirred mysteriously in the Prime Minister's mind in favour of a grand project. Subsequently she defended it by reference to having done something that will stand in memory of this administration.'[83] It would also, she argued, be a monument to what the private sector could do, as the Suez Canal had been in the nineteenth century. At 2 a.m., Mrs Thatcher proposed a toast to the tunnel.

After private investors were found, work began in December 1987 and the tunnel was eventually completed in 1993, at a cost for Britain of £12 billion and the lives of seven construction workers. The breakthrough came on 1 December 1990 when the two sides met fifty metres under the sea. Live on television, a smiling French construction worker called Phillippe Cozette became visible through a small borehole. He and his British counterpart, Graham Fagg, handed each other their national flags and embraced. It was an intensely moving moment, and one laden with irony. As the Prime Minister said 'No! No! No!' to Europe in the House of Commons, a few miles away under the sea Britain was being physically joined to the Continent for the first time since the Holocene period, around 6500 BC. The project which she had hoped would be a memorial to her rule instead became one to her downfall. For Thatcher, it was a bitter blow. The directors of the construction company TML implored her to attend the opening of the tunnel. She refused, but hung in her study a piece of rock from the breakthrough which TML had had mounted and sent to her.

Did the tunnel have an effect on British national identity? Undoubtedly. The opening conveniently took place a month after the ninetieth anniversary of the signing of the Entente Cordiale and the French press declared that the tunnel would end British insularity and begin a new era of Franco-British cooperation. André Fontaine, a former editor of *Le Monde*, argued that the two nations had much in common as former imperial powers searching for a new future; unless they grasped it through the European Union, both would become little more than attendants in a museum for American and Japanese tourists. Some of their British counterparts agreed. In a special joint edition of the *Guardian* and the left/liberal French paper *Libération*, the *Guardian*'s editor argued that in fifty or a hundred years' time the date of the tunnel's opening would be stamped on people's memories, while that of the Normandy landings would be an obscure anniversary.[84] The initial signs were promising. In 1994, 9 million Britons travelled to France – double the previous annual figure – while only 2.78 million French people travelled to the UK.[85]

There were doubters. On the French side, the social historian François Bédarida argued that the rivalries between the two went so deep into their respective national identities that 'the train of prejudice' was, so to speak, 'still on the rails'. If so, then the TGV was at least moving faster. When passenger trains started running in December 1994, they sped through the French countryside. But after emerging from the Tunnel at Folkestone in Kent, they chugged at a leisurely pace because the government had refused to invest in new track. It was symbolic, because although few Britons actually opposed the tunnel, they were less enthusiastic about it than the French. The Times felt it necessary to point out that 'France is, in fact, the friend, ally and partner of Great Britain, and not her enemy'.[86] The inauguration of the tunnel by the Queen and President Mitterrand on 6 May 1994 was televised continuously on one French channel from 8.30 a.m. to 6.55 p.m. and heralded as an epochal event. The BBC treated it as just another news item and broadcast only half an hour live in the morning and afternoon. And while President Mitterrand declared that the tunnel would reinforce European Union, the Queen pointedly did not.

Furthermore, the fiftieth anniversary of D-Day a month after the tunnel was formally opened showed how little had changed. The event received far more coverage in the British media than the tunnel had. Like the men who crossed the Channel to liberate France on 6 June 1944, the Queen travelled by sea for the event; the Germans (to Chancellor Kohl's anger) were not allowed to go; and Franco-British relations were strained, with each being unable to agree who had won the war except mutually to downgrade the role of America and the Soviet Union. A poll taken by Le Figaro concluded that 90 per cent of the French thought Free French forces had played a major part in the liberation of 1944–5; another for Le Monde showed that half the country thought the resistance had done as much as the Allies to win the war. All of this demonstrated how successful de Gaulle had been in implanting the myth of self-liberation in the French mind.[87]

It would therefore be wrong to claim that the British came to see themselves as European in the 1980s. However tasty spaghetti bolognese might be, eating it does not necessarily make an individual well disposed towards Italy, any more than drinking lager induces a fondness for Germans or eating a curry turns a racist into a champion of multiculturalism. The British still felt a greater cultural affinity towards the US than they did towards the Continent. But there were signs that a sympathetic *awareness* of the Continent was starting to develop which cannot be ignored if we are to reach an accurate conclusion about British attitudes to Europe in the late twentieth century. A growing number of people in Scotland and Wales were once again looking to Europe as a counterweight to the power of England. In Britain as a whole, foreign travel was now seen as a normal activity and Continental customs and products as a welcome addition to the British way of life. Football was beginning to provide a genuinely popular link with the Continent and not simply an opportunity for nationalist hooligans to replay old enmities. Popular acceptance and use of the Channel Tunnel demonstrated that Europe was no longer seen as a military threat. And though it is too soon to asses, the overall impact of the tunnel on national identity, the fact that Britain had been physically rejoined to the Continent could only diminish the island mentality of the British in the long run. As one senior British diplomat remarked in 1973, the project was one of 'very deep psychological significance'.[88]

Statistical evidence bears out these conclusions. In 1991, one poll for the *Daily Mail* showed 43 per cent in favour of joining a federal Europe, with only 31 per cent opposed. A more instructive example is the result of the regular surveys carried out by the EU on the attitude of its members towards the Union. In 1991, 57 per cent of Britons thought the Community was a good thing. This compared to 21 per cent in the depths of the recession of 1981. It also compared favourably to opinion in referendum year (50 per cent) and the year of the accession (31 per cent). The figure temporarily fell again to 36 per cent in 1997 as a result of the propaganda unleashed by the Eurosceptic wing of the Tory Party in the wake of Mrs Thatcher's removal from office. But overall, these figures show that despite closer integration and Mrs Thatcher's vocal resistance to it, support for Europe had grown. Her long-term effect was merely to harden opposition among those who were already sceptical rather than substantially to increase their number.

The British attitude to the European Union was not dissimilar to the Scottish attitude to the UK. There was continual grumbling about the power of the Union's largest member and there was acute dissatisfaction with the democratic unaccountability of the Union's political elite and their failure to reverse economic decline, yet few wanted to leave and become a wholly independent nation state once again. The comparison is compelling until one remembers one essential difference. Whereas the Scots were kept in the UK largely by the threat of how much it would cost them to leave, the reason most Britons wanted to stay in the EU was also because they felt an affinity with the Continent. It was fragile, and easily shaken by concerted attacks on the EU. Nonetheless, there emerged in this period a cultural foundation for the fostering of dual national/European identities in Britain which a bold Prime Minister of the future could build on to complete the postwar transformation of Britishness.

8. A brief period of celebration

In a letter to a Swedish admirer not long before his death in 1983, Sir Kenneth Clark wrote, 'I . . . regard Mrs Thatcher as an aberration.'[89] He was right to do so. She left a profound mark on the country's economic, social and political life which Britons live with every day and in almost every area of their lives in the twenty-first century. But she did not transform national identity in Britain and where she did it was more by default than intent. With Victorian economic liberalism as her weapon she sought to revive militant nineteenth-century British nationalism, presenting the self-reliant individual as the microcosm of a proud, self-reliant nation. 'Economics are the method,' she said in 1981, 'the object is to change the heart and soul.' When, after her departure, Mrs Thatcher was asked what she had changed, she replied, 'Everything.' She exaggerated.

The Falklands spirit was discredited and largely forgotten; hardcore Euroscepticism was mocked as an archaic and dangerous nationalist movement. Thanks in part to her own policies, Thatcher's beloved Union was in even greater crisis than when she had come to power. A growing majority in both of England's partner nations were rejecting the dual national identity with which the Union had been maintained for so long. Indeed, the whole idea of British democracy as it had been understood for over a century was now questioned by enough Britons to put the constitutional integrity of the United Kingdom in serious danger.

What, then, was left? The answer is, very little except the monarchy. The biggest new romantic party of all during the 1980s was the marriage of twenty-year-old Diana Spencer to the Prince of Wales on 29 July 1981. Beautiful and sexy in a gauchely vulnerable way, Diana looked the part of the fairy-tale princess which the Palace and the press wrote for her. The Archbishop of Canterbury, Robert Runcie, privately knew it to be an arranged marriage. Publicly, he opened his wedding sermon with the words, 'This is the stuff of which fairy tales are made.' It was the first time that an heir to the British throne had married a British woman. Much was made of this fact in order to emphasize once again how thoroughly un-European the monarchy really was (royalists even pointed out that Diana worked at a kindergarten called 'Young England').[90] Like the Silver Jubilee four years earlier, the monarchy's power to unite the nation during a crisis was strongly emphasized. The country was already in the middle of a recession, and the worst rioting of the century had occurred that year in Brixton in April and only a fortnight earlier in Bristol and Liverpool. The Ska band the Specials captured the mood of Britain's inner cities with their No. 1 single 'Ghost Town'. Inside St Paul's Cathedral the music was by Purcell, Elgar, Vaughan Williams, Britten and Tippett; the congregation sang 'I vow to thee my country' and the official programme said:

> For the monarchy, it means that a direct succession is almost certainly assured. For the people of Britain, it offers a brief period of celebration in difficult times – the romantic marriage of the eldest son of a beloved Royal Family to a charming and beautiful English girl. To the countless millions of people beyond our shores who will watch on their television screens the splendour and magnificence of a state ceremony that only Britain could stage, the Prince and Princess of Wales will symbolise qualities which are too frequently decried in this increasingly materialistic and irreligious world.[91]

A million people lined the streets of the capital and an estimated 750 million worldwide watched the event on TV. Despite cultivating royal connections for over a decade, Roy Strong was not invited to the wedding; instead, he went home to his country house in Herefordshire where he mused on the cult of monarchy. His diary recorded:

> We fled London on the eve of the Royal Wedding. We are indeed sunk beneath a marriage morass: T-shirts, mugs, towels, silver, plates, medals, bibles, books – it cascades forth. So does the press: every glance, thought and look of both bride and groom are

scrutinised and recorded. It is exactly as one predicted. As things get worse and worse the royalist cult accelerates. This event in a way leaves even the Silver Jubilee behind.[92]

But the portents for the royalist cult were not good. As Runcie guessed, Prince Philip had orchestrated the marriage to perpetuate the Windsor dynasty, and at the altar in St Paul's, Diana vowed fidelity to *Philip* Charles Arthur George by mistake. 'She's married my father!' exclaimed Prince Andrew to a companion. She might as well have. Asked on TV if he loved Diana, Charles famously replied, 'Yes, whatever love means.'[93] Like the new romantic pop bands of the time, all the make-up and lace in the world could not disguise a lack of substance in the relationship of the couple and in the institution which their union was supposed to prop up. Most Britons regarded the event as little more than an enjoyable spectacle. It came at a time when history, like sex, could sell almost anything. The royal wedding offered both.

Mrs Thatcher's relationship with the Queen highlighted the underlying tension between Crown and country. At first glance, the historic coincidence of Britain having a female head of state and a female premier augured well. Mrs Thatcher was not only an ardent monarchist; as a young MP in the early 1950s she had been inspired by the prospect of a woman on the throne. When she became Prime Minister, the admiration was returned. The Queen Mother sang Thatcher's praises to Woodrow Wyatt – journalist and confidant of both women. In his diary for 1986, Wyatt reported: 'She [the Queen Mother] says the Royal Family when they're alone together often drink a toast at the end of dinner to Mrs Thatcher. She adores Mrs Thatcher and thinks she is very brave and has done tremendous things.'[94] Like most British monarchs since the evolution of party politics in the eighteenth century, Elizabeth II was an instinctive Tory and she broadly supported the Thatcher Revolution. On board the royal yacht *Britannia* in 1991, she gave Ronald Reagan this insight into the problems facing the world: 'You see, all the democracies are bankrupt now because, you know, because of the way that the services have been planned for people to grab.'[95] The Queen was uneasy about social unrest in Britain, but then so were all except the most crazed political extremists of the time. She also disliked the fact that Mrs Thatcher was indifferent to the Commonwealth. But the Queen knew there was little to separate Thatcher from her recent predecessors at 10 Downing Street on this issue, other than the fact that Thatcher took less trouble to hide her indifference. The tension in the relationship of these two extraordinary women did not, therefore, spring from fundamental political differences.

The root of the trouble was more personal. The Queen disliked Mrs Thatcher's regal style of government. As the Prime Minister established her position as the most powerful and successful British leader of the postwar period she began to adopt monarchical habits, notably in her regular use of the royal 'we'. When she emerged from No. 10 to announce the birth of her son's child, she announced 'We are a grandmother.' This embarrassing incident offended the British sense of democracy, embedded as it still was in a belief in constitutional monarchy. The British people, as much as the Queen herself, disliked the royal position being usurped in this way and they disliked the fact that a prime minister should be so powerful as to feel able to do so. Concluding his assessment of the Thatcher years, Peter Hennessy has written: 'At its cruellest, history reduces the Ozymandias effect to a single one-liner . . . Surely [hers is] that immortal use of the royal "we". But, as history showed in November 1990, the British constitution has room for only one Queen, the one who lived at the western, not the eastern, end of St James's Park.'[96] True. But Mrs Thatcher's removal was a pyrrhic victory for the monarchy, the constitution and Britishness as a whole. As the nation entered the final decade of the twentieth century, the Crown was fatally wounded by two things: the Celtic nationalism it had helped to keep at bay for so long but which became unstoppable as a result of Thatcherism, and Princess Diana's public exposure of the royal family's personal inadequacies, which lost it support even in an England whose people were desperately clinging on to the last vestiges of Britishness. At the eastern end of St James's Park, no less than at its western end, the British were about to reject one of the last pillars of their national identity. Soon, the question would be asked, 'Who are the British?' and the pauses before a reply came would become longer and longer until eventually the silence was deafening.

PART II

MODERNIZERS

This is the patriotic party because it is the people's party.

Tony Blair, 1997

Since Mr Blair has decided to let Scotland go its own way we in England have said sod you, we'll go our own way too, we'll look after ourselves. I think England is discovering a sense of itself.

Patrick Tripp (flag-maker to the Crown), 1997

1. A nation of long shadows

In the final decade of the twentieth century, the decline of Britishness accelerated to such an extent that even the most complacent unionists were forced to admit that the British nation state was in grave danger and that something should be done to save it. So began a concerted effort to reform the political structure of the Union and to repair the national identity which had underwritten it for nearly three centuries. This project was accompanied by the most sustained critical inquiry into the nature of Britishness since the aftermath of the Suez crisis.

British politics in the 1990s were dominated by a battle between the Conservative and Labour parties to secure the Thatcherite Revolution by softening its ideological edges, especially those which the Lady had sharpened in the final, megalomaniac phase of her rule. Prime Ministers John Major (1990–7) and Tony Blair (1997–) attempted to move their parties into the centre ground while retaining her central tenets of free enterprise, family values and moderate Euroscepticism. In the advertising argot of the 1980s, they sought to create 'Thatcher Lite'. Major lost the struggle for three reasons: first, his mismanagement of the economy; second, his party's bitter civil war over Europe which a more ruthless man than he could not have stopped; and third, his failure to halt the haemorrhaging of popular unionism in Scotland and Wales.

By the time of Thatcher's fall, the Scots and Welsh had lost so much faith in their union with England that a constitutional revolution, accompanied by a reconstruction of British national identity, was vital, or so it seemed to most observers. The Conservatives' response was to shoot the messenger, blaming the Labour Party for destabilizing the Union by advocating devolution. The Conservative alternative was to continue defending the archaic version of Britishness that Mrs Thatcher had championed. For right-wing Eurosceptics, the indivisible sovereignty of the Westminster Parliament remained the basis of Britishness. In 1995, Charles Moore the editor of the *Daily Telegraph*, explained how to be British in an eponymous pamphlet:

The British nation state is a coherent, working entity which has not been seriously disputed for nearly 300 years except in relation to Ireland. Our capacity to be British, our idea of ourselves and our sense of worth are built round this history. And it follows that our Parliament is crucial to our sense of worth as the Bundestag is not for the Germans or the Assemblée Nationale for the French . . . A break-up would occur if the economic and monetary union provided for in [the EU treaty signed at] Maastricht, or the political union aimed for in it, did take place. So anyone who is interested in being British should oppose both these things.[1]

John Major promised to place Britain 'at the heart of Europe', and was coruscated by his party for attempting to do so, but his vision of Britishness was just as backward-looking. Not for nothing did he create the Department of National Heritage. One of its incumbents, Stephen Dorrell, said that its purpose was 'to express something of the excitement of what it means to be British at the end of the twentieth century'.[2] The nation was not excited.

Major's most famous definition of Britishness was delivered on the eve of St George's Day 1993, in a speech in London to the Conservative Group for Europe. He began with a contemporary picture of cultural exchange. 'It is no longer an oddity for British students to spend a year in France or to see a German student rowing in the boat-race for Cambridge . . . Little England steps out . . .' But, he concluded:

Fifty years from now Britain will still be the country of long shadows on county [cricket] grounds, warm beer, invincible green suburbs, dog lovers and pools fillers and – as George Orwell said – 'old maids bicycling to Holy Communion through the morning mist' and – if we get our way – Shakespeare still read in school. Britain will survive unamendable in all essentials.[3]

He later explained, 'I was not rhapsodising about the sort of country I wanted to create . . . My intention was to remind listeners that Britain's involvement in Europe did not threaten our national distinctiveness.'[4] That may be so. But what he wanted to preserve said much about the cultural and political myopia of the party he was leading.

Of course, the Scots and Welsh love beer, the pools, suburbs, dogs and church no less and no more than the English. But the nation which Major's imagery primarily conjured up – and the one he undoubtedly had in mind – was England and not Britain. Moreover the *kind* of England which it conjured up was redolent of Stanley Baldwin in the 1930s. Major admitted that Baldwin was his greatest influence, and the comparisons between the two are clear. Both men sought to create a conservative consensus following a period in which the nation had been bitterly divided (in Baldwin's case, after the General Strike). Major's declared wish to create 'a nation at ease with itself' was pure Baldwin; so too was his attempt to construct a patriotism based on the idea of England as a gentle, peaceful nation which minded its own business. Little England had 'stepped out'. But in his mind it rarely went further than the patio doors.

Major launched a spirited defence of the British polity. In one speech during the 1992 general election campaign, he said: 'If I could summon up all the authority of this office, I would put it into this single warning – the United Kingdom is in danger. Wake up, my fellow countrymen! Wake up now before it is too late!'[5] His surprise victory was partly attributable to this strategy. But those who heeded the call were almost entirely English. So too were those who responded to the celebrations his government organized to mark the fiftieth anniversary of VE Day, on 8 May 1995. The 1990s offered a spate of wartime anniversaries, of which this was the most significant. It was designed by the government to provide a reassuring picture of Britain as a united, self-contained island nation. It turned into the swan-song of the war culture which had been so central to British national identity for half a century.

The mastermind of the celebrations was the king of the heritage industry, Pruno Peek. They culminated with a three-day jamboree in Hyde Park from 6 to 8 May. A moving Ceremony of Peace and Reconciliation attended by the Queen and heads of state was held on the 7th. But the predominant tone was one of patriotic nostalgia. The *Sun* launched a successful campaign to reverse the government's decision to allow members of the German army to march through the capital. It congratulated itself with the headline 'THE SUN BANS THE HUN', followed by an adaptation of the *Dad's Army* theme tune 'So who do you think you are kidding, Mister Major? / We are the boys who have stopped your little game.'[6]

The Queen Mother was ever-present as the woman who had faced down the Blitz. Churchill's great-great-granddaughter lit the first of 100 beacons which ringed the island. As well as gun displays, people were treated to jitterbug classes, 'Sandy Lee's Nostalgic Fashion Show' and the Church Lads and Lasses Marching Band. In the official programme for the event, the Prime Minister wrote, 'The nation had to mobilise itself against a regime that was inherently evil. Had we failed, Parliamentary government would have died in this same country which gave it birth.'[7] Alongside his message were the lyrics for a mass sing-along that took place outside Buckingham Palace on 8 May. Led by Sir Cliff Richard, the songs ranged from 'Rule, Britannia' to 'The White Cliffs of Dover'. It was rounded off with Cliff serenading the Queen Mother with his own hit, 'Congratulations', while she beamed from the balcony on which she had stood with Churchill and George VI fifty years before.

The *Daily Telegraph* suggested that the event proved all was well with the UK:

> The British in 1940 were more admired by those who shared their values than any other free people have ever been in the history of the world ... Britain today preserves, despite all the fault-finding of the nation's professional critics, its national essence vital and intact. It is still a country of freedom, common decency and, where material concerns preoccupy, of energy, skills and creativity. It would not be so without the war generation's courage and achievements ... The 50 years since 1945 has [sic] been a hard peace. Imperial glory has withered, prosperity has been fitful, doubt ever present. This is a time to banish doubt ... The era of dictators and mad ideologies is over. The widest areas of the world are at peace. It is a peace the British did much to bring. Let us take pride and celebrate.[8]

The British had not forgotten the people who made their freedom possible.

However, there was a growing feeling, even in conservative quarters, that it was time for the country to move on and that 1995 should be the last major celebration of its kind. The veterans themselves wanted it to be so. The British Legion objected to what it saw as the trivialization of its members' sacrifice. It also suspected that the echoing patriotism of 1940–45 was being hijacked by the Conservative Party, just as that of the Falklands conflict had been during the 1980s. A government proposal for 'Home Front-style' Spam fritters to be cooked for revellers in Hyde Park caused particular offence to veterans. The British Legion protested and the Department of National Heritage was forced to abandon the idea. The *Guardian* posed the question 'WE'LL NOT MEET AGAIN SO TIME TO START ROLLING BACK THE BARREL?'

It was as much an attempt to recapture some sort of community spirit as it was a commemoration of war or nationalism. All kinds of fragments of Britishness found themselves caught up in the event. Just why it was thought appropriate that the fiftieth anniversary of the death of Hitler should be marked by Cliff Richard leading the massed crowds in the Mall in a rendition of 'We're All Going on a Summer Holiday' remains elusive ... It was one of those curious one-off events in British public life which most of us will remember in some way and which some found genuinely fulfilling. It was good that it happened – and it is good that it will not happen again.[9]

For once, this was not traditional left/liberal carping about the perils of patriotism per se. It was an accurate assessment of the nation's ambivalence towards a particular form of patriotism that had run its course.

For many English people the Second World War was a means of clinging on to their Anglo-British identity and they failed to notice that few celebrations of VE Day were held in Scotland and Wales. They also failed to notice that in Scotland and Wales the annual two-minute silence on Armistice Day, 11 November, was not as well observed. This tradition, which had lapsed during the 1940s, was successfully revived in England during the 1990s, following a campaign by the British Legion which featured Vera Lynn and the Spice Girls. The people of Ulster joined the English in honouring the dead, but those in the north and west of the mainland were less moved by what seemed to many an archaic ritual. The fading memory of the Second World War was a key factor in the decline of Britishness during the late twentieth century. The war had reinvigorated British national identity because the people who experienced it were aware that they had defended an island under siege which could ill afford national divisions. The wartime generation, whether Scots, Welsh or English, therefore felt most attached to the Union. As that generation died out, sentimental loyalty to the Union based on the Second World War died with them. Moreover, the fact that the war had been memorialized in a predominantly English way began to tell among a younger generation of Scots and Welsh, who came to see the Finest Hour as a largely English battle.

In the summer of 1996, John Major returned the Stone of Scone on the seven hundredth anniversary of its theft by Edward I. It appeared to be a master stroke. The Stone had been a focus of the nationalist revival in the early postwar period. Yet, as the Queen's property, it could be returned to Westminster Abbey for coronations, thus appeasing the Scots while preventing it becoming a symbol of separatism. In the House of Commons, the announcement was welcomed by Tony Blair: 'The return of the stone . . . is a welcome recognition of how we celebrate the unity of the United Kingdom while being distinct and proud nations with differing traditions, histories and cultures.'[10] The Scots were certainly pleased to have the Stone back. It was piped across the border on St Andrew's Day in an army Land Rover then taken to Edinburgh Castle, where it was displayed alongside the Scottish Crown Jewels.

If Churchill had followed the advice of his Secretary of State and returned the Stone in 1952, it might have had a positive effect on opinion. By 1996, the gesture was a futile one, seen for what it was: a substitute for rather than the fulfilment of Scottish nationality. In the House of Commons, the former Liberal leader Sir David Steel said, 'It is the settled view of people in Scotland that they want not just the symbol, but the substance of the return of democratic control over our internal affairs in Scotland.'[11] In an ironic echo of the chant which heralded the reawakening of English nationalism at Euro '96, the *Scotsman*'s front page declared 'IT'S COMING HOME'. Inside, this normally moderate paper said:

> It was a patronising publicity stunt by a government which can't disentangle myth from reality . . . Scots are proud of their history and as protective as anyone of symbols of nationhood. But they can tell tartan tokenism when it is shoved in their faces. It speaks volumes for the attitude of Westminster to the Scottish question that they should expect Scotland to be grateful for being awarded this useless lump of Sandstone in lieu of self-government.[12]

Major did not learn from this failure. A White Paper of 1997 on the constitution flatly proclaimed, 'We must reaffirm our faith in the Union and work to ensure that it flourishes in its fourth century.'[13] The Conservative election campaign of that year was one of 'Safety First'. Against a picture of Horatio Nelson on a Union Jack backdrop, the party's manifesto read: 'In a world where people want security, nothing could be more dangerous than to unravel a constitution that binds our nation together and the institutions that bring us stability.'[14] Not surprisingly, the Scots and the Welsh rejected this in 1997 even more vehemently than they had five years before. So did the English. They were either so disillusioned with Major they didn't care, or they were beginning to accept that devolution was the only way to save the Union.

The British rejected the cardigan that John Major placed around their shoulders just as they had rejected the corset with which Mrs Thatcher had nearly suffocated them. Major's fatal error was in believing that what the British desired was a period of calm when in fact what they wanted was further revolution placed within a more progressive framework and presented in a more stylish way. The Scots and the Welsh wanted devolution. And most Britons (especially the English) wanted a free-market enterprise culture. But they wanted its sleazy stubble shaved off by governmental rectitude, its raw, unforgiving skin moisturized with cash injections for health and education, and its bad xenophobic breath sweetened by a more open approach to multicultural Britain and to Europe. The Thatcher governments may have destroyed what was left of the postwar liberal consensus, but there was an underlying consensus for it to be destroyed. Britons simply wanted the job done more tactfully and less stridently than before, with pain caused to fewer people. And where pain was unavoidable, they wanted it to be less visible. In short, what the British wanted was a new national consensus to be constructed around the Thatcher Revolution. In Tony Blair, they found their man.

2. Hi! Good to see you!

The election of Tony Blair as Prime Minister on 1 May 1997 with a majority of 177 was the biggest Labour victory to date and the worst election result for the Conservative Party since 1832. Promises by Andrew Lloyd Webber and Frank Bruno to leave the country if the Tories lost did not sway the British electorate. This was especially true of Scotland and Wales. For the first time in history, not a single Conservative MP was elected in either land. The Conservatives were now truly the party of One Nation – England. Touchingly, Major demonstrated his party's Englishness by going to the Oval to watch his beloved Surrey beat the Combined Universities on 2 May. The long shadows of the late afternoon crept over flannelled cricketers and manicured grass in what *The Times* described as 'Mr Major's eternal England'.[15] Outside the Oval, Surrey was not faring so well. Tony Blair arrived in Downing Street to an ecstatic welcome from a crowd of Labour Party workers waving Union Jacks with a clear mandate from virtually the whole island. For all the stage-management of the scene, it demonstrated how successful Labour had been in recapturing British patriotism from the right after nearly two decades of Conservative hegemony. How had they done it?

The 'Third Way' has been described by one of its apologists as the mastery of 'political competence'.[16] It was much more than that. Blair did not simply move the Labour party to the right to win the votes of Middle England. He offered affluent and aspirant Britons everywhere absolution of the guilt they felt for welcoming (secretly or otherwise) the essentials of the Thatcherite Revolution. Like a charismatic priest leaning out of a richly decorated confessional, his smooth hands, warm smile and twinkling eyes beckoned a nation to the polling booths in 1997. 'Come,' he said, 'confess your desire for lower taxes, privatization and welfare reform, but be assured that you are the same decent, fair-minded people you always were. Receive this blessing, and go forth into the world confident in your Britishness.' Blair not only offered himself as confessor to the nation. As *Private Eye*'s portrayal of him as a trendy Anglican vicar so brilliantly illustrated, he attempted to get the nations, classes and races of Britain worshipping together again by redesigning the structure of the church.

There are clear comparisons between Blair and Harold Wilson. Their manipulation of the media could be as laughable as it was necessary (in Blair's case, the wearing of make-up at all times so that cameras never caught him looking tired). Blair's incessant, managerial talk of 'modernization' and his particular stress on technology (in his case computing) was another link with Wilson. So too was his courting of Britain's pop aristocracy in an attempt to appear hip – of which more later. However, Blair's language of patriotism ultimately owed most to the Attlee era even though his programme of reform was nothing like as radical. In 1995, he told the Labour Party conference, 'This is the patriotic party because it is the people's party.'[17] The equating of the nation with 'the people' was an attempt to co-opt the Continental rhetoric of popular, as opposed to Parliamentary, sovereignty which had dominated European political discourse since the French Revolution. By doing so, he not only appeared to be a radical democrat; he also shifted the focus of British patriotism away from the Parliament which he was poised to reform.

There were differences between Blair's language of patriotism and Attlee's. As a keen European, Blair made no effort to set the Labour Party apart from Europe. Peter Mandelson wrote:

> Old Labour . . . had an instinctive dislike of what was felt to be a continental cartel of capitalist-oriented Christian democrats . . . Labour has now totally rejected these outdated attitudes . . . New Labour has the self-confidence in Britain's values not to fear loss of national identity in this process of European co-operation. In contrast the Conservatives can only manage a crude and empty assertion of nationhood bordering at times on xenophobia. Because they have no real appreciation of the value of people working together for the public good – from neighbourhood council to European co-operation – because for them community is essentially an empty concept, they readily revert to flag waving nationalism as the only emotion that can bind us together.[18]

Blair's emphasis on the 'people' allowed him to construct a patriotism that appeared to be classless, or 'inclusive', as New Labour had it. As in the mid-1940s, this had two functions. On the one hand, it reassured left/liberals that the nation would once again include the poor and vulnerable. On the other hand, it reassured the conservative middle classes that they were to be part of the 'New Britain' and not its victims. Like Attlee's patriotism, it owed a lot to nineteenth-century British radicalism. Peter Clarke has rightly likened Blair's 'moral populism' to Gladstone's.[19] Although the Prime Minister was careful not to make any exclusive claim to Christianity, he did assert that his socialism was 'a moral purpose to life' in which 'I am my brother's keeper. I will not walk by on the other side.' Again, this appealed to both Labour traditionalists and liberal modernizers. As Clarke put it, 'this was . . . a politics of conscience rather than class . . . forming an ideological legacy to both Liberals and Labour.'[20]

But the new Prime Minister was careful not to historicize his ideology. Unlike Mrs Thatcher's rhetoric of Britishness, Blair's 'people' were timeless. Their values were pinpointed not as Victorian or Churchillian but as simply and ineffably British. Blair's elucidation of Britishness was also less nation-specific; that is to say, unlike John Major's litany of county cricket grounds, it did not draw specific pictures of national culture in the mind which might prejudice its appeal to Scotland, Wales or, for that matter, England. In short, the appellation of 'the people', of governing for 'the many not the few', could be applied to almost anything. This was a language of patriot-

ism which resembled Esperanto. It offered to break down the barriers
between different groups in society and when spoken it was plausible,
but ultimately meaningless. As Maurice Saatchi pointed out to the
disgruntled readership of the *Daily Telegraph*, a large part of
Labour's success was in dominating political language. 'In the last
election, the Conservative Party took its mind off the key battleground of *language*. Labour was allowed to control the meaning of
one word, "new" . . . You need search for no more lengthy explanation of Labour's victory.'[21] On the morning of Sunday 31 August
1997, New Labour's patriotic Esperanto found its most potent
expression in the championing of a 'People's Princess'. But before
examining the significance of Diana's death, we must first scrutinize
the sorry history of the British monarchy in the years leading up
to it.

3. Everywhere you look the country's institutions seem to be falling apart

By the early 1990s, monarchism was virtually all that was left of
Britishness. Yet, at the very moment when the Crown was more than
ever needed to prop up the Union, the institution entered its most
profound crisis of legitimacy since the republican revival of the
1870s. The ostensible cause of the crisis was that the marriages of
Elizabeth II's three eldest children all failed, her two sons' in sleazy,
undignified circumstances which made a mockery of the monarchy's
claim to be the moral guardian of the nation. A nadir was reached
with photos of the Duchess of York bending topless (and far from
erotically) over her American lover by a swimming pool. The twice-
married novelist A. N. Wilson was among those who criticized the
younger royals for letting down the British way of life by their
behaviour:

> It looks perilously as if the monarchy is going to be one of those
> things, like . . . the language of the old English Church which is
> simply allowed to go because no one can think of a good word to
> say for it . . . More than the House of Windsor will fall if the

Monarchy is allowed to be hounded out by bullies and brutes. It will be a symptom of the general coarsening of life in Britain today, in which the brashly new inevitably defeats the old, in which the ugly always overcomes the beautiful, and everything of which the British used to be proud is cast down and vilified. It is too much to hope in modern Britain – filthy, chaotic, idle, rancorous modern Britain – that sweetness and light could ever triumph over barbarism. The Queen is the only individual in British public life who has held out some hope that decency might survive. By failing the trust which she put in them, her children have failed us all. The lights have not quite gone out. But they are guttering in their sockets.[22]

In another sense, of course, the lights were blazing. But it was the blaze of paparazzi flashbulbs.

The royal PR revolution set in motion by the televising of the Coronation in 1953 had come full circle with disastrous consequences, as Winston Churchill had predicted it would. What began as a successful exercise in modernizing the monarchy by making it more transparent ended with that transparency revealing the human contradictions which lie at the heart of any family, particularly those with the money and leisure to indulge them. Three Australians played a significant part in the drama. The Queen's Press Secretary from 1969 to 1973, William Heseltine, increased the media's access to the monarchy; Rupert Murdoch's press took advantage of that, scrutinizing the private lives of the royal family to an unprecedented extent; and the Australian Premier, Paul Keating, began a debate on whether his country should become a republic which helped to kick-start the debate in Britain itself. Keating also made a dramatic break with protocol during Elizabeth II's Antipodean tour of 1992 by putting an arm around her waist while introducing her to a row of dignitaries. Until 1992, the Queen was relatively untouched by the crisis. Indeed, to some extent she benefited from it. The infidelities which had blighted her own marriage remained a no-go area to the press, allowing her and the Duke of Edinburgh to appear as figures of probity. She was the one reassuring link with a more moral national past which conservatives fondly imagined had once existed. Among liberal Britons, the Queen still basked in the equally mistaken perception that she had been ideologically opposed to the Thatcher Revolution. But then came what she called her 'Annus Horribilis'.

On 20 November 1992, a large section of Windsor Castle burnt down. When Heritage Secretary Peter Brooke suggested that the taxpayer should foot the bill (estimated at £60 million) the British were outraged (an appeal for public donations raised only £25,000 in three months). In a desperate attempt to atone for the mistake, the Queen agreed to pay some income tax on her personal fortune (estimated at £6 billion). She also took minor royals off the Civil List. This left herself, her husband and her mother to manage on £7.9 million a year plus £50 million which she got from the Treasury to pay for their food, transport and accommodation. Public discontent was not assuaged. Britons felt that the Queen was giving away too little and for the wrong reasons. The *Daily Mirror* ran the brutal headline 'H.M. THE TAX DODGER', next to a cartoon of her staring meanly at a calculator.[23]

Despite some heated parliamentary debates on the subject in the 1940s and the 1960s, Civil List republicanism never won many converts. The significance of the criticism on this occasion is that it highlighted the problem faced by reformers overtaken by events: how to appear to be changing out of a desire for change rather than as a calculated attempt to save one's skin. So palpably conservative a monarch as Elizabeth II would never succeed in convincing the nation her motive was the latter rather than the former. To make matters worse, on 2 November 1993 John Major told a packed House of Commons that the Prince and Princess of Wales were formally separating. His contention that this affected neither the latter's right to be Queen nor, apparently, the monarchy's position as a whole, drew audible gasps from a chamber used to the Prime Minister presenting wishes as facts.

The fact was that neither the royal family's personal misdemeanours nor the media's exposure of them were really to blame for the crisis. Royal scandal is nothing new (it is worth noting that Camilla Parker Bowles is the granddaughter of one of Edward VII's mistresses, Alice Keppel). The public's appetite for royal gossip had grown since the decline of class deference. But that in itself was not a cause of the crisis. If anything, the Windsors' chosen role as moral exemplars to the nation contributed to the decline of their popularity. Although Britons disliked the undignified way that royal peccadilloes were exposed, most did not object to the behaviour itself. Like the sexual scandals which troubled the political elite, what Britons objected to was the hypocrisy of national figureheads not practising what they preached, hence the public's acceptance of Diana's relationship with Dodi Al Fayed and, later, that of Charles and Camilla. Having been liberated from the economic and moral imperative of procreation and domesticity, Britons valued the pursuit of happiness at least as highly as the acceptance of duty in their personal lives. They therefore condoned unorthodox royal relationships on the grounds that if they made the individuals happy, they were good for them and for the country. The choice between love and power which Edward VIII had faced in 1936 was seen sixty years later as an unnecessary one.

Scandal, then, was merely the catalyst of the crisis. What caused it was the Windsors' more serious failure to fulfil the monarchy's difficult twin role as a symbol of ancient *and* modern Britain, defining not only where the British had come from but where they presently stood and pointing to where they should be going. As our examination of New Elizabethanism showed, the monarchy was still an avatar of modernity, its younger members associated with the latest developments in the arts, science, commerce and entertainment. As Britain and Britishness began to fragment in the 1960s, the royal family and the politicians who were advising them allowed the Crown to ossify. A study of opinion polls shows a slow but sure decline in the monarchy's popularity from the 1960s onwards, with the numbers of those wanting it to be reformed rising steadily.

In the short term, the ageing Queen, her conservative outlook and moral rectitude served a purpose because, amid the maelstrom of the 1970s, what Britons wanted was the security of an immutable nationhood. But in the long run, the strategy backfired because the monarchy ceased to be a symbol of Britishness and instead became a memorial to it. The Crown's pomp and circumstance still had the power to attract tourists, as traditionalists never tired of pointing out. In 1994, the Marketing Director of the English Tourist Board said, 'People come here for our "heritage", our arts, our fashion and our countryside. Royalty is a branding device that pulls those attractions together.'[24] But branding devices do not a nation make. Nor does heritage, a point illustrated by the public reaction to the Windsor fire.

Because postwar attempts to modernize the monarchy failed, it seemed conservative, fusty and downright alien to a people who, on the whole, had embraced the social changes of the era. Therefore, far from being an example of British decline, popular scepticism about the Crown was a sign of progress, proof of the fact that the British had moved on since the Second World War. In 1957, John Osborne claimed that the Crown was 'the gold filling in a mouthful of decay'. Forty years later, it would be more accurate to observe that it was one of the last rotten teeth not to have been extracted from a mouth that was getting progressively healthier. As if in reply to the English Tourist Board, the Conservative MP George Walden sounded this warning against complacency in 1994: 'Anyone in authority who does not understand that huge swathes of the country, mostly those under forty and by no means on the left, have had it up to here with royalty, is putting the future of the monarchy at risk.'[25] What made the institution not simply alien to the British but actually unpopular was the Princess of Wales.

Diana managed to play the roles of traditional fairy-tale princess and modern girl-about-town – able to tango with a head of state one minute and go to a pop concert the next. She also paraded her social conscience. Since the reign of George III, one of the ways in which the British monarchy had justified its existence was by patronizing charities – what one historian has called 'the making of a welfare monarchy'. In 1994, Elizabeth II donated a total of £208,345 from her personal fortune to various charities.[26] But the manner in which most of the royal family carried out their charitable activity was as formal as the way they carried out other duties. Diana, on the other hand, visibly made an emotional, tactile compact with those she helped, whether hugging AIDS victims or consoling homeless youths.

At first, she injected new life into the institution but by the 1990s it had become painfully apparent that the rest of the royal family were incapable of following her. The result was that she had a negative effect on the institution, her glamour and compassion serving only to highlight how moribund and out of touch it had become. This had already occurred by the time the collapse of her marriage became public knowledge, but her more direct and personal exposure of the monarchy's failings from 1992 to 1997 put even greater distance between Crown and people. Charles' infidelity, her subsequent mental breakdown and the Palace's attempt to prevent Diana making capital out of the story turned her from a popular maverick into the biggest focus of anti-Establishment sentiment in Britain since John Lennon and it made her fatal collision with the Establishment almost inevitable. Her battle with the royal family culminated in the loss of her royal status and a forced reduction of her public duties. But hers was the moral victory. The 1996 BBC interview in which she warned that she would 'not go quietly' and staked a claim to be 'Queen of people's hearts' was a declaration of war. Traditionalists came to loathe her. A. N. Wilson, for example, claimed that she did 'more damage to the British monarchy than Oliver Cromwell'.[27]

Such ridiculously exaggerated reactions showed how worried the Establishment was about the monarchy in the 1990s. In 1993, an anonymous government minister observed, 'We are losing our reference points. Everywhere you look, the country's institutions seem to be falling apart.'[28] The panic was just as apparent within the liberal elite as it was among conservatives. They too were culturally disorientated by the decline of Britishness because they too perpetuated their power and status through the national institutions which ordinary Britons appeared now to disdain. One positive result of this alarm was that British intellectuals constructively re-engaged with the question of national identity after a period of more than ten years when most of them had done little except bleat about Thatcherite nationalism. In the *Independent on Sunday*, Ian Jack noted, 'Nothing seems to work as it used to: government, trains, banks, courts, the economy, the monarchy. Now even a royal palace blazes in the night. Fate frowns down.'[29] If there was no leadership, there was at least an attempt at crisis management. At a speech at the Guildhall, in the City of London, Elizabeth II announced the belated start of the modernization of the British monarchy. Through gritted teeth she declared, 'No institution – City, Monarchy, whatever – should expect to be free from the scrutiny of those who give it their loyalty.' It was fitting that the Guildhall was the venue for this admission, because it was from there that Sir Kenneth Clark had launched commercial TV in 1955; and with it the media revolution which the Windsors had spectacularly failed to manipulate. In January 1993, the *Mail on Sunday* revealed exclusively that a royal think-tank was being set up. A courtier was quoted as saying: 'the cement of our society is trust. When the police are trusted as little as politicians, and the morale of the Church of England is so low and the monarchy itself might be in jeopardy, it is time to ask ourselves, "What are we doing wrong?"'[30]

A year later, at the Queen Elizabeth II Conference Hall, Westminster, Charter 88 held a conference on the future of the monarchy, to which it invited a cross-section of opinion-formers. Formed in 1988 on the tercentenary of the Glorious Revolution, the organization was a worthy but ineffective pressure group for constitutional reform, a CND for its time. But the speeches made at its 1994 conference showed that for the first time in the twentieth century the future of the British monarchy was considered to be in serious doubt. The weight of the speakers' opinion mirrored public opinion, falling into three categories. A minority believed there was no need for any reform. Charles Moore concluded, 'By far the biggest present assault on our rights comes not from the Crown of the Windsors but from the strong diadem of European Union.'[31] A majority believed that the institution should be reformed, among them the authors Will Hutton and Marina Warner. Suggestions put forward included abolishing the clause in the 1688 Bill of Rights which forbids the heir to the throne from marrying a Catholic. More generally, moderates argued that far from threatening Britishness, the European Union might be the vehicle for its revival – not only offering subjects the chance to become citizens under an EU Bill of Rights, but also offering the royal family a chance to renew the Crown by mimicking their lower-profile Continental cousins like Queen Beatrix of the Netherlands.

A small group of speakers argued for a republic. They accepted that they were a minority in Britain as a whole, but tried to explain why this might not always be the case. The playwright David Hare argued that the nation simply lacked the courage of its convictions: 'We know in our hearts that the monarchy is a historical absurdity. But because we lack the courage to abolish it . . . We shall mock them till they wish they had never been born.'[32] Like most republicans he lacked the courage of his own convictions, and accepted a knighthood when it was offered to him by Tony Blair in 1997, dutifully bowing at the feet of a Queen he had once urged Britons to mock mercilessly. The veteran Scottish republican Tom Nairn likened the situation to the end of a romantic novel:

> We are only debating the future of the monarchy because it has none. 'Modernisation' – the chorus of the salvationists already means something uncomfortably close to resurrection . . . What is it that has died? Not the sovereign or the institution, but the enchantment – a near-universal romance with the Crown, coloured by adulation and protected by a strong emotional taboo . . . Suddenly it appears to have reached the end of the tale. Sighing deeply, it rubbed its eyes as if waking up, and threw the book away.[33]

Sadly, there was to be a dramatic epilogue which allowed a compelling sequel to be written.

4. A very British girl who transcended nationality

The death of Diana, Princess of Wales was the most traumatic British bereavement of the twentieth century, comparable in scale to that experienced by the United States in 1963 when President Kennedy was assassinated. Although the grief displayed at the funerals of George VI, Winston Churchill and Earl Mountbatten was not cauterized, Diana's prompted an arterial explosion of feeling. Unlike those august men, she died when she was still young, at the height of her fame, and she had a larger base of support – one that included what her brother, Earl Spencer, described as 'a constituency of the rejected'. In a post-modern medley of comparisons, journalists compared her to Marilyn Monroe, Princess Grace of Monaco, Eva Perón, Mother Teresa and Princess Caroline of Brunswick. But, in the end, none of these historical comparisons struck as much of a chord with the British as Diana's contemporaneity, one fixed in the national consciousness by the Prime Minister's description of her as the 'People's Princess'. Blair's memorable phrase did two things. First, it co-opted Diana's popularity for New Labour, just as the Falklands conflict had been co-opted by Margaret Thatcher fifteen years earlier. Second, it confirmed Diana's reputation as the only royal to whom ordinary Britons could relate. But the most important thing about Blair's speech was that it formed a prelude to a concerted effort to rescue the British monarchy from itself.

Two major themes emerged: whether the monarchy had a future, and what the public's response to the death of Diana said about British society as a whole. Some commentators claimed that the sea of candles and flowers and weeping in the streets of the capital showed that Britain had become a more Mediterranean country, its Protestant, northern European reserve undermined by mass grief. Others detected a feminization of British culture. Both claims were bogus. The sight of Prince Charles and Diana's brother, Earl Spencer, crossing themselves during the funeral procession would have caused uproar a generation earlier. But the fulsome, variegated religiosity of the event only highlighted changes that had already taken place in the patterns of British worship. As for the wobbling of the stiff upper lip, this too was nothing new. VE Day showed that the British were quite capable of letting their hair down. So too did major sporting occasions and the pop and rock festivals which became such a feature of British life after the 1960s. There *was* a reformation of British manners in the postwar period but it was apparent at least thirty years before Diana's death.

Some believed that Diana's death had plunged the monarchy into its deepest crisis yet. In the extraordinary week between the Princess's death and her funeral, there were some grounds for thinking this. The level of grief clearly took the Windsors by surprise. Secluded at Balmoral, they appeared yet again to be remote from the nation which they claimed to embody. Their forced return to London by popular demand (whipped up, of course, by the tabloid press) recalled Louis XVI's return to Paris from Versailles before the French Revolution. The move was not a runaway success. Greeting mourners outside Buckingham Palace who everyone knew had been queuing for several hours, the Duke of Edinburgh asked, 'Have you been here long?' The Queen did not fare well either. The broadcast from Buckingham Palace in September in which she belatedly celebrated Diana's life was about as moving as her annual Christmas broadcast. In the months that followed, she was visibly more pained at the decommissioning of the royal yacht *Britannia* than she had been at the Princess of Wales' funeral. But more than anything, the funeral itself revealed just how badly the British monarchy had got it wrong since the 1960s.

The high point was the speech made by Earl Spencer in Westminster Abbey. In the long tradition of the aristocracy providing constructive criticism of the Crown, Spencer used it to launch a blistering attack on the House of Windsor.

> Diana was the very essence of compassion, of duty, of style, of beauty. All over the world she was a symbol of selfless humanity. All over the world, a standard bearer for the rights of the truly downtrodden, a very British girl who transcended nationality. Someone with a natural ability who was classless and who proved in the last year that she needed no royal title to continue to generate her particular brand of magic.[34]

Spencer condemned the press's hounding of his sister, pointing to the irony that Diana, named after the mythical goddess of hunting, came to be 'the most hunted person of the modern age' (a point originally made by the American feminist Camille Paglia).[35] He concluded by attacking not the press but the stifling, unreal world of the Windsors, pledging to defend the Princes against it. In St James's Park, where thousands were watching on specially erected screens, a wave of applause swelled, then rolled down the Mall and Whitehall to the crowds outside the Abbey. After a visibly awkward pause as the congregation inside wondered what to do, the applause broke through the great doors of the Abbey, swept up the aisle and crashed around the Windsors, who were seated, angry and bewildered, before the high altar. The next day, press and people were virtually unanimous. The British monarchy had got to change, and change fast. 'The nation unites against tradition', said the *Observer*.[36]

Mohammed Al Fayed's claims that his son and Diana were assassinated by MI6 on the instructions of the Duke of Edinburgh have to be treated with as much caution as the curse of any Egyptian pharaoh whose pyramid is robbed. But the contempt with which the allegations were dismissed displayed a conceit about British democracy which the Americans as well as the Egyptians found risible. Whatever the truth about her death, it cannot be denied that it was eerily convenient. The prospect of the heir to the British throne having as his stepfather (and possibly stepbrother) a Muslim from a family of Middle Eastern businessmen was removed overnight. And whatever the outcome of that particular relationship might have been, Diana's death removed a woman who had challenged the assumptions on which the institution had been based since the late nineteenth century.

From her throne in the House of Lords, Elizabeth II opened the 1998–9 parliamentary session with the words, 'My government's second legislative programme, like the first, will focus upon the modernisation of the country.'[37] Her own rehabilitation effectively began a year earlier with carefully staged celebrations of her golden wedding anniversary in September 1997. The central event was a 'People's Banquet' at the Banqueting Hall in Whitehall in which ordinary Britons like nurses sat next to royalty and politicians. Though no one noticed it at the time, the venue was an appropriate one, for it was from that Hall that Charles I had stepped out onto the scaffold to meet his death in 1649.

The first two Labour Party leaders, Keir Hardie and George Lansbury, were both avowed republicans. In 1924, the latter had threatened George V with the spectre of Cromwellian regicide should the King not allow Labour to form its first, minority government;

and Lansbury was rewarded with threats of assassination for what royalists saw as a treasonable outburst. However, from the mid-1920s onwards, Labour leaders, from Ramsay MacDonald through to James Callaghan, were ardent champions of the crown. They actively stifled republicanism in the party, most adherents of which were intellectuals (Attlee once dismissed republicans as 'bourgeois radicals'). When dealing directly with the royal family, Labour politicians were even more unctuous than their Conservative counterparts. The last senior figure to doubt publicly whether Britain should be governed in this way was Stafford Cripps in 1934, not long before he was expelled from the party. Labour leaders distanced themselves from nineteenth-century republicanism because they knew it was electoral suicide not to and because, as Labour became a party of government, many simply fell in love with the grandeur of the institution.

Tony Blair faced a different problem. In 1997, the future of the crown, not that of the Labour Party, was at stake. Genuflecting at weekly audiences, Privy Council meetings and garden parties might forge an alliance between the Palace and No. 10 from which a rescue operation could be launched. But much more was needed for it to be successful. If British national identity was to be resurrected in the twenty-first century, if the island's people were once more to have a sense of cultural community, then their faith in the last bastion of Britishness had to be restored. It was a task which required all the verve which Tony Blair had brought to the resurrection of the Labour Party. For inspiration, he turned to the Conservative Prime Minister from whom he had already borrowed the promise to build 'One Nation', the man who had rescued the monarchy over a century earlier: Benjamin Disraeli. In a toe-curling speech at the 'People's Banquet', Blair looked a clearly embarrassed sovereign in the eye and promised to be her Disraeli. In the years that followed, the Windsor relaunch was assisted by a chastened and more quiescent tabloid press and by obsequious TV reporting. Following on from the People's Banquet, the Queen and the Duke of Edinburgh were presented as a caring, friendly and down-to-earth couple. Both the futility and the danger of doing this was demonstrated on many occasions – particularly when the Duke made reactionary comments about immigrants and foreigners at public engagements, forcing the Palace to issue hurried disclaimers.

The Queen's inadequacies were just as apparent. In July 1999 she visited the home of a working-class Glaswegian family. It was not the first time that she had taken tea on a housing estate, but it may turn out to be the last. The Palace distributed a picture of the encounter to the press. Taken by David Cheskin, it captured the fragility of the British monarchy as surely as Van Dyck had captured it in the mid-seventeenth century. Among the portraits of Elizabeth II's own reign, the most telling comparison is with Cecil Beaton's Coronation study of her. Set against the backdrop of Westminster Abbey, orb and sceptre in hand, Beaton captured the majesty of Elizabeth II at a moment when the British monarchy seemed assured of a happy and glorious future. Cheskin's Glasgow portrait, on the other hand, reveals a sovereign who is distant from her subjects, uneasy in their company and frankly bewildered at the requirement thrust upon her to draw closer to them. She is divided from the housing official and the resident, Susan McCarron, by a formally laid out table. Tea and biscuits are untouched. The Queen looks into the middle distance, a smile fixed on her face (what Amanda Foreman has called the 'Regal rictus') while her two subjects return the smile with deadpan expressions, looking not in awe but indifference.[38] Also worth noting is the position of Mrs McCarron's son James. Children were central to the iconography of Diana. Usually shown cuddling her, they highlighted the Princess's maternal warmth and general affinity with the vulnerable. In addition, they associated her with youth and, therefore, the nation's future. The Glasgow portrait, on the other hand, shows the Queen's lady-in-waiting talking to James on the sofa at the rear of the picture. Picking his nose while looking away, he seems even more indifferent than his mother to what is being said; no physical contact is taking place, and the Queen is completely separate from, indeed almost oblivious to, the child's presence. All in all, the contrast with the Princess of Wales could not have been more pointed nor more poignant. The event was, as the *Daily Mail* cleverly put it, 'TEA FOR ONE'.[39] The government had more luck with Diana's elder son, William. Blessed with his mother's looks and style, he reportedly combined the Windsors' legendary gravitas with her ability to communicate with ordinary people.

Most Britons wanted the monarchy to be modernized; they did not want it to be abolished. Around three quarters hoped it would continue but in a more democratic and approachable form. Between 1953 and 1977, the number of Britons favouring a republic rose from 9 per cent to only 10 per cent, with brief fluctuations of between 16 and 19 per cent in the period 1964–71.[40] But after all

the royal scandal during the crisis years 1992–7, by the end of the
century republicans still made up a mere 20 per cent of the British
population, of whom only 8 per cent were judged to be a hard core
of committed ideologues.[41] The 400-strong Movement Against the
Monarchy issued amusing slogans like 'The monarchy debate: do we
hang them or shoot them?' but they failed to impinge on the public
consciousness. Furthermore, the person most Britons cited as the best
potential President was Princess Anne. It was hardly a ringing
endorsement of republicanism. In January 1999, the three hundred
and fiftieth anniversary of the execution of Charles I went unnoticed
by the British people. In November that year, Australians – the
people who for so long had warned the Windsors to adapt or die –
voted in a referendum to retain the Queen as Head of State. Figures
on British expectations of the future showed some uncertainty. A
poll taken by Gallup a week after Diana's death showed a rise in the
number of people who thought the monarchy would survive into the
next century; up to 71 per cent from 65 per cent in 1994. By 1999,
this had fallen again to 47 per cent.[42]

But whatever the eventual outcome, another problem Blair faced
which his predecessors had not was that by the time he came into
office the monarchy was seen as an English institution. A minor fillip
had been given to its standing in Wales by the Investiture of the
Prince of Wales in 1969, but it had had no lasting effect. In Scotland,
the situation was worse. The survey cited above also looked at the
components of national identity and discovered that the monarchy
did not even register in England's partner nations. The closest that
either nation came to expressing royal sentiment was that 40 per cent
of Scottish respondents cited William Wallace as a source of pride.[43]
The so-called 'Floral Revolution' of September 1997 had even less
effect on Scottish opinion than the lump of sandstone that John
Major delivered to the borders in 1996. Though the media gave no
indication of different responses to the death of Diana, mourning for
the Princess of Wales was nowhere near as intense nor as extensive
in Scotland as it was elsewhere on the island. It was more of a truce
than a reunification, in which national differences on the island were
briefly forgotten. The Scottish historian Christopher Harvie has
written, 'The contrast between a decorous truce in the north and
uninhibited orgies of grief in London suddenly seemed to crystallise
civic differences, growing for so long.'[44] Those differences were not
helped by the fact that Diana's death highlighted the Englishness of

the monarchy. Strident calls for the Queen to leave Balmoral and 'rejoin her people' by returning to London irritated Scots, as did Elton John's farewell to 'England's Rose'.

It is important not to exaggerate the effect of the monarchy's survival on national identity in Britain. The survival of an institution does not mean that it still commands the active affection of a people; still less that it acts as a bond between them, helping to define who they are as a nation. Were a poll to be taken, few in Scotland, Wales or England would wish their churches to be abolished. But, as we have repeatedly seen, although Protestantism remained a feature of Britain's cultural landscape, it was no longer a mainstay of national identity. Nor would most people want the BBC to take advertising, but that does not stop them watching ITV and satellite television in droves. Similarly, Britons may not have wanted to leap into the republican light, but few now saw the monarchy as anything other than a soap opera that was periodically given some gravitas by pageantry and social work. However much they were 'modernized', the royal family were now regarded as the curators of one particularly colourful aspect of the island's heritage.

The Diana cult waned quickly. The decline of the British monarchy was confirmed by the lukewarm public response to the marriage of Prince Edward to Sophie Rhys-Jones in 1999. Tabloid pictures of the new duchess having her breasts exposed in the back of a car by a disc jockey and game-show host demonstrated that admitting a woman into the royal family whose profession was public relations was a mixed blessing. The public's response was predominantly one of amusement. The couple's choice of title – the Earl and Countess of Wessex – was borrowed from a defunct Anglo-Saxon kingdom which until then was best known as a marketing device by the tourist industry of western England. It seemed to confirm that even a self-consciously modern royal couple could not, or did not wish to, shed the Ruritanian image of the British monarchy. Far more public interest was shown in the wedding of David Beckham to Victoria 'Posh Spice' Adams the same year. A footballer and a pop star, they represented the modern focal points of national identity in Britain, and as celebrities well versed in the art of showmanship they did it so much better. The main picture of the couple's wedding reception, in which they were seated on ornate, gilded thrones, highlighted the extent to which the Windsors had been removed from theirs in the popular imagination.

In 1985, the Poet Laureate, Ted Hughes, wrote these startling lines to celebrate the Queen Mother's eighty-fifth birthday:

> It was an eerie vision! The Land of the Lion!
> Each clear creature, crystal-bright,
> Honey-lit with lion-light,
> All dreaming together the Dream of the Lion.
> But now the globe's light hardens. The dreams go.
> And what is so is so.
> The awakened lands look bare.
> A Queen's life is hard. Yet a Queen reigns
> Over the dream of her people, or nowhere.[45]

Poetically the best of the postwar laureates, Hughes was also the most passionate royalist of them all. His view of the crown and its role in British society was related to his vision of the natural world. He saw society, like nature, as a brutal world, its violence sanctioned yet also contained by an organic, hierarchical order. As beast, the Lion was king of the animal world; as an emblem of the crown it represented the British nation. Like Enoch Powell, Hughes recognized that the life of a nation is lived largely in the imagination. He saw what it was in a mass democracy that maintained a people's faith in such an archaic and profoundly undemocratic institution: the dream of a united nation in which all its contradictions were resolved in an idealized image of the monarch.

Hughes also saw how fragile that relationship was. Daylight comes; dreams go. Whatever constitutional experts might say, Elizabeth II no longer reigned effectively over the British because she no longer reigned over their dream of who they were as a people. The political establishment might do everything at its disposal to protect the institution around which the British state was constructed – even, perhaps, disposing of the one person whom its citizens truly loved. But what the Establishment could not do was to restore Britons' *love of the institution of monarchy*. The comments made by republican intellectuals at the Charter 88 conference therefore bear repeated examination. The clearest indication of this was the plummeting viewing figures for the Queen's Christmas message to the nation. From the first TV broadcast in 1958 through to 1988, it attracted an average of 30 million domestic viewers. By 1993 this had fallen to 16 million and by 2001 it had virtually halved again, to 8.7 million.

Some commentators compared the decline of the monarchy to the collapse of communism in the Soviet Union. In the *Sunday Express*,

Diana's amanuensis, Andrew Morton, observed: 'Essentially, people in Britain are coming to terms with the collapse of this strand of ideology . . . in the same way the Russians are coming to terms with the collapse of communism.'[46] Yes. Except that the British were coming to terms with the collapse much less easily than the Russians were with theirs. And among the people of the UK, none more so than the English. The English clung on to the crown longer than the Scots and Welsh, just as they clung on to the legends of the Second World War. This was demonstrated by the continuing passion with which Wembley crowds sang the national anthem at England football matches a quarter of a century after the Scots and the Welsh had stopped doing so when their teams were playing. But although the monarchy was more popular in the south, it *was* in decline there too, particularly among the young. A survey of English teenagers commissioned by the *Sunday Times* in the autumn of 1997 found that 30 per cent regarded the national anthem as something 'which defines your nationality'. But only 14 per cent thought that the royal family did, compared to 36 per cent for the nation's football team and 17 per cent for *Coronation Street* and *EastEnders*. The monarchy may have become a soap opera, but even in that inglorious context the scriptwriters' conference established by the Blair government was clearly not pulling in viewers (intriguingly, despite a century in which the Windsors had desperately tried to shed their German connections, a full 10 per cent thought that the Queen was German).[47]

Because the crown had formed such an integral part of Anglo-Britishness, the decline of the monarchy meant that the English had less to fall back on in order to rebuild their shattered sense of self. Since the 1970s, Tom Nairn had been making a provocative link between constitutional monarchism and racist nationalism, arguing that the lack of a truly democratic narrative of Englishness explained why the country lurched from the worship of 'a semi-divine Constitution and the Mother of Parliaments to the crudest racialism'.[48] In 1994, he reiterated the claim:

> The Royal Family was the symbolic ethos of a state structurally at risk from genuine ethnicity . . . [In particular] the Windsor monarchy has been a glorious conjuring trick for sublimating the entrails of Englishness. Over-identification with the monarchy carried England into an odd neglect of the native self. Neglect can be a form of repression and repression breeds its own return. A nation defined at one end by the Royal Household has the Chelsea

Casuals and Essex Man at the other. Ask any representatives of Black Britain as they know all about the latter.[49]

Nairn did not address the question of why Continental republics like France had a worse record than any British nation when it came to political extremism. But he was undoubtedly right to posit the decline of monarchism as a largely English *problem* even though it had serious implications for the whole island. Before discussing the English Question, we must first look more closely at the haemorrhaging of Britishness in Scotland and Wales, and the transfusion which the Blair government administered in a desperate attempt to prevent the death of the Union.

5. We are the creative workshop of the world

One solution to the crisis of British national identity that was briefly in vogue among the English metropolitan elite in this period was the 're-branding of Britain'. The idea was that government and business should cooperate to jazz up the island's image in order to help British companies sell their goods abroad and to rebuild national unity at home. It was first mooted by the liberal think-tank Demos, in a pamphlet by one of its researchers, Mark Leonard. *Britain: Renewing Our Identity* argued:

> Britain's identity is in flux. Renewed national confidence in the arts, fashion, technology, architecture and design has coincided with the departure from Hong Kong, devolution, further integration with Europe and the imminence of the millennium. Around the world, however, Britain's image remains stuck in the past. Britain is seen as a backward-looking has-been, a theme park world of royal pageantry and rolling green hills, where a draught blows through people's houses . . . The old stereotypes of Britain having bad weather, poor food and stand-offish people still dominate perceptions. . . . British products are seen as low tech and bad value; British business is seen as strike-ridden and hostile to free trade . . . Renewing Britain's identity will be a slow burn not a quick fix. But, if we start now, it will not be long before some of

the benefits start to flow and within a generation we could again be seen as one of the world's pioneers rather than as one of its museums.[50]

Listing at length recent British achievements, the pamphlet offered 'six stories' as 'a toolkit for a new identity'. What they all came down to was the idea of a 'Creative Island'.[51] It didn't get very far. British Airways were criticized by Mrs Thatcher for replacing the Union Jack on their tailfins with a range of 'ethnic' designs and in 1999 were forced to return to red, white and blue due to public demand.

The aspect of rebranding which briefly caught the public imagination was 'Cool Britannia'. The term was originally the title of a song by the Sixties British group the Bonzo Dog Doo-Dah Band; it was then borrowed by the hippy Californian ice-cream manufacturers, Ben and Jerry, as a name for their strawberry and cream flavour product. In its New Labour incarnation, 'Cool Britannia' was used to describe the idea that Britain was a uniquely creative nation. It went hand in hand with Tony Blair's attempt to draw pop stars, designers, actors, and comedians into the New Labour project. More than that, it reprised the 1960s idea of a Britishness based less on ancient institutions and landscapes and more on a meritocracy of creative talent. In the spring of 1998, four silver pods appeared, like spaceships landed from Mars, in Horse Guards Parade in London. Normally, Horse Guards was the scene of Trooping the colour – a relic of late imperial Britishness and the UK's equivalent of the Kremlin march past. The pods housed a temporary exhibition called 'Powerhouse UK', designed to parade creative Britain and to demonstrate how economically important it was. In the exhibition leaflet, the Minister for Trade and Industry, Margaret Beckett, asserted, 'We can say we are the "creative workshop of the world".'[52] Not surprisingly, those who found themselves at the centre of all this attention liked it at first. The artist Tracey Emin told the *Guardian*: 'It's a good time to be British, especially for an artist. I wouldn't say I'm proud to be British, but for the first time, I'm not ashamed to be British. Britishness is looking out of a bus window, seeing sexy, stylish people laughing.'[53] Although Continental magazines were full of articles on 'Cool Britannia', the British were less impressed.

The idea failed for the same reasons that its progenitor had during the 1960s. Conservatives believed that traditional Britishness was being rubbished. The left were offended by the fact that rebranding had a strong commercial element to it and accused the project of further 'dumbing down' British culture. The contempt for mass democracy which had dogged the reformation of Britishness since the war, from commercial television to the heritage industry, showed itself to be in fine fettle. But above all, the idea failed to register in Scotland and Wales. Britishness had primarily been undermined by the economic decline of both countries and no amount of rebranding could make good the deficit. By 1999, British music accounted for a fifth of the world market, making it the nation's biggest export after whisky. British films amounted to a tiny proportion of those produced in the English-speaking world yet won on average a third of the Oscars.[54] But however much the creative industries were worth, they were based almost entirely in the south-east and the wealth they generated benefited few outside the region. The idea of 'Creative Britain' was therefore associated in Scotland and Wales with the rich, self-regarding southern elite whom they blamed for their troubles.

The fiasco of the Millennium Dome highlighted the strengths and the weaknesses inherent in Blair's attempt to resuscitate Britishness. Its site, on the Meridian Line in Greenwich, was not simply a geographically appropriate place to celebrate the millennium. The meridian, in use by the British since 1767, had been universally adopted in 1884 as the measurement for longitude. It thus recalled an era when Britain was, by international agreement, the commercial centre of the world. The Millennium Commission was set up in February 1994 under the National Lottery Act of 1993 with the intention of using Lottery money to mark 2000. In a speech in 1995, the Tory Heritage Minister, Virginia Bottomley, foresaw the project as a continuation of the VE Day celebrations:

> We believe there should be a single shared national experience in the year 2000 ... We can go forward into that new century positively, with excitement and high ambitions and as one nation ... The lesson of all national monuments, all national celebrations, is that people want the sense of congregation, of coming together ... The Millennium Exhibition will deliver that shared celebration. It will have mass appeal. It will embrace the whole nation. It will be uplifting. It will be fun. It will be the best in the world.[55]

Unifying, uplifting, fun and the best in the world. These were precisely the themes that Herbert Morrison had outlined when he announced the Festival of Britain in 1947. But unlike the Festival, the Millennium Experience did not have mass appeal, except in the sense that for a few hours it added some extra excitement to the New Year's Eve parties of 1999. The reason why the event failed to live up to Bottomley's expectations is that British national identity had declined to such an extent that even the most brilliant exhibition was incapable of fostering that 'sense of congregation' that would once more add meaning to the words United Kingdom.

It was not until Tony Blair came to power and gave it his personal seal of approval that the project got the kick-start it needed. In a speech at the Festival Hall in February 1998, he declared, 'This is our Dome, Britain's Dome. And believe me, it will be the envy of the world.' Promising 'the most exciting day out in the world', he appealed to British–German rivalry. 'Greenwich', said Blair, 'is the place the millennium begins . . . if it was Berlin Mean Time, don't you think the Germans would do likewise?'[56] From the very start, left- and right-wing commentators hounded the government. Nostalgic for a time when Protestantism united the UK, Church leaders criticized it for playing down the religious significance of the millennium. It was, after all Jesus' birth which defined the event. The 'Faith Zone' erected in the Dome did not allay criticism by displaying all nine major religions practised in the UK. At the South Bank in 1951 there had been no separate religious display of any kind because Christianity was thought to be so integral to British life.

In her preface to the exhibition guide, Elizabeth II wrote:

> The great national exhibition housed in the Dome on the Meridian Line at Greenwich is a demonstration of our confidence and commitment to the future. Within the largest enclosed space on earth are many examples of the country's inventiveness and imagination. The Millennium Experience, in the same tradition as its predecessors, the Great Exhibition of 1851 and the Festival of Britain in 1951, provides a focus for the nation's celebrations at an important moment in our history, bringing together people from communities throughout the United Kingdom and from many other countries.[57]

The Queen was absolutely right. The Dome was, as she concluded, 'an inspiring vision of life in Britain in the new millennium'.[58] Its architecture and design were stunning; most of the exhibits achieved a fine balance between thought-provoking artistic installation and entertaining interactive technology. In a spirit of ambiguity, irony and pluralism, the Dome subtly conveyed a pride in British life, eschewing the patriotic bombast of its predecessors. Yet that was ultimately why it failed.

Unlike in 1851 or 1951, in 2000 Britishness could no longer be presented as a homogeneous national identity. Nor could the corresponding 'island story' be told using a straightforward linear narrative of progress. The section of the Dome which confronted Britishness was a testament to how much had changed in the half-century since the bulldozers moved in to demolish Herbert Morrison's South Bank site. 'Self-Portrait' was a huge drum on which were placed 400 pictures of things considered to be essentially British. These images were far more diverse than those in the Festival of Britain's 'Lion and Unicorn' pavilion and they were displayed in a more random way. Moreover, unlike the Festival, they were chosen by ordinary Britons (following a survey conducted among 13,000 individuals and groups) rather than by the exhibition's organizers. Inside the drum was a small exhibition summing up the main features of Britishness. The guide described it as follows:

> We encounter a display of what the UK people feel are their best assets – qualities including the 'British' sense of humour, creativity, inventiveness, culture and tradition. Within this a series of larger-than-life sculptures . . . offers a more critical view of the national persona and the weaknesses of society. The figures are in the tradition of British satire, from a comment about addiction, to an indictment of hidden racism.[59]

To the Dome's opponents, the mention of 'hidden racism' was less unsettling than the fact that the word British was encased in quote marks. Those little marks stuck two post-modern fingers up at the certain idea of Britishness which had framed the patriotism of previous generations.

The Dome's most serious failing was that it conveyed no sense of what it meant to be English, Scottish, Welsh or Northern Irish. Like most of the unionist Establishment, its organizers seemed not to understand that Britishness could not be revived simply by making vague statements about creativity. The island's core national identities had to be engaged with and, ultimately, celebrated. Even the Attlee government, which had been no friend of devolution, successfully used the Festival of Britain to celebrate the UK's constituent nations. The result was that the Scots, Welsh and Northern Irish regarded the Dome as an exercise in pragmatic vacuity even more than the English did. They stayed away in their millions. Officially it was the most popular attraction in the UK in 2000, with 6.5 million people visiting it during the course of the year, of which 88 per cent pronounced themselves satisfied. But that was a third of the number who had seen the Festival of Britain in 1951, and only a quarter of the number who had visited the British Empire Exhibition in 1924. Indications are that most visitors to the Dome were English or foreign. In the spring of 2000, the *Daily Record* gleefully reported that fewer than 400 tickets had been sold in the whole of Scotland.[60]

Like the Dome, the rebranding of Britain deserved to be taken more seriously than it was. As its exponents pointed out, no one was suggesting that something as complex as a nation could update its national identity merely by playing with its symbols as if they were corporate logos. Nor were they suggesting that Britain's heritage should be junked. Like the idea of Swinging Britain, that of Creative Britain was a laudable attempt to get to grips with the disparity between modern British society and the archaic symbols and narratives which still dominated official notions of Britishness. But in the end, both concepts lacked substance. Here is an example. In the *New Statesman*, the intellectual guru of the 'Third Way', Anthony Giddens, wrote:

> Social democrats ordinarily have had little interest in the idea of the nation, which they have regarded with some scepticism as a threat to international solidarity. Neoliberals, on the other hand, have tended to mix an assertive and isolationist nationalism with their advocacy of free markets. The Third Way seeks to find a new role for the nation in a cosmopolitan world . . . The cosmopolitan nation is an active nation . . . Nations in the past were in some large part propelled to unity through antagonism to others . . . Today national identities need to be sustained in a more open and discursive way, in cognisance not only of their own complexities but of the other loyalties with which they overlap. Implied is a more reflexive construction of national identity, a modernising project par excellence.[61]

It is hard to question the good intentions behind Giddens' position nor the quality of his thought as a whole. But in practice, statements like 'The cosmopolitan nation is an active nation' were as likely to galvanize Britishness as Ben and Jerry's strawberry and cream flavour.

6. I believe in Britain

The main reason for saving the British monarchy was to save the Union. Surveys carried out in the last few years of the century by political scientists confirmed what cultural observers had been saying for years: that Britishness was in serious, if not terminal decline. In 1995, a study sponsored by the Joseph Rowntree Reform Trust asked people to describe their nationality. It found that 64 per cent of Scots and 41 per cent of the Welsh thought themselves *more* Scottish and Welsh than British or *not* British at all. This compared to only 25 per cent of the English.[62] The prospect of devolution did little to stabilize the trend, never mind reversing it. A survey carried out by a special unit at Nuffield College, Oxford, at the end of 1997 detected a slight rise in the number of people whose Britishness was weak or non-existent: 66 per cent of Scots, 43 per cent of the Welsh and 26 per cent of the English.[63] There were three more worrying factors for unionists.[64]

First, the Nuffield study found that when asked what best described their nationality, regardless of economic considerations, the numbers returning to their core nationalities rose still further – 85 per cent of Scots, 63 per cent of Welsh and 34 per cent of the English. Second, when asked about the focal points of their nationality, the Scots and the Welsh all cited things which were exclusive to them. Each nation's countryside came first, with 84 and 72 per cent respectively. In Wales the national rugby team came second with 49 per cent (strangely, the Scots were not asked about football, though the likely figure would have been as high). This was followed by national folk music/male voice choirs (40 and 46 per cent) and community spirit (40 and 45 per cent).

The third cause for concern was the influence which age and class had on national identity. Nuffield found that those whose Britishness was rock solid tended to be over fifty, thus confirming that the bastion of unionism was the ever-shrinking wartime generation. The working classes were losing their sense of Britishness faster – 68 per cent declared themselves to be Scottish compared to 51 per cent of the middle classes. In England the difference between them was negligible. This reflected the fact that the poorest were the people worst affected by the weakness of the Scottish and Welsh economies.

It also confirmed Nuffield's key finding that economics continued to be a major factor in determining national identity, simultaneously undermining Britishness *and* limiting the desire for independence because of fears that Scotland and Wales would be even worse off on their own.[65]

The constitutional reforms made by the first Blair government were its greatest and most radical achievement. The policy was inherited from John Smith. Unlike his predecessor, Blair was not a devolutionist in principle – like most British politicians, he simply saw it as a means of holding the Union together – but his conviction on the subject was no less passionate for being pragmatic. However, it did mean that he was determined to control the new Parliament/Assemblies from London and prevent them deviating from the New Labour agenda. He also had to reassure Middle England that the Union was not under threat. In the Labour Party manifesto of 1997 he stated:

> I believe in Britain. It is a great country with a great history . . . The United Kingdom is a partnership enriched by distinct national identities and traditions. Scotland has its own systems of education, law and local government. Wales has its language and cultural traditions . . . A sovereign Westminster Parliament will devolve power to Scotland and Wales. The Union will be strengthened and the threat of separatism removed . . . The United Kingdom Parliament is and will remain sovereign in all matters.[66]

White Papers on Scottish and Welsh devolution were presented to the House of Commons in July 1997. They provided for a 129 seat Scottish parliament with law-making powers, the ability to raise or lower the tax rate by 3p in the pound and control over virtually all home affairs. Wales got a 60 seat Welsh Assembly with the power to do little except discuss and dispense the principality's annual Treasury grant. Fifty-six seats in the former and twenty in the latter were elected by proportional representation. Referenda were held on 11 and 18 September in Scotland and Wales respectively.

The 'Yes' campaigns were overshadowed by Diana's death on 31 August. But unlike 1979, they were supported by a majority Labour government at the height of its popularity and heavily committed to the cause. Whether by chance or design, 11 September was the seven hundredth anniversary of William Wallace's victory over the English at the Battle of Stirling. The Scots voted by three to one in favour of devolution – 74.3 per cent of the votes cast on a turnout of 60.4 per cent.[67] The Welsh result was embarrassingly close – 50.3 per cent in favour on a turnout of 51.3 per cent, with 6,000 votes the difference between the two sides. An electorate the size of a rugby crowd on a wet afternoon had brought devolution to the principality after a century of debate. Home Rulers could take heart from the fact that there had been a swing of 30 per cent in favour since 1979 (compared to 23 per cent in Scotland). However, the referenda results and those of the elections that followed demonstrated two essential truths about the national identities of each country in the late twentieth century – that the Scots wanted independence but had no wish to pay for it, and that the Welsh were content to have their Welshness recognized by the rest of the UK without taking substantial control over their own affairs.

In 1998, the SNP was riding high. Polls showed that at least 50 per cent of Scots wanted complete independence, the highest figure ever recorded. In the eighteen to thirty-four age group, it rose to 63 per cent. Moreover, most Scots thought that their country would be independent within fifteen years.[68] But during the course of the election campaign in 1999 the SNP's support slumped. The party's most famous backer, Sean Connery, flew in from the US. Connery exchanged his tuxedo for tartan but found rallying Scotland a tougher assignment than saving Britain from the likes of Goldfinger and Blofeld. On 6 May 1999, Labour won 38.8 per cent of the vote and formed a coalition with the Lib Dems, on a disgracefully low turnout of 58 per cent of the electorate. The SNP became the country's second largest party and official opposition, but with only with 28.8 per cent of the vote, lower than it achieved in 1974. Despite playing down their ultimate goal of independence, national- ists were scuppered mainly because they admitted that independence would not come cheap, even if Scotland obtained the bulk of North Sea oil revenue. One estimate put the start-up cost at £10 billion, with taxes having to rise to 38p in the pound to pay for it.[69]

At the opening of the Scottish Parliament on 1 July 1999, unionists breathed a collective sigh of relief. Symbols of Scotland's links with the rest of Britain abounded. The Parliament was temporarily housed in the General Assembly of the Church of Scotland while a new one was built. The Queen appeared in a fetching tartan outfit and was welcomed by Scotland's First Minister, Donald Dewar, 'not only as Queen of the United Kingdom but also with warmth and affection as Queen of Scots'. In the Queen's speech, Scottishness was defined along Blairite lines as 'entrepreneurial flair'. She concluded:

Scotland is all this and so much more: the grit, determination and humour, the forthrightness and above all the strong sense of identity of the Scottish people – qualities which contribute so much to the life of the United Kingdom. And these qualities reflect a Scotland which occupies such a special place in my own and my family's affections.

But in most respects, the ceremony emphasized the nation's autonomy. The Scottish crown was borne to the Parliament from Edinburgh Castle by the Duke of Hamilton, as it had been before the Union. The Queen presented MSPs with a mace – symbol of parliamentary authority since the twelfth century – which had been made specially. Folk singer Sheena Wellington sang Burns' radical poem 'A Man's a Man for a' That'. The thrust of the event was continuity with the pre-Union era. Winnie Ewing, victor of Hamilton in 1967 and the oldest MSP, began the chamber's business by declaring 'the Scottish Parliament which adjourned on 25 March in the year 1707 is hereby reconvened'.[70] The effect of this comment and others like it in the press was to perpetuate the myth that Scottish democracy had been interrupted by union with England and Wales, when in fact Scotland's eighteenth-century oligarchic rule had been replaced by parliamentary democracy during and partly because of that union.

For most Scots, the Parliament was a symbol of their nationality rather than the start of a new polity which they stood to gain from materially. Three-quarters thought that it would increase national pride and give them more say in how their country was governed, but only 50 per cent thought it would increase their standard of living. They were not far wrong, because the tax-raising powers of the Scottish Parliament were not utilized by the New Labour/Lib Dem regime to pay for greater public investment and because the jobs which devolution spawned – in the civil service, media and lobbying industries – largely benefited the professional classes.[71] So, if the getting of a Parliament was more important than what it did, were attitudes towards the English improved as a result? Sadly not.

Scottish intellectuals waxed lyrical about 'civic nationalism'. But in housing estates, pubs, factories and offices, the reality was rather different. One survey of young Scots found that 75 per cent felt antipathy towards their southern neighbours, commonly describing them as arrogant, aggressive, and untrustworthy, and 43 per cent felt that throughout the population, this sentiment was getting worse as a result of devolution.[72] The media began to report stories of English people resident in Scotland (of whom there were 1 million in total) who experienced vicious Anglophobia amounting to racism. Such behaviour had been a feature of Scottish and Welsh society since the 1970s. But thanks to groups like 'Settler Watch', Anglophobia became more organized in the 1990s and it began to be taken more seriously. In 1997, the Commission for Racial Equality finally agreed to consider complaints from English expatriates which, it reported, made up three-quarters of all cases north of the border (the rest were Asians attacked by Scots). The Scots were so fond of their new identity as a more liberal nation than England that most denied such racism existed – even when it apparently led to the murder of a nineteen-year-old boy in Balerno, his assailants shouting 'English bastard' as they kicked him to death.[73]

The Australian actor/director Mel Gibson stoked up Anglophobia with *Braveheart* (1995), allowing the SNP to use it in its election publicity. The film was a box-office hit because it circumvented the history of the Union and offered Scots a simple medieval tale of dastardly English villains and macho Scottish heroes assisted by sympathetic Irishmen. For some reason, Mary Queen of Scots – a female bon viveur who took an Italian lover – offered less of a rallying point. The comedian and actor Billy Connolly was one of the few public figures to attack the Balkanization of Scotland's national identity.

> *Braveheart* is pure Australian shite . . . William Wallace was a spy, a thief, a blackmailer – a cunt, basically. And people are swallowing it. It's part of a new Scottish racism, which I loathe – this thing that everything horrible is English. It's conducted by the great unread and the conceited wankers in the SNP, those dreary little pricks in Parliament who rely on bigotry for support.[74]

It is also worth pointing out that the main issue to vex the Scots immediately after devolution was the British Government's proposal to repeal Clause 28. A campaign, funded by millionaire SNP supporter Brian Soutar, culminated in an unofficial referendum which found that 87 per cent of the country was against the legislation – on the grounds, he said, that 'the Scottish Parliament was not elected to change the traditions and morals of the nation'.[75] Scottish homophobia in 1997 echoed that of 1967 when the country opposed Westminster's legalization of homosexual acts. After forty years of saying they were oppressed by the uncaring, narrow-minded English, how did the Scots proclaim their new autonomy? By opposing a mature, pastoral discussion of sexuality as part of their children's social education, on the grounds that it would encourage buggery in an otherwise heterosexual nation. In a 1999 lecture entitled 'Scotland's Shame', the composer James MacMillan attacked the survival of anti-Catholic prejudice, denouncing his native land as 'Northern Ireland without the guns and bullets'.[76] That such prejudice existed is beyond doubt. But, given the fact that Brian Soutar's main support came from Scotland's Catholic leaders, the words 'pot' and 'kettle' inevitably spring to mind.

The irony of MacMillan's comment was that Scottish national identity had come to resemble that of southern Ireland in the first half of the twentieth century: bitter, obsessed with its past and, despite protestations of Europeanness, deeply parochial. The notion that Scotland is the last English colony was not confined to tartan epics like *Braveheart*. The film of Irvine Welsh's novel *Trainspotting* (1996) was justly celebrated as a rambunctious portrait of urban life replete with sex, drug-taking and thieving. But though it had no time for Highland romanticism, *Trainspotting* captured a self-loathing in the Scottish psyche, born out of the same feeling of victimhood which Mel Gibson had pandered to. When the protagonist, Renton, is led into the countryside by his fellow junkies in a bid to escape the squalor of their lives, he tells them:

> I hate being Scottish. We're the lowest of the fucking low, the scum of the earth, the most wretched, servile, miserable, pathetic trash that was ever shat into civilisation. Some people hate the English, but I don't. They're just wankers. We, on the other hand, are colonized by wankers. We can't even pick a decent culture to be colonized by. We are ruled by effete arseholes. It's a shite state of affairs and all the fresh air in the world will not make any fucking difference.[77]

It was a far cry from *Whisky Galore* fifty years before. In Compton Mackenzie's story, the addiction was alcohol not heroin and the English were seen by a self-confident Scottish community as pompous but ultimately redeemable comrades who just needed to lighten up a bit.

Although Scotland had a generally lower standard of living than England and Wales, the Union had benefited the Scots throughout its 300-year history. Had it not occurred, Scotland (like its partners) would have been poorer, her Enlightenment less vigorous, her industrial revolution slower and her empire less extensive. With the exception of the Highland Clearances, ordinary Scots endured no

major injustice that the English did not endure between 1707 and
2000. No meaningful comparison can therefore be made with the
Irish experience of Union, in which millions were starved and killed
and repeated attempts were made to extinguish their religion, culture
and way of life – a task which the Scots had happily assisted the
English with.

The reinvention of Scottishness gave people north of the border a
more coherent ideological framework with which to demand redress
from a complacent British political Establishment. But the tortured
tartanry of the late twentieth century hampered Scotland's long-term
aim of becoming one of Europe's modern nations. Concluding his
monumental history of Ireland, Roy Foster wrote, 'If the claims
of cultural maturity and a new European identity advanced by
the 1970s can be substantiated, it may be by the hope of a more
relaxed and inclusive definition of Irishness, and a less constricted
view of Irish history.'[78] The same applies to Scotland. For, while
it could be said that the Scots went into the Union with their
eyes wide open, they looked set to come out of it with them half
closed.

Welsh national identity was settled in comparison. In a 1998
interview, Nicky Wire, guitarist of the Welsh group Manic Street
Preachers, said, 'there is a bitterness in the Welsh that is different
from anywhere else in the world'.[79] Different perhaps, but less
pronounced than in Scotland. The length and depth of Wales' union
with England prevented discontent from spilling over into mass
dislike of the English and a paranoid belief that all the principality's
ills were due to its larger neighbour. And because a Welsh parliament
had never negotiated a treaty with England, the two countries could
alter their constitutional relationship with fewer historical memories
troubling the negotiations. By 1997, the large measure of cultural,
economic and political autonomy which the principality had won
since the 1880s appeared finally to have blunted the appeal of Home
Rule and independence. The Welsh had flirted with nationalism and
got what they wanted from it.

At the opening of the Welsh Assembly on 26 May 1999, thirty
years after his investiture as Prince of Wales, Charles Windsor
praised the fact that Wales had survived the political storms of more
than 1,000 years 'like a grand and sturdy tree'.[80] Wales was a more
relaxed nation than Scotland. *Twin Town*, a similar but superior film
to *Trainspotting* released in 1997, told the story of a Swansea family
of odd-jobbers, junkies and wastrels who live in a caravan on waste

ground. With ingenuity and black humour the family triumph against corrupt businessmen and policemen. This exchange is typical:

DODGY (A London drug dealer): I won't keep you from your coal mine, lads. Fuck me! Everyone's got shoes on their fucking feet . . . and not a rugby ball in sight.
GREYO (A Swansea policeman): Yeah. And I been picking leeks all fucking morning . . . boyo! Two world wars and one world cup they won and you'd never fucking believe it.[81]

Twin Town eschewed the sentimental clichés of mid-century Welshness. Its tart refusal to humour the English and the Scots demonstrated a national self-confidence that was missing when Welsh leaders told Clement Attlee 'dread and fear of the future are widespread' and audiences cried their eyes out to *How Green Was My Valley*.

The Welsh were the first Britons, remnants of the Celtic tribes who inhabited the island before invading Romans, Saxons and Danes pushed them west. This lies behind the principality's oldest joke, that the Welsh are the Irish who couldn't swim. Gwyn A. Williams concluded his history of the country thus: 'Britain as we have known it appears to have started its own long march out of history. This history of the Welsh may close with the intriguing thought that the Welsh, First of the British, look like being the Last.'[82]

But did they have the last laugh? They certainly got no thanks for their loyalty. Surveying the principality in 2000, the English (and a good many Scots) concluded that the vigorous postwar assertion of Welsh nationality had been an extended exercise in petulant vanity by a people who had almost entirely fabricated their culture. In 1895, the *Encyclopædia Britannica* had the following entry: 'For Wales – see England'. The Welsh were no longer the forgotten people of Britain. But they were still regarded with appalling condescension by their fellow Britons. In 1989, the Welsh Affairs Committee of the House of Commons concluded that the rest of the UK saw the principality as a land of 'short dark men singing hymns in the shadow of slag heaps'.[83] A decade later, that was still largely true.

But when the Welsh decided independence was not in their interest it did not make them less of a nation. It simply made them, like the Scots, a canny one. Welsh national identity had fundamentally changed since 1945. Not only had its Victorian components like chapel-going and mining disappeared; more importantly, Britishness was now a minority sentiment and was secondary even for those who still felt it. Britishness in Wales was therefore vulnerable to further erosion, as the Blair government soon discovered. Assuming that Welsh loyalty could now be taken for granted, Blair put forward a decent but nondescript placeman, Alun Michaels, as First Minister. The Welsh wanted Rhodri Morgan, a maverick MP passionately committed to his homeland. This flouting of national wishes, coupled with disillusionment with Blair's conservatism, resulted in Plaid Cymru becoming the second largest party in the country. At elections for the Welsh Assembly in June 1999, it took 28 per cent of the vote on a turnout of 46 per cent. This was more than double the Party's previous best performance of 11.5 per cent in 1970 and placed it on an electoral par with the SNP for the first time in its history. Where that will lead is unclear. But the result was a sharp reminder that if the Welsh people were not taken seriously, they could reprise the embarrassments inflicted on earlier governments.

New Labour also had a moderately successful go at resolving the Irish Question. The Good Friday Agreement reached in Easter 1998 was, said deputy SDLP leader Seamus Mallon, 'Sunningdale for slow learners'.[84] It recommended a power-sharing executive and a Northern Ireland Assembly elected by PR. But it went further than Sunningdale because the Republic of Ireland gave up its constitutional claim to the province in return for a cross-border Council of Ireland. And this time the Agreement got the crucial support of Sinn Fein/IRA and Loyalist paramilitary groups. A referendum held on 22 May 1998 resulted in 71.1 per cent approving the deal. One was simultaneously held in the republic, making it the first time that the whole island of Ireland had voted together since the general election of 1918 just before partition (94 per cent of the republic were in favour). Power was devolved back to the province after twenty-five years of direct rule.

Serious problems remained. Only 52 per cent of unionists voted yes, a level of support which declined sharply, despite the IRA's belated and partial decommissioning of its weapons. One expert on Northern Irish identity, Steve Bruce, made this observation: 'There is no Northern Ireland "problem". The word "problem" suggests that there is a "solution": some outcome which will please almost everybody more than it displeases almost everybody. Conflict is a more accurate term . . . Conflicts have outcomes, not solutions. Somebody wins and somebody loses.'[85] The sad truth of this conclusion meant that the conflict on Britain's doorstep continued for some time after, even if it cost fewer lives than before and reached TV screens less often.

The tragedy of the Protestant majority in Northern Ireland was that even in a period of relative peace which had not been seen since the early 1960s, Britons did not renew their affections for the province. The UK had simply changed too much. Scottish, Welsh and English nationalists were too busy with their own struggles. Even those who still considered themselves to be Britons saw the province at best as an ethnographic museum of mid-twentieth-century Britishness. After thrashing out the Good Friday Agreement, Tony Blair hoped that 'today . . . the burden of history can be lifted from our shoulders'.[86] It was. But the shoulders which straightened up most were on the mainland.

In 2000, the Labour government announced that in 2007 there would be an official celebration of 300 years of union between Scotland, Wales and England. In reply to a question in the House of Lords by the Ulster Unionist peer Lord Laird about what events were planned to mark the bicentenary of the Union of Britain and Ireland in 1801, Foreign Office minister Baroness Scotland said 'None'. An irate Lord Laird told the press:

> Most countries would use their bicentenary as an opportunity to do something, but the only answer I've had is a four-letter word . . . I would have thought that, at the very least, there could be an official stamp . . . Look at the events the Americans and French organised for their bicentenaries. A country which forgets its history is doomed.[87]

The noble lord had suffered an attack of amnesia himself. The Union of 1801 had effectively ceased to exist in 1922 when Ireland was partitioned. The fact that he considered it to be in existence nearly eighty years later said much about the outlook of the Northern Irish majority, namely their lingering view that the South were rebels in Her Majesty's realm. Yet one has to feel for a people who officially remained part of the United Kingdom but whose history that state seemed content to erase because they were seen to be troublesomely anachronistic. However, Ireland was the least of Tony Blair's problems. England, having been left out of the vast constitutional changes of 1997–9, was at last getting restless about its own future.

7. Thirty years of hurt never stopped me dreaming

Surveying the national identities of the British people in 1942, Ernest Barker concluded that the English were the hardest to fathom: 'It is far from easy to discover the mind of the English or to know what an Englishman is. One can describe the *perfervidium ingenium* of Scotland, or the fire of Wales, or the stern sanity of Ulster; one is baffled by the riddle of England.'[88] That did not stop Barker continuing his quest to solve the riddle. In *The Character of England*, published in 1947, he said: 'We have taken into our stock, and accepted into our minds, many strains and many treasures. Yet there is an identity behind the mixture, which has made the mixture possible. We are more than an amalgam and more than a crucible.'[89] So what was the identity behind the mixture? Barker concluded that it contained five interlocking elements: the cult of the amateur and that of the gentleman; the voluntary habit; eccentricity; social harmony; and an eternal youthfulness.

By youthfulness he meant an ability to constantly recreate what England was: a fluidity which lay at the heart of democratic nationalism. Challenging Arthur Bryant's idea of a seamless, metaphysical 'union in space and time', he wrote: 'Not only is national character made; it continues to be made and re-made. It is not made once and for all; it always remains ... modifiable. A nation may alter its character in the course of its history to suit new conditions or fit new purposes'.[90] Barker was born in Lancashire, into a Nonconformist, Liberal-voting working-class family. When he taught political science at Oxford in the 1900s, one of his pupils was the young Clement Attlee, who counted Barker as the tutor who had the most influence upon him. Did that influence stop with Attlee? To some extent, yes. Few English people in the late twentieth century thought amateurism and gentlemanliness were national traits. But millions who had never heard of Ernest Barker began to share his belief that recreating English national identity was desirable as well as necessary. Or, as Julian Barnes put it in his 1998 novel *England, England*, 'So England comes to me, and what do I say to her? I say, "Listen baby, face facts. We're in the third millennium and your tits have dropped. The solution is not a push-up bra" '.[91]

By the end of the century, it was at last dawning on the English that their national identity was no longer reciprocated by most of their partners in the United Kingdom. Although Ulster Protestants were now thoroughly alien to the English, the two did have something in common with each other. Like the Northern Ireland majority, the English were the victims of unrequited love, puzzled as to why former compatriots had rejected what seemed to them to be a fruitful relationship. The English found that the island which they inhabited was fast becoming – against their will – a piece of rock they shared rather than a national community they lived in.

In 1994, the playwright Dennis Potter was dying from pancreatic cancer. He recorded a moving last interview with Melvyn Bragg in which he said:

> I find the word British harder and harder to use – we English tend to deride ourselves far too easily because we've lost so much confidence, because we lost so much of our own sense of identity, which had been subsumed in this forced Imperial identity which I obviously hate. But we were at the same time, both a brave and a steadfast people, and we shared an aim, a condition, a political aspiration if you like, which was shown immediately in the 1945 General Election, and then one of the great governments of British history . . . I love England, and when I'm abroad I genuinely feel homesick . . . I've always loved my country, but not flags and drums and trumpets and billowing Union Jacks and busby soldiers and the monarchy and the pomp and circumstance and all that, but the real – something about our people that I come from and therefore respond to.[92]

From 1994 onwards, national newspapers began to be filled with correspondence from the public calling for the English to respond to the challenge of Scottish and Welsh nationalism by rediscovering their own nationality, and celebrities from Ray Davies and David Bailey to Jimmy Hill lined up to tell the press what they liked about being English. The columnist and former Tory MP Matthew Parris commented, 'far from having been overtaken or destroyed, English nationalism is actually the most potent of the four nationalisms found on our island . . . I have a hunch that their secret nationalism will resurface powerfully in the century ahead'.[93]

How did the English rediscover themselves? Not only had the

institutions of Anglo-Britishness fallen into disrepute, vital elements of the national character had also been thrown into doubt. The belated acceptance that for half a century English society had been profoundly racist made it harder to celebrate tolerance as a virtue. Also, the greed of the Thatcher era made it harder for them to claim that they were a people with a social conscience. Pop music offered one sanctuary. In 1994 the Britpop group Blur explained that their songs were 'about Englishness rather than being British'. Lead singer Damon Albarn said:

> There was a time when pop music wouldn't have been able to explain what being English was all about, but that's changed now. If you draw a line from the Kinks in the Sixties, through The Jam and The Smiths, to Blur in the Nineties, it would define this thing called Englishness as well as anything.[94]

The trouble was that pop groups, more than any other participants in 'Cool Britannia', were unwilling to harness themselves to a definite cultural movement. They were even less inclined to be associated for too long with any political party, for fear that they would lose their street credibility and with it their record sales. Instead, the English found a sense of direction in football.

The national football team had become steadily more important to the English since 1954, but as late as the World Cup of 1990, the patriotism it generated was still contained within a British identity. During the European Championships of 1996 the sport began to be recognized as the focal point of a new, self-conscious and separatist Englishness, and football patriotism acquired a sharper political edge than it had during the emotive debates in the 1980s about hooliganism. Shortly before the tournament began, the historian David Starkey wrote an article in *The Times* bemoaning 'The Death of England'. Pointing to the public indifference to St George's Day, he said, 'England itself has ceased to be a mere country and become a place of the mind . . . England, indeed, has become a sort of vile antithesis of a nation.'[95] Two months later, it was clear that most people were in fact conscious of belonging to a country called England; an England that was not to them a vile antithesis of a nation but a vibrant one trying to rediscover itself by synthesizing the cultural changes of the postwar years.

Euro 96 was the first major tournament to be held in Britain since the World Cup exactly thirty years before, and from the start it resonated with history. The Chief Executive of the FA, Graham

Kelly, declared, 'Euro 96 will be a festival, not only of football but of the English way of life.' The ITV coverage of the tournament began each night with shots of the white cliffs of Dover accompanied by 'Jerusalem'. Wembley was a sea of St George's crosses and red-and-white-painted faces. There is no more potent symbol of how the English shed their Britishness than the comparison between the flags waved in 1966 and those waved in 1996. The anthem that the English sang during the tournament was also significant. 'God Save the Queen' gave way to a pop song – 'Football's Coming Home' – composed by the Liverpudlian Britpop band the Lightning Seeds, with words by the comics David Baddiel and Frank Skinner. Commissioned by the FA, the song showed how important 1966 was to the English. When questioned about its blokey nationalism, Baddiel and Skinner said that it was a reply to 'people who knock England'.[96] But the song also revealed how much football now provided the English with a crucial sense of being an underdog. Whereas previous tournament songs had blithely assured the nation that the team were going all the way, 'Football's Coming Home' captured England's sense of departed glory and a bittersweet yearning for a different future.

The semi-final clash against Germany seemed to prove that the new Englishness was little more than a new vehicle for old hatreds. The *Sun* led with the headline 'LET'S BLITZ FRITZ!'; the *Star* followed with 'MEIN GOTT! BRING ON THE KRAUTS!', while the *Mirror* carried pictures of Paul Gascoigne and Stuart Pearce wearing tin helmets on its front page next to the headline 'ACHTUNG! SURRENDER! FOR YOU FRITZ, ZE 1996 EURO CHAMPIONSHIP IS OVER!' Inside, the paper's editor, Piers Morgan, couched his leading article in the style of Neville Chamberlain's BBC broadcast announcing the start of the war:

> I am writing to you from the Editor's office at Canary Wharf, London. Last night the *Daily Mirror*'s ambassador in Berlin handed the German government a final note stating that unless we heard from them by 11 o'clock that they were prepared at once to withdraw their team from Wembley, a state of soccer war would exist between us. I have to tell you that no such undertaking has been received and that consequently we are at soccer war with Germany. It is with a heavy heart we therefore print this public declaration of hostilities . . . May God bless you all. It is evil things that we shall be fighting against – the brute force, the high tackle, the unfair penalty, the Teutonic tedium of their tactics and the

pretence of injury after a perfectly legitimate English tackle.
Against these evils I am sure that inside right will prevail.[97]

The BBC was not immune to the jokey jingoism of the press. Radio
Five Live advertised its coverage of the match with the caption
'PREPARE FOR SOME AERIAL BOMBARDMENT'. The match was
watched by 26.2 million people, the highest ever for a British sports
broadcast and considerably more than the 25.21 million who
watched the Italia 90 semi-final against Germany. Given that most
of these people were English, that audience represents a significant
proportion of England's 49 million inhabitants. They were not all
driven by testosterone. Women and girls began to follow football in
substantial numbers for the first time. They made up approximately
15 per cent of attendances at club matches; many more watched the
sport on TV and a larger number (as yet unquantified) watched
England matches with all the patriotic fervour of men and boys.
'MICHAEL OWEN'S ENGLAND SHIRT TO BE WON! (UNWASHED!)'
proclaimed the girl's magazine *Sugar* in March 1997. By the mid-
1990s, they could buy the national team strip as a dress if they
preferred. Men did not object. Englishness therefore became a less
masculine identity than before; its popular focal point male in origin
but now leavened with feminine influence and the patriotism it
generated now a bond between the sexes rather than a gulf between
them.[98]
    Despite losing again to Germany in 1966, England won the FIFA
Fair Play award and the Press Complaints Commission ruled that
coverage of the event was 'part of a proud tradition' of British
nationalism which was leavened by humour and tolerance.[99] Not
surprisingly, Germans took offence. In 1999, the German Minister
for Culture, Michael Naumann, said: 'England is obsessed with the
war. It is the only nation in the world that has decided to make the
Second World War a sort of spiritual core of its national self,
understanding and pride.'[100] The Tory press erupted. The *Daily
Telegraph* was grateful that the war was now 'so deeply embedded
that it seems likely never to depart our national consciousness'.[101]
Both were wrong. In the space of four years since the VE Day
anniversary celebrations, England's obsession with the war was
waning almost as rapidly as elsewhere in the UK. Beating Germany
still mattered to the English. When they finally managed to do so, at
Wembley in 2000 and again, spectacularly, in Munich the following
year, there were delirious public celebrations throughout England.

But victory mollified the nasty, insecure nationalism which had surrounded the fixture since the 1960s. Moreover the really interesting thing about Euro '96, and the pointer to *why* English national identity was changing, is not to be found in vestigial Germanophobia but in what the tournament revealed about the country's attitudes to Scotland.

Polls showed that 75 per cent of Scots did not support England, while 40 per cent would prefer *any* team other than England to win the tournament.[102] The English began to accept this as the natural state of things and they reciprocated by refusing to support the Scots in any of their matches. The reality of devolution in 1997 shook all but the most myopic out of their complacency and it began a fundamental shift in their national identity. Patrick Tripp, sales director of the firm Turtle and Pearce, which had been making flags for state buildings since 1871, observed: 'Since Mr Blair has decided to let Scotland go its own way we in England have said sod you, we'll go our own way too, we'll look after ourselves. I think England is discovering a sense of itself.'[103] The English realized that not only were they detested by a great many Britons, but also that they were paying for the privilege. The system by which the Scots and Welsh received more in subsidy per head than they did had barely registered in the English consciousness for most of the postwar period. Now it became firmly lodged. So too did the fact that a large proportion of Britain's governing classes were Scots (in 1997, the four senior Cabinet posts were held by Scots and a further five Cabinet ministers hailed from north of the border). Whatever the justification for such prejudices, the important point is that they revealed a change in Englishness, which is necessary for most nationalist movements to thrive: that is, a sense that you are an oppressed, voiceless people. For the first time in several centuries, the English perceived *themselves* to be victims of injustice at the hands of their fellow islanders.

In 1998, the *Sun* launched a campaign to revive St George's Day. On the day itself, the newspaper published a special supplement which listed '100 REASONS WHY IT'S GREAT TO BE ENGLISH'. Top of the list of personalities was the Queen Mother. She was followed by the Beatles, Barbara Windsor, Shakespeare and Michael Caine, the last of whom was deemed 'the coolest English actor to step in front of a movie camera'. National customs listed included 'the great English cuppa', red phone boxes, Radio 4's *Today* programme, bingo, Wimbledon, fish and chips and Lancashire hot-pot. Among the more contemporary icons, Oasis were hailed as 'proof that

England is the home to the best rock 'n' roll'. Capping it all was a shot of the busty blonde page-three girl Melinda Messenger in a pink bikini on the white cliffs of Dover with the caption PEAKS OF PERFECTION. The *Sun* said:

> [This] is the day when we should all pay homage to the land of our birth. But how many will be wearing a red rose today? How many buildings will fly the flag of St George? What is it about the English that makes them so complacent about their birthright? In Wales, Scotland and Ireland they celebrate their saints' days. The French raise a glass or two on Bastille Day. The Americans have a ball on July the Fourth. But England? It's almost as if we are embarrassed to feel proud.[104]

For the first time since the Edwardian era, St George's Day became a feature of the English calendar.

By 2000, local authorities, assisted by the English Tourist Board, organized events all over the country, often on a grand scale. In 1995 the UK's largest greetings card retailer, Clintons, began selling St George's Day cards. The range was a mixture of new designs and reproductions of Edwardian cards. By 2000, it was selling 50,000 a year, with the number rising at a rate of 20 per cent each year. The Royal Society of St George, in decline since the 1940s, watched its membership quadruple to 20,000 in 1999. In the same year the ETB changed its name to the English Tourism Council and used the opportunity to change its official logo from an innocuous red rose to a fluttering St George's cross. Explaining its reason for doing so, the Council said:

> We were looking for an icon to take us into the twenty-first century and chose St George because he is emerging from the shadows after decades of neglect. As power is devolved to Scotland, Wales and Northern Ireland we are seeing a revival of English nationalism. The combination of the mythology of St George slaying dragons and his contemporary significance in a changing England makes him an ideal icon.[105]

A survey of English teenagers commissioned by the *Sunday Times* in the autumn of 1997 found that 66 per cent regarded themselves as English rather than British – twice the adult level at that time.[106]

Had the English become 'ninety-minute patriots', as Jim Sillars once described the Scots? Were they a people whipped into a frenzy when their team was playing, but incapable of translating their patriotism into a coherent national identity? Or were they finding a new voice that would provide the basis and inspiration for long-term political aspirations? All the evidence points towards the latter. By the end of the century, it was clear that the new Englishness was there to stay and that it was no longer confined to the irregular passions of football tournaments.

8. Emerging from the shadows

The revival of Englishness was not left to the *Sun*. Jeremy Paxman's brilliant anecdotal study *The English: A Portrait of a People* (1998) concluded:

> The English are simultaneously rediscovering the past that was buried when 'Britain' was created, and inventing a new future. The red-white-and-blue is no longer relevant and they are returning to the green of England. The new nationalism is less likely to be based on flags and anthems. It is modest, individualistic, ironic and solipsistic . . . based on values that are so deeply embedded in the culture as to be almost unconscious. In an age of decaying nation states, it might be the nationalism of the future.[107]

Interviewed in 1999, the novelist Will Self rejected what he called the 'white, middle class threnody of decline' of recent years.[108] He too celebrated the pluralism of Englishness:

> It is a culture of profound and productive oppositions . . . Is English culture bigoted or liberal? It is both. Is it hermetic and introverted or expansive and cosmopolitan? It is all of these . . . The youth of just about any English provincial city look infinitely cooler – to my mind – than their contemporaries in either Seattle or Turin . . . While the old idea of a monocultural landscape is impossible to sustain, England as the centre of that great rolling, post-colonial ocean of cultural ferment is alive and kicking. So I say: English culture is dead – long live English culture![109]

This was not merely wishful thinking. The clearest sign that the nation's identity was changing was its growing acceptance that to be English you did not have to be white.

By the century's end, half of the adult Afro-Caribbean and a third of the Asian population had been born in the UK. And over 78 per cent of children from all ethnic minorities were British by birth. Most maintained dual national identities – to England and to the country of origin of themselves or their older relatives. It was this which offended racists. Even the most Neanderthal accepted that black Britons were there to stay and could – despite Enoch Powell – be integrated. What they could not accept was that integration did not necessarily mean assimilation – that is, a complete and unquestioning of adoption of established notions of Englishness. In 1990 the Conservative politician Norman Tebbit put forward what he called the 'cricket test' as a way of defining Englishness. He argued that if black and Asian people wanted to be accepted by whites they had to support the English cricket team and no other. What Tebbit said, in other words, was that ethnic minorities could not have dual identities.[110] In July 1995, an article in *Wisden Cricket Monthly* – 'Is It In The Blood?' – went further. The author, Robert Henderson, was a former tax inspector, living on welfare in King's Cross, London. Henderson doubted whether 'an Asian or negro raised in England will . . . feel exactly the same pride and identification with the place as a white man'. 'A coloured England-qualified player' would have the same 'resentful and separatist mentality [as] the general West Indian-derived population' and would therefore be unlikely to play with the same commitment as someone who was 'unequivocally English'. Henderson concluded that blacks and Asians would never pass the cricket test and that consequently they should not be selected to play for the national team.[111] The dual identity of Jews who felt a simultaneous loyalty to Israel was not seen as a problem. Nor was that of the Scots and the Welsh, despite the fact that in many sports they had their own teams which were the source of anti-English feeling.

This bilious nonsense failed to register with most people for two reasons. First, because cricket was no longer a major component of Englishness. Thanks to the poor quality of the national team and corruption scandals worldwide, the sport was neither a source of patriotic pride nor a symbol of fair play. Second, the game which now captivated the nation – football – was one of the main public arenas where racial integration was clearly discernible. Black men have graced British football ever since Arthur Wharton, a Ghanaian with Caribbean and Scottish ancestry, turned out to play for the Staffordshire club Cannock in the 1883–4 season. At national level, Wales selected their first black player in 1930, and Scotland theirs in

1975. But it was not until 1979 that Viv Anderson became the first black man to play for the England team (the Republic of Ireland followed suit with Paul McGrath in 1985). Throughout the Isles hostility towards them was intense. But between 1985 and 1997, the number of black players in the English league doubled, and so talented were they that a disproportionately high number played in the Premiership.[112] The breakthrough came in November 1997, when Paul Ince became the first black Englishman to captain his national side, in a crucial World Cup qualifying match against Italy in Rome. Interviewed shortly afterwards, arms around team-mates David Beckham and Tony Adams, he told the millions watching, 'I'm English and I did it for my country.' It was a moment which did more for race relations than a dozen earnest reports by the Commission for Racial Equality.[113] After the 1998 World Cup, Spurs fans sang this tribute to the black England defender Sol Campbell to the tune of 'Qué Será, Será' – 'Sol Campbell, Campbell, he done his country proud, and now we're singin' loud, Sol Campbell, Campbell.' Lyrically, it may not have been a great addition to the canon of English popular song. But it was a far cry from the racist chants (often accompanied by bananas thrown on to the pitch) endured by footballers a decade or two earlier.

Examples could be drawn from all areas of national life. The influence of black music on British popular culture is inestimable. By the end of the century it had established a symbiotic relationship with white music. The English language changed, as whites began to incorporate West Indian patois into their speech. In the inner cities, this was often the result of peer pressure when white children were outnumbered by blacks. But peer pressure does not explain why words like 'wicked' (meaning 'great') crept into the football commentary of the BBC's John Motson, a man who once observed that it was difficult to tell black players apart.[114] By 1998, Indian cuisine was officially more popular than fish and chips. The Asian food industry had 8,000 outlets with a turnover of £2.5 billion per annum, employing (perhaps not surprisingly) more people than coal, steel and shipbuilding put together.[115] The local shop – that bastion of Englishness since the eighteenth century – was predominantly run by Asians, placing them at the heart of many local communities. By the end of the century, 70 per cent of independently owned grocery stores and newsagents in the UK were owned by south Asians alone. And finally, Trevor MacDonald, anchorman on ITN's *News at Ten*, became the nation's most popular newsreader, a trusted voice of authority who each weekday night sent millions to bed reassured that the world had not come to an end.

But the central point is this: not only were ethnic minorities producing national figureheads and customs that were accepted as English, whites were also starting to accept that ethnic minorities had as much right to dual identities as any other citizens of the UK. There was no backlash, for example, when the Anglo-Yemeni boxer Prince Naseem declared after one victory, 'I've carried the flag for England and the Arab world.'[116] And while the thought of a daughter bringing home a black or Asian boyfriend could still produce visceral clutch in many parents, miscegenation began to be more acceptable. By 2000, half of all British black men and a third of all Asian men had a white partner, while a third of women from both ethnic backgrounds were in mixed relationships.[117] These were some of the highest figures of any country in the western world, and they far outstripped the United States where miscegenation was still a taboo with harsh social consequences for those of any race who broke it.

Of course, this did not mean that brotherly love was breaking out everywhere. Unemployment among Afro-Caribbean Britons during the 1990s averaged 33 per cent; 27 per cent for Pakistanis/Bangladeshis; and 12 per cent for Indians – compared to 8 per cent for whites.[118] The situation was worst among young black males, many of whom saw no point in gaining educational qualifications. But defeatism does not account for the 130,000 incidents of racial abuse reported each year in the UK – that's one every four minutes.[119] In 1996, boys shouted racial abuse at the Anglo-Trinidadian goalkeeper Shaka Hislop until they realized who he was and asked for his autograph as if nothing had happened.[120] The incident demonstrated the extent to which black people were accepted only if they were celebrities. Not surprisingly, many black people still felt uncomfortable about supporting the England team (65 per cent according to one survey).[121] More dramatically, the murder of Stephen Lawrence, its bungled investigation and the right-wing hostility to the public inquiry condemnation of institutionalized racism showed how little had changed. The journalist Darcus Howe flatly declared, 'Englishness is invariably white and nationalistic'.[122]

However, these developments do signify something positive. Despite centuries of endemic and often vicious racism, ethnic minorities did not, on the whole, see themselves as victims. With what can only be described as a bulldog spirit, they forced their way into the

English consciousness as citizens who enriched the life of the nation. Many black and Asian people acknowledged that changes were afoot within the white population. Yasmin Alibhai-Brown wrote:

A substantial number of white Britons today see Stephen as their son. The *Daily Mail* saw him as their cause. We have a Home Secretary who decided that the nation should hear the truth . . . Racism has been lethally damaged. The blood of Stephen Lawrence has changed something for ever. Many more Britons today are convinced that the difference between the tribes is bridgeable, must be bridged and shall be bridged.[123]

In 1970, the South African political activist Steve Biko wrote: 'Differences grow on trees, but if we can ever expect whites to understand blacks, I think the British people will be the first to start such co-operation'.[124] The racial divisions within ethnic minorities (particularly that between Afro-Caribbeans and Asians) remained a taboo subject, for fear that scrutinizing 'internecine' conflict would play into the hands of racists. Another taboo subject was the violently illiberal attitudes to women and homosexuals that were present in almost every immigrant culture. However, Biko's optimism about relations with the white majority did start to be echoed within the black and Asian intelligentsia. They started to realize that the whole-sale condemnation of English national culture was as unproductive as the naive embrace of it by immigrants in the 1950s who had been reared on colonial school curricula. Mike Phillips, for example, stated, 'I despise that invented black culture which is stitched out of reggae, rap and red, green and yellow caps [and which rejects] the complete British heritage'.[125]

To some extent, English national identity in 2000 resembled that of the eighteenth century. There was the same resentment of Scots, based on a contradictory but mutually reinforcing view of them as parasitical on the one hand and too influential on the other. And the English had a reluctance to define themselves as British which their Hanoverian forebears would have recognized and applauded. One could also argue that, as a response to Scottish and Welsh national-ism, it mirrored the late Victorian revival of Englishness which Irish nationalism had provoked. But in another fundamental sense Englishness had changed. The singer Billy Bragg put his finger on why. In 1999, he observed that the country's future lay in realizing that there is a hyphen in Anglo-Saxon.[126]

The new Englishness was primarily about breathing life into a narrative of liberal democracy which evolved in the nineteenth and twentieth centuries but which, tied to Empire and Union, had never been fully realized. The English were legitimizing an extant identity rather than going back to the psychological drawing-board. This process was in itself a revolutionary one. But it seemed more dramatic than it actually was because the English had clung for so long to a vision of themselves which marginalized whole sections of society. Like the bulging in-tray of an office worker returning from holiday, the work that needed to be done was not that difficult; it was simply that a period of concentrated effort was required to shift the backlog. In 1963, Colin MacInnes accused the English of 'not seeing what our country *is*'. In the twenty-first century they were finally beginning to do just that.

What was the Blair government's response? It set about reforming the House of Lords to show how modern the nation had become. The Lords certainly needed to be reformed. It was the only non-elected second chamber in Europe. Labour's expulsion of hereditary peers in 1999 was a good start and it met with public approval. However, like Harold Wilson's abortive attempt to reform the Lords in 1969, Blair's tinkering was not of any consequence to the people. What they cared about was reform of the Commons. But Labour ministers were openly dismissive of the English Question. Home Secretary Jack Straw offered this assessment of the national character in 2000:

> The English are potentially very aggressive, very violent. [We have used this] propensity to violence to subjugate Ireland, Wales and Scotland. Then we used it in Europe and with our empire, so I think what you have within the UK is three small nations ... who've been over the centuries under the cosh of the English. Those small nations have inevitably sought expression by a very explicit idea of nationhood. You have this very dominant other nation, England, 10 times bigger than the others, which is self-confident and therefore has not needed to be so explicit about its expression. I think as we move into this new century, people's sense of Englishness will become more articulated and that's partly because of the mirror that devolution provides us with and because we're becoming more European at the same time.[127]

Straw's claim that the English were an innately aggressive people was not only tactless, it was profoundly ahistorical, pandering as it did to the myth that the Scots and Welsh had been the victims of an English empire rather than partners in a British one. Worse still, the only consolation New Labour offered the English was a form of self-government they had no liking for.

9. Because I'm English, it's my right to be Burgundian!

Since Andrew Fletcher of Saltoun told the Scottish Parliament of 1707 that instead of Union with Scotland, England should consider regional government for itself, the Scots have been lecturing the English on the subject. And in all that time, the English have shown precious little enthusiasm for it. In 1973, the Kilbrandon Report on the Constitution concluded, 'There are . . . social and cultural differences within England almost as great as those which distinguish England or its individual regions from the other countries which make up the United Kingdom . . . [But] there is no public demand for English regional assemblies with legislative powers, whether under a federal system or otherwise.'[128] Labour politicians no less than Conservative ones have always seen it as a foreign idea, the bastard nephew of Celtic and Continental attempts to undermine the United Kingdom. In 1976 Harold Wilson told the House of Commons that regional government would insert 'theologising [and] legalistically-inspired findings . . . into the whole of our economic and social life'.[129]

But then a strange thing happened. In 1995 New Labour began to reassess the idea. John Major denounced it as 'one of the most dangerous propositions ever put before the British nation'.[130] Few agreed. But neither did they flock to town halls demanding to be governed as Yorkshiremen or Essex men. In 1998, a Campaign for a Northern Assembly was begun by businessmen and civic leaders angry that the British economy was still being run for and by the south-east instead of for and by them. By 2000, the luminaries of five out of eight designated English regions had established Constitutional Conventions to campaign for devolution in their own areas. In May 1998 their protests grew louder when the south-east became the only part of England with its own directly elected assembly when 72 per cent of Londoners voted for a mayoral body on a turnout of

34 per cent. In the elections that followed a year later, they chose as their first mayor Ken Livingstone – a hardline socialist whose cross-party popularity rested on a cultivated image of a cheeky Cockney.

But these were exceptions that proved the rule. Throughout the 1990s, polls consistently showed that regionalism had no popular support. One will suffice: in September 1995, a MORI survey for the Joseph Rowntree Trust found that 62 per cent of English citizens opposed 'giving greater powers of government' to the regions, and a further 13 per cent were utterly indifferent to the idea.[131] In a *New Statesman* interview, the minister responsible for the regions, Richard Caborn, said, 'If you've got an identity it's helpful, but not a prerequisite.'[132] His remark revealed the weakness of New Labour's case, which was a tendency to see regionalism almost solely in administrative and political terms with little regard for the complex historical cultures which had developed over the course of a millennium. The main reasons for public hostility and apathy have been discussed in earlier chapters, but a new one appeared in the 1990s.

As the English rediscovered their nationhood, regionalism came to be seen for what it mostly was: a pragmatic attempt by politicians on the left and in the centre to placate English resentment about Celtic devolution without further undermining the Union. In other words, it was a version of the equally pragmatic establishment of Parliamentary Assemblies in Scotland, Wales and Northern Ireland. And it had the opposite effect to the one intended. Treating England as a mere collection of regions inflamed English nationalist sentiment in the same way that the earlier tendency of the British political elite to regard Scotland and Wales as regions inflamed nationalist opinion in those countries. In a St George's Day discussion of Englishness on *Newsnight* in 1998, the athlete Linford Christie told Jeremy Paxman and his fellow panellists, 'We're a nation too, you know, not just a bunch of regions.'[133]

In Ealing Studios' *Passport to Pimlico* (1949) an ancient charter is discovered which shows that Pimlico is actually part of the medieval kingdom of Burgundy. Seeing a chance to empower themselves against an over-mighty state, the local people declare independence from the rest of England. When Whitehall protests, Pimlico's new Prime Minister – a local shopkeeper, Mr Pemberton – declares, 'You can't push the English around like a sack of potatoes. I'm English and because I'm English, it's my right to be Burgundian!' Within Pemberton's gloriously chopped logic lies the essence of the nation's attitude to devolution in the twentieth century. Local cultures continued to exist, and in some cases flourished. But whatever loyalties the English felt to their cities, counties or regions, those loyalties overwhelmingly strengthened their national identity. And it was through that identity, whether Anglo-British or English, that they articulated their political consciousness. Despite all temptations, the English remained reluctant Burgundians.

10. Why does New Labour hate the English?

New Labour's reluctance to properly address the English Question led to resentment. The English felt that they were being prevented from expressing their own national identity, a feeling that naturally enough led to a greater determination to do so. Popular resentment was fuelled by the Tory press, eager to latch on to any sign of discontentment with an otherwise popular administration. Straw's comment drew this bombastic headline from the *Daily Mail*: 'WHY DOES NEW LABOUR HATE THE ENGLISH?' Newspapers also began to carry regular stories (most of them accurate) about how Labour-controlled local authorities were attempting to suppress English nationalism: council workers forbidden to fly the St George's cross on their vehicles, pubs granted late licences for St Patrick's Day but not St George's Day.[134] It may be true, as P. G. Wodehouse once remarked, that 'it is never difficult to distinguish between a Scotsman with a grievance and a ray of sunshine'.[135] But to their credit, the Scots (and the Welsh) were in favour of some constitutional redress for the English. Since the 1950s, their political and intellectual leaders had warned of an English backlash to Celtic nationalism.[136] If only for pragmatic reasons, they continued to do so. The Blair government remained unmoved.

This was a dangerous position to take, especially given how much the English already felt their rights were being eroded by the European Union: 70 per cent of the English people were opposed to joining a single currency and only 20 per cent were in favour. Apathy towards the European Parliament was at an all-time low, with only

22.6 per cent of the English electorate bothering to vote in the European Parliament elections of 1999. Blair had to take care.[137]

For the time being, unionist politicians could afford to be complacent. Like the governments of 1940 to 1997 faced with the rise of Scottish and Welsh nationalism, those tackling the English variety from 1997 onwards thought they were dealing with a cultural phenomenon, one that could be handled by Arts Council grants and knighthoods for football players. Politically, English nationalism was embryonic, and dominated by right-wingers hostile in principle to Scottish and Welsh devolution and to the EU, who wanted to reassert England's power rather than establish a progressive equilibrium. The English Parliament Movement, founded in 1996, mounted a weekly vigil outside the Houses of Parliament waving St George's flags and distributing leaflets.

Like the SNP and Plaid Cymru in their early years, the EPM's membership was tiny, but by the end of the century 38 per cent of the English population wanted their own Parliament and the figure was rising slowly but steadily.[138] So too were the number of people who defined themselves as English rather than British – up from 34 per cent in 1997 to 43 per cent in 2001. In 1998 the English Question began to be taken seriously by the Conservative Party. At the party conference in Bournemouth that year, the Tory leader, William Hague, came under pressure from Thatcherites to come out for an English Parliament, and at Westminster Teresa Gorman MP had introduced a Private Member's Bill to that effect.[139] It was talked out, of course. The *Spectator* supported the move, arguing that a Parliament would help win back Middle England from New Labour. 'To discuss, and even to embrace, an Anglo-Nationalism is not to argue for English independence, or even to question the value of the Union. Far from it. Instead, it is to acknowledge that English nationalism may well become, in the early years of the new millennium, a powerful influence in British politics. If England awakes, then it can be as a force for good.'[140]

Others went further, urging the party to drop its historic commitment to unionism and work for English independence. They argued that if England was freed of its unprofitable partnership with the two anti-Tory nations on its borders, the natural conservatism of the English would be allowed to breathe properly again, leading to a national renaissance. A rash of polemics appeared on the subject. Some, like Peter Hitchens' *The Abolition of Britain* (1999) and Roger Scruton's *England: An Elegy* (2000), were idiotic reactionary tracts which lamented that the last forty years of British history had happened at all. Though written from a Powellite perspective, Simon Heffer's *Nor Shall My Sword* was at least more forward-looking. It concluded:

> Something stirs deep in the blood of the English. The whole notion [of devolution] stimulates, and offends, their atavistic sense of fair play and decency . . . If there is writing on Hadrian's Wall it reads that the English should leave Scotland to its own devices . . . The new English nation that must be forged must . . . be one as free as possible from the meaningless trappings of sentiment. The new English will be first and foremost a mercantile people, whose relations with the world are those primarily of a business partner . . . The English have every reason to believe that this can be a prosperous and constructive future in which England is a force for good, moderation and sanity, and in which the English State serves first and foremost the interests of the English people.[141]

Heffer had the same realistic attitude towards the Union that Powell had once displayed towards the Empire. And underlying his realism was the same bitterness of a lover spurned rather than a positive acceptance of change.

At the time of writing it was all in vain. Like Labour, the Conservative Party baulked at the idea of Home Rule for England. Torn between the desire to win back support in Scotland and Wales by accepting devolution and the need to appease resentment about it in England, William Hague decided that his best bet was to fudge the issue. In July 1999, after a lengthy policy review, he announced:

> These are not theoretical problems. They are alive and real, a ticking time bomb under the British constitution . . . The signs of an emerging English consciousness are all around us. Try to ignore this English consciousness or bottle it up and it will turn into a more dangerous English nationalism that can threaten the future of the United Kingdom.[142]

Fighting talk. But the solution he proposed was simply that Parliamentarians should come to some arrangement by which Scottish and Welsh MPs should be forbidden to vote on matters that only concerned England.

Conservatives also failed pitifully to locate cultural sources of English patriotism beyond traditional institutions like the Church and the monarchy. The *Daily Telegraph* reported England's 1998 World Cup defeat by Argentina with the front-page headline 'ENG-

LAND LIONS GO DOWN FIGHTING', and it paid tribute to 'a band of brothers' whose gritty performance 'made a country proud'.[143] Alan Clark MP even celebrated the 'martial spirit' of the few men who rioted during the tournament and compared hooliganism to the Eton wall game.[144] But there remained an underlying regret that Englishness had come to this: eleven working-class men kicking a ball about on a bit of grass. Simon Heffer stated, for example, that the 'civilised and educated classes' were best fitted to lead England into its brave new world and not the 'spiky-haired louts with red and white faces'.[145]

But the alternatives failed to inspire. A Tory ginger group, the Countryside Alliance, brought 284,000 Barbour-clad landowners and assorted hoorays to London on 1 March 1998 to protest about, well, everything. T-shirts issued by the Alliance – 'Say no to the urban jackboot' – recalled mid-century rhetoric about townspeople as foreign invaders. The protesters claimed to care about rural unemployment, but they forgot to mention that the main reason why 80 per cent of farm labourers had been laid off since 1950 was the intensive farming methods landowners used to maximize their profits.[146] The Roast Beef of Old England which some protestors cooked and held aloft in the capital had been BSE-poisoned by those same methods. A retired lieutenant colonel from Wiltshire captured the true aim and spirit of the event in a letter to the *Daily Telegraph*:

> Sir – On Sunday morning, for the first time in my life, I took to the streets to protect something I feel very strongly about: the right to hunt, shoot and fish freely in the countryside. Of those marching with me, 95% seemed to be addressing themselves to the support of field sports. The sound of hunting horns was met by cheers, shouts and whistles.[147]

Such was the Blair government's fear of Middle England that one Downing Street official privately admitted that there had been almost as many high-level meetings to discuss the event as there had been to discuss the Iraqi crisis.[148] However, most of the British people greeted the sound of hunting horns with either hostility or indifference.

Despite postwar government attempts to democratize land by granting public access to it, and despite the aristocracy's attempt to present itself as curator of the nation's heritage, the English still related landowning to class privilege, whereas for the Scots and Welsh the countryside was a source of Highland heroes. F. M. L. Thompson has reminded us why landowners were able to bring so many middle-class admirers to Trafalgar Square in 1998: 'It is a prestige', he says, 'rooted in the continuing control of a great deal of land, not a consolation prize for the loss of former pre-eminence.'[149] The public's response to the rural revolt against Blair not only revealed the continuing town–country divide in English society but also the fact that rural romanticism, once a central component of Englishness, was in decline. In stark contrast to the Scots and Welsh, the English did not regard their countryside as an important part of their identity (it didn't even register in the 1997 *Sunday Times* survey of teenage attitudes). England was the first nation to industrialize and the first to romanticize the land. But it was also the first to recover its senses.

There was one last thing that traditional patriots still cheered about: The Last Night of the Proms. This event consciously echoed the Anglo-British nationalism of the imperial age. When the BBC first televised it in 1953, it immediately gained a much larger audience. Indeed, the response among some sections of the public was so zealous that the conductor Sir Malcolm Sargent remarked: 'if people can get as enthusiastic about music as they do about football that is all to the good'.[150] Since the 1950s, the patriotic songs, balloons and Union Jacks which filled the Albert Hall every September had made the Last Night a national institution of sorts, and occasional attempts to tone down the jingoism of the event had failed. Finally, in 2001, Prommers were humbled when, in tribute to the 5,000 victims of Islamist attacks on the United States, the Last Night programme was changed to include American music. The decision was a testament to the Special Relationship that existed between Britain and her former colony across the Atlantic. But it was also a testament to how much that relationship had changed. Considering the twentieth-century history of Britain and the United States, it was poignantly fitting that Elgar's *Land of Hope and Glory* should give way to Barber's *Adagio*, and under the baton of an American conductor, Leonard Slatkin.

The late-twentieth-century crisis of English national identity sprang from two things. First, as a result of their appalling complacency between the 1920s and the 1980s, the English were forced to reconsider who they were in an unstable, unpredictable political situation over which they had little control. Used to being in command of their destiny on the island of Britain, with the space and time to evolve an understanding of themselves, their pride was badly hurt by the success of Scottish and Welsh nationalism. English confusion was made worse by the fact that they had never developed a sufficiently democratic narrative of their national identity with which to launch themselves into a post-Union world. Despite periodic attempts to understand the democratic potential of nationalism in the mid-twentieth century, the left remained congenitally suspicious of it, while the right understood it all too well. The English were therefore faced not only with a stubborn, self-serving political elite, but also with a myopic intellectual elite, unwilling to weave England's many-splendoured features into a coherent, progressive picture around which the country could unite. England, the last stateless nation in the United Kingdom, was leaderless and adrift. 'For England – see Britain'.

Conclusion

The British were never as immune to nationalism as they liked to pretend. What they called patriotism in the eighteenth, nineteenth and twentieth centuries was often, in fact, a militant drive to assert their superiority over the rest of the world. British nationalism differed from Continental variants only in that it was cloaked more heavily in the phoney internationalism of the imperial mission. From 1940 to the millennium, as Union Jacks were lowered around the world and the country turned in on itself, the people of Britain became more nationalistic in the conventional sense. That is, with their world mission at an end and their post-imperial economy failing to live up to expectations, the English, Scots and Welsh returned to their core nationalities, once more defining themselves against rather than with each other.

The United Kingdom was primarily established to further the quest for Empire. When the Empire disappeared, the original raison d'être of the United Kingdom disappeared too. So too did most of the ideologies and institutions around which Britishness had been constructed since the eighteenth century. The monarchy was regarded with amusement, contempt or indifference. Most Britons had no wish for it to be abolished, and nor did they feel much animosity towards individual members of the Royal Family. It seemed unlikely that when Elizabeth II died, the public would pelt her coffin with excrement as they did during the State funeral of George IV. But the Crown had ceased to be a focal point of national identity in Britain. As the country prepared itself for the state celebrations of the Queen's Golden Jubilee in 2002, the monarchy looked rather like the wreck of a pleasure boat in the corner of a harbour. Nobody could be bothered to tow away it because it did not block harbour traffic and at low tide it was a rather picturesque addition to the sea-front. But it played no significant part in people's lives.

Protestantism had become the private pursuit of a minority. Besieged by secular humanism and by competition from other faiths, the Churches' role was reduced to staging the rituals which marked an individual's journey through life. The British God was truly 'just the ordinary one': omnipresent at thousands of weddings and funerals every week but incapable of mobilizing the nation in war or peace.

The British still thought of themselves as a democratic people, but this was now more of a generic moral outlook than a unifying patriotic faith with an institutional focal point. The 'Mother of Parliaments' at Westminster was not venerated except by a few right-wing English nationalists. After fifty years of Scottish and Welsh discontent, Westminster's sovereignty had finally been split by devolution, but done in a partial and pragmatic way that left none of the four nations satisfied and which structurally created a succubus for further constitutional crisis. In addition, the Scots and Welsh began to look favourably towards the European Union as an alternative polity to the UK. This trend widened the gulf between them and the more Euro-sceptical English, who regarded the EU as a threat to their way of life and a co-conspirator in the detachment of Scotland and Wales from the UK.

Economically, the Union no longer offered a good return for the Scots and the Welsh on the sovereignty they pooled into it. The notion that they were endowed with unique communitarian virtues in contrast to the more individualistic English became a part of Celtic national identity as a way of explaining their relative economic decline. This had an effect on the way that the welfare state was viewed. Having once been a set of institutions and provisions which morally united the British, it came instead to be one of the battle-grounds between the English and their partners and another way in which they defined themselves as nations with different values.

The racial definition of Britishness which the imperial age bequeathed was also on the wane. The white population had not only accepted that a multicultural society was a fact of life; they were also coming to believe that that coloured people had a right to belong to the UK. But this failed to reunite the four nations of the island because the vast majority of black and Asian Britons resided in England, and race was primarily a part of the English experience. Therefore, rainbow Britain could not unite the UK as the idea of white Britain had previously done, except in the most abstract philosophical terms.

The countryside, once worshipped as a source of racial purity, was still a source of patriotic pride. But it was something which the Scots, Welsh and English viewed as part of their own distinct national cultures. The idea of the *British* countryside continued to have little emotive appeal. What is more, throughout the Isles few people believed that land contained the sole essence of their nationality. Now at ease with the modern world, the British viewed the country-side in more functional terms, as a source of food, energy and leisure. Its inhabitants, far from being authentic Britons, were thought by many to be strange and backward people, disconnected from the mainstream of national life.

More modern transmitters of Britishness were no longer able to reach a mass audience. The BBC lost its place as the arbiter of national culture. Its broadcasting monopoly was broken by a fissiparous media revolution, and like the Churches' its moral authority was undermined by a more sceptical and impatient population. The British cinema never recovered the ability to rival Hollywood at home which it had enjoyed from the 1930s to the 1960s. Though films occasionally captured a British zeitgeist, they were few and far between and never achieved a consistent expression of national identity as the American or French cinema did. Pop music was a transient medium, and its stars – no less than poets, composers and artists – were reluctant to be harnessed to any organized attempt to promote Britishness. Football was a shared passion, but at international level it had become a focus for the conflicting nationalisms of the Scots and English because it provided an outlet for tensions and hatreds denied them by other pursuits.

Finally, the Second World War lost its patriotic allure. The war had re-invigorated Britishness in the mid-twentieth century, but by 2000 it was no longer a source of pride for the Isles as a whole. When the generation who had defended the UK from German invasion passed away, their collective memory of the geopolitical need for British unity went with them. All that remained were the Anglocentric legends of the Finest Hour, which to younger generations of Scottish and Welsh people seemed to be another example of English arrogance. England's continuing obsession with the war hampered the UK's involvement in the European Union and further highlighted the different view which the Scots, Welsh and English had of the Continent. Eventually, the Second World War also began to lose its grip on the southern imagination as people began to adopt Continental habits and patterns of consumption. But England's continuing political distrust of the EU still distinguished and separated it from other British nations.

Could it all have been different? Not much. The English tendency to take the loyalty of the Scots, Welsh and Northern Irish for granted, and the countless political blunders that resulted from that outlook, profoundly alienated the smaller nations of the Isles and hastened the demise of British national identity. Had the English realized sooner the depth of their partners' discontent, the fragmentation of the United Kingdom would probably have occurred in the early twenty-first century rather than in the late twentieth, and with less ill-feeling. But it would still have occurred as a result of the long-term and largely irreversible historical trends described above.

So, what of the future? There were many at the end of the twentieth century who looked down at the wheezing body of the British nation state and announced its imminent death. The chances are that the death will be much longer and more painful. Why? Because so much stands in the way of a radical reformation of the Isles.

The Scots will not readily pay for the cost of independence, however much they dislike the English and want to be rid of them. The Scottish ruling classes entered the Union on pragmatic grounds, primarily for financial gain, and the same criteria apply in today's democracy. The cost of leaving, rather than fondness for the English and Welsh, keeps them on board. There is a residual British sentiment in Scotland. But it is weak and getting weaker; and in the end, whether the Scots choose to remain in the UK or not will depend on whether they can find the courage to endure the start-up costs of independence. At the moment, they do not possess that courage. Most of the Welsh do not want rid of the Union at all, however much they make a song and dance about their culture. It is quite possible that their minds will change. They have had a taste of autonomy and seem to like it. But demand for more will be a long time coming. Until the early 1960s, the Scots merely wanted their culture to be respected by the English. It took several generations and further economic decline for hurt pride to develop into a desire for political autonomy. The same applies to the Welsh. The Protestant majority in Northern Ireland are even less inclined than the Welsh to leave the Union. Thankfully, they have started to forge a better relationship with the Republic and with Catholics in the North. The Loyalists have been a distinctive people for five centuries and there is no reason why Ireland should be completely reunified any more than Britain should be, although Protestants may one day feel confident enough of their unique British-Irish nationality to be part of an independent Northern Irish state. However, that too will take time.

Finally, what of the English? There is no sign that they want independence. Dazed and confused by the changes which have taken place, they are not sure what they want. Many, if not most, are simply indifferent to constitutional issues. However, they have woken up en masse to the fact that their blithe unionism is no longer reciprocated and that their seamless Anglo-British identity is effectively redundant. Devolution has forced the English to do what their partners did in the second half of the twentieth century – to reconsider who they are as a people. The task is more difficult for them, for two reasons: first, because their national identity was subsumed within the Union for so long, and second, because they are doing it by default. The English must grasp the political opportunities presented by the changes thrust upon them. In one of J. B. Priestley's last books, published in 1973, he wrote: 'Englishness is still with us. But it needs reinforcement, extra nourishment, especially now when our public life seems ready to starve it'.[1] That is truer today than it was then. The English need a sense that their own unique nationality is respected; and that, for all their past sins and present faults, they still have something valuable to offer the UK.

Those who predict the imminent break-up of Britain should also remember that the vast majority of the island's economic and political elite are opposed to it happening. Like most reform carried out in Britain since 1832, the constitutional changes of the late 1990s, however radical they might be, are not designed to usher in a new order but to maintain a broader status quo. Over the coming decades, *everything* possible will be done to ensure the survival of the British state, some of which we shall never know about. The Empire may have gone, but capitalism – the economic system which helped to give birth to it – remains in existence. So too does the matrix of power relationships which evolved out of that economic system. It is highly unlikely that those who benefit most from capitalism would lose their privileges if Britain were to break up. But very few are prepared to take that chance. There is life in Britannia yet, pox-ridden and toothless though she now is. As Winston Churchill once said in a different context, 'This is not the end. It is not even the beginning of the end. But it is, perhaps, the end of the beginning.'[2]

What we are now entering is a period of history in which the battle to save the United Kingdom will intensify both behind closed doors and in public as unionists struggle to convince people that their interests are best served in a United Kingdom.

Linda Colley has argued that Britons should move away from the emotive debate about national identity and address the question of citizenship. Speaking to the Prime Minister and an audience of 100 VIPs at Downing Street in December 1999, she said:

> Instead of being mesmerised by debates over British identity, it would be far more productive to concentrate on renovating British citizenship, and on convincing all of the inhabitants of these islands that they are equal and valued citizens irrespective of whatever identity they may individually select to prioritise ... Power becomes something not just done to and for the people, but which the people themselves participate in.[3]

Even in the unlikely event of this occurring, the British Question would not be solved because citizenship does not exist in a tidy, rational world of its own. 'Intransigent issues of Britishness' cannot, as she suggested, be left 'to look after themselves'. It is precisely because a complacent unionist elite took that view for so long that Britain came so close to breaking up in the 1990s. But further constitutional change and the putting out of more flags would not guarantee the survival of the UK either. There would have to be a reasonable distribution of wealth across the country so that differences between the nations cease to be iniquities. The Scots and Welsh may continue to be bought off by Treasury subsidies for some time yet, but unless Britain's financiers can be persuaded to invest properly in the economy of the whole island the day will surely come when pride, if nothing else, makes independence seem a more attractive option than the begging bowl. Despite half a century of disproportionately large state subsidy to the north and west of Britain, income levels in those parts of the island remain lower, while mortality rates and crime are correspondingly higher. Scotland and Wales may be much better off than they were in 1940. But the disparity between them and England remain in place, and it is upon that issue that the question of Britishness will continue to turn. Rekindling Britishness will take at least a generation to achieve. Given the rate at which it is now declining, it is hard to see how the time which has been so complacently thrown away since 1945 can be made up before the situation reaches breaking point. There is a third thing – perhaps the only thing – which could restore a popular sense of Britishness: a world war in which the whole island and its way of life are threatened by a foreign invader, forcing the four nations together once again in order to survive.

So what is the future of the British? My conclusion is that the United Kingdom will survive for a long time to come. But I doubt whether it will last for more than another century, never mind another three. If the current rhetoric about the British being a creative people is to have any meaning, it is that they must be prepared to see that no nation state is immutable. All the signs are that they do realize this and are mentally preparing for further change of a kind which was familiar to their forebears a few centuries ago but which was lost from view in the fog of Victorian hubris. Assuming that the monarchy survives, the most likely outcome is a modern adaptation of the polity which existed between 1603 and 1707. That is to say, England and Scotland will be independent nation states with their own Parliaments and armed forces but will be nominally united by a common Crown. The Welsh Assembly will become a Parliament with tax-raising powers of the kind which Scotland has recently won but it will remain attached to England in all other respects. But, reader! Do not fear!

Whatever system evolves, it will not mean the end of the British way of life. Attempting to sum up the English people in 1940, George Orwell asked what it was that a nation – any nation – has in common with its past. He wrote: 'What can the England of 1940 have in common with the England of 1840? But then, what have you in common with the child of five whose photograph your mother keeps on the mantelpiece? Nothing, except that you happen to be the same person.'[4] Like all metaphysical depictions of a national community, that is not strictly true. In emotional and intellectual terms, most adults are not the same people that they were at the age of five. Britain has changed incredibly since Orwell wrote those lines. Little of what Orwell identified as making the English 'different from a European crowd' is now recognizable:

> Bad teeth and gentle manners ... the clatter of clogs in the Lancashire mill towns, the to and fro of lorries on the Great North Road, the queues outside the Labour Exchanges, the rattle of pin-tables in the Soho pubs, the old maids biking to Holy Communion through mists of autumn morning ... solid breakfasts and gloomy

Sundays, smoky towns and winding roads, green fields and red pillar-boxes.[5]

And yet, Orwell had a point. Despite the vast changes which the British people experienced in the twentieth century, a cultural continuum is apparent.

Even if Scotland, Wales, England and Northern Ireland become independent nation states, their inhabitants will still have a special relationship with each other. In a fundamental sense, they will not cease to be British, any more than the people of Ulster ceased to be Irish after choosing to remain in the United Kingdom when the South won its independence. Britishness may not inhabit the hearts of these islanders as it once did but it will remain at the back of their minds, and, like an acid flashback, it will periodically return to the fore. Islanders who no longer call themselves Britons will find that intense memories of Union are triggered unexpectedly from within some remote synapse by the slightest sight, smell or sound of the present day. Nor will Britishness just survive in the minds of the generation who lived through the last days of the Union. Thanks to historians, future generations will read about the United Kingdom and the benefits which for a time it brought each of the nations that belonged to it. In short, there may be no love lost between the Scots, Welsh, English and Northern Irish but it is unlikely that their interconnecting histories will ever be forgotten.

Why this optimism? Because after more than a millennium inhabiting the same island and several centuries of political unification it would be impossible for the Scots, Welsh, English and Northern Irish *not* to have a special relationship. Think of the bonds which Britons still have with America and the Republic of Ireland despite the geographical distance of the former and the bitter history of the latter. A shared past will not be the only thing which the peoples of Britain have in common. The four nations will maintain a contemporary bond through culture and trade, both of which are oiled by a common language. They will still share the same ironic sense of humour; will still be sentimental about animals; will still grumble about the weather and trains not running on time. They will still drink, dance and make love together; still enjoy the world's best pop music; still garden, DIY and go to football or rugby matches to watch teams with players from all over Britain. Businessmen, scientists, poets and scholars will still meet and share their knowledge.Schools and the media will still give priority to British subjects.

Tourists will still journey from around the Isles to enjoy the scenery of the Highlands, Brecons and Lakes or the metropolitan splendour of Edinburgh and London (perhaps even Cardiff or Belfast if the planners get it right). Above all, people will still migrate around the island in significant numbers, as the Irish continue to do from across the water. The friendships, romances and family ties formed by those migrations and by myriad other connections will endure.

We must also keep the subject in perspective. The British way of life is more at risk from global warming and Muslim fanatics than it is from devolution and federalism. The peoples of Britain must complete the comprehensive re-examination of who they are and how they relate to each other which they began in the 1940s. But in the twenty-first century they must do more than that. It is time for the Scots, Welsh, English and Northern Irish to look outward again and re-engage with the world; not as imperialists this time, but as Europeans. The British will always be happiest on their little islands, and rightly so. But they must learn to work more closely with other nations – not only to create a more equitable, peaceful and sustainable planet, but also for their own sake. If they swallow their pride, the European Union could act as a kind of social service, providing counselling and alternative accommodation for the dysfunctional family on its western reaches. Then, and only then, will they lay to rest the ghosts of their extraordinary past. Since it was a Frenchman who devised the European Union, it is right that a Frenchman should have the last word on the subject. In 1950 the existentialist writer Albert Camus made the following plea to the British in a BBC broadcast:

> Your country will have earned an even greater right to the gratitude of free men when its virtues are no longer exercised in isolation. Europe, because of its very disorder, has need of Britain; and wretched as this continent may seem, it is certain that Britain will not find salvation apart from Europe. The attitude of prejudice or indifference which your politicians often cultivate toward the continent may be legitimate; it is nonetheless regrettable. Mistrust may be a useful method, but it is an odious principle: a moment always comes when the principle conflicts with the facts. The facts affirm that, for better or worse, Britain and Europe are bound up together. It may seem an unfortunate marriage. But as one of our moralists said: marriage may sometimes be good but never delightful. As our marriage is not a delightful one, let us at least try to make it a good one, since divorce is out of the question.[6]

Camus's plea could also be applied to relations between the four countries of the United Kingdom. Their marriage today seems an unfortunate one, and separation an attractive and viable solution. But divorce for them is also out of the question.

Notes

INTRODUCTION

1 David Daiches, *Scotland and the Union* (1977) 161.
2 Roy Foster, *Modern Ireland 1600–1972* (1988) 283.
3 Linda Colley, *Britons: Forging the Nation, 1707–1837* (1992) 53–4.
4 Richard J. Finlay, *A Partnership For Good? Scottish Politics and the Union Since 1880* (1997) 28–9.
5 G. J. Renier, *The English: Are They Human?* (1931) 18.
6 A. L. Morton, *In Search of England* (1927) 186–7.
7 Ian McBride, 'Ulster and the British Problem', in Richard English and Graham Walker (eds), *Unionism in Modern Ireland: New perspectives on Politics and Culture* (1996) 6.
8 Colley, op. cit., 29.
9 Esme Wingfield-Stratford, *The Foundations of British Patriotism* (1940) 406–7.
10 J. B. Priestley, *English Journey* (1934; reprinted 1984) 300.
11 Ibid., 301.
12 Edwin Muir, *Scottish Journey* (1935; reprinted 1996) 244.
13 Stefan Collini, *Matthew Arnold: A Critical Portrait* (1994) 86.
14 Ernest Renan, *Qu'est-ce qu'une nation?* (1882) 65.
15 Anthony D. Smith, *National Identity* (1991) 71.
16 David Cannadine, 'Penguin Island Story: planning a new history of Britain', *Times Literary Supplement*, 12 March 1993.

1. WARRIORS

1 David Cannadine, *Blood, Toil, Tears and Sweat: Winston Churchill's Famous Speeches* (1989) 151. The italics are mine.
2 PRO: INF1/175, Harold Nicolson, 'Propaganda', broadcast 1 June 1940.
3 The higher number of registered conscientious objectors in the Second World War not only reflected the growth of the peace movement since 1918, it also reflected a greater official tolerance of objectors and a consequent readiness to consider their claims more generously. Also, those whose claims were accepted were treated better. In the First World War,

one in ten were imprisoned; in the Second World War, the figure was one in a hundred.

4 Angus Calder, *The People's War: Britain 1939–45* (1969) 53.

5 Fred Taylor (ed.), *The Goebbels Diaries, 1939–1941* (1982) 69.

6 John Erickson (ed.), *Invasion 1940: The Nazi Invasion Plan for Britain by SS General Walter Schellenberg* (2000) xxix.

7 Ibid., 142.

8 Martin Gilbert, *Winston S. Churchill: Finest Hour 1939–1941* (1983) 559. De Gaulle believed that 'one could not, by an exchange of notes, even in principle fuse England and France together, including their institutions, their interests and their Empires, supposing this was desirable . . . But the offer [of Franco-British Union] did involve a manifestation of solidarity which might take on a real significance.' See General de Gaulle, *War Memoirs*, vol. 1: *The Call to Honour 1940–1942* (1955) 80–81.

9 John Colville, *Footprints in Time* (1976) 88–9.

10 Gilbert, op. cit., 561.

11 Cannadine, op. cit., 177–8.

12 John Wolffe, *God and Greater Britain: Religion and National Life in Britain and Ireland 1843–1945* (1994) 260.

13 Ibid., 250.

14 PRO: PREM5/276, Churchill to Temple, 11 February 1942.

15 Wolffe, op. cit., 251.

16 W. R. Matthews, *Memories and Meanings* (1969) 282.

17 Wolffe, op. cit., 254.

18 Keith Robbins, 'Britain, 1940 and Christian Civilisation', in his *History, Religion and Identity in Modern Britain* (1993) 200.

19 Martin Gilbert (ed.), *The Churchill War Papers*, vol. 2: *Never Surrender, May 1940–December 1940* (1994) 847.

20 Arthur Mee, *Nineteen-Forty: Our Finest Hour* (1941) Preface; 98–100; 211.

21 Leonard Miall, *Inside the BBC: British Broadcasting Characters* (1994) 80. The governor who wrote that statement was H. A. L. Fisher, Warden of New College, Oxford, and former President of the Board of Education, who introduced university scholarships in the Education Act of 1918.

22 F. A. Iremonger, *William Temple, Archbishop of Canterbury: His Life and Letters* (1948) 419–20.

23 Ibid., 567. For a contemporary Jewish appreciation of the ideological links between Protestant Zionism and liberal democracy, see Hans Kohn, 'The Genesis and Character of English Nationalism', *Journal of the History of Ideas*, vol. 1, no. 1, January 1940.

24 Edward Norman, *Church and Society in England 1770–1970: A Historical Study* (1976) 394.

25 Robert Rhodes James, *A Spirit Undaunted: The Political Role of George VI* (1998) 210.

26 Piers Brendon and Philip Whitehead, *The Windsors: A Dynasty Revealed* (1994) 113.

27 Odhams Press, *The Royal Family in Wartime* (1945) 9–11.

28 Calder, op. cit., 77.

29 Edward Bliss (ed.), *In Search of Light: The Broadcasts of Ed Murrow 1938–61* (1968) 237.

30 John Davies, *Broadcasting and the BBC in Wales* (1994) 137.

31 PRO: INF1/168, Studies in Broadcast Propaganda no. 22, 26 October 1940.

32 BBCWAC/R34/622, Policy: 'Projection of Britain 1941–46', Alan Bullock et al., 'The Projection of Britain', 1 December 1942.

33 Humphrey Jennings (dir.), *The Heart of Britain* (Crown Film Unit, 1941). It should also be noted that during the war the BBC received regular complaints from the public that it played too much German and Italian music.

34 BBC Board Paper G28/42, 1 April 1942, drafted by Sir Arthur Bliss, cited in Lewis Foreman (ed.), *From Parry to Britten: British Music in Letters 1900–1945* (1987) 273–4.

35 Vera Lynn, *Vocal Refrain: An Autobiography* (1975) 99.

36 Ibid., 93–4.

37 Attlee Papers, MS.Eng.C.4793/3, Clement Attlee to Tom Attlee, 19 May 1943.

38 BBCWAC/910/E. M. Forster, Jean Rowntree (Assistant Talks) to Forster, 4 June 1944.

39 William Temple, *The Resources and Influence of English Literature* (1943) 24.

40 BBC: WAC/R34/622, John Green (Director European Broadcasts) to Harman Grisewood (Controller European Service), 17 December 1942.

41 BBC: WAC/R34/622, Sir Richard Maconachie (Controller Home Service) to Basil Nicholls (Director Talks), 8 March 1943.

42 Antonia White, *BBC at War* (1941) 26.

43 Jeffrey Richards, *Films and British National Identity: From Dickens to Dad's Army* (1997) 89.

44 Ibid.

45 Graham Payn and Sheridan Morley (eds), *The Noël Coward Diaries* (1982) 6–7.

46 Richards, op. cit., 108.

47 PRO: BW69/5, Reith to Lloyd, 6 February 1940.

48 PRO: EL1/2, Memorandum in Support of an Application to the Treasury for Financial Assistance to the Arts, 6 March 1940.

49 *Listener*, vol. 23, no. 585, 28 March 1940.

50 Robert Hewison, *Under Siege: Literary Life in London 1939–45* (1977) 23.

51 Bernard Miles, *The British Theatre* (1948) 44.

52 John Piper, *British Romantic Artists* (1946) 7.

53 Margaret Garlake, *New Art New World: British Art In Postwar Society* (1998) 84.

54 *Daily Herald*, 5 February 1942.

55 See John Summerson, *50 Years of the National Buildings Record 1941–1991* (1991). Parliament had passed the first Ancient Monuments Protection Act in 1882 and Royal Commissions (one each for Scotland, Wales and England) had been set up in 1908. But the inventories they prepared from then until 1941 were not exhaustive and were limited to pre-1700 structures.

56 See David Mellor, Gill Saunders and Patrick Wright, *Recording Britain: A Pictorial Domesday of pre-war Britain* (1990).

57 Stanley Baldwin, 'The Englishman', in British Council, *British Life and Thought* (1941) 446–7.

58 Christian Mawson (ed.), *Portrait of England* (1942) 50.

59 George Orwell, *The Lion and the Unicorn: Socialism and the English Genius* (second edn, 1982) 63–5.

60 PRO: INF1/848, Policy Committee 10th Meeting, 15 March 1940, Item 9.

61 John Lehmann, *I Am My Brother: Autobiography II* (1960) 31.

62 *New Statesman*, vol. 20, no. 496, 24 August 1940.

63 Calder, op. cit., 494–5.

64 Quentin Bell, *Virginia Woolf: A Biography*, vol. 2 (1972) 212.

65 Hewison, op. cit. 51.

66 PRO: INF1/848, Policy Committee 15th Meeting, 23 May 1940, Item 1.

67 Arthur Koestler, 'The Intelligentsia', *Horizon*, vol. 9, no. 51, March 1944.

68 Hewison, op. cit., 52.

69 Robert Pagan, 'A Dodo In Every Bus', *Penguin New Writing*, no. 4, March 1941, 97.

70 *Listener*, vol. 28, no. 703, 2 July 1942.

71 Jack Lindsay, *British Achievement in Art and Music* (1945) 12.

72 Cannadine, op. cit., 203.

73 Russell Galbraith, *Without Quarter: A Biography of Tom Johnston, 'The Uncrowned King of Scotland'* (1995) 245. For further detail, see Johnston's *Memories* (1952).

74 Charles Stuart (ed.), *The Reith Diaries* (1975) 300–301, entry for 25 March 1943.

75 PRO: HO45/21644, A Petition from the Welsh Parliamentary Party to the Prime Minister, 28 October 1943.

76 T. S. Eliot, *Notes Towards the Definition of Culture* (1948) 55.

77 Davies, op. cit., 129.

78 *Listener*, no. 577, 1 February 1940.

79 Sian Nicholas, *The Echo of War: Home Front Propaganda and the BBC, 1939–45* (1996) 231.

80 Davies, op. cit., 129.
81 Foreman (ed.), op. cit., 232, Boult to Vaughan Williams, 9 September 1940.
82 Arthur Bryant, *English Saga 1840–1940* (1940) 334.
83 Esme Wingfield-Stratford, *The Foundations of British Patriotism* (1940) 218.
84 See David Scott Fox, *St. George: The Saint with Three Faces* (1983).
85 *The Times*, 20 October 1942.
86 BBC: WAC/R34/238/1/1A, Basil Nichols, Note for file, 10 June 1943.
87 BBC: WAC/R34/238/2, Leonard Cottrell to Leslie Stokes, 8 February 1944.
88 Peter Donnelly (ed.), *Mrs. Milburn's Diaries: An Englishwoman's day-to-day reflections, 1939–1945* (1989) 210.
89 Tim Pat Coogan, *Eamon De Valera: The Man Who Was Ireland* (1993) 608.
90 Nigel Nicolson (ed.), *Harold Nicolson, Diaries and Letters 1939–45* (1967) 217–18.
91 Candida Lycett Green (ed.), *John Betjeman, Letters Volume One: 1926 to 1951* (1994) 200.
92 Brian Girvin and Geoffrey Roberts, 'The Forgotten Volunteers of World War II', *History Ireland*, vol. 6, no. 1, Spring 1998.
93 PRO: AIR9/447, War Ministry, Plans Division, 'Eire', 31 May 1940.
94 Brian Barton, 'The Impact of World War II on Northern Ireland and on Belfast–London Relations', in Peter Catterall and Sean McDougall (eds), *The Northern Ireland Question In British Politics* (1996) 47.
95 James Loughlin, *Ulster Unionism and British National Identity Since 1885* (1995) 126.
96 Ibid., 123.
97 Louis MacNeice, *Selected Poems* (1988) 95.
98 Alfred Noyes, 'The Sea', in Hugh Kingsmill (ed.), *The English Genius* (1939) 164–170.
99 Angus Calder, *The Myth of the Blitz* (1991) 30.
100 Ibid., 30–31.
101 See Ian McLaine, *Ministry of Morale: Home Front Morale and the Ministry of Information in World War II* (1979) 223–4.
102 Angus Calder, *The People's War: Britain 1939–45* (1969) 159.
103 Ibid., 160.
104 J. B. Priestley, *Postscripts* (1940) 4. Broadcast 5 June 1940.
105 Christopher Marsden, *The English at the Seaside* (1947) 48.
106 Nigel Rose, 'Dear Mum and Dad: An RAF Pilot's Letters to His Parents, June–December 1940', in Paul Addison and Jeremy A. Crang (eds), *The Burning Blue: A New History of the Battle of Britain* (2000) 149.
107 Drew Middleton, *The British* (1957) 246.
108 Paul Richey, 'Fighter Pilot', *Youth At War* (1944) 88.

109 Calder, op. cit., 419–20.

110 Hesketh Pearson, 'Humour', in Kingsmill, op. cit., 54–5; see also J. B. Priestley, *English Humour* (1929).

111 *Listener*, vol. 22, no. 560, 5 October 1939.

112 Calder, op. cit., 357.

113 John Burnett, *Liquid Pleasures: A Social History of Drinks in Modern Britain* (1999) 66.

114 Calder, *Myth of the Blitz*, 14.

115 *The Times*, 23 June 1942.

116 Calder, *Myth of the Blitz*, 171.

117 Sean Glynn and Alan Booth, *Modern Britain: An Economic and Social History* (1996) 91, 284.

118 Galbraith, op. cit., 244.

119 John Davies, *A History of Wales* (1993) 600.

120 D. Hywel Davies, *The Welsh Nationalist Party 1925–1945: A Call to Nationhood* (1983) 231.

121 Galbraith, op. cit., 247.

122 H. E. Bates, 'The English Countryside', in Anthony Weymouth (ed.), *The English Spirit* (1942) 38.

123 Calder, *People's War*, 422.

124 Richard Harman (ed.), *Countryside Mood* (1943) 5. The Mosleyite novelist Henry Williamson was among the contributors to this volume.

125 Vita Sackville-West, *The Women's Land Army* (1944) 14.

126 Nicola Tyrer, *They Fought In The Fields, The Women's Land Army: The Story of a Forgotten Victory* (1996) 103.

127 Harry Batsford, *How to See the Countryside* (1942) 44. The series – which also included *How to Grow Food* and *How to Look at Old Buildings* – was produced by Batsford's own publishing company. The company made its name during the 1930s when its guidebooks to the isles (rural and urban) catered to a growing demand for accessible, patriotic topography among holidaymakers.

128 J. B. Priestley, *Out of the People* (1941) 31–2.

129 Paul Addison and Jeremy A. Crang, 'A Battle of Many Nations', in Addison and Crang, op. cit., 249.

130 John Brophy, *Britain's Home Guard: A Character Study* (1945) 5–9.

131 Richards, op. cit., 113.

132 Janice Winship, 'Women's Magazines: Times of War and Management of the Self in *Woman's Own*', in Christine Gledhill and Gillian Swanson (eds), *Nationalising Femininity: Culture, Sexuality and British Cinema in the Second World War* (1996) 130.

133 Penny Summerfield, 'The Girl That Makes the Thing That Drills the Hole That Holds the Spring: Discourses of Women and Work in the Second World War', in Gledhill and Swanson, op. cit., 41.

134 Penny Summerfield, 'Women in Britain since 1945: companionate

marriage and the double burden', in James Obelkevich and Peter Catterall (eds), *Understanding Post-War British Society* (1994) 60–61.

135 Pat Thane, 'Women since 1945', in Paul Johnson (ed.), *20th Century Britain: Economic, Social and Cultural Change* (1994) 401.

136 Summerfield, op. cit., 50.

137 Calder, op. cit., 153–4.

138 Andrew Roberts, *Eminent Churchillians* (1994) 214.

139 (Anonymous), *You and the Empire*, BWP 16, March 1944 in *The British Way and Purpose: Consolidated Edition* (Directorate of Army Education, 1944) 461. For a history of ABCA and its predecessors, see S. P. Mackenzie, *Politics and Military Morale: Current Affairs and Citizenship Education in the British Army 1914–1950* (1992).

140 C. B. Fawcett, 'The Setting', BWP 6, April 1943, *The British Way and Purpose*, 187; 190.

141 Peter Fryer, *Staying Power: The History of Black People in Britain* (1984) 363.

142 Colin Holmes, *John Bull's Island: Immigration & British Society, 1871–1971* (1988) 168.

143 Ibid., 366.

144 Ibid., 362.

145 Ibid., 201.

146 Calder, *Myth of the Blitz*, 63.

147 The anti-Semitic riots of 1947 were also a reaction to the killing of British soldiers in Palestine by Zionist guerrillas.

148 Calder, *The People's War*, 499.

149 J. B. Priestley, *Out of the People*, 104.

150 John Betjeman, *Coming Home: An Anthology of Prose* (1997) 109–10.

151 Rose Macaulay, *Life Among the English* (1942) 48.

152 Priestley, *Postscripts*, 38.

153 Tom Harrison, *Living Through The Blitz* (1990).

154 Odhams Press, *Ourselves in Wartime* (1944) 84.

155 Ludovic Kennedy, 'Sub-Lieutenant', *Youth At War* (1944) 157.

156 Anthony Irwin, 'Infantry Officer', ibid., 211.

157 Adrian Gregory, *The Silence of Memory: Armistice Day 1919–1946* (1994) 213–14.

158 Bernard Law Montgomery, *The Memoirs of Field Marshal Montgomery* (1958) 487.

159 Jose Harris, *William Beveridge: A Biography* (1977) 419.

160 Peter Hennessy, *Never Again: Britain 1945–51* (1992) 76.

161 Bliss, op. cit., broadcast 10 September 1940.

162 Frank Harper, Camberwell air-raid warden, interview with the author, 10 June 1997.

163 *The Times*, 21 September 1943. Bernays was killed in January 1945 when the aircraft he was travelling in was shot down by an impolite Messerschmitt.

164 A. H. Halsey (ed.), *Trends in British Society Since 1900* (1972) 127.

165 *The Times*, 5 December 1942.

166 Cannadine, op. cit., 271.

167 Paul Addison, *The Road to 1945: British Politics and the Second World War* (second edn, 1994) 290.

168 Orwell, op. cit., 48, 52.

169 Ibid., 54.

170 *New Republic*, 22 October 1945.

171 Labour Party, *Let Us Face the Future* (1945), reprinted in Iain Dale (ed.), *Labour Party General Election Manifestos 1900–1997* (2000) 53.

172 John Strachey, *Why You Should Be a Socialist* (1944) 55–6.

173 Kenneth Harris, *Attlee* (1982) 257.

174 Robert Hewison, *Culture and Consensus: England, Art and Politics since 1940* (1995) 15.

175 Eric W. White, *The Arts Council of Great Britain* (1975) 68. Keynes moved the Arts Council from the umbrella of the Board of Education to the Treasury because if it had stayed at Education the Council would have been split up, since the Scots ran their own education. Keynes knew that the Treasury would prove a less sympathetic champion but he was so determined to see off nationalism that he took the risk.

176 PRO: EL2/20, Vaughan Williams to Mary Glasgow, 31 July 1943.

177 Ivor Brown, 'A Plan for the Arts', in Gilbert and Elizabeth McAllister (eds), *Homes, Towns and Countryside: A Practical Plan for Britain* (1945) 140.

178 *Picture Post*, vol. 18, no. 1, 2 January 1943.

179 Brown, op. cit., 140.

180 PRO: EL2/40, Keynes to Mary Glasgow, 7 November 1945.

181 PRO: EL2/139, Keynes to Stepanov, 7 May 1945. He was trying to impress Stepanov in order to obtain the Bolshoi for Covent Garden's opening season. Nonetheless, the comment is revealing.

182 PRO: EL2/14, Esher to Keynes, 4 March 1942.

183 Brown, op. cit., 142.

184 *Listener*, vol. 34, no. 861, 12 July 1945.

185 Calder, *The People's War*, 103.

186 *Parliamentary Debates (Commons)*, vol. 411, 1482–3, 12 June 1945.

187 *Listener*, vol. 34. no. 861, 12 July 1945.

188 LPA: RD/284, Philip Noel-Baker, 'Facilities for Popular Entertainment and Culture', March 1945.

189 Ian Britain, *Fabianism and culture: A study in British socialism and the arts, 1884–1918* (1982) 154.

190 Dale, op. cit., 58.

191 S. Baron (ed.), *Country Towns in the Future England: A Report of the Conference Representing Local Authorities, Arts and Amenities*

*Organisations and Members of the Town and Country Planning
Association on 23 October 1943* (1944).

192 George Orwell, *Collected Essays, Journalism and Letters* (1970), vol. 2,
      337–46.

193 Hewison, op. cit., 172.

194 Ibid., 165.

195 Baron, op. cit., 98.

196 Orwell, op. cit., 337.

197 Hugh David, *The Fitzrovians: A Portrait of Bohemian Society 1900–1955*
      (1988) 222.

198 Ibid., 222–3.

199 CCC: Haley/13/5, Diary entry, 16 August 1945.

200 A. L. Rowse, *The English Spirit: Essays in History and Literature* (1944)
      51.

201 Calder, *People's War*, 490.

202 Ibid., 491.

203 John Costello, *Love, Sex and War: Changing Values 1939–45* (1985) 333.
      The incidence of rape by British and American troops was very low
      compared to that of the Red Army.

204 Kate Dunn (ed.), *Always and Always: Wartime Letters of Hugh and
      Margaret Williams* (1995) 257.

205 William Beveridge, *The Price of Peace* (1945) 50–51.

206 John Kendle, *Federal Britain: A History* (1997) 112.

207 Gilbert, op. cit., 847.

208 Asa Briggs, *The History of Broadcasting in the United Kingdom*, vol. III:
      The War of Words (1970) 209.

209 Robert J. Wybrow, *Britain Speaks Out, 1937–87: A social history as seen
      through the Gallup Data* (1989) 8.

210 Matthews, op. cit., 267.

211 *Daily Express*, 8 May 1945.

212 *Parliamentary Debates (Commons)*, vol. 411, 1867–9, 8 May 1945.

213 Martin Gilbert, *The Day the War Ended: VE Day 1945 in Europe and
      around the World* (1995) 208.

214 *Birmingham Mail*, 8 May 1945.

215 Robin Cross, *VE Day: Victory in Europe 1945* (1995) 128–9.

216 Jonathan Dimbleby, *Richard Dimbleby: A Biography* (1975) 202.

217 *Daily Telegraph*, 5 May 1945.

218 *Daily Telegraph*, 7 May 1945.

219 Richard Buckle (ed.), *Self Portrait with Friends: The Selected Diaries of
      Cecil Beaton 1926–1974* (1979) 165, Diary entry 11 November 1944.

220 Helen Jones (ed.), *Duty and Citizenship: The Correspondence and Papers of
      Violet Markham 1896–1953* (1994) 185–6, VM to Nan Carruthers, 1 June
      1945.

221 Nigel Nicolson (ed.), *Harold Nicolson, Diaries and Letters 1945–62* (1968) 265, VSW to HN, 14 September 1954.

222 Leonard Miall (ed.), *Richard Dimbleby, Broadcaster* (1966) 44.

223 Dunn, op. cit., 252.

224 Ibid., 255.

225 Interview for *Execution At Camp* 21, transcript, Channel Four, 21 November 1999.

226 Adrian Hastings, *A History of English Christianity 1920–1985* (1986) 385.

227 David Eccles (ed.), *By Safe Hand: The Letters of Sybil and David Eccles* (1983) 380, SE to DE, 17 May 1942.

228 Roy Denman, *Missed Chances: Britain and Europe in the Twentieth Century* (1996) 182–4.

229 Jean Monnet, *Mémoires* (1976) 362.

230 R. C. F. Maugham, *Jersey under the Jackboot* (1946) 110–11. Because Channel Island women were forbidden to marry Germans, illegitimacy rates shot up – from 5.4 per cent of births in 1938 to 21.8 per cent in 1944.

231 Ibid., dust-jacket notes.

232 P. M. H. Bell, *France and Britain 1940–1994: The Long Separation* (1997) 62. Another example of French Anglophilia in this period is Georges Bernanos, *Lettre aux Anglais* (1946).

233 Pierre Maillaud, *The English Way* (1945) 215.

234 Mervyn Jones, *Michael Foot* (1994) 85–6.

235 A. L. Rowse, *The English Spirit* (1944) 35.

236 Eccles, op. cit, 130.

237 Orwell, op. cit., 324.

238 'Cato', *Guilty Men* (1940) 11–12. The journalists Frank Owen and Peter Howard contributed to the book.

239 Jones, op. cit., 84.

240 Ibid., 90.

241 Wybrow, op. cit., 2, 6.

242 William Gerhardie, 'Climate and Character', in Kingsmill, op. cit., 65.

2. CITIZENS

1 Hugh Dalton, *The Fateful Years: Memoirs 1931–45* (1957) 468–9.

2 Harry Hopkins, *The New Look: A Social History of the Forties and Fifties in Britain* (1963) 73.

3 Peter Hennessy, *Never Again: Britain 1945–51* (1992) 144.

4 *Picture Post*, vol. 43, no. 10, 4 June 1949.

5 Sonia Orwell and Ian Angus (eds), *The Collected Essays, Journalism and Letters of George Orwell*, vol. 4: *In Front of your Nose 1945–50* (1970) 328–9.

6 Nigel Nicolson, *Harold Nicolson, Diaries and Letters 1939–45* (1967) 449.

7 This phrase belongs to Secretary of State Arthur Woodburn in PRO: CAB129, CP(47) 323, 'Scottish Demands for Home Rule or Devolution', 6 December 1947.

8 Conservative Party, *Scottish Control, Scottish Affairs: Unionist Policy* (1949) 1.

9 Angus Calder, *The Myth of the Blitz* (1991) 342.

10 Kenneth O. Morgan, *Rebirth of a Nation: Wales 1880–1980* (1981) 376.

11 PRO: HO45/21645, statement by the Welsh Parliamentary Labour Party to the Prime Minister, 6 March 1946.

12 Ibid.

13 PRO: PREM8/658, John Taylor (Secretary, Scottish Council of the Labour Party) to Herbert Morrison, 16 June 1947.

14 PRO: HO45/25177, Cabinet Committee on the Machinery of Government, M.G. (45) 11th Meeting, 25 October 1945.

15 PRO: CAB129, CP(46) 21, 'The Administration of Wales and Monmouthshire', 27 January 1946.

16 *The Times*, 15 October 1946.

17 H. T. Edwards, *Hewn From the Rock* (1967) 125.

18 PRO: PREM8/658, Attlee to Morrison, 23 June 1947.

19 PRO: PREM8/658, Morrison to Joseph Westwood, 25 July 1947.

20 Cmnd 7308, *Scottish Affairs* (1948).

21 PRO: CAB129, CP(47) 323, 'Scottish Demands for Home Rule or Devolution', 6 December 1947.

22 Ian Finlay, *Scotland* (1945) 130. See also his *Art In Scotland* (1948).

23 David Mellor, Gill Saunders and Patrick Wright, *Recording Britain: A Pictorial Domesday of pre-war Britain* (1990) 52–6.

24 Hugh MacDiarmid, 'Two Scots who Like the English' (1949), in Angus Calder, Glen Murray and Alan Riach (eds), *Hugh MacDiarmid, The Raucle Tongue, Hitherto Uncollected Prose*, vol. 3 (1998) 202–6. MacDiarmid was reviewing *A Small Stir: Letters on the English* by James Bridie and Moray Maclaren, which expressed qualified admiration for the English.

25 *Times Literary Supplement*, 29 August 1952.

26 Jack Brand, *The National Movement in Scotland* (1978) 246.

27 Kenneth Young (ed.), *The Diaries of Sir Robert Bruce Lockhart*, vol. 2: *1939–1965* (1980) 710–11.

28 PRO: CAB129, CP(50) 101, 'Scottish Affairs', 11 May 1950.

29 PRO: CAB128, CM(50) 31st Conclusions, Minute 4, 15 May 1950.

30 PRO: CAB129, CP(50) 150, 'Scottish Affairs', 30 June 1950.

31 Scottish National Congress, *Sangs o' the Stane* (1951). The SNC was a left-wing republican group with links to the SNP. Inspired by the tactics of the Indian National Congress, it advocated non-violent direct action

against the British state. It was declared a prohibited organization by the SNP in 1958 after it asked the Soviet government to present Scotland's case to the UN. When it ceased to exist in 1964, many of its members joined the SNP.

32 Ian Hamilton, *Taking of the Stone of Destiny* (1952) 23.

33 *Glasgow Herald*, 26 December 1950.

34 Hamilton, op. cit., 11.

35 Ibid.

36 Alexander Mackendrick (dir.), *Whisky Galore* (1949).

37 *Daily Telegraph*, 28 December 1950.

38 *Daily Mirror*, 27 December 1950.

39 *Guardian*, 27 December 1950.

40 PRO: CAB128, CM(51) 29th Conclusions, Minute 4, 19 April 1951.

41 PRO: CAB129, CP(51) 111, 'The Stone of Scone', 17 April 1951.

42 *Parliamentary Debates (Lords)*, vol. 171, 833, 9 May 1951.

43 PRO: CAB129, CP(51) 117, 'The Stone of Scone', 26 April 1951.

44 PRO: PREM8/1516, Brook to Attlee, 2 May 1951.

45 *Sunday Dispatch*, 23 April 1951. See also Lawrence Whistler's *English Festivals* (1947), which said the English had become 'a little slack' in celebrating their nationhood. 'The Union Jack . . . denotes the union of four countries and the pomp of Empire, but . . . simpler and lovelier are the emblems of St. George'.

46 Kathleen Paul, *Whitewashing Britain: Race and Citizenship in the Postwar Era* (1997) 21.

47 Ibid.

48 See Stephen Howe, *Anticolonialism in British Politics: The Left and the End of Empire 1918–1964* (1993).

49 Paul, op. cit., 22.

50 Ibid., 85.

51 Ibid., 67.

52 Ibid., 114.

53 Ibid., 116.

54 Ibid., 127.

55 Ibid., 118.

56 Ian R. G. Spencer, *British Immigration Policy Since 1939: The Making of Multi-Racial Britain* (1997) 90.

57 Paul, op. cit., 149.

58 Mike Phillips and Charlie Phillips, *Notting Hill in the Sixties* (1991) 33.

59 Panikos Panayi (ed.), *Racial Violence in Britain in the Nineteenth and Twentieth Centuries* (2nd edn, 1996) 174.

60 PRO: PREM8/1222/1, Note by Sir John Maffey, 3 August 1946.

61 PRO: CAB129, C(46) 381, Lord President, 'Éire and Northern Ireland', 16 October 1946.

62 PRO: CAB21/1843, Rugby to Attlee, 17 November 1948.

63 *Parliamentary Debates (Commons)*, vol. 456, 1415–18, 25 November 1948.

64 *Manchester Guardian*, 18 October 1948.

65 Paul, op. cit., 108.

66 Ibid., 29.

67 Mark Amory (ed.), *The Letters of Evelyn Waugh* (1980) 373.

68 PRO: PREM8/1466, Attlee to Viscount Hall, Personal Minute M.8/51, 30 January 1951; Note of a Meeting with the Irish Republic Ministerial Delegation, 24 January 1951. The Foreign Secretary did not attend the meeting because Anglo-Irish relations were still dealt with by the Commonwealth Office due to Ireland's retention of its special status.

69 David H. Hume, 'Empire Day in Ireland 1896–1962', in Keith Jeffrey (ed.), *An Irish Empire? Aspects of Ireland and the British Empire* (1996) 162–3.

70 Steve Bruce, *The Edge of the Union: The Ulster Loyalist Political Vision* (1994) 39.

71 Ian McBride, *The Siege of Derry in Ulster Protestant Mythology* (1997) 72.

72 E. Estyn Evans, *About Britain no. 13: Northern Ireland* (1951) 7–8. This was part of a series published by Collins in conjunction with the Festival of Britain and sponsored by the government and the Brewers Society. Another example of the province's high standing was its incorporation in the British 'County' guidebook series: Hugh Shearman, *Ulster* (1949).

73 Political and Economic Planning, *The Arts Enquiry: The Visual Arts, A Report Sponsored by the Dartington Hall Trustees* (1946) 27. Cole's conclusion was a direct quote from Herbert Read's *Education Through Art* (1943).

74 *Listener*, vol.14, no. 357, 13 November 1935, 882.

75 *Parliamentary Debates (Commons)*, vol. 421, 1840, 9 April 1946.

76 *Parliamentary Debates (Commons)*, vol. 463, 1485–6, 31 March 1949.

77 David Cannadine, *G. M. Trevelyan: A Life in History* (1993) 159.

78 Eric Parker, *Britain Advance: Landmarks Given to the People* (1943) 13. The Scottish National Trust had to be bailed out by a reluctant Stafford Cripps in 1948. While it did not enjoy the same level of support as its English counterpart, the growing nationalist sentiment north of the border after 1947 would not have been placated by its disappearance. Accordingly, when the Scottish Office predicted 'a great outcry in Scotland' unless the Treasury found the money, it duly did so. See PRO: T226/38, Sir Charles Cunningham to Sir Bernard Gilbert, 21 July 1948.

79 NTA: 319/1, Mallaby to Executive Committee, 28 December 1945.

80 NTA: 319/2, Executive Committee Minutes, Item 3 (a), 11 January 1946. Mallaby had previously been Secretary to the Joint Planning Staff at

Potsdam before joining the Trust. After serving as Secretary to the Brussels Treaty Defence Organisation (1948–50), he concluded his career as an under-secretary at the Cabinet Office (1950–54).

81 James Lees-Milne, *Caves of Ice* (1983) 5.

82 James Lees-Milne, *Midway on the Waves* (1985) 28.

83 NTA: 36/3, Memorandum submitted to the Gowers Committee, undated.

84 NTA: Publicity/Special Collections/Acc.45, 'The National Trust: Past Achievements and Present Activities', BBC Third Programme, 10 August 1947.

85 HM Treasury, *Houses of Outstanding Historic or Architectural Interest: Report of a Committee* (1950) 3.

86 PRO: HLG126/18, Memorandum to the Gowers Committee, 6 November 1950. Maclagan was an adviser to the Ministry of Town and Country Planning on the listing of buildings.

87 PRO: CAB128/19, CM(51) 30, 23 April 1951, Item 2.

88 National Trust, *Annual Report, 1946–7*, 7.

89 PRO: HLG71/1753, Herbert Gatliff, Minute, 1 July 1945.

90 *Spectator*, 18 November 1949. This complaint was still being made nearly a decade later, in the Trust's Annual Report for 1958.

91 NTA: 319, A. A. Martineau to Admiral Bevir, 28 March 1949. The former was the Trust's solicitor; the latter succeeded Mallaby as Secretary.

92 NTA: 319, Standing Committee on National Parks, 'Accommodation in National Parks for Visitors', 9 February 1945.

93 Howard Newby, *Country Life: A Social History of Rural England* (1987) 176.

94 C. E. M. Joad, *The Untutored Townsman's Invasion of the Country* (1946) 223.

95 *Times Literary Supplement*, 1 March 1948.

96 *First Report of the National Parks Commission* (1950) 5.

97 Peter Mandler, *The Fall and Rise of the Stately Home* (1997) 396.

98 This memorable phrase belongs to my agent, Giles Gordon, coined in 1998 during one of our conversations about this book.

99 *Parliamentary Debates (Commons)*, vol. 512, 2209, 6 February 1953.

100 Stuart Laing, 'Images of the Rural in Popular Culture, 1750–1990', in Brian Short (ed.), *The English Rural Community: Image and Analysis* (1992) 146.

101 See Georgina Boyes, *The Imagined Village: Culture, Ideology and the English Folk Revival* (1993) 220–21.

102 See Paul Oliver, Ian Davis and Ian Bentley, *Dunroamin: The Suburban Semi And Its Enemies* (second edn, 1994). Standish Meacham, *Regaining Paradise: Englishness and the Early Garden City Movement* (1999) is also instructive.

103 David Matless, 'Taking Pleasure in England: landscape and citizenship in the 1940s', in Richard Weight and Abigail Beach (eds), *The Right to*

Belong: Citizenship and National Identity in Britain, 1930–1960 (1998) 181.

104 James Lees-Milne, 'Who Cares for England?', *Listener*, 19 March 1964.

105 F. M. Levanthal, 'The Best for the Most: CEMA and State Sponsorship of the Arts in Wartime, 1939–1945', *Twentieth Century British History*, vol. 1, no. 3, 317.

106 PRO: ED136/196A, Wilkinson to Keynes, 27 August 1945.

107 *The Times*, 9 May 1946.

108 Sir John Rothenstein, 'The Re-opening of the Tate Gallery', *Listener*, 11 April 1946.

109 *Observer*, 14 April 1946.

110 TGA: TG20, 'Speech by the Foreign Secretary at the Re-Opening of the Gallery', 10 April 1946. Bevin's attendance was secured by the Tate's purchase of a bust of him by Jacob Epstein.

111 Geoffrey Whitworth, *The Making of a National Theatre* (1951) 232.

112 J. B. Priestley, *Theatre Outlook* (1947) 16–17.

113 Aneurin Bevan, *In Place of Fear* (1952) 50–51.

114 Arts Council of Great Britain, *Plans For An Arts Centre* (1945) 7.

115 *Parliamentary Debates (Lords)*, vol. 160, 987–88, 17 February 1949.

116 Jack Lindsay, *British Achievement in Art and Music* (1945) 8.

117 *Parliamentary Debates (Lords)*, vol. 160, 998, 17 February 1949.

118 Alistair Horne, *Macmillan 1891–1956 , Volume i of the Official Biography* (1988) 160.

119 PRO: EL4/45, Ralph Vaughan Williams, 'Nationalism or Internationalism?' Arts Council Paper No. 206A, 29 January 1946.

120 Arnold Haskell, *The National Ballet: A History and Manifesto* (1943) 33.

121 *Picture Post*, vol. 27, no. 3, 30 June 1945.

122 Robert Stradling and Meirion Hughes, *The English Musical Renaissance 1860–1940: Construction and Deconstruction* (1993) 242.

123 Cmd 6852, *Broadcasting Policy* (1946) 81.

124 CCC: Haley, 13/6, Diary entry 11 August 1950.

125 Anthony Smith, *British Broadcasting* (1974) 78–9.

126 William Haley, 'What the Third Programme Aims At', *Listener*, 3 October 1946.

127 *Picture Post*, 30 November 1946.

128 Hennessy, op. cit., 120.

129 *Observer*, 22 September 1946.

130 T. S. Eliot, *Notes Towards the Definition of Culture* (1948) 112.

131 *Times Literary Supplement*, 28 September 1946.

132 CCC: Haley/16/52, Sir William Haley, 'The Responsibilities of Broadcasting: The Lewis Fry Memorial Lectures delivered in the University of Bristol 11, 12 May 1948', 10–11. See also his 'Moral Values in Broadcasting: Address to the British Council of Churches on 2 November 1948', in which he outlined a similar approach to religious broadcasting.

133 G. D. H. Cole, *Local and Regional Government* (1947) 154–5.

134 Michael Young, *Small Man, Big World* (1952) 17.

135 Asa Briggs, *The History of Broadcasting in the United Kingdom*, vol. 4: *Sound and Vision* (1979) 95. Regional broadcasting was partly designed as a form of internal competition within the BBC, in an attempt to stave off the introduction of commercial broadcasting.

136 Ibid., 110. The phrase originated at Yorkshire's cricket ground, Headingly, where spectators tired of a plodding batsman would shout out, 'For God's sake, have a go!'

137 *Listener*, vol. 34, No. 861, 12 July 1945.

138 Priestley, *Theatre Outlook*, 59.

139 Eliot, *Notes Towards the Definition of Culture*, 52. Eliot had another reason for supporting regionalism. Although an American exile, he believed that people should remain where they were born as this cemented family and class ties. For Eliot, the maintenance of a high level of culture depended upon class stratification, so regionalism was a means of achieving that.

140 Ibid., 31.

141 Ibid., 58.

142 Arts Council of Great Britain, *The First Aldeburgh Festival of Music and the Arts* (1948).

143 *Times Literary Supplement*, 27 July 1948.

144 David Reynolds, *Rich Relations: The American Occupation of Britain 1942–1945* (1995) 434–5.

145 Ibid.

146 Ross McKibbin, *Classes and Cultures: England 1918–1951* (1998) 523.

147 Clive Ponting, *1940: Myth and Reality* (1990) 233–4.

148 Noël Annan, *Changing Enemies: The Defeat and Regeneration of Germany* (1995) 159.

149 MRCW: Gollancz/MSS157/3/GE/2/f.14.

150 BBCWAC/E1/109, 'American Material in Programmes', R. J. F. Howgill (Controller Entertainment), Note for File, 6 September 1946.

151 Paul Swann, *The Hollywood Feature Film in Postwar Britain* (1987) 2.

152 Board of Trade, *Tendencies towards Monopoly in the Cinematograph Industry* (1944) 12.

153 The Arts Council could not help because Keynes did not consider film to be an art and had refused to include it in the organization's remit.

154 LPA: RD/43, 'The Enjoyment of Leisure', February 1947. A report by the left/liberal thinktank Political and Economic Planning, *The Factual Film* (1947), reached the same conclusion.

155 Swann, op. cit., 22.

156 Ben Pimlott, *Harold Wilson* (1992) 120.

157 Robert Murphy, *Realism and Tinsel: Cinema and Society in Britain 1939–48* (1989) 231.

158 Quoted in Charles Barr, *Ealing Studios* (second edn, 1993) 60.

159 Ibid., 44.

160 J. P. Mayer, *British Cinemas and Their Audiences: Sociological Studies* (1948) 239.

161 Ibid., 231.

162 Ibid., 241.

163 Michael Davie (ed.), *The Diaries of Evelyn Waugh* (1976) 650. Entry for 8 June 1946.

164 *Picture Post*, vol. 31, no. 12, 22 June 1946.

165 *Times Literary Supplement*, 8 March 1947.

166 Richard Findlater (ed.), *The Complete Guide to the National Theatre* (1977) 44.

167 *Horizon*, vol. 16, no. 90, July 1947.

168 *Horizon*, vol. 12, no. 81, September 1946.

169 Robert Hewison, *In Anger: Culture in the Cold War 1945–60* (1981) 22.

170 J. B. Priestley, *The Arts under Socialism* (1947) 14.

171 CCC: Haley/13/6, Diaries, 1948–51, Entry for 28 August 1949.

172 PRO: EL3/60, Cyril Wood to Mary Glasgow, 8 December 1947.

173 B. Seebohm Rowntree and G. R. Lavers, *English Life and Leisure* (1951) 370–71.

174 Charles Landstone, *Off Stage: A Personal Record of the First Twelve Years of State-Sponsored Drama in Great Britain* (1953) 60. The most generous figures appear in a poll of 1947. Carried out for the Musicians Union by Gallup, it estimated that 31 per cent of Britons were more interested in classical music than before the war as a result of CEMA's work.

175 PRO: EL4/46, Arts Council Paper No.221, Michael Macowan, 'Drama Policy', 26 October 1946.

176 PRO: EL4/62, *British Theatre Conference: Summary of the Proceedings, 5–8 February 1948*.

177 PRO: EL 3/60, Cyril Wood to Mary Glasgow, 8 December 1947.

178 Ivor Brown, *Edinburgh Festival: Review of the First Ten Years 1947–56* (1957) 9.

179 PRO: EL4/47, 'Edinburgh Festival', Arts Council Paper no. 234, 8 September 1947.

180 *Glasgow Forward*, 16 February 1952.

181 Paul Ferris, *Sir Huge: The Life of Huw Wheldon* (1990) 73–4.

182 Ibid., 74.

183 PRO: EL2/17, Lord Harlech to Mary Glasgow, 11 July 1948.

184 PRO: EL4/47, Mary Glasgow, 'Audiences for the Arts', Arts Council Paper no. 240, 29 October 1947.

185 LPA: RD43, 'The Enjoyment of Leisure', February 1947, 120.

186 PRO: EL4/55, W. E. Williams, 'Financial Estimates, 1952–3: Notes for a Preliminary Discussion', 24 July 1951.

187 PRO: EL4/85, 'Report of a conference between Regional Directors of the Arts Council of Great Britain and Local Authorities', 12 December 1952.

188 Michael Frayn, 'Festival', in Michael Sissons and Philip French (eds), *Age of Austerity* (1963) 324.

189 BBC WAC/R34/364, *The Heritage of Britain* (BBC Transcription Service Pamphlet, 1951).

190 J. B. Priestley, 'On with the Festival!', *Listener*, vol. 45, no. 1158, 10 May 1951.

191 PRO: EL6/1, excerpt from the Ramsden Report, 17 December 1945.

192 Herbert Read, 'Britain Can Make It', *Listener*, vol. 36, no. 925, 3 October 1946.

193 *The Times*, 29 September 1951.

194 Mary Banham and Bevis Hillier (eds), *A Tonic To The Nation: The Festival of Britain 1951* (1976) 32.

195 PRO: CAB124/1220, Lord Ismay, Speech made in the presence of Princess Elizabeth at the opening meeting of the Festival Council, 31 May 1948.

196 PRO: INF12/302, Minutes of Festival Overseas Publicity Committee, Item 5 (iv), 13 November 1950.

197 Noël Coward, *The Lyrics of Noël Coward* (1965) 343–6.

198 *Radio Times*, 27 April 1951.

199 PRO: EL6/133, Gerald Barry, Press Conference, 14 October 1948.

200 Michael Frayn, 'Festival', in Michael Sissons and Philip French (eds), *Age of Austerity* (1963) 319–20.

201 Robert Hewison, *Culture and Consensus: England, art and politics since 1940* (1995) 58.

202 Paul Addison, *Now The War Is Over: A Social History of Britain 1945–51* (1985) 208–9.

203 Banham and Hillier, op. cit., 80.

204 PRO: INF12/302, Minutes of Overseas Publicity Committee, Item 2(b), 14 October 1949.

205 Gerald Barry, 'The Festival of Britain 1951', *Journal of the Royal Society of Arts*, vol. 100, no. 4880, 2 August 1952, 693.

206 Banham and Hillier, op. cit., 170.

207 PRO: EL6/1, Memorandum by the Lord President, 'Proposals Regarding the 1951 Exhibition'.

208 PRO: CAB124/1220, C. G. Costley-White (CRO) to Lord President's Office, 24 June 1948.

209 G. C. Lawrence (ed.), *Official Guide, British Empire Exhibition* (1925) 89.

210 PRO: CAB124/1220, Note of a meeting between the Foreign Office and Colonial Relations Office at the Festival of Britain headquarters, 26 July 1949.

211 Barry, op. cit., 697.

212 LPL/Fisher/85/51, Barry to Fisher, 13 February 1950.

213 *The Official Book of the Festival of Britain* (1951) 20.

214 Ibid., i.

215 *Illustrated London News*, 12 May 1951, 764.

216 PRO: EL6/133, *Festival Newsletter*, 12 November 1949.

217 Ian Cox, *The South Bank Exhibition: A Guide to the Story It Tells* (1951) 8–9; see 'The Country', 17–19, with its headings 'Science and the Land', 'Livestock and Breeding', 'Mechanisation', and 'Planning the Use of the Land'.

218 Ibid., 82.

219 Ian Cox, *Festival Ship Campania: A Guide to the Story It Tells* (1951) 31.

220 Jacob Bronowski, *Exhibition of Science, South Kensington: A Guide to the Story It Tells* (1951) 5

221 Ibid., 7.

222 Banham and Hillier, op. cit., 177.

223 Ismay, *The Memoirs of General Lord Ismay* (1960) 451.

224 LPL/Fisher/85/51, Festival Advisory Committee of the British Council of Churches, *A Form of Divine Service for Use during the Festival of Britain.*

225 Geoffrey Fisher, 'The Closing of the Festival of Britain', *Listener*, vol. 46, no. 1179, 4 October 1951.

226 Kevin Jackson (ed.), *The Humphrey Jennings Film Reader* (1993) 172–7.

227 PRO: HO45/24406, George Tomlinson, 'Notes for Speech at Central Conference on Juvenile Delinquency, Central Hall Westminster, 2 March 1949'.

228 Cox, op. cit., 5.

229 PRO: CAB124/1221, Festival of Britain Meeting of Heads of Local Government, Text of a speech by Gerald Barry, 8 June 1949.

230 HMSO, *The Festival of Britain* (1951) 26. The Northern Ireland Festival Committee was entirely drawn from the Protestant landowning, commercial and professional elite.

231 *The Times*, 3 May 1951.

232 PRO: CAB124/1221, Festival of Britain Meeting of Heads of Local Governments, text of a speech by Gerald Barry, 8 June 1949.

233 Fisher, op. cit.

234 Ferris, op. cit., 77.

235 Banham and Hillier, op. cit., 81.

236 Frayn, op. cit., 335.

237 Banham, op. cit., 177–8.

238 Frayn, op. cit., 338.

239 Ibid., 166.

240 Harold Nicolson, 'After the Festival: A Note for Posterity', *Listener*, vol. 46, no. 1183, 1 November 1951.

3. VIEWERS

1 *Parliamentary Debates (Commons)*, vol. 495, 960–62, 11 February 1952.
2 PRO: CAB21/3730, Eccles to R. A. Butler, 5 May 1952.
3 Ibid., Eccles to Butler, 3 May 1952.
4 David Eccles' obituary, *Daily Telegraph*, 26 February 1999.
5 David Cannadine, 'The Context, Performance and Meaning of Ritual: The British Monarchy and the Invention of Tradition, c. 1820–1977', in Eric Hobsbawm and Terence Ranger (eds), *The Invention of Tradition* (1983) 217.
6 Lavinia, Duchess of Norfolk's obituary, *Daily Telegraph*, 12 December 1995. The phrase belongs to the journalist Robert Harris.
7 LPL/Fisher/123/53, Diary entry, 16 February 1953. The Duke of Norfolk rejected Attlee's proposal on the rather dubious ground (thought Fisher) that the entire Commonwealth would have to be consulted.
8 *The Coronation of Her Majesty Queen Elizabeth II: Approved Souvenir Programme* (1953) 8.
9 LPL/Fisher/123/53, Ratcliff to Fisher, 21 December 1952.
10 Arthur Bryant, *English Saga 1840–1940* (1940) 9.
11 *Daily Mirror*, 3 June 1953.
12 PRO: CAB21/3732, Osbert Cheke to Alan Lascelles, 1 July 1953.
13 *Sunday Dispatch*, 7 June 1953.
14 *Picture Post*, vol. 59, no. 4, 25 April 1953.
15 Ibid.
16 PRO: CAB129, CP (52) 26, 'The Stone of Scone', 8 February 1952.
17 PRO: PREM11/252, Jock Colville to Lady Airlie, 1 April 1952.
18 Cmd. 9212, *Royal Commission on Scottish Affairs* (1954) 12.
19 *Parliamentary Debates (Commons)*, vol. 536, 915–19, 1 February 1955.
20 PRO: CAB129, C(58) 105, 'Special Stamps: Robert Burns', 12 May 1958. Marples added that the United States, which had introduced commemorative stamps in 1956, had to deal with two thousand applications for twelve issues in that year and had found it 'a very controversial and thankless task'.
21 PRO: CAB128, CC(58) 45th Conclusions, Minute 5, 22 May 1958.
22 *The Conservative Policy for Wales and Monmouthshire* (1949) 10.
23 Cited in Alan Butt Philip, *The Welsh Question: Nationalism in Welsh Politics, 1945–1970* (1975) 296.
24 PRO: BD24/302, Sir Edward Bridges to Sir Frank Newsom, 23 October 1952.
25 The Prince was chosen by the Legitimist Jacobite League, a short-lived organization established during the Home Rule campaigns of the late nineteenth century.

26 Jeffrey Richards, *Films and British National Identity: From Dickens to Dad's Army* (1997) 186. Alexander Korda's *Bonnie Prince Charlie* (1948) was the only film of this genre not to be a success, thanks to the hopeless miscasting of David Niven in the lead role.

27 See Murray G. H. Pittock, *The Invention of Scotland: Stuart Myth and the Scottish Identity, 1638 to the Present* (1991).

28 Graham Walker and Tom Gallagher, 'Protestantism and Scottish Politics', in Graham Walker and Tom Gallagher (eds), *Sermons and Battle Hymns: Protestant Popular Culture in Modern Scotland* (1990) 90.

29 LPL/Fisher 123/53, Dean of Westminster to Fisher, 16 February 1952.

30 LPL/Fisher/123/53, Diary entry, 2 June 1953.

31 Philip Ziegler, *Crown and People* (1978) 124.

32 Edward Shils and Michael Young, 'The Meaning of the Coronation', *The Sociological Review* (New Series) vol. 1, No. 2, December 1953, 67.

33 Adrian Hastings, *A History of English Christianity 1920–1985* (1986) 447.

34 Ibid., 454.

35 The Bishop of Chichester, G. K. A. Bell, *The English Church* (1942) 7.

36 Edward Carpenter, *Archbishop Fisher: His Life and Times* (1991) 351.

37 Hastings, op. cit., 469.

38 John Highet, *The Scottish Churches: A review of their state 400 years after the Reformation* (1960) 156.

39 Ibid., 158.

40 LPL/Fisher/252, f.206, Thomas Hannay (Bishop of Argyll & the Isles and Primus of the Scottish Episcopal Church) to Fisher, 17 July 1959.

41 LPL/Fisher/252, f.212, Fisher to Hannay, 28 June 1960.

42 Minutes of the Proceedings of the General Assembly of the Church of Scotland, 11 October 1960, *The Principal Acts of the Church of Scotland* (1961) 135. The last monarch to address the Assembly was James VI, shortly before the Union of the Crowns.

43 *Sunday Dispatch*, 10 February 1953.

44 *Sunday Graphic*, 17 February 1952.

45 *Listener*, vol. 49, no. 1266, 4 June 1953.

46 *The Coronation of Her Majesty Queen Elizabeth II: Approved Souvenir Programme*, 30.

47 PRO: PREM11/529, Prime Minister's Personal Minute, No. M391, 16 July 1952.

48 PRO: CAB128/25, CC106 (52) Item 4, 18 December 1952.

49 BL: CPA/CCO4/5/109, Stephen Pierssené (Director, Central Office) to Central Office Agents, 15 July 1952.

50 *The Times*, 2 June 1953.

51 Richard Dimbleby, *Elizabeth our Queen* (1953) 171–2.

52 *The Times*, 3 June 1953.

53 CCC: Haley/1/1, Grisewood to Haley, 3 June 1953.

54 PRO: CAB21/3730, Salisbury to Thorneycroft, 18 June 1953. The Cabinet concurred on 20 June.

55 *Parliamentary Debates (Commons)*, vol. 499, 719, 24 April 1952.

56 *Daily Telegraph*, 17 June 1953.

57 Kenneth and Valerie McLeish (eds), *Long To Reign Over Us: Memories of Coronation Day and Life in the 1950s* (1992) 178–9.

58 *Daily Express*, 3 June 1953.

59 See Gordon T. Stewart, 'Tensing's Two Wrist-Watches: The Conquest of Everest and Late Imperial Culture in Britain 1921–1953', *Past and Present*, no. 149, November 1995.

60 Kenneth and Valerie McLeish, op. cit., 103.

61 *Listener*, vol. 49, no. 1266, 4 June 1953.

62 Tom Fleming (ed.), *Voices out of the Air: The Royal Christmas Broadcasts 1932–1981* (1981) 73–4.

63 *Sunday Express*, 8 June 1952.

64 Duke of Windsor, *The Crown and the People 1902–1953* (1953) 39–40.

65 PRO: PREM11/34, Brook to Churchill, 24 October 1952.

66 *Daily Express*, 27 October 1952.

67 *Manchester Guardian*, 27 October 1952.

68 *Parliamentary Debates (Commons)*, vol. 505, 1742–3, 28 October 1952.

69 *Listener*, vol. 49, no. 1267, 11 June 1953, 956.

70 *News Chronicle*, 3 June 1953.

71 *Evening Standard*, 3 June 1953.

72 LPL/Fisher/123/53, Fisher to George Barnes (Director of Television), 9 June 1953.

73 Lord Harewood, *The Tongs and the Bones* (1981) 134.

74 *Journal of the Royal Society of Arts*, vol. XCVI, no. 4755, 21 November 1947.

75 Robert Hewison, 'Happy Were He: Benjamin Britten and the *Gloriana* story', in Paul Banks (ed.), *Britten's Gloriana: Essays and Sources* (1993) 13.

76 William Plomer, 'Let's Crab an Opera', *London Magazine*, vol. 3, no. 7, October 1965.

77 *The Times*, 14 February 1951.

78 Bod/BAAS, Prince Philip to Sir Harold Hartley, 3 January 1951.

79 *The Times*, 3 March 1954.

80 *Picture Post*, 2 June 1952.

81 *Sunday Dispatch*, 25 August 1955.

82 BBC: WAC/R9/10/3, Audience Research Special Reports, '*Britain in Decline*', 9 January 1956. For more on the debate, see C. P. Snow, *The Two Cultures and A Second Look* (1963); F. R. Leavis, *Two Cultures? The Significance of C. P. Snow* (1962) and Ian MacKillop, *F. R. Leavis, A Life in Criticism* (1995), 314–29. In intellectual circles, Snow came off worse. A novelist, civil servant and scientist, he argued that the gulf

between science and the arts in Britain sprang partly from a snobbish anti-materialism among the literary intelligentsia, and that mouths had to be fed before souls could sing. Leavis was a Cambridge academic, for whom English literature was a medium for the national spirit. His ferocious attack on Snow's theory, and the support he received for making it, proved yet again that mass democracy was still an acquired taste among Britain's intellectuals.

83 Communist Party of Great Britain, *Coronation* (1953) 5.

84 G. J. Renier, 'The Queen and Her People', *Listener*, vol. 49, no. 1265, 28 May 1953.

85 Ziegler, op. cit., 101.

86 Shils and Young, op. cit., 3.

87 James Joll, 'On Being an Intellectual', *Twentieth Century*, vol. 157, June 1955.

88 Shils and Young, op. cit., 56.

89 J. H. Huizinga, *Confessions of a European in England* (1958) 207–9.

90 Asa Briggs, *The BBC: The First Fifty Years* (1985) 239.

91 *Parliamentary Debates (Commons)*, vol. 522, 45, 14 December 1953.

92 Ibid., 65.

93 Paul Ferris, *Sir Huge: The Life of Huw Wheldon* (1990) 83–4.

94 Christopher Mayhew, *Dear Viewer* (1953) 1.

95 Bernard Sendall, *Independent Television in Britain*, vol. 1: *Origin and Foundation 1946–62* (1982) 16.

96 H. H. Wilson, *Pressure Group: The Campaign for Commercial Television* (1961) 114.

97 William Clark, 'The Future of Television', *Twentieth Century*, vol. 154, July 1953.

98 Nicolson, op. cit., 245.

99 *Parliamentary Debates (Commons)*, vol. 528, 1069–70, 22 February 1955.

100 Ibid.

101 John Springhall, *Youth, Popular Culture and Moral Panics: Penny Gaffs to Gangsta-Rap 1830–1996* (1999) 142.

102 Only one prosecution was ever made under the Act but it remains on the statute book today.

103 Asa Briggs, *History of Broadcasting in the United Kingdom*, vol. 4, 471–2.

104 Mayhew, op. cit., 6.

105 *Parliamentary Debates (Lords)*, vol. 188, 355–6, 1 July 1954.

106 *Economist*, 15 August 1953.

107 *Parliamentary Debates (Commons)*, vol. 522, 47, 14 December 1953.

108 Ibid., 74.

109 Ibid., 65.

110 Briggs, op. cit., 911.

111 Kathleen Tynan (ed.), *Kenneth Tynan, Letters* (1994) 196–7.

112 Ibid., 166.

113 Sendall, op. cit., 127.

114 TGA: Clark Papers/8812.2.2.10121, ITV opening night speech, 22 September 1955.

115 Bernard Sendall, *Independent Television in Britain*, vol. 1: *Origin and Foundation 1946–62* (1982) 112.

116 Kenneth Clark, *The Other Half: A Self-Portrait* (1977) 138.

117 TGA: Clark Papers/8812.2.2.10124, Clark to Robert Heller, 30 December 1959.

118 Sir Robin Day, *Grand Inquisitor: Memoirs* (1989) 82.

119 John Montgomery, *The Fifties* (1965) 287–8.

120 *News Chronicle*, 2 December 1955.

121 TGA: Clark Papers/8812.2.2.1021, undated interview, c. 1955.

122 John Corner (ed.), *Popular Television in Britain: Studies In Cultural History* (1991) 15.

123 Sendall, op. cit., 36.

124 Bernard Sendall, *Independent Television in Britain*, vol. 2: *Expansion and Change 1958–68* (1983) 28–9.

125 W. H. Macdowell, *The History of BBC Broadcasting in Scotland 1923–1983* (1992) 84.

126 Corner, op. cit., 44.

127 Humphrey Carpenter, *The Envy of the World: Fifty Years of the BBC Third Programme and Radio 3, 1946–1996* (1996) 68.

128 Harry Hopkins, *The New Look: A Social History of the Forties and Fifties in Britain* (1963) 49.

129 Lord Aberdare, Foreword to Gordon Winter, *Games for Court and Garden* (1947) 5.

130 John Smith, *The Auld Enemy: A Century of England v. Scotland* (1997) 24.

131 Neville Cardus, *English Cricket* (1945) 9.

132 Richard Holt, *Sport and the British: A Modern History* (1989) 345.

133 Dennis Compton, *End Of An Innings* (second edn, 1988) 198–9.

134 Jack Williams, 'Cricket', in Tony Mason (ed.), *Sport In Britain: A Social History* (1989).

135 Vita Sackville-West, 'Outdoor Life', in Ernest Barker (ed.), *The Character of England* (1947), 410.

136 Stanley Matthews, *The Way It Was: My Autobiography* (2000) 213.

137 See Peter J. Beck, *Scoring For Britain: International Politics and International Football 1900–1939* (1999).

138 H. F. Moorhouse, 'One State, Several Countries: Soccer and Nationality in a United Kingdom', *International Journal of the History of Sport*, vol. 12, August 1995, no. 2, 70.

139 *Daily Express*, 3 September 1947.

140 *The Times*, 26 November 1953.

141 Richard Holt, *Sport and the British: A Modern History* (1989) 273.

142 Denzil Batchelor, *Soccer: A History of Association Football* (1954) 149–51.
143 Williams, op. cit., 122.
144 Ibid., 126.
145 Tony Mason, 'Football', in Mason, op. cit., 149.
146 Roy Denman, *Missed Chances: Britain and Europe in the Twentieth Century* (1996) 196.
147 Ibid., 199.
148 PRO: FO371/116040, Jebb to Macmillan, 15 June 1955.
149 Denman, op. cit., 198–9.
150 Ibid., 171.
151 PRO: PREM11/39, Brook to Churchill, 9 February 1952.
152 J. H. Huizinga, *Confessions of a European in England* (1958) 211.
153 John Mather (ed.), *The Great Spy Scandal: The Inside Story of Burgess and Maclean* (1955) 179.
154 Kim Philby, *My Silent War* (1968) vii.
155 Ibid., 445.
156 Bernard Porter, *Plots and Paranoia: A History of Political Espionage in Britain 1790–1988* (1989) 187.
157 *Spectator*, 23 September 1955.
158 *Daily Herald*, 20 September 1955.
159 Mather, op. cit., 133.
160 Robert Cecil, *A Divided Life: A Biography of Donald Maclean* (1988) 194.

4. SHOPPERS

1 Brian Brivati, *Hugh Gaitskell* (1996) 277.
2 Russell Braddon, *Suez: Splitting of a Nation* (1973).
3 PRO: PREM11/1138, Note by Eden, 28 December 1956.
4 Edward Heath, *The Course of my Life* (1998) 178.
5 BBC TV, *The Suez Crisis*, transcript, 22 October 1996.
6 Harold Macmillan, *Riding the Storm 1956–1959* (1971) 319.
7 Nigel Nicolson, *Harold Nicolson, Diaries and Letters 1945–62* (1968) 314, 323–4.
8 Graham Payn and Sheridan Morley (eds), *The Noël Coward Diaries* (1982) 349.
9 Fintan O'Toole, 'Imagining Scotland', *Granta*, No. 56, 1997, 54.
10 John M. Mackenzie, 'David Livingstone: the construction of the myth', in Graham Walker and Tom Gallagher (eds), *Sermons and Battle Hymns: Protestant Popular Culture in Modern Scotland* (1990) 37–40.
11 Isobel Lindsay, 'Migration and Motivation: A Twentieth Century

Perspective', in T. M. Devine (ed.), *Scottish Emigration and Scottish Society* (1992).

12 Peter Hennessy, *Muddling Through: Power, Politics and the Quality of Government in Postwar Britain* (1996) 99.

13 PRO: PREM11/2204, Brooke to Macmillan, 25 November 1957.

14 PRO: PREM11/2204, Macmillan to Huw T. Edwards, 11 December 1957.

15 PRO: BD24/86, Edwards to Gwilym Lloyd George, 23 July 1956.

16 PRO: BD24/86, Speech by Henry Brooke at the opening of the Festival of Wales, Cardiff, 18 July 1958. Prince Philip attended the opening.

17 Huw T. Edwards, 'What The Festival Is All About', *Festival of Wales Official Souvenir Programme* (Cardiff, 1958) 2.

18 PRO: BD25/5, Speech by Harold Macmillan at the unveiling of the statue to David Lloyd George in Cardiff, 8 July 1960.

19 PRO: BD25/5, Speech by Harold Macmillan, Cardiff City Hall, 8 July 1960.

20 PRO: HO45/25177, Howard to Home Office, 24 May 1945.

21 PRO: BD24/308, Minutes of the Committee of the Privy Council on Welsh Arms, 1 December 1952.

22 *Western Mail*, 13 May 1957.

23 PRO: PREM11/4441, Brooke to Macmillan, 16 June 1958.

24 PRO: BD24/313, A. E. Jones (Recorder of the Gorsedd of the Bards of Wales) to Lord Brecon (Minister of State for Welsh Affairs), 20 June 1958.

25 PRO: PREM11/2879, Brooke to Macmillan, 13 February 1959.

26 James Morris, *Farewell The Trumpets: An Imperial Retreat* (1978) 474.

27 A. H. Halsey (ed.), *Trends in British Society Since 1900* (1972) 568.

28 BBC TV, op. cit.

29 Ibid.

30 Ibid.

31 Braddon, op. cit., 189–90.

32 Denis Healey, *The Time of my Life* (1989) 283.

33 Macmillan, op. cit., 297.

34 *Guardian*, 1 December 1961.

35 John Osborne, *Damn you, England: Collected Prose* (1994) 193–4.

36 John Osborne, *The Entertainer* (1957) 32–3.

37 See Anthony Aldgate, *Censorship and the Permissive Society: British Cinema and Theatre 1955–1965* (1995) 66–72.

38 PRO: PREM11/2601, Hogg to Macmillan, 23 May 1957.

39 PRO: PREM11/3933, Hill to Macmillan, 30 April 1958. Hill, the Postmaster-General, pointed out that between 1950 and 1958 the amount of money government spent on promoting the Empire to UK residents fell from £125,000 to £3,000 per annum.

40 PRO: PREM11/2601, Lennox-Boyd to Macmillan, 30 May 1957.

41 Ibid., Brook to Macmillan, 18 June 1957.

42 PRO: PREM11/3933, Macmillan to Hill, 4 May 1958.

43 Ibid., Sandys to Alec Douglas-Home, 'Extract of a Report on Commonwealth Weeks', 8 March 1962.

44 Ibid.

45 Bernard Porter, *The Lion's Share: A Short History of British Imperialism 1850–1995* (3rd edn, 1996) 369.

46 Private information.

47 Acheson was speaking at West Point on 5 December 1962.

48 Andrew Roberts, *Eminent Churchillians* (1994) 230.

49 Ibid., 215.

50 Ibid., 225.

51 Ian R. G. Spencer, *British Immigration Policy Since 1939: The Making of Multi-Racial Britain* (1997) 90.

52 Edward Pilkington, *Beyond the Mother Country: West Indians and the Notting Hill White Riots* (1988) 119.

53 This briefly had a political basis, when the British created the West Indian Federation in 1958. But inter-island rivalries quickly undermined it and it was dissolved in 1962. Between then and 1983, the islands became independent states.

54 PRO: CO1032/196, 'Press Comment on Race Riots', September 1958.

55 Colin MacInnes, *Absolute Beginners* (1959, reprinted 1980) 190.

56 Paul, op. cit., 139–41. Among the sociological studies which upheld this claim were Anthony Richmond, *The Colour Problem* (1954) and E. J. B. Rose et al., *Colour and Citizenship* (1969).

57 Philip Gibbs, *How Now England?* (1958) 44.

58 Ibid., 37.

59 Lord Elton, *The Unarmed Invasion: A Survey of Afro-Asian Immigration* (1965) 7. See his *St George or the Dragon: Towards A Christian Democracy* (1942).

60 Ibid., 85.

61 Colin MacInnes, *England, Half English* (1961) 30.

62 Colin MacInnes, *Out of the Way: Later Essays* (1979) 100.

63 PRO: CAB129/102/1, C. (60) 128, 'Coloured Immigration', Memorandum by the Home Secretary, 19 July 1960.

64 *Parliamentary Debates (Commons)*, vol. 649, 693, 16 November 1961.

65 From 1951 to 1981, the total number of UK emigrants outstripped the number of immigrants by 614,000. See Zig Layton-Henry, *The Politics of Race in Britain* (1984) 25.

66 *Parliamentary Debates (Commons)*, vol. 649, 693, 16 November 1961.

67 *The Times*, 15 November 1961.

68 PRO: CAB21/4774, Norman Manley to Macmillan, 17 November 1961.

69 Braddon, op. cit., 182.

70 Christopher Booker, *The Neophiliacs: A Study of the Revolution in English Life in the Fifties and Sixties* (second edn, 1993) 117.

71 Braddon, op. cit., 179.

72 PRO: PREM11/1809, David Eccles to Anthony Eden, 6 June 1956; C. P. (56) 278, 'A Further Advance In Education', Memorandum by the Minister of Education. Eccles held his post from 1954–57 and again from 1959–62. But it was only during his second term under Macmillan that he was given the financial resources to make a real difference.

73 David Eccles' obituary, *Daily Telegraph*, 26 February 1999.

74 PRO: PREM11/3930, 'Transcript of Prime Minister's Remarks to the Cabinet', 28 May 1962.

75 Cmnd 2165, *Higher Education* (1963) para. 28, 7.

76 Eric Hopkins, *The Rise and Decline of the English Working Classes 1918–1990: A Social History* (1991) 124.

77 *Evening News*, 7 July 1960.

78 PRO: PREM11/3930, 'Transcript of Prime Minister's Remarks to the Cabinet', 28 May 1962.

79 Payn and Morley, op. cit., 349.

80 Kathleen Tynan, *Kenneth Tynan: Letters* (1994) 220–26.

81 *Daily Mail*, 5 September 1956.

82 *Daily Mail*, 4 September 1956.

83 PRO: HO300/8, LCC Children's Department, 'West End Jazz and Dance Clubs', Note for meeting with Home Secretary and Minister of Health, 15 September 1964.

84 Anthony Sampson, *Anatomy of Britain* (1962) 108–9. Though he understood why many Britons were aggrieved about US power, Gaitskell was not himself anti-American. See his critical essay 'Anti-Americanism in Britain', in Phillip Williams, *The Diary of Hugh Gaitskell* (1983) 316–20.

85 J. B. Priestley, *Thoughts In The Wilderness* (1957) 122.

86 Richard Hoggart, *The Uses of Literacy: Aspects of Working-Class Life With Special Reference To Publications and Entertainments* (1957) 204–5.

87 I am grateful to Lawrence Black for this reference and for all the material in the section on left-wing attitudes to youth culture. It comes from his excellent unpublished essay 'Socialists and Social Change in 1950s Britain' (1998).

88 Doris Lessing, *Walking in the Shade* (1995) 24.

89 See John and Mary Postgate, *A Stomach For Dissent: The Life of Raymond Postgate, Writer, Radical Socialist and Founder of The Good Food Guide* (1994).

90 Labour Party, *Take It from Here* (1956) 6.

91 *The Memoirs of Field-Marshal Montgomery* (1958) 427–8.

92 Nicholas Crowson, 'Citizen Defence: the Conservative Party and its Attitude to National Service, 1937–57', in Richard Weight and Abigail Beach (eds), *The Right to Belong: Citizenship and National Identity in Britain, 1930–1960* (1998) 214.

93 Ibid., 216.

94 See for example David Eccles, 'Popular Capitalism', *Objective*, no. 20,

January 1955, in which he argued: 'The barriers . . . are coming down . . . National Service brings boys from every kind of home into contact with each other and gives them experience of a common discipline.'

95 Crowson, op. cit., 214.

96 Trevor Royle, *The Best Years of their Lives: The National Service Experience 1945–63* (1986) 275.

97 Ibid., 276.

98 Major T. B. Beveridge, *A Guide for the National Service Man* (1953) 10–11.

99 Royle, op. cit., 250.

100 Alistair Horne, *Macmillan 1957–1986: Volume II of the Official Biography* (1989) 51.

101 Royle, op. cit., 306.

102 Ibid., 307.

103 Stephen Martin, 'Our Country Needs You: Attitudes Towards National Service in Britain 1945–63', *Oral History*, vol. 25, no. 2, Autumn 1997, 68.

104 Ibid., 71.

105 Royle, op. cit., 308.

106 Ibid., 273.

107 Andrew Sinclair, *Arts and Cultures: The History of the 50 Years of the Arts Council of Great Britain* (1995) 123.

108 PRO: PREM11/2950, Note by Macmillan, 29 December 1959.

109 BL: CPA/CRD2/52/13, PCRAS/61, 'The Use of Leisure', 1959.

110 TCC: RAB: G34/4, 'Proceedings of a Conference on the Prevention of Delinquency', 2 February 1959, 3.

111 Ibid., 6.

112 Ibid., 5.

113 Ibid., 10–11.

114 Ibid., 2.

115 Richard Hoggart, *An Imagined Life: Life and Times* (1992) 18–22.

116 Peter Laurie, *The Teenage Revolution* (1965) 43.

117 Ibid., 45.

118 John Hill, 'Television and Pop', in John Hill (ed.), *Popular Television in Britain: Studies in Cultural History* (1991) 89.

119 Ibid., 93.

120 Asa Briggs, *The History of Broadcasting in the United Kingdom*, vol. 5: *Competition 1955–1974* (1995) 264.

121 Bernard Sendall, *Independent Television in Britain*, vol. 2: *Expansion and Change 1958–68* (1983) 317.

122 Ibid., 365.

123 Reginald Bevins' obituary, *Daily Telegraph*, 19 November 1996.

124 Ibid.

125 *Sunday Pictorial*, 1 July 1962.

126 Raymond Williams, *Communications* (1962) 79.

127 *Young Elizabethan*, vol. 6, no. 9, September 1953.

128 BL: CPA/CCO4/5/108, 'The League of Empire Loyalists and the Elizabethan Party', Confidential Circular to MPs and Constituency Agents, 1 February 1955.

129 Robert Hewison, *Culture and Consensus: England, Art and Politics since 1940* (1995) 86.

130 John Grigg (Lord Altrincham), 'The Monarchy Today', *English and National Review*, vol. 149, August 1957, 61–6.

131 Malcolm Muggeridge, 'Royal Soap Opera', *New Statesman*, vol. 50, no. 1285, 22 October 1955, 499.

132 Tom Harrisson (ed.), *Britain Revisited* (1961) 249–50.

133 *Daily Mirror*, 22 May 1962.

134 Ibid.

135 Tom Fleming (ed.), *Voices out of the Air: The Royal Christmas Broadcasts 1932–1981* (1981) 97.

136 Kingsley Martin, *The Crown and the Establishment* (1962) 16.

137 I. Q. Hunter, 'The Strange World of the British Science Fiction Film', in I. Q. Hunter (ed.), *British Science Fiction Cinema* (1999) 7.

138 Horne, op. cit., 55.

139 Ibid., 57.

140 Stephen Constantine, 'Amateur Gardening and Popular Recreation in the 19th and 20th Centuries', *Journal of Social History*, vol. 14, no. 3, Spring 1981.

141 PRO: CAB21/4965, 'Recreational Trends in Britain', May 1963.

142 Harry Roberts, 'English Gardens', in Edmund Blunden (ed.), *The Englishman's Country* (1954) 207–8.

143 *Daily Express*, 2 March 1954.

144 Ross McKibbin, *The Ideologies of Class: Social Relations in Britain 1880–1950* (1990) 182.

145 David Lean (dir.), *This Happy Breed* (1944).

146 Ernest Barker (ed.), *The Character of England* (1947) 553.

147 John H. Tobe, *Garden Glimpses: Random Thoughts of an Enthusiastic Gardener* (1957) 12–13.

148 Geoffrey Gorer, *Exploring English Character* (1955) 213.

149 Clive Emsley, 'The English Bobby: An Indulgent Tradition', in Roy Porter (ed.), *Myths of the English* (1992) 128. For more detail see Emsley, *The English Police: A Political and Social History* (second edn, 1996).

150 Robert Shepherd, *Iain Macleod: A Biography* (1994) 160–1. The observation was made by Cub Alport.

151 Denman, op. cit., 208.

152 PRO: FO371/150369, Maxwell Fyfe to Heath, 14 December 1960.

153 *Encounter*, vol. 19, no. 6, December 1962.

154 Ibid.

155 R. T. Howard, *Ruined and Rebuilt: The Story of Coventry Cathedral, 1939–62* (1962) 123.

156 English Counties Periodicals, *Cathedral Reborn* (1962) 28.

157 Basil Spence, *Phoenix at Coventry: The Building of a Cathedral* (1962) 8–9.

158 Howard, op. cit., 120.

159 Humphrey Carpenter, *Benjamin Britten: A Biography* (1992) 408.

160 Ibid., 409.

161 Ibid.

162 Ibid., 410.

163 Private information.

164 CCC: Haley/5/11, Note of a meeting with the Prime Minister, 14 June 1961.

165 *Guardian*, 1 August 1961.

166 *Parliamentary Debates (Commons)*, vol. 661, 581, 6 June 1962.

167 Ibid., 718–20, 7 June 1962.

168 Harold Macmillan, *At The End Of The Day, 1961–63* (1973) 45.

169 Brian Brivati, *Hugh Gaitskell* (1996) 21.

170 Ibid., 414.

171 Ibid., 423.

172 Denman, op. cit., 220.

173 PRO: PREM11/4415, Iain Macleod, 'Public Opinion and the Common Market', 18 September 1962, 1–3.

174 Hugo Young, *This Blessed Plot: Britain and Europe from Churchill to Blair* (1998) 50–51.

175 Brivati, op. cit., 409.

176 *Encounter*, vol. 19, no. 6, December 1962.

177 *The Times*, 30 January 1963.

178 PRO: PREM11/4415, 'Public Opinion and the Common Market', 3.

179 *Daily Mirror*, 4 June 1962.

180 D. C. Watt, *Britain Looks to Germany: a study of British opinion and policy towards Germany since 1945* (1965) 147–51.

181 PRO: PREM11/4415, 'Public Opinion And The Common Market', 3–4.

182 Anne Chisholm and Michael Davie, *Lord Beaverbrook: a life* (1992) 517. He was at least consistent. Fifty years earlier, he had backed Bonar Law against Balfour on the issue of Tariff Reform, in defence of imperial economic unity.

183 *Daily Mirror*, 4 June 1962.

184 Heath, op. cit., 184.

185 Adrian Gregory, *The Silence of Memory: Armistice Day 1919–1946* (1994) 222.

186 PRO: CAB129, C.(60) 125, 'Battle of Britain Memorial', Memorandum by the Secretary of State for Air, 12 September 1960.

187 John Ramsden, 'Refocusing the People's War: British War Films of the

1950s', *Journal of Contemporary History*, vol. 33, No. 1, 37. See also Ramsden's forthcoming *Don't Mention The War* and Geoff Hurd (ed.), *National Fictions: World War II in British Films and Television* (1984).

188 *Victor*, No.157, 22 February 1964.

189 Ruth Winstone (ed.), *The Benn Diaries* (1995) 104, entry for 6 October 1963.

190 Ramsden, op. cit., 37.

191 Ramsden, op.cit., 41.

192 Ibid.

193 Ibid., 57.

194 John Osborne, 'They Call It Cricket', in Tom Maschler (ed.), *Declaration* (1957) 58–9.

195 Adam Sisman, *A. J. P. Taylor: A Biography* (1994) 299.

196 Ibid., 296.

197 Eva Haraszti Taylor (ed.), *A. J. P. Taylor: Letters To Eva, 1969–83* (1991) 4.

198 Michael Ignatieff, *Isaiah Berlin: A Life* (1998) 36.

199 Nikolaus Pevsner, *The Englishness of English Art* (second edn, 1964) 194.

200 *The Times* leader, 'The Englishness of Kunstgeshichte', 20 August 1983.

201 Pevsner, op. cit., 9; 198.

202 For a discussion of this point, see Colin Holmes, *John Bull's Island: Immigration and British Society, 1871–1971* (1988) 245–6. As in many countries, the Jewish population declined after the establishment of a homeland in the Middle East – falling from 450,000 in 1955 to 330,000 in 1985. See Geoffrey Alderman, *Modern British Jewry* (seond edn, 1998) 323.

203 PRO: PREM11/4415, 'Public Opinion And The Common Market', 4.

204 PRO: CAB128/35, CC(61) 42, 21 July 1961.

205 Harold Macmillan, *Britain, the Commonwealth and Europe* (1961) 5–10.

206 Athena Syriatou, 'Teaching European History in English Secondary Schools 1945–75', in Brian Brivati and Harriet Jones (eds), *From Reconstruction to Integration: Britain and Europe since 1945* (1993).

207 Ibid., 174.

208 Macmillan, op. cit., 7.

209 Alistair Horne, *Macmillan 1957–1986: Volume II of the Official Biography* (1989) 319.

210 Jean Lacouture, *De Gaulle: The Ruler 1945–1970* (1991) 358.

211 Charles de Gaulle, *Memoirs of Hope* (1971) 188.

212 *Daily Express*, 30 January 1963.

213 Heath, op. cit., 235.

214 Horne, op. cit., 449.

215 Harold Macmillan, *At the End of the Day, 1961–63* (1973) 368.

216 Roy Hattersley, *Fifty Years On* (1996) 152.
217 *Encounter*, vol. 19, no. 6, December 1962, 59.

5. SWINGERS

1 Jonathon Green, *All Dressed Up: The Sixties and the Counter Culture* (1998) ix.
2 Labour Party, *Let's Go with Labour for the New Britain: The Labour Party's Manifesto for the 1964 General Election* (1964) 24.
3 Harold Wilson, *THE NEW BRITAIN: Labour's Plan Outlined: Selected Speeches 1964* (1964) 9–10.
4 Gordon Heald and Robert J. Wybrow, *The Gallup Survey of Britain* (1986) 234.
5 C. A. R. Crosland, *The Future of Socialism* (1956) 520.
6 Peter Thompson, 'Labour's Gannex Conscience? Politics and Popular Attitudes in the Permissive Society', in R. Coopey, S. Fielding and N. Tiratsoo (eds), *The Wilson Governments 1964–1970* (1993) 138.
7 Jeffrey Weeks, *Sex, Politics and Society: The regulation of sexuality since 1800* (1981) 252.
8 Christopher Booker, *The Neophiliacs: A Study of the Revolution in English Life in the Fifties and Sixties* (second edn, 1993) 10.
9 PRO: FO371/1234, Clark Kerr to Pembroke, 6 April 1943. Unusually among the upper echelons of the diplomatic service, Clark Kerr (1882–1951) was a left-leaning anti-imperialist. As British Ambassador to the US from 1946 to 1948 he was Donald Maclean's boss, and though he was not implicated in Maclean's defection, his premature death was hastened by it.
10 George Mikes, *How To Be A Brit: A George Mikes Omnibus* (1984) 35. Mikes said that of all his observations, that about sex received the most agreement among readers who corresponded with him.
11 Nina Epton, *Love and the English* (1960) 371–2.
12 Ibid., 374.
13 Cmnd. 2152, *John Profumo and Christine Keeler* (abridged edn, 1999) 215.
14 Charlotte Mosley (ed.), *Love From Nancy: The Letters of Nancy Mitford* (1993) 421; Letter to Sir Hugh Jackson, 11 October 1963.
15 Anne Billson, *My Name Is Michael Caine: A Life in Film* (1991) 42–3.
16 Michael Caine, *What's It All About? The Autobiography* (1992) 134.
17 Sara Maitland (ed.), *Very Heaven: Looking Back at the 1960s* (1988) 47–58.
18 Sue Harper, *Women in British Cinema: Mad, Bad and Dangerous to Know* (2000) 98.
19 Maitland, op. cit., 171.

20 Christine Geraghty, 'Women and Sixties British Cinema: The Development of the "Darling" Girl', in Robert Murphy (ed.), *The British Cinema Book* (1997) 162.

21 Ken Russell, *Fire Over England: The British Cinema Comes Under Friendly Fire* (1993) 140.

22 Maitland, op. cit., 210–14.

23 Philip Norman, *Shout! The True Story Of The Beatles* (second edn, 1993) 193.

24 Thompson, op. cit., 142.

25 Michael Schofield, *The Sexual Behaviour of Young Adults* (1973) 179.

26 David McGillivray, *Doing Rude Things: The History of the British Sex Film 1957–1981* (1992) 20.

27 Ibid., 27.

28 Joan Littlewood, *The Best of British*, tx: BBC1, 5 November 1998.

29 Peter Mandler, *The Fall and Rise of the Stately Home* (1997) 374.

30 Patrick Higgins, *Heterosexual Dictatorship: Male Homosexuality In Postwar Britain* (1996) 17.

31 Sebastian Faulks, *The Fatal Englishman: Three Short Lives* (1996) 241.

32 Ibid.

33 *Sunday Mirror*, 28 April 1963. Hugh David, *On Queer Street: A Social History of British Homosexuality 1895–1995* (1997) 198.

34 Higgins, op. cit., 137–8.

35 Ibid., 141–2.

36 Geoffrey Gorer, *Sex and Marriage in England Today* (1973) 255.

37 When equalizing the gay age of consent to sixteen was being discussed by Parliament in 1998, an ICM poll showed 56 per cent of Britons found homosexuality morally acceptable; 52 per cent thought it was also compatible with holding public office. *Guardian*, 10 November 1998.

38 Thompson, op. cit., 141.

39 NAS: HH41/1748, Church of Scotland to Secretary of State for Scotland, 3 March 1966. Before 1967, prosecutions for homosexual acts were actually lower than in England and Wales, but only because Scottish law demanded a higher standard of proof. It is also worth noting that the only member of Wolfenden's Committee to dissent from its recommendation in 1957 was James Adair, the Procurator Fiscal of Glasgow.

40 Stephen Jeffrey-Poulter, *Peers, Queers and Commons: The Struggle for Gay Law Reform from 1950 to the Present* (1991) 48–9.

41 *Sunday Pictorial*, 16 August 1953.

42 Penny Summerfield, 'Women in Britain since 1945: companionate marriage and the double burden', in James Obelkevich and Peter Catterall (eds), *Understanding Post-War British Society* (1994) 67. Women's pay – on average half that of men's in 1945 – was still only three-quarters of men's by the end of the century. As for professional opportunities, less than 10 per cent of higher professionals were women. Middle management

was little better. For example, 70 per cent of office staff were women but only 14 per cent were office managers.

43 Cate Haste, *Rules of Desire, Sex in Britain: World War I To The Present* (1992) 256–7.

44 Miles Jebb (ed.), *The Diaries of Cynthia Gladwyn* (1995) 363.

45 J .D. Scott, *Life In Britain: A Guide To British Institutions, Traditions and Contemporary Life* (1956) 7–12.

46 David Cannadine, *Class in Britain* (1988) 160.

47 Brian Simon, *Education and the Social Order: British Education since 1944* (1991) 324.

48 Susan Crosland, *Tony Crosland* (1982) 148. In theory, education north of the border was autonomous; but this did not stop successive Secretaries of State for Scotland from inflicting comprehensives on their country.

49 Eric Hopkins, *The Rise and Decline of the English Working Classes, 1918–1990* (1991) 156–7. The numbers of middle- and upper-class Britons in higher education rose by 25 per cent during the 1960s – over ten times the figure for the working classes.

50 Hopkins, op. cit., 156–7. The numbers of middle and upper class Britons in higher education rose by 25 per cent during the 1960s – over ten times the figure for the working classes.

51 PRO: CAB128/43/2, CC (68) 36, 18 July 1968, Item 4. The report recommended that prior to the municipal takeover of public schools, half of their places should be made available to state-funded pupils and that the schools' charitable status should be abolished.

52 David Frost and Antony Jay, *To England With Love* (1967) 87.

53 Robert McCrum, William Cram and Robert MacNeil, *The Story of English* (1986) 30.

54 Ibid.

55 Green, op. cit., 73.

56 Caine, op. cit., 159.

57 Billson, op. cit., 49–50.

58 Robert Colls, *Geordies: Roots of Regionalism* (1992) 7.

59 Blake Morrison, *The Movement: English Poetry and Fiction of the 1950s* (1980) 58.

60 Ibid.

61 *Encounter*, vol. 19, No. 6, December 1962.

62 John Hill, *Sex, Class and Realism: British Cinema 1956–1963* (1986) 204.

63 James Curran and Jean Seaton, *Power Without Responsibility: The Press and Broadcasting in Britain* (fourth edn, 1991) 215.

64 Cited in Read, *The English Provinces*, 254. Bernstein was defending himself at the Pilkington inquiry when he made this statement.

65 Raphael Samuel, *Island Stories: Unravelling Britain* (1998) 165.

66 Graham McCann, *Morecambe and Wise* (1998) 11.

67 Ibid.

68 Robert Hewison, *Culture and Consensus: England, Art and Politics since 1940* (1995) 46.

69 *Punch*, 20 July 1966.

70 Leonard Miall, *Inside the BBC: British Broadcasting Characters* (1994) 107.

71 *New Musical Express*, 7 October 1967.

72 Miall, op. cit., 224.

73 Charles Stuart (ed.), *The Reith Diaries* (1975) 509–10; entry for 12 September 1963.

74 Green, op. cit., 64.

75 Patricia Hollis, *Jennie Lee: A Life* (1997) 252.

76 Ibid., 308.

77 Cmnd. 2601, *A Policy For The Arts: The First Steps* (February 1965), paras. 14 and 99.

78 Ibid., paras. 59, 60 and 100.

79 Lord Goodman, *Not For The Record: Selected Speeches & Writings* (1973) 138; Speech in the House of Lords, 19 April 1967.

80 Green, op. cit., 418.

81 The Kinks, 'Waterloo Sunset' (1967) Pye 7N 17321.

82 *Daily Telegraph*, 30 December 1995.

83 *New Musical Express*, 3 January 1964; 6 January 1968.

84 *The Mod*, No. 9, November 1964. For more on the cult see Richard Barnes, *Mods!* (second edn, 1991) and Terry Rawlings, *Mod: A Very British Phenomenon* (2000).

85 George Melly, *Revolt Into Style: The Pop Arts* (second edition, 1989) 148.

86 *New Musical Express*, 25 June 1965.

87 Arthur Marwick, *The Sixties: Cultural Revolution in Britain, France, Italy and the United States, c.1958–c.1974* (1998) 456.

88 *New Musical Express*, 22 October 1965.

89 Jeff Stein (dir.), *The Who: The Kids Are Alright* (1979) The interview in which Townshend originally expressed this view was filmed c. 1969.

90 Hewison, op. cit., 66.

91 *The Times*, 23 December 1963.

92 Geoffrey and Brenda Giuliano (eds), *The Lost Beatle Interviews* (1995) 45.

93 *New Musical Express*, 7 February 1965.

94 *The Times*, 1 July 1967.

95 *Melody Maker*, 8 July 1967.

96 Philip Norman, *The Stones* (1989) 243–5.

97 Philip Norman, *Shout! The True Story Of The Beatles* (second edition, 1993) 76.

98 Ibid., 287.

99 Peter Laurie, *The Teenage Revolution* (1965) 23.

100 Jock Colville, *The New Elizabethans* (1960) 275–6.

101 John Crosby, 'London, The Most Exciting City In The World', *Weekend*

Telegraph, 16 April 1965, reprinted in Ray Connolly (ed.), *In The Sixties: The Writing That Captured A Decade* (1995) 77–82.

102 Caine, op. cit., 236.

103 James Chapman, *Licence To Thrill: A Cultural History of the James Bond Films* (1999) 1. For a more conventional reading of the genre as imperial escapism see David Cannadine, 'James Bond and the Decline of England', *Encounter*, vol. 53, No. 3, November 1979.

104 Ibid., 4.

105 Chapman, op. cit., 64.

106 Donald Read, *The English Provinces c.1760–1960: A Study in Influence* (1964) 274. By the time of the *Guardian's* title change, two-thirds of its readers were from outside the Manchester area, and in the three years after, sales rose by a third, from 183,000 to 260,000.

107 *Daily Worker*, 27 October 1965.

6. NATIONALISTS

1 Kenneth Morgan, *Rebirth Of A Nation: Wales 1880–1980* (1981) 317. The UK census of 1971 showed that for the first time since 1881, more people worked on the land in Wales than in industry.

2 Philip Whitehead, *The Writing On The Wall: Britain In The Seventies* (1985) 287.

3 Christopher Harvie, *No Gods and Precious Few Heroes* (3rd edn, 1998) 56.

4 PRO: PREM11/4451, Freddie Erroll to Macmillan, 24 January 1963.

5 PRO: PREM11/4451, Macmillan to Norman Brook, 23 June 1962.

6 PRO: PREM11/4451, Noble to Macmillan, 21 January 1963.

7 See Vernon Bogdanor, *Devolution in the United Kingdom* (1999) 243–9. The figures given here are those for 1979 after the Barnett formula was fixed, but they correspond to the figures of the late 1960s.

8 Simon Heffer, *Nor Shall My Sword: The Reinvention of England* (1999) 71–2.

9 PRO: PREM11/2204, Brooke to Macmillan, 25 November and 11 December 1957.

10 Harold Wilson, *The Labour Government 1964–1970: A Personal Record* (1971) 9.

11 Richard Crossman, *The Diaries of a Cabinet Minister*: vol. 1, *Minister of Housing 1964–66* (1975) 117.

12 Cmnd. 3334, *Wales: The Way Ahead* (1967).

13 Crossman, op. cit., 317, Entry for 18 April 1967.

14 PRO: BD24/87, Note of discussion between Idris Evans (Chief Regional Officer for Wales) and J. H. Macmillan (Director of Publications, COI) 14 October 1953.

15 Butt Phillip, op. cit., 102.

16 Christopher Harvie, *No Gods and Precious Few Heroes: Twentieth-Century Scotland* (3rd edn, 1998) 61.

17 Ian Hamilton, *The Taking of the Stone* (1952), Preface.

18 *Scotsman*, 4 November 1967.

19 Ibid.

20 *Guardian*, 23 June 1965.

21 NAS: HH1/2786, Gordon Wilson (National Secretary, SNP) to all Scottish Members of Parliament, 21 January 1965.

22 NAS: ED48/2094, Department of Education Memorandum no. 12/66, 4 July 1965.

23 NAS: ED48/2094, Willie Ross to Richard Crossman, 12 July 1965.

24 *Scotsman*, 7 June 1965.

25 *Scotsman*, 4 November 1967.

26 Morgan, op. cit., 387.

27 Alan Butt Philip, *The Welsh Question: Nationalism in Welsh Politics, 1945–1970* (1975) 125–34.

28 *Sunday Times*, 17 November 1963. John Morgan, Assistant Editor of the *New Statesman*, wrote the article.

29 D. Elliston Allen, *British Tastes: An enquiry into the Likes and Dislikes of the Regional Consumer* (1968) 217.

30 Ibid., 101.

31 Tim Williams, 'The anglicisation of South Wales' in Raphael Samuel (ed.), *Patriotism: The Making and Unmaking of British National Identity*, vol. 2: *Minorities and Outsiders* (1989), 195.

32 Jonathan Dimbleby, *The Prince of Wales: A Biography* (1994) 119. The daffodil had initially been championed as a national symbol by Lloyd George in the Edwardian era.

33 Philip, op. cit., 120.

34 *Western Mail*, 2 August 1966.

35 Philip, op. cit., 132.

36 Ibid., 189.

37 Dimbleby, *Prince of Wales* 119.

38 PRO: PREM11/4441, Harold Macmillan to Freddie Bishop, 25 June 1958.

39 Ibid.

40 See John S. Ellis, 'The Prince and the Dragon: Welsh National Identity and the 1911 Investiture of the Prince of Wales', *Welsh History Review*, vol. 18, no. 2, December 1996.

41 Dimbleby, *Prince of Wales*, 118.

42 Ibid., 123.

43 PRO: PREM13/2360 Hughes to Wilson, 3 August 1968.

44 PRO: PREM13/2359, Meeting between the Secretary of State for Wales and Welsh Church Representatives at the Welsh Office, 13 July 1967.

45 Dimbleby, *Prince of Wales*, 129.

46 Philip Ziegler, *Crown and People* (1978) 161–2.

47 Dimbleby, *Prince of Wales*, 131.

48 Ibid., 132.

49 PRO: PREM13/2360, Minutes of the Investiture Committee, 3rd Meeting, 9 October 1968.

50 Ben Pimlott, *The Queen: A Biography of Elizabeth II* (1996) 391.

51 Dimbleby, *Prince of Wales*, 136.

52 *Daily Mirror*, 2 July 1969.

53 *Western Mail*, 3 July 1969.

54 Richard Aldous, 'Perfect Peace? Macmillan and Ireland', in Richard Aldous and Sabine Lee (eds), *Harold Macmillan: Aspects of a Political Life* (1999) 131–2.

55 Ibid., 137.

56 Thomas Hennessey, *A History of Northern Ireland 1920–1996* (1997) 107.

57 PRO: CAB129/123/1, C.(65) 175, Secretary of State for Commonwealth Affairs, 'Negotiations of a Free Trade Agreement with the Irish Republic', 8 December 1965.

58 PRO: PREM13/1167, Anthony Halls to Wilson, 8 July 1966.

59 Terence O'Neill, *Ulster At The Crossroads* (1969) 137. Speech made to the Unionist Society, 28 October 1968.

60 Ben Pimlott, *Harold Wilson* (1992) 549.

61 O'Neill, op. cit., 137.

62 Ibid., 145.

63 PRO: CAB134/2697, DS 2 (68) , Memorandum by the Secretary of State for Wales, 'Further Constitutional Changes in Wales', 22 February 1968.

64 PRO: PREM13/2151, John Morris to Wilson, 17 June 1968.

65 PRO: CAB128/43, CC44 (68), Item 3, 29 October 1968.

66 PRO: CAB134/2697, DS 23 (68), Conclusions of the Ministerial Committee on Devolution, 30 May 1968.

67 PRO: PREM13/2151, Crossman to Wilson, 25 June 1968.

68 Although Wilson promised to make the victor of Smethwick, Peter Griffiths, 'a parliamentary leper', he was never repudiated by the Conservative Party.

69 Opponents of immigration had been reluctant to press the matter because it was thought that by allowing women to follow their menfolk to Britain miscegenation might be reduced.

70 PRO: PREM13/1170, N. E. Costar to Arthur Bottomley, 16 March 1966. Bottomley was an East End trade unionist who had previously been Mayor of Walthamstow. In the year of Powell's 'Rivers of Blood' speech Wilson appointed him Chairman of the Select Committee on Race Relations, a position he held until 1970.

71 Ibid.

72 *Parliamentary Debates (Commons)*, vol. 711, Col. 953, 3 May 1965.

73 Ibid., 955.

74 Andy Medhurst, Introduction to Therese Daniels and Jane Gerson (eds), *The Colour Black: Black Images in British Television* (1989) 15.

75 Johnny Speight, *The Thoughts Of Chairman Alf: Alf Garnett's Little Blue Book or Where England Went Wrong* (1973) 11.

76 Ibid., 72–3.

77 *London Evening Standard*, 21 February 1968.

78 See Johnny Speight, *It Stands To Reason* (1974).

79 BBC2: *Odd Man Out: A Portrait of Enoch Powell*, transcript, 11 November 1995.

80 John Wood (ed.), *A Nation Not Afraid: The Thinking of Enoch Powell* (1965) 144–5.

81 Simon Heffer, *Like The Roman: The Life of Enoch Powell* (1998) 456.

82 Labour Party, News Release, 5 May 1968. The government did not, however, prosecute Powell for inciting racial hatred. On 2 May, the Attorney General, Sir Elwyn Jones, claimed that his intent could not be proved, although it is more likely that Wilson decided not to add to Powell's popularity by making a martyr of him.

83 *The Times*, 22 April 1968.

84 *Odd Man Out*. Simon Heffer dismisses such claims as 'anecdotal'. However, he is happy to cite racist letters Powell received containing anecdotal claims about 'uncivilised' immigrants as evidence of the legitimate 'concern' of the white population: op. cit., 463.

85 Ian MacDonald, *Revolution In The Head: The Beatles Records and the Sixties* (second edn, 1997) 267. The song was initially written about the plight of Kenyan Asians.

86 Private information.

87 Richard Crossman, *Diaries*, Vol. 3: *Secretary of State for Social Services 1968–1970* (1977) 28–9, Entry for 27 April 1968.

88 Paul Gilroy, 'Frank Bruno or Salman Rushdie?', in Onyekachi Wambu (ed.), *Empire Windrush: Fifty Years of Writing About Black Britain* (1998) 248–9.

89 *Illustrated London News*, 28 June 1969.

90 Wybrow, op. cit., 73.

91 *Daily Mirror*, 3 July 1969.

92 *Parliamentary Debates (Commons)*, vol. 76, 725, 16 November 1961.

93 Bashir Man, *The New Scots: The Story of Asians in Scotland* (1992) 205.

94 *Encounter*, vol. 20, no. 1, January 1963.

95 Adrian Hastings, *A History of English Christianity 1920–1985* (1986) 533.

96 Wybrow, op. cit., 69.

97 Ibid., 421.

98 Owen Chadwick, *Michael Ramsey: A Life* (1990) 114.

99 *Daily Mirror*, 28 May 1963.

100 Jeffrey Weeks, *Sex, Politics and Society: The regulation of sexuality since 1800* (1981) 275.

101 PRO: CAB129/96, C(59) 8 (Annexe) Duke of Norfolk to Harold Macmillan, 1 November 1958.

102 PRO: CAB129/96, C(59) 8, 'Representation of the Vatican in the United Kingdom', Memorandum by the Foreign Secretary, 20 January 1959.

103 PRO: CAB128/39, CC(65) 69/6, 9 December 1965.

104 PRO: PREM13/1907, Jenkins to Wilson, 6 June 1966.

105 *Daily Mirror*, 30 September 1965.

106 *Liverpool Weekly News*, 28 October 1965.

107 PRO: PREM13/1907, Chief Constable of the Metropolitan Police to Sir Charles Cunningham, 26 October 1965; Chief Constable of Liverpool to Cunningham, 2 November 1965.

108 PRO: PREM13/1907, Burke Trend to Wilson, n.d.

109 Ramsey's approach paid off. A *Daily Mirror* survey published on 29 May 1963 found that while British teenagers rejected much of the Churches' teachings, 60 per cent of them thought that religious leaders were beginning to understand them better.

110 Dilip Hiro, *Black British White British* (third edn, 1991) 32.

111 PRO: BD25/186, Christian Churches of the Vale of Clwyd to Henry Brooke, 5 May 1961.

112 PRO: BD24/320, Wrexham Baptists to Harold Macmillan, 12 December 1960.

113 PRO: BD24/320, Wales and Monmouthshire Sunday Opening Council to Rab Butler, 13 October 1960.

114 *Western Mail*, 2 November 1961.

115 Butt Philip, op. cit., 237.

116 Peter Clarke, *Hope and Glory: Britain 1900–1990* (1996) 346.

117 *Sunday Times*, 4 October 1981.

118 Geoffrey and Brenda Guiliano (eds), *The Lost Beatles Interviews* (1995) 60.

119 Ibid.

120 Ibid.

121 Grace Davie, *Religion in Britain since 1945: Believing without Belonging* (1994) 1.

122 Richard Lester (dir.), *A Hard Day's Night*, United Artists/Proscenium (1964).

123 Graham Payn and Sheridan Morley (eds), *The Noël Coward Diaries* (1982) 501.

124 Ibid., 543–5.

125 David Cannadine, 'The Context, Performance and Meaning of Ritual: The British Monarchy and the Invention of Tradition, c. 1820–1977', in Eric Hobsbawm and Terence Ranger (eds.), *The Invention of Tradition* (1983) 157.

126 *Observer*, 31 January 1965.

127 Richard Crossman, *The Diaries of a Cabinet Minister*: vol. 1, *Minister of Housing 1964–66* (1975) 142–3.

128 *The Times*, 25 January 1965.

129 Henry Fairlie, 'His Vision of England', *Sunday Telegraph*, Special Supplement 1, 31 January 1965.

130 Jonathan Dimbleby, *Richard Dimbleby: A Biography* (1975) 384.

131 *The Times*, 25 January 1965.

132 Laurie Lee, 'Farewell to Greatness', *Sunday Telegraph*, Special Supplement 2, 31 January 1965.

133 Martin Gilbert, *Never Despair: Winston Churchill 1945–1965* (1988) 1, 363.

134 Dimbleby, op. cit., 386.

135 *Daily Telegraph*, 1 February 1965.

136 *Sunday Times*, 31 January 1965.

137 *Sunday Telegraph*, 31 January 1965.

138 Colin MacInnes, 'The Week He Died', *Sunday Telegraph*, Special Supplement, 31 January 1965.

139 PRO: CAB129/122, C(65) 119, 'Policy Towards Germany', Memorandum by the Foreign Secretary, 5 August 1965.

140 PRO: PREM13/326, Sir Patrick Reilly to Foreign Office, Telegram no. 363, 22 May 1965.

141 Michael Stewart, *Life & Labour: An Autobiography* (1980) 164.

142 PRO: CAB129/122, C(65) 119, 'Policy Towards Germany', Memorandum by the Foreign Secretary, 5 August 1965.

143 Alf Ramsey, Obituary, *Daily Telegraph*, 1 May 1999.

144 Niall Edworthy, *The Second Most Important Job In The Country* (1999) 68.

145 *Daily Mail*, 30 July 1966.

146 *Observer*, 24 July 1966.

147 Ibid.

148 Kenneth Wolstenholme, *They Think It's All Over: Memories Of The Greatest Day In English Football* (1996) 119.

149 Dave Hill, *England's Glory: 1966 And All That* (1996) 180.

150 Roger Hutchinson, . . . *it is now! The Real Story of England's 1966 World Cup Triumph* (1995) 179.

151 Hill, op. cit., 198.

152 Dave Bowler, *A Biography of Sir Alf Ramsey* (1998) 222.

153 Ibid., 203–4.

154 *FA News*, vol. 16, no. 1, July 1966, 486–95.

155 Kenneth Wolstenholme, *The Boy's Book of the World Cup* (1966) 11.

156 *Sun*, 1 August 1966.

157 Ibid.

158 George Orwell, 'The Sporting Spirit', in Sonia Orwell and Ian Angus (eds), *The Collected Essays, Journalism and Letters of George Orwell*, vol. 4: *In Front of your Nose 1945–50* (1970) 63.

159 *Sunday Express*, 31 July 1966.

160 *FA News*, vol. 16, no. 2, September 1966, 47. The likely author of this article was Lord Harewood.

161 *Sunday Express*, 31 July 1966.

162 Crossman, *Diaries*, vol. 1, 594, entry for 31 July 1966.

163 *Sun*, 1 August 1966.

164 Hutchinson, op. cit., 204.

165 PRO: CAB128, CC(67) 66, Cabinet minutes, 16 November 1967.

166 Wolstenholme, *They Think It's All Over*, 118.

167 Reprinted in *FA News*, vol. 16, no. 2, September 1966, 3.

168 Hutchinson, op. cit., 203.

169 *Observer*, 31 July 1966.

170 PRO: CAB128/2, C(67) 33 Appendix, Meeting between the Prime Minister and President de Gaulle, 24 January 1967.

171 Ibid., Meeting held on 25 January 1967.

172 PRO: CAB128/2, C(67) 33, Note by the Prime Minister, 'The Approach to Europe', 16 March 1967.

173 Crossman, *Diaries*, vol. 2, 456.

174 PRO: CAB129/133/1, C(67) 159, 'Approach to Europe', Speech by Lord Chalfont to the Consultative Assembly of the Council of Europe, Strasbourg, 26 September 1967.

175 Peter Collinson (dir.), *The Italian Job* (Paramount/Oakhurst, 1969).

176 Nicholas Cull, 'The Great Escape of the Self-Preservation Society: Englishness in popular war and crime films', British Council Conference, 'Looking Into England: English identities in the Context of UK Devolution', University of Warwick, 12–18 December 1999.

177 Roy Denman, *Missed Chances: Britain and Europe in the Twentieth Century* (1996) 229.

178 PRO: PREM13/504, Statement by Jean Monnet, 20 December 1967.

179 TGA: Clark/8812.1.4, Lees-Milne to Clark, 16 May 1969.

180 Kenneth Clark, *The Other Half: A Self-Portrait* (1977) 222.

181 Roy Lewis and Angus Maude, *The English Middle Classes* (1950) 212.

182 MacDonald, op. cit., 22.

183 Robert Hewison, *Too Much: Art and Society in the Sixties, 1960–75* (1986) 65.

7. SCEPTICS

1 Francis Wheen, 'The Stagnant Years', *The Modern Review*, March 1998, 25.

2 'Going into Europe – Again? A Symposium, Part 1', *Encounter*, vol. 36, no. 6, June 1971.

3 Roy Denman, *Missed Chances: Britain and Europe in the Twentieth Century* (1996) 237.

4 Hugo Young, *This Blessed Plot: Britain and Europe from Churchill to Blair* (1998) 234.

5 Ibid., 239.

6 Ibid.

7 *Parliamentary Debates (Commons)*, vol. 821, 1552, 21 July 1971.

8 Private information.

9 Uwe Kitzinger, *Diplomacy and Persuasion: How Britain Joined the Common Market* (1973) 415.

10 Private information.

11 Conservative Party, *Europe and You: Sovereignty in the Common Market* (1971).

12 Cmnd. 4715, *The United Kingdom and the European Communities* (1971) 17.

13 *Observer*, 6 October 1974, reprinted in *Damn you, England: Collected Prose* (1994) 197.

14 *The Times*, 27 July 1971, reprinted in Kathleen Tynan, *Kenneth Tynan: Letters* (1994) 497–8.

15 *Encounter*, vol. 36, no. 6, June 1971.

16 *Encounter*, vol. 37, no. 1, July 1971.

17 Tom Fleming (ed.), *Voices out of the Air: The Royal Christmas Broadcasts 1932–1981* (1981) 124.

18 Ruth Winstone (ed.), *The Benn Diaries* (1995) 423–4, entry for 5 July 1977.

19 Cmnd. 4715, *The United Kingdom and the European Communities* (1971) 8.

20 European Community (UK Press and Information Office), *Europe's Tomorrow* (1971).

21 Interview for *The Last Europeans, Part Two: Party & Country*, Brook Associates for Channel Four, transcript, 15 November 1995.

22 Ibid.

23 Ibid.

24 Young, op. cit., 273.

25 Cited in Denman, op. cit., 240.

26 *Parliamentary Debates (Commons)*, vol. 823, 2202–12, 28 October 1971.

27 Roy Jenkins, *A Life at the Centre: Memoirs of a Radical Reformer* (1991), 309.

28 *The Last Europeans, Part Two: Party & Country*, Brook Associates for Channel Four, tx., 15 November 1995.

29 Ibid.

30 Audrey Hilton (ed.), *This England, 1968–1974: Selections from the 'This England' column of the New Statesman* (1974). This report originally appeared in the *Daily Telegraph*.

31 Cmnd. 3164, *Decimal Currency in the United Kingdom*, December 1966, 1. Apart from the obvious commercial benefits, decimalization was also

seen to have educational benefits, because time would no longer be wasted teaching children about the arithmetical structure of British currency.

32 Cmnd. 2145, *Report of the Committee of Inquiry on Decimal Currency*, September 1963.

33 'Foam Truths', *Sunday Times*, 13 October 1996.

34 Report by the Department of Local Government Affairs, European Commission, 12 January 2001. The figures given here include non-EU European countries such as Russia. In addition, there were 24 Chinese, 7 Japanese, 14 South American and 8 Israeli towns twinned with UK ones. For more on Coventry's leading role in this matter, see George Hodgkinson, *Sent To Coventry* (1970).

35 Anthony Sampson, *The New Europeans: A guide to the workings, institutions and character of contemporary Western Europe* (1968) 257.

36 Richard S. Grayson, 'Britain and the Channel Tunnel', *Twentieth Century British History*, vol. 7, no. 3, 1996, 387. For an extensive history of the earlier period see Keith Wilson, *Channel Tunnel Visions, 1850–1945: Dreams and Nightmares* (1994).

37 Grayson, op. cit., 387.

38 Cmnd. 5256, *The Channel Tunnel Project* (1973) 3.

39 Private information.

40 Barbara Castle, *The Castle Diaries 1974–76* (1980) 281, entry for 16 January 1975.

41 *Daily Express*, 1 January 1973.

42 Interview for *The Last Europeans*, op. cit.

43 *Daily Express*, 1 January 1973.

44 European Community (UK Press and Information Office), *Europe's Tomorrow* (1971).

45 *Encounter*, vol. 20, no. 1, January 1963.

46 Sean Greenwood (ed.), *Britain and European integration since the Second World War* (1996) 151.

47 *Parliamentary Debates (Commons)*, vol. 845, 1189, 9 November 1972.

48 *Parliamentary Debates (Commons)*, vol. 846, 1507, 23 November 1972.

49 *The Times*, 2 January 1973.

50 Interview for *The Last Europeans*, op. cit.

51 *Sunday Times*, 7 January 1973.

52 Anthony Gishford and Victor Caudery (eds), *Fanfare for Europe: Official Programme Book* (1973) 152–3.

53 Anthony Sampson, *The New Europeans: A guide to the workings, institutions and character of contemporary Western Europe* (1968) 305–8.

54 Ibid., 243–4.

55 Gishford and Caudery, op. cit., 143.

56 *New Musical Express*, 20 January 1973.

57 *New Musical Express*, 13 January 1973.

58 A. H. Halsey (ed.), *Trends in British Society Since 1900* (1972) 549–50.

59 Office For National Statistics, *Social Trends* 29 (1999) 219.

60 John Benson, *The Rise of Consumer Society in Britain 1880–1980* (1994) 88.

61 Piers Brendon, *Thomas Cook: 150 Years of Popular Tourism* (1991) 312.

62 Office For National Statistics, op. cit., 209.

63 Office For National Statistics, *Britain 1999: The Official Yearbook of the United Kingdom* (1998) 529.

64 Brendon, op. cit., 291.

65 Gishford and Caudery, op. cit., 23.

66 Ibid., 25; 33.

67 Miriam Akhtar and Steve Humphries, *Some Liked It Hot: The British on holiday at home and abroad* (2000) 124–5.

68 Piers Brendon, *Thomas Cook: 150 Years of Popular Tourism* (1991) 290.

69 Ibid.

70 Sue Read, *Hello Campers! Celebrating 50 Years of Butlins* (1986) 170.

71 Akhtar and Humphries, op. cit., 121.

72 Ibid., 121–2.

73 See Paul Fussell, *Abroad: British Literary Travelling Between the Wars* (1980).

74 Richard Hoggart, *The Way We Live Now* (1995) 202.

75 PRO: FO371/109713, F. Barnes to F. Warner, 17 July 1954.

76 *The Times*, 1 January 1973.

77 *The Times*, 2 January 1973.

78 *Guardian*, 1 January 1973.

79 David Butler and Uwe Kitzinger, *The 1975 Referendum* (1976) 156. The support of farmers' unions for membership helped to secure the narrow 'Yes' votes in Scotland and Ulster.

80 *Sunday Times*, 8 June 1975.

81 Young, op. cit., 292.

82 Butler and Kitzinger, op. cit., 90.

83 Young, op. cit., 291.

84 Butter and Kitzinger, op. cit., 279–80.

85 Private information.

86 Denman, op. cit., 250.

87 Ibid.

8. STRIKERS

1 George Orwell, *The Lion and the Unicorn: Socialism and the English Genius* (second edn, 1982) 41.

2 Sir Walter Citrine, *British Trade Unions* (1947) 47–8.

3 Peter Stead, 'I'm All Right, Jack', *History Today*, vol. 46, January 1996.

4 Jack Jones, *Union Man: An Autobiography* (1986) 215.

5 Robert J. Wybrow, *Britain Speaks Out, 1937–87: A social history as seen through the Gallup Data* (1989) 92–3.

6 John Campbell, *Edward Heath: A Biography* (1993) 572–3.

7 Hughie Green, obituary, *Daily Telegraph*, 5 May 1997.

8 Janie Hampton (ed.), *Joyce and Ginnie: The Letters of Joyce Grenfell and Virginia Graham* (1997) 422.

9 Eric Silver, *Victor Feather, TUC: A Biography* (1973) 192.

10 John Burnett, *Liquid Pleasures: A Social History of Drinks in Modern Britain* (1999) 67.

11 *The Times*, 21 December 1973.

12 *The Times*, 7 September 1970.

13 Robert Taylor, 'The Heath government and industrial relations: myth and reality', in Stuart Ball and Anthony Seldon (eds), *The Heath Government 1970–74: A Reappraisal* (1996) 177.

14 Private information.

15 Paul Arthur and Keith Jeffery, *Northern Ireland since 1968* (second edn, 1996) 99.

16 Conor Cruise O'Brien, *Memoir: My life and themes* (1998) 335.

17 Lord Grey of Naunton, obituary, *Daily Telegraph*, 19 October 1999.

18 *The Times*, 9 February 1972.

19 *Evening Standard*, 6 October 1974.

20 Thomas Hennessy, *A History of Northern Ireland 1920–1996* (1997) 248–9. While the British identity of Protestants intensified, the number of Catholics who thought themselves to be Northern Irish rather than Irish rose from zero in 1968 to 28 per cent in 1989. This was a result of political reform in the North and a realization that the republic would not go to war on their behalf.

21 Private information.

22 Kenneth O. Morgan, *Callaghan: A Life* (1997) 349.

23 Hennessy, *Northern Ireland*, 160.

24 Ibid., 162.

25 Desmond Bell, *Acts of Union: Youth Culture and Sectarianism in Northern Ireland* (1990) 146–7. A rare exception to this trend was the continuing cross-community management and support of Derry City Football Club. A plan to rename it Derry Celtic was vetoed on the grounds that it went against the club's tradition.

26 PRO: CAB129, C(46) 381, Lord President, 'Eire and Northern Ireland', 16 October 1946.

27 Wybrow, op. cit., 104.

28 Steve Bruce, 'The Ulster Connection', in Graham Walker and Tom Gallagher (eds), *Sermons and Battle Hymns: Protestant Popular Culture in Modern Scotland* (1990) 253.

29 Graham Walker, 'Scotland and Ulster: Political Interactions Since the Late Nineteenth Century and Possibilities of Contemporary Dialogue', in John

Erskine and Gordon Lucy (eds), *Cultural Traditions in Northern Ireland*, vol. 4, *Varieties of Scottishness: Exploring the Ulster Scottish Connection* (1996) 104.

30 Panikos Panayi, *The impact of immigration: A documentary history of the effects and experiences of immigrants in Britain since 1945* (1999) 151.

31 Roy Jenkins, *A Life at the Centre: Memoirs of a Radical Reformer* (1991) 373–4.

32 Dervla Murphy, *A Place Apart* (1978). Murphy's excellent book was a rare attempt by a Southern Irish citizen to empathetically understand the majority culture and identity of Ulster.

33 Hennessy, *Northern Ireland*, 229.

34 Heath, op. cit., 478.

35 John Taylor, *War Photography: Realism in the British Press* (1991) 148.

36 Confidential interview.

37 Confidential interview.

38 Douglas Hurd, *An End To Promises: Sketch Of A Government 1970–74* (1979) 131.

39 Campbell, op. cit., 589.

40 Cecil King, *The Cecil King Diary, 1970–74* (1975) 332.

41 Francis Wheen, 'The Stagnant Years', *The Modern Review*, March 1998, p. 25.

42 Trevor Griffiths, *Oi! For England* (1982) 24–5.

43 Zig Layton-Henry, *The Politics of Immigration: Race and Race Relations in Postwar Britain* (1992) 142–3. The real figures were much higher because the state only tabulated criminal cases like assault, murder and violent robbery. Many of these crimes went unreported because the black and Asian communities had lost faith in the police. Moreover, official figures did not take into account subtler forms of racial harassment.

44 Benjamin Bowling, 'The emergence of violent racism as a public issue in Britain, 1945–81', in Panikos Panayi (ed.), *Racial Violence in Britain in the Nineteenth and Twentieth Centuries* (second edn, 1996) 199.

45 Kathleen Paul, *Whitewashing Britain: Race and Citizenship in the Postwar Era* (1997) 183.

46 Michael Abdul Malik, *From Michael De Freitas to Michael X* (1968) 31.

47 Onyekachi Wambu (ed.), *Empire Windrush: Fifty Years of Writing About Black Britain* (1998) 211–13.

48 Andrew Fountaine, obituary, *Daily Telegraph*, 25 September 1997.

49 Bowling, op. cit.

50 Andrew Thorpe, 'Introduction' to Thorpe (ed.), *The Failure of Political Extremism in Inter-War Britain* (1989) 10.

51 *Daily Telegraph*, 25 September 1997.

52 Private information.

53 Edward Heath, *The Course of my Life* (1998) 462.
54 Candida Lycett Green (ed.), *John Betjeman, Letters Volume One: 1926 to 1951* (1994) 438.
55 Ibid., 439.
56 I owe this point to Christopher Booker, *The Seventies* (1980) 161–6.
57 Roy Strong, Introduction to Patrick Cormack, *Heritage in Danger* (1978) 10.
58 Booker, op. cit., 44.
59 Philip Ziegler, *Crown and People* (1978) 176.
60 Ben Pimlott, *The Queen: A Biography of Elizabeth II* (1996) 452.
61 *The Times*, 8 June 1977.
62 Ziegler, op. cit., 172–4.
63 *Daily Express*, 8 June 1977.
64 Ibid.
65 *Daily Mirror*, 2 June 1977.
66 *Daily Mirror*, 7 June 1977.
67 *The Times*, 8 June 1977.
68 Ziegler, op. cit., 187.
69 Ibid.
70 Pimlott, *The Queen*, 447.
71 *Guardian*, 8 June 1977.
72 James Loughlin, *Ulster Unionism and British National Identity Since 1885* (1995) 206.
73 Pimlott, op. cit., 449. For more on the Queen's reception in Northern Ireland, see Loughlin, op. cit., 206–7.
74 Ziegler, op. cit., 191.
75 Ibid., 192.
76 Tony Peake, *Derek Jarman* (1999) 245.
77 Dick Hebdige, *Subculture: the meaning of style* (1979) 87.
78 Peake, op. cit., 244.
79 Ronald Allison, *Britain In The Seventies* (1980) 215.
80 Ziegler, op. cit., 190.
81 *The Times*, 8 June 1977.
82 Jock Colville, *The New Elizabethans* (1977) 313–14.
83 *Daily Express*, 8 June 1977.
84 Hobsbawm and Ran David Cannadine, 'The Context, Performance and Meaning of Ritual: The British Monarchy and the Invention of Tradition, c. 1820–1977', in Eric Hobsbawm and Terence Ranger (eds), *The Invention of Tradition* (1983) 160.
85 *The Times*, 8 June 1977.
86 Douglas Hurd and Andrew Osmond, *Scotch on the Rocks* (1971).
87 Private information.
88 Private information.

89　Mike Wilson, *Don't' Cry For Me Argentina: Scotland's 1978 World Cup Adventure* (1998) 167.

89　*Guardian,* 12 November 1999.

91　Adrian Thrills, *You're Not Singing Anymore!: A riotous celebration of football chants and the culture that spawned them* (1998) 109.

92　*Daily Mirror,* 6 June 1977.

93　Cmnd. 5460, *Royal Commission on the Constitution 1969–1973 , volume 1: Report* (1973) 137; 102–3.

94　Under the terms of the Irish Free State (Agreement Act) 1922, Northern Ireland was allocated thirteen seats (reduced to twelve in 1948 when university seats were abolished) instead of the seventeen which it was entitled to according to the size of its population. See Vernon Bogdanor, *Devolution In The United Kingdom* (1999) 69–81.

95　Christopher Harvie, *Scotland and Nationalism: Scottish Society and Politics, 1707–1994* (1994) 191.

96　Cmnd. 6348, *Our Changing Democracy: Devolution for Scotland and Wales* (1975).

97　Kenneth O. Morgan, *Callaghan: A Life* (1997) 361.

98　Ibid., 631.

99　Ibid., 677.

100　Harvie, op. cit., 183.

101　John Davies, *A History of Wales* (1993) 677.

102　John Osmond, *The Divided Kingdom* (1988) 127.

103　Roy Strong, *The Roy Strong Diaries: 1967–1987* (1997) 209.

104　Adam Sisman, *A. J. P. Taylor: A Biography* (1994) 373.

105　Philip Whitehead, *The Writing on the Wall: Britain in the Seventies* (1985) 230.

106　Robert Taylor, *The Trade Union Question in British Politics: Government and Unions since 1945* (1993) 370–71.

107　Wheen, op. cit., 27, diary entry for 22 January 1979.

108　Morgan, *Callaghan,* 673.

109　John Goodwin (ed.), *Peter Hall's Diaries: The Story of a Dramatic Battle* (1983) 429; 434.

110　Paul Bailey, *An English Madam: The Life and Work of Cynthia Payne* (1982) 102.

9. HUSTLERS

1　John O'Farrell, *Things can only get better: Eighteen miserable years in the life of a Labour supporter 1979–1997* (1998) 19.

2　Hugo Young, *One of Us: A Biography of Margaret Thatcher* (second edn, 1991) 224.

3　Ibid.

4 For a more detailed discussion of the comparison with Gaullism, see David Marquand, 'The Paradoxes of Thatcherism', in Robert Skidelsky (ed.), *Thatcherism* (1988) 159–72.

5 Peter Hennessy, *Muddling Through: Power, Politics and the Quality of Government in Postwar Britain* (1996) 296–7.

6 When the 1968 Race Relations Act 1968 was under consideration, the Police Federation lobbied hard for the force to be exempted, and continued to do so in subsequent years. See PRO: CAB129/139, C (68) 122, 'Race Relations – The Police', Memorandum by the Home Secretary, 6 November 1968. 'Their views are intense and deep seated', wrote the Home Secretary. '[If we acted] there would be . . . a considerable outcry by them . . . at a time when we are dependant on the loyalty of the police in dealing with civil unrest'.

7 Andrew Adonis and Stephen Pollard, *A Class Act: The Myth of Britain's Classless Society* (1997) 3–4.

8 Eric J. Evans, *Thatcher and Thatcherism* (1997) 43.

9 Gordon Heald and Robert J. Wybrow, *The Gallup Survey of Britain* (1986) 257.

10 Evans, op. cit., 411.

11 Ibid.

12 *New Statesman*, 10 April 1983.

13 Tony Parsons, 'The Tattooed Jungle: The Decline of the Working Class', in Dylan Jones (ed.), *Ten Years of Arena* (1996) ; originally published September 1989.

14 Julie Burchill, 'McLaren's Children', *20/20 Magazine*, 1990; reprinted in Burchill, *Sex and Sensibility* (1992) 95–6.

15 Eric Jacobs, *Kingsley Amis: A Biography* (1995) 336–7.

16 Raphael Samuel, 'Continuous National History', in Samuel (ed.), *Patriotism: The Making and Unmaking of British National Identity*, vol. 1: *History and Politics* (1989) 9.

17 Ibid.

18 Geoffrey Elton, *The English* (1992) 234.

19 Kenneth Baker, *The Turbulent Years: My Life In Politics* (1993) 205.

20 Ibid., 193.

21 Margaret Thatcher, *The Downing Street Years* (1993) 596.

22 Gallup for the *Daily Telegraph*, 27 August 1996.

23 Carolyn Steedman, 'True Romances', in Samuel (ed.), *Patriotism*, Vol. 1, 26.

24 Ibid.

25 *Scotsman*, 2 December 1960.

26 The Munn Committee of 1977 accelerated the growth of a more tartan curriculum. See Cameron Harrison, 'How Scottish is the Scottish Curriculum?', in Margaret M. Clark and Pamela Munn, *Education in Scotland: policy and practice from pre-school to secondary* (1997).

27 Robert Hewison, *The Heritage Industry: Britain in a Climate of Decline* (1987) 128.

28 David McCrone, Angela Morris and Richard Kiely, *Scotland – the Brand: The Making of Scottish Heritage* (1995) 2.

29 Robert Hewison, 'Commerce and Culture', in John Corner and Sylvia Harvey (eds), *Enterprise and Heritage: Cross-currents of National Culture* (1991) 165–6.

30 Hewison, *The Heritage Industry*, 32.

31 Robert Hewison, 'Making History: Manufacturing Heritage', John Iddon (ed.), *The Dodo Strikes Back* (1998) 9.

32 Andrew Higson, 'The Heritage Film and British Cinema', in Higson (ed.), *Dissolving Views: Key Writings on British Cinema* (1996) 248.

33 Cairns Craig, 'Rooms Without A View', *Sight and Sound*, no. 59, January 1990.

34 Higson, op. cit., 243.

35 Peter York and Charles Jennings, *Peter York's Eighties* (1996) 35.

36 *Observer*, 8 November 1987.

37 Hewison, *The Heritage Industry* 146.

38 *The Times*, 12 June 1999.

39 Magnus Magnusson, Foreword to Jenni Calder (ed.), *The Wealth of a Nation in the National Museums of Scotland* (1989) viii–ix.

40 Joyce McMillan, 'Fabric of a Nation', in Alan Taylor (ed.) *What A State! Is Devolution For Scotland The End Of Britain?* (2000) 185.

41 Nick Merriman, 'Museum Visiting as a Cultural Phenomenon', in Peter Vergo (ed.), *The New Museology* (1989) 156.

42 John Iddon (ed.), *The Dodo Strikes Back* (1998) 14.

43 Raphael Samuel, *Theatres of Memory*, vol. 1: *Past and Present in Contemporary Culture* (1994) 265.

44 Bruce Robinson, *Withnail And I: The Original Screenplay* (second edn, 1995) 13.

45 *The Times*, 13 May 1987.

46 Christopher Harvie, *Fool's Gold: The Story of North Sea Oil* (1994) 288–90.

47 Alec Cairncross, *The British Economy Since 1945* (second edn, 1995), 315.

48 Jeffrey Richards, *Films and British National Identity: From Dickens to Dad's Army* (1997) 228.

49 Christopher Harvie, *Scotland and Nationalism: Scottish Society and Politics, 1707–1994* (1994) 119.

50 John Osmond, *The Divided Kingdom* (1988) 141.

51 R. Merfyn Jones, 'Beyond Identity? The Reconstruction of the Welsh', *Journal of British Studies*, No. 31, October 1992, 354–5. Welsh Office responsibilities grew steadily in the 1970s and 1980s. Health was added in

1970, economic development in 1975, agriculture and education in 1979, local authority funding in 1980 and higher education in 1991.

52 Ibid., 335.

53 Ibid., 341.

54 Hugo Young, *One of Us: A Biography of Margaret Thatcher* (second edn, 1991) 622.

55 Margaret Thatcher, *The Downing Street Years* (1993) 624.

56 Ibid., 618.

57 Young, op. cit., 425. See also Henry Clark, *The Church Under Thatcher* (1993).

58 Ibid., 622. Apparently not. Half the Scottish population did not pay the tax, the highest level of refusal in the UK.

59 Ibid., 618.

60 Ibid., 51.

61 Cairncross, op. cit., 314–16.

62 Ibid., 316–17.

63 Raphael Samuel, *Theatres of Memory*, Vol. 2: *Island Stories: Unravelling Britain* (1998) 166.

64 See Alan Tomlinson, 'North and South: the rivalry of the Football League and the Football Association', in John Williams and Stephen Wagg (eds), *British Football and Social Change: Getting into Europe* (1991).

65 See for example, D. Hobbs, *Doing the Business: Entrepreneurship, the Working Class and Detectives in the East End of London* (1988).

66 It was appropriate that George Cole, who played Daley, had originally made his name playing the spiv in the 'St. Trinian's' films made by Ealing in the 1950s.

67 John Osmond, *The Divided Kingdom* (1988) 55.

68 Christopher Harvie, 'English Regionalism: The Dog That Never Barked', in Bernard Crick (ed.), *National Identities: The Constitution of the United Kingdom* (1991).

69 See J. W. Burrow, *Victorian Historians and the English Past* (1981). For an original example, see Esme Wingfield-Stratford, *The History of English Patriotism* (1913): he wrote of the Conquest, 'the English nation was dying for lack of discipline and this was just what the Normans were qualified to give', vol. 1, 9.

70 Harvie, op. cit., 110.

71 Ibid.

72 John Wood (ed.), *A Nation Not Afraid: The Thinking of Enoch Powell* (1965) 145.

73 Cited in Donald Read, *The English Provinces c.1760–1960: A Study in Influence* (1964) 241.

74 John Osmond, *The Divided Kingdom* (1988) 56.

75 See Harvie, op. cit. As a Scottish nationalist and Europhile based in Germany, it could be said that Chris Harvie embodies everything that makes the English suspicious of regionalism!

76 Michael Hechter, *Internal Colonialism: The Celtic fringe in British national development, 1536–1966* (1975) 64–5.

77 William Borlase's *Antiquities Historical and Monumental of the County of Cornwall* (1754, revised edn, 1769) was the most influential text of the British/Cornish movement. See Amy Hale, 'A History of the Cornish Revival', in Tim Saunders (ed.), *The Wheel: An Anthology of Modern Poetry in Cornish 1850–1980* (1999) 19–27.

78 Bernard Deacon, 'And Shall Trelawney Die? The Cornish Identity', in Philip Payton (ed.), *Cornwall Since The War* (1993) 206–7.

79 Andrew Anthony, 'Passport to Padstow', *Observer*, 3 January 1999.

80 Hale, op.cit., 19–27.

81 Mebyon Kernow, *For Cornwall – A Future!* (1977) 11–12.

82 Anthony, op. cit.

83 The Lord Warden of the Stannaries, appointed by the Duke of Cornwall, also presides over the Council of the Duchy. However, the Duchy does not conform to Cornish territorial boundaries, owning 130,000 acres across twenty-three counties.

84 See, for example, *Western Morning News*, 6 September 1996.

85 The announcement in 1978 that Cornwall and Plymouth would form one of the large constituencies for the new European Parliament provoked seventy-six petitions from Cornish parishes, compared to a total of eighteen for all the similar cases in the rest of England. Even the Liberals were guilty of this. Jeremy Thorpe's *Power to the Provinces* (1968) initiative, which attempted to revive some of the ancient region/kingdoms like Mercia, only offered an assembly to 'Westcountry'.

86 Taylor, op. cit., 128–9.

87 Alan Clark, *Diaries* (1993) 99.

88 John Taylor, *War Photography: Realism in the British Press* (1991) 129.

89 Thatcher, op. cit., 385.

90 John Taylor, op. cit., 128–9.

91 Roy Foster, *History and Identity in Modern Ireland: The Eighth Annual Bindoff Lecture, Delivered at Queen Mary and Westfield College, University of London, 12 March 1997* (1997) 1.

92 H. V. Morton, *In Search of Ireland* (1930) v.

93 E. Estyn Evans, *About Britain No. 13: Northern Ireland* (1951) 7.+9

94 Steve Bruce, *The Edge of the Union: The Ulster Loyalist Political Vision* (1994) 150.

10. TUNNELLERS

1 Mervyn Hughes, *Michael Foot* (1994) 483.
2 Robert Cecil, *A Divided Life: A Biography of Donald Maclean* (1988) 182.
3 Max Hastings and Simon Jenkins, *The Battle for the Falklands* (1983) 72.
4 Ibid., vii.
5 *Daily Express*, 26 July 1982.
6 Nicholas Henderson, *Mandarin: The Diaries of An Ambassador, 1969–1982* (1994).
7 *Parliamentary Debates (Commons)*, vol. 21, 649, 3 April 1982.
8 Lord Carrington, *Reflect on Things Past* (1988) 370.
9 Lucy Noakes, *War And The British: Gender and National Identity, 1939–91* (1998) 110.
10 Ruth Winstone (ed.), *The Benn Diaries* (1995) 532, 537, diary entries for 3 April and 8 June 1982.
11 Bernard Porter, *The Lion's Share: A Short History of British Imperialism 1850–1995* (3rd edn, 1996) 365–6.
12 *The Times*, 5 April 1982.
13 *Daily Express*, 19 May 1982.
14 *Parliamentary Debates (Commons)*, vol. 21, 649, 3 April 1982.
15 Noakes, op. cit., 113.
16 Ibid., 125–8.
17 *The Times*, 15 June 1982.
18 Noakes, op. cit., 111.
19 *The Times*, 5 April 1982.
20 *The Times*, 15 June 1982.
21 Alasdair Milne, *DG: The Memoirs of a British Broadcaster* (1988) 89.
22 Ibid., 92.
23 BBC 1: *Question Time*, 6 June 1983.
24 Alan Bennett, *Writing Home* (1994) 123, diary entry for 15 June 1982.
25 Cecil Woolf and Jean Moorcroft Wilson (eds), *Authors Take Sides On The Falklands* (1982) 170.
26 Ibid., 174.
27 Winstone, op. cit., 534, diary entry for 23 April 1982.
28 Anthony Barnett, *Iron Britannia: Why Parliament waged its Falklands War* (1982) 75.
29 Madge Dresser, 'Britannia', in Raphael Samuel (ed.), *Patriotism: The Making and Unmaking of British National Identity*, vol. 3: *National Fictions* (1989) 41.
30 *New Statesman*, 17 June 1982.
31 Conversation with the author, Institute of Historical Research, London, 12 April 1994.

32 Robert Shepherd, *Enoch Powell: A Biography* (1996) 487.

33 Noakes, op. cit., 114.

34 Ibid., 124.

35 John Wolffe, *God and Greater Britain: Religion and National Life in Britain and Ireland 1843–1945* (1994) 264.

36 Humphrey Carpenter, *Robert Runcie: The Reluctant Archbishop* (1996) 256–8.

37 Ibid., 57.

38 Matthew Engel, *Tickle the Public: One Hundred Years of the Popular Press* (1996) 275.

39 Barnett, op. cit., 150–53.

40 Ibid., 150.

41 *The Times*, 15 June 1982.

42 Margaret Thatcher, *The Downing Street Years* (1993) 173.

43 Peter York and Charles Jennings, *Peter York's Eighties* (1996) 113.

44 Eric J. Evans, *Thatcher and Thatcherism* (1997) 98.

45 Paulo Filo della Torre, *Viva Britannia: Mrs. Thatcher's Britain* (1985) 90–91.

46 The survey did not distinguish between Scottish, Welsh and English opinion. Gordan Heald and Robert J. Wybrow, *The Gallup Survey of Britain* (1986) 276.

47 Nicholas Henderson, *Mandarin: The Diaries of Nicholas Henderson* (1994) 459. Entry for 16 May 1982.

48 Noakes, op. cit., 104.

49 Hugo Young, *One of Us: A Biography of Margaret Thatcher* (second edn, 1991) 282–3.

50 Michael Bilton and Peter Kosminsky, *Speaking Out: Untold Stories From The Falklands War* (1989) 292–3.

51 Thatcher, op. cit., 11–12.

52 Denman, op. cit., 259.

53 Thatcher, op. cit., 791.

54 Young, *One of Us*, 360–61.

55 Ibid., 408.

56 Ibid.

57 *Spectator*, 12 July 1990.

58 John Williams, 'Having an away day: English football spectators and the hooligan debate', in John Williams and Stephen Wagg (eds), *British Football and Social Change: Getting into Europe* (1991) 164.

59 Ibid., 166.

60 Ibid., 171.

61 Ibid., 166.

62 Richard Holt, *Sport and the British: A Modern History* (1989) 343.

63 I am grateful to Rachel Cutler for this reference.

64 Irvine Welsh, 'England is Dead, Long Live England', *Big Issue*, no. 296, 10–16 August 1998.

65 Denman, op. cit., 264.

66 Thatcher, op. cit., 743.

67 Ibid., 745.

68 Ibid., 838–9.

69 *Sun*, 1 November 1990.

70 Basil Skinner, 'Scotland – Cultural Links With Europe', in Athony Gishford and Victor Caudery (eds), *Fanfare for Europe* (1972) 62.

71 Peter Lynch, *Minority Nationalism and European Integration* (1996) 81.

72 Ibid., 38.

73 John Burnett, *Plenty and Want: A social history of diet in England from 1815 to the present day* (1966) 277.

74 Ibid., 280.

75 Anthony Sampson, *The New Europeans: A guide to the workings, institutions and character of contemporary Western Europe* (1968) 222.

76 *Daily Mirror*, 1 January 1973.

77 Lisa Chaney, *Elizabeth David: A Mediterranean Passion* (1998) 347.

78 I am extremely grateful to Bridget Williams, Director of the Sainsbury Archive, for this information. See her *The Best Butter In the World: A History of Sainsbury's* (1994).

79 Ibid., 353.

80 Office for National Statistics, *Social Trends* 29 (1999) 215.

81 George Orwell, *The Lion and the Unicorn: Socialism and the English Genius* (second edn, 1982) 63.

82 Sarah Curtis (ed.), *The Journals of Woodrow Wyatt*, vol. 1 (1998) 344.

83 David Dickinson, '12 Billion Pounds Under the Sea', *Independent on Sunday*, 18 January 1998.

84 P. M. H. Bell, *France and Britain, 1940–1994: The Long Separation* (1997) 286.

85 Ibid., 295.

86 *The Times*, 9 April 1994.

87 Bell, op. cit., 287.

88 Private information.

89 TGA: Clark Papers, 8812.1.4, f.99, Clark to Swede, 10.5.82.

90 George VI married a Scot, Elizabeth Bowes-Lyon, in 1923, but he was not then heir to the throne.

91 Royal Jubilee Trusts, *The Royal Wedding: Official Souvenir* (1981) 2.

92 Roy Strong, *The Roy Strong Diaries, 1967–1987* (1997) 284.

93 Julie Burchill, *Diana* (1998) 70.

94 Curtis, op. cit., 100, entry dated 13 March 1986. When Wyatt informed Thatcher of the Queen Mother's remarks, she was apparently 'very touched'; ibid., 101.

95 Peter Hennessy, *The Hidden Wiring: Unearthing the Constitution* (1995) 48.

96 Peter Hennessy, *Muddling Through: Power, Politics and the Quality of Government in Postwar Britain* (1996) 297.

11. MODERNIZERS

1 Charles Moore, *How To Be British* (1995) 17.

2 *Daily Telegraph*, 27 July 1994.

3 *Conservative Party News*, 'Speech by the Prime Minister to the Conservative Group for Europe', 22 April 1993.

4 John Major, *The Autobiography* (1999) 376.

5 James Mitchell, 'Contemporary Unionism', in Catriona M. Macdonald (ed.), *Unionist Scotland, 1800–1997* (1998) 128.

6 *Sun*, 24 March 1994.

7 *The VE Day Celebrations Souvenir Programme* (1995) 7.

8 *Daily Telegraph*, 8 May 1995.

9 *Guardian*, 9 May 1995.

10 *Parliamentary Debates (Commons)*, vol. 284, 973, 3 July 1996.

11 Ibid.

12 *Scotsman*, 4 July 1996.

13 Cmnd. 1591, *Scotland in the Union* (1997) 13.

14 Conservative Party, *You Can Only Be Sure With the Conservatives* (1997) 51.

15 *The Times*, 3 May 1997.

16 Brian Brivati, 'Earthquake or watershed? Conclusions on New Labour in Power', in Brivati and Tim Bale (eds), *New Labour in Power: Precedents and Prospects* (1997) 183.

17 Peter Clarke, *A Question of Leadership: From Gladstone to Blair* (second edn, 1999) 344.

18 Peter Mandelson and Roger Liddle, *The Blair Revolution: Can New Labour Deliver?* (1996) 27–8.

19 Clarke, *Question of Leadership* 344.

20 Ibid., 345.

21 *Daily Telegraph*, 22 November 1997.

22 A. N. Wilson, *The Rise and Fall of the House of Windsor* (1993) 201.

23 *Daily Mirror*, 12 February 1993.

24 Robert Hewison, *Culture and Consensus: England, Art and Politics since 1940* (1995) 8.

25 Anthony Barnett (ed.), *Power and the Throne: The Monarchy Debate* (1994) 169.

26 Frank Proschaska, *Royal Bounty: The Making of A Welfare Monarchy* (1995) 277.

27 Wilson, *House of Windsor*, caption to plate 13.

28 Hewison, *Culture and Consensus* 2.

29 Ibid., 3.

30 Barnett, op. cit., 16.

31 Ibid., 59.

32 Ibid., 209–10.

33 Ibid., 151.

34 *Observer*, 7 September 1997.

35 See 'Diana Regina' in Camille Paglia, *Vamps and Tramps: New Essays* (1995) 163–171.

36 *Observer*, 7 September 1997.

37 *Independent*, 25 November 1998.

38 Amanda Foreman, 'Uncommon Touch', *Guardian*, 9 July 1999.

39 *Daily Mail*, 8 July 1999.

40 Philip Ziegler, *Crown and People* (1978) 127.

41 Antony Taylor, *British Anti-monarchism and Debates about Royalty since 1790* (1999) 233.

42 Frank Prochaska, *The Republic of Britain 1760 to 2000* (2000); *Daily Telegraph*, 'British institutions: will they still be here in 2100?', 31 December 1999.

43 John Curtice, 'Is Scotland a nation and Wales not?', in Bridget Taylor and Katarina Thomson, *Scotland and Wales: Nations Again?* (1999) 127.

44 Christopher Harvie, *No Gods and Precious Few Heroes: Twentieth Century Scotland* (third edn, Edinburgh, 1998) 183.

45 Ted Hughes, *Rain-Charm for the Duchy* (1989) 23.

46 *Sunday Express*, 15 November 1992.

47 *Sunday Times*, 21 September 1997.

48 Tom Nairn, *The Break-up of Britain* (second edn, 1981) 294.

49 Barnett, op. cit., 153–4.

50 Mark Leonard, *Britain: Renewing Our Identity* (1997) 8.

51 Ibid., 48–62.

52 Department of Trade and Industry, *Powerhouse UK* (1998), Introduction by Margaret Beckett, President of the Board of Trade.

53 Frank Prochaska, *The Republic of Britain 1760 to 2000* (2000) 213.

54 *Daily Telegraph*, 14 July 1999. The music industry generated 130,300 full-time jobs, of which 42,000 were composers' and performers'.

55 Millennium Commission, *Marking the Millennium: A Speech by the Rt Hon Virginia Bottomley JP MP, Chairman of the Millennium Commission, 30 October 1995* (1995) 15.

56 *Guardian*, 25 February 1998.

57 Millennium Commission, *Millennium Experience: The Guide* (2000) 4.

58 Ibid., 7.

59 Ibid., 31.

60 *Daily Record*, 1 March 2000.

61 *New Statesman*, 1 May 1998.

62 'State of the Nation: The 1995 Joseph Rowntree Memorial Trust/Mori Survey', *Scottish Public Opinion*, September 1995.

63 Curtice, op. cit., 125. The survey was carried out by CREST (Centre for Research and Election Trends). Sadly, it did not examine corresponding English attitudes.

64 Anthony Heath, Bridget Taylor, Lindsay Brook and Alison Park, 'British National Sentiment', *British Journal of Political Science*, vol. 29, no. 1, January 1999.

65 Alice Brown, David McCrone, Lindsay Patterson and Paula Surridge, *The Scottish Electorate: The 1997 General Election and Beyond* (1999) 62–3. In England the class differences among those losing their sense of Britishness and those doggedly clinging on to it were minimal: 27 versus 25 per cent in the former category and 64 versus 63 per cent in the latter.

66 Cmnd. 3658, *Scotland's Parliament* (1997), paras 42 and 5.12.

67 Scots were asked to vote separately on whether they wanted their parliament to have tax-raising powers. Slightly less – 63 per cent – were in favour.

68 Simon Heffer, *Nor Shall My Sword: The Reinvention of England* (1999) 1.

69 *Scotland on Sunday*, 25 April 1999. The estimate was made by the Centre for Economic and Business Research.

70 Brian Taylor, *The Scottish Parliament* (1999) 7.

71 Curtice, op. cit., 140.

72 NOP, *Sunday Times*, 28 June 1998.

73 'New Nation, Old Bigotry', *Observer*, 15 August 1999.

74 *Guardian*, 17 April 1996.

75 *Daily Telegraph*, 31 May 2000.

76 James MacMillan, 'Scotland's shame', in M. Devine (ed.), *Scotland's Shame? Bigotry and Sectarianism in Modern Scotland* (2000) 13–24.

77 John Hodge, *Trainspotting & Shallow Grave* (1996) 46.

78 Roy Foster, *Modern Ireland, 1600–1972* (1988) 596.

79 *Guardian*, 18 September 1998.

80 *Guardian*, 27 May 1999.

81 Kevin Allen and Paul Durden, *Twin Town* (1997) 21.

82 Gwyn A. Williams, *When Was Wales?* (1985) 303.

83 R. Merfyn Jones, 'Beyond Identity? The Reconstruction of the Welsh', *Journal of British Studies*, No. 31, October 1992, 332.

84 *Daily Telegraph*, 5 May 1998.

85 Steve Bruce, *God Save Ulster! The Religion and Politics of Paisleyism* (1986) 268.

86 *Guardian*, 11 April 1998.

87 *Daily Telegraph*, 11 February 2000.

88 Ernest Barker, *Britain and the British People* (1942) 16.

89 Ernest Barker (ed.), *The Character of England* (1947) 552.

90 Ernest Barker, *National Character And The Factors In Its Formation* (fourth edn, 1948) 7–8.

91 Julian Barnes, *England, England* (1998) 37.

92 Dennis Potter, *Seeing the Blossom: Two Interviews and a Lecture* (1994) 8–9.

93 *The Times*, 7 February 1994.

94 Jon Wilde, 'Listening to England', *Livewire*, September 1994.

95 *The Times*, 20 April 1996.

96 Ben Carrington, 'Football's coming home but whose home? And do we want it?: Nation, football and the politics of exclusion' in Adam Brown (ed.), *Fanatics! Power, Identity and Fandom in Football* (1998) 112.

97 Emma Poulton, 'Fighting Talk From the Press Corps', in Mark Perryman (ed.), *The Ingerland Factor: Home Truths From Football* (1999) 126.

98 Dave Russell, *Football and the English: a social history of association football in England 1863–1995* (1997) 226. For more on women's attitudes to and participation in the sport, see John Williams and Jackie Woodhouse, 'Can play, will play: women and football in Britain', in John Williams and Stephen Wagg (eds.), *British Football and Social Change: Getting Into Europe* (1991).

99 *Sun*, 17 February 1999.

100 *Daily Telegraph*, 16 February 1999. For a more reasoned response, see Antony Beevor, 'Tom and Jerry', *Guardian*, 16 February 1999.

101 Gallup for the *Daily Telegraph*, 30 June 1998.

102 *Observer*, 28 June 1998.

103 Ibid.

104 *Sun*, 'St. George's Day Special', 23 April 1999.

105 *Daily Telegraph*, 19 July 1999.

106 'Youth rallies to English flag', *Sunday Times*, 21 September 1997.

107 Jeremy Paxman, *The English: A Portrait of a People* (1998) 265–6.

108 Jason Cowley, 'Searching For England', *The Waterstone's Magazine*, vol. 19, Summer 1999.

109 Will Self, 'UK Identity Part Four: Birth of the Cool', *Weekend Guardian*, 6 August 1994.

110 *Daily Mail*, 20 April 1990. Tebbit made his infamous remark in an interview for the *Los Angeles Times* the day before. What prompted it was his opposition to the Government's Hong Kong Bill. This permitted around 50,000 Hong Kong Chinese professionals to assume British citizenship and enter the UK after the handover of Hong Kong itself and the Crown Colony to China in 1997.

111 *Wisden Cricket Monthly*, July 1995. Although the editor of *WCM* stood by Henderson in the face of writs from black cricketers, Tebbit publicly disowned him.

112 Phil Vasili, *Colouring Over The White Line: the History of Black*

Footballers in Britain (2000) 190. 15 per cent of English professional players are black, but 33 per cent of them play in the Premiership.

113 See Mike Ticher, 'When In Rome', *When Saturday Comes*, December 1997, no. 130.

114 *Daily Mail*, 5 January 1998. Despite protests from leading black footballers, Motson denied that his remarks were racist.

115 BBC1: *Business Breakfast*, transcript, 13 February 1999.

116 BBC Radio One: Simon Mayo, transcript, 8 October 1998.

117 Yasmin Alibhai-Brown, *Who Do We Think We Are? Imagining The New Britain* (2000) 2.

118 Adonis and Pollard, op. cit., 256.

119 Ibid., 253–4.

120 Shaka Hislop, Foreword to Phil Vasili, op. cit., 10.

121 Simon Woolley, 'Who Did You Cheer For?', *New Nation*, 13 July 1998.

122 'England, Whose England?', *New Statesman Special Supplement*, 24 February 1995, 37

123 Alibhai-Brown, op. cit., 274.

124 Alan Grace, *This Is The British Forces Network: The Story of Forces Broadcasting in Germany* (1996) 124. Biko had just broadcast a message of encouragement to British troops stationed in Germany.

125 Alibhai-Brown, op. cit., 258.

126 British Council, 'Special Report, Looking Into England: English identities in the context of UK devolution', *British Studies Now*, no. 13, Summer 2000, 25. Bragg was speaking on 17 December 1999 at the University of Warwick conference on which the report was based. See also Billy Bragg, 'Two World Wars and One World Cup', in Perryman, op. cit., 37–43.

127 *Daily Telegraph*, 18 July 2000.

128 Cmnd. 5460, *Royal Commission On The Constitution, 1969–1973*, vol. 1 (September 1973) 57, para. 181; 353, para. 1188. Kilbrandon observed that Cornwall was the only exception and recommended that more should be made of the Duchy's title in the affairs of the county in order to emphasize its unique constitutional status. See paras. 221, 329 and 1211.

129 John Kendle, *Federal Britain: A History* (1997) 167.

130 John Mawson, 'English Regionalism and New Labour', in Howard Elcock and Michael Keating (eds), *Remaking the Union: Devolution and British Politics in the 1990s* (1998) 166.

131 'State of the Nation: The 1995 Joseph Rowntree Reform Trust/MORI Survey', *Scottish Public Opinion*, September 1995. I am grateful to Bob Worcester for this information.

132 'Sowing the seeds of English devolution', *New Statesman Special Supplement*, 26 June 1998, iv.

133 BBC1; *Newsnight*, transcript, 23 April 1998.

134 See the *Sun*, 'An Insult By George', 25 March 1999, for the refusal to

grant extended pub licences on St George's Day, and *Daily Telegraph*, 10 July 1999, for the pensioner forbidden to fly his flag.

135 Alan Taylor (ed.), *What A State!: Is Devolution For Scotland The End of Britain?* (2000) 210.

136 Polls consistently showed majority support in Scotland and Wales for English constitutional reform.

137 MORI for the *Daily Telegraph*, 26 June 2000. This is a conservative estimate, since figures include Scottish, Welsh and Northern Irish opinion, which is more sympathetic to a single currency. The average turnout in the rest of the UK at the 1999 European elections was 36.9 per cent.

138 Gallup for the *Daily Telegraph*, 15 April 1999.

139 *Parliamentary Debates (Commons)* vol. 304, 589–660, 16 January 1998.

140 *Spectator*, 19 September 1998.

141 Heffer, *Nor Shall My Sword* 132–3. For the moderate, Unionist view on the need for an English Parliament, see Kenneth Baker, 'Speaking For England', *Spectator*, 1 August 1998.

142 William Hague, Speech to the Centre for Policy Studies, 15 July 1999, reprinted in the *Guardian*, 16 July 1999.

143 *Daily Telegraph*, 1 July 1998.

144 *Daily Telegraph*, 18 June 1998.

145 Heffer, *Nor Shall My Sword*, 133.

146 Philip Lowe, 'The rural idyll defended: from preservation to conservation', in G. E. Mingay, *The Rural Idyll* (1989) 126.

147 *Daily Telegraph*, 2 March 1998. A MORI poll showed that despite Alliance claims that it represented ordinary country people, 47 per cent were in the AB bracket and only 5 per cent in DE. 79 per cent voted Conservative and their largest concern was, as the Colonel said, Labour's proposal to ban hunting with hounds in England.

148 *Sunday Telegraph*, 1 March 1998.

149 F. M. L. Thompson, 'English Landed Society in the Twentieth Century IV: Prestige Without Power?', *Transactions of the Royal Historical Society*, 6th Series, vol. 3, 1993, Presidential Address, read 20 November 1992.

150 David Cox, *The Henry Wood Proms* (1980) 173.

CONCLUSION

1 J. B. Priestley, *The English* (1973) 246–8.

2 Winston Churchill, Speech at the Mansion House, London, 10 November 1942, in Churchill, *The End of the Beginning* (1943) 214.

3 *Observer*, 12 December 1999.

4 George Orwell, *The Lion and the Unicorn: Socialism and the English Genius* (second edn, 1982) 37.

5 Ibid.

6 Albert Camus, 'Britain After the Election: Two French Views', *Listener*, vol. 36, no. 1186, 22 November 1951. The other view was given by Raymond Aron. While agreeing that Europe should move closer together, he reminded readers that it was thanks to American capitalism that Britain and the Continent were recovering from the war.

Bibliography

Explanatory Note

Because the British are so obsessed with their national identity, space has dictated that this bibliography is not comprehensive. Much of the material I consulted only appears in the endnotes to the text. This includes contemporary studies of the various cultures and identities of the Isles, for example Esme Wingfield-Stratford's *The Foundation of British Patriotism* (1940), references to public records (major manuscript collections are listed below as a general guide), newspapers, journals and periodicals (sixty different titles were examined), and biographies, memoirs and letters, whose individual commentaries on British life put some flesh on the bones of the above. All of this has allowed me to give more space to recently published works. The first part of the bibliography lists works devoted entirely or predominantly to the subject of national identity. This is split into seven sections so that readers particularly interested in, say, the identity of black Britons can find what they want more easily (it should be noted that some books in the section 'Britain' include specific studies of Scotland, Wales etc. as well as studies of Britishness tout court). The second part of the bibliography is more general. Split into two sections, Culture and Politics, it lists works that range across every area of national life, from football to fish and chips. The histories in these books are the criss-crossing beams upon which national identity in Britain rests. Throughout, place of publication is London unless otherwise stated.

List of Abbreviations

BBCWAC	British Broadcasting Corporation, Written Archives Centre, Reading
BL	Bodleian Library, Oxford
BLPES	British Library of Political and Economic Science, London
BTA	British Travel Association, London
BUL	Birmingham University Library
CCC	Churchill College, Cambridge
CERC	Church of England Record Centre, London
IWM	Imperial War Museum, London
LP	Lambeth Palace Library, London
LPA	Labour Party Archive, Manchester

MO   Mass Observation, University of Sussex
MRW Modern Records Centre, University of Warwick
NAS   National Archives of Scotland, Edinburgh
NLS   National Library of Scotland, Edinburgh
NLW National Library of Wales, Cardiff
NTA   National Trust Archive, London
PRO   Public Record Office, London
TCC   Trinity College, Cambridge
TGA   Tate Gallery Archive, London
UCL   University College, London

Manuscripts

Arts Council of Great Britain (PRO)
Clement Attlee (BL)
Gerald Barry (BLPES)
British Association for the Advancement of Science (BL)
British Broadcasting Corporation (BBCWAC)
British Council (PRO)
British Travel Association (BTA)
R. A. Butler (TCC)
Campaign for Nuclear Disarmament (MRW)
Church of England (CERC)
Church of Scotland (NLS)
Sir Kenneth Clark (TGA)
Conservative Party (BL)
Anthony Eden (BUL)
Hugh T. Edwards (NLW)
English Football Association, Lancaster Gate, London
European Movement (British Section), Europe House, London
Geoffrey Fisher (LP)
Victor Gollancz (MRW)
William Haley (CCC)
Labour Party (LPA)
Hugh MacDiarmid (NLS)
Mass Observation (MO)
National Trust for England and Wales (NTA)
George Orwell (UCL)
Plaid Cymru (NLW)
Michael Ramsey (LP)
Scottish Football Association (NLS)
Scottish National Party (NLS)
Scottish Office, National Archives of Scotland, Edinburgh (NAS)

Tate Gallery (TGA)
William Temple (LP)
Trades Union Congress (MRW)
War Artists' Advisory Committee, Imperial War Museum London (IWM)
Welsh Office (NLW and PRO)

Published Material – 1. National Identity

I GENERAL

Peter Alter, *Nationalism* (1989)
Benedict Anderson, *Imagined Communities: Reflections on the Origin and
    Spread of Nationalism* (second edn, 1991)

Ernest Gellner, *Nations and Nationalism* (1983)
– *Nationalism* (1997)
Liah Greenfeld, *Nationalism: Five Roads to Modernity* (1992)

Adrian Hastings, *The Construction of Nationhood: Ethnicity, Religion and
    Nationalism* (1997)
E. J. Hobsbawm, *Nations And Nationalism Since 1780: Programme, Myth and
    Reality* (second edn, 1992)
John Hutchinson and Anthony D. Smith (eds), *Nationalism* (1994)

David McCrone, *The Sociology of Nationalism: Tomorrow's Ancestors* (1998)

Tom Nairn, *Faces of Nationalism: Janus Revisited* (1997)

Anthony D. Smith, *National Identity* (1991)

Maurizio Viroli, *For Love of Country: An Essay on Patriotism and
    Nationalism* (1995)

II BRITAIN

Peter Bennett, 'Britpop and National Identity', *Journal for the Study of British
    Cultures*, vol. 5, no. 1, 1998, pp. 13–26
Vernon Bogdanor, *Devolution and the United Kingdom* (1999)
Michael Burgess, *The British Tradition of Federalism* (1995)
Ian Buruma, *Voltaire's Coconuts or Anglomania in Europe* (1999)

Linda Colley, *Britons: Forging The Nation 1707–1837* (1992)
– 'Britishness and Otherness: An Argument', *Journal of British Studies*, vol. 31,
    no. 4, 1992, pp. 309–29
Reginald Coupland, *Welsh and Scottish Nationalism: A Study* (1954)

Bernard Crick, *National Identities: The Constitution of the United Kingdom* (1991)

Norman Davies, *The Isles: A History* (1999)
Philip Dodd, *The Battle Over Britain* (1995)

Owen Dudley Edwards, Gwynfor Evans and Hugh MacDiarmid, *Celtic Nationalism* (1968)
Howard Elcock and Michael Keating, *Remaking the Union: Devolution and British Politics in the 1990s* (1998)

Brian Foss, 'Message and Medium: Government Patronage, National Identity and National Culture in Britain 1939–45', *The Oxford Art Journal*, vol. 14, no. 2, 1991, pp. 52–72

Patricia L. Garside and Michael Hebbert (eds), *British Regionalism 1900–2000* (1989)
J. H. Grainger, *Patriotisms: Britain 1900–1939* (1986)
Alexander Grant and Keith J. Stringer (eds), *Uniting the Kingdom? The Making of British History* (1995)

Anthony Heath et al., 'British National Sentiment', *British Journal of Political Science*, vol. 29, no. 1, pp. 155–75
Michael Hechter, *Internal Colonialism: The Celtic fringe in British national development, 1536–1966* (1975)
Eric Hobsbawm and Terence Ranger (eds), *The Invention of Tradition* (1993)
Roger Hooker and John Sargent (eds), *Belonging to Britain: Christian Perspectives on Religion and Identity in a Plural Society* (1991)

Daniel Jenkins, *The British: Their Identity & Their Religion* (1975)

Hugh Kearney, *The British Isles: A History of Four Nations* (1989)
John Kendle, *Federal Britain: A History* (1997)

Brian P. Levack, *The Formation of the British State: England, Scotland and the Union 1603–1707* (1987)
Wm. Roger Louis, *Adventures With Britannia: Personalities, Politics and Culture in Britain* (1995)
– *More Adventures With Britannia: Personalities, Politics and Culture in Britain* (1998)

Andrew Marr, *The Day Britain Died* (2000)
Charles Moore, *How To Be British* (1995)
H. F. Moorhouse, 'One State, Several Countries: Soccer and Nationality in a "United" Kingdom', *International Journal of the History of Sport*, vol. 12, no. 2, 1995, pp. 55–74
Alexander Murdoch, *British History 1660–1832: National Identity and Local Culture* (1998)

Tom Nairn, *The Break-Up of Britain: Crisis and Neo-Nationalism* (second edn, 1981)
– *The Enchanted Glass: Britain and its Monarchy* (1988)
Lucy Noakes, *War And The British: Gender And National Identity 1939–91* (1998)

John Osmond, *The Divided Kingdom* (1988)

Jeffrey Richards, *Films and British National Identity: From Dickens to Dad's Army* (1997)
Keith Robbins, *Nineteenth Century Britain: Integration and Diversity* (1988)
– *History, Religion and Identity in Modern Britain* (1993)
– *Great Britain: Identities, Institutions and the Idea of Britishness* (1998)

Raphael Samuel (ed.), *Patriotism: The Making and Unmaking of British National Identity* (3 vols., 1989)
– *Theatres of Memory* (1994)
– *Island Stories: Unravelling Britain* (1998)
Peter Scott, 'British Regional Policy 1945–51: A Lost Opportunity', *Twentieth Century British History*, vol. 8, no. 3, 1997, pp. 358–82
Christopher Shaw and Malcolm Chase (eds), *The Imagined Past: History and Nostalgia* (1989)
David Smith, *North and South: Britain's Economic, Social and Political Divide* (second edn, 1994)

Bridget Taylor and Katarina Thomson, *Scotland and Wales: Nations Again?* (1999)

Richard Weight, 'State, Intelligentsia and the Promotion of National Culture in Britain, 1939–45', *Journal of Historical Research*, vol. 30, no. 1, February 1996
– and Abigail Beach (eds), *The Right To Belong: Citizenship and National Identity in Britain 1930–1960* (1998)
Patrick Wright, *On Living In An Old Country: The National Past In Contemporary Britain* (1985)

III MINORITY BRITAIN

Geoffrey Alderman, *Modern British Jewry* (1992)
Yasmin Alibhai-Brown, *Who Do We Think We Are? Imagining the New Britain* (2000)

Charlotte Benton, *A Different World: Émigré Architects In Britain 1928–1958* (1995)
Gunter Berghaus, *Theatre And Film In Exile: German Artists in Britain, 1933–1945* (1989)

Therese Daniels and Jane Gerson (eds), *The Colour Black: Black Images in British Television* (1989)

Peter Fryer, *Staying Power: The History of Black People in Britain* (1984)

Paul Gilroy, *There Ain't No Black In The Union Jack* (1987)
Amy Zahl Gottlieb, *Men Of Vision: Anglo-Jewry's Aid To Victims Of The Nazi Regime 1933–1945* (1998)
Jonathon Green, *Them: Voices from the Immigrant Community in Contemporary Britain* (1990)

Dilip Hiro, *Black British White British* (third edn, 1991)
Gerhard Hirschfeld (ed.), *Exile In Great Britain: Refugees from Hitler's Germany* (1984)
Colin Holmes, *Immigration & British Society, 1871–1971* (1988)

Miriam Kochan, *Britain's Internees In The Second World War* (1983)

Zig Layton-Henry, *The Politics of Race in Britain* (1984)
– *The Politics of Immigration* (1992)
Gisela C. Libzelter, *Political Anti-Semitism In England 1918–1939* (1978)
Louise London, *Whitehall And The Jews 1933–1948* (2000)

Kwesi Owusu (ed.), *Black British Culture & Society* (2000)

Panikos Panayi, *Immigration, ethnicity and racism in Britain 1815–1945* (1994)
– (ed.), *Racial Violence In Britain In The Nineteenth And Twentieth Centuries* (second edn, 1996)
Kathleen Paul, *Whitewashing Britain: Race and Citizenship in the Postwar Era* (1997)
Mike and Charlie Phillips, *Notting Hill In The Sixties* (1991)
Mike and Trevor Phillips, *Windrush: The Irresistible Rise Of Multi-Racial Britain* (1998)
Edward Pilkington, *Beyond The Mother Country: West Indians And The Notting Hill Riots* (1988)
Jim Pines (ed.), *Black and White in Colour: Black People in British Television Since 1936* (1992)

Paul B. Rich, *Race and Empire in British Politics* (second edn, 1990)

Ian R. G. Spencer, *British Immigration Policy: The Making of Multi-Racial Britain* (1997)

Phil Vasili, *Colouring Over The White Line: The History of Black Footballers in Britain* (2000)

Onyekachi Wambu (ed.), *Empire Windrush: Fifty Years Of Writing About Black Britain* (1998)

IV ENGLAND

Clive Aslet, *Anyone For England? A Search for British Identity* (1997)

Georgina Boyes, *The Imagined Village: Culture, Ideology and The English Folk Revival* (1993)
Michael Bracewell, *England is mine: Pop Life in Albion from Wilde to Goldie* (1997)
J. W. Burrow, *A Liberal Descent: Victorian Historians and the English Past* (1981)

Stefan Collini, *English Pasts: Essays in History and Culture* (1999)
Robert Colls and Philip Dodd (eds), *Englishness: Politics and Culture 1880–1920* (1986)
– and Bill Lancaster (eds), *Geordies: Roots of Regionalism* (1992)

C. Dellheim, 'Imagining England: Victorian Views Of The North', *Northern History*, vol. 22, no. 2, 1986, pp. 216–30
Brian Doyle, *English and Englishness* (1989)

David Edgerton, *England And The Aeroplane: An Essay on a Militant and Technological Nation* (1991)
Geoffrey Elton, *The English* (1992)

Dave Scott Fox, *Saint George: The Saint With Three Faces* (1983)

Amy Hale, 'A History of the Cornish Revival', in Tim Saunders (ed.), *The Wheel: An Anthology of Modern Poetry in Cornish 1850–1980* (1999)
Dave Haslam, *Manchester England: The Story of The Pop Cult City* (1999)
Simon Heffer, *Nor Shall My Sword: The Reinvention of England* (1999)
Richard Holt, 'Cricket and Englishness: The Batsman as Hero', *International Journal of the History of Sport*, vol. 13, no. 1, 1996, pp. 48–70

Helen M. Jewell, *The North–South Divide: The Origins of Northern Consciousness in England* (1994)

Hans Kohn, 'The Genesis And Character Of English Nationalism', *Journal of the History of Ideas*, 1 (1940), pp. 69–94

Paul Langford, *Englishness Identified: Manners and Character 1650–1850* (2000)
Alison Light, *Forever England: Femininity, Literature and Conservatism Between The Wars* (1991)
David Lowenthal, 'British National Identity and the English Landscape', *Rural History*, vol. 2, no. 2, 1991, pp. 205–30
John Lucas, *England and Englishness: Ideas of Nationhood in English Poetry 1688–1900* (1990)

Peter Mandler, 'Against Englishness: English Culture And The Limits To Rural Nostalgia 1850–1940', *Huntingdon Library Journal*, vol. 12, no. 1, 1993.

Mark Marqusee, *Anyone But England: Cricket, Race and Class* (second edn, 1998)

Blake Morrison, *The Movement: English Poetry and Fiction of the 1950s* (1980)

Gerald Newman, *The Rise of English Nationalism: A Cultural History 1740–1830* (1987)

Jeremy Paxman, *The English: A Portrait Of A People* (1998)

Mark Perryman (ed.), *The Ingerland Factor: Home Truths from Football* (1999)

Philip Peyton (ed.), *Cornwall Since The War* (1993)

Roy Porter (ed.), *Myths of the English* (1992)

Donald Read, *The English Provinces 1760–1960: a study in influence* (1964)

Edward Royle (ed.), *Issues of Regional Identity* (1998)

Dave Russell, *Football and the English*: *a social history of association football in England 1863–1995* (1997)

Roger Scruton, *England: an elegy* (2000)

Gareth Stedman Jones, 'The cockney and the nation, 1780–1988', in David Feldman and Gareth Stedman Jones (eds), *Metropolis London: Histories and Representations Since 1800* (1989)

Robert Stradling and Meirion Hughes, *The English Musical Renaissance 1860–1940: Construction and Deconstruction* (1993)

D. J. Taylor, *After the War: The Novel and England Since 1945* (1993)

Miles Taylor, 'John Bull And The Iconography of Public Opinion In England c. 1712–1929', *Past And Present*, no. 134, 1991.

Frank Trentmann, 'Civilisation and its Discontents: English Neo-Romanticism and the Transformation of Anti-Modernism in Twentieth-Century Western Culture', *Journal of Contemporary History*, vol. 29, 1994, pp. 583–625

Martin J. Weiner, *English Culture And The Decline Of The Industrial Spirit 1850–1980* (1981)

Michael Wood, *In Search of England: Journeys Into The English Past* (1999)

Patrick Wright, *The Village that Died for England: The Strange Story of Tyneham* (1995)

V SCOTLAND

Chris Bambery (ed.), *Scotland: class and nation* (1999)

Lynn Bennie, Jack Brand and James Mitchell, *How Scotland Votes* (1997)

Jack Brand, *The National Movement in Scotland* (1978)

Dauvit Broun, R. J. Finlay and Michael Lynch, *Image and Identity: The Making and Re-making of Scotland Through the Ages* (1998)

Alice Brown, David McCrone and Lindsay Paterson, *Politics and Society in Scotland* (second edn, 1998)

– *The Scottish Electorate: The 1997 General Election and beyond* (1999)

Keith M. Brown, *Kingdom or Province? Scotland and the Regal Union 1603–1715* (1992)

George Bruce, *Festival In The North: The Story of the Edinburgh Festival* (1975)

Patrick Cadell and Anne Matheson (eds), *For the Encouragement of Learning: Scotland's National Library* (1989)

Angus Calder, *Revolving Culture: Notes From the Scottish Republic* (1994)

Alan Cameron, *Bank of Scotland: A Very Singular Institution, 1695–1995* (1995)

Alan Clements, Kenny Farquharson and Kirsty Wark, *Restless Nation* (1996)

David Daiches, *Scotland & the Union* (1977)

T. M. Devine, (ed.), *Scottish Emigration And Scottish Society* (1992)

– *The Scottish Nation 1700–2000* (1999)

– (ed.), *Scotland's Shame? Bigotry and Sectarianism in Modern Scotland* (2000)

– and R. Finlay (eds), *Scotland in the 20th Century* (1996)

Richard J. Finlay, 'Pressure Group or Political Party? The Nationalist Impact on Scottish Politics, 1928–1945', *Twentieth Century British History*, vol. 3, no. 3, 1992, pp. 274–97

– 'National Identity in Crisis: Politicians, Intellectuals and the 'End of Scotland', *History*, vol. 79, no. 256, 1994, pp. 242–59

– *A Partnership For Good? Scottish Politics and the Union Since 1880* (1997)

Alasdair Gray, *Why Scots Should Rule Scotland* (1997)

Forsyth Hardy, *Scotland and Film* (1990)

Marjory Harper, *Emigration from Scotland between the wars* (1998)

Christopher Harvie, *Fool's Gold: The Story of North Sea Oil* (1994)

– *Scotland and Nationalism: Scottish Society and Politics 1707–1994* (1994)

– *No Gods and Precious Few Heroes: Twentieth Century Scotland* (third edn, 1998)

– *Travelling Scot: Essays on the history, politics and future of the Scots* (1999)

Grant Jarvie and Graham Walker, *Scottish Sport in the Making of the Nation: Ninety-Minute Patriots?* (1994)

Michael Keating and David Bleiman, *Labour and Scottish Nationalism* (1979)

Arnold Kemp, *The Hollow Drum: Scotland Since the War* (1993)

C. H. Lee, *Scotland and the United Kingdom: The economy and the Union in the twentieth century* (1995)

Ian Levitt, *The Scottish Office: Depression and Reconstruction 1919–1959* (1992)

Bashir Maan, *The New Scots: The Story of Asians in Scotland* (1992)
Colin McArthur (ed.), *Scotch Reels: Scotland in Cinema and Television* (1982)
– 'Scotland and the *Braveheart* Effect', *Journal for the Study of British Cultures*, vol. 5, no. 1, 1998, pp. 27–40
David McCrone, Angela Morris and Richard Kiely, *Scotland – the Brand: The Making of Scottish Heritage* (1995)
Catriona Macdonald, *Unionist Scotland 1800–1997* (1998)
W. H. McDowell, *The History of BBC Broadcasting in Scotland 1923–1983* (1992)
James Mitchell, *Conservatives and the Union: A Study of Conservative Party Attitudes to Scotland* (1990)

Tom Nairn, *After Britain: New Labour and the Return of Scotland* (2000)

Fintan O'Toole, 'Imagining Scotland', *Granta*, No. 56, 1997.

Lindsay Paterson (ed.), *A Diverse Assembly: The Debate on a Scottish Parliament* (1998)
Murray G. H. Pittock, *The Invention of Scotland: The Stuart Myth and the Scottish Identity, 1638 to the Present* (1991)
George Pottinger, *The Secretaries of State For Scotland 1926–76* (1979)

Paul H. Scott (ed.), *Scotland: A Concise Cultural History* (1993)

Alan Taylor (ed.), *What A State! Is Devolution for Scotland the End of Britain?* (2000)
Brian Taylor, *The Scottish Parliament* (1999)
Angela Tuckett, *The Scottish Trades Union Congress: The First 80 Years, 1897–1977* (1986)

Graham Walker and Tom Gallagher (eds), *Sermons and Battle Hymns: Protestant Popular Culture in Modern Scotland* (1990)

VI WALES

David Berry, *Wales & Cinema: The First Hundred Years* (1994)

David Cole (ed.), *The New Wales* (1990)
Tony Curtis (ed.), *Wales, The Imagined Nation: Essays In Cultural & National Identity* (1986)

D. Hywel Davies, *The Welsh Nationalist Party 1925–1945: A Call To Nationhood* (1983)
John Davies, *Broadcasting and The BBC in Wales* (1994)
– *A History of Wales* (1994)

John S. Ellis, 'The Prince and the Dragon: Welsh National Identity and the 1911 Investiture of the Prince Of Wales', *Welsh History Review*, vol. 18, no. 2, 1996, pp. 272–94

Pyrs Gruffudd, 'Remaking Wales: nation-building and the geographical imagination, 1925–50', *Political Geography*, vol. 14, no. 3, pp. 219–39

J. Graham Jones, 'The Parliament For Wales Campaign, 1950–1956', *Welsh History Review*, vol. 16, no. 2, 1992, pp. 207–36

R. Merfyn Jones, 'Beyond Identity? The Reconstruction of the Welsh', *Journal of British Studies*, no. 31 (October 1992) pp. 330–57

Kenneth O. Morgan, *Wales in British Politics 1868–1922* (1970)

– *Wales: Rebirth of A Nation 1880–1980* (1981)

– *Modern Wales: Politics, People and Places* (1995)

Jan Morris, *Wales: Epic Views of A Small Country* (1998)

Alan Butt Philip, *The Welsh Question: Nationalism in Welsh Politics 1945–1970* (1975)

Gwyn A. Williams, *When Was Wales?: A History of the Welsh* (1985)

VII IRELAND

Desmond Bell, *Acts of Union: Youth Culture and Sectarianism in Northern Ireland* (1990)

D. George Boyce, *Nationalism In Ireland* (second edn, 1991)

Steve Bruce, *The Edge of the Union: The Ulster Loyalist Political Vision* (1994)

R. Cathcart, *The Most Contrary Region: The BBC in Northern Ireland 1924–80* (1984)

Peter Catterall and Sean McDougall (eds), *The Northern Ireland Question in British Politics* (1996)

Richard English and Graham Walker, *Unionism in Modern Ireland: New Perspectives on Politics and Culture* (1996)

John Erskine and Gordon Lucy, *Cultural Traditions in Northern Ireland: Exploring the Ulster-Scottish Connection* (Belfast, 1997)

Stephen Evans, 'The Conservatives and the Redefinition of Unionism, 1912–21', *Twentieth Century British History*, vol. 9, no. 1, 1998, pp. 1–27

Roy Foster, *Modern Ireland 1600–1972* (1988)

– *Paddy & Mr. Punch: Connections in Irish and English History* (1993)

– 'History and Identity in Modern Ireland', *The Eighth Annual Bindoff Lecture, Queen Mary College London* (1997)

Brian Girvin and Geoffrey Roberts, 'The Forgotten Volunteers of World War II', *History Ireland*, vol. 6, no. 1, 1998, pp. 46–51.

Thomas Hennessey, *A History of Northern Ireland 1920–1996* (1997)

Keith Jeffery (ed.), *An Irish Empire? Aspects of Ireland and the British Empire* (1996)

James Loughlin, *Ulster Unionism and British National Identity Since 1885* (1995)

Ian McBride, *The Siege of Derry in Ulster Protestant Mythology* (1997)

Martin McLoone (ed.), *Broadcasting in a Divided Community: Seventy Years of the BBC in Northern Ireland* (1996)

Deirdre McMahon, *Republicans & Imperialists: Anglo-Irish Relations in the 1930s* (1984)

Nicholas Mansergh, *The Unresolved Question: The Anglo-Irish Settlement and Its Undoing, 1912–72* (1991)

David Miller (ed.), *Rethinking Northern Ireland: Culture, Ideology and Colonialism* (1998)

Dervla Murphy, *A Place Apart* (1978)

Eunan O'Halpin, *Defending Ireland: The Irish State And Its Enemies Since 1922* (1999)

Kevin Rockett, Luke Gibbons and John Hill, *Cinema and Ireland* (1987)

A. T. Q. Stewart, *The Narrow Ground: Aspects of Ulster 1609–1969* (1977)

John Sugden and Alan Bairner, *Sport, Sectarianism And Society In A Divided Ireland* (1993)

Peter Taylor, *Provos: The IRA and Sinn Fein* (1997)

Sabine Wichart, *Northern Ireland Since 1945* (1991)

Published Material – 2. National Life

I CULTURE AND SOCIETY

Paul Addison, *Now The War Is Over* (1985)
– and Jeremy A. Crang (eds), *The Burning Blue: A New History of the Battle of Britain* (2000)
Andrew Adonis and Stephen Pollard, *A Class Act: The Myth of Britain's Classless Society* (1997)
Anthony Aldgate, *Britain Can Take It: The British Cinema In The Second World War* (1986)
– *Censorship And The Permissive Society: British Cinema & Theatre 1955–1965* (1995)
– and Jeffrey Richards, *Best of British: Cinema and Society from 1930 to the Present* (second edn, 1999)

Maggie Andrews, *The Acceptable Face of Feminism: The Women's Institute as a Social Movement* (1997)

Noël Annan, *Our Age: Portrait Of A Generation* (1990)

Brian Appleyard, *The Pleasures of Peace: Art and imagination in post-war Britain* (1989)

Roy Armes, *A Critical History of British Cinema* (1978)

Victor Bailey, *Delinquency and Citizenship: Reclaiming the Young Offender 1914–48* (1987)

Michael Balfour, *Propaganda in War 1939–1945: Organisations, Policies and Publics in Britain and Germany* (1979)

Mary Banham and Bevis Hiller (eds), *A Tonic To The Nation: The Festival of Britain 1951* (1976)

Richard Barnes, *Mods!* (second edn, 1991)

Charles Barr (ed.), *All Our Yesterdays: 90 Years of British Cinema* (1986)

– *Ealing Studios* (second edn, 1993)

Peter J. Beck, *Scoring For Britain: International Football and International Politics 1900–1939* (1999)

François Bédarida, *A Social History Of England 1851–1990* (second edn, 1991)

John Benson, *The Rise Of Consumer Society In Britain 1880–1980* (1994)

Katherine Bentley Beauman, *Partners In Blue: The story of women's service with the Royal Air Force* (1971)

Virginia Berridge, *Opium and the People: Opiate Use and Drug Control Policy in Nineteenth and Early Twentieth Century England* (second edn, 1999)

Eugenio F. Biagini, *Citizenship and community: Liberals, radicals and collective identities in the British Isles 1865–1931* (1996)

Christopher Booker, *The Seventies: Portrait Of A Decade* (1980)

– *The Neophiliacs: A Study Of The Revolution in English life in the Fifties And Sixties* (second edn, 1993)

Joanna Bourke, *Working-Class Cultures In Britain 1890–1960: Gender, Class and Ethnicity* (1994)

Stephen Bourne, *Brief Encounters: Lesbians and Gays in British Cinema 1930–1971* (1996)

Piers Brendon, *Thomas Cook: 150 Years of Popular Tourism* (1991)

– and Philip Whitehead, *The Windsors: A Dynasty Revealed* (1994)

Asa Briggs, *The History of Broadcasting In The United Kingdom*, vol. I: *The Birth of Broadcasting* (1961)

– *The History of Broadcasting In The United Kingdom*, vol. II: *The Golden Age of Wireless* (1965)

– *The History of Broadcasting In The United Kingdom*, vol. III: *The War of Words* (1970)

– *The History of Broadcasting In The United Kingdom*, vol. IV: *Sound & Vision* (1979)

– *The History of Broadcasting In The United Kingdom*, vol. V: *Competition* (1995)
– *Governing The BBC* (1979)
– *The BBC: The First Fifty Years* (1985)
Ian Britain, *Fabianism and culture: A study in British socialism and the arts 1884–1918* (1982)
Colin John Bruce, *War in the Air 1939–1945* (1991)
– *War at Sea 1939–1945* (1993)
– *War on the Ground 1939–1945* (1995)
Peter Buitenhuis, *The Great War Of Words: Literature as Propaganda 1914–18 and After* (1989)
Michael Bunce, *The Countryside Ideal: Anglo-American Images of Landscape* (1994)
Madeleine Bunting, *The Model Occupation: The Channel Islands Under German Rule 1940–1945* (1995)
John Burnett, *Plenty & Want: A Social History of Food In England From 1815 To The Present Day* (third edn, 1989)
– *Liquid Pleasures: A Social History of Drinks in Modern Britain* (1999)
Alan Burton, Tim O'Sullivan and Paul Wells, *Liberal Directions: Basil Dearden and Postwar British Film Culture* (1997)
– *The Family Way: The Boulting Brothers and Postwar British Film Culture* (2000)
Ivan Butler, *To Encourage The Art Of The Film: The Story Of The British Film Institute* (1971)

Angus Calder, *The People's War: Britain 1939–45* (1969)
– *The Myth Of The Blitz* (1991)
– and Dorothy Sheridan, *Speak For Yourself: A Mass-Observation Anthology 1937–1949* (1984)
David Cannadine, *The Pleasures Of The Past* (1989)
– *The Decline And Fall Of The British Aristocracy* (1990)
– *Aspects of Aristocracy: Grandeur and Decline in Modern Britain* (1994)
– *Class In Britain* (1998)
– *History In Our Time* (1998)
John Carey, *The Intellectuals And The Masses: Pride and Prejudice Among The Literary Intelligentsia 1880–1939* (1992)
Humphrey Carpenter, *The Brideshead Generation: Evelyn Waugh and his Friends* (1989)
– *The Envy of the World: Fifty Years Of The BBC Third Programme And Radio 3* (1996)
– *That Was Satire That Was: The Satire Boom Of The 1960s* (2000)
Andrew Chandler, 'Munich and Morality: The Bishops of the Church of England and Appeasement', *Twentieth Century British History*, vol. 5, no. 1, 1994, pp. 77–99

James Chapman, *The British At War: Cinema, State and Propaganda 1939–1945* (1998)
– *Licence To Thrill: A Cultural History Of The James Bond Films* (1999)
Steve Chibnall and Robert Murphy (eds), *British Crime Cinema* (1999)
Ian Christie, *Arrows of Desire: The Films of Michael Powell and Emeric Pressburger* (second edn, 1994)
Mark Clapson, *A Bit of a Flutter: Popular gambling and English society, c. 1823–1961* (1992)
Margaret M. Clark and Pamela Munn (eds), *Education in Scotland: Policy and Practice from Pre-School to Secondary* (1997)
Tim Clayton and Phil Craig, *Finest Hour* (1999)
Matthew Collin, *Altered State: The Story of Ecstasy Culture and Acid House* (second edn, 1998)
Stefan Collini, *Public Moralists: Political Thought And Intellectual Life In Britain 1850–1930* (1991)
Bruce Collins and Keith Robbins (eds), *British Culture And Economic Decline* (1990)
Mark Connelly, *Christmas: A Social History* (1999)
Stephen Constantine, 'Amateur Gardening and Popular Recreation in the 19th and 20th Centuries', *Journal of Social History*, vol. 14, no. 2, 1981, pp. 387–406
Emmanuel Cooper, *People's Art: Working-Class Art from 1750 to the Present Day* (1994)
John Corner (ed.), *Popular Television In Britain: Studies In Cultural History* (1991)
John Costello, *Love, Sex & War: Changing Values 1939–45* (1985)
Maurice Cowling, *Religion and Public Doctrine in Modern England*, Vol. I: (1980)
– *Religion and Public Doctrine in Modern England*, vol. II: *Assaults* (1985)
David Cox, *The Henry Wood Proms* (1980)
William Crofts, *Coercion Or Persuasion? Propaganda in Britain after 1945* (1989)
David Crouch and Colin Ward, *The Allotment: Its Landscape and Culture* (second edn, 1997)
Nicholas John Cull, *Selling War: The British Propaganda Campaign Against American Neutrality in World War II* (1995)
James Curran and Jean Seaton, *Power Without Responsibility: The Press and Broadcasting in Britain* (fourth edn, 1991)
– and Vincent Porter (eds), *British Cinema History* (1983)

Martin Daunton, *Royal Mail: The Post Office Since 1840* (1990)
Hugh David, *The Fitzrovians: A Portrait of Bohemian Society 1900–55* (1988)
– *Heroes, Mavericks And Bounders: The English Gentleman From Lord Curzon to James Bond* (1990)

– *On Queer Street: A Social History of British Homosexuality 1895–1995*
    (1997)
Grace Davie, *Religion in Britain since 1945* (1994)
Frances Donaldson, *The British Council: The First Fifty Years* (1984)
Harriet Dover, *Home Front Furniture: British Utility Design 1941–1951* (1991)
Kirsten Drotner, *English Children And Their Magazines 1751–1945* (1988)
Raymond Durgnat, *A Mirror for England: British Movies From Austerity To
    Affluence* (1971)

Niall Edworthy, *The Second Most Important Job In The Country: England
    Managers From Winterbottom to Hoddle* (1999)
John Elsom and Nicholas Tomalin, *The History of the National Theatre* (1978)
Clive Emsley, *The English Police: A Political and Social History* (second edn,
    1996)
Lionel Esher, *A Broken Wave: The Rebuilding of England 1940–1980* (1981)

Paul Ferris, *Sex And The British: A Twentieth Century History* (1993)
Adrian Forty, *Objects of Desire: Design And Society Since 1750* (1986)
Conrad Frost, *Coronation June 2 1953* (1978)
Paul Fussel, *The Great War And Modern Memory* (1975)
– *Abroad: British Literary Travelling Between The Wars* (1980)
– *Wartime: Understanding and Behaviour In The Second World War* (1989)
Jim Fyrth, *Labour's Promised Land? Culture and Society in Labour Britain
    1945–51* (1995)

Juliet Gardner, *'Over Here': The GIs In Wartime Britain* (1992)
– *D-Day: Those Who Were There* (1994)
Alan D. Gilbert, *The Making of Post-Christian Britain: A History of the
    Secularization of Modern Society* (1980)
Martin Gilbert, *The Day The War Ended: VE Day 1945 in Europe and
    Around the World* (1995)
Mark Girouard, *The Return to Camelot: Chivalry And The English Gentleman*
    (1981)
Christine Gledhill and Gillian Swanson (eds), *Nationalising Femininity:
    Culture, Sexuality and British Cinema in the Second World War* (1996)
Frank Gloversmith (ed.), *Class, Culture and Social Change: A New View of the
    1930s* (1980)
Sean Glynn and Alan Booth, *Modern Britain: an economic and social history*
    (1996)
Andrew Graham-Dixon, *A History Of British Art* (1996)
Jonathon Green, *The Sixties and the Counterculture* (1998)
Paul Greenhalgh, *Ephemeral Vistas: The Expositions Universelles, Great
    Exhibitions and World's Fairs, 1851–1939* (1988)
Adrian Gregory, *The Silence of Memory: Armistice Day 1919–1946* (1994)

Miles Hadfield, *A History of British Gardening* (1979)

Dennis Hardy, *From Garden Cities To New Towns: Campaigning for town and country planning 1899–1946* (1991)
- *From New Towns to Green Politics: Campaigning for town and country planning 1946–1990* (1991)
Nicholas Harman, *Dunkirk: The Necessary Myth* (1980)
Sue Harper, *Women in British Cinema: Mad, Bad and Dangerous to Know* (2000)
John S. Harris, *Government Patronage Of The Arts In Great Britain* (Chicago 1970)
Martin Harrison, *Young Meteors: British Photojournalism: 1957–1965* (1998)
Tom Harrisson, *Living Through The Blitz* (second edn, 1990)
Adrian Hastings, *A History of English Christianity 1920–1985* (1986)
Dick Hebdige, *Subculture: The Meaning of Style* (1979)
Robert Hewison, *Under Siege: Literary Life In London 1939–45* (1977)
- *In Anger: Culture in the Cold War 1945–60* (1981)
- *Too Much: Art and Society in the Sixties* (1986)
- *The Heritage Industry: Britain In A Climate of Decline* (1987)
- *Culture & Consensus: England, Art and Politics Since 1940* (1995)
Patrick Higgins, *Heterosexual Dictatorship: Male Homosexuality In Post-War Britain* (1996)
Andrew Higson, *Waving The Flag: Constructing a National Cinema in Britain* (1995)
- (ed.), *Dissolving Views: Key Writing On British Cinema* (1996)
John Hill, *Sex, Class and Realism: British Cinema 1956–63* (1986)
- *British Cinema In The 1980s* (1999)
Mathew Hilton, *Smoking in British popular culture 1800–2000* (2000)
Richard Holt, *Sport and the British: A Modern History* (1989)
- (ed.), *Sport and the Working Class in Modern Britain* (1990)
Eric Hopkins, *The Rise and Decline of the English Working Classes 1918–1990: A Social History* (1991)
Harry Hopkins, *The New Look: A Social History Of The Forties And Fifties In Britain* (1963)
Alun Howkins, *Reshaping Rural England: A Social History 1850–1925* (1991)
- 'A Country at War: Mass Observation and Rural England, 1939–45', *Rural History*, vol. 9, no. 1, 1998, pp. 75–97
I. Q. Hunter (ed.), *British Science Fiction Cinema* (1999)
Malcolm Hunter (ed.), *Preserving The Past: The Rise of Heritage In Modern Britain* (1996)
Roger Hutchinson, *. . . it is now! The Real Story of England's 1966 World Cup Triumph* (1995)
Samuel Hynes, *The Auden Generation: Literature and Politics in England in the 1930s* (1976)

Ian Inglis (ed.), *The Beatles, Popular Music and Society: A Thousand Voices* (2000)

Christopher Innes, *Modern British Drama 1890–1990* (1992)

Alan A. Jackson, *The Middle Classes 1900–1950* (1991)

Stephen Jeffrey-Poulter, *Peers, Queers & Commons: The Struggle for Gay Law Reform from 1950 to the Present* (1991)

Jennifer Jenkins and Patrick James, *From Acorn To Oak Tree: The Growth of the National Trust 1895–1994* (1994)

Paul Johnson (ed.), *20th Century Britain: Economic, Social and Cultural Change* (1994)

Nicholas Joicey, 'A Paperback Guide to Progress: Penguin Books 1935–c. 1951', *Twentieth Century British History*, vol. 4, no. 1, 1993, pp. 25–36

Stephen G. Jones, *Workers At Play: A Social and Economic History of Leisure 1918–1939* (1986)

John Keating, 'Faith and Community Threatened? Roman Catholic Responses to the Welfare State, Materialism and Social Mobility, 1945–62', *Twentieth Century British History*, vol. 9, no. 1, 1998, pp. 86–108

Nicholas Kenyon, *The BBC Symphony Orchestra: 1930–1980* (1981)

Diana Rait Kerr and Ian Peebles, *Lords 1946–1970* (second edn, 1987)

Pat Kirkham and David Thoms (eds), *War Culture: Social Change and Changing Experience in World War Two* (1995)

Krishan Kumar, 'The Nationalization of British Culture', in Stanley Hoffman and Paschalis Kitromilides (eds), *Culture and Society in Contemporary Europe* (1981)

Antonia Lant, *Blackout: Reinventing Women for Wartime British Cinema* (1991)

K. Leech, *Youthquake: The Growth of a Counterculture Through Two Decades* (1973)

D. L. LeMahieu, *A Culture For Democracy: Mass Communication and the Cultivated Mind in Britain Between the Wars* (1988)

F. M. Levanthal, 'The Best for the Most: CEMA and State Sponsorship of the Arts in Wartime 1939–1945', *Twentieth Century British History*, vol. 1, no. 3, 1990, pp. 289–317

Bernard Levin, *The Pendulum Years: Britain and the Sixties* (1970)

Jane Lewis, 'Public Institution and Private Relationship: Marriage and Marriage guidance, 1920–1968', *Twentieth Century British History*, vol. 1, no. 3, 1990, pp. 233–63

– *Women in Britain since 1945* (1992)

Roger Lloyd, *The Church of England 1900–1965* (1966)

Jules Lubbock, *The Tyranny of Taste: The Politics of Architecture and Design in Britain 1550–1960* (1995)

Joseph McAleer, *Popular Reading and Publishing In Britain 1914–1950* (1992)

Robert McCrum, William Cran and Robert MacNeil, *The Story of English* (1987)

Ian Macdonald, *Revolution In The Head: The Beatles Records & The Sixties* (second edn, 1997)

Brian McFarlane, *An Autobiography Of British Cinema By the Actors and Filmmakers who made it* (1997)

David McGillivray: *Doing Rude Things: The History of the British Sex Film 1957–1981* (1992)

G. I. T. Machin, 'British Churches and Social Issues, 1945–60', *Twentieth Century British History*, vol. 7, no. 3, 1996, pp. 345–70

John M. MacKenzie, *Propaganda And Empire: The manipulation of British public opinion 1880–1960* (1984)

– (ed.), *Imperialism And Popular Culture* (1986)

Ross McKibbin, *The Ideologies of Class: Social Relations In Britain 1880–1950* (1989)

– *Classes and Cultures: England 1918–1951* (1998)

Ian McLaine, *Ministry of Morale: Home Front Morale and the Ministry of Information in World War II* (1979)

Geoffrey McNab, *J. Arthur Rank and The British Film Industry* (1993)

Patrick J. Maguire and Jonathan M. Woodham (eds), *Design and Cultural Politics in Postwar Britain: The Britain Can Make It Exhibition of 1946* (1997)

Peter Mandler, *The Fall And Rise Of The Stately Home* (1997)

J. A. Mangan and James Walvin (eds), *Manliness And Morality: Middle-Class Masculinity In Britain And America 1800–1940* (1987)

Gordon Marsden (ed.), *Victorian Values: Personalities and Perspectives in Nineteenth Century Society* (1990)

Jan Marsh, *Back To The Land: The Pastoral Impulse in Victorian England from 1880 to 1914* (1982)

Stephen Martin, 'Our Country Needs You: Attitudes Towards National Service in Britain 1945–63', *Oral History*, vol. 25, no. 2, Autumn 1997, pp. 67–73

Arthur Marwick, *The Deluge: British Society and the First World War* (1965)

– *Britain in the Century of Total War: War, Peace & Social Change 1900–1967* (1968)

– *The Home Front: The British And The Second World War* (1976)

– *Class: Image and Reality in Britain, France and the USA since 1930* (second edn, 1990)

– *The Sixties* (1998)

Tony Mason (ed.), *Sport In Britain: A Social History* (1989)

David Mellor (ed.), *A Paradise Lost: The Neo-Romantic Imagination in Britain 1935–55* (1987)

– Gill Saunders and Patrick Wright, *Recording Britain: A Pictorial Domesday of pre-war Britain* (1990)

George Melly, *Revolt Into Style: The Pop Arts in the 50s and 60s* (second edn, 1989)

Mandy Merck (ed.), *After Diana: Irreverent Elegies* (1998)

Peter Miles and Malcolm Smith, *Cinema, Literature & Society: Elite and Mass Culture in Interwar Society* (1987)

David Miller, *That Noble Cabinet: A History Of The British Museum* (1973)

G. E. Mingay (ed.), *The Rural Idyll* (1989)

– *Land and Society in England 1750–1980* (1994)

Janet Minihan, *The Nationalization of Culture: The Development of State Subsidies to the Arts in Britain* (1977)

David Morgan and Mary Evans, *The Battle For Britain: Citizenship and Ideology in the Second World War* (1993)

John Motson and John Rowlinson, *The European Cup 1955–1980* (1980)

Alan Munton, *English Fiction Of The Second World War* (1989)

Robert Murphy, *Realism and Tinsel: Cinema and Society in Britain 1939–48* (1989)

– *Sixties British Cinema* (1992)

– (ed.), *The British Cinema Book* (1997)

– *British Cinema of the 90s* (2000)

Howard Newby, *A Social History of Rural England* (1987)

– (ed.), *The National Trust: The Next Hundred Years* (1995)

Sian Nicholas, *The Echo of War: Home Front Propaganda And The Wartime BBC 1939–45* (1996)

Edward Norman, *Church and Society in England 1770–1970* (1976)

Geoff Nuttall, *Bomb Culture* (1968)

James Obelkevich and Peter Catterall (eds), *Understanding Post-War British Society* (1994)

John Oliver, *The Church and Social Order: Social Thought In The Church of England 1918–1939* (1968)

Paul Oliver, Ian Davis and Ian Bentley, *Dunroamin: The Suburban Semi And Its Enemies* (1981)

Bernard Palmer, *Gadfly For God: A History of the Church Times* (1991)

Geoffrey Pearson, *Hooligan: A History of Respectable Fears* (1983)

Susan Pedersen and Peter Mandler (eds), *After The Victorians: Private Conscience & Public Duty In Modern Britain* (1994)

George Perry, *Forever Ealing: A Celebration of the Great British Film Studio* (1981)

– *The Great British Picture Show* (second edn, 1985)

Roy Porter and Lesley Hall, *The Facts of Life: The Creation of Sexual Knowledge in Britain, 1650–1950* (1995)

Harry Potter, *Hanging In Judgement: Religion and the Death Penalty in England* (1993)

Jeremy Potter, *Independent Television in Britain*, vol. 3: *Politics and Control 1968–80* (1989)
– *Independent Television in Britain*, vol. 4: *Companies and Programmes 1968–80* (1990)
Frank Prochaska, *Royal Bounty: The Making of a Welfare Monarchy* (1995)
– *The Republic of Britain 1760–2000* (2000)
Nicholas Pronay and D. W. Spring (eds), *Propaganda, Politics and Film 1918–45* (1982)
Martin Pugh, *Women And The Women's Movement In Britain 1914–1959* (1992)

David Reynolds, *Rich Relations: The American Occupation of Britain 1942–1945* (1995)
Jeffrey Richards, *The Age Of The Dream Palace: Cinema And Society In Britain 1930–1939* (1984)
– and Dorothy Sheridan, *Mass-Observation At The Movies* (1987)
Adrian Rigelsford, *Carry On Laughing: A Celebration* (1996)
John Robb, *The Nineties: What The F**k Was That All About?* (1999)
James C. Robertson, *The British Board of Film Censors: Film Censorship in Britain 1896–1950* (1985)
Michael Roper and John Tosh (eds), *Manful Assertions: Masculinities in Britain since 1800* (1991)
Sheila Rowbotham, *A Century of Women: The History of Women In Britain and the United States* (1997)
Trevor Royle, *The Best Years Of Their Lives: The National Service Experience 1945–63* (1986)
W. D. Rubinstein, *Capitalism, Culture & Decline In Britain 1750–1990* (1993)
Dave Russell, *Popular Music in England 1840–1914: A Social History* (Manchester, second edn, 1997)
Deborah S. Ryan, *The Ideal Home Through The 20th Century* (1997)

Michael Sanderson, *From Irving To Olivier: A Social History of the Acting Profession 1880–1983* (1984)
Jon Savage, *England's Dreaming: Sex Pistols and Punk Rock* (1991)
Paddy Scannell and David Cardiff, *A Social History of British Broadcasting*, vol. 1: *Serving the Nation 1922–1939* (1991)
Bernard Sendall, *Independent Television in Britain*, vol. 1: *Origin and Foundation 1946–62* (1982)
– *Independent Television in Britain*, vol. 2: *Expansion and Change 1958–68* (1983)
Brian Short (ed.), *The English Rural Community: Image and Analysis* (1992)
K. R. M. Short, *Film and Radio Propaganda in World War II* (Tennessee, 1986)
Brian Simon, *Education and the Social Order: British Education since 1944* (1991)

Andrew Sinclair, *Arts and Cultures: The History of the 50 Years of the Arts Council of Great Britain* (1995)

Alan Sinfield, *Literature, Politics and Culture in Postwar Britain* (1989)

Frances Spalding, *British Art Since 1900* (1986)

– *The Tate: A History* (1998)

John Springhall, *Youth, Empire and Society: British Youth Movements 1883–1940* (1977)

– *Youth, Popular Culture and Moral Panics: Penny Gaffs to Gangsta-Rap 1830–1996* (1998)

Peter Stead, *Film and the Working Class: The Feature Film In British and American Society* (1989)

Lawrence Stone, *Road To Divorce: England 1530–1987* (1990)

Gordon T. Stewart, 'Tenzing's Two Wrist-Watches: The Conquest of Everest and Late Imperial Culture in Britain 1921–1953', *Past And Present*, no. 149, November 1995

Roy Strong, *The Spirit of Britain: A Narrative History of the Arts* (1999)

Penny Summerfield, *Women Workers in the Second World War* (1984)

Sir John Summerson, *50 Years of the National Buildings Record 1941–1991* (1991)

Paul Swann, *The Hollywood Feature Film In Postwar Britain* (1987)

Antony Taylor, *'Down With The Crown': British Anti-monarchism and Debates about Royalty Since 1790* (1999)

John Taylor, *War Photography: Realism in the British Press* (1991)

Philip M. Taylor, *The Projection of Britain: British Overseas Publicity and Propaganda 1919–39* (1981)

– (ed.), *Britain And The Cinema In The Second World War* (1988)

– *British Propaganda In The Twentieth Century: Selling Democracy* (1999)

Adrian Tinniswood, *A History of Country House Visiting* (1989)

Barry Turner and Tony Rennell, *When Daddy Came Home: How Family Life Changed Forever in 1945* (1995)

Nicola Tyrer, *They Fought In The Fields, The Women's Land Army: The Story of a Forgotten Victory* (1996)

Bernard Waites, Tony Bennett and Graham Martin (eds), *Popular Culture: Past and Present* (1982)

Alexander Walker, *Hollywood England: The British Film Industry In The Sixties* (1974)

– *National Heroes: British Cinema in the Seventies and Eighties* (1985)

John A. Walker, *Arts TV: A history of arts television in Britain* (1993)

John K. Walton, *Fish & Chips & The British Working Class 1870–1940* (Leicester, 1992)

– *The British Seaside: Holidays and resorts in the twentieth century* (2000)

– and James Walvin (eds), *Leisure In Britain 1780–1939* (1983)

James Walvin, *Leisure and Society 1830–1950* (1989)

– *The People's Game: The History of Football Revisited* (second edn, 1994)

Colin Ward and Dennis Hardy, *Goodnight Campers! The History of the British Holiday Camp* (1989)

Sadie Ward, *War In The Countryside 1939–45* (1988)

Chris Waters, *British Socialists and the Politics of Popular Culture 1884–1914* (1990)

Merlin Waterson, *The National Trust: The First Hundred Years* (second edn, 1997)

Jeffrey Weeks, *Sex, Politics and Society: The regulation of sexuality since 1800* (1981)

Paul Welsby, *A History of The Church of England 1945–1980* (1984)

Gary Werskey, *The Visible College: A Collective Biography of British Scientists and Socialists of the 1930s* (second edn, 1988)

Eric White, *The Arts Council of Great Britain* (1975)

Kate Whitehead, *The Third Programme: A Literary History* (1989)

Philip Whitehead, *The Writing On The Wall: Britain in the Seventies* (1985)

Alan Wilkinson, *The Church of England and the First World War* (1974)

– *Dissent or Conform? War, Peace and the English Churches 1900–1945* (1986)

John Williams and Stephen Wagg (eds), *British Football and Social Change: Getting Into Europe* (1991)

Janet Wolff and John Seed (eds), *The Culture Of Capital: art, power and the nineteenth-century middle class* (1988)

John Wolffe, *God & Greater Britain: Religion and National Life in Britain and Ireland 1843–1945* (1994)

Kenneth Wolffe, *The Churches And The British Broadcasting Corporation 1922–1956* (1984)

Peter York and Charles Jennings, *Peter York's Eighties* (1996)

Philip Ziegler, *Crown and People* (1978)

– *London At War 1939–1945* (1995)

II POLITICS AND ECONOMY

Paul Addison, *The Road to 1945: British politics and the Second World War* (second edn, 1994)

Richard Aldous and Sabine Lee (eds), *Harold Macmillan: Aspects Of A Political Life* (1999)

Stuart Ball and Anthony Seldon, *The Heath Government 1970–74* (1996)

Anthony Barnett (ed.), *Power And The Throne: The Monarchy Debate* (1994)

– *This Time: Our Constitutional Revolution* (1997)

Correlli Barnett, *The Collapse of British Power* (1972)

- *The Audit of War: The Illusion & Reality of Britain As A Great Nation* (1986)
- *The Lost Victory: British Dreams, British Realities* (1995)
Francis Beckett, *Enemy Within: The Rise and Fall of the British Honours System* (1995)
P. M. H. Bell, *France And Britain 1900–1940: Entente and Estrangement* (1995)
- *France And Britain 1940–1994: The Long Separation* (1997)
Jeremy Black, *Convergence or Divergence? Britain and the Continent* (1994)
Vernon Bogdanor, *The Monarchy And The Constitution* (1995)
- *Power And The People: A Guide To Constitutional Reform* (1997)
- and Robert Skidelsky (eds), *The Age of Affluence* (1970)
Andrew Boyle, *Climate of Treason: Five Who Spied for Russia* (1979)
Brian Brivati and Harriet Jones (eds), *From Reconstruction To Integration: Britain And Europe Since 1945* (1993)
- *What Difference Did The War Make?* (1993)
- and Tim Bale (eds), *New Labour in Power: Precedents and prospects* (1997)
Stephen Brooke, *Labour's War: The Labour Party during the Second World War* (1992)

Alec Cairncross, *The British Economy since 1945* (second edn, 1995)
Peter Clark, *Hope And Glory: Britain 1900–1990* (1996)
- *A Question Of Leadership: From Gladstone to Blair* (second edn, 1999)
Chris Cook, *A Short History of the Liberal Party 1900–1997* (fifth edn, 1998)
R. Coopey, S. Fielding and N. Tiratsoo, *The Wilson Governments 1964–1970* (1993)

John Darwin, *Britain and Decolonisation: The Retreat From Empire In The Post-War World* (1988)
- *The End of the British Empire: The Historical Debate* (1991)
Roy Denman, *Missed Chances: Britain And Europe In The Twentieth Century* (1996)
John Dickie, *'Special' No More: Anglo-American Relations: Rhetoric And Reality* (1994)
Michael Dintenfass, *The Decline of Industrial Britain 1870–1980* (1992)

David Edgerton, 'The Prophet Militant and Industrial: The Peculiarities of Correlli Barnett', *Twentieth Century British History*, vol. 2, no. 3, 1991, pp. 360–79
- 'The White Heat Revisited: The British Government and Technology in the 1960s', *Twentieth Century British History*, vol. 7, no. 1, 1996, pp. 53–82
Eric J. Evans, *Thatcher and Thatcherism* (1997)

Stephen Fielding, Peter Thompson and Nick Tiratsoo, *England Arise! The Labour Party and popular politics in 1940s Britain* (1995)

Martin Francis and Ina Zweiniger-Bargielowska, *The Conservatives and British Society 1880–1990* (Cardiff 1996)

Derek Fraser, *The Evolution of the British Welfare State* (second edn, 1984)

Jim Fyrth, *Labour's High Noon: The Government and the Economy 1945–51* (1993)

Martin Gilbert (ed.), *The Churchill War Papers*, Vol. 1: *At the Admiralty, September 1939–April 1940* (1992)

– *The Churchill War Papers*, Vol. 2: *Never Surrender, May 1940–December 1940* (1994)

Ian Gilmour and Mark Garnett, *Whatever Happened To The Tories? The Conservatives Since 1945* (1997)

Richard S. Grayson, 'Britain and the Channel Tunnel', *Twentieth Century British History*, vol. 7, no. 3, 1996, pp. 382–8

Philip Hall, *Royal Fortune: Tax, Money & The Monarchy* (1992)

Max Hastings and Simon Jenkins, *The Battle For The Falklands* (1983)

Peter Hennessy, *Whitehall* (1989)

– *Never Again: Britain 1945–1951* (1992)

– *The Hidden Wiring: Unearthing The British Constitution* (1995)

– *Muddling Through: Power, Politics and the Quality of Government in Postwar Britain* (1996)

Stephen Howe, *Anticolonialism In British Politics: The Left and the End of Empire 1918–1964* (1993)

Lawrence James, *Imperial Rearguard: Wars of Empire 1919–85* (1988)

Peter Jenkins, *Mrs. Thatcher's Revolution: The Ending of the Socialist Era* (1987)

Harriet Jones and Michael Kandiah (eds), *The Myth of Consensus: New Views On British History 1945–64* (1996)

Dennis Judd, *Empire: The British Imperial Experience from 1765 to the Present* (1996)

Dennis Kavanagh, *Thatcherism and British Politics: The End of Consensus?* (second edn, 1990)

Uwe Kitzinger, *Diplomacy and Persuasion: How Britain Joined The Common Market* (1973)

Richard Lamb, *The Failure of the Eden Government* (1987)

– *The Macmillan Years 1957–1963: The Emerging Truth* (1995)

T. O. Lloyd, *The British Empire 1558–1983* (1984)

Lord Longford, *A History Of The House of Lords* (second edn, 1999)

Rodney Lowe, *The Welfare State in Britain since 1945* (second edn, 1999)

W. Scott Lucas, *Divided We Stand: Britain, the US and the Suez Crisis* (1991)

Peter Lynch, *Minority Nationalism & European Integration* (Cardiff 1996)

S. P. Mackenzie, *Politics And Military Morale: Current Affairs and Citizenship Education in the British Army 1914–1950* (1992)

David McKie and Chris Cook, *The Decade of Disillusion: British Politics in the Sixties* (1972)

Janet P. Morgan, *The House Of Lords And The Labour Government 1964–1970* (1975)

Kenneth O. Morgan, *Labour in Power 1945–51* (1984)

– *Labour People, Leaders and Lieutenants: Hardie to Kinnock* (1987)

– *The People's Peace: British History 1945–1989* (1990)

Ritchie Ovendale, *Anglo-American Relations In The Twentieth Century* (1998)

Henry Pelling, *A History of British Trade Unionism* (fifth edn, 1992)

Bernard Porter, *Plots And Paranoia: A History of Political Espionage In Britain 1790–1988* (1989)

– *The Lion's Share: A Short History of British Imperialism 1850–1995* (third edn, 1996)

John Ramsden, *The Age of Churchill and Eden 1940–1957* (1994)

– *The Winds of Change: Macmillan to Heath 1957–1975* (1996)

David Reynolds, *Britannia Overruled: British Policy & World Power In The 20th Century* (1991)

L.V. Scott, *Conscription And The Attlee Governments: The Politics and Policy of National Service: 1945–1951* (1993)

Anthony Seldon, *Churchill's Indian Summer: The Conservative Government 1951–55* (1981)

Michael Sissons and Philip French (eds), *Age Of Austerity* (1963)

Alan Sked, *Britain's Decline: Problems and Perspectives* (1987)

– and Chris Cook, *Post-War Britain: A Political History* (second edn, 1984)

Robert Skidelsky (ed.), *Thatcherism* (1988)

Lesley M. Smith (ed.), *The Making of Britain: Echoes of Greatness* (1988)

Philip Stephens, *Politics And The Pound: The Tories, the Economy and Europe* (1996)

Peter M. R. Stirk (ed.), *European Unity In Context: The Interwar Period* (1989)

A. J. P. Taylor, *English History 1914–1945* (1965)

Richard Taylor and Nigel Young (eds), *Campaigns For Peace: British peace movements in the twentieth century* (1987)

Robert Taylor, *The Trade Union Question in British Politics: Government and Unions since 1945* (1993)

Andrew Thorpe (ed.), *The Failure of Political Extremism In Inter-War Britain* (1989)

Richard Thurlow, *Fascism in Britain: From Oswald Mosley's Blackshirts to the National Front* (second edn, 1998)

Nick Tiratsoo, *Reconstruction, Affluence And Labour Politics: Coventry 1945–60* (1990)
– (ed.), *The Attlee Years* (1991)
– (ed.), *From Blitz to Blair: A New History of Britain Since 1939* (1997)
Isobel Tombs, 'The Victory of Socialist Vansittartism: Labour and the German Question 1941–5', *Twentieth Century British History*, vol. 7, no. 3, 1996, pp. 287–309

John Walker, *The Queen Has Been Pleased: The Scandal Of The British Honours System* (1986)
Martin Walker, *The National Front* (1977)
Ian Ward, *A State of Mind? The English Constitution and the Popular Imagination* (2000)
D. C. Watt, *Britain Looks To Germany: A study of British opinion and policy towards Germany since 1945* (1965)
Kevin Wilson and Jan van der Dussen, *The History of the Idea of Europe* (second edn, 1995)

Hugo Young, *This Blessed Plot: Britain And Europe From Churchill To Blair* (1998)
Ken Young and Nirmala Rao, *Local Government since 1945* (1997)

Index